A PRACTITIONER'S GUIDE
TO THE
EUROPEAN CONVENTION
ON HUMAN RIGHTS

AUSTRALIA
Law Book Co.
Sydney

CANADA and USA
Carswell
Toronto

HONG KONG
Sweet & Maxwell Asia

NEW ZEALAND
Brookers
Wellington

SINGAPORE and MALAYSIA
Sweet & Maxwell Asia
Singapore and Kuala Lumpur

A PRACTITIONER'S GUIDE TO THE EUROPEAN CONVENTION ON HUMAN RIGHTS

BY

KAREN REID

THOMSON

™

SWEET & MAXWELL

First edition 1998
Reprinted 2003
Second edition 2004

Published in 2004 by Sweet & Maxwell Ltd
100 Avenue Road
London NW3 3PF
(http://www.sweetandmaxwell.co.uk)

Typeset by LBJ Typesetting Ltd, Kingsclere
Printed and bound by Athenaeum Press, Gateshead, Tyne and Wear

No natural forests were destroyed to make this product;
only farmed timber was used and replanted.

ISBN 0 421 87590 9

A CIP catalogue record for this book is available
from The British Library

ACKNOWLEDGMENTS

To Sebastian and Joshua, now teenagers, who barely noticed that I was working on this edition but were tolerant when they did.

To the Registry of the Court, still a remarkable, if motley, crew, over-crowded and much-abused, of which I am privileged to be a member.

To Sir Nicolas Bratza, to whose contribution to the Court's jurisprudence and to shoring up the morale of said Registry I am unable to do justice.

DISCLAIMER

The views expressed in this book are solely those of the author and do not represent those of the Court.

CONTENTS

CONTENTS

CONTENTS

TABLE OF CASES

TABLE OF CASES

TABLE OF CASES

TABLE OF CASES

TABLE OF CASES

TABLE OF CASES BEFORE THE EUROPEAN COURT OF HUMAN RIGHTS

TABLE OF CASES BEFORE THE EUROPEAN
COMMISSION OF HUMAN RIGHTS

TABLE OF LEGISLATION

International Treaties and Conventions

INTRODUCTION

PURPOSE OF THIS BOOK

This is intended to be a practical book. It will not offer solutions or theories or an exhaustive study. It will, hopefully, indicate the range of situations and legal problems which may fall within the scope of the European Convention of Human Rights ("the Convention") and its Protocols. And it aims to explain the what, when, how and why of a particular procedure, that of introducing applications before the European Court of Human Rights ("the Court").

WHAT

The basic subject matter of this procedure is human rights. This is a concept which is trammelled with popular misconceptions, false expectations and knee-jerk prejudices. In this book, the term means solely those rights and freedoms expressly guaranteed under the Convention and its Protocols. The competence of the Court is defined by the Convention. Every complaint must base itself squarely on the Convention's provisions and comply with its requirements. Essentially, the provisions of the Convention cover classic civil and political rights: economic and social rights are only covered indirectly, if at all. Part II: Problem Areas highlights the situations and disputes, which fall, or may fall, within the ambit of Convention rights.

HOW

An application begins, simply, with a letter to the Court, setting out the substance of the complaint.

The procedures which follow do require some explanation (see Part I: Practice and Procedure). However, there are a minimum of formalities and no fees which reflects the fact the system is meant to be open to everyone, legally represented or not and that a significant number of applications are pursued by individuals who have no access to, no means to pay or no inclination to use, lawyers.

WHEN

A strict time-limit applies. An application must be made within six months of the final decision relating to the subject-matter of the complaint where domestic remedies exist or within six months of the act or event complained of where no domestic remedies exist. Limited exception arises where there can be said to be a continuing situation (see Part IB: Admissibility Checklist).

INTRODUCTION

WHY

The responsibility of Governments to adhere to minimum standards of fair and proper conduct in exercising their powers in respect of their own citizens and any others within their jurisdiction is acknowledged on domestic and international level. In ratifying the Convention, the United Kingdom Government has expressly pledged by way of treaty obligation to ensure the observance of fundamental rights and freedoms guaranteed in that instrument. It has, as a result, accepted the rights of individuals, groups of individuals, non-governmental organisations and private companies to introduce complaints against it (and all public authorities under its responsibility) under the implementation system provided in Strasbourg. Since this is a supranational instance, it offers the possibility of remedies where a domestic system cannot. No national legal system is free from *lacunae*, historical anomalies, cultural biases or blindspots. While the United Kingdom seems, sometimes unfairly, to be subject to unfavourable scrutiny in Strasbourg, it is a compliment to the Government, which allows free, unhindered access to the system and co-operates fully and fairly in the procedures; to the applicants who are prepared to fight for justice against the weight of the State; and to the lawyers who bring a common law approach and British trained legal expertise to the process.

In the proceedings, applicants can obtain a limited but not negligible range of remedies. It is possible that the Government will offer to settle the case: providing specific reparation (for example, right of entry to the United Kingdom, grant of planning permission); or a change of legislation or administrative practice; *ex gratia* payment of compensation; and reasonable legal costs. A binding judgment may make public declaration of the State's breach accompanied by a monetary award of just satisfaction and the payment of legal costs (Part III). Following such a judgment, the State is required to comply with the Court's findings which may also lead to a specific result such as legislative change or other step necessary to remedy whatever failing has been identified.

Besides rendering a successful outcome for a particular individual, an application can be seen in a wider context. It is a method of achieving law reform and improving or maintaining civil rights standards. It participates in furnishing a system of model standards contributing to worldwide developments. In that context, practitioners, prepared to represent applicants, play a significant and creative role in identifying those cases which can usefully be dealt with in Strasbourg and in developing the case law under the Convention by the arguments and principles which they advocate in pleading.

YES, BUT. . .

There are drawbacks. The admissibility threshold is high: at most one in ten cases succeeds in crossing it (see Pt IB: Admissibility Checklist). But it is possible to be selective and successful. Some practitioners from the United Kingdom have a high success rate in reaching the admissibility stage, and subsequent friendly settlement or findings of violation by the Court.

There is delay. Ironically, for an institution which sits in judgment on allegations that domestic courts have failed to decide cases within a reasonable time, it may take more than three years for a successful case to conclude before the Court. (Less successful cases are generally disposed of more summarily and often as quickly as within three to six months.) The reasons for the delay are several: the backlog of applications which increases with every new country that joins the system, long series of cases generated by systemic problems, the inherent openness of the system which allows, and requires decisions in, large numbers of unmeritorious or hopeless complaints; shortage of staff and resources. The Court is sensitive to the problem, constantly reviewing its procedures, introducing such modifications as are compatible with its powers but the situation has long been unsatisfactory. Further fundamental reforms, following Protocol No.11 in 1998, are imminent in the latest Protocol No. 14 which has yet to come into force but proposes to allow single judges to take decisions in clearly inadmissible cases; for committees of three judges to declare admissible cases which follow established case law and issue a judgment on the merits; and the creation of a new inadmissibility criteria allowing rejection of cases where an applicant has not suffered a significant disadvantage.

There are also inequalities as regards the position of the applicant. Governments enjoy certain procedural advantages in addition to obvious superiority of resources.

No international system can be perfect, immune to error. All who have worked with the Court have had experience off cases that were, in their view, disappointing, regrettable, if not worse. But these are, on the whole, outweighed by the successes. The Convention system is a tool of remarkable possibilities. While the continuing rise in the volume of cases has practical disadvantages, it has also contributed to dynamic trends in interpretation as the case law extends into new areas and adapts to changing climates and perceptions. As a final and hopefully persuasive illustration, the following changes in UK legislation and practice resulted from, or were contributed to, by cases dealt with in Strasbourg: the Security Service Act 1989; Interception of Communications Act 1985; end of blanket censorship of prisoners' letters; change in practice regarding the grant of legal aid on appeal in Scotland; the Children Act 1989; end of criminalisation of homosexual relationships between consenting adults over 16; regular review by a tribunal of the continued detention of mental health patients and life sentence prisoners; end of corporal punishment in schools and birching on the Isle of Man; revision of the court martial system; the Special Immigration Appeals Commission Act 1997, providing for legal representation of applicants to be deported in the interests of national security and review by the special tribunal of the evidence basing the decision; and introduction of a new code of conduct lifting the ban on gays serving in the military.

PART I: PRACTICE AND PROCEDURE

A. PROCEDURE BEFORE THE EUROPEAN COURT OF HUMAN RIGHTS

1. The Court

On November 1, 1998, pursuant to Protocol No.11, the single permanent Court   I–001
replaced the previous Convention organs, the European Commission of Human
Rights ("the Commission") and the old Court. Both bodies had sat on part time
basis. The Commission had acted as a quasi-judicial, fact-finding and filter
mechanism, its files and hearings not open to the public. It had dealt with the bulk
of applications, applying the admissibility criteria to decide which cases could
eventually be referred to the Court which held public hearings and issued binding
judgments, monitored by the Committee of Ministers of the Council of Europe.[1] The
new Court now examines both admissibility and merits.

Membership of the Court

The qualifications for the new Court remain the same as the old Court, namely, that   I–002
the judges must be of high moral character and possess the qualifications required
for appointment to high judicial office or be jurisconsults of recognised competence.[2]
Protocol No.11 added an age-limit of 70, after which a judge can no longer sit. The
judges are also under an obligation not to engage in any activity incompatible with
full time office, the intention being that the judges should live in Strasbourg and sit
on a permanent basis. *Ad hoc* judges may be appointed by a Contracting State in
particular cases where the national judge withdraws.[3]

   The appointment procedure, in brief, is that each member State nominates three
suitable candidates for their national seat. They are encouraged to find women
candidates. They may or may not indicate their preference. A committee of the
Parliamentary Assembly of the Council of Europe (made up of representatives of the
legislatures of member States) interviews all candidates and reports to the Assembly
which elects the judge for each seat by majority vote.

   The Court is headed by a President, two Vice-Presidents (who act also as
Presidents of Sections) and two additional Presidents of Sections, each elected for a
three year period. They may be re-elected.[4] The President of the Court has the
power to issue practice directions (Art.32).[5]

---

[1] The Committee of Ministers consists formally of the Foreign Ministers of the member States of the
Council of Europe, but generally its functions are carried out by deputies attached to the various
embassies and representations in Strasbourg.
[2] Currently, amongst the Court, there figure members of the judiciary from their home countries, ex-
practising lawyers, ex-ambassadors or Government Agents and a fair sprinkling of academics specialising
in international law.
[3] r.29, *e.g.* where a judge has or had a connection with a case on the domestic level.
[4] r.8 of the Rules of Court.
[5] Three practice directions have issued: on interim measures, the institution of proceedings and written
pleadings. See Annex 6.

Organisation of the Court

I–003   There are four types of composition: committees of three, Chambers (Sections), the Grand Chamber and the Plenary Court.

The **Plenary** Court has a primarily internal administrative function.

Committees of three may reject as inadmissible or strike out cases by unanimous vote. The vast majority of cases are rejected in this manner (in 2002, 96 per cent of decisions taken on admissibility were reached in committees).

Chambers consist of seven judges. There is no quorum and substitute judges sit to maintain the numbers. There are at the moment four Sections from which the Chambers are composed. Two are headed by Vice-Presidents and the others by Presidents of Section. Cases not dealt with in committee are examined in Chamber. Where a Chamber considers that the case raises a serious question affecting the interpretation of the Convention or protocols, or where the resolution of a question might have a result inconsistent with a judgment previously delivered by the Court (Art.30), it may relinquish jurisdiction to the Grand Chamber, unless within one month one of the parties to the case objects.[6] After the Chamber gives judgment on the merits, the parties may within three months in exceptional cases request that the case be referred to the Grand Chamber (Art.44). A panel of the Grand Chamber (five judges including the President, the Presidents/Vice Presidents of the Sections not previously involved in the case and a judge designated in rotation) may accept the request if the case raises a serious question affecting the interpretation and application of the Convention or a serious issue of general importance (Art.43).

The **Grand Chamber** (17 judges including the President, Vice-Presidents and Presidents of the Sections and the national judges for any respondent State) examines cases where the Chambers have relinquished jurisdiction or those referred by the Panel after request by one of the parties after a Chamber judgment. It may also issue advisory opinions (Arts 47–49) at the request of the Committee of Ministers concerning legal questions on the interpretation of the Convention. To date it has received only one request which it declined as outside its competence.[7]

2. Outline of Procedure

I–004
- Lodging of application
- Preliminary contacts with the Court's Registry

Admissibility stage

- Registration of the case in the list of pending cases
- Appointment of a *judge rapporteur*
- First examination of the case by either a Committee or a Chamber or by a Chamber President

---

[6] r.72(2) refers to a "duly reasoned objection" and stipulates that an objection which does not fulfil the criteria will be considered invalid. This perhaps leaves scope for discounting objections which do not contain sound objections, as well as those containing no reasons at all.

[7] Decision on the competence of the Court to given an advisory opinion, June 2, 2004: concerning possible conflict between the European Convention system and the human rights treaty drawn up by the Commonwealth of Independent States.

- Communication of the case by a Chamber or Chamber President to the respondent Government
- Filing of observations on admissibility (and merits)
- Oral hearing (in a minority of cases)
- Admissibility decision

Merits stage

- Establishment of the facts
- Friendly settlement
- Oral hearing (in a minority of cases)
- Judgment on the merits by a chamber
- Referral to Grand Chamber (subject to grant of leave by the Panel)

1. Lodging of application[8]

Introduction of an application may be done by letter or fax. To stop time running for the purposes of the six month rule, any preliminary letter, pending submission of a detailed application, must contain a brief outline of the facts and complaints sufficient to convey the substance of the application.[9]

I–005

A full application must be made on the application form provided by the Registry and include the information specified in r.47—principally, details identifying the applicant (name, date of birth, nationality, sex, occupation and address); the Contracting Party/Parties; a succinct Statement of facts; a succinct Statement of alleged violations; an explanation as to compliance with the six month rule and rule of exhaustion of domestic remedies; the object of the application; accompanied by any relevant supporting documents, in particular the decisions, whether judicial or not, relating to the complaints. Failure to comply with these requirements may result in the application not being examined by the Court, namely it will not be included on the list of pending cases.[10]

An applicant's name is public, unless, on request, supported by adequate reasons, the President of the Chamber authorises anonymity. This is commonly done in cases involving children or sexual abuse victims. The President may, in such cases, order anonymity of his or her own motion.[11]

A period of six weeks is usually indicated in the first letter from the Registry as the time within which an application form should be returned. This is not a formal rule derived from the Convention but a practice to prevent long lapses in time in registering a case for examination by the Court: it is possible, if necessary and not unreasonable in the circumstances, for longer time to be taken (see Admissibility, Six months). A gap of more than a year in correspondence will now result in the file being destroyed.[12]

A legal representative must provide a letter of authority signed by the applicant authorising the lawyer to represent him before the Commission.

[8] See Practice Direction on Institution of Proceedings, Annex 6.
[9] r.47(5).
[10] r.47(4).
[11] r.47(3).
[12] See Practice Direction on Institution of Proceedings, para.11, Annex 6.

2. Preliminary contacts with the Registry

I–006 The Registry, staffed by lawyers from Contracting States, manage applications as follows. A file is opened with each new complaint/letter. It is allotted to a case-lawyer within an applications division who has the relevant linguistic and legal expertise. The Registry will send the application form and inform an applicant whether he has omitted any necessary information or supporting documentation. As a general rule, it will not register a case for examination until all information or documents have been provided. The Registry are authorised to draw to applicants' attention any apparent problems as to admissibility, though due to the increasing work load of the Court this is no longer done as a matter of course. However, any points raised by the Registry, even if disagreed with, should be answered. Since clearly inadmissible cases can be rejected in summary fashion (Committees of three judges), it is advisable to establish that the case does not fall into that category.

Admissibility stage

3. Registration of the application

I–007 Once the case file is ready, the application is included in the list of cases awaiting examination by the Court. The speed with which it receives its first examination will depend on the pressure of work and complexity of the case (varying from three to 18 months). Cases may be given priority under r.41 by a Chamber or a President (*e.g.* where an applicant has serious health problems[13] or children are involved). The case is allotted to a Section (generally the section in which the national judge sits).

4. Appointment of a judge rapporteur

I–008 The President of the Section appoints in each case a *judge rapporteur*—a judge charged with presenting the case to the Court.[14] Exceptionally, more than one judge rapporteur may be appointed to the case. The identity of the *rapporteur* is never disclosed and it cannot be assumed that it is the national judge. It is the *rapporteur*, with the assistance of the case-lawyer from the Registry, who makes proposals to the Court as to the procedure, decisions and texts to be adopted in respect of a case. Before submitting a case to the Court, a *rapporteur* may request factual information or documentation from one or more of the parties.[15]

5 First examination

(a) *Examination by Committee*

I–009 Cases which the *rapporteur* considers to be clearly inadmissible or appropriate to be struck out are listed for examination by committees of three judges.[16] A one page

---

[13] *Pretty v UK*, April 29, 2002, ECHR 2002–III.
[14] r.49 (concerning individual applications under Art.34). However, in inter-state cases under Art.35, it is the Chamber that appoints the *rapporteur(s)* (r.48).
[15] r.49(2)a(i).
[16] Art.28.

decision letter is sent to the applicant recording in brief terms the date and ground of inadmissibility. This procedure, which enables the Court to reject large numbers of cases swiftly, is a key means for dealing with its huge work load. Committees are used not only to reject hopeless or misconceived applications but also cases which, albeit factually or procedurally complex, interesting or well-argued, can nonetheless be rejected under the admissibility criteria.[17]

Although the national judge does not always sit on the committee dealing with the cases from his/her country, copies are provided in advance and he/she may make his/her views known. A committee must be unanimous in rejecting a case. If the committee does not agree with the proposal, it is adjourned and brought before the Chamber.

(b) *Examination by Chamber*

On first examination, or on adjournment from a committee, a Chamber may reject a   **I–010** case as inadmissible or strike it out. It may, on occasion, request further information (issues of fact or domestic law or particular documents).[18] Where, however, a Convention issue is considered to arise requiring examination, the complaint is communicated to the respondent Government for observations on admissibility and merits (see further below).

The Chamber will not declare a case admissible without first inviting the Government's comments.

A Chamber may, at any stage, relinquish jurisdiction of a case to the Grand Chamber (Art.30). It must consult the parties first and where a party objects it must continue the examination of the case.[19] An objection must, however, comply with Art.30 and r.72 of the Rules of Court. In particular, it must be lodged within one month of notification of the Chamber's intention to relinquish and constitute "a duly reasoned objection". An objection which does not comply with these conditions is invalid. For the moment, there is no indication of the grounds on which a Chamber could discount an objection as lacking due reasoning or invalid. Chambers will often wait until after admissibility to pass a case to the Grand Chamber and have so far not shown themselves over-zealous in giving up jurisdiction themselves.[20]

6. Communication by a Chamber or Chamber President

Where a Convention issue is considered to arise requiring further examination, the   **I–011** respondent Government is invited to submit observations on admissibility and merits. Questions are generally put, indicating the areas of concern. The parties may also be directed that no submissions are required on other points, which is generally an indication that they are regarded as inadmissible. The questions put to the parties should be addressed or risk going by default.

The Government is generally given three months to reply. A copy is sent to the applicant for his response. A shorter time-limit of a month is standard. However,

---

[17] In 2003, of 17,530 decisions on admissibility, 16,364 were rejected in committee.
[18] r.54(2)a.
[19] *e.g. Pellegrini v Italy*, July 20, 2001, ECHR 2001–VIII, where the applicant objected.
[20] *e.g. Pretty*, n.13 above, which raised new points of interpretation of Convention law, was kept in Chamber, perhaps with a view to the more expeditious procedures available. Grand Chambers, made up of 17 judges and extra substitutes, tend to attract problems of timetabling and involve more cumbersome procedures.

applications can be made for an extension in the time-limit, which should be received by the Court before the expiry of the time-limit. Submissions sent after the expiry of the time-limit may not be accepted.[21] An applicant is advised to reply to any arguments raised by the Government on inadmissibility, whether non-exhaustion, six-months or manifestly ill-founded. While the Court is perfectly capable of rejecting Government arguments on its own knowledge of domestic and Convention case law, well-prepared argument by applicants is of valuable assistance to a thorough and accurate examination of the issues. The form and contents of pleadings, including the requirement where submissions are over 30 pages for a short summary to be provided, are subject to a practice direction.[22]

A recent change in the rules provides that the President of a Chamber may communicate a case to the respondent Government.[23] This was instituted to allow for more expeditious treatment of applications which are clearly communicable, in particular, as they are part of a series of cases.[24] The President cannot declare any part of the application inadmissible. Partial decisions (partly inadmissible, partly adjourned for observations) continue to be decided by the Chamber.

6a. Abbreviated procedure

I–012 Generally, applications which result in a judgment go through a two-stage examination—admissibility and merits, with the opportunity for two rounds of observations. Art.29, para.3 of the Convention however allows the Court to decide both stages together. To do this, the Chamber on communicating to the respondent Government puts the parties on notice that it may proceed to determine admissibility and merits together in a judgment and to that end require the parties to put forward their submissions on just satisfaction. This procedure may be used increasingly by the Court in the future to fight its backlog.

7. Oral hearings

I–013 Before declaring a case admissible, the Court may, in exceptional cases, hold an oral hearing on admissibility and merits. A hearing may also be held on the merits alone after a decision on admissibility. Hearings only tend to occur where a novel or complex point of law arises on which oral argument may provide assistance or, on occasion, where a case may, in the view of the Government, have fundamental effects on an important area of domestic law or practice. The vast majority of cases are decided without an oral hearing.

When a oral hearing is decided, the Court sends the parties a list of questions to be addressed. This indicates its primary concerns and other issues are addressed at the risk of being regarded as irrelevant. An opportunity is provided to supplement any oral observations with further written materials submitted by a fixed time-limit shortly before the hearing. This may be useful for providing relevant background information, further factual developments or subsidiary arguments.

---

[21] r.38 is formulated in strict terms—it is necessary for the President to decide to accept late submissions.
[22] Practice Direction on Written Pleadings, see Annex 6.
[23] r.54(2)b as amended.
[24] *e.g.* length of civil or criminal proceedings, or, from the UK, cases dealing with court martials, discrimination in allowances/pensions payable to widowers, etc.

Parties are also requested to provide a copy of their speech at least one day in advance. This is solely to assist the interpreters (English-French, the two official languages of the Court). Adjustments may be made to the speech as required. Speakers should bear in mind the interpretation process and avoid talking fast. Court hearings are in public, unless in exceptional circumstances the Chamber decides otherwise.[25]

The procedure for the hearing is notified to the parties beforehand, the timing being subject to strict regulation. The standard hearing held in a morning, or in an afternoon, consists of 30 minutes each for the Government and the applicant, questions put by the judges, a 20–30 minute adjournment, a final round of 15 minutes each for Government and applicant, to address the questions and make final points (including response to the other side's oral pleadings). The average hearing is over in two hours. Exceptionally, complex cases or cases joined and being heard together, will be allocated further time, but this generally does not exceed 90 minutes total for each party.

Lawyers make their submissions standing and are not required to, and generally do not, wear robes.

After the hearing is closed, the Court proceeds to deliberate and will generally reach a decision on admissibility or merits the same day. However, no advance notice is given and the parties must wait until the adoption of the relevant written decision or judgment.

8. Decisions on admissibility

Where the Court declares a case inadmissible, whether in a committee or Chamber, I–014 there is no provision for appeal. The text of the decision indicates whether the decision was unanimous or by a majority without specifying the exact votes. No dissenting opinions by judges are given on admissibility.

Where admissible, the friendly settlement and merits stage follow.

A case may be restored to the list (Art.37, para.2 of the Convention, r.43(5)). This is not the same thing as an appeal, and only occurs in the most exceptional circumstances, such as the Court's clear mistaken reliance on an erroneous fact (such as the date of introduction).

Merits stage

9. Establishment of the facts

The Court has power to take evidence and hear witnesses (see Annex to the Rules I–015 concerning investigations).

It is rare that the Court is unable sufficiently to determine the factual basis of an application on the documentary material provided by the parties. Where a matter has been adjudicated in a domestic system, at first instance and on appeal, it is likely that the crucial facts have become common ground between the parties or that the differences between them unlikely to be resolved further. The Court, as the

---

[25] r.63. Press and public may be excluded in the interest *inter alia* of the protection of private life or juveniles or in special circumstances where publicity would prejudice the interests of justice (r.63(2)). Very few hearings have been held even partly in camera, mostly involving children.

Commission before it, occasionally carries out fact-finding missions where the location is of particular relevance, for example, conditions of detention cases.[26] Where there are no apparent effective investigations at the domestic level and disagreement between the parties as to the basic facts, the Court has also been forced to take on the role of hearing witnesses, following the practice of fact-finding missions conducted by the Commission from 1995–1999 in cases from the State of emergency region in south-east Turkey.

On such missions, hearings are generally conducted before a delegation of three judges. Witnesses are heard on oath and the parties are present and able to put questions after the judges have done so. An inquisitorial, rather than adversarial approach, is adopted.[27]

10. Friendly settlement procedure and striking out

I–016   The Court informs the parties when it sends the decision on admissibility that it is at their disposal to assist a friendly settlement. It does not however follow the previous practice of the Commission in giving an indication of its provisional opinion of the merits with a view to encouraging settlements. The Registrar of the relevant Chamber will however consult with the parties in appropriate cases concerning the possibility of settlement. The Court does not generally intervene in any formal or direct manner as regards making proposals.

Friendly settlement negotiations are confidential and not referred to in the judgment. Nor are the documents concerning settlement accessible in the file.[28]

The Court is not bound to strike a case out where the parties agree to settle. It is required to continue the examination of the case where human rights so require.[29] However, it has accepted the vast majority of settlements or requests from the applicant to withdraw.[30] In a system of individual applications, it would take very exceptional circumstances for the Court to continue a case where the individual claiming to be a victim of the breach no longer wished, of his free will, to pursue it further.

Where agreement is reached, the parties are generally required to make declarations to that effect and undertake not to seek to refer the case to the Grand Chamber. The Court adopts a judgment striking the case out, which is public and sent to the Committeee of Ministers. The parties are generally left to arrange payment of compensation and reasonable costs between themselves.

The Convention organs, struggling under an ever-increasing workload, have always been favourable towards settlements. Where a lead case has established the Convention position on an issue or a breach is acknowledged and appropriate redress is offered, it might be considered an ineffective use of the Court's time and resources to proceed to a judgment on the merits. Some applicants, understandably, look more to the principle of their cause and prefer to obtain a public, binding judgment against the Government concerned. In *Paez v Sweden*,[31] the old Court struck the case

---

[26] *e.g. Valasinas v Lithuania*, July 24, 2001, ECHR 2001–VIII.
[27] See Annex to the Rules concerning investigations.
[28] r.33(1).
[29] Art.37(1).
[30] The only exceptions appear to be *Tyrer v UK*, April 25, 1978, Series A, No.26, paras 24–27 and *Karner v Austria*, 40016/98, July 24, 2003, ECHR 2003–IX, where the applicant died and the next-of-kin declined to continue the case.
[31] October 30, 1997, R.J.D. 1997–VII.

out under previous r.51, paras 1 and 4 finding that the circumstances disclosed a "fact of a kind to provide a solution of the matter". The Swedish Government had granted the applicant residence permit and the Court considered the matter resolved. Impliedly it saw no point in continuing the case on the basis of the applicant's claims for compensation, the essential object of his complaints about the risk of expulsion to Peru having been met. It also found no necessity to continue the examination of the case from the point of view of clarifying the application of the Convention, previous cases specifying the nature and extent of the State's obligations under Art.3 in such cases.

The applicable provisions for striking out may now be found in Art.37, para.1. Paragraph 1(a) applies where the applicant expresses an intention to withdraw his application. The applicant's consent has not been held necessary when striking out under the other limbs of Art.37. In an expulsion case, where the extradition order against the applicant could no longer be enforced, the new Court proceeded to strike the case out under Art.37, para.1(b) on the basis that the matter had been resolved, notwithstanding the applicant's objections.[32]

The Court has also developed a practice of striking an application out under Art.37, para.1(c) (circumstances rendering it no longer justified to examine the case) where the Government makes a unilateral declaration which acknowledges the breach and provides redress. This will depend on whether, in the circumstances, the Court considers that the unilateral declaration offers a sufficient basis for finding that respect for human rights does not require the continued examination of the case. In *Akman v Turkey*,[33] where the applicant's son had been shot by security forces, the case was struck out on the basis of the unilateral declaration by the Government which expressed regret at the use of excessive force in the case and accepted that this disclosed a breach of Art.2, undertaking to issue appropriate instructions and take necessary measures in future (including effective investigations) as well as to pay the applicant £85,000. The Grand Chamber has since clarified in *Tahsin Acar v Turkey*[34] that in cases of disappearance and killings by unknown perpetrators, where the facts are disputed by the parties, there must as a minimum be an acknowledgement by the Government of a failure to furnish an effective investigation and an undertaking to provide a Convention compliant investigation as redress. Applicants, who in future reject a Government proposal to settle a case on the basis of a concession of a breach and compensation or other form of adequate redress, therefore run the risk of having the case struck out on the basis of a unilateral declaration to the same effect.

Where the Court strikes out a case under any of the above heads, it may award costs to the applicant under r.43, para.4.[35]

11. Judgment on the merits

The Chambers may put specific questions for written observations on the merits or hold an oral hearing on the merits (see Oral Hearings above) before proceeding to adopt a judgment. The procedure at any hearing is largely identical to hearings prior

I–017

---

[32] *Bilasi-Ashri v Austria*, 3314/02, (Dec.) November 26, 2002, ECHR 2002–X; see also *Perna v Italy (Striking Out)*, October 24, 2002, paras 42–50, where the applicant's conviction had been quashed after hearing a witness not previously heard.

[33] June 26, 2001: ECHR 2001–VI.

[34] May 6, 2003, ECHR 2003–VI.

[35] Previously r.44(4), *e.g. Kalantari v Germany*, October 11, 2001, paras 61–64; *JM v UK*, 41518/98, (Dec.) September 28, 2000, ECHR 2000–X.

to admissibility, save that in hearings on the merits the applicant addresses the Court first.

The applicant is invited at this stage (or on communication of the application to the respondent Government in the abbreviated procedure) to submit his claims for just satisfaction at the same time as any further submissions on the merits. The heads of claim—pecuniary, non-pecuniary and costs and expenses—must be covered and details given. A failure to submit claims within the time-limit may result in no award being made.[36] A failure properly to quantify claims may also lead to no award.[37] Occasionally, in cases involving complex financial or property claims, the question of just satisfaction is adjourned and the matter addressed in a separate judgment.

Judges who vote against the majority may, and generally do, give dissenting opinions. Concurring and separate opinions also occur where a judge agrees with the result but not necessarily the reasoning.

Few judgments are delivered in public in Strasbourg, though important Grand Chamber judgments are read out in extract by the President. It is considered sufficient to deliver them in writing and to have them available the same day on the Court's web site.

Chamber judgments become final within three months of delivery, unless one of the parties before the expiry of this time period have requested referral to the Grand Chamber (Art.43, para.1). A panel of five judges of the Grand Chamber examines the referral request and are required by Art.43, para.2 to grant it where the case raises a serious question affecting the interpretation or application of the Convention or a serious issue of general importance. To date they have not given published reasons showing how they approach this assessment. They are however showing extreme restraint in granting requests, from interests of legal certainty and to prevent the referral system becoming an automatic appeal system.[38] No appeal lies to the Grand Chamber from the decision of the panel.[39] Once a case is referred, the Grand Chamber enjoys the full range of judicial powers conferred on the Court and its examination is not necessarily confined to the points of concern raised by the referring party.[40]

A party may within one year from delivery of the judgment request *interpretation of the judgment* (r.79).[41] The request must state precisely the point or points in the operative part of the judgment (the conclusion of the judgment setting out the Court's votes on each part of the case) on which interpretation is required. Where

---

[36] *Ferrantelli and Santangelo v Italy*, August 7, 1996, R.J.D. 1996–III, No.12.

[37] *Ausiello v Italy*, May 25, 1996, R.J.D. 1996–III, No.10.

[38] For recent examples of referred cases, *e.g. Hatton v UK*, July 8, 2003, ECHR 2003–VIII; *Ezeh and Connors v UK*, October 9, 2003, ECHR 2003–X.

[39] *Pisano v Italy (Striking Out)*, October 24, 2002, paras 26–27.

[40] *ibid.*, paras 27–28. This includes admissibility points.

[41] *e.g. Ringeisen v Austria (No.3)*, June 23, 1973, Series A, No.16, para.13; *Allenet de Ribemont v France (interpretation)*, August 7, 1998, R.J.D. 1996–III, No.12, where the Commission asked the Court whether any sum awarded as just satisfaction should be paid without attachment, the Court found that this was an abstract point of interpretation and outside the rule. As regarded the second question as to how the global figure awarded for pecuniary and non-pecuniary damage should be distinguished, it stated that it had not distinguished any percentage, did not need to do so and had no intention of so doing— its judgment was clear and to hold otherwise was modification, not clarification.

the Chamber accepts the request, the other party is invited to make written submissions. A hearing may be held.

A party can also request *revision of a judgment* in the event of discovery of a fact which might have a decisive influence but was not known to the Court at the time and could not reasonably have been known to that party.[42] Such request must be lodged within six months of discovery of the fact. Where the Chamber accepts the request, the other party is invited to make written submissions. A hearing may be held. Strict scrutiny is applied to such requests, the Court taking the view that legal certainty weighs against granting revision requests on anything but an exceptional basis.[43]

12. Intervenors

The Contracting State of which the applicant is a national (if not the respondent State) may intervene as party in the proceedings as a matter of right (Art.36, para.1).[44] The State is informed of its right to intervene in a particular case when the case is communicated to the respondent State and given twelve weeks to inform the Court of its intentions. It may submit written observations and participate in an oral hearing.

Others require the leave of the President, or the invitation of the Court (Art.37, para.2).[45] Requests should be lodged within twelve weeks of the communication to the respondent State, although the President may exceptionally fix different time-limits.[46] Generally, leave is limited to the submission of written observations of a specified maximum length which deal with domestic and international law issues, without arguing the facts and merits of the case. It is very much rarer for non-State intervenors to be given leave to participate in an oral hearing.[47]

I–018

13. Length of Court proceedings

Time taken depends on the current state of the Court's work load, the number of applications pending from a particular country, the complexity of the case and any requirements for gathering further evidence. Cases to which priority have been given have been known to take under a year to reach judgment, under six months in the case of *Pretty v the United Kingdom*. On average, cases fall within the following range:

I–019

---

[42] Revision was granted in *Pardo v France (revision)* July 10, 1996, R.J.D. 1996–III, No.11, where the applicant had produced two letters, previously unobtainable, one of which had been referred to expressly by the Court in the context of lack of substantiation of his complaint. See also *Gustafsson v Sweden (revision)*, R.J.D. 1998–V, No.84.

[43] e.g. *McGinley and Egan v UK* (revision), ECHR 2000–I, para.30.

[44] e.g. Turkey intervened in *Sen v Netherlands*, December 21, 2001.

[45] The Voluntary Euthanasia Society and the Catholic Bishops' Conference of England and Wales were permitted to intervene in *Pretty*, n.13 above, while Liberty made submissions, *inter alia*, in *Christine Goodwin v UK*, (GC), July 11, 2002, ECHR 2002–VI. In *TI v UK* (43844/98, (dec.) March 7, 2000, ECHR 2000–III) concerning the safety of deporting the Tamil applicant from the UK to Germany where a previous asylum application had been refused, the Court invited both the German Government and the UNHCR to make written submissions before deciding on admissibility.

[46] r.44(2).

[47] See *V v UK*, December 12, 1999, ECHR 1999–IX, where permission was given for the lawyers of the parents of the victim, murdered by the applicant, to address the Court briefly.

Committee case	3–12 months
Decision to communicate	3–12 months
Case rejected as inadmissible after communication	15–24 months
Case decided on the merits in a judgment	24–36 months

14. Monitoring compliance

I–020   Pursuant to Art.46, para.2, the Committee of Ministers[48] supervises execution of Court judgments. Its role is to oversee what action is taken by Governments in response to a finding of a violation. When the case is placed on its agenda, it invites the State to inform it of the measures taken, and the matter is automatically recalled on the agenda at intervals of not less than six months. When it is satisfied that a Government has complied, it issues a resolution recording the position and declaring that it has exercised its function. Since the Court rarely hints at what steps would remedy a violation,[49] the Committee of Ministers operates largely independently. It has received criticism not only for the length of time taken to issue a resolution and complete the monitoring process but also in respect of its position in, on occasion, accepting a lack of positive action by a Government as sufficient response.[50] Thus in *Brogan v United Kingdom*, the Committee of Ministers accepted the Government's derogation under Art.15 as complying with the judgment finding a breach of Art.5, para.3.[51] In other cases, it has found it enough for the State to publicise the judgment and draw it to the attention of the relevant authorities.

Under the Committee of Ministers' rules, an applicant may make communications about failure to receive compensation awarded by the Court or any other matter relating to execution.

3. Interim Relief

I–021   Under r.39, the Court may *indicate* that a measure be taken in the interests of the parties or the proper conduct of the proceedings. Though the equivalent measure previously applied by the Commission was not regarded as binding,[52] the Court has recently found in *Mamatkulov and Askarov v Turkey* that a Contracting State subject to a r.39 indication is required to comply and refrain from any act or omission that might prejudice the integrity and effectiveness of the Court's final judgment.[53] Though no violation of Art.3 was found on the merits, the failure to comply with

---

[48] See n.1 above.

[49] It considers that this is outside its role—see, *e.g. Akdivar v Turkey* (Art.50), April 1, 1998, R.J.D. 1998–II, No.69, para.57; *Finucane v UK*, July 1, 2003, para.89.

[50] See, *e.g.* "The Committee of Ministers" by Adam Tomkins, European Human Rights Law Review, Launch issue.

[51] November 29, 1988, Series A, No.145–B E.H.R.R. 117, Resolution DH (90) 23.

[52] *Cruz Varas v Sweden*, March 20, 1991, Series A, No.201, para.102.

[53] Judgment of February 6, 2003, where, notwithstanding the Chamber's indication under Rule 39, Turkey extradited to Uzbekistan two men who had claimed that they would be at risk of torture or inhuman treatment. The Court had regard to international practice, *inter alia*, the International Court of Justice, the Inter-American Court and the UN Committee against torture. Pending before the Grand Chamber.

the request to suspend the extradition of the applicants was found to breach the obligation imposed by Art.34 not to hinder the effective exercise of the right of individual petition.

As the Court nonetheless relies on the good will and co-operation of the Contracting States, it is careful not to abuse this procedure by intervening in domestic affairs without pressing reason. In practice, requests are only made where there is an apparent real and imminent risk of irreparable harm to life and limb (Art.2 or 3 cases). It may be said that as a result there is a very high compliance rate by Contracting States. Most typically, the interim measure requested is the suspension of expulsion of an applicant to a country where there is a risk of serious ill-treatment, for example, a Tamil to Sri Lanka,[54] a deserter to Iran[55], a girl to Tanzania where she claimed to be at risk of female genital mutilation[56] and more recently, suspected Chechen terrorists from Georgia to Russia.[57] While there is a certain presumption that Contracting States provide the necessary guarantees against ill-treatment, the Court has applied r.39 to Turkish Kurds threatened with return to Turkey, while the Commission applied its version of the procedure to an expulsion from France to Spain of a suspected ETA member.[58] The Court may also request information from the Contracting State, for example, regarding guarantees available or request, as in *Ocalan v Turkey*, that the applicant's lawyers be given full access to a detainee.[59]

Rule 39 has also been applied where the risk derives from the effect on health of the measure *per se*, for example where the applicant facing expulsion was in the later stages of a difficult pregnancy with a history of miscarriages[60] and where the applicant AIDS sufferer, who was very ill, would have no access to treatment on deportation from the UK to St Kitts.[61]

While the procedure has been invoked in respect of other types of cases, *e.g.* adoption of children, which may arguably be of an irreparable nature, r.39 has not been applied. Matters of detention, interference with property, for example, are not regarded as necessitating interim measures.[62]

If an applicant intends to request a measure, it is necessary to submit the facts of the case in an outline application, detailing the complaints. It should be shown that domestic remedies have been exhausted (r.39 may not be applied if there are any pending procedures unless these do not have suspensive effect)—copies of the decisions should be provided.[63] The expulsion must also be *imminent*—the date should be provided or it should be be pointed out that removal can lawfully take place without further warning. Any materials substantiating the alleged risk to life or of ill-treatment should be provided, such as medical reports concerning past

---

[54] *Venkadajalasarma v Netherlands*, 58510/00, (Dec.) July 9, 2002.

[55] *Amrollahi v Denmark*, July 11, 2002.

[56] *Lunguli v Sweden*, 33692/02, (Dec.) July 1, 2003.

[57] *Shamayev and 10 others v Georgia and Russia*, 36378/02, (r.39) October 4, 2002.

[58] *e.g. Avcisoy v UK*, 49277/99, (Dec.) February 19, 2002; 31113/96, (Dec.) December 5, 1996.

[59] March 12, 2003, paras 5, 246–242.

[60] 26985/95 (Dec.) May 15, 1996.

[61] *D v UK*, May 2, 1997, R.J.D. 1997–III, No.37.

[62] See however 25849/94 (Dec.) November 16, 1994, where the Commission applied interim measures to a woman allegedly faced with the risk of strict house arrest and other ill-treatment from her husband's family on return to Lebanon.

[63] In UK cases, this generally means the decision of the Secretary of State refusing asylum, the decision of the Adjudicator and Immigration Appeal Tribunal, and the decisions of the courts (High Court and Court of Appeal) on judicial /statutory review application.

incidents of torture, up-to-date reports on conditions in the receiving country (Amnesty International, UNHCR, US State Department country reports, etc.).

Rule 39 requests are dealt with urgently. Assuming there is no time for the matter to be put before a Chamber, the decision is taken by the President of the Section to which the case is allocated. As much time however as possible should be given to allow the necessary procedure to be instituted by the Registry. It is wise to fax the request, with "Rule 39—Urgent" prominently on the first page, and to telephone the Registry either to warn of the arrival of the request or to verify its receipt. If the request is granted, the Government is informed immediately and the matter put before the Chamber for review at an early opportunity. If the request if refused, the case may nonetheless proceed for examination on admissibility and merits in the normal manner. The Practice Direction on Requests for Interim Measures,[64] warns that a failure to make a request with the appropriate expedition or to supply relevant documents, in particular domestic court decisions and any material substantiating the applicant's allegations, may result in the Court being unable to examine the request properly or in good time. It also specifies that in cases of expulsion or extradition, details should be given of the expected date and time of removal as well as the applicant's place of detention and case or reference number.

Measures are generally applied for limited, but renewable periods. Since they rely on the continued existence of the risk, they will not be renewed if that risk disappears.[65] Rule 39 may also be applied to the applicant. This is rare but has occurred in hunger strikes where the Commission or Court requested an applicant to give up the strike until the proceedings have been resolved.

4. Legal Aid and Representation

Procedure

I–022   Legal aid only becomes available when a case is communicated by the Court to the respondent Government.[66] At that stage, declaration of means forms are sent to applicants who have either requested legal aid or it is considered appropriate. Other applicants are informed of the opportunity to apply. The declaration of means must be certified by the relevant domestic authority. This is a formality required by the Rules of Court and insisted on rigidly by some Contracting States. Currently, the certifying body in the UK is the Legal Services Commission, which applies the standard of eligibility for domestic civil legal aid—which is not strictly relevant to Convention proceedings in Strasbourg.

When the Court receives the means form and certification, it sends copies to the Government for comment. Once the Government's comments have been received, or the time-limit expired, and the observations from the Government on admissibility have also been received or the time-limit expired, the President of the Chamber proceeds to decide the application. If granted, offers of legal aid are sent at each stage of the procedure. The applicant's lawyer must sign and return them.

---

[64] See Annex 6.

[65] For example, due to steps taken by the Government or due to the receipt of guarantees against the risk alleged as in the *Shameyev* case, n.57 above, where the Russian Government gave guarantees of unhindered access to medical treatment, legal advice and to the Court and undertook not to apply the death penalty and to protect the applicants' health and safety.

[66] r.91.

When the work covered by the offer has been done, a claim form is sent to the lawyer, requiring bank details. On its return, the Registry forwards the paperwork to the Council of Europe finance division, which has the amounts sent by bank transfer.

The conditions for the grant of legal aid

The Rules of Court impose a condition of financial necessity (*i.e.* the applicant has insufficient means to meet all or part of the costs—r.92(a)). Though there is another criterion, that it is necessary for the proper conduct of the case before the Chamber (r.92(b)), provision of legal aid to needy applicants is generally regarded as axiomatic. However, in cases which form part of a long series on identical issues, legal aid may be granted at a lower, even minimal rate. There are no written guidelines as to what insufficient means are and the Court takes a flexible approach. It is aware that the cost of legal representation is likely to be prohibitive to any person of moderate income and that, where an applicant is pursing a human rights issue, it is in the general interest that it be facilitated. A person on income support or a prisoner with no income is certainly covered. Low to middling salaries may also attract legal aid, as in the case of *Goodwin*, a working journalist. The extent to which other family members' income and means are taken into account is not subject to guidelines. It is only likely to be relevant where a parent/spouse is wealthy and can be reasonably be expected to contribute.   I–023

In practice, it is rare for the UK Government to comment negatively on applications and rare for the Court to refuse.

Level of legal aid

In the vast majority of cases a standard grant of legal aid is made by way of set contributions for specified items of work or costs incurred (see Annex 5, Legal Aid Rates). The rate awarded is generally the maximum amount allowable but may be reduced for submissions which are of particular brevity or concern cases based on an established precedent. The amounts are not generous compared with the level of UK professional fees and are intended rather to be a contribution towards costs and expenses.   I–024

Hearings

For representation at oral hearings, generally a fee for pleading and expenses for one lawyer are paid. Exceptionally, for the UK, expenses for two lawyers, counsel and solicitor, are paid, though only one fee. Applicants will generally be granted expenses for attending. Additional counsel/legal advisers may attend if given leave, uncovered by legal aid needless to say.   I–025

Additional items

Legal aid is not given in respect of any work done without specific request from the Court. Any specific additional items, *e.g.* costs of obtaining transcripts, fees for translations, medical opinions must obtain prior approval.   I–026

Legal representation

I–027   The Rules of Court require that an applicant must be represented by an appropriate lawyer once the case has been communicated to the Government and at any stage where there is an oral hearing (r.36, paras 2 and 3). Generally, a legal representative must be a lawyer resident and qualified to practise in one of the Contracting States.[67] This covers barristers and solicitors from the UK. Anyone else purporting to represent an applicant, for example, an academic or legal officer, must obtain leave from the President. A lawyer who fails to comply with Court procedures or who is otherwise regarded as unsuitable can be refused permission to act in Court proceedings.[68]

While an applicant may introduce his own application therefore, he must generally obtain a lawyer once the case is communicated. He may apply for leave to represent himself or to obtain authorisation for assistance from another person. However, leave is unlikely to be granted by the President where an oral hearing is held. The rule is less rigidly applied in cases following a lead judgment where arguably no further legal argument is required. The Court does not recommend lawyers. Nor does it have any list of approved firms or representatives. An applicant who does not have a lawyer and wishes to instruct one will be generally directed to contact the domestic bar association or its equivalent.

Lawyers should be able to address oral or written submissions to the Court in one of the official languages, French or English. Leave is required to use another language. Applicants in person may use an official language of a Contracting State until the case is communicated and thereafter must also obtain leave if they are unable to switch to English or French.[69]

Unrepresented applicants

I–028   Applicants who obtain leave to represent themselves will only be reimbursed expenses. No claim can be made for hours worked by analogy to legal fees.

---

[67] There is no bar on an applicant from one Contracting State using a lawyer from another, *e.g.* UK lawyers represented Turkish applicants in many of the factfinding cases conducted 1996–2000, despite the objections of the Turkish Government that this inflated the amount of legal costs (*e.g. Kurt v Turkey*, May 25, 1998, R.J.D 1998–III, No.74, para.179).

[68] *e.g. Manoussos v the Czech Republic*, 46488/99, (Dec.) September 7, 2002.

[69] r.36(5).

B. ADMISSIBILITY CHECKLIST

Cases must comply with the grounds of admissibility identified below. A case may   **I–029**
also be struck out before or after admissibility under Art.37 (see below).

Governments are required to raise objections before the decision declaring a case admissible and will be estopped from raising them afterwards. Rule 55 provides "[a]ny plea of inadmissibility must, in so far as its character and the circumstances permit, be raised by the respondent Contracting Party in its written or oral observations on the admissibility of the application . . .". Where however an applicant changes the nature of the application or complaints after the decision on admissibility, or where a new legally relevant procedural event subsequently occurs, estoppel may not apply.[1]

1. Six months[2]

Principle of rule: legal certainty and avoidance of stale complaints[3]

The rule cannot be waived, either by the Court or a respondent Government.[4] Even   **I–030**
if a Government does not raise it, the Court will do so of its own motion.[5]

The Court has stated however that it will not apply the rule with undue formalism which would run counter to the purpose of the Convention as a mechanism for providing effective protection of human rights.[6]

1. When time runs from

(a) *Where there are domestic remedies*

- Time begins running from the day after the final decision in the process of   **I–031**
  exhaustion of domestic remedies in respect of each complaint (see below).

---

[1] *Malama v Greece*, March 1, 2001, ECHR 2001–II, para.40; *NC v Italy*, December 18, 2002, ECHR 2002–X, paras 44–47.

[2] Art.35, para.1 (formerly Art.26).

[3] *e.g.* 10626/83, (Dec.) May 7, 1985, 42 D.R. 205; *Karabardak v Cyprus*, 76575/01, (Dec.) October 22, 2002; *Bulut and Yavuz v Turkey*, 73065/01, (Dec.) May 18, 2002.

[4] *e.g.* 10416/83, (Dec.) January 9, 1995, 38 D.R. 158; *Hay v UK*, 41894/98, (Dec.) October 17, 2000, ECHR 2000–XI where the Government had settled a case in domestic proceedings "without prejudice" to an application to Strasbourg); *Ipek v Turkey*, 39706/98, (Dec.) November 1, 2000.

[5] *Walker v UK*, 34979/97, (Dec.), January 25, 2000, ECHR 2000–I—where the Government made no objection on six months, the Court dismissed it on that basis nonetheless.

[6] *e.g. Fernandez-Molina Gonzalez v Spain*, 64359/01, (Dec.), October 8, 2002—where the applicants could only invoke Art.14 in their *amparo* appeal, it would have been artificial to require them to bring their Art.1 of Protocol No.1 complaints based on the same facts before these proceedings had ended.

The date of the final decision is that when the judgment is rendered orally in public.[7] Where, pursuant to domestic law and practice, the applicant is entitled to be served *ex officio* with a written copy of the judgment, time starts to run on the date the judgment is received.[8] Where it is not announced in public and there is no provision for service, the relevant date is that when the applicant or his lawyer are informed of the final decision.[9] The date is however taken from the notification of the lawyer, even if the applicant becomes aware later.[10] Where the reasons for the decision are relevant for the application to the Court, time runs from the date on which the full text is received, rather than the serving of the operative parts of the decision.[11]

(b) *Where there are no domestic remedies*

I–032

- Where the complaints relates to a specific act or omission:
  from the date of the act or omission, or from the date of knowledge of that act or its effect or prejudice on the applicant.[12]
- Where there is sequence of events linked in time and place:
  from the end of the episode, depending on whether it is practical to expect complaint earlier.[13]
- Where the applicant makes use of a remedy which later proves to be ineffective for the purposes of exhaustion of domestic remedies:
  from the moment that he becomes aware or should reasonably have become aware of this situation.[14]

2. When time stops running

I–033

- Date of introduction of the application before the Court—this is in general that communication[15] which sets out, even summarily, the object of the application.[16] In practice to introduce an application, a qualifying communi-

---

[7] *e.g. Loveridge v UK*, 39641/98, (Dec.) October 23, 2001.

[8] *Worm v Austria*, August 29, 1997, Reports 1997–V, No.45, para.33.

[9] *e.g.* 21034/92, (Dec.) January 9, 1995, 80–A D.R. 87. See also *Haralambidis v Greece*, 36706/97, March 29, 2001, para.38, where the date ran from the finalisation and signature of the judgment as in Greece there was no provision for service of the judgment.

[10] *e.g.* 14056/88, (Dec.) May 28, 1991, 70 D.R. 208; *Keskin v Turkey*, 36091/97, (Dec.) September 7, 1999.

[11] *e.g.* 9299/81, (Dec.) March 13, 1984, 36 D.R. 20; 34728/97, (Dec.) October 20, 1997. See also cases where decisions only become final at a later date, *e.g.* 12077/86, (Dec.) December 9, 1991, 71 D.R. 13.

[12] *e.g.* 8440/78, (Dec.) July 16, 1980, 21 D.R. 138 (actual effect of measure); 12015/86, (Dec.) July 6, 1988, 57 D.R. 108 (date of knowledge); *Finucane v UK*, 29178/95, (Dec.) July 2, 2002 (date of knowledge of new information about alleged security force collusion); *Dennis v UK*, 76573/01, (Dec.) July 2, 2002 (date of knowledge of relatives of victims of the Marchioness tragedy that the bodies had been mutilated).

[13] 22280/93, (Dec.) January 9, 1995, where the six-month time limit ran from the end of the raid of the village (which took place over a three-day period).

[14] 23654/94, (Dec.) May 15, 1995, 81–A D.R. 76: while the applicant applied to the public prosecutor in May 1993, he had received advice that this remedy was ineffective and he should have introduced his complaints when he became aware of this situation. See, conversely, *Paul and Aubrey Edwards v UK*, 46477/99, (Dec.) June 7, 2001: the applicants became aware of the non-availability of remedies after publication of the inquiry report into their son's death.

[15] Although the word used in r.47, para.5 is "communication", the Convention organs have not held in any decision that an application may be introduced by telephone. It is unlikely that this would be the

cation must identify the applicant, the factual basis of each complaint and the violations of the Convention alleged to result.[17] Failure to specify all complaints in the introductory communication may lead to application of the six month time limit to those raised at a later stage.[18]

The date taken is, according to the practice in UK cases[19]:

- the date written on the letter (an undue gap between this date and arrival will be regarded with caution)[20];
- where the letter is undated, from the postmark on the envelope;
- if post mark illegible, date of arrival at the Court (stamped in Registry);
- the date of arrival of the fax version at the Court.

3. Effect of undue delay

- An unreasonable or unexplained delay in communications after the original introductory letter may result in the first letter ceasing to be regarded as introducing the application.[21] The date of introduction is then taken from the later communication in which the applicant re-affirms his intention to revive or continue the case.

I–034

A holding introductory letter will only serve its purpose if the application is pursued actively. If there are intervening domestic events which render the case premature, it is only possible to keep the file active in the Court for a limited period. It will either have to be pursued regardless or where effective domestic remedies are

case, save in an extreme emergency excluding the possibility of written notification. See 34728/97, (Dec.) October 20, 1997, 91–A D.R. 85, where a purported introduction of an application by telephone was not accepted.

[16] r.47(5), *e.g. Baumann v Austria*, 39917/98, (Dec.) September 4, 2001.

[17] There is a certain flexibility, *e.g.* a reference to interference with freedom of expression is enough without mentioning Art.10. See however *Latif v UK*, 72819/01, (Dec.) January 29, 2004, where a bald reference to a trial and appeal was not sufficient to indicate the object of the application under the Convention.

[18] See *Allan v UK*, 48539/99, (Dec.) August 28, 2001, where the first communications which raised specific allegations under Art.6 did not mention the drawing of inferences from silence under police questioning. The general reference to unfairness was not sufficient to introduce this aspect.

[19] The Court has yet to rule definitively in a case in which the different possibilities make a decisive difference. There is an argument, based on analogy with r.38, para.2 which concerns the submission of written pleadings, that the date of the letter is irrelevant and that the material date is "the certified date of dispatch of the document or, if there is none, the actual date of receipt at the Registry."

[20] See *Arslan v Turkey*, 36747/02, (Dec.) November 11, 2002, ECHR 2002–X—the letter was dated 12 April and postmarked April 19, whereas the six-month time limit expired on April 13, the Court dismissed the complaint as out of time, there being no explanation for the delay in submitting the letter to the post office.

[21] r.47, para.5 *in fine* referring to "good cause" for changing the date of introduction: this practice is to prevent an application lying dormant and thus bypassing the spirit and purpose of the six-month rule. See 10626/83, n.3 above; *Chalkley v UK*, 63831/00, (Dec.) September 26, 2002, where the Government objected to the long periods of delay in the applicant's communications but the Court did not find that the applicant's representatives had acted in an abusive or unreasonable manner overall and considered that they kept in touch with the Court with sufficient regularity to prevent any appearance of the matter lying dormant; *Gaillard v France*, 47337/99, (Dec.) July 11 2000, where a ten month lapse in returning the application form led to a change in the introduction date; *Nee v Ireland*, 52787/99, (Dec.) January 30, 2003, gap of one year in returning application form led to later date being taken as date of introduction.

being exhausted, be re-introduced within six months of the final effective decision in those proceedings.

4. Special circumstances suspending the period

I–035   Only very limited circumstances of *force majeure* are regarded as suspending the running of the period:

- illness and mental incapacity have not been accepted in any case[22];
- detention is not sufficient in itself, unless it is proved that outside contact with others was totally barred;
- ignorance of the Convention or its case law is not enough. In particular, time is not suspended by applications to non-effective remedies such as the Parliamentary Commissioner of Administration or applications for discretionary or exceptional remedies (*e.g.* requests to the Home Secretary for a reference to the Court of Appeal, applications to *ex gratia* criminal injuries compensation funds or supervisory review procedures instigated after a "final" decision[23]).

5. Continuing situations

I–036   Where there is a continuing situation, act or omission or state of affairs, *e.g.* a state of legislation which continuously affects the exercise of a guaranteed right or freedom,[24] the six month time limit does not apply. A distinction must be drawn between a situation disclosing a situation of ongoing violation and the after-effect or consequence of a breach which occurred and ended at a particular point in time.[25]

2. Exhaustion of domestic remedies[26]

1. Principle of the rule

I–037   Before an international jurisdiction decides whether a State has violated a human right, the State should have the opportunity to remedy the matter itself. The Strasbourg organs should primarily be a supervisory last resort and the main business of enforcing human rights should be done by domestic authorities who are in the best position to do so.[27]

---

[22] 6317/73, July 10, 1975, 2 D.R. 87: mere reference to a bad state of health was insufficient; 25435/94 (Dec.) February 20, 1995 where the applicants both suffered from mental illness, this did not prevent them from complying with the six-month time limit given that they were able to pursue domestic proceedings at that time.

[23] *e.g.* concerning supervisory review, *Sardin v Russia*, 69582/01, (Dec.) February 12, 2004.

[24] *e.g. Dudgeon v UK*, October 22, 1981, Series A, No.45; 4 E.H.R.R. 149 (legislation banning adult consensual homosexual acts); *Malama*, n.1 above, para.35 (ongoing failure to pay compensation); *Loizidou v Turkey*, March 23, 1995, Series A, No.310; 23 E.H.R.R. 513, (continuing interference with property rights of the legal owner of the land).

[25] *e.g.* 25681/94, (Dec.) April 1, 1996, 85–A D.R. 134 where the traumatic personal suffering of the families of the victims of "Bloody Sunday" did not constitute a continuing situation; *Posti and Rahko v Finland*, September 24, 2002, para.40; *Malhous v Czech Republic*, 33701/96, (Dec.) December 12, 2000 where deprivation of ownership rights was regarded as an instantaneous act.

[26] Art.35, para.1.

[27] *e.g. Akdivar v Turkey*, September 16, R.J.D., 1996–IV, No.15, para.65.

2. Application of the rule

- The burden is on the Government invoking the rule to prove the existence I–038 in theory and practice of available and sufficient remedies at the relevant time.[28] However once this burden of proof has been satisfied it falls to the applicant to establish that the remedy was in fact exhausted, was for some reason not effective or adequate in the circumstances of the case[29] or there existed special circumstances absolving him from the requirement.[30]

- A Government may not use arguments which are incompatible with those which they relied on in domestic court proceedings.[31]

- A Government must generally invoke the rule prior to the Court's decision on admissibility.[32] Failure by the Government to respond to communication of complaints may result in the matter going be default and any issues as to effectiveness of remedies being dealt with on the merits, where relevant.[33] The Convention organs have nonetheless on occasion relied on an argument of non-exhaustion which has not been raised by the Government.[34]

- The applicant is generally required to raise in substance in the domestic proceedings the complaints made in Strasbourg and in compliance with the formal requirements and time-limits imposed by domestic law.[35] This includes any procedural means which might have prevented a breach of the Convention.[36] It is sufficient for the substance of the Convention complaint to be put before the domestic courts, even if it is not formulated expressly.[37]

---

[28] *e.g. Deweer v Belgium*, February 27, 1980, Series A, No.35, para.26; *Horvat v Croatia*, July 26, 2002, ECHR 2002–VIII, para.45, where a constitutional application relied on by the Government could not be regarded with sufficient certainty as an effective remedy; *Zhu v UK*, 36790/97, (Dec.) September 12, 2000, where there was no established authority indicating damages for breach of duty lay in such a case and the mere possibility of such a remedy was "too speculative" to be deemed an effective remedy.

[29] *Grisankova and Grisankovs v Latvia*, 36117/02, (Dec.) February 13, 2003, ECHR 2003–II; *Caldas Ramirez de Arrellano v Spain*, 68874/01, (Dec.) January 28, 2003, ECHR 2003–I.

[30] *Akdivar*, n.27 above, para.68, where the total passivity of the national authorities in the face of serious allegations of misconduct by state agents was given as such a factor and shifted the burden of proof rendering it incumbent on the Government to show what they had done in response to the scale and seriousness of the matters complained of. See also *Aksoy v Turkey*, December 18, 1996, R.J.D. 1996–IV, No.26; 23 E.H.R.R. 553 where the applicant was exempted in view of the failure by the State prosecutor to react to his injuries incurred during custody; and *Selmouni v France*, July 28, 1999, ECHR 1999–V, paras 78–81, where delays and inaction in the investigation rendered the alleged remedy ineffective.

[31] *e.g.* 23892/94, (Dec.) October 16, 1995, 83–A D.R. 57 (citing *Kolompar v Belgium*, September 24, 1992, Series A, No.235; 16 E.H.R.R. 197).

[32] See r.55; *Malama*, n.1 above; *NC v Italy*, n.1 above, where the Government were estopped from raising a non-exhaustion point based on a fact arising after the decision on admissibility due to undue delay in bringing it to the attention of the Court.

[33] *e.g. Ergi v Turkey*, 23818/94, (Dec.) March 2, 1995, 80–A D.R. 157.

[34] 20946/92, (Dec.) August 8, 1994, where the applicant had not applied for judicial review in respect of complaints of opening by a Scottish prison of his letters from his solicitor, following the English Court of Appeal decision holding *ultra vires* a prison rule allowing such interference on wider grounds than merely to ascertain if they *were bona fides* communications. Also on the first examination of applications, clear cases of non-exhaustion will be rejected by the Court of its own motion.

[35] *Cardot v France*, March 3, 1991, Series A, No.200; 13 E.H.R.R. 853. Concerning procedural mistakes, *e.g.* 18079/91, (Dec.) December 4, 1991, 72 D.R. 263. The shortness of time-limits for submitting evidence could, arguably, render compliance with procedural rules unrealistic, *e.g.* in asylum cases (see *Bahaddar v Netherlands*, February 19, R.J.D. 1998–I, para.45).

[36] *e.g. Barbera, Messegue and Jabardo v Spain*, December 6, 1988, Series A No.146; 11 E.H.R.R. 360.

[37] *Gasus Dosier-unde Förder technick GmbH v Netherlands*, February 23, 1995, Series A, No.306–B; 20

- The rule does not apply to administrative practice of violation, since in the face of State connivance or acquiescence the system will be considered globally ineffective.[38]

Convention approach

I–039

- Remedies must be real and practical and not theoretical or illusory,[39] *e.g.* genuine fear of reprisals, intimidation.
- Account will be taken not only of the personal circumstances of the applicant, but the general legal and political context in which the alleged remedies operate.[40]
- An unduly formalistic approach is not to be taken by the Convention organs which will apply a certain degree of flexibility.[41]

Remedies must:

- be effective, *i.e.* capable of providing redress for the complaint (*e.g.* power to recommend is not enough as in the Parole Board dealing with post-tariff life sentences, the Board of Visitors, ombudsmen[42]); the speed of the procedure may also be relevant to its effectiveness;[43] the remedy must be capable of remedying directly the state of affairs[44];
- form part of the normal process of redress and involving normal use of the remedy, *e.g.* not cover exceptional or discretionary remedies such as requests for *ex gratia* compensation or for re-opening of judicial proceedings[45];

E.H.R.R. 403, where the applicant had not relied on Art.1 of Protocol No.1 expressly before Dutch courts, relying rather on Art.6, the Court was not impressed by the fact that the applicant had not invoked Art.1 of Protocol No.1 since in any event it did provide the courts with the opportunity of preventing or putting right the alleged violation of that provision. The purpose of the rule is to allow the Contracting States the opportunity of putting right violations (para.48).

[38] *e.g. Donnelly v UK*, 5577–5583/72, (Dec.) December 15, 1975, 4. D.R. 4. See Pt IIB: Torture, inhuman and degrading treatment.

[39] *Akdivar*, (Dec.) October 19, 1994, n.27 above.

[40] *Akdivar*, n.27 above, para.69.

[41] *Cardot*, n.35 above, para.34.

[42] *e.g.* 11192/84, (Dec.) May 14, 1987, 52 D.R. 227; *Lehtinen v Finland*, 39076/97, (Dec.) October 14, 1999, ECHR 1999–VII.

[43] 15530–1/89, (Dec.) October 10, 1992, 72 D.R. 169; *Tomé de Mota v Portugal*, 32082/96, (Dec.) December 2, 1999, ECHR 1999–IX; *Pallanich v Austria*, January 30, 2001, para.30.

[44] 12724/87, (Dec.) May 3, 1989, 61 D.R. 206; 15404/89, (Dec.) April 16, 1991, 70 D.R. 262; *Civet v France*, September 28, 1999, ECHR 1999–VI, para.43.

[45] 7729/76, (Dec.) December 17, 1976, 7 D.R. 164; 8850/80, (Dec.) October 7, 1980, 22 D.R. 232; 19117/91, (Dec.) January 12, 1994, 76–A D.R. 70 (request for re-trial not included unless domestic law establishes that this provides an effective remedy); 14545/89, (Dec.) October 9, 1990, 66 D.R. 238 (request for exercise of ministerial discretion to award compensation not included); 20348/92, (Dec.) March 3, 1994 (where power of Secretary of State shown to have been rarely exercised); *Reilly v UK*, 53731/00, (Dec.) June 26, 2003 (application to the Criminal Cases Review Commission not generally regarded as an effective remedy: though in this case where the applicant had not appealed after his trial and the Court of Appeal had subsequently clarified domestic law and reviewed similar cases, it was expected that the applicant apply to have the matter brought to the Court of Appeal via the CCRC). Normal use of remedies, *e.g.* 16278/90, (Dec.) May 3, 1993 74 D.R. 93; 19092/91, (Dec.) October 11, 1993, 75 D.R. 207.

- be accessible[46]: it may be relevant if an applicant is barred from taking action due, for example, to lack of money or legal representation, where these are practically essential[47];
- offer reasonable prospects of success[48]; the Commission has long stated that a mere doubt as to the prospect of success in going to court does not exempt from exhaustion. Where case-law is unclear, contradictory or in the process of ongoing interpretation, an applicant may be expected to pursue an action or appeal which allows the courts to rule on the issues.[49] Where a statute provides new provisions, it may be necessary to put them to the test even where their scope or application is untried and unknown. Counsel's opinion that there is no prospect of success may be enough to indicate that a remedy or appeal would not be effective.[50] The fact that an identical claim has been dismissed may be sufficient to indicate that there is no prospect of success;

Also
- if there is more than one remedy available, an individual is not required to try more than one[51];
- an applicant is generally not required to try the same body again by way of a repeated request or application.[52]

(a) *Particular remedies in the UK*

Note: these are generally required but will always be subject to the principles above and to the provisions or practice of domestic law as it develops.

(I) CRIMINAL

- Application for permission to appeal against conviction and/or sentence to the Court of Appeal, renewing application from single judge to the full court[53]; it is generally assumed that appeal to the House of Lords is an

I–040

---

[46] *e.g.* 14545/89, n.45 above; 12604/86, (Dec.) July 10, 1991, 70 D.R. 125; 14986/89, (Dec.) July 3, 1991, 70 D.R. 240 (where remedies brought to attention of foreign detainee in language she did not understand).

[47] The Convention organs have generally expected applicants to take proceedings themselves where they have been refused legal aid; in very complex proceedings, as in *Airey v Ireland*, October 9, 1979, Series A, No.32; (1979–80) 2 E.H.R.R. 305, lack of legal aid could conceivably form a ground of exemption.

[48] *Akdivar*, n.27 above, para.68.

[49] 20357/92, (Dec.) March 7, 1994, 76–A D.R. 80; concerning constitutional testing, *e.g.* 18760/91, (Dec.) December 1, 1993.

[50] *e.g.* 10000/82, July 4, 1983, 33 D.R. 247; 24196/94, (Dec.) January 22, 1996, 84–A D.R. 72—where counsel advised no hopes of success and it was accepted that this indicated the remedy was ineffective; see however 10789/84, (Dec.) October 11, 1984, 40 D.R. 278 where counsel's doubts did not absolve the applicant from applying to the House of Lords, especially where the Court of Appeal gave leave in a similar case shortly afterwards; *Mogos v Germany*, 78084/01, (Dec.) March 27, 2003.

[51] *McCann and others*, (Dec.) September 3, 1993; 19092/91, n.45 above; *Sargin and Yagci v Turkey*, 14116–7/88 (Dec.), May 11, 1989, 61 D.R. 250; *France*, 14838/89, (Dec.) March 5, 1991, 69 D.R. 286. Where there is a choice of remedies, the selection of the appropriate one is primarily for the applicant— *Airey*, n.47 above, para.23; *Hilal v UK*, 45276/99, (Dec.) February 8, 2000, the applicant's decision to pursue one avenue of appeal rather than another was not unreasonable and did not exclude the courts from examining the relevant issues.

[52] *Granger v UK*, (Dec.) May 9, 1988; 7729/76, n.45 above.

[53] *e.g. Reilly*, n.45 above.

exceptional remedy though there might be in a particular case a point of
law of general public importance which might be reasonably be expected to
be pursued[54];

(II) CIVIL

I–041

- Generally in a civil case, the highest avenue of appeal where there is a
prospect of success is the Court of Appeal; whether it is necessary to go to
the House of Lords may depend on the nature of the claims and the existing
state of case law[55];
- child care cases:
  - appeal may not be required to the Court of Appeal due to its limited
  intervention on the assessment of facts but will depend, *inter alia*, on
  nature of the complaints about the proceedings, counsel's opinion as to
  the existence of grounds of appeal, whether the Court of Appeal has
  intervened in the exercise of the particular type of discretion by a first
  instance judge before.
- prisoners:
  - for matters of internal discipline and regulation, petition to the prison
  authorities/Secretary of State in relation to the application of norms is
  expected though not in respect of the content of those norms[56]; the
  Board of Visitors generally is not effective as without binding powers
  of decision; judicial review may not be effective due to its limited scope
  of review but this may depend on the nature of the claims made and
  the existence of case law showing the complaints show a prospect that
  the court will examine them in substance[57]; in respect of assault, ill-
  treatment, negligence, the appropriate civil proceedings are generally
  expected;
- planning:
  - appeal is from Inspectors and decisions of the Secretary of State to the
  High Court, notwithstanding the limited scope of review, where the
  matters of complaint may arguably be considered by the court in some
  manner[58];
- immigration and expulsion:
  - appeals to adjudicators, immigration appeal tribunal where such lie;
  judicial or statutory review may be required where risk to life or limb
  is concerned (see Part IIB section Immigration and expulsion) or in
  other cases, depending on whether the nature of the complaints falls
  within the scope of the limited review and having regard to previous
  precedents.[59]

---

[54] *e.g.* 10789/84, n.50 above.
[55] *e.g.* 20075/92, (Dec.) August 31, 1994: there were conflicting decisions of the Court of Sessions and
Court of Appeal, which could have been ruled on by the House of Lords on appeal.
[56] *Silver v UK*, March 25, 1983, Series A, No.61; 5 E.H.R.R. 347.
[57] *e.g.* 13669/88, (Dec.) March 7, 1990, 65 D.R. 245; 20946/92, n.34 above.
[58] *e.g. Bryan v UK*, November 22, 1995, Series A, No.335–A; 21 E.H.R.R. 342.
[59] *e.g.* 14507/89, (Dec.) April 2, 1990, 65 D.R. 296, judicial review ineffective for discretionary decision
refusing entry of non-national wife.

3. Manifestly ill-founded[60]

- Complaint unsubstantiated or unsupported by the material submitted; I–042
- The facts complained of do not disclose an interference in the enjoyment of the right invoked.[61]
- Act or decision complained of discloses *prima facie* an interference but justified on grounds contained in the provisions of the Convention, *e.g.* child removed from parents but circumstances support the view that it is necessary to protect the rights of the child.
- the applicant has ceased to be a victim.[62] An individual may no longer claim to be a victim of a violation of the Convention where the national authorities have acknowledged, either expressly or in substance,[63] the breach of the Convention and afforded redress.[64] Also, where, for example, an applicant accepts a sum of compensation in settlement of the civil claim before the domestic courts and thereby renounces further use of local remedies, he or she can no longer claim to be a victim.[65]

4. Incompatibility

1. Incompatibility *ratione temporis*[66]

- Where the complaint relates to events which occurred before a Contracting I–043
State's acceptance of the right of individual petition under Art.34 (before 1 November 1998, former Art.25 for cases introduced before the Commission or former Art.46 for the acceptance of the old Court's jurisdiction) it must be rejected as incompatible *ratione temporis* where the State has specified that its ratification is prospective only.[67] Without such stipulation it will be regarded as retrospective and the Convention organs will be competent to examine the complaints, subject to the other admissibility criteria.[68]

Note: where a complaint is about the length of proceedings covering a period before and after acceptance of the right of individual petition, the prior period may

---

[60] Art.35, para.3 (formerly Art.27, para.2).

[61] *e.g.* 24875/94 (Dec.) September 6, 1996, 86–A D.R. 74, where the operation of child support legislation was not such as to disclose any lack of respect for family life.

[62] *e.g.* there was unfairness at trial but a later acquittal on appeal (*e.g. Doubtfire v UK*, 31825/96, (Dec.) April 23, 2002, where the applicant had the possibility of applying for compensation for the conviction and detention served). This head is to be distinguished from the head of incompatibility *ratione personae* below—where the applicant is found not to be a victim of the alleged interference.

[63] The acknowledgement must be sufficiently clear, *e.g. Jensen v Denmark*, (Dec.) September 20, 2001, ECHR 2001–X, where the court reduced the applicant's sentence to reflect the delay in proceedings but refused to acknowledge any breach of Art.6. In *Labita v Italy*, April 6, 2000, ECHR 2000–IV, para.143, the Court referred to lack of any acknowledgment, express or implied, by the court, when awarding compensation, that the pre-trial detention was excessive.

[64] *Eckle v Germany*, July 15, 1982, Series A, No.51, para.66; *Dalban v Romania*, ECHR 1999–VI, para.44; *Posokhov v Russia*, March 4, 2003, ECHR 2003–IV; *Rechachi and Abdelhafid v UK*, (Dec.) June 10, 2003–IV, where the applicants received substantial *ex gratia* payments for detention without proper legal basis.

[65] *e.g. Caraher v UK*, 41894/98, (Dec.) January 11, 2000, ECHR 2000–IX; *Hay v UK*, 41894/98, (Dec.) October 17, 2000, ECHR 2000–XI.

[66] Art.37, para.3 (former Art.27 para.2).

[67] *e.g. Veeber v Estonia* (No.1), July 11, 2000, paras 54–55—the Court would retain jurisdiction in situations of continuous breach extending beyond the relevant date.

[68] *e.g.* 9559/81, (Dec.) May 9, 1983, 33 D.R. 158.

be taken into account in assessing the reasonableness of the later period (see Part IIB: Fair trial, Length of proceedings).

2. Incompatibility *ratione loci*[69]

I–044   • Where complaints are based on events in a territory outside the Contracting State and there is no link between those events and any authority within the jurisdiction of the Contracting State.[70]

3. Incompatibility *ratione personae*[71]

I–045   This includes:
- complaint against a State which has not signed the Convention or the relevant protocol;
- complaint against an individual or body for which the State is not responsible[72];
- where the applicant is not a victim of the events or measures which base the allegations.[73] A person may claim to be a victim where he is directly affected by a measure—it is not necessary to show damage.[74]

4. Incompatibility *ratione materiae*[75]

I–046   This includes:
- where a person invokes a right not included in the Convention[76];

---

[69] Art.35, para.3 (former Art.27, para.2).

[70] This is likely to arise only where an applicant complains of matters within an overseas territory for which the Contracting State has not extended its acceptance of the right of individual petition under Art.56 (former Art.63): *e.g. Yonghong v Portugal*, 50887/99, (Dec.) November 25, 1999, ECHR 1999–IX, concerning Macao.

[71] Art.35, para.3 (former Art.27, para.2).

[72] *e.g.* lawyers (unless there is an issue that a State-appointed lawyer failed to assure the defence of an accused in circumstances for the which the domestic courts should have taken responsibility—see Pt IIA: Fair Trial, Legal representation in criminal proceedings) or, commonly, neighbours or private employers (assuming no positive obligation arose on the State to prevent the interference by the private person or body).

[73] *e.g.* where a person complains on behalf of another without the necessary authority; where the person cannot claim to be affected by the measures (*e.g. Agrotexim v Greece*, October 24, 1995, Series A, No.330; 21 E.H.R.R. 250: shareholders cannot claim to be victims of interferences with the rights of the company in the absence of direct effect on the property rights in the shares). Where organisations bring applications in their own name, their own rights have to be affected, *e.g.* 15404/89, n.44 above, the trade union was not affected by the broadcasting restrictions though its members were.

[74] *e.g. Dudgeon*, n.24 above, para.41, referring to continuous and direct effect on private life from legislation prohibiting adult homosexual acts irrespective of the fact that the applicant had not been subject to a measure of implementation; *Wassink v Netherlands*, September 27, 1990, Series A, No.185-A: status of "victim" may exist even where there is no damage, which is relevant rather to the application of Art.41 (just satisfaction for pecuniary or non-pecuniary damage).

[75] Art.35, para.3 (former Art.27, para.2).

[76] *e.g.* right to a job, or to minimum wage, or certain standard of living (*e.g.* 6807/75, (Dec.) December 10, 1975, 3 D.R. 153; 11776/85, (Dec.) March 4, 1986, 46 D.R. 251) right to driving licence (7462/76, (Dec.) March 7, 1977 9 D.R. 112), to obtain a prosecution against another person, right to political asylum (21808/93, (Dec.) September 8, 1993, 75 D.R. 264), free choice of doctor (19898/92, (Dec.) August 30, 1993, 75 D.R. 223), right to conscientious objection (17086/90, (Dec.) December 6, 1991, 72 D.R. 245).

- where the person's complaints fall outside the scope of particular rights invoked.[77]

5. Substantially the same[78]

- Where the complaints are substantially the same as a matter which has already been examined:
- by the Court; or
- by another procedure of international investigation or settlement[79]; and
- it contains no new, relevant information.

I–047

New, relevant facts may include: further lapse of time in the length of proceedings already examined by the Court[80] continuation of a period in remand[81]; where an application was rejected for non-exhaustion and the applicant has terminated the domestic proceedings; the discovery of new evidence relevant to the previous complaints.[82] They do not include legal arguments concerning the interpretation of the Convention that the applicant did not submit in the prior application.[83]

6. Abuse of petition[84]

It may be applied in cases of:
- forgery; fraud; deliberate misrepresentation;
- vexatious and repeated applications of a similar nature[85];
- claim based on facts for which the applicant is himself responsible[86];

I–048

---

[77] *e.g.* where the applicant complains of the fairness of proceedings under Art.6 which do not involve the determination of a criminal charge or civil rights (*e.g. Maaouia v France*, October 5, 2000, ECHR 2000–X, Art.6 not applicable to asylum or expulsion proceedings); no right to adopt contained in Art.12 (*Frette v France*, 36515/97, (Dec.) June 12, 2001).

[78] Art.35, para.2(b) (former Art.27, para.1(b)).

[79] *e.g.* 11603/85, (Dec.) January 20, 1987, 50 D.R. 228 (where it was not the applicants who had brought the complaints before the ILO); 16358/90, (Dec.) December 10, 1990, 73 D.R. 214 (where the complaints were substantially the same as those examined by an organ of the ILO); 17512/90, (Dec.) July 6, 1992, 73 D.R. 214 (applicants' complaints substantially the same as those brought by them before the UN Human Rights Committee 'HRC'); *Smirnova v Russia*, 46133/99 and 48183/99, (Dec.) October 3, 2002 (where the complaint before the Court was wider in scope than that brought by one applicant before the HRC).

[80] 8233/78, (Dec.) October 3, 1979, 17 D.R. 122.

[81] 9621/81, (Dec.), October 13, 1983, 33 D.R. 217.

[82] *e.g.* 23956/94, (Dec.) November 28, 1994, concerning new information about the applicant prisoner's security status relevant to his previous complaints about transfer/visiting restrictions.

[83] 8206/78, (Dec.) July 10, 1981, 25 D.R. 147.

[84] Art.35, para.3 (former Art.27, para.2).

[85] *e.g.* 13284/87, (Dec.) October 15, 1987, 54 D.R. 214 abuse found on the fifth application. The Commission held that it was not its function to deal with a succession of ill-founded and querulous complaints, which created unnecessary work incompatible with its function of ensuring the implementation of the Convention and which hindered it in that function.

[86] *e.g.* where the applicant complained of the length of extradition proceedings, the Commission considered that this was largely the result of the applicant jumping bail and going into hiding to avoid arrest (*Ireland*, 9742/82, (Dec.), March 2, 1982, 32 D.R. 251)

- deliberate, flagrant breach of procedural rules[87];
- abusive contents of submissions.[88]

Political motivations

The fact that applicants may be pursuing a political goal or purpose of some kind is generally not sufficient to disclose abuse. The Convention organs have not found it abusive for applicants to use the Strasbourg procedure as part of a pressure campaign or publicity to put pressure on a State or to influence public opinion subject to the proviso that the complaints are based on true facts, not unsupported by the evidence or concerning matters outside the scope of the Convention.[89]

7. Striking out

I–049   The Court may proceed to strike a case from its list under Art.37 (former Art.30) where:

- the applicant does not intend to pursue his application.[90] This includes withdrawal by the applicant, where there has been an informal settlement with the Government[91] or where the applicant has lost interest in pursuing the case[92];
- where the matter has been resolved, for example, by a settlement between the parties or the situation about which the applicant is complaining has ceased to place him at risk of a violation[93]; in the latter circumstance, it is not relevant that the applicant wishes to continue with his complaints, as the Court will examine whether there remains any objective justification for pursuing the application, namely whether the circumstances complained of directly by the applicant still obtain and whether the effects of a possible violation of the Convention on account of those circumstances have been redressed[94];
- where for any other reason the Court finds it no longer justified to continue the examination of the application[95]; where, for example, the applicant has

---

[87] e.g. revealing to the press confidential documents. Minor inadvertent breaches are likely to attract a warning.

[88] *Stamoulakatos v UK*, 27567/95, (Dec.) April 9, 1997; *Duringer v France*, 61164/00, (Dec.) February 4, 2002, where the applicants made repeated insulting accusations against Court judges, Registry lawyers and State officials.

[89] e.g. 8317/78, (Dec.) May 15, 1980, 20 D.R. 44 and 11208/84, (Dec.) March 4, 1986, 46 D.R. p.182—where the Government alleged the prisoners' complaints were part of a concerted campaign to get political status. Also *Akdivar*, n.27 above, para.54, where the Government alleged applications by Kurds were abusive as part of a propaganda campaign by the PKK to undermine the State.

[90] Art.37, para.1(a).

[91] *Swaby v UK*, 65822/01, (Dec.) May 23, 2002, where the applicant withdrew application on *ex gratia* award from Government.

[92] e.g. failure to respond to requests for information, observe time-limits without reasonable explanation, notify a change of address or keep in contact with legal representative (e.g. *Feal-Martinez and Pearson v UK*, 1309/02, (Dec.) July 1, 2003).

[93] Art.37, para.1(b), e.g. *Tsavachidis v Greece*, January 21, 1999, where a friendly settlement was reached on the basis of compensation and an assurance of no further surveillance of jehovahs' witnesses on grounds of their religion; *Abdouni v France*, February 27, 2001, where the applicant was no longer at risk of expulsion.

[94] *Pisano v Italy*, October 24, 2002, para.42: pending the Court's examination of complaints about an unfair trial, including failure to hear a witness B., the applicant's conviction was quashed following a retrial at which B. was heard. He was also able to apply for compensation for the wrongful conviction.

[95] Art.37, para.1(c).

died[96]; there has been a unilateral declaration by a Government acknowledging the breach and providing adequate redress[97]; or where the circumstances are such that the Court is unable to continue an effective examination[98]; where there has been deliberate and manipulative breach of confidentiality rules.[99]

The Court may nonetheless continue the examination of a case in any of the above where respect of Human Rights requires such a course. In theory, an applicant cannot be bought off by a Government leaving a situation where similar violations may continue to occur.[100] However there have only been two cases where the Convention organs have continued a case in the absence of an applicant, with the exception of certain cases where the Commission was not satisfied that the applicant's expression of intention to withdraw was genuine.[101]

In *Tyrer v United Kingdom*, the Court continued examination of complaints under Art.3 about birching of a juvenile, even though the applicant himself had withdrawn on reaching his majority.[102] More recently, in *Karner v Austria*,[103] even though the applicant had died and no relative wished to continue the application, the Court proceeded to find a violation of Art.14 in conjunction with Art.8 in respect of the applicant's inability, as homosexual partner of a deceased tenant, to succeed to the tenancy. It observed that while Art.34 required the existence of a victim to engage the protection mechanism of the Convention, this criterion did not apply rigidly during the proceedings. As human rights cases had a moral importance transcending the individual applicant, it was in accordance with the purpose of the Convention to continue with the case in absence of the applicant, where as in this case an important question of general interest arose not only for Austria but for Contracting States generally. Unlike other cases struck out on the death of the applicant, it may be noted that the principal issue at stake had not been resolved, or examined in other similar, recent cases and it was possible to carry out an effective examination of the case without the participation of the applicant, *e.g.* no questions of factual dispute or credibility.

8. Appeal against admissibility decisions or re-opening

There is no appeal by an applicant against a decision declaring his application or part of his application inadmissible.[104] Pursuant to Art.37, para.2, the Court may restore an application to the list. The practice is only do so where the Court has

I–050

---

[96] *e.g. Skoutaridou v Turkey*, December 17, 1999, where the Court noted that there were numerous other pending cases raising similar issues; *Gladkowski v Poland*, March 14, 2000.

[97] *Akman v Turkey*, June 26, 2001, ECHR 2001–VI; *cf. Tahsin Acar v Turkey*, May 6, 2003, concerning inadequate unilateral declarations.

[98] *e.g.* 22057/93, (Dec.) January 13, 1997, 88–A D.R. 17; *Sevgi Erdogan v Turkey*, April 29, 2003, para.38).

[99] *e.g.* 20915/92, (Rep.) March 3, 1995, where the lawyer of the applicant company had submitted to the Supreme Court in support of his appeal a confidential Commission letter informing him of the provisional opinion on the merits, which was a serious breach of its rules for which there was no justification.

[100] *e.g. Tsavachidis*, n.93 above, para.25, where the Court noted that it had already clarified the nature and extent of the Contracting States' obligations in similar surveillance situations.

[101] *e.g. Kurt v Turkey*, 24276/94, (Dec.) May 22, 1993, 81–A D.R. 112.

[102] April 25, 1978, Series A, No.26, paras 24–27.

[103] July 24, 2003, ECHR 2003–IX.

[104] Governments however may raise fresh admissibility objections even after the case is declared admissible. See second paragraph on estoppel at the beginning of this chapter.

made a factual error in the decision which is of relevance to its conclusions, for example, where it overlooked a letter introducing the application which affected the calculation of the six-month time-limit or where it relied in its reasoning on a fact which was not correct. It might also be possible that re-opening might occur where it appears that the Government has failed to comply with a settlement[105]; or where new circumstances arose enabling the Court to resume its examination.[106]

9. Standing

I–051

- An individual, group of individuals or non-governmental organisation claiming to be a victim of a violation of the Convention or other person (friend, relative, etc. as well as lawyer, NGO representative) who has authority to act (by means of signed letter of authority specifying that the applicant wishes him/her to act in the proceedings before the Court) may present an application. Domestic rules on standing are not decisive.[107]
- Municipal bodies or public law corporations performing official duties cannot bring an application.[108]
- An application cannot be brought in the name of a deceased person. A person with required standing as next-of-kin or as heir of the estate may bring the application in his/her own name as a victim.[109] Where an applicant dies during the proceedings, it may continue where a spouse or appropriate close relative with a legitimate interest adopts it. This has been permitted in most cases.[110] However, when the applicant in *Scherer v Switzerland*[111] died, the Court proceeded to strike the case out as there was no close relative wishing to continue, only an executor, and it found, in light of the change in legislation and case-law, that there was no reason of public policy to examine the case further.

---

[105] e.g. 16266/90, (Dec.) May 22, 1993, 65 D.R. 337.
[106] e.g. an applicant who failed to make contact with his lawyer renewed his complaints with a convincing reason for the lapse (e.g. intimidation).
[107] e.g. *Scozzari and Giunta v Italy*, July 13, 2000, ECHR 2000–VIII, paras 138–139, concerning representation of children.
[108] e.g. 25978/94, (Dec.) January 18, 1996, 84–A D.R.129 the status of the BBC has been left open; *Ayuntamiento de Mula v Spain*, 55346/00, (Dec.) February 1, 2001, ECHR 2001–I.
[109] e.g. *Yasa v Turkey*, September 2, 1998, R.J.D. 1998–VI, No.88, paras 63–66, where the Court rejected the Government's objection to a nephew bringing a complaint about the killing of his uncle.
[110] e.g. *Lukanov v Bulgaria*, March 20, 1997, R.J.D. 1997–II, No.34 (wife of deceased applicant continued complaints of unlawful arrest and detention); *Laskey, Jaggard and Brown v UK*, February 19, 1997, R.J.D. 1997–I, No.29 (father of deceased continued complaints about private life interference); *Stretch v UK*, June 24, 2003 (son continued complaints about deprivation of property).
[111] March 25, 1994, Series A, No.287; 18 E.H.R.R. 276.

C. CONVENTION PRINCIPLES AND APPROACH

Applying the Convention involves a special perspective distinct from national law. There is a set of interlocking principles governed by its international and human rights context. The Court intends to lay down certain minimum international standards. [1] It is not seeking to identify the most appropriate way to protect human rights, recognising the diversity in the Contracting States. It identifies at most the minimum which a particular legal system should attain.

I–052

It must also be noted that, as a treaty, the Convention falls to be interpreted in light of the rules of the Vienna Convention of May 23, 1969 on the Law of Treaties. Accordingly, the Court must take account of any relevant rules of international law applicable in the relations between the parties and the Convention must be interpreted as far as possible in harmony with the other rules of international law of which it forms a part. That said, the Court places precedence on the special character of the Convention as a human rights treaty and has not owned itself necessarily bound by other international law norms.[2]

1. Subsidiarity

The Court is primarily a supervisory body and subsidiary to the national systems safeguarding human rights.[3] Pursuant to Art.1 of the Convention the Contracting States have undertaken to "secure to everyone within their jurisdiction the rights and freedoms" set out in the Convention. It is therefore first and foremost the role of the State to protect human rights. Article 13 imposes the obligation on the State to provide a remedy to all those who claim, arguably, that their rights under the Convention have been violated, while Art.35, para.1 requires the exhaustion of domestic remedies as a precondition which reflects the fact that coming to Strasbourg is meant to be very much the last resort.[4]

I–053

---

[1] *Belgian Linguistics Case (No.1)*, February 9, 1967, Series A, No.5; 1 E.H.R.R. 241.
[2] See *Al-Adsani v UK*, November 21, 2001, ECHR 2001–XI, para.55 (concerning State immunity and access to court); *Bankovic v Belgium and 16 other Contracting States*, 52207/99, (Dec.) December 19, 2001, ECHR 2001–XII, para.55–58 (concerning "within 'Contracting State's' jurisdiction" in Art.1; *Witold Litwa v Poland*, April 4, 2000, ECHR 2000–III, paras 57–59 (concerning the meaning of "alcoholics" in Art.5, para.1(e)).
[3] *e.g. Handyside v UK*, December 7, 1996, Series A, No.24; 1 E.H.R.R 737, para.48; *Eckle v Germany*, July 15, 1982, Series A, No.51, 5 E.H.R.R. 1, para.61; *Akdivar v Turkey*, September 16, 1996, R.J.D. 1996–IV, No.15, para.65; *Z v UK*, May 10, 2001, ECHR 2001–V, para.103.
[4] There is also the practical consideration that the Court has neither the time nor resources to decide on the merits all human rights cases in Europe. It is not particularly geared to do the fact finding tasks commonly fulfilled by domestic courts, with no compellable powers over witnesses or discovery of documents.

2. Fourth instance

I–054   The Convention organs are not, as the Commission was fond of saying, a court of appeal from domestic courts and cannot intervene on the basis that a domestic court has come to the "wrong" decision or made a mistake. Their role is to ensure compliance with the provisions of the Convention by the Contracting States.

    The Court will, generally, not rehear cases, except to the extent that factual or legal issues arise under the Convention similar to those in domestic proceedings. Its factfinding function is limited. While the Court may be required to make findings of fact in disputed cases, its examination is almost entirely limited to the written submissions of the parties and the documents provided. Its hearings are generally on points of applicable domestic law and the scope of Convention rights: it only rarely hears witnesses or even sees the applicant, its procedures being largely in writing. In the vast majority of cases, where a case has been thoroughly examined on the domestic level, the facts have been thrashed out and the Court cannot hope to do any better in resolving disputed elements.[5] In most cases, the essential facts are not in dispute or do not have to be resolved since the examination undertaken under the Convention often focusses on the procedural safeguards, the decision-making procedure, the applicable standards.[6] If it is alleged that the Court relies too heavily on domestic courts findings, this is a reflection of nature of the exercise that is being undertaken. The Court will not redecide whether or not a decision to remove children was in fact the correct decision, but will assess whether the manner of decision-making and implementation failed in some way to protect the parents' rights. In a case of suspicious killing by an unknown assassin, the Court cannot seriously attempt to identify the culprit and thereby whether the State was directly responsible as alleged. What it can do is examine whether the victim was sufficiently protected beforehand—by the standards imposed by law, or, if applicable the necessary safeguards—and whether afterwards the incident was properly investigated in such a way as to indicate the rule of law is in force.[7] Consequently, much of Convention case law turns on procedural considerations.

    That said, there is a general overview of the merits taken in the Court's requirement that decisions and measures taken are supported by "relevant and sufficient" reasons[8] and in the context of Art.14, objective and reasonable justification. This is a means both of verifying that decisions are in fact in pursuit of the alleged aims and that they are not arbitrary or in abuse of power.

3. Margin of appreciation

I–055   The domestic authorities have always been recognised by the Convention organs as generally being in the best position either to reach a decision in a particular case or

[5] *Stocke v Germany*, March 19, 1991, Series A, No.199; 13 E.H.R.R. 839, where the applicant alleged connivance by police officers with an informer who tricked him onto a plane to Germany where he was arrested. The Commission heard witnesses but was unable to come any different conclusion than the domestic courts.

[6] There is also the frequently used technique of reaching conclusions "even assuming" a particular state of affairs, to avoid the necessity of settling doubtful factual matters.

[7] *e.g. Yasa v Turkey*, September 2, 1998, R.J.D. 1998–VI, No.88.

[8] In the context of the necessity for measures, *e.g. Olsson v Sweden*, March 24, 1988, Series A, No.130, 11 E.H.R.R. 259 (Art.8) the reason must be pertinent to the interference and justify the extent or nature of the interference; *Lingens v Austria*, July 8, 1986, Series A, No.103; 8 E.H.R.R. 103 (Art.10).

to decide on the measures necessary in a particular area, whether it be expropriation of property to build a new road, banning blasphemous videos or the distribution of sex education books.[9] In this context frequent reference is made to the "margin of appreciation" to be accorded to Contracting States. This is a term which is not subject to, or perhaps capable of, precise definition and smacks somewhat of a "let out" to Governments, particularly in those cases, where there is a *prima facie* interference with a right, arguments either way as to whether such interference is necessary and the case is resolved by pulling the term "margin of appreciation" out of the hat.[10]

The fact that customs, policies and practices vary considerably between Contracting States is sometimes used to support the existence of a margin of appreciation. Where there is no uniform conception, for example, of morals, there is accepted to be a number of possible solutions or approaches in such areas.[11] In *Dudgeon v United Kingdom*,[12] the Court referred to different moral and social conditions which can apply in different areas and commented that because a restriction was not seen as necessary elsewhere did not mean it was unacceptable in one particular area. However in that case the Court considered that notwithstanding the margin of appreciation, it was for the Convention organs to make the final evaluation and it came to the conclusion that the prohibition of adult homosexual activities was not necessitated in the conditions of Northern Ireland to maintain moral standards or protect vulnerable members of society. The cost was disproportionately high on the individual with correspondingly little concrete gain for the community.

In other controversial areas, the Court has relied on the lack of consensus or common ground as indicating that it cannot impose obligations on Contracting States.[13] This shows a more cautious approach, since it might be argued that it is in such difficult areas that the Convention areas should assist a consensus to emerge. On the other hand, where there is a wide agreement in member States as to particular standards to apply, this will generally be a material consideration, as in the case of judicial corporal punishment in *Tyrer v United Kingdom*[14] and concerning the legal recognition of gender re-assignment for transsexuals in *Christine Goodwin v United Kingdom*.[15]

The scope of the margin of appreciation will differ according to the context.[16] It has been held by the Court to be particularly wide in the areas of national security[17];

---

[9] *e.g. Muller v Switzerland*, May 24, 1988, Series A, No.133; 13 E.H.R.R. 212, para.35: as being in direct and continuous contact with the vital forces of their countries.

[10] *e.g. Handyside v UK*, n.3 above, paras 48, 54 and 57 (seizure and forfeiture and conviction in relation to "Little Red Schoolbook"); *Stubbings v UK*, October 22, 1996, R.J.D. 1996–IV, No.18, para.74 (different time-limits imposed on persons claiming injuries); *Buckley v UK*, September 25, 1996, para.84 (refusal of planning permission to gypsy family); *Wingrove v UK*, November 25, 1996, R.J.D. 1996–V, No.23, para.64 (banning of a video film as blasphemous).

[11] *Handyside*, n.3 above, para.48.

[12] October 22, 1981, Series A, No.45.

[13] See the early transsexual *cases, e.g. Rees v UK*, January 24, 1986, Series A, No.106; 9 E.H.R.R. 56, para.37; *Cossey v UK*, September 27, 1990, Series A, No.184; 13 E.H.R.R. 622, para.40; *B. v France*, March 25, 1992, Series A, No.232–C; 16 E.H.R.R., para.48 where there was reference to insufficient scientific, medical, legal and social consensus on the phenomenon.

[14] April 25, 1978, Series A, No.26; 2 E.H.R.R. 1, paras 31 and 38: vast majority of States had not used such methods for years; reference to "commonly accepted standards". See also *Dudgeon*, n.12 above, para.60, where the majority of States no longer considered it appropriate to apply criminal sanctions to consensual adult homosexual acts.

[15] July 11, 2002, ECHR 2002–VI.

[16] *Sunday Times v UK*, April 26, 1979, Series A, No.30, para.59; *Dudgeon*, n.12 above, para.52.

[17] *Leander v Sweden*, March 26, 1987, Series A, No.116; 9 E.H.R.R. 433.

planning policies;[18] matters such as transsexualism or artificial insemination by donor (AID) when perceived to be controversial.[19] As regards the area of the protection of morals, the Court in *Dudgeon*[20] did not accept that the margin was wide as a general proposition, stating that it was not only the aim of the measures which affected the scope of the margin of appreciation but the nature of the activities involved. Since *Dudgeon* concerned interference with an intimate area of private life, the balance tipped towards applicants in requiring "particularly serious reasons" for interferences.

In practice, the margin of appreciation operates as a means of leaving a State freedom of manoeuvre in assessing what its society needs and the best way to achieve those needs, and even the timing of policies.[21] There is not only one way of protecting children from abuse or of fighting drugtrafficking. In multicultural Europe, with its morasse of local traditions, the Convention cannot, should not attempt to impose uniformity or detailed and specific requirements.[22] In its supervisory capacity however, the Court can require legitimate aims and that the State does not step beyond certain boundaries. For example, in the field of nationalisation and expropriation, where issues of the national economy may be in play, the Court gives the general and public interest a wide meaning and will respect the State's assessment unless manifestly without reasonable foundation.[23] Nonetheless, generally, provision should be made to compensate the persons affected. In the field of education, though without express mention of the margin of appreciation, the Court referred to limits which should not be exceeded. Thus, while the setting and planning of a school curriculum falls in the first place for the State to settle and the State is not prevented from imparting information or knowledge of a religious or philsohical kind, it cannot step over the line into indoctrination.[24]

Procedural safeguards available to the individual will be especially material in determining whether the respondent State has, when fixing the regulatory framework, remained within its margin of appreciation. In areas where there is a wide margin of appreciation, the Court's examination tends to focus on whether the decision-making process leading to measures of interference was fair and such as to afford due respect to the interests safeguarded to the individual by Art.8.[25]

---

[18] *Buckley*, n.10 above, para.75: in the planning area, the authorities have to exercise a discretion involving a multitude of factors.

[19] *X, Y and Z v UK*, April 22, 1997, R.J.D. 1997–II, No.35, where there was no common ground as to parental and family rights in relation to children born by AID.

[20] n.12 above, para.52.

[21] *e.g.* 11089/84, (Dec.) November 11, 1986, 49 D.R. 181, where the Commission noted that the margin of appreciation applies to when a State decides to change a system. The fact that the UK modified its tax system did not indicate a previous lack of objective and reasonable justification since goals could legitimately changes from time to time. Also *Petrovic v Austria*, March 27, 1998, R.J.D., 1998–II, No.67, paras 41–43, gradual evolution of entitlement to paternity leave.

[22] *e.g. Sunday Times*, n.16, para.61.

[23] *e.g. Lithgow v UK*, July 8, 1986, Series A, No.102 (nationalisation); *James v UK*, February 21, 1986, Series A, No.98 (sweeping leasehold reform); *Pressos Compania v Belgium*, November 20, 1995, Series A, No.30 (legislative intervention in pending tort claims).

[24] *Kjeldsen, Madsen and Pedersen v Denmark*, December 7, 1976, Series A, No.23; 1 E.H.R.R. 711, para.53.

[25] *e.g. Buckley*, n.10 above, pp.1292–93, para.76, *Chapman v UK* [GC], January 18, 2001, ECHR 2001–I, para.92.

4. Autonomous concepts

When it comes to interpreting the extent or application of the substantive rights   I–056
and freedoms under the Convention, the Court looks very much to the substance of
the right protected. It is not to be distracted by how a Contracting State chooses in
domestic law to interpret a term or principle, which is, at most, a starting point.[26]
Whatever the domestic label, it will examine the matter in form, substance and
procedure before reaching its own decision.

The Court thus maintains that the terms contained in the Convention are
autonomous concepts and that it is free to assess their application to particular
situations in domestic systems. This covers the concepts of "civil rights and
obligations", "criminal charge", "witness", etc. It will determine the scope of the
rights guaranteed under the Convention and Contracting States cannot limit or
redefine them by formal classifications and definitions in their own domestic law.
But even where the Court does not refer to autonomous concepts, it approaches
notions of "family", "private life" by looking at the substance of what is at stake
without being governed by the meaning given to the term in the particular
State.

5. Effectiveness

The Convention is a system for the protection of human rights. This renders it of   I–057
crucial importance that it is interpreted and applied in a manner which renders these
rights practical and effective, not theoretical and illusory.[27] A State cannot therefore
escape its obligations by protecting a right in a superficial or self-defeating manner.
For example, it is not enough to appoint a lawyer for a trial, the assistance given
must be effective[28]; a State cannot disclaim responsibility in expelling an individual
to a country where he faces a real risk of treatment contrary to Art.3[29]; the use of
deliberate lethal force by State agents must be subject to the most careful scrutiny,
and attract some form of effective official investigation[30]; and the protection
provided to associations under Art.11 must cover not only their founding but extend
to their entire life[31]; and the rules governing the eligibility of candidates for election
to the legislature conform with criteria framed to prevent arbitrary decisions and
abuse of power.[32]

---

[26] *e.g. Chassagnou v France*, April 29, 1999, ECHR 1999–III, para.100, concerning the term "association"
under Art.11.
[27] *Artico v Italy*, May 13, 1980, Series A, No.37; 3 E.H.R.R. 1, para.33.
[28] *Artico*, n.27 above, para.33; *Campbell and Fell v UK*, June 28, 1984, Series A, No.80; 7 E.H.R.R. 165,
access by a prisoner to a lawyer was not effective where conducted within hearing of prison officers.
[29] *Soering v UK*, July 7, 1989, Series A, No.161; 11 E.H.R.R. 439.
[30] *McCann v UK*, September 27, 1995, Series A, No.324; 21 E.H.R.R. 97.
[31] *United Communist Party v Turkey*, January 30, 1998, ECHR R.J.D. 1998–I, No.62, para.33.
[32] *Podkolzina v Latvia*, April 9, 2002, ECHR 2002–II, para.35. See also *Matthews v UK*, February 18,
1999, ECHR 1999–I, para.33, concerning Government responsibility for European, as well as domestic,
elections under Art.3 of Protocol No.1; *Conka v Belgium*, February 5, 2002, ECHR 2002–I, para.46,
concerning the realistic possibility of using remedies against arbitrary detention.

6. Strict limitations

I–058 Exceptions to the rights guaranteed under the Convention are to be strictly construed.[33] Thus, case law indicates the importance of physical freedom or liberty and emphasises that exceptions are exhaustively limited to those set out in the sub-paragraphs of Art.5, para.1. If the detention does not fall within any of these categories then it cannot be justified under Art.5, para.1, however useful the aim might be.[34]

7. Essence of the right

I–059 In assessing the impact of restrictions or interferences the Convention organs sometimes have regard to the "essence" of the right, whether it has been effectively destroyed or an acceptable scope for its exercise remains. This originated in cases of access to court where limitations even if proportionate and pursuing reasonable aims must not impair the essence of the right[35] but has been used in other contexts.[36] In the cases of *CR* and *SW v United Kingdom*, where the applicants challenged the decision of the House of Lords as retrospectively abolishing the marital immunity to rape, the Court found that the decisions, having regard to the manifestly debasing character of rape, could not be said to be at variance with the object and purpose of Art.7, which was to prevent arbitrary prosecution, conviction and punishment.[37]

8. Rule of law

I–060 The rule of law is one of the key principles underlying the Convention. It implies that an interference by the authorities with an individual's rights should be subject to effective control, especially so where the law bestows on the executive wide discretionary powers.[38] Where in *Stran Greek Refineries v Greece* there was legislative interference with judicial process, the Court emphasised several times the idea of rule of law which Greece undertook to respect in joining the Coucil of Europe and ratifying the Convention.[39] In *Al-Nashif v Bulgaria*, the concepts of lawfulness and the rule of law in a democratic society required that measures affecting fundamental human rights, even in the sensitive area of national security, must be subject to

---

[33] *e.g. Van Mechelen v Netherlands*, April 23, 1997, R.J.D. 1997–III, No.36, para.58: limits to defence rights must be restricted to those "strictly necessary".

[34] *e.g. Ciulla v Italy*, February 22, 1989, Series A, No.148, para.41: arrest and detention pending the order of preventive measures fell outside the permitted exceptions of Art.5, despite the acknowledged importance of the fight against the mafia. See also *Engel v Netherlands*, June 8, 1976, Series A, No.22, para.57, where the claim of special exclusion for military discipline was not accepted.

[35] *Ashingdane v UK*, May 28, 1985, Series A, No.93, para.57.

[36] Under Art.12, the essence of the right should not be hampered by national laws (see Pt IIB: Marriage); under Art.3 of Protocol No.1, see *Matthews*, n.32 above, paras 63–65; concerning positive obligations under Art.10, *Appleby v UK*, May 6, 2003, ECHR 2003–VI, para.47; delays in executions of judgment, *e.g. Burdov v Russia*, May 7, 2002, ECHR 2002–III, paras 34–35.

[37] November 22, 1995, Series A, Nos 335–B and C.

[38] *e.g. Silver v UK*, March 25, 1983, Series A, No.61; 5 E.H.R.R. 347, para.90; *Rotaru v Romania*, February 4, 2000, ECHR 2000–V, para.59.

[39] See also *Hornsby v Greece*, March 19, 1997, R.J.D. 1997–II, para.40 where the Court emphasised the rule of law in the effective implementation of judicial decisions by the authorities.

some form of adversarial proceedings before an independent body competent to review the reasons for the decision.[40]

A State may interfere with citizens' rights or regulate their freedom to act for specified legitimate aims but if it does so it must do so by law, and a norm cannot be classified as a law unless it is accessible and also foreseeable to a reasonable degree in its application and consequences.[41] This is the approach generally taken wherever the word "law" or "lawful" appears as a requirement.[42] Article 2 in addition makes reference to protection by law,[43] while Art.6 deals with a detailed procedural code for the operation of courts of law and Art.7 expressly prohibits retrospective imposition of criminal offences and heavier penalties. The requirement of effective access to court, and the scrutiny of any attempt to remove court jurisdiction over claims, can be said to derive from this fundamental concept.[44]

Lawfulness has been interpreted to refer to two elements. Firstly, the measure in issue must have some basis in domestic law;[45] secondly, it must possess the quality of law, namely, that it is accessible and enables the individual to foresee with reasonable degree of certainty the consequences of his actions or the circumstances in which and the conditions on which authorities may take certain steps.[46] These elements are applied with a view principally to ensuring that safeguards against arbitrary abuse of power are in place in the domestic law itself. Powers to interfere with the rights of individuals must be subject to defined limitations as to their subject-matter, duration, methods of implementation, having regard to the practical consideration that absolute certainty is neither possible or desirable and that many laws are inevitable couched in terms which are to some extent vague and whose interpretation and application are questions of practice.[47] The Court is interested in ensuring certain minimum standards and a wide discretion, and partially defined concepts will not necessarily offend.[48]

Matters of interpretation and application of domestic law itself are primarily for the national courts, and the Court is not likely to contradict their findings.[49] Nonetheless since compliance with domestic law is an integral part of the obligations of Contracting States, the Court has stated its competence to satisfy itself of such compliance where relevant, subject to its inherent limits in the European

[40] June 20, 2002, para.123—although appropriate procedural limitations on the use of classified information might be conceivable.

[41] e.g. Sunday Times, n.16 above.

[42] "in accordance with law" (Art.8); "prescribed by law" (Arts 9, 10 and 11); procedure prescribed by law (Art.5, para.1; "lawful" as precondition for every sub-para of Art.5; conditions provided for by law (Art.1, Protocol 1).

[43] See McCann, n.30 above, (Rep.) para.92: reference to rule of law requiring effective oversight of the use of force by agents of the State to avoid the arbitrary abuse of power; Avsar v Turkey, July 10, 2001, ECHR 2001–VII, paras 393–5 and 404—concerning the importance of accountability and maintaining public confidence in the maintenance of the rule of law.

[44] Fayed v UK, September 21, 1994, Series A, No.294–B; 18 E.H.R.R. 393.

[45] e.g. Malone v UK, August 2, 1984, Series A, No.82; 7 E.H.R.R. 14.

[46] For general principles, see Sunday Times, n.16 above, para.49 ; Malone, n.45 above, paras 67–68 ; also findings of violation : Kruslin v France, April 24, 1990, Series A, No.176–B; 12 E.H.R.R. 547; Amuur v France, June 25, 1996, R.J.D. 1996–III, No.11; Rotaru, n.38 above.

[47] Sunday Times, n.16 above, para.49; changes in case-law through judicial development are compatible with "lawfulness" criteria where reasonably foreseeable, if necessary with the assistance of a lawyer (see Pt IIA: Retrospectivity).

[48] See, e.g. cases concerning Surveillance and Interception of Communications (Pt IIB).

[49] e.g. Casada Coca v Spain, February 24, 1994, Series A, No.285; 18 E.H.R.R. 1, para.43.

system of protection.[50] In particular, where deprivation of liberty is concerned, it may verify that domestic law is not interpreted or applied in an arbitrary manner, since no arbitrary detention can ever be regarded as "lawful".[51] In practice, this gives a certain leeway to domestic systems but might also be said to avoid breaches which are technical and lacking in merit.[52]

The Court has also referred to the fundamental principle of the separation of powers, in particular where the executive enjoys a decision-making power in a procedure to which judicial guarantees should apply.[53] The Court has stated that this is not a matter of form but detracts from a necessary guarantee against the possibility of abuse.[54] This notion has also been accepted as a reason justifying the immunity of Members of Parliament from being sued in the courts in relation to their functions in Parliament.[55] However, the principle is to be applied in the context of the requirements of the Convention and does not require States to adopt any particular constitutional arrangements.[56]

9. Democratic values

I–061   In addition to the rule of law, reliance in interpretation and application of Convention rights is placed on "democratic values".[57] These involve recognition of the importance of rights to a fair trial[58] and the fundamental rights guaranteed by Art.2 (right to life) and Art.3 (prohibition of torture and inhuman and degrading treatment).[59] States are required to adopt a certain tolerance and broadmindedness and to accept a certain pluralism and diversity.[60] A democracy does not mean that the majority always prevails: a balance must be achieved which ensures the fair and proper treatment of minorities and avoids abuse of a dominant position.[61] States must also afford protection to the media, which acts in democratic society as a "watchdog" (see, Pt IIB: Freedom of expression) and governments must expect to bear more criticism than others and react with restraint.[62] The link between the protection of human rights and democracy is such, however, that a State may, where necessary, take steps to defend its democratic order and institutions which limit the exercise of fundamental rights.[63]

[50] *Lukanov v Bulgaria*, March 3, 1997, R.J.D. 1997–II, No.34, paras 41–43 where the Court found that the applicant ex-minister's participation in a collective decision to send aid to the Third World did not constitute a criminal offence under Bulgarian law at the time.

[51] *Winterwerp v Netherlands*, October 24, 1979, Series A, No.33; 2 E.H.R.R. 387, paras 39 and 45.

[52] *e.g.* 9997/82, (Dec.) December 7, 1982, 31 D.R. 145.

[53] *Stafford v UK*, May 28, 2002, ECHR 2002–IV, para.78; *Easterbrook v UK*, June 12, 2003, para.28.

[54] *Benjamin and Wilson v UK*, September 26, 2002, para.36.

[55] *A v UK*, December 17, 2002, ECHR 2002–X, para.73.

[56] *Kleyn v Netherlands*, May 6, 2003, ECHR 2003–VI, para.193, where the Court was sensitive to the existence of bodies in a number of countries, which can play a judicial and legislative role.

[57] *e.g. Soering*, n.29 above, para.87: "any interpretation of the rights and freedoms guaranteed had to be consistent with the general spirit of the Convention, an instrument designed to maintain and promote the ideals and values of a democratic society" citing *Kjeldsen*, n.24 above, para.53.

[58] *e.g. Ait-Mouhoub v France*, October 28, 1998, R.J.D. 1998–VIII, No.96, para.52.

[59] *Soering*, n.29 above, para.88; *McCann*, n.30 above, para.147.

[60] *Dudgeon*, n.12 above, para.53 concerning homosexual acts but see *Laskey, Jaggard and Brown v UK*, February 19,1997, R.J.D. 1997–I, No.29, where the applicants' plea for toleration and broadmindedness was not successful in relation to group sado-masochistic activities of a certain severity.

[61] *Young, James and Webster v UK*, August 13, 1981, Series A, No.44; 4 E.H.R.R. 38, para.63.

[62] *e.g. Castells v Spain*, April 23, 1992, Series A, No.236; 14 E.H.R.R. 445, para.46.

[63] *e.g. Refah Partisi v Turkey*, February 13, 2003, ECHR 2003–III, paras 102–103; *Zdanoka v Latvia*, June 17, 2004, paras 78–81.

10. Necessity

Where interferences under the Convention may be justified in pursuit of specified
legitimate aims, the requirement that these interferences nonetheless be "necessary"
appears to place a burden on the State. The Court has laid down the element that
an interference with a right has to be justified by "a pressing social need".[64]
However, in practice, this is not applied in such a manner as to require a
Government to establish, for example, that the measure is of any particular urgency
or unavoidable, or that there is no other way of achieving the goal with lesser
impact on individual rights. The findings of the Convention organs are phrased less
demandingly in terms that, having regard to the various relevant factors, the
interference may be considered as necessary in a democratic society.[65] The principle
of proportionality is more decisive (see below).

I–062

11. Proportionality

Proportionality is a dominant theme underlying the whole of the Convention. It is an
ingredient of the requirement of the necessity of the measure under Arts 2 and 8 to
11 and has been imported into other provisions—in the context of objective and
reasonable justification for difference in treatment under Art.14, as regards restrictions
on access to court under Art.6, and the framework of property rights under Art.1 of
Protocol No.1 as well as part of the basis in finding States under a positive obligation
to act. It requires a reasonable relation between the goal pursued and the means
used.[66] It is also used in the sense of finding a balance between the applicant's interests
and those of the community.[67] Many issues centre on the conflict between an
individual and the good of the general amorphous mass of society: roads; taxes;
airports; preservation of the countryside are objectively to everyone's benefit.
Proportionality examines whether providing them places too much of a burden on
certain individuals. Whether this burden has been mitigated by procedures or forms of
relief will be relevant to whether the State has struck the right balance.

I–063

The consideration of whether the State could achieve the goal in another way may
be asked under proportionality but can only go so far.[68] Since the Convention is not
setting ideal standards, it is not enough to establish a violation that, for example,
other methods could be used or are used in another State.[69] The method used must
fail the proportionality test and fall outside the margin of appreciation having regard
to the particular circumstances of the case.

---

[64] *Handyside*, n.3 above, para.48; *Sunday Times*, n.16 above, para.59: "necessary" identified as less than
"indispensable" but not as flexible as "useful" "reasonable" or "desirable".
[65] e.g. *Laskey*, n.60 above, para.50: "the national authorities were entitled to consider that the
prosecution and conviction of the applicants were necessary in a democratic society for the protection of
health. . .".
[66] *James v UK*, n.23 above.
[67] *Sporrong and Llonroth v Sweden*, September 23, 1982, Series A, No.52; 5 E.H.R.R. 35, para.69.
[68] In *Inze v Austria*, October 28, 1987, Series A, No.126; 10 E.H.R.R. 394—the fact that the law about
inheritance changed did not show that there had been a violation but did indicate that there were other
ways of achieving the Government's aim of maintaining farms.
[69] e.g. *Mellacher v Austria*, December 19, 1989, Series A, No.169, para.53; see however *Chahal v UK*,
November 15, 1996, R.J.D. 1996–V, No.22, para.131 where in finding a violation of Art.5, para.4, the
Court attached significance to the method applied in Canada to permit courts to review sensitive security
material.

12. Positive obligations

I–064   The provisions of the Convention impose primarily negative obligations on States, namely, to refrain from taking steps infringing fundamental rights and freedoms. Increasingly however, rights are being interpreted in such a manner as to impose positive obligations on States to take steps to protect the enjoyment of rights from interferences from other sources.[70] In this area, limitations on the imposition of obligations derive from the consideration of the factors identified above in the context of the margin of appreciation dominated by the perception that this trespasses more acutely in matters of State policy, priorities and allocation of resources.[71] In assessing whether the State is under an obligation to take a particular step, the Court examines whether a fair balance has been struck between the interests of the individual and those of the community. It has also referred to examining whether the essence of the right is destroyed or effective exercise of the right barred in the absence of positive measures.[72] In striking the balance, where Art.8 is concerned for example, the legitimate aims adverted to in the second paragraph may be relevant. The interests of the general community perhaps start out heavier in the balance, with a certain burden on the individual to establish that his interests clearly predominate.[73] The cases indicate that where an important individual right is at stake, the applicant suffering significant effects, a positive obligation may arise.[74] However, where the individual interest is not perceived as suffering material prejudice, or an important State interest is at stake, this is less likely.[75]

13. Individual rights

I–065   The Convention is based on the right of individual petition. An applicant must claim to be a victim of a violation of one of the guaranteed rights. The Court will not entertain complaints by way of *actio popularis* or *in abstracto*. Its examination will generally be restricted to the measures as they affect the individual in his situation. It does not respond with enthusiasm to an invitation to look at the global position, as in the case of gypsies, who may well be suffering from unfavourable social and legal trends over the last 50 years but can only complain with any hope of success to Strasbourg of measures which can be shown to effect them directly and concretely.[76] Arguments which focus on the general injustice or unfairness of a policy or measure

---

[70] Obligations found first, and most commonly, under Art.8; now also under Arts 2, 3, 10 and 11.

[71] *Abdulaziz v UK*, May 28, 1985, Series A, No.94; 7 E.H.R.R. 471, para.67; *Osman v UK*, October 28, 1998, R.J.D. 1998–VIII, No.95, para.91.

[72] *Appleby*, n.36 above, para.47.

[73] See, *e.g.* X, *Y and Z*, n.19 above, para.47, where the Court stated that, while it had not been shown that recognition of the filiation of a child born by AID was contrary to the interests of the community, it had not been established as necesary to the welfare of the child either.

[74] *e.g. B v France*, n.13 above (transsexual applicant suffered daily humiliation and the civil register system did not require radical alteration); *Gaskin v UK* , July 7, 1987, Series A, No.160 (vital interest of the applicant, in care almost all his childhood, to have access to information about his past in social security files).

[75] *e.g. Abdulaziz*, n.71 above, (immigration policy); *Rees* and *Cossey*, n.13 above (UK transsexuals not considered to suffer significant hardship such as would require the State to change its entire registration system); *Appleby*, n.36 above, where the applicants, barred from a shopping centre, could exercise their freedom of expression elsewhere.

[76] See Pt IIB, Gypsies.

will be of limited assistance unless relevant to explaining or setting in context the impact on the individual applicant.

14. Living instrument

The Convention is seen as a living instrument, to be interpreted in light of present day conditions.[77] As a result, notwithstanding the possible intentions of the drafters of the Convention 50 years ago, the Court will have regard to developments in Contracting States in applying the rights guaranteed in the Convention. Thus changing attitudes to homosexuality,[78] children born out of wedlock,[79] equality of the sexes,[80] transsexuals,[81] the acknowledged priority of eradicating racism[82] have played a role in decision-making. There must however apparently be a general acceptance of the changing conditions before this can be decisive, as shown by the transsexual cases, where the Court kept the matter under review for a number of years and noted the evolving consensus.[83] The almost complete abandonment of the death penalty in peace time by Contracting States (through the ratification of Protocol No.6) led the Court to express the view that Art.2 had thereby been modified to exclude capital punishment as an exception and that its imposition would also be inhuman punishment contrary to Art.3.[84]

I–066

The contents of domestic and constitutional law, Council of Europe texts, other international treaties and human rights jurisprudence may be of relevance in establishing developments or evolving principles. This can be in relation to specific changes or more general trends, as in *Selmouni v France*, where the Court considered that the increasingly high standard being required in the area of the protection of human rights and fundamental liberties correspondingly required greater firmness in assessing breaches of the fundamental values of democratic societies.[85]

As part of this theme, the notion of flexibility can be identified. The Court's case-law develops progressively and has overruled earlier decisions.[86] In the area, particularly, of domestic remedies, it intends to apply the Convention flexibly, avoiding excessive formalism.[87] A failure to evolve case law in light of changing

---

[77] *e.g. Tyrer v UK*, April 25, 1978, Series A, No.26, 2 E.H.R.R. 1, para.31; *Johnston v Ireland*, December 18, 1986, Series A, No.112; 9 E.H.R.R. 203, para.53; *Inze*, n.67 above, para.41

[78] *e.g. Dudgeon*, n.12 above.

[79] *e.g. Johnston*, n.77 above; *Inze*, n.68 above.

[80] *e.g. Schuler-Zgraggen v Switzerland*, June 24, 1993, Series A, No.263; 16 E.H.R.R. 405, para.67; *CR v UK*, n.37 above, para.60.

[81] *Christine Goodwin*, n.15 above, para.75, where the Court stated that it was examining the case in light of present day conditions.

[82] *Sander v UK*, May 9, 2000, ECHR 2000–V, para.23. Also emphasis in *Menson v UK*, 47916/99, (Dec.) May 6, 2003, ECHR 2003–V, concerning particular need for vigour in investigating racially-motivated attacks.

[83] See also *L and V v Austria*, January 9, 2003, ECHR 2003–I, para.47, noting consensus on equality of ages of consent between girls and boys.

[84] *Ocalan v Turkey*, March 12, 2003, paras 195–198, though it did not express a firm opinion as it decided the case on other grounds.

[85] July 28, 1999, ECHR 1999–V, para.101 where the Court lowered the threshold for treatment falling within the prohibition of torture in Art.3.

[86] *e.g. Borgers v Belgium*, October 30, 1991, Series A, No.214; 15 E.H.R.R 92, para.24, overruling *Delcourt v Belgium*, Januuary 17, 1970, Series A, No.11; 1 E.H.R.R. 355, in light of the growing importance of public confidence in administration of justice.

[87] *Akdivar*, n.3 above, para.69.

conditions might, it has noted, render the Court a bar to progress within Contracting States.[88]

Dynamic interpretation cannot however in principle extend so far as to create rights not intended to be included in the Convention.[89]

15. Convention approach to evidence and burdens of proof

I–067   There are no rules of admissibility of evidence. Parties may present such documentary evidence as they think appropriate and are not bound to comply with required domestic forms of presentation or content.[90] In the hearing of witnesses, there is no prohibition of hearsay. Nor is there any formalised theory of burden and standard of proof. The Convention organs take the approach of a free assessment of the available evidence, including matters taken *proprio motu*.

In practice however, an applicant must present an application which provides *prima facie* substantiation of an interference with his rights and an arguable basis for eventual violation. It will only be in exceptional cases, complaints raising serious issues against a background that provides justification for failure to present factual substantiation, that the application will be considered as meriting further examination by communication to the respondent Government.[91]

As regards admissibility criteria, the Government bears a burden of establishing the existence of available and effective remedies for the purpose of the exhaustion of domestic remedies under Art.35 para.1 (see Pt IB: Admissibility Checklist). In other contexts, it may seen that once an interference with rights is established, the burden shifts practically onto the Government to provide convincing justification.[92] However, where public and individual interests are more finely balanced, due either to the nature of the claims or the fact that it is a positive obligation in issue, it appears that the applicant faces the onus of substantiating the degree of prejudice alleged.

In relation to disputed factual situations, where there are allegations of torture, inhuman and degrading treatment contrary to Art.3, the Court has used the standard of proof beyond a reasonable doubt. The first judgment in which it appeared was in an interstate case, where dozens of witnesses were heard concerning practices used in interrrogation in Northern Ireland. It was rarely used again until the Convention organs undertook witness hearings in Turkey concerning allegations under Arts 2 and 3, about ill-treatment and deaths at the hands of security forces.[93] Outside this

---

[88] *Stafford v UK*, May 28, ECHR 2002–IV, paras 67–68: noting developments in domestic and Convention case-law since the previous judgment on similar complaints, the Court found Art.5, paras 1 and 4 could now apply to mandatory life prisoners' detention after expiry of tariff. See also *Mamatkulov and Askarov v Turkey*, February 6, 2003, para.105 (evolving interpretation of Court's power to issue interim measures); and *Société Colas Est v France*, April 16, 2002, ECHR 2002–III, para.41 (extending Art.8 protection to the head office and agencies of a company).

[89] Where later provided in the protocols (*ne bis in idem*; freedom of movement) or otherwise, *e.g. Johnston*, n.77 above, para.53, concerning the Court's refusal to evolve interpretation of Art.12 to include a right to divorce clearly not intended by the drafters. There is therefore a distinction to be drawn, possibly fine, between the creation of new rights and the extension by interpretation of existing ones.

[90] Though it is not infrequent for parties submit statements by way of affidavit and this may be taken into account as part of the weighing of the credibility of the evidence.

[91] *e.g.* the cases brought by villagers from South-East Turkey, where serious allegations were made and no documentary substantiation was allegedly possible due to the ineffective nature of domestic remedies. There was independent confirmation of village destruction in other international texts and NGO reports.

[92] *e.g. Dudgeon*, n.12 above; freedom of expression cases.

[93] *e.g. Aydin v Turkey*, September 25, 1997, R.J.D. 1997–VI, No.50, para.73; see also *Poltoratskiy v Ukraine*, April 29, 2003, ECHR 2003–V, paras 122–123.

context, the establishment of the facts is generally carried out without any reference to standards and burden of proof. Presumptions of or inferences of fact may be made where a Government has hindered the fact finding process or failed to provide any, or any satisfactory, explanation, concerning a situation within their particular knowledge, *e.g.* injuries or deaths in custody.[94] A shift of the burden of proof has been found to occur in the context of allegations of violence motivated by racial discrimination, where the Government have failed to pursue lines of inquiry in that regard.[95]

It is perhaps worth mentioning that there is a certain presumption in practice that Governments act in good faith, that the authorities comply with important domestic rules and that legal processes work in the way laid down by law. For example, judges are presumed very strongly to abide by their oaths and duties[96] and statutory systems of protection to function as intended.[97] Any allegations alleging abuse or misuse of power tend to require a certain level of substantiation.

16. Structured approach

In any complaint of substance, the Convention organs analyse the application of the invoked provision with regard to each ingredient. This involves generally an examination of whether the complaint falls within the scope of the right claimed (applicability) and whether any interference with the right conforms with its conditions (compliance). While this may vary concerning the subject-matter, the general approach for the most commonly-invoked provisions is set out below: I–068

Article 5, para.1

- is there a deprivation of liberty?   I–069
- is it in conformity with lawfulness considerations?
- is it for a ground permitted under para.1? Does it comply with its conditions?

Article 6

Criminal:

- do the proceedings relate to a criminal charge? (see Pt IIA : Fair trial,   I–070
  Criminal Charge)
- if so, have the guarantees been complied with?

Civil:

Do the proceedings relate to: I–071
- a right or obligation recognised in domestic law;

---

[94] *e.g. Salman v Turkey*, June 27, 2000, ECHR 2000–VII, para.100. See Pt IIB: Hindrance in the exercise of the right of individual petition.
[95] *Nachova v Bulgaria*, February 26, 2004, para.169.
[96] See *Kraska v Switzerland*, April 19, 1993, Series A, No.254–B (where a judge announced that he had not read the applicant's documents).
[97] See, *e.g.* Pt IIB: Interception of communications and Surveillance and secret files; also *Goddi v Italy*, April 9, 1984, Series A, No.76; 6 E.H.R.R. 457, para.76, where in the absence of substantiation of a factual point from either side, the Court was not prepared to find the Government at fault.

- is there a genuine and serious dispute (*"contestation"*) about the right or obligation (which includes the consideration whether the proceedings are directly decisive for that right or obligation)?
- is the right or obligation "civil" in character?
- have the guarantees under para.1 been complied with?

Articles 8–11

I–072   *First paragraph*:

- applicability: whether the complaint falls within the scope of the right?
- existence of an interference: whether the matters complained of infringe the right.

Second paragraph: justification for any interference:

- lawfulness criteria;
- legitimate aim;
- necessity, including considerations of "pressing social need", margin of appreciation, proportionality, procedural safeguards and relevant and sufficient reasons for any decisions involved.[98]

Where positive obligations are concerned the examination does not extend into the second paragraph but the considerations of aim and proportionality are transposed into a general balancing exercise as to the existence of the obligation.

Article 13

I–073
- is the claim in relation to an alleged violation of a substantive provision?
- is it arguable?
- is there any effective remedy?

Article 14

I–074
- is there a substantive right in issue?
- is there a difference in treatment?
- between persons in relevantly similar positions;
- based on grounds of personal status;
- without objective and reasonable justification (including consideration of legitimate aim, proportionality and margin of appreciation)?

Article 1 of Protocol No.1

I–075
- are "possessions" involved which fall within this provision?
- if so, does the measure constitute a deprivation, a control of use or an interference with peaceful enjoyment?
- compliance: legitimate aim (whether specified as general or public interest), lawfulness, margin of appreciation and proportionality (including procedural safeguards, compensation) are relevant to all heads in some degree.

---

[98] So far the latter criterion has been almost wholly applied in Arts 8 and 10 cases, although it has also been applied to Art.11, *e.g. Sidiropoulos v Greece*, July 19, 1998, R.J.D. 1998–IV, No.79, para.40 and Art.9, *e.g. Leyla Sahin v Turkey*, June 29, 2004, para.103.

1. Court judgments and decisions

Available:

- *on the internet: http://www.echr.coe.int*—the site includes all judgments,   I–076
  monthly information notes on cases, press releases on recent hearings and
  judgments and a search programme "HUDOC".[1]
- *official series: texts of judgments:*
  - until 1996, Series A Nos.1–338;
  - 1996–1998, yearly volumes of Reports, published as *Reports of Judg-
    ments and Decisions* (cited by the Court as *Reports* 1997–. . .);
  - from 1999, yearly volumes of Reports of the new Court's judgments
    and decisions (cited by the Court as ECHR 2000–. . .)

These contain the entire text of the court judgment in English and French with
any separate opinions and also, in respect of cases sent to the Court before 1
November 1998, save where the length was prohibitive, the "Opinion" part of the
Commission report on the merits, again with separate opinions.[2]

There is no formal doctrine of precedent binding the Court. The Court obviously
pays attention to relevantly similar cases decided by itself but may choose if it
considers it appropriate or timely to depart expressly or impliedly from previous
positions.[3] Therefore authority from the Court in support of a proposition is one of
the most convincing arguments, although not necessarily conclusive.

2. Commission cases

Principal sources:

- *on the internet: http://www.echr.coe.int*: Commission decisions on admissibility   I–077
  and reports on the merits from 1986 which have been made public are
  accessible in the HUDOC search programme;
- *Decisions and reports*: from 1974, the principal publication of Commission
  cases published in numerical volumes DR 1–94. Volumes 1–75 contained

---

[1] Only judgments and decisions chosen for publication in the official series are translated into both of the
Court's working languages, English and French.There is some delay before the translation is placed on
the site. Unpublished judgments and decisions are to be found only in one language on the web site.
[2] There is no official index for Series A or the subsequent Report series.
[3] Procedurally however any change in case law should be conducted by a Grand Chamber. A Chamber
should not depart from the previous cases since this is a ground on which the case should be relinquished
to a Grand Chamber (r.72). See, e.g. *Stafford v UK*, May 28, 2000, ECHR 2002–IV, paras 68–69, where
the Court departed from its reasoning in *Wynne v UK*, July 18, 1994, Series A 294–A.

each extract in both English and French. To diminish the time taken for publication, there were subsequently two versions of volumes 76–94: volume A contains the text in the original language, and volume B contains the translation into the other official language. Indexes by name and number, and summaries by article and keyword, were produced at intervals of every 15–20 volumes.

Supplementary sources:

- *Collection of Decisions* consists of 46 volumes covering 1955–74, including selected decisions, with indexes for 1–30 and 32–43 only. These include cases of interesting historical significance *e.g.* Commission decisions in *Ireland v United Kingdom* interstate case;
- *Yearbook of the European Convention of Human Rights* published annually, containing general institutional information and statistics and cases which tended to reproduce those in DR, although some material may be included which is not published elsewhere. There is no complete index to the Yearbook.
- *Digest of Strasbourg case law* (1982), (arranged by chunks of relevant texts of decisions and reports under each Article of the Convention in five volumes). It is not regarded as an official source of published case law and it is not cited as a source as a matter of practice. Looseleaf supplements have brought it up to 1990 for decisions and reports and up to 1992 for judgments.

It is only recently that the Court has openly given weight to Commission precedent. It is therefore not irrelevant to refer the Court to Commission case law which is particularly persuasive or was based on its special expertise on issues of admissibility.

3. Procedure

I–078   The Rules of Court govern Court procedure (latest version, November 2003). They are available on the Court web site.

Until recently, there was no equivalent of practice notes, with the result that there is no official published source of authority for Court practice in granting interim measures, legal aid, rights of audience or effects of delays in submitting written pleadings. The Rules of Court however do now provide in r.32 for the President to issue Practice Directions. At the date of writing, three practice directions have been issued (Annex 6). The first, concerning interim measures under r.39, deals with the way in which requests should be lodged rather than giving any explanation as to how the Court exercises its discretion. The other two set out technical requirements for the institution of proceedings and written pleadings.

Basic notes are given for guidance to parties before oral hearings and brief explanatory letters sent by the Registry with each procedural step. As a result the main source of information about procedural matters is generally the Registry. Enquiry by letter or telephone is possible.

4. Institutional and statistical information

The Court publishes annual surveys of statistical information, and summaries of   I–079
principal case law, which are also available on the website. Information about judges
is available on the internet. See also the Yearbooks (Section 2 above).

5. Journals and periodicals

- *European Human Rights Reports* (Sweet and Maxwell).   I–080
- *European Human Rights Law Journal* (Sweet and Maxwell): bi-monthly, which
  includes articles, a bulletin of information, including pending hear-
  ingsproviding casenotes of judgments and decisions reached in the previous
  two or three months.
- *Human Rights Practice*: looseleaf.

6. Relevant external sources of human rights materials

The following may be relevant, in particular as indicative of existing or emerging   I–081
international human rights standards:

- the state of law in other Contracting States on certain points (with a view to
  indicating any European consensus on a particular standard or approach);
- Council of Europe materials: Parliamentary Assembly, Committee of
  Ministers, European Committee for the Prevention of Torture (CPT);
- case law of the European Court of Justice;
- European Parliament recommendations;
- other European or international treaty provisions;
- United Nations sources, *e.g.* General Assembly, Convention and treaty
  provisions (*e.g.* I.C.C.P.R.), cases from the Human Rights Committee,
  reports from the UNHCR, ILO texts;
- Inter-American reports and judgments;
- constitutional law material from outside Europe, *e.g.* US Supreme Court or
  Commonwealth jurisdictions.

PART II: PROBLEM AREAS

General Principles: Fairness

Key provisions:

Article 6, para.1 (fair and public hearing in the determination of criminal charges   IIA–001
and civil rights and obligations, within a reasonable time, before an independent and
impartial tribunal); para.2 (presumption of innocence); para.3(a) (information about
the charge); para.3(b) (adequate time and facilities for preparation); para.3(c) (right
to be present and represented); para.3(d) (right to call and examine witnesses);
para.3(e) (right to interpretation).

Key case law

Albert and Le Compte v Belgium, February 10, 1982, No.58; 5 E.H.R.R. 533, para.39;
Artico v Italy, May 13, 1980, Series A, No.37; 3 E.H.R.R. 1; *Barbera, Massegué and
Jabardo v Spain*, December 6, 1988, Series A, No.146; 11 E.H.R.R. 360; *Kamasinski
v Austria*, December 19, 1989, Series A, No.168; 13 E.H.R.R. 36; *Kraska v
Switzerland*, April 19, 1993, Series A, No.254–B; 18 E.H.R.R. 188; *V v UK*,
December 16, 1999, ECHR 1999–IX.

1. General principles

Complaints about court proceedings form a major percentage of the cases before the   IIA–002
Convention organs, reflecting that it is in court that most people are likely to come
into contact, in a significant manner, with the power and authority of the State as it
administers civil and criminal justice. However, justice is not the word that is
highlighted by the Convention or the Convention organs. The key principle
governing Art.6 guarantees is fairness.[1] Paragraphs 2 and 3 are constituent
elements, or specific aspects of the fair trial guaranteed in paragraph 1. Further,
while the sub-paras 3(a)–(e) exemplify the notion of fair trial in typical procedural
situations, their intrinsic aim is always to ensure or contribute to ensuring the
fairness of the proceedings as a whole.[2] Though they are expressed as applying to
criminal proceedings, they have also been considered by the Court to be implicit
requirements in fairness outside the criminal sphere, applying *mutatis mutandis* in
civil proceedings.[3] While the "fairness" principle applies to both criminal and civil

---

[1] *Kamasinski*, para.62; *Hadjianastassiou v Greece*, December 16, 1992, Series A, No.252–A; 16 E.H.R.R.
219, para.31; *Hamer v France*, August 7, 1996, R.J.D. 1996–III, No.13.
[2] The sub-paragraphs are often considered in conjunction with para.1, *e.g. Can v Austria*, (Rep.) July 12,
1984, Series A, No.96; 8 E.H.R.R. 121.
[3] *Albert and Le Compte*, para.39.

proceedings, a special importance is attached to the rights of the defence in criminal proceedings and where civil litigation is involved national authorities enjoy greater latitude.[4] Nonetheless, in general the same principles of equality of arms, adversarial proceedings, etc. described below apply, if not with the same force, in civil cases.

The right to a fair trial is seen as holding so prominent a place in democratic society that the Court has stated that there is no justification for interpreting Art.6, para.1 restrictively.[5]

As to fairness, it is perhaps simpler to say what it does not mean. The Commission frequently stated, and the Court continues to emphasise, that the Convention organs are not courts of appeal from domestic courts and cannot examine complaints that a court has made errors of fact or law or reached the wrong decision or that a person was, for example, wrongly convicted.[6] They will not enter into the merits of decisions. For this reason, complaints concerning miscarriages of justice are unlikely to succeed before them.[7]

Domestic courts are in the best position to assess the evidence before them, to decide what is relevant or admissible. Matters of appreciation of domestic law and the categorisation of claims in domestic law are also primarily for the appreciation of domestic courts.[8] In this area the Convention organs exercise only a limited supervisory jurisdiction, guided by the overriding principle of fairness. While more recently developments have indicated that the Court will require that reasons be given and that a lack of reasons on key points may disclose unfairness, it is unlikely that it will intervene on substantive matters, *i.e.* the decision itself, unless there is some gross unreasonableness or arbitrariness. This would appear to mean that there is something striking and palpable on the face of the decision.[9]

From the Convention point of view it is not so much the result that is in question but the process of "hearing". An applicant should be "heard", given an adequate and effective opportunity to present his case. Domestic courts are under a duty to conduct a proper examination of the submissions, arguments and evidence adduced by the parties, without prejudice to their assessment of whether they are relevant to its decision.[10] Basing a decision on a clearly inaccurate finding may disclose a failure by the court to ensure an applicant receives a fair hearing,[11] as may an oversight or omission that means an applicant's pleadings are not taken into account.[12]

---

[4] *e.g. Niderost-Huber v Switzerland*, February 18, 1997, R.J.D. 1997–I, No.29, para.28.

[5] *Moreira de Azevedo v Portugal*, October 23, 1990, Series A, No.189, para.66.

[6] *e.g. Sawoniuk v UK*, 63716/00, (Dec.) May 29, 2001, ECHR 2001–VI, where the trial procedures examining offences committed some 50 years earlier were fair, notwithstanding the lapse of time.

[7] *e.g.* 14739/89, (Dec.) May 9, 1989 69 D.R. 296: where the Birmingham Six, alleging wrongful conviction, focussed on the failure to hold a jury trial to rehear the new evidence instead of the Court of Appeal, these matters did not reveal unfairness—juries are not standard features of criminal trials in Europe as a whole and no right to a re-trial is contained in the Convention.

[8] *e.g.* 10153/82, (Dec.) October 13, 1986, 49 D.R. 67.

[9] *e.g. Canela Santiago v Spain*, 60350/00, (Dec.) October 4, 2001: the Court did not exclude that a domestic court refusal to make an Art.177 reference to the European Court of Justice might raise fairness issues if tainted by arbitrariness; *Van Kuck v Germany*, June 12, 2003, para.46, where the Court would not substitute its interpretation of domestic law for that of the domestic courts "in the absence of arbitrariness" and paras 53–57, where it found that their interpretation of "medical necessity" and evaluation of evidence was "not reasonable".

[10] *e.g. Barbera*, para.68; *Kraska*, para.30.

[11] *Fouquet v France*, (Rep.) October 12, 1994, R.J.D. 1996–I (settled before the Court), where the *Cour de Cassation* based itself, erroneously, on the finding that the applicants had admitted fault in their pleadings.

[12] *Quadrelli v Italy*, January 11, 2000, where the Court of Cassation made no reference to the applicant's submissions in its decision and no copy was later found in the file.

2. Aspects of fairness

A number of subsidiary principles have been identified. *Equality of arms* between the parties, or a "fair balance" must be achieved. This means that each party must be afforded a reasonable opportunity to present his case—including his evidence—under conditions which do not place him at a substantial disadvantage *vis-à-vis* his opponent.[13] As the primary purpose of procedural rules is to provide the accused with *protection against abuse of authority*, they should be laid down by law with sufficient clarity and certainty.[14]

IIA–003

Proceedings should also be *adversarial* in character, with an opportunity for the parties to a criminal or civil trial to have knowledge of and comment on all evidence adduced or observations filed even by an independent member of the national legal service with a view to influencing the court's decision[15] or material obtained at the court's own motion.[16] They should also respect the *principle of immediacy*, namely, that witnesses be heard in the presence of the judges who ultimately decide the case.[17]

The importance of ensuring *the appearance of the fair administration of justice* is adverted to in a number of contexts. Foremost, there are the objective requirements of independence and impartiality but there is also the importance of public hearings which allows for public scrutiny of the processes of justice and maintains confidence in the administration of justice.[18]

An accused, and in civil proceedings the parties, must be able to *participate effectively* in proceedings.[19] Measures taken in the conduct of a criminal trial must be reconciliable with an *adequate and effective exercise of the rights of the defence*.[20] The importance of securing defence rights in criminal proceedings has been identified as a fundamental principle of democratic society and in this respect Art.6 must be interpreted to render them practical and effective rather than theoretical and illusory.[21] States are expected to exercise diligence in ensuring defence rights[22] and

---

[13] *e.g. Dombo Beheer BV v Netherlands*, October 27, 1993, Series A, No.274, para.33.

[14] *Coeme v Belgium*, June 22, 2000, ECHR 2000–VII, paras 102–3.

[15] *e.g. Ruiz-Mateos v Spain*, June 23, 1993, Series A, No.262, para.63; *Belziuk v Poland*, March 25, 1998, R.J.D. 1998–II, No.67, para.37(iii). It may apply to proceedings ancillary to the main proceedings, *e.g.* in *Mantovanelli v France*, March 18, 1997, R.J.D. 1997–II, No.32, concerning the expert report procedure. See also Pt IIA: Equality of arms.

[16] *Krcmar v Czech Republic*, March 3, 2000, paras 40–46.

[17] *Pitkanen v Finland*, March 9, 2004, para.58: normally a change in composition of the court after the hearing of an important witness should lead to the rehearing of the witness.

[18] *Bulut v Austria*, February 22, 1996, R.J.D. 1996–III, No.5, para.47; *Borgers v Belgium*, October 30, 1991, Series A, No.214–B, para.24; *Krcmar*, n.16 above, para.43.

[19] *e.g. V v UK*, paras 85–91, where child accused was unable to participate effectively in the public and formal criminal trial procedures in a case attracting intense media attention and public emotion; *SC v UK*, June 15, 2004 (see however strong dissent from the President and Vice-President of the Section, distinguishing this case from *V* as the child was not subject to a traumatic atmosphere and the court had properly considered whether he was able to participate).

[20] *e.g. Ludi v Switzerland*, June 15, 1992, Series A, No.238; 15 E.H.R.R. 173.

[21] *Artico*, para.33.

[22] See, *e.g. Colozza v Italy*, February 12, 1985, Series A, No.89; 7 E.H.R.R. 516, para.28; *Hamer v France*, n.1 above, para.28 where Court objected to the appeal system putting the onus on convicted appellants to find out when an allotted period of time expired; *Vaudelle v France*, January 30, 2001, ECHR 2001–I, paras 52–66, where the courts should have taken additional steps to ensure the attendance of the applicant, who had mental disabilities, at a psychiatric examination and at the hearing; *Frette v France*,

any measures restricting them should be strictly necessary.[23] Thus while an applicant's own conduct will be relevant domestic courts must still ensure the requirements of Art.6, para.1 are met.[24]

The standard applied, however, is not one of perfection. The proceedings are looked at as a whole and one restriction on the defence may be insufficient to render the proceedings as a whole unfair. The Court will examine whether any other opportunities were offered to remedy or make up for some shortcoming. Defects in a trial may be remedied by subsequent procedures before appeal courts.[25] The Convention organs have also had a pragmatic approach to difficulties of criminal justice, in particular to drug-trafficking, organised mafia-type crime and terrorism, and where good reasons exist to keep witnesses anonymous or where circumstances make it impossible for the authorities to act otherwise, allowance is generally made notwithstanding the undesirable effects on defence rights.[26]

Whether or not the "unfairness" alleged has an effect on the outcome of the proceedings is a factor which generally is not, or should not be of relevance.[27] However, occasionally, it is taken into account whether some factor had the possibility of effecting the course of proceedings or outcome and whether the applicant has shown whether it was capable of such effect to distinguish material factors from extraneous or trivial ones.

3. Aspects of conduct of the proceedings

(a) *Conduct of the judge*

IIA–004   Besides the requirements of independence and impartiality, the conduct of the judges in the proceedings must in principle comply with the standard of fairness. However, the cases have so far revealed a certain reluctance to find judges at fault. In *Colak v Germany*, the Court found no unfairness in an alleged assurance to defence counsel from the President of the Assize Court that the only basis for conviction would be grievous bodily harm although subsequently his client was convicted of attempted murder.[28] While in *Kraska v Switzerland*, where in appeal proceedings in a fraud case one of the five judges had stated in open court that he had been unable to read the file, the Court, even while noting the importance of appearances in the

---

February 26, 2002, ECHR 2002–I, para.49, where the burden should not have been on the applicant to contact the *Conseil d'Etat* constantly to discover when his case was listed.

[23] *Van Mechelen v Netherlands*, April 23, 1997, R.J.D. 1997–III, No.36, para.58—if a less restrictive measure can suffice then that measure should be applied.

[24] *Barbera*, para.75—lack of fair trial notwithstanding the applicants' lawyers' failure to make objection to documents not being read out which led to a drastically brief trial; *Kerojärvi v Finland*, July 19, 1995, Series A, No.322, para.42—it was irrelevant that the unassisted applicant made no complaint about non-communication of documents—the Supreme Court should have made them available itself.

[25] *e.g. Edwards v UK*, December 16, 1992, Series A, No.247–B; 15 E.H.R.R. 417. See Pt IIA: Appeals.

[26] *e.g. Ferrantelli and Santangelo v Italy*, August 7, 1996, R.J.D. 1996–III, No.12, where the applicants were unable to question a key witness who had died before an opportunity had been given; *Baegen v Netherlands*, October 27, 1995, Series A, No.327–B (inability to question abuse victim); *Doorson v Netherlands*, March 26, 1996, R.J.D. 1996–II, No.6 (drug trafficking).

[27] *e.g. Artico*, para.35.

[28] December 6, 1988, Series A, No.147; 11 E.H.R.R. 513: the Court noted that the formal position was clear as to the charge before the court and counsel should have known that the court would only rule after its deliberations.

administration of justice, found that the applicant's standpoint was not decisive and any misgivings must also be objectively justified. It found that there was no evidence to suggest that the members of the court failed to examine the appeal with due care before taking their decision and though the judge's comments were open to criticism it did not give rise to any reasonable misgivings.[29] In *CG v United Kingdom*, the judge's interruptions of defence counsel's examination were "excessive and unduly blunt" but since the applicant's counsel was never prevented from continuing his line of defence and his closing speech lasted 45 minutes, with only one brief interruption, the Court assessed that the interruptions were not such as to render the trial, viewed as a whole, unfair.[30]

A failure by a court to comply with domestic procedural rules will not necessarily be fatal either. Where a judge failed as required by law to record his comments to the jury, the Commission noted that Art.6 did not lay down any requirements regarding internal court procedures which were primarily a matter for the domestic courts although it did not exclude that non-observance of such national rules could raise an issue.[31]

(b) *Appearances and incidents in the conduct of the proceedings*

While the conformity of a trial with the requirements of Art.6 must be assessed on the basis of the trial as a whole, a particular incident may assume such importance as to constitute a decisive factor in the general appraisal of the trial overall. In this context there have been occasional incidents where witnesses have been arrested in open court, a dramatic intervention which might be considered to influence the views of juries in particular.[32] Where the applicant's main witness was arrested as an accomplice during the hearing, the Commission noted that the matter of the arrest had been debated before the jury which considered that it did not feel influenced and was able to continue and that the applicant had not been prevented from questioning the witness by the action taken.[33]

As regards the potentially adverse effect of the handcuffing of defendants during criminal trials, the Commission criticised the practice as undesirable in public but never found the issue decisive. Where an applicant was handcuffed during his appeal, no problem of appearances arose and the Commission did not consider that it prevented him presenting his own appeal adequately.[34] Where a defendant sat in a glass cage, the Commission did not accept this stigmatised him before the court and jury as it was a permanent security feature; nor did it place him at a disadvantage as he was able to communicate with his lawyer freely.[35] In *Welch v*

IIA–005

---

[29] See the minority which stressed that in a democratic society the courts must inspire confidence in the public and above all the parties: the judge had indicated that he wanted to read the memorial which he regarded as pertinent and there was accordingly a doubt, which should have been decisive, that the applicant's observations had been not been properly considered by one member of the court.

[30] December 19, 2001.

[31] 13926/88, (Dec.) October 4, 1990, 66 D.R. 209: though the Commission noted sound reasons for the rule, having regard to proceedings as a whole, it concluded that they were not conducted so as to place the applicant at any disadvantage *vis-à-vis* the prosecution.

[32] See Pt IIA: Juries. See also *GB v France*, October 2, 2001, ECHR 2001–X, paras 69–70, where there was a dramatic *"volte face"* by an expert witness during the trial which the applicant was not given opportunity to counter and which could have lent the evidence particular weight with the jury.

[33] 9000/80, (Dec.) March 11, 1982, 28 D.R. 27.

[34] 12323/86, (Dec.) July 13, 1988, 57 D.R. 148.

[35] 11837/85, (Rep.) June 7, 1990, 69 D.R. 126.

United Kingdom, where there was a heavy security presence at the applicant's trial, which was alleged to overdramatise his dangerousness, the Commission considered that the security arrangements had not been shown to be unnecessary or to have been stage-managed, and referring to the practical view that otherwise no trial could be held in security-risk cases, held that the precautions may have led a jury to deduce that the police considered an accused to be dangerous but that this was not the same as a presumption of guilt.[36]

Similarly, in theory, a virulent press campaign may adversely affect the fairness of a trial by influencing public opinion and consequently a jury, although to date it has yet to be shown that a campaign was likely to sway the outcome of a trial.[37]

4. Extent of the applicability of fairness

IIA–006   Fairness applies not only to the immediate conduct of proceedings before the domestic courts *inter partes* but to the proceedings as a whole. Thus the intervention of the legislature to determine the outcome of pending proceedings by passing a law may violate the principle of equality of arms[38], while intervention by other State authorities in obtaining the overturning of final judgments violates the principle of legal certainty which is part of the rule of law.[39] Execution of judgments also falls within the notion of "trial".[40]

---

[36] See also security precautions strapping accused to a stretcher in *Meerbrey v Germany*, 37998/97, (Dec.) January 12, 1998, which were not considered to suggest that he was guilty.

[37] *e.g. Wloch v Poland*, 27785/95, (Dec.) March 30, 2000, *Pullicino v Malta*, 45441/99, (Dec.) June 15, 2000; *Papon v France (No.2)* 34896/97, (Dec.) November 15, 2001, ECHR 2001–XII, where the Court noted the role of the press in contributing to the publicity of proceedings etc, although they should not overstep the bounds imposed in the interests of the administration of justice; *Craxi v Italy (No.2)*, 34896/97, (Dec.) December 5, 2002, severe press criticism of the morality of senior government figures was accepted as inevitable but professional judges could be expected not to be unduly influenced by the debate.

[38] *Stran Greek Refineries v Greece*, December 9, 1994, Series A, No.301–B, para.49.

[39] *e.g. Brumarescu v Romania*, October 28, 1999, ECHR 1999–VIII. See Pt IIA, Access to Court, Setting aside of final judgments.

[40] *Hornsby v Greece*, March 19, 1997, R.J.D. 1997–II, No.33. See Pt IIA, Access to Court, Lack of enforcement.

General Principles: Criminal charge

Key provisions:

Article 6, paras 1, 2 and 3.

Key case law:

Engel v Netherlands, July 8, 1976, Series A, No.22; 1 E.H.R.R 706; *Öztürk v Germany*, February 21, 1984, Series A, No.73; 6 E.H.R.R. 409; *Campbell and Fell v UK*, June 28, 1984, Series A, No.80; 7 E.H.R.R. 165; *Agosi v UK*, October 24, 1996, Series A, No.108; 9 E.H.R.R. 1; *Weber v Switzerland*, May 22, 1990, Series A, No.177; 12 E.H.R.R. 508; *Demicoli v Malta*, August 27, 1991, Series A, No.210; 14 E.H.R.R. 909; *Société Stenuit v France*, February 27, 1992, Series A, No.232–A; 14 E.H.R.R. 509; *Ravnsborg v Sweden*, March 23, 1994, Series A, No.283–B; 18 E.H.R.R. 38; *Raimondo v Italy*, February 22, 1994, Series A, No.281–A; 18 E.H.R.R. 237; *Bendenoun v France*, February 24, 1994, Series A, No.284; 18 E.H.R.R. 54; *Air Canada v UK*, May 5, 1995, Series A, No.316–A; 20 E.H.R.R. 150; *Gradinger v Austria*, October 23, 1995, Series A, No.328–C; *Putz v Austria*, February 22, 1996, R.J.D. 1996–I; *Garyfallou AEBE v Greece*, September 24, 1997, R.J.D. 1997–V, No.49; *Pierre-Bloch v France*, October 22, 1997, R.J.D. 1997–VI, No.53; *Malige v France*, September 23, 1998, R.J.D. 1998–VII, No.93; *Janosevic v Sweden*, July 23, 2002. ECHR 2002–VII; *Ezeh and Connors v UK*, October 9, 2003, ECHR 2003–X.

IIA–007

1. General considerations

In determining the existence of a "criminal charge" for the purposes of applying Art.6, paras 1–3, *Engel v Netherlands* established the three criteria to be read in light of the autonomy of the concept under the Convention—the classification of the offence in domestic law, the nature of the offence and the severity of the penalty. It suffices that the offence in question is "criminal" by its nature from the Convention perspective or that the person is liable to a sanction which is of a nature or severity to fall within the "criminal" sphere.[1] However, where the separate analysis of each criterion does not make it possible to reach a clear conclusion, the Court may adopt a cumulative approach.[2]

IIA–008

2. Autonomous concept

The Court will not allow the Contracting States to re-categorise offences at will to avoid the application of Art.6 guarantees. It reserves supervisory jurisdiction over whether an offence is properly designated as disciplinary but has commented that a State would be free to designate as a criminal offence an act or omission not constituting the normal exercise of one of the rights that the Convention protects since such a choice renders applicable Arts 6 and 7.[3] Although in *Öztürk v Germany*

IIA–009

---

[1] The *Engel* criteria were confirmed by the Grand Chamber in *Ezeh and Connors*, para.82.

[2] *Bendenoun*, para.47; *Garyfallou AEBE*, para.33.

[3] *Engel*, para.81; *Societe Stenuit*, paras 60–61 where domestic law was alleged to exclude fines on corporate bodies from being criminal.

the Court was not in theory opposed to decriminalisation of traffic offences to "regulatory" matters, it considered that it must nonetheless ensure that States do not act against the object and purpose of Art.6. Similarly notwithstanding the special context of military or prison discipline, the guarantee of a fair hearing under Art.6 is one of the fundamental principles of a democratic society and any dividing line between the "disciplinary" and "criminal" sphere has to be consistent with that provision.[4]

3. The Engel criteria

(a) *Classification of the offence in domestic law*

IIA–010   This has not proved an important criterion in practice and is only a starting point.[5] It is also subject to comparison with the applicable legislation in other Contracting States.

(b) *Nature of the offence*

IIA–011   This is a factor of "greater import".[6] The Court has regard to factors such as how the offence is regarded in other Contracting States, the procedures applied, and their connection or similarity to criminal offences and procedures[7] and whether the subject-matter constitutes an offence because of its context or because of general prohibition in the public interest.[8] The imposition of liability on objective grounds without the need to establish any criminal intent or neglect does not deprive an offence of its criminal character however.[9]

Regarding "disciplinary" offences, a distinction is drawn between offences applicable to persons under a specific regime and those affecting potentially the whole population. For example, criminal offences were at stake in *Weber v Switzerland*, where contempt of court, applied to a journalist unconnected with the trial, was not regarded as part of the internal functioning of the court and in *Demicoli v Malta*, where breach of privilege, applied to a journalist's external publication about a member of the legislature, was not a matter of internal parliamentary discipline. In *Ravnsborg v Sweden*, however, the Court noted that the applicant was fined as a party in domestic proceedings, which contempt provisions

---

[4] *Engel*, paras 81–82; *Campbell and Fell*, para.69; *Ezeh and Connors*, para.88.

[5] *e.g.* taxation surcharge cases such as *Janosevic*, para.66.

[6] *Engel*, para.82; *Ezeh and Connors*, para.91.

[7] *e.g. Gradinger*, where the terminology of administrative "criminal" offences was noted; *Steel v UK*, September 23, 1998, R.J.D. VII, No.91, para.48, where breach of the peace was not classed as criminal but the nature of the proceedings, with the applicable penalties, rendered it such.

[8] In *Campbell and Fell*, the Court examined whether the conduct was only an offence because committed in prison or whether it was also prohibited by the criminal law (*e.g.* mutiny and incitement was akin to conspiracy) which could give a "certain colouring" beyond that of a purely disciplinary matter; *Societé Stenuit*, (Rep.) para.62, where the ministerial imposition of a heavy fine on a company was for infringement of economic legislation which affected the general interests of society normally protected by criminal law; *Bendenoun*, where tax penalties applied to all citizens under a general rule. Conversely in 7341//76, (Dec.) March 4, 1978, 15 D.R. 35 a refusal to obey an order (fatigues) was clearly a disciplinary matter, based on internal operating rules of the armed forces as was 5 days' isolation as punishment of a soldier for late return—7754/77, (Dec.) May 9, 1977, 11 D.R.. 216.

[9] *Janosevic*, para.68.

did not apply to persons making statements outside those proceedings. Sanctions imposed on persons participating in proceedings pursuant to court powers to ensure the orderly conduct of the proceedings are therefore likely to fall outside the criminal sphere[10] unless the penalty is severe enough to attract the guarantees of Art.6 nonetheless. Disciplinary proceedings against lawyers and doctors accordingly will not become criminal, where confined to an essentially disciplinary context even where the fine can be described as punitive in size.[11]

Where tax surcharges are not intended as pecuniary compensation for any costs incurred as a result of the taxpayer's conduct but are predominantly punitive and deterrent, they have been found to disclose a criminal character.[12]

The lack of seriousness of minor offences, as in careless driving in Öztürk, may not divest offences of their criminal character.[13] In Öztürk, the Court had regard to the character of the rule, noting that it was still criminal in other countries and aimed at the public generally.[14]

(c) *Severity of the penalty*

The Court looks at the nature and purpose of the penalty "liable to be imposed" on the applicant. While the actual penalty imposed is stated to be relevant, this is not seen as diminishing the importance of what was initially at stake.[15] Regard is had to the nature and purpose of the penalty, in particular whether it is intended to be deterrent and punitive.[16] **IIA–012**

Deprivation of liberty as a penalty (excepting measures which by length or nature are not appreciably detrimental[17]) generally belongs to the criminal sphere, bearing in mind the seriousness of what is at stake and the importance attached to physical liberty.[18] The threat of imprisonment may also be decisive. In *Engel*, the fact an applicant received a penalty not occasioning deprivation of liberty did not affect the Court's assessment since the final outcome of the appeal could not diminish the importance of what was initially at stake.[19] In *Campbell and Fell v United Kingdom*, loss of remission of almost three years, even though remission was a privilege rather

---

[10] *Putz*, para.33—concerning fines imposed on applicant by a court for disrupting the proceedings, which conduct in principle fell outside Art.6.

[11] e.g. *Irving Brown v UK*, 38644/97, (Dec.) November 24, 1998, where a solicitor was fined £10,000.

[12] *Janosevic*, para.68.

[13] See also *Ezeh and Connors*, para.104—the criminal nature of the offence does not necessarily require a certain degree of seriousness, while the severity of the penalty falls under the third criteria.

[14] See also *Schmautzer v Austria*, October 23, 1995, Series A, No.328–A (fine for not wearing seatbelt); *Umlauft v Austria*, October 23, 1995, Series A, No.328–B (refusal to give breath sample); *Malige* (loss of points on driving licence).

[15] *Ezeh and Connors*, para.120.

[16] *Öztürk*, para.53; *Steel* (Rep.), n.7 above, para.67, where proceedings for breach of the peace leading to binding over were criminal in nature, as deterrent (requiring the person to keep the peace) and punitive (since if person did not agree he was imprisoned).

[17] *Engel*, where for one applicant a risk of 2 days' strict arrest for absence without leave was considered too short a duration and for another, four days' light arrest did not constitute deprivation of liberty; *Brandao Ferreira v Portugal*, 41921/98, (Dec.) September 28, 2000, ECHR 2000–X—five days' simple arrest where the applicant continued to discharge most of his duties.

[18] *Engel*, para.82 ; *Campbell and Fell*, para.72.

[19] *Engel*, where three applicants faced risk of 3–4 mths committal to disciplinary unit; *Demicoli*, where the applicant, though only fined for breach of privilege, risked imprisonment of 60 days; *Weber*, where the applicant was at risk of fine for contempt of 500 swiss francs convertible in certain circumstances into a period of imprisonment; *Gradinger*, a fine for drink driving with prison in default.

than a right, was taken into account since it had the effect of extending the expected period of detention and came close to deprivation of liberty. The Court found that the object and purpose of the Convention required that imposition of a measure of such severity attracts guarantees of Art.6. This approach has been reinforced in *Ezeh and Connors v United Kingdom*, where the imposition of additional days on prisoners for punitive reasons after a finding of culpability, was found to be a criminal penalty in nature and degree, notwithstanding that it did not increase a prisoner's sentence as a matter of law but affected the calculation of the release date. It referred to the test of whether the effective deprivation of liberty was "appreciably detrimental" in nature and found that the maximum period of 42 days imposable, and the actual penalty of 40 and 7 days, respectively crossed this threshold.

Where fines are concerned, consideration is given to whether they are intended as pecuniary compensation for damage or essentially as a punishment to deter re-offending.[20] In Öztürk, where the applicant was only fined 60 DM, the Court referred to the purpose of the penalty being to deter and punish. In other cases, where considerations as to the nature of the offence weigh more heavily, larger fines have not been decisive[21] and there is some authority that minor taxation surcharges will not be serious enough to bring administrative fiscal procedures within the scope of Art.6.[22] Forfeiture measures have not been regarded as criminal penalties[23] nor have preventive measures or the application of personal security measures.[24] Confiscation orders, which are conditional on criminal convictions, and are deterrent in nature and purpose, rather than preventive, have been found to constitute "penalties" under Art.7, which prohibits retrospective criminal penalties.[25] A payment order imposed on an electoral candidate for exceeding the limit on campaign expenses was found by the Court to be a payment to the community of the sum by which the applicant improperly took advantage to seek votes and thus not a criminal penalty akin to a fine.[26]

The docking of points from a licence imposed in the context of, and as the outcome of criminal proceedings, was seen as punitive and deterrent in character and also, impliedly, serious as it could lead in time to the invalidation of the licence.

---

[20] *e.g. Benedoun*, para.47, where tax penalties were not intended as compensation for pecuniary damage but as punishment to deter re-offending; *Société Stenuit*, para.64, where sanctions were imposable on a company up to 5% of its turnover indicated that it was intended to be deterrent; *cf. Shirley Porter v UK*, 15814/02, (Dec.) April 8, 2003, where the surcharge imposed on the applicant for wilful misconduct as leader of a council reflected the loss suffered by the local authority.

[21] *Ravnsborg*, which involved three fines of 1000 kroner for contempt, convertible to imprisonment by the court in limited circumstances when the applicant would be summoned to an oral hearing in separate proceedings—also the fines were not registered on police files as other criminal "fines" were; *Putz*, fines were convertible but only up to 10 days, not entered on the record and appeals were possible; *Bendenoun*, where the substantial fines of 4–500,000 FRF were not decisive in themselves; *Shirley Porter*, n.20 above, where the sheer size of the surcharge (millions of pounds) did not render it criminal.

[22] *Morel v France*, 54559/00, (Dec.) June 3, 2003, concerning 10% increase of 4450 FRF.

[23] *Agosi* (seizure and forfeiture of kruegerrands by Customs); *Air Canada* (Customs seizure an aircraft, released on payment of £50 000). Where property or pecuniary rights are concerned however Art.6 in its civil aspect is likely to apply.

[24] *e.g. Raimondo*, para.43 (special supervision, including confiscation of property of the applicant on grounds of suspicion of membership in a mafia-type organisation); *Riela v Italy*, 52349/99, (Dec.) September 4, 2001 (preventive and confiscatory measures); *Guzzardi v Italy*, November 6, 1980, Series A, No.39, para.108 (compulsory residence requirements).

[25] *Welch v UK*, February 9, 1995, Series A, No.307–A; 20 E.H.R.R. 247.

[26] *Pierre-Bloch*, para.58.

Art.6 therefore applied to the procedure.[27] Educational measures imposed on drivers, involving costs and loss of licence in case of failure to comply were not criminal, where imposed separately from criminal proceedings and independently of any conviction.[28]

4. Proceedings excluded from Article 6 "criminal aspect"

The following have not been found "criminal":

IIA–013

- proceedings which relate to issues of lawfulness of detention where the *lex specialis* is Art.5[29] or to the execution of sentences[30];
- decisions to deport an alien[31] or to exclude an alien, even where imposed in the context of criminal proceedings, are regarded as special preventive measures of the purposes of immigration control[32];
- decisions by courts on extradition requests, even where there is an assessment as to whether there is a case to answer[33];
- restrictions placed by Secretary of State on activities in running insurance companies[34];
- proceedings ancillary or associated with criminal proceedings which are not decisive for the determination of the criminal charge, *e.g.* applications for legal aid[35] or Constitutional Court proceedings which are not capable of affecting the outcome[36];
- applications for re-opening of proceedings, retrial, nullity or amnesty[37];
- proceedings under s.4A of the Criminal Procedure (Insanity) Act 1964 where the applicant has been found unfit to plead and the procedure, aimed at establishing the facts, cannot result in a conviction[38];
- proceedings under the Local Government Finance Act 1982, reclaiming as surcharges the amount of money lost by the local authority due to an officer's wilful misconduct.[39]
- imposition of interest for late tax payments[40];
- administrative fines for carrying out work on a house without planning permission.[41]

---

[27] *Malige*, paras 38–40. Contrast *Escoubet v Belgium*, October 28, 1999, ECHR 1999–VII; where Art.6 was not applicable to the short term provisional withdrawal of a driving licence prior to the applicant being charged with an offence.

[28] *Blokker v Netherlands*, 45282/99, (Dec.) November 7, 2000.

[29] *e.g.* review of an order for detention on remand—6541/74, (Dec.) December 18, 1974; 1 D.R. 82.

[30] *Aydin v Turkey*, 41954/98, (Dec.) September 14, 2000.

[31] *e.g. Agee v UK*, 7729/76, (Dec.) December. 17, 1976, 7 D.R. 64.

[32] *Maaouia v France*, October 5, 2000, ECHR 2000–X, para.39.

[33] 10479/83, (Dec.) March 12, 1984, 37 D.R. 158; *Penafiel Salgado v Spain*, 65964/01, (Dec.) April 16, 2002.

[34] 7598/76, (Dec.) July 17, 1980 21 D.R. 5.

[35] *Gutfreund v France*, June 12, 2003—the procedure was separate from the criminal trial and did not involve the establishment of guilt, the fixing of sentence or establishment of facts.

[36] *Gast and Popp v Germany*, February 25, 2000, ECHR 2000–II, paras 63–68.

[37] *e.g. Fischer v Austria*, 27569/02, (Dec.) May 6, 2003 (retrial or plea of nullity); *Montcornet de Caumont v France*, 59290/00, (Dec.) May 13, 20000 (amnesty).

[38] *Antoine v UK*, 62960/00, (Dec.) May 13, 2003.

[39] *Shirley Porter*, n.20 above.

[40] *Boofzheim v France*, 52938/99, ECHR 2002–X.

[41] *Inocencio v Portugal*, 43862/98, (Dec.) January 11, 2001.

Cross-reference

Part IIA: Length of proceedings (duration of "criminal charge")
Part IIA: Retrospectivity (penalties)
Part IIB: Army, Discipline

General Principles: Civil rights and obligations

Key provision:

Article 6, para.1.

Key case law:

Lecompte, Van Leuven and De Meyere v Belgium, June 23, 1981, Series A, No.43; 4   **IIA–014**
E.H.R.R. 1; *Sporrong and Llönnroth v Sweden,* September 23, 1982, Series A, No.52;
5 E.H.R.R. 35; *Benthem v Netherlands,* October 23, 1985, Series A, No.97; 8
E.H.R.R. 1; *Feldbrugge v Netherlands,* May 29, 1986, Series A, No.99; 8 E.H.R.R.
425; *Deumeland v Germany,* May 29, 1986, Series A, No.100; 8 E.H.R.R. 448; *Van
Marle v Netherlands,* June 26, 1986, Series A, No.101; 8; E.H.R.R. 483; *W v UK,*
July 8, 1987, Series A, No.121; 10 E.H.R.R. 29; *Pudas v Sweden,* October 27,
1987, Series A, No.125; 10 E.H.R.R. 380; *H v Belgium,* November 30, 1987,
Series A, No.127; 10 E.H.R.R. 339; *Tre Traktorer v Sweden,* July 7, 1989, Series A,
No.159; 13 E.H.R.R. 309; *Allan Jacobsson v Sweden (No.1),* October 25, 1989,
Series A, No.163; 12 E.H.R.R 56; *Fredin v Sweden (No.1),* February 18, 1991,
Series A, No.192; 13 E.H.R.R. 784; *Kraska v Switzerland,* April 19, 1993, Series
A, No.254–B; 18 E.H.R.R. 188; *Ruiz-Mateos v Spain,* June 23, 1993, Series A,
No.262; 16 E.H.R.R. 505; *Schuler-Zraggen v Switzerland,* June 24, 1993, Series A,
No.263; 16 E.H.R.R. 405; *Schouten and Meldrum v Netherlands,* December 9, 1994,
Series A, No.304; 19 E.H.R.R. 432; *Procola v Luxembourg,* September 28, 1995,
Series A, No.326; 22 E.H.R.R. 193; *Masson and Van Zon v Netherlands,* September
28, 1995, Series A, No.327–A; 22 E.H.R.R. 491; *Süssman v Germany,* September
16, 1996, R.J.D. 1996–IV, No.15; *Georgiadis v Greece,* May 29, R.J.D. 1997–III,
No.38; *Rolf Gustafsson v Sweden,* August 1, 1997, R.J.D. 1997–IV, No.41; *Pierre-
Bloch v France,* October 22, 1997, R.J.D. 1997–VI, No.53; *Pellegrin v France,*
December 8, 1999, ECHR 1999–VIII; *Maaouia v France,* October 5, 20000,
ECHR 2000–X; *Z v UK,* May 10, 2001, ECHR 2001–V; *Ferrazzini v Italy,* July
12, 2001, ECHR 2001–VII.

1. General considerations

Outside the criminal sphere, the guarantees of fair trial under Art.6, para.1 apply   **IIA–015**
only to proceedings which involve the determination of "civil rights and
obligations". This includes a number of considerations: the rights or obligations
must at least on arguable grounds exist in domestic law; there must be a dispute
or "contestation" about those rights and obligations of a "genuine and of a serious
nature"and which is decisive for those rights; and the rights claimed must be
"civil" in nature.

Interpretation has been progressive in this area. Matters which once were
considered as outside the scope of Art.6, para.1, such as welfare benefits, now
generally fall inside the scope of "civil rights and obligations". The concepts
applied are wide and capable of application to almost any type of significant
dispute.

2. Basis in domestic law

IIA–016   Article 6 does not guarantee any particular content for "rights and obligations" in the substantive law of Contracting States. There must at least on arguable grounds be a basis for the right in domestic law,[1] while matters at the total discretion of the authorities may not disclose a "right".[2]

Where in child care cases the Government claimed that parental rights resolutions had the effect in domestic law of extinguishing parental rights of access, the Court noted that the effect of the measures did not extinguish all parental rights in respect of a child, which in any event would hardly have been compatible with fundamental rights of family life under Art.8, and having regard to statutory recognition that parental access was desirable, found that there was at least on arguable grounds a right of access in domestic law. It would seem that where parental- child relationships are concerned the Convention organs will be reluctant to find no right existing in domestic law, on an underlying assumption that such matters are of fundamental importance.[3] Similar considerations might apply where proceedings concern serious interferences with other fundamental rights guaranteed under the Convention.

3. Dispute or "contestation" concerning rights and obligations

IIA–017   This element which is derived from the French text of Art.6 is not to be construed too technically, and given a substantive rather than formal meaning.[4] A tenuous connection or remote consequences between the dispute and the right does not suffice.[5] Civil rights or obligations must be the object or one of the objects of the dispute and the result of the proceedings must be directly decisive for such a right.[6] A dispute can for these purposes concern not only the actual existence of the right but the scope of the right or its manner of exercise.[7] It may concern both questions of fact and law.[8]

The dispute must also be of "genuine and serious nature".[9] For example, where an applicant complained about the amount of child maintenance imposed by the Child Support Agency, the Commission noted that there was no provision for the costs of access visits to be taken into account as the applicant claimed and that he did not deny that the assessment had been correctly made under the legislation. Thus there was no dispute, or any dispute of a genuine or serious nature about any

---

[1] *e.g. Z v UK*, paras 87 and 98.

[2] *e.g. Masson and Van Zon*, where compensation for costs in criminal proceedings ending in an acquittal were at the discretion of the courts; 16484/90, (Dec.) January 17, 1991 where the applicant could not claim a right to obtain a licence in Gibraltar to operate a fast launch; 11098/84, (Dec.) July 1, 1985, 43 D.R. 198 where compensation for criminal injuries was *ex gratia*. Contrast *Rolf Gustafsson*, where the Court found domestic law conferred a right to compensation where certain conditions were fulfilled.

[3] See however *Price v UK*, 12402/86, (Dec.) July 14, 1988, 55 D.R. 224: no rights in domestic law were found in favour of grandparental access to children.

[4] *Lecompte*, para.45.

[5] *ibid.*, para.47.

[6] *ibid.*, para.47. *Balmer-Schafroth v Switzerland*, August 26, 1997, R.J.D. 1997–IV, No.43, para.32.

[7] *e.g. Lecompte*, para.47: thus Art.6 applied even though the right to practise medicine was not removed but only briefly suspended.

[8] *e.g. Pudas*, para.31.

[9] *Benthem*, para.32.

civil right or obligation.[10] In *Van Marle v Netherlands*, the Court found no dispute, where the applicants had been refused registration as certified accountants following an examination of their competence. It considered that there were no claims of irregularity in the procedure and that assessments involving the evaluation of knowledge and experience for carrying on a profession were akin to school or university examinations and as such were removed from normal judicial functions. Conversely, in *H v Belgium*, where the applicant had been struck off from the Bar and refused reinstatment, the Court found a dispute capable of judicial assessment, having regard to the terms of the regulations which allowed reinstatement in "exceptional circumstances" which left scope for a variety of interpretations and under which the applicant could arguably claim the right to practise at the Bar since he fulfilled the conditions.

The Court has stated that Art.6, para.1 can be relied on where an applicant claims that an interference with the exercise of a civil right is unlawful.[11] Thus in cases where notwithstanding the wide discretion imposed on public authorities in the imposition of measures, applicants who are able to challenge the lawfulness of the measures in the most general sense may claim a dispute. This was where the authorities' discretion was not unfettered since they were bound by generally recognised legal and administrative principles.[12]

4. Civil nature of the right or obligation

The concept of "civil rights and obligations" is not to be interpreted solely by reference to the respondent State's domestic law but is an autonomous notion based on the character of the right.[13] Article 6, para.1 also applies irrespective of the status of the parties, the character of the legislation which governs how the dispute is to be determined and the character of the authority which is invested with jurisdiction in the matter, the key point being whether the outcome of the proceedings is decisive for private rights and obligations.[14]

The Court has regard to the private and personal nature of the right, whether it is connected with contractual relationships,[15] connected with the exercise or enjoyment of property rights[16] or the exercise of commercial, business or professional

IIA–018

---

[10] 24875/94, (Dec.) September 9, 1996, 86–A D.R. 74.

[11] *Lecompte*, para.44.

[12] *Pudas*, para.34; *Allan Jacobsson*, para.69; para.28, *Tre Traktorer*, paras 39–40: *e.g.* where applicants alleged improper motives by the authorities, departure from longstanding practice, failure to take their interests into account, discrimination, abuse of power, which was regarded as raising issues of lawfulness.

[13] *e.g. Konig v Germany*, June 28, 1978, Series A, No.27, paras 88–89; *Baraona v Portugal*, July 8, 1987, Series A, No.122, paras 42–43: it was not decisive that Portugese law distinguished between acts of private and public administration, where the right in issue was a personal property right.

[14] *Ringeisen*, para.94; *Editions Periscope v France*, March 26, 1992, Series A, No.234, para.40, where it was not decisive that the dispute originated in the State's functions in imposing tax and was dealt with in the administrative courts.

[15] *Lecompte*, para.48, where a profession is conducted by means of private relationships with clients on a contractual or quasi-contractual nature, regardless of whether the profession is exercised in the public interest with special duties, *e.g.* medical profession.

[16] *e.g. Baraona*, n.13 above, para.44; property cases, *e.g. Sporrong and Llonroth* (imposition of expropriation permit), para.79; *Fredin* (revocation of permit to exploit gravel pit), para.63; *Ortenberg v Austria*, November 25, 1994, Series A, No.295–B; 19 E.H.R.R. 193; (public law objections to planning permission granted by authorities to owners of neighbouring land).

activities[17] or whether the subject-matter of the action is pecuniary in nature and founded on infringement of rights of a pecuniary nature.[18] For example, in *Pudas v Sweden*, where the applicant taxi-driver's taxi licence was revoked this was clearly civil, having regard to its connection with his business activities, carried out with the object of earning profits and based on contractual relationships with customers. State regulation of certain activities in the public interest, *e.g.* transport or sale of alcohol or the practice of law may bestow features of public law but will not suffice to exclude private commercial activities from the category of civil rights.[19]

Proceedings for compensation generally have a private law character even where derived from public law or criminal proceedings.[20] Where the outcome of constitutional or public law proceedings may be decisive for civil rights and obligations, such proceedings, even if before the Constitutional Court, will fall within the scope of Art.6, para.1. In *Ruiz-Mateos v Spain*, the Court noted that the constitutional proceedings challenging a law was the sole means available to the applicants to complain of an interference with their property rights by an expropriation decree. Application to the *Conseil d'Etat* for the annulment of orders fixing milk quotas in *Procola v Luxembourg* was closely connected by its possible outcome to the pecuniary rights and economic activities of the applicant agricultural association.[21]

In the areas of social security or State benefits, the Court's examination previously centred on whether the private law or public law features are of greater significance.[22] Particular weight has been given to the similarity between social security schemes and private insurance as lending a private law character. Links with contracts of employment have also been emphasised. In the cases so far considered by the Court, these private law features have outweighed the public law elements present, such as the character of the legislation, assumption of responsibility by public authorities, the compulsory nature of the schemes.[23] In *Schuler-Zgraggen v Switzerland* the Court stated that as a general rule Art.6, para.1 applied in the field of social insurance and that the most important consideration militating in favour of applicability was that the applicant had suffered an interference with her means of subsistence and was claiming "an individual, economic right flowing from the specific rules laid down in domestic law".[24] While this approach was stated not to

---

[17] *Benthem*, para.36, concerning the refusal to the owner of a garage of a licence to install LPG storage tank to supply motor vehicles; *Tre Traktorer*, para.43, finding that revocation of a restaurant licence to serve alcohol had adverse effects on the goodwill and value of the business and that the serving of alcohol was a private commercial activity based on the earning of profits and contractual relationships; *H v Belgium*, right to practise as an advocate.

[18] *e.g.* *Editions Periscope*, n.14 above. However this is to be distinguished from proceedings which merely have an economic aspect, *e.g.* *Pierre-Bloch*, para.51.

[19] *e.g.* *Pudas*, para.37, *Tre Traktorer*, para.43; *H v Belgium*, where advocates were part of the judicial system and subject to public law regulation, they still exercised an independent profession and their chambers and clientèle constituted property interests.

[20] *e.g.* *Georgiadis*, para.35: claims for compensation for detention following acquittal; *Beaumartin v France*, November 24, 1994, Series A, No.296–B; 19 E.H.R.R. 485; where the compensation claim for expropriated property in Morocco derived from an international agreement between France and Morocco—notwithstanding the treaty and State prerogative aspects, French nationals could claim a share pursuant to a decree and the right was pecuniary in nature based on property rights.

[21] See also *Kraska* (public law proceedings concerning practice of the medical profession); *Sussman* (Constitutional Court proceedings concerning amendments to civil servant pension schemes).

[22] *e.g.* *Schouten and Meldrum*, paras 40–60.

[23] *e.g.* *Feldbrugge*, *Deumeland*, *Salesi v Italy*, February 26, 1993, Series A, No.257–E.

[24] para.46.

apply automatically to obligations to pay contributions as opposed to claims to entitlements, Art.6 was still found to apply to disputes about the amount of contributions to be paid in *Schouten and Meldrum v Netherlands* (See Pt IIB: Welfare benefits).

The status of European community "rights" for the purposes of Art.6, para.1 has been considered in a few cases. The Commission found that "civil rights" included rights arising under directly applicable European community law[25] but however where the character of the right was perceived to be public Art.6 was excluded.[26]

The following have been found to be covered : the proceedings relating to the costs of proceedings[27]; measures confiscating property of suspected organised crime members[28]; procedures for changing surnames[29]; civil-party interventions in criminal proceedings.[30]

Areas falling outside Art.6 are principally matters relating to deprivation of liberty which fall to be dealt with under the *lex specialis* of Art.5[31]; proceedings relating to asylum, expulsion and nationality[32] or extradition.[33] The Court also decided in *Pellegrin v France*, applying a functional test unrelated to domestic classification, that matters relating to the employment or dismissal of public officials or civil servants who exercise the authority of the State and enjoy a special bond of trust and loyalty fall outside Art.6.[34] This covers the armed forces and the police[35] and has also excluded disputes about salaries by senior judges[36] and by diplomats and senior Foreign Ministry officials.[37] It is possible that disputes about pension rights which are not directly related to the exercise of public powers could still fall within Art.6.[38]

---

[25] 24960/94, (Dec.) January 11, 1995, where nonetheless the applicant *avocat stagiaire* in Rome did not enjoy the status under EEC provisions to claim the right to practise law in Greece.

[26] 28979/95 and 30343/96, (Dec.) January 13, 1997, where the applicants claimed freedom of movement within the European Union, the Commission noted the origin and general nature of the Maastricht provision, and the lack of personal, economic or individual aspects characteristic to the private law sphere.

[27] See Fair trial guarantees, Costs in court.

[28] *e.g. Riela v Italy*, 52439/99; (Dec.) September 4, 2001.

[29] *Mustafa v France*, June 17, 2003.

[30] *Perez v France*, February 12, 2004.

[31] *e.g.* 6541/74, (Dec.) December 18, 1974, 1 D.R. 82.

[32] *e.g. Maaouia*, paras 36–41 (Art.6 not applicable to decisions concerning the entry, stay and deportation of aliens); *Katani v Germany*, 67679/01, (Dec.) May 31, 2001 (not applicable to asylum procedures).

[33] *Salgado v Spain*, 65964/01, (Dec.) April 16, 2002 (extradition proceedings).

[34] *Pellegrin*, overruling *Neigel v France*, March 17, 1997, R.J.D. 1997–II, No.32. This definition of public official does not cover nursery school, secondary school or university teachers (*Volkmer v Germany*, 39799/98, *Petersen v Germany* 39793/98 and *Knauth v Germany*, 41111/98, (Decs.) November 11, 2001, ECHR 2001–XII), low-level civil servants (*Devlin v UK*, October 30, 2001), school caretakers (*Procaccini v Italy*, March 30, 2000), director of a district medical-pedagogical centre (*Satonnet v France*, August 2, 2000); a ministry technical adviser sent under contract to work overseas (*Frydlender v France*, June 27, 2000, ECHR 2000–VII).

[35] *Pellegrin*, para.66; *Batur v Turkey*, 38604/97, (Dec.) July 4, 2000 (dismissal of army officer).

[36] *Kajanen v Finland*, 36401/97, (Dec.) October 19, 2000; *Pitkevich v Russia* 47936/99, (Dec.) February 8, 2001.

[37] *Martinez Caro v Spain*, 36401/98, (Dec.) March 7, 2000; also excluded in *Pellegrin* was a senior civil servant exercising considerable responsibilities in public finances which entailed participating directly in the exercise of powers conferred by public law and the performance of duties designed to safeguard State interests.

[38] See *Massa v Italy*, August 24, 1993, Series A, No.265–B; 18 E.H.R.R. 266, (claim for pension by surviving spouse) and, *mutatis mutandis*, *Martinez Caro*, n.37 above (concerning salaries and special allowances).

Matters relating to the obligation to pay tax will generally fall outside the scope of civil rights,[39] save where relating to pecuniary claims with a foundation in private law (see Pt IIB: Tax). Claims relating to electoral or political matters will be excluded (See Pt IIB: Electoral rights). Nor is there any right to have other persons prosecuted or sentenced for a criminal offence.[40]

Cases have also held Art.6, para.1 inapplicable to the right to report on a public trial[41]; refusal to issue a passport;[42] right not to be denied elementary education[43]; unilateral decision of the State to compensate the victims of a natural disaster;[44] proceedings before a Parliamentary Commission.[45]

Cross-reference

Part IIA: Access to court
Part IIA: Costs in court
Part IIB: Electoral rights
Part IIB: Pensions
Part IIB: Tax
Part IIB: Welfare benefits

---

[39] *Ferrazzini*; *Vidacar and Obergrup SL v Spain*, 41601/98 and 41775/98, (Dec.) April 20, 1999, ECHR 1999–V.
[40] *Perez*, n.30 above, para.70.
[41] 23868–23869/94, (Dec.) February 24, 1995, 80 D.R. 162.
[42] 19583/92, (Dec.) February 20, 1995, 80 D.R. 38.
[43] 14688/89, December 4, 1989, 64 D.R. 188.
[44] 14225/88, (Dec.), December 3, 1990, 69 D.R. 223.
[45] *Montera v Italy*, 64713/01, (Dec.) July 9, 2002.

Access to court

Key provision:

Article 6, para.1.

Key case law:

Golder v UK, February 21, 1975, Series A, No.18; 1 E.H.R.R. 524; *Campbell and* IIA–019
Fell v UK, June 28, 1984, Series A, No.80; *Ashingdane v UK*, May 28, 1985, Series
A, No.93; 7 E.H.R.R. 528; *Powell and Rayner v UK*, February 21, 1990, Series A,
No.172; 12 E.H.R.R. 355; *Philis v Greece (No.1)*, August 27, 1991, Series A,
No.209; 13 E.H.R.R. 741; *Hennings v Germany*, December 16, 1992, Series
A, No.251–A; 16 E.H.R.R. 83; *De Geouffre de la Pradelle v France*, December 16,
1992, Series A, No.253; *Zumtobel v Austria*, September 21, 1993, Series A, No.268–
A; 17 E.H.R.R. 116; *Fayed v UK*, September 21, 1994, Series A, No.294–B; 18
E.H.R.R. 116; *Air Canada v UK*, May 5, 1995, Series A, No.316–A; 20 E.H.R.R.
150; *Bellet v France*, December 4, 1995, Series A, No.333–B; *Bryan v UK*,
November 22, 1995, Series A, No.335–A; 21 E.H.R.R. 342; *Stubbings v UK*,
October 22, 1996, R.J.D. 1996–IV, No.18; *Hornsby v Greece*, March 19, 1997,
R.J.D. 1997–II, No.33; *Canea Catholic Church v Greece*, December 16, 1997, R.J.D.
1997–VIII, No.60; *Tinnelly and McElduff v UK*, July 10, 1998, R.J.D. 1998–IV,
No.79; *Osman v UK*, October 28, 1998, R.J.D. 1998–VIII, No.95; *Brumarescu v
Romania*, October 28, 1999, ECHR 1999–VIII; *Z v UK*, May 10, 2001, ECHR
2001–V; *Al-Adsani v UK*, November 21, 2001, ECHR 2001–I; *A v UK*, December
12, 2002, ECHR 2002–X. *Ryabykh v Russia*, July 24, 2003, ECHR 2003–IX.

1. General considerations

The interpretation of Art.6, para.1 to confer an effective right of access to court in IIA–020
the determination of civil rights and obligations is one of the most significant and
creative steps taken by the Convention organs. In *Golder v United Kingdom*, where a
prisoner had been refused permission to contact his solicitor with a view to bringing
a civil action for libel against a prison officer, the Court, faced with the question as
to whether Art.6, para.1 was limited to guaranteeing the right to a fair trial to
pending legal proceedings or whether in addition it secured a right of access to court
for persons wishing to bring an action concerning their civil rights and obligations,
found in favour of the latter. The Court noted that otherwise a Contracting State
would be free to abolish its courts or remove jurisdiction over particular classes of
action, which would bring in the danger of arbitrary power and the denial of the
principles of justice.[1]

The right of access to court is not absolute however but subject to limitations. By
its very nature, the Court has said, it calls for regulation by the State, which may
vary in time and in place according to the needs and resources of the community

---

[1] Re-iterated since, *e.g. Fayed*, para.63, *A v UK*, para.63, to the effect that it would not be consistent with
the rule of law if States could, without restraint or control by the Convention organs, remove from the
jurisdiction of the courts a whole range of civil claims or confer immunities from civil liability on large
groups or categories of persons.

and individuals.[2] The State has a margin of appreciation in making such regulations but the limitations applied must not restrict or reduce the access left to the individual in such a way as or to such an extent that the very essence of the right is impaired. In addition, a limitation will not be compatible with Art.6 if it does not pursue a legitimate aim and if there is not a reasonable proportionality between the means employed and the aim sought to be achieved. These criteria are sometimes referred to as the "*Ashingdane* principles".[3]

2. Applicability

IIA–021   Access to court can only apply in respect of *contestations* (disputes) over civil rights and obligations which can be said, at least on arguable grounds, to be recognised under domestic law; it cannot in itself guarantee any particular content for those rights.[4]

An applicant's complaint of denial of access must relate to a right which has a basis in domestic law. In *Powell and Rayner v United Kingdom,* where a statute provided that nuisance and trespass would not lie in respect of the ordinary incidents of flights of aircraft which conformed with reasonable height requirements and navigation regulations, the Court found that as a result of this exclusion of liability the applicant houseowners could not claim to have a substantive right under English law to obtain relief for for exposure to aircraft noise in those circumstances.[5]

Whether a limitation on a claim constitutes a procedural bar restricting access to court or forms part of the substantive definition of the right in domestic law may in some cases be difficult to distinguish and the matter has been left open by the Court in a number of cases. Difficulties have arisen particularly as the operation of special defences, privileges and immunities (see section 4: Defences, privileges and immunities, below).

3. Procedural and practical restrictions

IIA–022   Procedural and practical impediments may contravene the Convention where they operate to bar effective access to court.[6]

(a) *Obstacles in obtaining access*

IIA–023   Refusal of permission to prisoner to contact his solicitor with a view to suing a prison officer in libel deprived him of access to court: it was not for the Secretary of State to take the role of determining whether or not such a claim had prospects of success.[7] Inability for a prisoner to have confidential out of hearing consultations with a solicitor was also considered to deny effective access to court.[8]

---

[2] *Golder*, para.38.
[3] *Ashingdane*, para.57.
[4] *e.g. W v UK*, July 8, 1987, Series A, No.121; 10 E.H.R.R. 29; *Z v UK*, para.98.
[5] See also 12810/87, (Dec.) January 18, 1989, 59 D.R. 172; 14324/88, (Dec.) April 19, 1991, 69 D.R. 227.
[6] *Golder*, para.26.
[7] *Golder, ibid.*
[8] *Campbell and Fell v UK.* See also *McComb v UK*, 10621/83, (Dec.) March 11, 1985 (complaints of

If the authorities, without cause, prevented applicants from gaining access to documents in their possession which would assist them in their claims, or falsely denied the existence of such documents, the Court stated, in *McGinley and Egan v United Kingdom*[9] that problems of fairness or effective access to court could arise. In that case however there was a procedure available for applying for access to relevant records and it had not been shown that the State had prevented access to any relevant evidence.

(b) *Limitations on categories of litigant and legal standing*

Limitations on access as regards minors and persons of unsound mind, bankrupts IIA–024
and vexatious litigants have been acknowledged as pursuing legitimate aims. However the *Ashingdane* principles still apply, though so far restrictions examined have generally not been found incompatible with them.[10] In *Luordo v Italy*, the bar on a bankrupt's ability to litigate was considered to pursue the aim of protecting the rights of others, including the creditors and only fell foul of Art.6 due to the disproportionate length of time (over 14 years) that the incapacity was lasted.[11]

Where a claim belonging to an individual may only be pursued by another person or body, in the absence of any incapacitating feature as those above, it may be harder for the restriction to be justified. In *Philis v Greece (No.1)*, the applicant engineer's claim for remuneration for work done could only be pursued by the Technical Chamber of Greece pursuant to decree. While this might have provided engineers with the benefit of experienced legal representation for little expense, the Court found it insufficient to justify removing the applicant's capacity to pursue and act in his own claim.

The removal or denial of legal capacity to take proceedings may also impair the substance of the right to a court, as in *Canea Catholic Church v Greece*, where a court ruling that the applicant church did not have legal personality led to the dismissal of actions brought to assert its property rights.

(c) *Time-bars and prescription periods*

Time-limits imposed on the bringing of claims are acceptable in the interests of IIA–025
good administration of justice, pursuing the legitimate aims of preventing stale claims and injustice to defendants faced with evidential difficulties in contesting allegations relating to distant events and of promoting legal certainty.[12] The Convention organs have accepted final time-limits which cannot be waived, even when new facts have arisen after the expiry of the time-limit[13] or where knowledge

opening of legal correspondence between a prisoner and solicitor were declared admissible under Art.6 but settled on change of practice); *Hodgson v UK*, 11392/85, (Dec.) March 4, 1987 (restrictions on prisoners' direct correspondence with domestic courts).
[9] June 9, 1998, R.J.D. 1998–III, No.76.
[10] *cf. Winterwerp v Netherlands*, October 24, 1979, Series A, No.33, paras 73–76 where there was a breach of Art.6, para.1, where proceedings by which a person committed to mental detention had the automatic effect of divesting him of all capacity to administer his property but did not afford him the opportunity to appear or be represented.
[11] July 17, 2001.
[12] *Stubbings*, para.51.
[13] 9707/82, (Rep.) October 6, 1982, 31 D.R. 223 where the applicant had three years from the birth of the child to contest paternity but did not discover that he could not be the father till 24 years later.

of the cause of action only arose after the time-limit.[14] A three year time-limit was found to be reasonable for paternity proceedings[15] and six years for assault and trespass to the person, including sexual abuse.[16]

Where a time-limit is so short as to render it practically impossible to act within time it may effectively deprive the applicant of access to court.[17] In *Hennings v Germany*, where the applicant claimed of the one-week notice given by the prosecution summons, the Court found that his main excuse for not reacting to the notice was the claim that he had no key to his mailbox, which he could reasonably have been expected to obtain and for which failure to do so the authorities were not responsible.

(d) Coherent procedures

IIA–026   Although leeway is given to domestic courts in applying and interpreting procedural rules, applicants may claim a right to procedures which are "coherent" and afford a clear, practical and effective opportunity to challenge administrative acts which affect their rights.[18] Thus where the law was considered to be extremely complex, and an applicant could not be expected to realise time for appealing ran from the official publication of the decree rather than the serving of the notice, there was a denial of effective access to court.[19] A court rejection of an applicant's claim for damages for HIV infection from a blood bank on the basis that he had accepted compensation from a special fund was found to constitute a restriction on access to court since the applicant reasonably relied on the wording of the applicable legislation in bringing his claim and the system was not sufficiently clear or sufficiently attended by safeguards to prevent misunderstanding as to the procedures for making use of available remedies and the restrictions stemming from the simultaneous use of them.[20] Overly strict or arbitrary interpretation of procedural rules in rejecting claims, in particular for errors for which the applicants are not to blame, has also disclosed a disproportionate hindrance on access to court.[21]

---

[14] In *Stubbings*, the applicants (sexual abuse victims) complained that it was not possible to comply with an inflexible time-limit (suppressed memories, etc.). The Court found that a six year time-limit from the age of majority did not impair the essence of right of access to court, noting no general principle of flexibility in time-limits (*i.e.* from date of knowledge) in Contracting States.

[15] 9707/82, n.13 above.

[16] *Stubbings*.

[17] See *Perez de Rada Cavanilles v Spain*, October 28, 1998, R.J.D. 1998–VIII, No.96, where the applicant sent his appeal by recorded delivery within the three day time-limit but it was rejected as received outside that time—he could not have reasonably been expected to act quicker.

[18] *De Geouffre de la Pradelle*, para.34.

[19] *ibid.*, *i.e.* the time-limit expired the day before the Prefect served the notice of the decree. Also *Miragall Escalano v Spain*, 38366/97 etc., (Dec.) January 25, 2000, ECHR 2000–I, overly strict interpretation of a procedural rule where the one year time-limit ran from a decision not served on the applicants; *mutatis mutandis*, *Geffre v France*, 51307/99, (Dec.) January 23, 2003 where the system of publishing a decree in several ways gave sufficient opportunity to make appropriate applications.

[20] *Bellet*; *FE v France*, October 30, 1998, R.J.D. 1998–VIII, No.97.

[21] *Garcia Manibardo v Spain*, 38695/97, (Dec.) February 15, 2000, ECHR 2000–II, refusal of an applicant's appeal for failure to pay into court the damages awarded at the first instance where persons granted legal aid were exempt but the applicant's application for legal aid was granted too late for her to make use of it; *Leoni v Italy*, October 26, 2000, where it was the fault of the lower court that the appeal documents were not transmitted within the time-limit; *Sotiris and Nikos Koutras Attee v Greece*, November 16, 2000, ECHR 2000–XII, where a claim was dismissed for a procedural error committed on lodging

(e) Costs

Prohibitive levels of court costs may raise issues of denial of access to court. See Part IIA: Costs in court.

IIA–027

(f) Arbitration

While it is compatible with Art.6 for parties to regulate their civil disputes by submitting them to arbitration proceedings in place of the courts, as this pursues the aim of encouraging non-judicial settlements and relieving the courts of an excessive burden, issues may arise where the procedure is not voluntary or part of a contractual arrangement to which the applicant can be considered have agreed.[22] While some degree of court supervision of arbitration procedures may be required, Contracting States enjoy considerable discretion in regulating the grounds on which an arbitral award should be quashed.[23]

IIA–028

(g) Denial of legal aid

Lack of legal aid may constitute a denial of access to court. See Pt IIA: Legal Representation in civil proceedings.

IIA–029

(h) Lack of enforcement

Execution of a judgment is an integral part of the "trial" for the purposes of Art.6, para.1, the guarantees of which would become illusory if a domestic legal system allowed a final, binding judicial decision to remain inoperative to the detriment of one party. Failure by the authorities for more than five years to take the necessary steps to comply with a final enforceable decision was therefore found in *Hornsby v Greece* to deprive Art.6, para.1 of all useful effect and disclose a violation. Subsequent case law establishes that decisions taken by the authorities which effectively prevent, invalidate or unduly delay the enforcement of a judicial decision

IIA–030

the application by public officials; *Platakou v Greece*, January 11, 2001, ECHR 2001–I, para.39, failure of the court bailiff to serve a notice within time, and paras 43–44, concerning the Court of Cassation's overly rigid application of rules on contents of appeal notice; *Zvolsky and Zvolska v the Czech Republic*, November 12, 2002, concerning overly strict, and little known requirement that applicants should lodge appeals simultaneously with the Supreme Court and Constitutional Court. *Mutatis mutandis*, *Canete de Goni v Spain*, October 15, 2002, where it was not considered arbitrary to apply constructive notice of proceedings to a third party, where the applicable case law was published, accessible and sufficiently precise that the applicant, if necessary with skilled legal advice could have determined what steps she should have taken to join the case; *Ivanova v Finland*, 53054/99, (Dec.) May 2002, not arbitrary to require claims in an official language; *Grof v Austria*, 25046/94, (Dec.) April 4, 1998, not overly formalistic to reject appeal for failure of the lawyer to provide signed copies of documents for service.

[22] *e.g.* 11960/86, (Dec.) July 13, 1990 concerning a private contractual relationship providing for arbitration.

[23] 23173/94, (Dec.) October 22, 1996; 28101/95, (Dec.) November 27, 1996 where the Commission implied that some court review of arbitration was required but that arbitral bodies did not need to comply with Art.6, para.1 and strict conditions could be imposed for the quashing of an arbitral award; *Suovaniemi v Finland*, 31737/96, (Dec.) February 23, 1999, where the applicants were found to have waived their right to a court and the arbitration was attended by sufficient guarantees.

may be regarded as undermining the decision and depriving the applicant of the right to have the dispute decided by a court.[24] Lack of funds for honouring a judgment debt is not a sufficient excuse by the authorities.[25]

(i) *Setting aside of final judgments*

IIA–031   There was a denial of access to court in *Brumarescu v Romania*, where after final judgment had been given and executed in a property case, the Procurator-General, who was not a party to the proceedings, exercised a power to bring the case before the Supreme Court which held that the courts had not jurisdiction to decide civil disputes such as the applicant's. The procedure allowing the quashing of a final judgment was also found to infringe the principle of legal certainty and deprive the applicant of a fair hearing.[26] The procedure of supervisory review was also found in *Ryabykh v Russia* to deprive the applicant of right to a court and infringe legal certainty. The Court commented that the right to a court would be illusory if the Contracting State's legal system allowed a judicial decision which had become final and binding to be quashed by a higher court on an application made by a State official.[27]

4. Defences, privileges and immunities

IIA–032   Potential problems arise where an immunity or special defence has the effect of bringing court proceedings to an end, without consideration of the applicant's substantive claims.

In *Ashingdane* (concerning an immunity in statute barring civil actions by mental patients against staff or health authorities without leave on grounds of bad faith or lack of reasonable care) and in *Fayed v United Kingdom* (concerning the privilege of Department of Trade inspectors from suit in defamation) the Court found it unnecessary to decide whether these limitations defined the content of the right or imposed a restriction on access, since in any event the essence of the right to a court was not impaired nor the principle of proportionality transgressed. In *Ashingdane*, it found that the applicant could nonetheless take proceedings for negligence, whereas in *Fayed*, it found that any restriction pursued a legitimate aim (ensuring the proper conduct of the affairs of public companies) in a proportionate manner and that in producing their report the Inspectors were bound by a duty to act fairly and were subject to judicial review where they exceeded the bounds of their function.

This distinction, between elements that relate to the existence of a right in domestic law or which act as procedural bars to obtaining determination of a right, has proved difficult to apply in practice in UK cases. In *Osman v United Kingdom*,

---

[24] *e.g. Immobiliare Saffi v Italy*, July 28, 1999, ECHR 1999–V (prefectoral stay of enforcement for more than six years of order for possession in landlord-tenant dispute); *Antonakopoulos v Greece*, December 14, 1999 (refusal of State Treasurer to comply with judgment of the Audit Court); *Jasiuniene v Lithuania*, March 6, 2003, where the Government contested the judgment and imposed additional obligations on the applicant to obtain enforcement.

[25] *Burdov v Russia*, May 7, 2002, ECHR 2002–III, para.35—some delay may be justified but not such as to render Art.6 devoid of purpose (some four years in this case).

[26] See also *Vasilescu v Romania*, May 22, 1998; R.J.D. 1998–III, No.73.

[27] See also *Timofeyev v Russia*, October 23, 2003, where delays in executions and adjournments caused by the interference of supervisory-review authorities together violated Art.6 on lack of enforcement grounds.

which concerned the public policy immunity from suit in negligence for the police acting in an investigative or preventative capacity, the Court considered that there was a common law right to sue in negligence and that the domestic law approach in excluding a duty of care on public interest considerations acted an automatic immunity from suit that was a disproportionate restriction on access to court. Where a similar exclusion of a duty of care for suing social services for negligence regarding their duties in child protection arose later in *Z v United Kingdom*, the Court acceded to the Government's arguments that the domestic court ruling that no duty of care arose in such circumstances could not be regarded as either an exclusionary rule or an immunity which deprived the child applicants of access to court. While a novel point of interpretation of negligence law arose for determination attracting the application of Art.6, the striking out procedure, in which the applicants were represented and able fully to argue their claims for extending a duty of care, did not therefore disclose a restriction on access to court.[28]

Privileges and immunities in other contexts have been treated as acting as bars on access to court which require justification under the *Ashingdane* principles. Privilege from suit in defamation attaching to documents produced in criminal proceedings or investigations,[29] immunity from suit of the official receiver for alleged misstatements made in the exercise of his functions[30] and the application of the *ex turpi causa* rule to strike out the applicant's claims in tort[31] have been found to pursue legitimate aims in a proportionate manner. In the context of the privilege preventing members of Parliament from being sued in defamation, the Court found it unnecessary in *A v United Kingdom* to settle whether the privilege was a matter of substantive content or procedural bar, although it noted that Art.9 of the Bill of Rights was framed not in terms of a substantive defence to civil claims but rather as a procedural bar to the determination of the court. In any event, it found the restriction on access justified by the fundamental importance of protecting free debate in Parliament.[32] Immunity given to a magistrate from civil claims in damages was found justified in *Ernst v Belgium*, although in that case the Court appeared to place particular weight on the existence of other means by which the applicants could protect their interests.[33]

In the context of international law and international organisations, immunities preventing the litigation of issues in domestic courts have also been characterised as restrictions on access to court. So far however they have been justified as pursuing legitimate aims in a proportionate manner, with sometimes decisive weight being

---

[28] The Court took the view that the problem was one of effective remedies rather than access to court, finding a violation of Art.13 instead. Similar approach in *TP and KM v UK*, May 10, 2001, ECHR 2001–V; *DP and JC v UK*, October 10, 2002, namely to the extent a dispute about the existence of a right arose, the applicants had adequate access to court to put their claims.

[29] *Taylor v UK*, 49589/99, (Dec.) June 10, 2003 (statements by Serious Fraud Office officials); *Mahon and Kent v UK*, 70434/01, (Dec.) July 8, 2003 (documents submitted to The Securities Association concerning share fraud).

[30] *Mond v UK*, 49606/99, (Dec.) June 10, 2003, accepting that fear of vexatious actions would render seriously impede performance of duties and the administration of justice.

[31] *Clunis v UK*, 45049/98, (Dec.) September 11, 2001.

[32] Immunities were disproportionate in *Cordova v Italy (No.1)*, January 30, 2003, where it was not appropriately linked to the ongoing performance of legislative functions (*i.e.* it applied for life to certain politicians); *Cordova v Italy (No.2)*, January 30, 2003 (where it applied to speech outside Parliament or parliamentary duties).

[33] July 15, 2003—paras 53–56, the applicants could have sued anyone else involved in the allegedly abusive search and seizure and were able to lodge a claim for damages against the State.

placed on the vital public or international law interests.[34] In *Al-Adsani v United Kingdom*, where the applicant sought to sue the Government of Kuwait for torture in English courts, the Court noted that the applicant was claiming damages for personal injury, a cause of action well known to English law and that the action against Kuwait was not barred *in limine* since if the defendant State waived immunity it would proceed to hearing and judgment—Art.6 therefore applied. It found however that the principle of sovereign immunity pursed the legitimate aim of comply with international law to promote comity and noting that the Convention had to be interpreted as far as possible to harmonise with other rules of international law, considered that measures taken by a High Contracting Party reflecting generally recognised rules of public international law could not be in principle regarded as imposing disproportionate restriction on access to court.[35]

5. Limitations in the scope of review of the court

IIA–033   Where claims may only be put before a court which does not have full jurisdiction over the facts and legal issues in the case, there may be a denial of access to court.[36] Relevant factors here relate to the subject-matter of the dispute; whether the court may, even with limited competence, adequately review the disputed issues; the manner in which that decision was arrived at, and the content of the dispute, including the desired and actual grounds of the action or appeal.[37]

In childcare cases, where parents sought to access or custody of their children in local authority care, judicial review, which was confined to issues of illegality, unfairness or irrationality, was not sufficient, the Court finding that Art.6, para.1 required that local authority decisions be reviewed by a tribunal having jurisdiction to examine the merits.[38]

Where executive certificates remove a court's jurisdiction to examine the applicant's claims on a particular point, this may render access to court ineffective. In *Tinnelly and McElduff v United Kingdom*, where statutory provisions against discrimination in employment did not apply where an act was done, *inter alia*, to safeguard national security, the Court found that the serving of a certificate by the Secretary of State as conclusive evidence that national security applied was a disproportionate restriction on access to court. The applicants should have been able to argue and present evidence to show that the act did not pursue national security purposes and the court able freely to assess the issue.

---

[34] See, *e.g. Waite and Kennedy v Germany*, February 18, 1999, ECHR 1999–I, immunity from suit enjoyed by the European Space Agency in an employment case pursued the legitimate aim of ensuring the proper functioning of such organisations free from government interference; *Prince Hans-Adam II of Liechtenstein v Germany*, July 12, 2001, ECHR 2001–VIII, where the German courts declared inadmissible a claim for restitution of a painting confiscated in 1946 in former Czechoslovakia, the Court emphasised the vital public interest in Germany regaining sovereignty which was behind the post-war Settlement Convention.

[35] See also *McElhinney v Ireland*, November 21, 2001 (state immunity applied in Irish courts in a claim for damages for assault by a British soldier); *Fogarty v UK*, November 21, 2001 (state immunity applied to US Government in a labour dispute with an embassy employee); *Kalogeropoulou v Greece and Germany*, 59021/00, December 12, 2002, ECHR 2002–X (state immunity applying to enforcement of judgment against German property in Greece).

[36] Where a court appears to deprive itself of jurisdiction over crucial aspects of a dispute, it may also be regarded as depriving the applicant of access to a "tribunal" satisfying the requirements of Art.6 para.1 as having jurisdiction to examine all questions of fact and law relevant to the dispute before it, *e.g. Terra Woningen BV v Netherlands*, December 17, 1996, R.J.D. 1996–VI, No.25.

[37] *Bryan*, para.45.

[38] *W v UK*, n.4 above, para.82; see in employment context, *Koskinas v Greece*, June 20, 2002.

In administrative areas of a more technical nature, restricted review of decisions by the courts has been accepted as a common feature in Contracting States. In *Zumtobel v Austria* where there was dispute over expropriation of property and the appropriate compensation, with expert assessments of property values, etc., the Court referred to a notion of expediency, *i.e.* that courts may legitimately restrict their review of decisions by the administrative authorities on grounds of expediency. In *Bryan v United Kingdom*, concerning enforcement proceedings for breach of planning controls in respect of the applicant's "barns", appeal to the High Court restricted to points of law was not a problem even though its jurisdiction over the facts was limited. The Court emphasised the specialised character of planning, considered to be a typical example of the exercise of discretionary judgment in the regulation of citizen's conduct and this was found to render it reasonable to restrict the intervention of courts *vis-à-vis* the factual application of this discretion, the realm of the executive. The manner in which the decision was reached, in particular that the planning enquiry beforehand was run on fair, adversarial lines, was also a relevant factor in finding the limited review compatible with Art.6. [39]

Where a court effectively limits the scope of its powers by deferring to the view of an external authority, issues of lack of independence and as to its status as a "tribunal" satisfying the requirements of Art.6 may arise (see Pt IIA—Tribunal).

Cross-reference

Part IIA: Costs in court
Part IIA: Legal representation in civil proceedings
Part IIA: Legislative interference in judicial process
Part IIA: Tribunal

---

[39] *e.g. Air Canada*, where H.M. Customs confiscated an aircraft and released it on payment of a sum of money, the Court rejected the applicant's arguments that the scope of judicial review would have been too narrow to allow any meaningful challenge of the very broad discretion bestowed on the customs by statute; 32788/96, (Dec.) April 9, 1997 where, having regard to the special statutory context, judicial review satisfied the requirements of Art.6 for the complaints of a foster carer about deregistration by a social services fostering panel; *X v UK*, 28530/95, (Dec.) January 19, 1998, the scope of review of the Secretary of State's decision declaring the applicant unfit to be chief executive of an insurance company was adequate; *Chapman v UK*, January 18, 2001, ECHR 2001–I, applying the *Bryan* approach to applications for judicial review of decisions refusing gypsies planning permission to station caravans on their own land; *Potocka v Poland*, October 4, 2001, ECHR 2001–X, adequate scope of review by the Supreme Administrative Court of lawfulness of an administrative decision on land ownership.

Adequate time and facilities

Key provision:

Article 6, para.3(b) (adequate time and facilities for preparation of defence).

Key case law:

IIA–034   *Campbell and Fell v UK*, June 28, 1984, Series A, No.80; 7 E.H.R.R. 165; *Bricmont v Belgium*, July 7, 1989, Series A, No.158; 12 E.H.R.R. 217; *Hadjianastassiou v Greece*, December 16, 1992, Series A, No.252–A; 16 E.H.R.R. 219; *Melin v France*, June 22, 1993, Series A, No.261–B; 17 E.H.R.R. 1; *Kremzow v Austria*, September 21, 1993, Series A, No.268–B; 17 E.H.R.R. 322; *Domenchini v Italy*, November 15, 1996, R.J.D. 1996–V, No.22; 32 E.H.R.R. 68; *Vacher v France*, December 17, 1996, R.J.D., 1996–V, No.25; 24 E.H.R.R. 482; *Foucher v France*, March 18, 1997, R.J.D. 1997–II, No.33; 25 E.H.R.R. 234; *Pelissier and Sassi v France*, March 25, 1999, ECHR 1999–II; 30 E.H.R.R. 715; *Fitt v UK*, February 16, 2000, ECHR 2000–II; 30 E.H.R.R. 480; *Rowe and Davies v UK*, February 16, 2000, ECHR 2000–II; 30 E.H.R.R. 1; *Zoon v Netherlands*, December 7, 2000, ECHR 2000–XII; *Sadak v Turkey*, July 2, 2001, ECHR 2001–VII; *GB v France*, October 2, 2001, ECHR 2001–X; *Ocalan v Turkey*, March 12, 2003, pending before the Grand Chamber.

1. General considerations

IIA–035   The provisions of Art.6, para.3 depend on a criminal charge having been brought, though the Court has commented that these elements are implicit in the notion of fair trial in civil matters *mutatis mutandis*.[1] The case-law indicates that they are aspects of the general principle of fairness guaranteed in the first paragraph, to be assessed not on the basis of an isolated incident or element but having regard to the proceedings as a whole. Thus while the sub-paragraphs of Art.6, para.3 exemplify the notion of fair trial in typical procedural situations, their intrinsic aim is always to ensure or contribute to ensuring the fairness of the proceedings as a whole.[2] Frequently, therefore, complaints under Art.6, para.3 are considered in conjunction with Art.6, para.1.

    Where non-criminal cases are concerned, questions of adequate time and facilities are dealt with under Art.6, para.1, having regard to fairness and other applicable principles such as equality of arms, adversariality and the ability to participate effectively in the proceedings.[3]

    In criminal cases, applicants' access to evidence, facilities and lawyers is restricted to what is necessary for the defence.[4] In *Lamy v Belgium*, the applicant's inability to consult the investigation file in the first 30 days did not affect the preparation of his defence and the Commission found that Art.6, para.3(b) was not applicable.[5]

---

[1] *Albert and Le Compte v Belgium*, February 10, 1983, Series A, No.58, 5 E.H.R.R. 533, para.39.

[2] *Can v Italy*, 9300/81, (Rep.) July 12, 1984, Series A, No.96 (settled before the Court).

[3] See Pt IIA: Fair Trial Guarantees, General Principles, Fairness.

[4] *e.g.* 8463/78, (Dec.) July 9, 1981, 26 D.R. 24, no right to unrestricted access to lawyer; 11396/85, (Dec.) December 11, 1986, 50 D.R. 179 where there were practical limits to the legal research materials prison authorities could be expected to provide.

[5] (Rep.) October 8, 1987, Series A, No.151.

2. Victim status

A person acquitted in criminal proceedings may not complain of alleged difficulties in preparing his defence.[6] An accused who declares that he will not take any further part of the proceedings cannot complain either.[7]

IIA–036

3. Adequate time

Where time for preparation of trial is concerned, short periods have been found acceptable. It is also expected that applications for adjournment are made where there is an alleged problem. Thus, in *Campbell and Fell v United Kingdom*, concerning prison disciplinary proceedings, five days notice of charges and notice of the report given the day before were found by the Court to be sufficient in the circumstances, noting that no request was made for an adjournment.[8] On that basis, the Commission appeared to accept the UK practice of briefing counsel at short notice, presuming that by training they were able to cope and that if they could not, they had the possibility to apply for an adjournment.[9] In *Kremzow*, the Court found a period of three weeks was sufficient for counsel to draft a reply to a 49 page document.[10] However in *Ocalan v Turkey*, a period of two weeks given to trial lawyers to prepare a 17,000 page file was not sufficient time, together with other restrictions, rendering it difficult for the applicant to exercise the defence rights guaranteed under Art.6.

IIA–037

Where time-limits are imposed which, either by their brevity or vagueness, render the right of any appeal ineffective, violations have been found.[11] The rules by which courts function must be "sufficiently coherent and clear".[12] The Court has emphasised that States must ensure that everyone charged with a criminal offence benefits from the safeguards of Art.6, para.3. Putting the onus on convicted defendants to find out when an allotted time started to run or expire was not compatible with the diligence which the Contracting States must exercise to ensure

---

[6] 8083/77, (Dec.) March 13, 1980, 19 D.R. 223—applicant no longer a victim as the Court of Appeal quashed the charge of contempt.

[7] 8386/78, (Dec.) October 9, 1980, 21 D.R. 126 where counsel withdrew from the trial, embarassed by statements made by applicant contradicting his not guilty plea, the applicant refused offer of help from solicitors or to pursue questions himself or to call witnesses.

[8] Also *Kremzow*: where the Attorney General served documents three weeks before an appeal hearing, and the applicant could also have consulted the file beforehand, no violation; *Craxi v Italy (No.2)* December 20, 2002, where no complaint was made by the applicants' representatives at the time about the alleged difficulties arising from the close proximity of various hearing dates.

[9] Also *Twalib v Greece*, June 9, 1998, R.J.D., 1998–IV, No.77, paras 40–43, where counsel was given a "short interval" to prepare at the commencement of the trial but no complaint about lack of preparation time was made then or on appeal.

[10] para.48. See also *GB v France*, paras 60–63, where it was acceptable for the prosecution to file new evidence at the beginning of the trial, with the defence having three days until the conclusion of the proceedings to assimilate it.

[11] *Hadjianastassiou*: where the time-limit for lodging grounds of appeal expired before the applicant knew the substance of the court's decision convicting him, there was a violation since he was thus unable usefully to exercise his right of appeal. It was not enough, as the Government argued, for parts to be orally pronounced and for him to deduce the rest from the previous proceedings. See also *Vacher* below.

[12] *Melin*, para.24; *Vacher*, para.26.

that rights are enjoyed in an effective manner.[13] Where however a full judgment was not made available to an accused before the expiry of the period for appeal, this did not unduly affect defence rights as an abridged version had been served and the appeal process was not directed against the first instance judgment but against the charges and would involve a completely new assessment of facts and law.[14]

4. Facilities: access to evidence

IIA–038   The Court has held that the right to an adversarial trial, with equality between prosecution and defendant, means that the defence must be given the opportunity to have knowledge of and comment on the observations filed and evidence adduced by the prosecution. This requires that the prosecution should disclose to the defence all material evidence in their possession for or against the accused.[15]

There is no absolute right of access however, with acknowledgment to potentially superceding public interests such as national security, witness protection,[16] risk of reprisals, safeguarding police working methods.[17] The general principle that only restrictions on the rights of the defence which are strictly necessary are permissible tends to cede to the public interest as the Court leaves it to the domestic courts to assess the evidence in such cases but verifies instead whether the procedure followed by the judicial authorities sufficiently counter-balanced the limitations on the defence with appropriate safeguards.[18] It was therefore compatible with Art.6 for evidence to be withheld at trial on public interest grounds where the judge reviewed the evidence himself in light of the principle of ordering disclosure if it might further the defence[19] and not so compatible where the material was withheld at trial by the prosecution and only reviewed on appeal by the Court of Appeal *ex parte*.[20]

The right has also been stated to be restricted to those facilities which assist or may assist in defence, which may in some cases appear to put the burden on applicants to prove the relevance of material they have not seen.[21] The Commission also appeared to take the view that where information was available elsewhere or

---

[13] *Colozza v Italy*, February 12, 1985, Series A, No.89; 7 E.H.R.R. 516, para.28. See *Melin* and *Vacher*, concerning the practice of the *Cour de Cassation* not to inform appellants in person when the hearing of the appeal was listed or set time-limits for submissions. There was a violation where, in *Vacher*, the appeal was dismissed 8 days before lodging of the grounds of appeal; no violation in *Melin*, by a narrow majority: *Melin* was a lawyer who had worked at the bar and there was over a 4 month delay before the dismissal of the appeal, whereas in *Vacher* the period was two months shorter than the average time usually taken.

[14] *Zoon*, paras 45–51.

[15] *Fitt*, para.44; *Rowe and Davis*, para.60.

[16] 11219/84, (Dec.) July 10, 1985, 42 D.R. 287 where defence lawyer was barred from discussing with the applicant the statements of anonymous witnesses which would allow him to identify them.

[17] *e.g.* 29335/95, (Dec.) January 17, 1997 where evidence was not disclosed since it would uncover details of police informers.

[18] *Fitt*, paras 45–46; *Rowe and Davis*, paras 61–62.

[19] *Fitt*, paras 47–49.

[20] *Rowe and Davis*, paras 65–66: the procedure in the Court of Appeal could not remedy the defect at trial, as the appellate body was not in the same position as the trial judge to assess and monitor through the trial the relevance of the withheld material; *Dowsett v UK*, June 24, 2003—nor was it enough that the applicant could apply to the Court of Appeal for it to order disclosure to the defence as it would reach its decision without assistance from the defence or first-hand knowledge of the trial. In effect the onus is on the prosecution to obtain a judicial ruling on non-disclosure of potentially relevant material (see Sir Nicolas Bratza's concurring opinion).

[21] 8403/78, (Rep.) December 14, 1981, 27 D.R. 61.

within means of an applicant and lawyer to obtain, that this was sufficient by way of facilities, even if it might have been reasonably expected (as well as quicker and more efficient) for the prosecution to provide the information.[22] Lack of access to a file for a part of the period before the trial will not raise issues, if nonetheless access was possible for a sufficient time to prepare the defence.[23] Where there was more fundamental lack of access to the file, however, and no opportunity to make copies of documents at first instance, then the possibility to make application for access at the appeal stage did not prevent a violation of Art.6, para.3(b).[24] There was a violation in *Ocalan v Turkey* where the applicant did not obtain access to the investigation file and evidence produced by the prosecution until almost the end of his trial.

In the context of expert evidence, circumstances may require that courts accede to an accused's requests for expert opinion on a particular matter. In *GB v France*, the refusal to order a second expert opinion where a psychiatrist changed his opinion in a very adverse manner during questioning at trial violated Art.6, paras 1 and 3(b) though the Court emphasised that the mere fact that an expert changes an opinion would not *per se* infringe the principles of fairness (see further section Evidence, 6. Refusal to call expert evidence or take other investigative measures).

5. Facilities: overlap with access to legal advice

There is overlap with the right of access to a lawyer, since representation by a lawyer is often meaningless unless some prior consultation is included in the "facilities" provided to the defendant.[25] In *Domenchini v Italy*, monitoring of a prisoner's correspondence with his defence lawyer was a violation of Art.6, para.3(b) since the delay resulting in forwarding a letter led to the filing of grounds after the statutory time-limit. Similarly, the restriction on the number and length of the applicant's meetings with his lawyers in *Ocalan v Turkey* was one of the factors rendering difficult the preparation of his defence.[26]

IIA–039

6. Article 6, para.3(a)—information about the charge

Where an applicant has not been promptly informed of the charge, this may prevent him from properly preparing his defence at the same time.[27] The provision of information that an offence has been reclassified, or that the material facts at the base of the charge have been modified, is not enough since it has to be in good time and allow the opportunity to organise the defence in a practical and effective manner on the basis of the changes.[28]

IIA–040

---

[22] 8403/78, n.21 above. Also *Bricmont*: no violation for the authorities' failure to produce an exhibit which the applicants said would have enabled them to rebut charge, since they did not give details supporting this, nor violation from failure to obtain a special audit of accounts since they had never asked for one.

[23] *Padin Gestoso v Spain*, 39519/98, (Dec.) December 8, 1998, ECHR 1999–II.

[24] *Foucher*, para.32.

[25] *Campbell and Fell*.

[26] paras 152–157.

[27] e.g. *Chichlian and Ekindjian v France*, November 28, 1989, Series A, No.162–B.

[28] *Pelissier and Sassi*, para.62; *Mattocia v Italy*, July 25, 2000, ECHR 2000–IX, paras 71–72; *Sadak and others*, paras 57658; 24751/94, (Dec.) June 28, 1995, 82–A D.R. 85.

Cross-reference

Part IIA: General principles
Part IIA: Information about the charge
Part IIA: Legal representation in criminal proceedings

Appeals

Key provision:

Article 6, paras 1–3 (fair trial).

Key case law:

Delcourt v Belgium, January 17, 1970, Series A, No.11; 1 E.H.R.R. 355; *Pretto v Italy*, **IIA–041**
December 8, 1983, Series A, No.71; 6 E.H.R.R. 182; *Axen v Germany*, February 22,
1983, Series A, No.72; 6 E.H.R.R. 195; *Sutter v Switzerland*, February 22, 1984,
Series A, No.74; 6 E.H.R.R. 272; *Monnell and Morris v UK*, March 2, 1987, Series
A, No.115; 10 E.H.R.R. 205; *Ekbatani v Sweden*, May 26, 1988, Series A, No.134;
13 E.H.R.R. 504; *Kremzow v Austria*, September 21, 1993, Series A, No.268–B; 17
E.H.R.R. 322; *Brualla Gomez de la Torre v Spain*, December 19, 1997, R.J.D. 1997–
VIII, No.61.

1. General considerations

There is no right to appeal contained in the Convention itself (as opposed to the **IIA–042**
right provided for in Art.2 of Protocol No.7). However, where a judicial system
provides for appeals, the Court had held since *Delcourt v Belgium*[1] that the
fundamental guarantees provided in Art.6 will apply. Having regard, however, to
the fact that in many Contracting States higher instances take differing forms, this is
subject to the rider that the way in which Art.6 applies will depend on the special
features of the proceedings. This includes consideration of the functions, in law and
practice of the appellate body, its powers and the manner in which the interests of
the parties are presented and protected.[2]

There can therefore be no right either to provision of any particular kind of
appeal procedure or manner of dealing with appeals. For example, Art.6 does not
require that matters of new evidence raised on appeal should be remitted by the
Court of Appeal for rehearing by a jury.[3] Access to a final instance may be regulated
and include conditions such as the requirement to be represented by a lawyer or the
imposition of fines for abusive appeals.[4]

2. Application of Art.6 guarantees

Where an appeal lies, the provisions of Art.6 generally will apply. However there **IIA–043**
may be special features of the appellate body or its procedure which will affect the
way in which the guarantees apply.

One important distinction has been found to exist between appeal proceedings
proper and leave to appeal proceedings. In *Monnell and Morris v United Kingdom*, the
Court found it was not incompatible with fairness that the applicants were not

---

[1] paras 25–26.
[2] *Monnell and Morris*, para.56.
[3] *e.g.* 14739/89, (Dec.) May 9, 1989, 60 D.R. 296.
[4] 16598/90, (Dec.) November 16, 1990, 66 D.R. 260; 15384/89, (Dec.) May 9, 1994, 77–A D.R. 5.

present or represented in leave to appeal applications as they did not involve the rehearing of witnesses or re-examination of the facts, the issue being whether there were arguably grounds which would justify the hearing of an appeal. The principle of equality of arms was respected since the prosecution did not appear and the applicants had advice as to their prospects of appeal and the opportunity to submit written submissions. Where applicants had already been represented by counsel at trial, this was considered sufficient to safeguard their interests. In contrast, in *Granger v United Kingdom*, where full appeal proceedings were in issue, the failure to provide the accused with legal representation did disclose a violation of Art.6, para.3(c). The prosecution was present and the applicant could not be expected to present his case effectively.

Where appeal proceedings involve points of law only or a limited cassation procedure, the approach has been taken that lack of public hearing at second or third instances may be justified by these special features.[5] Where however, as in *Ekbatani v Sweden*, a court of appeal has to examine both facts and law and can not fairly or properly determine the issues without hearing the applicant or other witnesses in person, the denial of a public hearing or right to be heard in person may disclose a violation. Similarly, where an appeal raises issues as to the personality of the applicant, he may claim a right to be present and participate.[6] The Court has stated, however, that the personal attendance of accused at an appeal hearing does not take on the same crucial significance for an appeal hearing as it does for trial.[7]

The requirement for higher instance courts to render judgments publicly also has been interpreted in light of their role. Where their function is to confirm lower instances' judgments or give brief decisions, it has been considered sufficient if the lower instances' judgments are rendered publicly and "public" access to the superior court's decision is provided for by way of, for example, access to court registry records.[8]

Presumption of innocence may also cease to apply in appeal proceedings, due to the nature of those proceedings, after an accused has been convicted at first instance. It has therefore not been successfully argued that the Court of Appeal in England fails to comply with this requirement in the test which it applies in deciding whether or not to quash a conviction in light of new evidence.[9]

The Court has also found that conditions of access to superior appeal courts, in particular Supreme Courts, may be stricter and more formal. It found no deprivation of access to court in *Brualla Gomez de la Torre v Spain*, where an applicant's appeal to the Supreme Court was rejected due to an intervening change in the criteria for cases which it could deal with.[10] The applicant had, it noted, received two full

---

[5] *Axen; Sutter.*

[6] *Kremzow.*

[7] *Kamasinski v Austria*, December 19, 1989, Series A, No.168; 13 E.H.R.R. 36, para.107: where the Court also noted the difficulties that attach to the attendance of prisoners.

[8] *Pretto, Axen* and *Sutter.*

[9] 14739/89, n.3 above.

[10] See also *KDB v Netherlands*, March 27, 1998, R.J.D. 1998–II, No.68, where the Supreme Court gave the applicant no warning as to when it would consider his case but he had not shown that he had not had the opportunity to file his written grounds; *Berger v France*, December 3, 2002, ECHR 2002-X, acceptable limitations on access to higher instance by a *"partie civile"*; *De Ponte Nascimento v UK*, 55331/00, (Dec.) January 31, 2002, concerning the grounds on which the Court of Appeal should grant leave. See also Part IIA: Access to court.

hearings in lower instance courts. Where appeal lies however, procedural rules should not operate or be interpreted so strictly so as to block effective access.[11]

3. Curing defects at first instance

In criminal proceedings, the extent to which a higher court can cure defects in the trial is limited, though the possibility exists where the nature of the defect permits the effect of the shortcoming to be rectified.[12] An accused has a right to a fair trial at first instance with all the guarantees and it is no argument to state that, for example, the appellate body offers the independence lacking below.[13]

IIA–044

In civil proceedings however, proceedings lacking in conformity with Art.6, para.1 may be cured by subsequent review of the case by a tribunal offering the necessary guarantees and appropriate scope of review.[14]

---

[11] See, *e.g. Miragall Escolano v Spain*, January 25, ECHR 2000–I, concerning running of a time-limit from an event of which the applicants had no knowledge; *Annoni di Gussola v France*, November 14, 2000, ECHR 2000–XI, where the Court of Cassation struck out the applicants' appeals for failure to comply with the judgment below despite their impecunious circumstances; *Sotiris and Nikos Koutras Attee v Greece*, November 16, 2000, ECHR 2000–XII, where the applicant company's appeal to the Supreme Administrative Court was struck out for a excessively formalistic approach to a clerical error for which it was not responsible; *Beles v Czech Republic*, November 12, 2002, ECHR 2002–IX, application of procedural rule blocking effective access to Consitutional Court.

[12] *De Cubber v Belgium*, October 26, 1984, Series A, No.86, para.33; *Adolf v Austria*, March 26, 1982, Series A, No.49, paras 38–41, where the Supreme Court cleared of any finding of guilt an applicant in respect of whom the lower court had breached the presumption of innocence; *Edwards v UK*, December 16, 1992, Series A, No.247–B; 15 E.H.R.R. 417 where it was found that the review of a conviction by the Court of Appeal in light of material undisclosed to the defence by the police at the trial remedied the defects in the original trial.

[13] *Findlay v UK*, February 25, 1997, 1997 R.J.D. 1997–I, No.30, para.79, lack of independent and impartial tribunal at first instance court martial; *Foucher v France*, March 18, 1997, R.J.D. 1997–II, No.33, denial of access to the file at first instance not cured by the possibility of applying for access on appeal; *Rowe and Davis v UK*, February 16, 2000, ECHR 2000–II, para.65, where the trial judge should have assessed whether evidence should not be disclosed on public interest grounds and review by the Court of Appeal was not sufficient to remedy this; *Condron v UK*, May 2, 2000, ECHR 2000–V, para.63, where the review by the Court of Appeal of the safety of the conviction did not remedy the trial judge's failure to direct the jury not to draw any inference from the applicants' failure to answer police questions.

[14] *Le Compte, Van Leuven and De Meyere v Belgium*, June 23, 1981, Series A, No.43; 4 E.H.R.R. 1: where the proceedings before the Appeals Council were not in public and not cured by a public hearing before the Court of Cassation since it could not take cognisance of the merits of cases. See however in special contexts, *e.g. Bryan v UK*, November 22, 1995, Series A, No.335–A; 21 E.H.R.R. 342; and *Zumtobel v Austria*, September 21, 1993, Series A, No.268–A; 17 E.H.R.R. 116 where restricted scope of review was accepted; 18874/91, (Dec.) January 12, 1994, 76–A D.R. 44.

Costs in court

Key provisions:

IIA–045   Article 6, para.1 (access to court for fair trial); 6, para.2 (presumption of innocence); Art.1 of Protocol No.1 (peaceful enjoyment of possessions).

Key case law:

Airey v Ireland, October 9, 1979, Series A, No.32; 2 E.H.R.R. 305; *Tolstoy v UK*, July 7, 1995, Series A, No.316; 20 E.H.R.R. 442; *Masson and Van Zon v Netherlands*, September 28, 1995, Series A, No.327; 22 E.H.R.R. 491; *Robins v UK*, September 23, 1997, R.J.D. 1997–V, No.49; 26 E.H.R.R. 527; *Ait-Mouhoub v France*, October 28, 1998, R.J.D. 1998–VIII, No.96; 30 E.H.R.R. 382; *Kreuz v Poland*, June 19, 2001, ECHR 2001–VI.

1. General considerations

IIA–046   Problems have principally arisen as to the compatibility with the presumption of innocence of costs orders against acquitted accused; in the procedural context, the extent to which the guarantees of Art.6, para.1 apply to the costs proceedings following substantive litigation; and the impact which costs may have on effective access to court.

The obligation to pay "litigation costs" *per se* does not appear to involve any right under substantive provisions since they are "contributions" within the meaning of the second paragraph of Art.1 of Protocol No.1 and escape detailed supervision.[1] The Commission found that the basic rule that costs follow the event in civil litigation was reasonable as such, acting as a disincentive to unnecessary litigation and providing for at least the recovery of some of the successful litigant's costs.[2]

2. Costs orders against acquitted accused

IIA–047   See Pt IIA: Presumption of innocence.

3. Applicability of Art.6, para.1 to costs procedures

(a) *Criminal proceedings*

IIA–048   Whether proceedings concerning reimbursement of legal costs incurred in a criminal trial in which an applicant has been acquitted attracts the guarantees of Art.6 depends principally on whether there is a "right" to costs in domestic law. The grant to a public authority of a considerable measure of discretion may indicate that no right is recognised in domestic law, as in *Masson and Van Zon v Netherlands*, where the courts made awards where "reasons in equity" existed.

---

[1] 15434/89, (Dec.) February 15, 1990, 64 D.R. 232.
[2] *ibid.*

(b) *Civil proceedings*

Cost procedures following substantive proceedings were generally held by the Commission not to involve the civil rights of the individual.[3] This view was overruled by the Court in *Robins v United Kingdom*. It now appears established that, where the substantive proceedings involve civil rights and obligations, the cost proceedings, even if separately decided, must be seen as a continuation of the substantive litigation and falling within the scope of Art.6, para.1. Thus, four years taken in the costs proceedings in the *Robins* case disclosed a violation of the reasonable time requirement of that provision.[4] Considering the limited or technical nature of the issues arising in costs proceedings, it is perhaps doubtful that the guarantees of Art.6 will apply with full vigour, for example as regard the requirement for public hearings or the public rendering of decisions.

IIA–049

4. Access to court

The requirement to pay fees or costs in advance in connection with civil claims is not *per se* incompatible with Art.6, para.1.[5] However, although there is no right to free proceedings or right to repayment of costs and fees,[6] the high cost of proceedings could raise a problem with respect to right of access to court, if it can be shown to have a prohibitive effect depriving an applicant of the essence of the right having regard to the *Ashingdane v United Kingdom* principles.[7]

IIA–050

For example, there was lack of effective access to court in *Airey v Ireland*, where the costs for representation (legal aid not available) in a separation application were "very high" and the procedure so complex and subject matter entailing an emotional involvement such that the applicant could not be expected effectively to present her own case.

Where a precondition for appeal is the payment into court of security for costs, the cases indicate that such orders which pursue the legitimate aim of protecting one party from being faced with an irrecoverable bill for legal costs if the party appealing is unsuccessful, will disclose no problem if there has been a full and fair hearing at first instance and the court gives a fair chance to the applicant to argue that the interests of justice require an appeal to go on.[8] The Court has been stricter where significant security costs orders have been imposed as condition for the claim

[3] 8569/79, (Dec.) May 8, 1985, 42 D.R. 23 where the substantive action concerned public law; 21775/93, (Dec.) May 25, 1995, 81 D.R. 48 where the Commission found the question of costs was a subsidiary issue to the main civil proceedings and did not concern civil rights and obligations; majority Commission opinion in *Robins v UK*.
[4] See also *Beer v Austria*, February 6, 2001, para.13, affirming the *Robins* approach.
[5] *Kreuz*, para.60.
[6] *e.g.* 6202/73, (Dec.) March 16, 1975, 1 D.R. 66; 15488/89, (Dec.) February 27, 1995, 80–A D.R. 14.
[7] *i.e.* whether the essence of the right is impaired and whether the restriction pursues a legitimate aim in a proportionate manner, having regard to the proceedings as a whole. See Pt IIA: Access to court.
[8] See *Tolstoy*, where the applicant, the unsuccessful defendant in defamation proceedings (£1.5 million award) was required to pay £124,000 as security in costs in order to pursue his appeal. However, the applicant had had a full hearing at first instance; there was no indication that the sum was not a fair reflection of the likely costs and the Court of Appeal considered the merits of the case in deciding whether or not the measure would amount to a denial of justice, thereby showing no arbitrariness but basing itself on a full and thorough evaluation of the relevant factors. If the matter had been decided purely by the registrar of the court, the result might not be so obvious.

being processed at first instance, emphasising the prominent place held by the right to a court in a democratic society.[9] In *Ait-Mouhoub v France*, where 80,000 franc orders were imposed on an applicant seeking to bring civil actions against police officers for misconduct and who had no financial resources, the Court found that the sum was disproportionate and deprived him of access to court.[10] The merits of the complaints were apparently irrelevant, the Court not accepting the Government's claims that the orders were necessary to prevent wrongful claims being brought.

5. Penalty costs orders against lawyers

IIA–051   Wasted costs orders against lawyers in courts do not concern the determination of civil rights or obligations and thus do not attract guarantees of Art.6. Nor have they been found to involve the determination of a criminal charge.[11] Such orders are regarded as "contributions" within the meaning of second paragraph of Art.1 of Protocol No.1 and not an interference with possessions.[12]

---

[9] *e.g. Ait-Mouhoub*, para.52; *Kreuz*, paras 57 and 66.

[10] See also *Kreuz v Poland*, where a requirement to pay PLZ 100 million for lodging an action was considered excessive—the Court found the domestic court's view that the applicant could pay were based on assumptions and that they rejected his assertion of inability to pay without obtaining or considering any evidence on the point. See, conversely, *Sinko v Slovakia*, 33466/96, (Dec.) May 20, 1998, where the court fees were not considered excessively high and the applicant had been offered the chance to make instalments and had not shown that he could not afford them; *Reuther v Germany*, 74789/01, (Dec.) June 5, 2003, where fees (about EUR 750) for the Bavarian Constitutional Court were not considered excessive.

[11] 10615/83, (Dec.) July 3, 1984, 38 D.R. 213; *Tormala v Finland*, 41528/98, (Dec.) March 16, 2004.

[12] 7544/76, (Dec.) July 12, 1978, 14 D.R. 60; 7909/74, (Dec.) October 12, 1994 15 D.R. 160.

Double jeopardy

Relevant provisions:

Article 6, para.1 (fair trial); Art.4 of Protocol No.7 (no trial or punishment in same State for offence for which already acquitted or convicted).   IIA–052

Key case law:

Gradinger v Austria, October 23, 1995, Series A, No.328–C; *Oliveira v Switzerland*, July 30, 1998, R.J.D. 1998–V, No.83; 28 E.H.R.R. 289; *Franz Fischer v Austria*, May 29, 2001.

1. General considerations

The principle of "double jeopardy" or *non bis in idem* which prohibits that a person be tried twice for the same offence is not expressly contained in the Convention itself but subject to specific provision in Art.4 of Protocol No.7, which only came into force relatively recently for a number of Contracting States.[1]   IIA–053

2. Fairness

While it has not been clearly excluded that the trial of a person for the same offence in the same State could not raise separate issues of fairness under Art.6, para.1,[2] which would be of relevance where a State has not ratified Protocol No.7, such a possibility would be difficult to reconcile with the existence of the specific right in Protocol No.7, notwithstanding arguments as to the widespread recognition of the fundamental principle.   IIA–054

The Commission stated that in interpreting the provisions of the Convention it might be useful to take into account provisions contained in other international legal instruments, including the Brussels Convention which barred prosecution of a person in one State in respect of whom a trial had been finally disposed of in another State concerning the same facts. However, there was no question of lending provisions of the Convention a scope which the Contracting Parties expressly intended to exclude by means of a Protocol which applied only to prosecution of a person twice within the same State. Article 6 could not therefore be interpreted to imply a more extended right applying between States.[3]

3. Article 4 of Protocol No.7

The first paragraph of this provision establishes the principle that no one shall be liable to be tried[4] or punished in criminal proceedings under the jurisdiction of the   IIA–055

---

[1] The UK and Ireland have not ratified.

[2] 9433/81, (Dec.) December 11, 1981, 27 D.R. 233; 8945/80 (Dec.) December 13, 1983, 39 D.R. 43.

[3] 21072/92, (Dec.) January 1, 1995, 80–B D.R. 89: where the applicant had allegedly been tried in Denmark and Italy in respect of the same matters.

[4] See *Zigarelli v Italy*, 48154/99, (Dec.) October 3, 2002 —although a second set of proceedings was opened concerning the same offence, the Court avoided a literal interpretation and found that as the

same State for an offence for which he has already been finally acquitted or convicted. It does not cover imposition of several penalties flowing from one conviction, *e.g.* a prison sentence and fine by a court and withdrawal of the driving licence by an administrative body in respect of a drunken driving offence.[5]

There have been few significant cases. Those mainly establish that administrative proceedings which penalise the same conduct in issue in a criminal trial will offend the prohibition, notwithstanding the differing designations and the allegedly different purpose of the proceedings. In *Gradinger v Austria*, the applicant, who killed a cyclist while driving, was convicted of causing death by negligence rather than the more serious crime of being under influence of alcohol since his level was below the prescribed limit. The administrative authorities proceeded to fine him for driving under the influence of drink on the basis of a medical report which deduced that in fact he was over the limit. Since both decisions were based on the same conduct, there was a violation of Art.4 of Protocol No.7.[6]

However, the fact that a person is convicted of separate offences arising out of a particular event is not incompatible with this provision, where as in *Oliveira v Switzerland*, the applicant was convicted first of failing to adapt her speed to road conditions and in a separate procedure relating to the same road traffic accident of negligently causing injury. The Court commented however that it would have been more consistent with the principles governing the proper administration of justice for sentence in respect of the two offences to be passed by the same court in a single set of proceedings. This should be distinguished from the situation where the essential elements of two offences based on one act are the same, for example where one offence encompasses all the elements of the other plus an additional one, in which case two prosecutions will in fact concern the same essential elements and a violation will arise.[7]

---

courts had terminated those proceedings on recognition of the fact, no issue arose; nor did the provision apply where a public prosecutor had earlier discontinued proceedings, such not amounting to a conviction or an acquittal—*Smirnova v Russia*, 46133/99 and 48183/99, (Dec.) October 3, 2002.

[5] *RT v Switzerland*, 31982/96, (Dec.) May 30, 2000.

[6] The Commission had commented strongly that it would render Art.4 of Protocol No.7 ineffective if States could prosecute an individual under nominally different offences.

[7] *Franz Fischer*, violation where the applicant was fined by an administrative authority for drunken driving and convicted by a court for causing death by negligence while intoxicated—the problem was not resolved by reduction of his prison term to take into account the administrative fine; contrast *Ponsetti and Chesnil v France*, 36855/97 and 41731/98, (Dec.) September 14, 1999, ECHR 1999-VI, where the constitutive elements of the two offences (the fiscal penalties imposed for failure to make tax returns and the criminal offence of wilful tax evasion) were considered to be different, incompatible *ratione materiae*; *Goktan v France*, July 2, 2002, where the applicant was fined by customs for importation of contraband and convicted and imprisoned for drug trafficking offences, the Court found no violation, albeit with some reluctance.

Entrapment and agents provocateurs

Key provisions:

Article 6, para.1 (fair trial); Art.8 (private life).

IIA–056

Key case law:

Ludi v Switzerland, June 15, 1992, Series A, No.238; 15 E.H.R.R. 173; *Teixeira de Castro v Portugal*, June 9, 1998, 1998–IV, No.77.

1. General considerations

The fine line between entrapment, incitement and undercover investigation is a well-known problem. There have been few cases in Strasbourg. In the leading case to date, *Teixeira de Castro v Portugal*, the Court emphasised the need to limit the use of undercover agents and to put safeguards in place, holding that notwithstanding difficulties of fighting crime the public interest could not justify the use of evidence obtained as a result of police incitement.[1] Issues principally arise as to the fairness of proceedings where a person becomes involved in a crime which would otherwise not have been contemplated but for the suggestion of the agent provocateur, as to whether the use of evidence gathered undercover is compatible with the rights of the defence and potentially, respect for private life.

IIA–057

2. Relevance to fairness of trial

(a) *Incitement of offences*

The essential question appears to be whether the role played by the police officer concerned went beyond that of an undercover agent investigating in an essentially passive role and could be considered as instigating the offence. In *Teixeira de Castro v Portugal*, the Court noted that there had been no investigation or suspicion previously against the applicant and that there was nothing to suggest that without their intervention the applicant would have committed the offence of obtaining drugs for them. In contrast in *Radermacher and Pferrer*,[2] where the Commission found on the facts that the police informer had not initiated the offence but that a third person had come to him, bringing the one of the applicants, there was no violation, notwithstanding the active and important role of the police informer in the events leading to the delivery of counterfeit money. It also had regard to procedural safeguards in the proceedings, namely, the possibility of challenging the conviction and that the involvement of undercover agents was seen as a mitigating factor in sentencing.[3]

IIA–058

[1] para.36.
[2] 12811/87, (Rep.), October 11, 1990, Ybk of the ECHR p.274.
[3] Also *Calabro v Italy*, 59895/00, (Dec.) March 21, 2002, where the undercover agent had not provoked the offence—the applicant had contacted him and shown that he was part of a trafficking network—it was also noted that the conviction was not conclusively based on the agent's testimony, unlike *Teixeira de Castro*; similar reasoning in *Sequiera v Italy*, 73557/01, (Dec.) May 6, 2003.

Where an applicant was victim of "private entrapment" by a journalist who obtained evidence against him of drug dealing, the Court considered that the State's role was limited to the prosecution and it restricted its examination to the fairness of the use of evidence at trial.[4]

(b) *Use of evidence from undercover agents*

IIA–059   The principal consideration is whether the evidence in a trial is put forward in such a way that the proceedings are fair as a whole, including an adequate opportunity for the defence to challenge any evidence before the court. In *Ludi v Switzerland*, where evidence against the applicant included an undercover agent's report, the inability to challenge the agent's evidence in oral proceedings breached Art.6, para.3(d) taken together with the first paragraph, as the rights of the defence had been limited to an extent depriving him of a fair trial. The Court was not satisfied that a need for anonymity excluded all defence challenge of the agent, since matters could have been arranged so as to protect the legitimate police interest in using their agent again.[5]

3. Invasion of privacy complaints

IIA–060   Deliberate intervention in the affairs of suspects, involving the striking up of relationships and personal contact, might appear to involve an invasion of privacy and to raise problems of respect for private life under Art.8.

In *Ludi*, where an applicant was convicted on drugs charges on the basis of evidence of an undercover agent and telephone tapping, the Commission found an interference with private life from the involvement of the undercover officer together with telephone tapping, since the words intercepted had resulted wholly or in part from the relationship which the officer established with the suspect, gaining entry by subterfuge to the suspect's private life. That aspect was not in accordance with law as required by Art.8, para.2, there being insufficient safeguards against arbitrariness, in particular, the legislation did not specify in which cases undercover work was allowed, on whose authority, for what duration or using which methods. The Court did not rule on this aspect, however, since it found that the use of an undercover agent alone or in connection with the telephone interception did not affect private life. It observed that the undercover agent's actions took place within the context of a large cocaine deal, that the applicant must have been aware that he was engaged in a criminal acts and that he ran the risk of encountering an undercover police officer. There was apparently no interference with a protected right on the basis that the conduct concerned related to criminal activities, which is perhaps a strict approach.

While the conformity with "law" of telephone tapping and secret surveillance has been subject to review by the Convention organs, the only challenge to "lawfulness" of undercover activities has been *Ludi*. The nature of undercover work would however appear to render it less amenable than telephone tapping to detailed statutory regulation and it is arguable that the minimum would suffice.

[4] *Shannon v UK*, 67537/01, (Dec.) April 6, 2004.
[5] *Sequiera*, n.3 above, proceedings found fair where the two undercover agents were heard in court and the applicant was able to question them.

Cross-reference

Part IIA : Evidence
Part IIA: Witnesses
Part IIB: Interception of communications
Part IIB: Surveillance and secret files.

Equality of arms

Key provision:

IIA–061   Article 6, para.1 (fair trial).

Key case law:

Delcourt v Belgium, January 17, 1970, Series A, No.11; 1 E.H.R.R 355; *Bonisch v Austria*, May 6, 1985, Series A, No.92; 9 E.H.R.R. 191; *Monnell and Morris v UK*, March 2, 1987 Series A, No.115; 10 E.H.R.R. 205; *Brandstetter v Austria*, August 26, 1991, Series A, No.211; 15 E.H.R.R. 378; *Borgers v Belgium*, October 30, 1991, Series A, No.214; 15 E.H.R.R. 92; *Ruiz-Mateos v Spain*, June 23, 1993, Series A, No.262; 16 E.H.R.R. 505; *Schuler-Zgraggen v Switzerland*, June 24, 1993, Series A, No.263; 16 E.H.R.R. 405; *Dombo Beheer BV v Netherlands*, October 27, 1993, Series A, No.274; 18 E.H.R.R. 213; *Bendenoun v France*, February 24, 1994, Series A, No.284; 18 E.H.R.R. 54; *Van de Hurk v Netherlands*, April 19, 1994, Series A, No.288; 18 E.H.R.R. 481; *Hentrich v France*, September 22, 1994, Series A, No.296; 18 E.H.R.R. 440; *Stran Greek Refineries v Greece*, December 9, 1994, Series A, No.301–B; 19 E.H.R.R. 293; *Schouten and Meldrum v Netherlands*, December 9, 1994, Series A, No.304; 19 E.H.R.R. 432; *Lobo Machado v Portugal*, February 20, 1996, R.J.D. 1996–I, No.3; 23 E.H.R.R. 79; *Bulut v Austria*, February 22, 1996, R.J.D. 1996–II, No.5; 24 E.H.R.R. 84; *Vermeulen v Belgium*, February 20, 1996, R.J.D. 1996–I, No.3; 32 E.H.R.R. 513; *Ankerl v Switzerland*, October 23, 1996, R.J.D. 1996–V, No.19; 32 E.H.R.R. 1; *Mantovanelli v France*, March 18, 1997, R.J.D. 1997–II, No.32; 24 E.H.R.R. 370; *Kress v France*, June 7, 2001, ECHR 2001–VI.

1. General considerations

IIA–062   Equality of arms, as in the sense of "fair balance", is one of the long-established elements of fairness.[1] It is sometimes linked to considerations that proceedings must be adversarial. It implies that each party must be afforded a reasonable opportunity to present his case—including his evidence—under conditions which do not place him at a substantial disadvantage *vis-à-vis* his opponent.[2] This means in principle the opportunity for the parties to a criminal or civil trial to have knowledge of and comment on all evidence adduced or observations filed.[3] Particular importance is to be attached in this context to the appearance of the fair administration of justice.[4]

2. Aspects of equality of arms

(a) *Opportunity to receive and respond to submissions*

IIA–063   The right to adversarial trial has also been held to mean that in a criminal case both prosecution and defence must be given the opportunity to have knowledge of and

---

[1] *Delcourt*, para.28.
[2] *Dombo Beheer*, para.33; *Kress*, para.72.
[3] *Ruiz-Mateos*, para.63; *Lobo Machado*, para.31.
[4] *Bulut*, para.47; *Borgers*, para.24.

comment on the observations filed and the evidence adduced by the other party. While there are various ways by which national law may seek to achieve this, whatever method is chosen should ensure that the other party will know if observations are filed and will get a real opportunity to comment.[5] Where civil rights and obligations are concerned, even in the context of the special nature of Constitutional Court proceedings, parties must as a rule be granted free access to the observations of other participants and a genuine opportunity to comment on them.[6] This extends also to ancillary matters such as cost applications, where even if for reasons of judicial economy and efficiency the possibility to present factual and legal argument may be limited, as litigants' confidence in the workings of justice, which is based, *inter alia*, on the knowledge that they have had the opportunity to express their views on every document in the file, remains at stake.[7]

Where State legal officers such as *procureurs-general* participated in proceedings, the Court initially accepted that they could be regarded as neutral or impartial and therefore no breach of equality resulted from failure to give parties or an accused the opportunity to know the content of or respond to their interventions.[8] However the Court has since found that where a legal officer has recommended that an application be rejected or accepted, such an officer can no longer be regarded as neutral and the applicant should have the possibility of commenting on the officer's submissions.[9] The presence of such judicial officers during court deliberations has also disclosed inequality of arms, since even if their role is limited to neutral points of law, which may be doubted, an accused may legitimately fear that the opportunity is used to bolster arguments to obtain a particular result.[10]

It is not necessary for identifiable prejudice to flow from a procedural inequality. In *Bulut v Austria*, the Government's argument that the observations lodged by the

---

[5] *Brandstetter*, para.67, violation where the prosecutor's submissions were not communicated to the applicant: it was not enough that in the Austrian system the applicant could have anticipated something might have been submitted and applied to see the complete file nor that there was an indirect opportunity to answer prosecutor's points which had been adopted in the appeal court's judgment; *Kuopila v Finland*, April 27, 2000, where the prosecutor submitted an additional police report to the Court of Appeal on which the applicant had no opportunity to comment -it was irrelevant that the court did not refer to the report in its decision.

[6] *Ruiz-Mateos*: violation where State Counsel had filed observations on the validity of the impugned law and the applicants were not given the opportunity to reply; conversely, in *Van de Hurk*, no violation where the minister changed his ground of objection before the Tribunal, since the applicant had a genuine opportunity to respond.

[7] *Beer v Austria*, February 6, 2001, para.18.

[8] *Delcourt*.

[9] e.g *Bulut*; *Borgers*—while the Court still accepted the independence and impartiality of the *procureurs'* department, it referred to the evolution in its case law concerning the importance to be attached to appearances and to the increased sensitivity of the public to the administration of justice. Inequality disclosed by role of similar officers in criminal cases: *JJ v Netherlands*, March 27, 1998, R.J.D. 1998–II, No.68; *Reinhardt and Slimane-Kaid*, March 31, 1998, R.J.D. 1998–II, No.68, imbalance in procedure where the reporting judge's report and draft judgment was seen by advocate-general before the hearing whereas only part was disclosed to applicant during the hearing and the applicant also did not receive the advocate-general's submissions. See, however, *Kress v France*, para.76, where sufficient procedural safeguards were in place in respect of the submissions of the government commissioner made orally during the proceedings, as the parties' lawyers could ask in advance for an indication of the tenor of those submissions and put in a memorandum in reply for the deliberations.

[10] e.g. *Lobo Machado*, *Borgers*, *Vermeulen*; more recently, *KDB v Netherlands*, March 27, 1998, paras 42–44; *Kress v France*, paras 83–87, concerning the government commissioner in administrative court proceedings who attended the deliberations.

Attorney General with the Supreme Court (but not served on the applicant) merely recommended the court to deal with the case in a particular manner were rejected. It was for the defence to assess whether a submission deserved a reaction and it was therefore unfair for the prosecution to make submissions to a court without the knowledge of the defence.

(b) *Opportunity to present or give evidence*

IIA–064   Where a party is permitted to confine its submissions in a summary fashion which deprives the other party of an effective opportunity to counter them, there may be a breach.[11] Generally, a party may claim the right to give evidence in his own behalf, despite technical domestic rules.[12] It is compatible with fairness for an accused to be prevented from consulting his reference notes while giving evidence at his trial, even where it was alleged that prosecution witnesses were not subject to this restriction.[13]

(c) *Inequal status of witnesses*

IIA–065   The position of experts must be attended by a fair balance between the parties. The mere fact that official experts in expropriation proceedings worked for the administrative authority was not a ground in itself for justifying fears that they did not act with neutrality. Otherwise it would place unacceptable limits on the possiblity to obtain expert advice.[14] In respect of court appointed experts, potential problems may arise where the expert has been involved in the prosecution but whether a violation arises will depend on whether he in fact exercised a privileged role.[15]

Technical differences may be discounted, as in *Ankerl v Switzerland*, where the wife was not allowed to take an oath, but her evidence was nonetheless before the court.

---

[11] *e.g. Hentrich*, where in the proceedings to challenge the pre-emption by the Revenue of the applicant's purchase of property, she was unable to challenge the Revenue's assessment by adducing evidence to show that she had acted in good faith and that the proper market price had been paid—in addition the tribunals allowed the Revenue to confine its reasons for pre-emption to a summary and general statement.

[12] *Dombo Beheer*: violation found where the applicant company was in a civil dispute with a bank over an oral agreement but the applicant company director was barred from being a witness since he was identified with a party to the proceedings whereas the representative of the bank, who was involved in the transaction, could be a witness.

[13] *Pullicino v Malta*, 45441/99, (Dec.) June 15, 2000, where the Court took into account as offsetting any difficulty other safeguards such as the fact that the accused was represented and his counsel could fully cross-examine prosecution witnesses.

[14] *Zumtobel v Austria*, September 21, 1993, Series A, No.268–A; 17 E.H.R.R. 116, para.86: the applicants were free to submit their own expert opinions, which if disregarded, could be subject to appeal.

[15] *Bonisch*: violation of Art.6, para.1, since the expert whose report had lead to the applicant's prosecution was appointed court expert with powers to question whereas the applicant's expert was only subject to examination and had limited attendance possibilities; *Brandstetter*: no violation, since, even though the expert who initiated the proceedings was appointed court expert, there was no inequality as he did not question anyone and the defence, largely agreeing with the court expert, relied on matters on which he had made no submissions.

(d) *Procedural inequalities*

Potentially, issues might arise where one party enjoys by their position advantages over the conduct of the proceedings or access to material.[16] However, these may to some extent be unavoidable where State authorities are concerned and the Court seems to take a pragmatic approach as to whether the applicant has in fact been disadvantaged. For example, there was no prejudice from the fact that a time-limit was not imposed on the submission by the Attorney General of his position paper to Supreme Court[17]; there was no inequality of arms where the applicant complained of not being given copies of the contents of the file held by tax authorities in tax evasion proceedings, where the Court found that those documents were not among those relied on by the tax authorities and he did not put forward any reasons for seeking disclosure.[18] As to an alleged ability by a State authority to delay the proceedings, the Court found no substance in the allegations that the authority could choose the order of cases, since no preceding case prejudged his or prevented him putting his arguments.[19]

IIA–066

However where there was a procedural rule that time ceased to run against the State during judicial vacation, the Court found that the applicant had suffered inequality of arms since her application, rejected as out of time, would have not have been deemed outside the time-limit if the same rule had applied to her.[20] Where in expropriation proceedings the government commissioner played both role of party and expert, and enjoyed a dominant position with significant influence over the judge's assessment of value, this was also incompatible with the principle of equality of arms.[21] Power of the prosecution to decide whether not to disclose evidence to the accused at trial on public interest grounds disclosed unfairness and lack of equality of arms in a series of UK cases.[22]

(e) *Legislative interference*

Where a State intervenes by passing a law to ensure the favourable outcome of pending proceedings in which it is a party, there may be a striking inequality of arms. In those circumstances, it is not enough that in the proceedings before the domestic court a party is able to present all the arguments they wished, since fairness applied to the proceedings in their entirety, not merely the hearing *inter partes*. Such intervention infringes the principle that each party must be afforded a

IIA–067

---

[16] *e.g. Mantovanelli*: violation as regarded the applicants' lack of effective involvement in the preparation of the court expert report whereas the defendant hospital staff were involved (framed as infringement of the adversarial principle).

[17] *Kremzow*, para.75.

[18] *Bendenoun*; *Schuler-Zgraggen*, where there was no inequality of arms in relation to complaints of access to material—the applicant had access to the file and was able to make copies, while the report which she did not see was not part of the file, was summarised in another document she had seen and the courts did not have the full report either.

[19] *Schouten and Meldrum*.

[20] *Platakou v Greece*, January 11, 2001, paras 47–48.

[21] *Yvon v France*, April 24, 2003—the judge was required by law to keep within the limits of the valuation proposed by the commissioner in certain circumstances and had to give express reasons for not following the commissioner's conclusions.

[22] See Evidence, Failure to disclose evidence: the cases cited therein.

reasonable opportunity to present his case under conditions that do not place him at a substantial disadvantage *vis-à-vis* his opponent.[23]

Cross-reference

Part IIA: General Principles: Fairness
Part IIA: Evidence
Part IIA: Legislative interference in judicial process
Part IIA: Witnesses
Part IIB: Review of detention, Equality of arms (Art.5, para.4).

---

[23] *e.g. Stran Greek*, para.46.

Evidence

Key provision:

Article 6, paras 1–3 (fair hearing guarantees). IIA–068

Key case law:

Barbera, Messegué and Jabardo v Spain, December 6, 1988, Series A, No.146; 11 E.H.R.R. 360; *Schenk v Switzerland*, July 12, 1988, Series A, No.140; 13 E.H.R.R. 242; *H v France*, October 24, 1989, Series A, No.162; 12 E.H.R.R. 74; *Edwards v UK*, December 16, 1992, Series A, No.247–B; 15 E.H.R.R. 417; *Dombo Beheer BV v Netherlands*, October 27, 1993, Series A, No.274–A; 18 E.H.R.R. 213; *Ferrantelli and Santangelo v Italy*, August 7, 1996, R.J.D. 1996–III, No. 12; *Fitt v UK*, February 16, 2000, ECHR 2000–II; 30 E.H.R.R. 480; *Rowe and Davies v UK*, February 16, 2000, ECHR 2000–II; 30 E.H.R.R. 1; *Khan v UK*, May 12, 2000, ECHR 2000–V; 31 E.H.R.R. 1016; *GB v France*, October 2, 2001, ECHR 2001–X; *Allan v UK*, November 5, 2002, ECHR 2002–IX; *Edwards and Lewis v UK*, July 22, 2003, ECHR 2003–IX; *Papageorgiou v Greece*, May 9, 2003.

1. General considerations

The admissibility and assessment of evidence is, primarily, a matter for the domestic IIA–069 courts. Whether or not the courts have correctly assessed the evidence is largely outside the competence of the Court.[1] There has only been a limited supervision by the Convention organs, having regard to their position that they are not a fourth instance nor in an appropriate position to overrule the opinion of the local courts who have first-hand knowledge and experience.

The Court examines, in terms of the Convention, whether the requirements of Art.6, para.1 as to fairness have been complied with, including the way in which evidence was submitted.[2] This means generally that any alleged evidential imbalance or unfairness will be looked at in light of the proceedings as a whole and as to whether an applicant has been deprived of an ability to participate effectively in the proceedings or the position of the defence significantly impaired.[3] In criminal cases, the whole matter of the taking and presentation of evidence must also be looked at in light of the guarantees of paras 2 and 3. For example, in light of the presumption of innocence, when carrying out their duties, the members of a court should not start with the preconceived idea that the accused has committed the offence and the burden of proof is on the prosecution and any doubt should benefit the accused. It also follows that the prosecution must inform the accused of the case against him so that he may prepare and present his defence, and to adduce evidence sufficient to convict him.[4]

---

[1] 6172/73, (Dec.) July 7, 1975, 3 D.R. 77.
[2] *Barbera*, para.68.
[3] *e.g. Dombo Beheer*, para.33 (equality of arms): a party must have a reasonable opportunity to present his case, including evidence, under conditions not placing him at a substantial disadvantage vis-à-vis his opponent.
[4] *Barbera*, paras 76–77.

2. Presentation of evidence at trial

IIA–070   In principle, the evidence against accused should be presented in court publicly, subject to an adversarial procedure. In *Barbera, Messegué and Jabardo v Spain*, where a case of robbery and murder resulting in sentences of up to 36 years was examined in a trial lasting one day, the Court found a violation cumulatively on a number of defects but, particularly, in that very important pieces of evidence were not adequately adduced and discussed at the trial in the applicants' presence and under the public eye. This included material evidence such as weapons relied on by the prosecution but not produced in court; confessions which the applicants stated were given under duress and in which respect the Court had reservations since they were obtained during a long period of incommunicado custody; and lack of attendance at the trial of witnesses whose statements incriminated the applicants and whom the applicants has no prior possibility of examining. In *Pagageorgiou v Greece*, the failure to produce in court for examination in the presence of the accused key evidence, namely the originals of the allegedly forged cheques, rendered the applicant's trial and appeal unfair, where the first instance court had in fact ordered their destruction and relied on photocopies. Destruction or loss of evidence may not impinge on fairness however where the defence is not unduly handicapped as a result.[5]

There is a duty on courts to ensure they have evidence properly and fairly presented. Thus in *Barbera*, the Court held that even though the prosecution and defence had agreed to waive the oral presentation of documentary evidence at trial, this did not dispense the court from complying with the requirements of Art.6, para.1.

Regarding methods of presentation of evidence, the Commission criticised the practice where, before an appeal court, the statement of the witness was read out and he was asked if he maintained it, noting that it may reduce the value of the statements of a witness if he is reminded of what he said before. However since the parties were able to put further questions to the witnesses and to challenge the correctness of the evidence, the method was not of such a character that it rendered the hearing unfair.[6]

3. Admissibility of evidence

IIA–071   Article 6, para.1 does not lay down any rules as to the admissibility of evidence which is primarily a matter for the regulation under national law.[7] A failure by the applicant or his counsel to object to any evidence is an important, if not necessarily decisive factor, bearing in mind the courts' general duty to ensure the fairness of the proceedings of their own motion.[8] Also relevant are any aspects which might remedy or mitigate the alleged unfairness and whether the matter was subject to careful scrutiny by the appeal courts.

---

[5] *Sofri v Italy*, 37235/97, (Dec.) May 27, 2003—the Court regretted that administrative error had led to the destruction of evidence (clothing, car and bullets) in a murder case; however, the applicants had not shown that the lost clothing of the victim could have assisted the defence, reports existed on the state of the car and on bullets and the prosecution faced the same problems in carrying out further expert examinations.

[6] 10486/83, (Dec.) October 9, 1986, 49 D.R. 86.

[7] *e.g.* 12505/86, (Dec.) October 11, 1988, 58 D.R. 106.

[8] *e.g.* 7306/75, (Dec.) October 6, 1976, 7 D.R. 155; 8876/80, (Dec.) October 16, 1980, 23 D.R. 233.

(a) *Accomplices*

Issues of fairness may arise where an accomplice, who has been granted immunity, gives evidence against an applicant. However, where that fact was made known to the defence and the terms of the agreement explained to the jury, who were warned by the judge and the matter examined on appeal, no problem arose.[9] Where a guilty plea of a co-accused to tax evasion charges was admitted as evidence at the applicant's trial, this did not render the proceedings unfair, given, *inter alia*, the judge's warning to the jury of its limited relevance.[10]

IIA–072

(b) *Indirect or documentary evidence*

The Commission held that use of indirect evidence is not prohibited by the Convention. It had regard however to whether it was the sole evidence. In a German case, where the applicant complained that the evidence before the court was largely written statements of alleged witnesses it noted that the conviction was based primarily on the accused's own statements made before the first instance court.[11] Also relevant is whether an applicant has had an opportunity to challenge at some stage a witness whose written evidence was used against him.[12]

IIA–073

(c) *Hearsay*

The Commission considered that the rule excluding hearsay evidence is legitimately based on the aim of ensuring the best evidence before the jury, who can evaluate the credibility of witnesses before them and to avoid reliance on evidence untested by cross-examination. It is not, in principle, contrary to Art.6, para.1.[13]

IIA–074

(d) *Confessions and coercion*

Where convictions are based on confessions allegedly obtained by coercion, the Convention organs have still applied the principle that the assessment of the evidence is for the domestic courts. The Commission held that the guarantee of a fair trial required a procedure whereby the validity of such evidence could be examined. It found the process in English courts of a *voire dire* (adversarial trial-within-a-trial, including evidence and argument, before a judge in the absence of jury) which issued a ruling on admissibility and left the probative value to to the jury was sufficient safeguard and provided a fair trial.[14]

IIA–075

In *Ferrantelli and Santangelo v Italy*, where the applicants complained that they had been convicted on the basis of confessions obtained by coercion, the Court, noting that the question of ill-treatment was subject to specific investigation by the judicial authorities, who ruled no case to answer against the alleged perpetrators, found

[9] 73605/75, (Dec.) October 6, 1976, 7 D.R. 115; see also 17265/90, (Dec.) October 21, 1993, 75 D.R. 76.

[10] 28572/95, (Dec.) January 17, 1997.

[11] 8945/80, (Dec.) December 13, 1983, 39 D.R. 43.

[12] See Pt IIA, Witnesses.

[13] 12045/86, (Dec.) May 7, 1987, 52 D.R. 273.

[14] 9370/81, (Dec.) October 13, 1983, 35 D.R. 75.

insufficient material before it depart from the domestic findings. This appears to allow confessions to be used as long as the domestic courts investigate any allegations of ill-treatment. In the absence of this procedural guarantee, and where doubts arise due to prolonged periods in police custody without appearance before a judicial officer, issues as to the fairness of use of confession may arise.[15]

Methods of obtaining admissions from suspects may raise fairness issues even where involving subterfuge short of direct physical or mental ill-treatment in interrogation. In *Allan v United Kingdom*, where there were elements of oppression and entrapment in coaching an informer as cell-mate to obtain admissions from a detained applicant placed under deliberate pressure, the Court found use of the evidence effectively deprived the applicant of his right to silence to police questions.

(e) Unlawfully obtained evidence

IIA–076   The use of unlawfully obtained evidence is not excluded as a matter of principle. However the way the evidence was obtained and the role played at the trial will be examined in the context of ascertaining whether the trial as a whole was fair.[16] In practice, alleged unlawful elements have not been found to disclose unfairness, where the evidence was not obtained by means of oppression, entrapment or coercion and it has been subject to adversarial proceedings, with the applicant able to challenge it.[17] Thus in *Schenk v Switzerland*, the Court found that the use of a recording, unlawful insofar as it was not ordered by the investigating judge, did not render the trial automatically unfair or furnish a ground for violation *per se*. It examined the fairness factors, and it was sufficient that the applicant had knowledge of the tape and circumstances in which it was recorded and was able to challenge its use. Although the Court also attached weight to the fact in that case it was not the only evidence on which the conviction was based, in *Khan v United Kingdom*, where the taped telephone conversations obtained without any legal basis were the only evidence, the Court still found its use at trial was not unfair as procedures provided at two instances for the applicant to challenge its reliability and the fairness of its admission. The lack of proper legal authority for inventive police methods of obtaining evidence is considered by the Court rather as raising issues under Art.8's right to respect for private life than *per se* a fairness problem under Art.6.

4. Weight given to evidence

IIA–077   The probative value of evidence also falls essentially for the domestic instances to determine.[18] Thus in an Italian case, where the applicant, accused of instigating a murder, complained the conviction was based only on circumstantial evidence and presumptions, the Commission found it sufficient that the charges against him were presented and debated adversarially before the trial judges and the Court of

---

[15] *e.g. Barbera; Hazar v Turkey*, 16311–13/90, etc. (Dec.) November 11, 1991, 72 D.R. 200; (settled) (Rep.) December 10, 1992, 73 D.R. 111, where the applicants alleged torture in police custody during the 14 day period before being brought before a judicial officer and the confession obtained were used to obtain convictions.

[16] 12505/86, (Dec.) October 11, 1988, 58 D.R. 106.

[17] 12505/86, n.16 above; *PG and. JH v UK*, September 25, 2001, ECHR 2001–IX, para.78; *Perry v UK*, 63737/00 and *Chalkley v UK*, 63831/00, (Decs.) September 26, 2002.

[18] *e.g.* 12013/86, (Dec.) March 10, 1989, 59 D.R. 100.

Cassation. It did list the elements of indirect proof presumably implying that the "whole body of indirect evidence" on which the judges based their finding that the applicant ordered the execution was not unfair.[19]

5. Failure to disclose evidence

There is a requirement for the prosecution to disclose to the defence all the material evidence for or against the accused.[20] Whether or not a failure to do so discloses objectionable unfairness will depend on an assessment of the proceedings as a whole. In *Edwards v United Kingdom*, the failure to disclose that one of the witnesses had failed to identify the applicant from a police photograph album and the existence of fingerprints, not the applicant's, at the scene of the burglary, was a defect, but the Court found it was cured since when this was discovered there was an independent enquiry and the case was referred to the Court of Appeal where counsel had every opportunity to persuade the court to overturn the conviction, including the possibility to apply for police officers to be called as witnesses.

IIA–078

The entitlement to disclosure of relevant evidence is not, however, absolute. The Court has acknowledged that it may be necessary to withhold certain evidence, for example to protect the fundamental rights of another individual or to safeguard an important public interest, *e.g.* to protect national security or witnesses, keep secret police methods of investigation.[21] Restrictions must, in those situations, be limited to what is strictly necessary and the impact on the defence sufficiently counterbalanced by procedures. Thus, in *Rowe and Davis v United Kingdom*, the procedure whereby it was the prosecution which decided that public interest required non-disclosure of relevant evidence and the material was not reviewed by the first instance judge did not provide the necessary safeguards. In *Fitt v United Kingdom*, where the judge assessed whether the material should be disclosed in the interests of the defence and the matter was kept under review during the trial, there were sufficient safeguards.[22] Where however the material is of potential relevance to issues in the trial, the fact that the judge reviews it may not sufficiently protect the position of the defence which will not have been able to make submissions on it. In *Edwards and Lewis v United Kingdom*, the judge had ruled on non-disclosure of material on public interest grounds which seemingly might have had bearing on his later ruling rejecting the applicants' applications to exclude other police evidence on grounds of entrapment. The Court distinguished the *Fitt* line of cases by stating that in those the undisclosed material had formed no part of the prosecution case and was never put to the jury.

---

[19] 12013/86, n.18 above.
[20] *Jespers v Belgium*, 8403/78, ((Rep.) December 14, 1981, 27 D.R. 61; *Edwards*, para.36; *Rowe and Davis*, para.60.
[21] *Rowe and Davis*, para.61; *Fitt*, para.45.
[22] See also *Dowsett v UK*, June 24, 2003, para.50, where the material had not been disclosed to the trial judge by the prosecution, it was not sufficient that the defence could have applied for the Court of Appeal to review the material—this was not an adequate safeguard as the appellate court did not have the advantage of the trial judge of seeing and hearing the witnesses and would not be assisted by defence counsel's arguments as to relevance; *Atlan v UK*, June 19, 2001.

6. Refusal to call expert evidence or take other investigative measures

IIA–079   The Commission did not exclude that the refusal by a court to order an expert, hear a witness or to accept other types of evidence might in certain circumstances render the proceedings unfair. Since however it was for the national courts to decide what was necessary or essential to decide a case, it commented that only in exceptional circumstances would it conclude that a decision of a national court in such a matter violated the right to a fair hearing. It gave the example of where an applicant adduced some evidence which the court rejected outright, refusing to allow verification of it and without giving sufficient reasons for its refusal.[23] Although in *Elsholz v Germany*, the Court did find a violation arose where the domestic courts in child contact proceedings refused the applicant father's request for a psychological report on the 5–6 year old child's views on contact, the Grand Chamber has since re-iterated that as a general rule it is for domestic courts to assess the evidence before them, including the means to ascertain relevant facts: having regard in particular to the age and maturity of the child who was heard in the proceedings in that case, it found the courts well able to reach a reasoned decision on the issues without the expert evidence requested by the applicant.[24]

Although the mere fact that an expert changes his views during proceedings does not *per se* impinge on the fairness of a trial and require an opportunity for the defence to seek a second opinion, issues may also arise where this threatens to have undue influence on the jury.[25] In *GB v France*, where in oral examination an expert reacted to new evidence by abruptly changing his own opinion in a highly adverse manner to the accused, the Court could not exclude that this might had given the opinion particular weight in the eyes of the jury and fairness had required the defence have the opportunity to seek another expert opinion on the issue.

7. Admission of new evidence

IIA–080   Where new evidence following conviction appears, there is no right to retrial.[26] Nor where a case is re-opened, is there a requirement for a complete rehearing. In the Birmingham Six case, the Commission rejected the argument that the new evidence should have been put in front of a jury rather than reviewed by the Court of Appeal. The Commission noted that a jury trial was not essential to fairness[27] and it found the proceedings before the Court of Appeal fair, the Court of Appeal having stated

[23] *H. v France*, where the courts refused the applicant's application for a medical opinion for the purpose of proving the causal link between his medical treatment and his injury. The Commission noted, *inter alia*, that there had been medical expert evidence in the file and it was evident that the decision was reached after fairly detailed examination of the causation issue. The Court agreed, commenting adversely on the applicant's dilatoriness in taking proceedings. See however *Vidal v Belgium*, April 22, 1992, Series A, No.235, violation where the appeal court overturned an acquittal without hearing witnesses requested by the applicant and without giving reasons.

[24] *Sommerfeld v Germany*, July 8, 2003, ECHR 2003–VIII, (concerning failure to order expert opinion on the negative views to contact expressed by a 13 year old), where the Court's reasoning was under the procedural aspect of Art.8, with no separate issue arising under Art.6. Similar reasoning regarding the failure of the court to hear a 5 year old concerning contact, where there was expert evidence as to the undesirability of direct questioning—*Sahin v Germany*, July 8, 2003, ECHR 2003–VIII.

[25] *GB v France*, paras 68–70.

[26] 7761/77, (Dec.) May 8, 1978, 14 D.R. 171.

[27] Not all Contracting States rely on or admire the institution.

that, if there had been the least doubt that the verdicts were safe or satisfactory, it would quash the convictions.[28]

8. Judicial notice

The Commission accepted the German courts were able to take cognisance of   IIA–081
established historical fact. Thus there was no problem in a refusal to admit evidence concerning the existence of the gas chambers and extermination of the Jews since this was established fact.[29]

9. Assessment of evidence

Notwithstanding the general statements above, the Commission stated that it would   IIA–082
intervene where the assessment of evidence disclosed gross unfairness or arbitrariness.[30] What this means in practice has not been explored. It seems to indicate that there will be some verification that there is some evidence to support the decision. The fact that a judge prefers the evidence of particular witnesses is unlikely to be sufficient, unless his stated reasons for doing so disclose a fundamental unsoundness.[31] Where an applicant was convicted on the basis of a statement given in his absence by a witness who later retracted it, the Court considered it sufficient that the court had the opportunity to observe the demeanour of the witness at first hand and as it gave detailed reasons for its decision to attach weight to the accusatory statement, the verdict could not be deemed "arbitrary or manifestly unreasonable".[32]

Cross-reference

Part IIA: Entrapment
Part IIA: Presumption of innocence
Part IIA: Witnesses
Part IIB: Interception of communications

---

[28] 14739/89, (Dec.) May 9, 1989, 60 D.R. 296; see also *Edwards*; and *Oyston v UK*, 42011/98, (Dec.) January 22, 2002: where it was compatible with fairness for the Court of Appeal to assess the relevance of new evidence and decide whether the conviction should stand.

[29] 25096/94, (Dec.) September 6, 1995, 82–A D.R. 117.

[30] *e.g.* 7987/77, (Dec.) December 13, 1979, 18 D.R. 31, where an applicant company complained of the assessment of compensation for expropriated property, the Commission found that evaluation of the evidence could not be reviewed by it unless the judge had drawn grossly unfair or arbitrary conclusions from the facts before him—however the judge's findings of fact were supported by the higher court and the reasons on which the decisions were based sufficient to exclude any arbitrariness; 22909/93, (Dec.) September 6, 1995 82–B D.R. 25.

[31] *e.g. mutatis mutandis, Schuler-Zgraggen v Switzerland,* June 24, 1993, Series A, No.263, where the court relied on factors discriminatory on grounds of sex.

[32] *Camilleri v Malta*, 51760/99, (Dec.) March 16, 2000.

Independence and impartiality

Key provision:

IIA–083   Article 6, para.1 (fair trial by "independent and impartial tribunal").

Key case law:

Ringeisen v Austria, July 16, 1971, Series A, No.13; 1 E.H.R.R. 455; *Le Compte v Belgium*, June 23, 1981, Series A, No.43; 4 E.H.R.R. 1; *Piersack v Belgium*, October 1, 1982, Series A, No.53; 5 E.H.R.R. 169; *Sramek v Austria*, October 22, 1984, Series A, No.84; *Campbell and Fell v UK*, June 28, 1984, Series A, No.80; 7 E.H.R.R. 165; *Belilos v Switzerland*, April 29, 1988, Series A, No.132; 10 E.H.R.R. 466; *De Cubber v Belgium*, October 26, 1984, Series A, No.86; 7 E.H.R.R. 236; *Hauschildt v Denmark*, May 24, 1989, Series A, No.155; 12 E.H.R.R. 266; *Langborger v Sweden*, June 22, 1989, Series A, No.155; 12 E.H.R.R. 416; *Oberschlick v Austria (No.1)*, May 23, 1991, Series A, No.204; 19 E.H.R.R. 389; *Demicoli v Malta*, August 27, 1991, Series A, No.210; 14 E.H.R.R. 47; *Pfeiffer and Plankl v Austria*, February 25, 1992, Series A, No.227; 14 E.H.R.R. 692; *Nortier v Netherlands*, August 24, 1993, Series A, No.267; 17 E.H.R.R. 273; *Saraivo de Carvalho v Portugal*, April 22, 1994, Series A, No.286; 18 E.H.R.R. 534; *Van de Hurk v Netherlands*, April 19, 1994, Series A, No.288; 18 E.H.R.R. 481; *Debled v Belgium*, September 22, 1994, Series A, No.292–B; 19 E.H.R.R. 506; *Diennet v France*, September 26, 1995, Series A, No.325; 21 E.H.R.R. 544; *Procola v Luxembourg*, September 28, 1995, Series A, No.326; 22 E.H.R.R. 193; *Thomann v Switzerland*, June 10, 1996, R.J.D. 1996–III, No.11; 24 E.H.R.R. 553; *Ferrantelli and Santangelo v Italy*, August 7, 1996, R.J.D. 1997–I, No.30; 23 E.H.R.R. 288; *Findlay v UK*, February 25, 1997, R.J.D. 1997–I, No.30; 24 E.H.R.R. 221; *McGonnell v UK*, February 8, 2000; 30 E.H.R.R. 289; *Kingsley v UK*, November 7, 2000; *Kleyn v Netherlands*, May 6, 2003, ECHR 2003–VI; *Kyprianou v Cyprus*, January 27, 2004.

1. General considerations

IIA–084   This core element of the notion of a fair trial has generated many cases. The two aspects are often interlocked, a lack of independence coinciding with a lack of objective impartiality. Thus the two notions are frequently treated together. The basic principles were established early. The cases tend merely to illustrate their application to a diverse number of factual and procedural circumstances.

2. Independence

IIA–085   The tribunal or court must be independent of the executive and the parties[1] and also of the legislature or Parliament.[2] As to whether it satisfies the condition of

---

[1] *Ringeisen*, para.95.
[2] *e.g.* 8603/79, (Dec.) December 18, 1980, 22 D.R. 220; *Demicoli*, breach of privilege proceedings before the Maltese House of Representatives against a journalist for defamatory articles—the Commission found lack of independence, the Court found a lack of impartiality.

independence, regard is had to the manner of appointment of the members, the duration of their office, the existence of guarantees against outside pressure and the question whether the body presents an appearance of independence.[3]

Aspects and guarantees

(a) Composition

The presence of legally-qualified or judicial members is a strong indicator of independence, as in *Lecompte v Belgium* where on the Appeals Council the members were made up equally of medical practitioners acting in personal capacity and members of the judiciary, being chaired by one of latter.[4] Where, in *Sramek v Austria*, the regional authority in land disputes included three civil servants from the local government, which was a party in the proceedings, there was a legitimate doubt about their independence, since even though there was no indication that they were subject to instructions, they were subordinate to the officer acting for the local government in the proceedings. Where patents bodies were entirely made up of civil servants, who had no guarantees of irremovability and appointed from a pool to act at first instance and on appeal, the Commission found problems of structural independence.[5]

IIA–086

(b) Appointment and term of office

The mere fact that a minister appoints members does not pose a problem since in many systems judges are appointed on approval by ministers of justice.[6] Nor can exception be taken to appointment by Parliament either.[7] However, the irremovability of judges is in general a corollary of their independence although the lack of this guarantee is not necessarily fatal. For example, though there were no regulations or guarantees concerning Board of Visitors members, it was accepted that although the Home Secretary could require a member to resign this would be done in only the most exceptional circumstances.[8]

IIA–087

Fixed terms also tend to be regarded as a guarantee. In *Le Compte*, six-year terms for Appeals Council members furnished a safeguard. Three-year terms for Board of Visitor members in *Campbell and Fell v United Kingdom* were considered rather short but it was acknowledged that the posts were unpaid and it was difficult to get volunteers. Four year terms for military judges on the National Security Court in Turkey was questionable.[9]

---

[3] *Piersack*, para.27.
[4] *Campbell and Fell*, where the Board of Visitors' membership was generally half magistrates.
[5] *British American Tobacco v Netherlands*, November 20, 1995, Series A, No.331–A; 21 E.H.R.R. 409—the Court found it unnecessary to decide as in any event appeal lay to a normal court.
[6] 18781/91, (Dec.) July 6, 1998.
[7] *Filippini v San Marino*, 10526/02, (Dec.) August 26, 2003.
[8] *Campbell and Fell*, para.80; *McMichael v UK*, (Rep.) Series A, No.307–B, paras 61 and 114, where the Commission had doubts concerning removability of members of the Children's Panel by the Secretary of State.
[9] *Incal v Turkey*, June 9, 1998, R.J.D. 1998–IV, No.78, para.68; though in *Yavuz v Turkey*, 29870/96, (Dec.) May 25, 2000, four year terms appeared to be considered favourably.

(c) *Appearances*

IIA–088 While weight is given to the proper appearance of independence, suspicions have to be to some extent objectively justified. In *Campbell and Fell*, the Commission thought that the Board of Visitors did not give an appearance of institutional independence, since it fulfilled a number of administrative roles in prison and was associated by prisoners with prison management. The Court however found that the fact the Board had administrative roles was not decisive and it could still be independent. It also took the view that in a custodial setting certain sentiments by prisoners were inevitable but there was no indication that they would be reasonably entitled to think that the Board was dependent on the prison.

Where a police board acting in a judicial capacity was concerned however, appearances were found to be decisive in the context of determining whether it acted as a "tribunal" for the purposes of Art.6, para.1. In *Belilos v Switzerland*, a member of the police sat in his personal capacity on the Police Board, was not subject to orders, took an oath and could not be dismissed. Since, however, he was a civil servant who returned to other departmental duties and would tend to be seen as member of the police force subordinate to superiors and loyal to colleagues, this disclosed a situation which could undermine the confidence which courts should inspire.

(d) *Subordination to other authorities*

IIA–089 The tribunal must not be subject to instructions in its adjudicatory role although it may be compatible for a minister to issue general guidelines.[10] Where a minister had the power to set aside the decisions issued by the tribunal deciding on milk quota disputes, the Court found that the tribunal lacked the quality of independence, even though it seemed that the power was not exercised in practice. The power to give a binding decision which could not be altered by a non-judicial authority was identified as inherent in the guarantees of Art.6, as confirmed by the use of the term "determination".[11]

Where executive authorities intervened in judicial proceedings obtaining annulment of decisions and the setting aside of final judgments, the Court has found that the applicants have been deprived of hearing by "an independent and impartial tribunal".[12]

3. Impartiality

IIA–090 The Court distinguishes between subjective impartiality—the existence of actual prejudice on the part of a judge or tribunal- and objective impartiality—whether a judge offers guarantees sufficient to exclude any legitimate doubt in this matter.[13] Personal impartiality of a judge is to be presumed, until there is proof to the contrary.[14] In practice, this is a very strong presumption. The Court has commented

---

[10] *Campbell and Fell*, concerning the Board of Visitors.
[11] *e.g. Findlay*, where the convening officer had power to confirm the court martial decision.
[12] *e.g. Sovtransavto Holding v Ukraine*, July 25, 2002, where the Court found resulting infringements of the basic principles of the rule of law and legal certainty.
[13] *Piersack*, para.30.
[14] *Le Compte*, para.58.

that the fact that a judge takes a strongly negative view of an applicant's case or even character is not sufficient to disclose bias, and that unduly harsh or oppressive behaviour is not necessarily a reflection of personal prejudice.[15] The intemperate reaction of judges in imprisoning a lawyer for contempt of court was a rare example giving rise to a finding under the subjective element.[16]

In the context of *objective impartiality*, appearances are of a certain importance having regard to the confidence which the courts must inspire in the public in a democratic society, and above all in criminal proceedings, in the accused. The latter aspect was later qualified when the Court noted that the standpoint of the accused was important but not decisive. What was determinant was whether the fear could be considered as objectively justified.[17] The Court has also commented that any judge in respect of whom there is a legitimate reason to fear a lack of impartiality must withdraw.[18] Judges are also expected to exercise maximum discretion with regard to their cases in order to preserve their image as impartial judges, in particular refraining from using the press for comment even when provoked.[19] On the other hand, there is a strong presumption that professional judges by their training are not influenced by adverse media coverage or hostile public opinion against an accused.[20] They cannot however be presumed to be neutral as regards alleged contempts of court carried out in their presence when their personal feelings may be engaged.[21]

Major problems have arisen where a judge plays different procedural roles in the course of the proceedings; where the composition of a court coincides with another court which has been involved in some related aspect of the case or where the tribunal is not, as the traditional court, made up of trained legal or judicial members.

(a) *Differing roles of a judge*

This problem tends to arise where judges can have an investigating role or there is overlap between the prosecution (*e.g. procureur*) and the trial court. The mere fact that a judge has been involved in decisions before the trial is not sufficent to render him lacking in objective impartiality, special features being required beyond the judge's knowledge of the case file, the fact that he has looked at questions of risk on remand decisions or made assessment of the existence of a *prima facie* case.[22] It is necessary for the judge to have been squarely involved in deciding issues relevant to

IIA–091

---

[15] *e.g. Ranson v UK*, 14180/03, (Dec.) September 2, 2003.

[16] *Kyprianou*, paras 38–42. See also n.19 below, where in two cases judges made comments in the press which appeared to show prejudgment of issues: this was treated as undermining the impartiality of the tribunal.

[17] *Piersack*, para.30; *Morel v France*, June 6, 2000, ECHR 2000–VI, para.44; *Nortier*, para.33: objective test even where the applicant's apprehensions may be understandable.

[18] *Hauschildt*, para.48.

[19] See findings of lack of impartiality in *Buscemi v Italy*, September 16, 1999, ECHR 1999–VI, where a judge had responded to the applicant's comments in the press in a manner implying that he had already formed an unfavourable view of the applicant's case; *Lavents v Latvia*, November 28, 2002, paras 118–121, where a judge expressed views critical of the defence.

[20] *Craxi v Italy*, 34896/97, (Dec.) December 5, 2002.

[21] *Kyprianou*, paras 34–37.

[22] *Nortier; Saraivo de Carvalho; Morel v France*, n.17 above, concerning commercial court proceedings.

those in the trial or to have been involved in a prosecution capacity.[23] The fact that a judge has detailed prior knowledge of the case is not sufficient, attention being given to the scope and nature of any measures taken before the trial.[24] No problem arose where the judge had merely been head of the prosecution service at the time the applicant was being questioned by police about a different offence.[25]

Nor does any problem arise *per se* where a judge plays a role in a criminal case and then sits in an associated civil compensation claim.[26]

(b) *Judges' connections external to the proceedings*

IIA–092   While there is no problem as such arising from a judge acting as a lawyer, the Court found an applicant could legitimately fear that a judge, who was acting as lawyer for another party in proceedings involving the applicant, continued to view him as the opposing party.[27] Similarly, the fact that a judge had regular, close and financially lucrative links as a professor with the university sued by the applicant justified fears that he might lack impartiality.[28] Involvement of a judge in a financial agreement between her husband and a bank which was a party in proceedings in which she sat was considered to disclose links of "such a nature and amplitude" and was so close in time to the hearing of the case that the applicant could entertain reasonable fears that the court lacked the requisite impartiality.[29]

---

[23] See *Piersack*, where a judge had previously been the head of the public prosecutor's section which instituted the prosecution; *Hauschildt*, where the presiding judge had taken decisions on pre-trial detention, subject to a special feature that on nine occasions he referred to a "particularly confirmed suspicion" that the accused committed the offence *i.e.* the judge had to be convinced of a very high degree of clarity as to guilt, the difference with the issue to be settled at trial was tenuous; *Ferrantelli and Santangelo*, where the presiding appeal judge had convicted co-accused in a judgment referring to the applicants' participation in events and the appeal judgment cited extracts from that earlier judgment when convicting the applicants; *Oberschlick v Austria (No.1)*, where a judge who participated in the first instance judgment sat in the appeal hearing against that judgment; *Castillo Algar v Spain*, October 28, 1998, R.J.D. 1998–VIII, No.95 where two judges on trial court had previously rejected an appeal against the issuing of the criminal charge on the basis of "sufficient evidence" that a military offence had been committed; *Tierce v San Marino*, July 25, 2000, ECHR 2000–IX, violation found in successive role of *Commissario della Legge* as active investigating judge and trial judge; *Perote Pellon v Spain*, July 25, 2002, violation where military court judges had taken decisions to detain on the basis of findings of "solid" proof of guilt.

[24] *e.g.* no violation concerning an insolvency judge's varying interventions in *Morel v France*, n.17 above, and in *Delage and Magistrello v France*, 40028/98, (Dec.) January 24, 2002, ECHR 2002–II, or concerning cassation judges sitting on different applications in *Depiets v France*, February 10, 2004. Contrast violation in *Werner v Poland*, November 15, 2001, where the insolvency judge's ruling on a motion prejudged the final decision.

[25] *Mellors v UK*, 57386/00, (Dec.) January 30, 2003—the situation might have differed if the judge had not left the prosecution post before the applicant was charged, remanded or indicted on the murder charge on which the judge later sat in an appellate role.

[26] *Lie and Bernstenn v Norway*, 25130/94, (Dec.) December 16, 1999, where separate issues arose for determination; also *Kalogeropoulou v Greece*, 59021/00, (Dec.) December 12, 2002, where a judge acted on the merits and then in the execution procedure.

[27] *Wettstein v Switzerland*, December 12, 2000, ECHR 2000–XII—there was no material link between the two cases. It was the contemporaneous overlap of the proceedings that gave rise to objectionable appearances. The fact that an office colleague of two judges had also been a lawyer opposing the applicant would further confirm fears, though was of minor relevance by itself

[28] *Pescador Valero v Spain*, June 17, 2003.

[29] *Sigurdsson v Iceland*, April 10, 2003, para.45. However, the fact that two judges' daughters worked for the friend of the head of the bank in proceedings did not affect impartiality: *Academy Trading v Greece*, April 4, 2000, para.46.

On the other hand, the fact that a judge in a civil case had privately instructed the firm which also was representing one of the parties did not give rise to suspicion, where it concerned a will and a partner outside the litigation department.[30] The mere fact that a judge is a freemason is insufficient to cast doubt on his impartiality, even where a party or witness in the proceedings is also a freemason, at least in the UK. In *Salaman v United Kingdom*, the Court noted the Parliamentary inquiry into the matter and considered that there was no reason to doubt that a judge would regard his judicial oath as taking precedence over other obligations. Whether a judge should withdraw due to personal acquaintance with another freemason or due to the interests of a freemason being in issue would depend on the circumstances of the case.[31]

(c) Specialist tribunals

It is accepted that there may be good reasons in technical areas for opting for special adjudicatory bodies.[32] The mere existence of professional connections between an applicant and members of a tribunal is generally not sufficient to cast doubt on their impartiality, even if it may be assumed there is a potential for a conflict of interests.[33] More direct links between members and a party may be required to raise issues and once a legitimate doubt is raised, it may not be enough to point to the presence of judicial members or a judicial casting vote.[34] In *Gautrin v France*, for example, medical members of the tribunal could be regarded as having a connections with competitors of the applicant doctors "SOS Medecins" and with bodies who had lodged complaints against their alleged advertising infringements.[35]

In the military area, hierarchical dependence between court martial members and superior officers has caused problems and the Convention organs have required guarantees against any appearance of control or influence.[36] The Commission considered that the use of military tribunals over civilians *per se* raised problems of independence and impartiality.[37] In cases from Turkey, the Court has found that the

IIA–093

---

[30] *Lawrence v UK*, 74660/01, (Dec.) January 24, 2002 No grounds for doubt in *Sofianopoulos v Greece*, 1988/02, (Dec.) December 12, 2002, where a magistrates' association expressed public views on an issue in a case but the individual judges had not.

[31] 43505/98, (Dec.) June 15, 2000; see *Kiiskinen v Finland* 26323/95, (Dec.) June 1, 1998.

[32] *British American Tobacco*, n.5 above, concerning patents.

[33] Where, in *Le Compte*, the medical appeals council was made up of half doctors and half members of the judiciary, the Commission found that the former could not be deemed neutral since their interests were close to those of the parties. The Court disagreed, finding that the composition and the presence of a judicial chairman with casting vote was a definite assurance of impartiality (contrast *Langborger* below). In *Debled*, where the applicant doctor made numerous complaints concerning members of the medical appeals structure, the Court took a pragmatic approach, finding that the system generally acceptable as regarded structural objectivity; that the applicant threatened to paralyse the whole system if challenged members were excluded from all decisions; his complaints were general and abstract and not based on specific material facts showing any member was hostile towards him.

[34] *Langborger*, concerning the Housing and Tenancy Court, made up of two professional judges and two lay assessors nominated by property owners and tenants assocations and appointed by Government, where the lay assessors had close links with the two assocations which sought to maintain a clause the applicant was challenging—there being a legitimate fear that their interests were contrary to his own, it was not sufficient that the judicial president had the casting vote.

[35] May 20, 1998, R.J.D. 1998–III, No.72.

[36] See, *e.g. Findlay*, *Yavuz*, n.9 above. See Armed Forces, Military Justice.

[37] *Mitap and Müftüglu v Turkey*, (Rep.) December 8, 1994, R.J.D. 1996–II. See also the Court's comments in *Incal*, n.9 above, para.72.

inclusion of a military judge on the National Security Court which sat on civilian criminal cases concerning State security issues cast legitimate doubts on the court's independence and impartiality as the military judge belonged to the army which took orders from the executive and they remained subject to military discipline and assessment reports. The applicants tried before the court could legitimately fear that it might allow itself to be unduly influenced by considerations which had nothing to do with the case.[38]

(d) Dual roles

IIA–094 Where a body has dual roles, which conflict, its independence and impartiality as an adjudicating body may be undermined. In *Procola v Luxembourg*, concerning a milk quota dispute, four members of the *Conseil d'Etat* had performed successive advisory and judicial roles in the case. This was capable of casting doubt on structural impartiality of the judicial committee, giving rise to fears which were objectively justified and a legitimate doubt however slight that members might feel bound by their previous opinion.[39] In *McGonnell v United Kingdom*, the mere fact that the Deputy Bailiff who presided in the Royal Court in the determination of the applicant's planning appeal also presided over the States of Deliberation in adopting the development plan allegedly breached was enough to vitiate the impartiality of the court even though the doubt was perceived as slight.

The Court subsequently took a more cautious and nuanced approach. In *Kleyn v Netherlands*, it expressly refrained from criticising constitutional frameworks that provided for dual roles of particular bodies in conflict with the notion of separation of powers and applied the approach of examining whether in the facts of the particular case the successive legislative advisory and judicial roles of the Council of State gave the requisite appearances of independence and impartiality. As the advisory opinions given in that case on the general transport infrastructure and the subsequent appeals on a particular routing decision could not be regarded as involving the "same case" or "the same decision" fears of lack of independence and impartiality were not objectively justified.[40]

(e) Rehearings

IIA–095 Where a first instance decision is quashed on appeal and returned for a fresh decision, the fact that the same body, with or without the same membership, decides the matter again does not disclose legitimate fears of lack of impartiality.[41] Thus in *Diennet v France*, where the decision of a medical appeal tribunal was quashed by the Court of Cassation for a procedural error, the inclusion of three of same members in the second hearing which reached same conclusion, raised no ground for legitimate suspicion. Where in *Thomann v Switzerland*, an applicant was

---

[38] *e.g. Incal*, n.9 above, paras 72 and 78; *Sadak v Turkey (No.1)*, July 17, 2001, ECHR 2001–VIII.

[39] Four out of five had been involved in the advisory panel giving an opinion on the draft regulation under judicial challenge.

[40] para.200—this was the element identified, perhaps not very convincingly, as distinguishing the *Procola* and *McGonnell* judgments. See also *GL and SL v France*, 58811/00, (Dec.) March 6, 2003, where general complaints about the legislative and adjudicative roles of the *Conseil d'Etat* were insufficient to cast doubt on independence in that particular case.

[41] *Ringeisen*, para.97.

retried by the court which had convicted him *in absentia*, the Court considered that the judges would be aware that they had reached their first decision on limited evidence and would undertake fresh consideration of the case on a comprehensive, adversarial basis.

(f) *Juries*

These principles apply equally to juries (see Pt IIA: Fair Trial Guarantees, Juries). **IIA–096**

(g) *Court clerks and legal officers*

Where legal officers such as *advocates-general, procureurs* and government commissioners play a role in proceedings, acting in the public interest or to ensure coherence of case law, the Court has found that although their independence and impartiality are not in doubt as such, they cannot be regarded as part of the tribunal and since they issue opinions on the outcome of the case, they can no longer be regarded as neutral. Thus considerations of equality of arms apply, requiring that the applicant be afforded the opportunity to comment on any submissions made by them for example and giving rise to problems where the officer retires with the judges.[42] Court clerks, such as magistrates' clerks for example, may be regarded as part of the tribunal however and where they assist the court on points of law and evidence and do not have any duty with regard to influencing the decision one way or another, no problem arises where they retire with the court. However, as a result, such clerks must observe the requirements of impartiality and independence and should not, for example, exhibit bias when questioning accused on behalf of the tribunal.[43] **IIA–097**

4. Curing defects on appeal

Problems of independence and impartiality may be curable where a higher instance body provides a hearing with the necessary guarantees and adequate rehearing of the issues in civil cases.[44] In *Le Compte, Belilos* and *Kyprianou*, the higher instances did not have jurisdiction to re-examine the facts or merits and therefore their undoubted independence and impartiality was not sufficient. The review by the Court of Appeal of civil proceedings where the judge had descended into the arena to harry the applicant was sufficient, where the Court of Appeal exercised full jurisdiction and re-assessed the lower court's findings thoroughly.[45] Following judgments dealing with specialist administrative areas, less appears to be required by way of review by the judicial instances on grounds of expediency and the exercise of discretionary powers.[46] Thus, in *Kingsley v United Kingdom*, full court hearing on both facts and law **IIA–098**

---

[42] See, *e.g. Reinhardt and Slimane-Kaid*, March 31, 1998, R.J.D. 1998–II, No.68; see Fair Trial Guarantees, Equality of Arms.

[43] *Agnes Mort v UK*, 44564/98, (Dec.) September 6, 2001, ECHR 2001–IX.

[44] *De Cubber*, para.33.

[45] *Ranson v UK*, n.15 above; see also *Shirley Porter v UK*, 15184/02, (Dec.) April 8, 2002, where the Divisional Court's review of a local authority auditor's procedure cured any defect arising from his roles as investigator, prosecutor and judge.

[46] *Zumtobel v Austria*, September 21, 1993, Series A, No.268–A; 17 E.H.R.R. 116; *Bryan v UK*, November 22, 1995, Series A, No.335–A; 21 E.H.R.R. 342.

on appeal from the Gaming Board, which carried out a regulatory function in a classic exercise of administrative discretion, was not required, though the inability of the reviewing courts to quash and refer to an impartial tribunal deprived it of the requisite jurisdiction.

In criminal cases, it appears that an accused can claim to have the full guarantees of independence and impartiality at first instance.[47]

5. Waiver

IIA–099   The extent to which an accused may waive his right to an impartial tribunal by failing to challenge judges has not been clearly decided. To the extent that waiver may be possible, the Court has stated that this must be limited and minimum guarantees remain which cannot depend on the parties alone. In any event, the waiver must be established in an unequivocal manner. A failure to object in *Pfeiffer and Plankl v Austria* to two court judges who had been investigating judges and disqualified was not sufficient. The waiver argument also failed in *Oberschlick v Austria (No.1)* where the apppeal presiding judge had participated in previous proceedings and was disqualified under the Code of Criminal Procedure. Though the applicant did not challenge his presence, he was not regarded as waiving his right to impartial tribunal. The Court appeared to give weight in both these cases to the failure of the courts to abide by the domestic rules aimed at eradicating reasonable doubts as to impartiality.

Cross-reference

Part IIA: Fairness
Part IIA: Appeals
Part IIA: Juries
Part IIA: Tribunal established by law

---

[47] *Findlay.*

Information about the charge

Key provision:

Art.6, para.3(a).   IIA–100

Key case law:

Albert and Le Compte v Belgium, February 10, 1983, Series A, No.58; 5 E.H.R.R. 533; *Campbell and Fell v UK*, June 28, 1984, Series A, No.80; 7 E.H.R.R. 165; *Brozicek v Italy*, December 19, 1989, Series A, No.167; 12 E.H.R.R. 371; *Gea Catalan v Spain*, February 10, 1995, Series A, No.309; 20 E.H.R.R. 266; *De Salvador Torres v Spain*, October 24, 1996, R.J.D., 1996–V, No.19; 23 E.H.R.R. 601; *Pelissier and Sassi v France*, March 25, 1999, ECHR 1999–II; 30 E.H.R.R. 715; *Mattocia v Italy*, July 25, 2000, ECHR 2000–IX; *Dallos v Hungary*, March 1, 2001, ECHR 2001–II; *Sadak v Turkey*, July 2, 2001, ECHR 2001–VII.

1. Applicability

The context of Art.6, para.3(a) is criminal and it is to be seen as a particular aspect   IIA–101
of the right to fair trial.[1] Nonetheless in *Albert and Le Compte v Belgium*, concerning disciplinary proceedings against doctors, the Court commented that the civil and criminal aspects of Art.6, para.1 were not mutually exclusive and that Art.6, paras 2 and 3 were aspects of the notion of fair trial contained within para.1 in the civil context.

2. Information about the charge

This includes not only the cause of the accusation (the material facts which form the   IIA–102
basis of the accusation) but the nature of the accusation (the legal classification of these material facts).[2] Full, detailed information concerning the charges are considered an essential prerequisite for ensuring the proceedings are fair. This involves sufficient information as is necessary for the accused to understand fully the extent of the charges against him with a view to preparing an adequate defence.[3] Thus, any changes in the accusation, including changes in the material facts must be duly and fully communicated to the accused who must be provided with adequate time and facilities to adapt his defence to them.[4]

---

[1] *FCB v Italy*, August 28, 1991, Series A, No.208–B; 14 E.H.R.R. 909, para.29; *Can v Austria*, 9300/81, (Rep.) July 12, 1984, Series A, No.96 (settled before the Court).
[2] *Pelissier and Sassi* , para.51; the information should be detailed; *Gea Catalan*, following Commission case law, *e.g. Chichlian and Ekindjian v France*, (Rep.) March 16, 1989, para.65, Series A, No.162–B; 13 E.H.R.R. 553.
[3] *e.g. Mattocia* , paras 59–60; *Kyprianou v Cyprus*, January 27, 2004, paras 65–66.
[4] *e.g. Mattocia*, para.61: the Court found a violation as changes in key facts about the alleged rape were communicated when it was no longer possible for the accused to react and no allowances were made by the court for the difficulties caused to the defence confronted by another version of events.

Information must in fact be received by the person: a legal presumption of receipt is not enough.[5] No particular form of notification is required.[6]

Common sense and practicality are to be applied in determining whether there has been a change in the offence under consideration. Though the Commission in *Gea Catalan v Spain* found a violation where the prosecution referred in its submissions to aggravating factor one and the domestic court convicted on aggravating factor seven, the Court agreed with the domestic courts that it was a mere clerical error. The material facts relied on by the prosecution were the same relied on by the domestic court and factor seven was referred to expressly by the investigating judge on committal. In *De Salvador Torres v Spain*, though the offence of simple embezzlement had been in issue in the lower courts, the application by the Supreme Court of the aggravating factor of abuse of public office did not disclose a violation since it had been an underlying factual element throughout, the relevance of which the applicant could not claim to be unaware.[7]

Where however an offence has been reclassified in a substantive sense and this possibility has not been brought to the attention of the accused, a violation is likely to arise. In *Chichlian and Ekindjian v France*, the two applicants were acquitted of currency offence charged under s.7 of a decree and then convicted on appeal of the offence under s.1. The Commission noted that the material facts had always been known to the applicants but there was no evidence that the applicants had been informed by the relevant authority of the proposal to reclassify the offence before the appeal hearing.[8] Similarly, where in *Pélissier and Sassi v France* the appeal court convicted the applicants of aiding and abetting criminal bankruptcy rather than criminal bankruptcy and neither the prosecutor or the first instance court had ever made reference to that possibility, the Court found a violation as different ingredients made up the offence of aiding and abetting under the Criminal Code and it could not be considered an intrinsic element of the initial accusation known to the accused from the beginning of the proceedings.[9]

Subsequent proceedings in which the applicant is given the opportunity to advance his defence to a reformulated charge may cure defects in earlier procedures.[10]

---

[5] 10889/84, (Dec.) May 11, 1988, 56 D.R. 40 where notification by the investigating judge was delivered to the address, signed by some-one else and the applicant claimed that he did not receive it.
[6] *e.g. Pelissier and Sassi,* para.53; *Erdogan v Turkey,* 14723/89, July 9, 1992, 73 D.R. 81: the applicant complained that he was not formally served with the arrest warrant or indictment but the Commission considered that he was aware of the terms of the arrest warrant and the fact that he did not get the indictment was attributable to his own conduct.
[7] Also *Campbell and Fell,* where the applicant Campbell knew that he was accused of 'mutiny' following disturbances in prison, the Court rejected his claim that he was not able to understand precisely what this term meant; *Garner v UK,* 38330/97, (Dec.) January 26, 1999, where the substituted conviction was based on the identical facts and misconduct, the applicant could not claim to be unaware of the nature and cause of the action against him.
[8] n.2 above.
[9] Although the counsel of the *"partie civile"* had made reference to the possibility, it had never been referred to by the judges or prosecutor. See also *Sadak and others,* paras 56–58, where the modified charge of membership of an illegal organisation could not be considered as an element intrinsic to the original charge of treason against the integrity of the State.
[10] *Dallos,* para.52.

3. Language

The information about the charge must be in a language the applicant understands. In *Brozicek v Italy*, where the applicant was not Italian or resident in Italy and had clearly expressed his language difficulties to the court, the Court found that the authorities should have had the notification translated unless they were in a position to establish that he knew adequate Italian.[11]

IIA–103

4. Promptly

Though the requirement for information being provided is of promptness, the Convention organs have not been particularly demanding. Thus in one case, where there was a delay in notification of proceedings, the Commission noted that the applicant was not affected immediately. Also he was served with a notice four months before trial which was in good time for the preparation of his defence, which was the principal underlying purpose of the safeguard.[12] Similarly, in *Padin Gestoso v Spain*, no issue arose for the Court where the applicant had not been immediately informed of the investigations conducted by the investigating judge as he had not been directly affected by them and was informed in good time of the charges later preferred against him.[13]

IIA–104

5. Relationship with Art.6, para.3(b)

Where an applicant has not been promptly informed of the charge, it may well be that this has prevented him from properly preparing his defence at the same time, there being a logical connection between the two provisions.[14] Information about the nature and cause of the accusation must be adequate to enable a suspect to prepare his defence. In *Chichlian and Ekindjian*, the Commission commented that notification of the mere fact of reclassification of the offence is not enough, it has to be in good time and allow the opportunity to organise the defence on the basis of that reclassification.

IIA–105

6. Relationship with Art.5, para.2

Article 5, para.2 concerning reasons for arrest and detention generally requires less detail and is not as rigorous as Art.6, para.3(a).

IIA–106

Cross-reference

Part IIA: Adequate time and facilities
Part IIB: Reasons for arrest and detention

---

[11] The Government submitted that in the context it was clear he knew Italian.
[12] 10889/84, n.5 above.
[13] 39519/98, (Dec.) December 8, 1999, ECHR 1999–II; also *Ines v France*, 28145/95, (Dec.) May 25, 1998—it was not necessary for the applicant to be told at the earliest possible moment of the judgments *in absentia* against him—the moment of the extradition was enough.
[14] *Pelissier and Sassi*, para.54; *Sadak*, paras 58–59.

Interpretation

Relevant provision:

IIA–107   Art.6, para.3(e) (free assistance of an interpreter).

Relevant case law:

Luedicke, Belkacem and Koç v Germany, November 28, 1978, Series A, No.29; 2 E.H.R.R. 149; *Kamasinski v Austria*, February 21, 1984, Series A, No.73; 13 E.H.R.R. 36; *Cuscani v UK*, September 24, 2002.

1. General considerations

IIA–108   The ability to comprehend the proceedings in a criminal trial, guaranteed in Art.6, para.3(e), may be seen as another aspect of the importance for an accused to participate effectively in the proceedings.

For the right to be effective, the obligation of the authorities is not limited to the provision of an interpreter but may also extend to a degree of control over the adequacy of the interpretation provided.[1] Issues as to the standard of the interpretation could arise if it could be established as damaging to the accused's effective participation in the proceedings. Although a failure to complain at the time may be fatal to claims before the Court as generally domestic courts must be given an opportunity to remedy any inadequacy, the onus is nonetheless on the trial judge to treat an accused's interest with "scrupulous care" and take steps to ensure his ability to participate where problems are drawn to his attention.[2]

As the interpreter is not part of court or tribunal, there is no formal requirement of independence or impartiality as such, the key requirement being that the services of the interpreter provide the accused with effective assistance in conducting his defence and that his conduct not be of such a nature as to impinge on the fairness of the proceedings.[3]

2. Absolute nature of the right

IIA–109   The right is absolute, with no expressed qualifications and none implied.[4] Interpretation costs cannot be reclaimed from defendants after conviction as the Government argued in *Luedicke, Belkacem and Koç v Germany*. Similarly, the Commission found a

---

[1] *Kamasinski*, para.74; *Ucak v UK*, 44234/98, (Dec.) January 24, 2000.
[2] *Cuscani*, para.39, the judge, informed of the need for interpretation before the hearing, should have acted, notwithstanding applicant's counsel's readiness to do without proper interpretation; conversely, in *Ucak*, n.1 above, the applicant made no complaint about the interpretation during trial or appeal, even when invited to inform the court if he did not understand what was being said.
[3] *e.g. Ucak*, n.1 above, where the applicant complained that the interpreter came from a police list.
[4] See however 11311/84, *Fedele v Germany*, (Dec.) December 9, 1987 where the applicant failed to attend two hearings and was later charged the interpreters' fees: the Commission found that "assistance" must refer to an accused who is present and that only some-one who is present and cannot understand or speak the language used in court can be "assisted" by the interpreter; since the applicant was not present he could not claim free assistance of an interpreter.

violation even where an applicant who was required to pay costs of interpretation after conviction was covered by his legal insurance.[5]

The requirement for interpretation must, however, be genuine and necessary to the fair conduct of the proceedings. Where an applicant has sufficient understanding of the language of the proceedings, he cannot claim a cultural or political preference for another.[6] Once it is apparent that the applicant requires interpretation assistance, it is unlikely that informal and unprofessional assistance will be sufficient.[7]

3. Translation of documents

Article 6, para.3(e) has been held to cover documentary material and pre-trial matters but it does not extend to requiring translations of all documents in the proceedings.[8] It is sufficient if the applicant is assisted by interpreters, translations and the help of his lawyers so that he has knowledge of the case which enables him to defend himself, in particular by being able to put forward his version of events. If this standard is reached, a failure to provide all the translations an applicant might have wanted is not a problem.[9] An applicant would presumably have to indicate that the untranslated documents were material to his ability to defend himself and that he was refused or not permitted the necessary facilities.

IIA–110

Cross-reference

Part IIA: Adequate time and facilities
Part IIA: Information about the charge

---

[5] 11394/85, (Rep.) July 5, 1988.
[6] *e.g. Lagerblom v Sweden*, January 14, 2003, the applicant, mother-tongue Finnish, had sufficient street Swedish and could not claim that his counsel should be Finnish-speaking.
[7] *Cuscani*, where in the absence of the interpreter the court made do with the "untested language skills" of the accused's brother.
[8] *Kamasinski*, para.74.
[9] See 14170/88, (Dec.) November 13, 1987; 14106/88, (Dec.) December 6, 1991 where a British applicant tried in Sweden complained that the documents were in Swedish, the Commission noted that his lawyer understood English and that an interpreter was not refused when requested.

Juries

Key provision:

IIA–111   Article 6 (fair trial by an independent and impartial tribunal).

Key case law:

Holm v Sweden, November 25, 1993, Series A, No.279–A; 18 E.H.R.R. 79; *Remli v France*, April 23, 1996, R.J.D 1996–II, No.8; 22 E.H.R.R. 253; *Pullar v UK*, June 10, 1996, R.J.D. 1996–III, No.11; 22 E.H.R.R. 391; *Gregory v UK*, February 25, 1997, R.J.D. 1997–I, No.31; 25 E.H.R.R. 577; *Sander v UK*, May 9, 2000, ECHR 2000–V; 31 E.H.R.R. 1003.

1. Right to a jury

IIA–112   There is no right contained within Art.6, para.1 to trial by jury, not surprisingly since some Contracting States do not use juries. The Commission accordingly dismissed an Irish case in which the applicant complained of the special courts presided over by judges without a jury which were introduced for terrorist-related offences.[1] Similarly, when the Birmingham Six argued that new evidence should not have been considered by the Court of Appeal, submitting that they could not receive a fair trial unless the evidence in its entirety was heard by a jury, the Commission found no reason why new evidence could not be fairly and properly assessed by an appellate body of professional judges.[2]

2. Undue influence on the jury

IIA–113   Concerns are sometimes raised as to the susceptibility of untrained, lay jurors to suggestions or inferences that an accused person is guilty contrary to the presumption of innocence as well as impinging on the fairness of the trial.

A virulent press campaign may, the Court accepts, adversely affect the fairness of trial through its effect on the jury.[3] No finding of unfair trial has yet been found on this ground, press interest and sometimes critical commentary being accepted as inevitable in a democratic society and a corollary of freedom of the press.[4] It would take more than close media interest in a case to raise a serious issue and the fact that the jurors took oaths and were warned to discount news coverage would generally be regarded as sufficient to offset prejudice.[5]

Other aspects of the proceedings, relating to security measures which appear to label the accused as "guilty" in advance, have also been examined. However, even where the Commission has expressed reservations, it has taken the attitude that

---

[1] 8299/78, (Dec.) October 10, 1980, 22 D.R. 51.

[2] 14739/89, (Dec.) May 9, 1989, 60 D.R. 296.

[3] *e.g.* 8403/78, (Dec.) October 15, 1980, 22 D.R. 100; 10486/83 (Dec.) October 9, 1986, 49 D.R. 86; *Wloch v Poland*, 27785/95, (Dec.) March 30, 2000; *Priebke v Italy*, 48799/99, (Dec.) April 5, 2001.

[4] *e.g. Priebke v Italy*, n.3 above.

[5] *e.g. Noye v UK*, 4491/02, (Dec.) January 21, 2003, press coverage some time in the past and dealt with by adequate direction.

juries can distinguish between security measures based on assessments of "dangerousness" and the examination of the merits in the trial.[6]

3. Independence and impartiality

This requirement of a fair trial applies equally to lay jurors as to professional and lay judges (see Pt IIA: Independence and impartiality). In view of the fundamental importance that the courts inspire confidence in the public and, in criminal cases, the accused, the Court has stressed that a tribunal, including a jury, must be impartial from a subjective and objective view.[7]

I–114

Convention organs will presume the subjective impartiality of a judge and also that of unprofessional, untrained jurors.[8] The Commission in *Holm v Sweden* noted however that the unreasoned nature of a jury's verdict leads to a particular need for objective guarantees of impartiality and independence.

Objective independence and impartiality may be called in doubt by an exterior feature, for example, connection between a juror and a party to a civil case or a juror and prosecution witnesses. Regard is had to the nature of the connection and the safeguards in the system. In *Holm*, where five jurors out of nine were members of the political party which was the dominant shareholder in the defendant company and political overtones were of relevance since the alleged libel related to the applicant's activities in an organisation hostile to that party, the connection was of such a nature as to allow the applicant legitimately to fear that the jurors would be influenced by their political opinions. There was also the factor that there were no procedural ways of curing any defect in this case, the appeal court having limited jurisdiction where, as in this case, the jury acquitted.

However, in *Pullar v United Kingdom*, where the doubt arose from the discovery that one juror was an employee of a key Crown witness, the Court discounted the fact that the juror was disqualified in domestic law.[9] In its view it did not follow that because a member of a tribunal had personal knowledge of a witness he would be prejudiced in favour of that person's testimony. It was necessary rather to assess whether the familiarity was of such nature and degree to indicate lack of impartiality. Since the juror was a junior employee, unconnected with the events and had been given notice of redundancy it was not certain that he would be inclined to believe his employer rather than defence witnesses. It also noted other safeguards in the system, including the number of jurors (15), the sheriff's directions, and the oaths taken. This approach seemed to confuse considerations of the existence of actual bias with whether there were objective grounds for the applicant having doubts as to the impartiality of the jurors. The Commission found that it could be legitimately be feared that the juror, even if ignorant of of the facts of the case, would bring his own personal views of the Crown witness to bear on his own and the other jurors' assessment of the case.

---

[6] *e.g.* 12323/86, (Dec.) July 13, 1988, 57 D.R. 148 concerning use of handcuffs before juries; glass cages for accused did not "stigmatise" in 11837/85, (Rep.) June 7, 1990, 69 D.R. 126; also 17440/90, (Dec.) February 12, 1993, where the intense security at his trial was not found unnecessary (one trial had been abandoned due an attempt to influence a juror) or stage-managed, and the effect on the jury was not such as to violate the presumption of innocence.

[7] *e.g. Sander*, para.22.

[8] *Sander*, para.25.

[9] See however *Oberschlick v Austria*, May 23, 1991, Series A, No.204; 19 E.H.R.R. 389 where it took a different view when a disqualified judge sat on a case, finding that the failure to abide by the domestic rules aimed at eradicating reasonable doubts as to impartiality left the proceedings open to doubt.

Since then, the Court has stated concerning links between a juror and other individuals connected with the trial that it will depend on the facts of each case whether the familiarity in question is of such a nature or degree as to indicate a lack of impartiality. In *Simsek v United Kingdom*,[10] the fact that a juror was sister-in-law of a prison officer in the Category A block where the accused was detained disclosed no real doubts, the accused's misgivings being based on a number of weak suppositions. Since the Court of Appeal looked into the matter and it appeared that the prison officer had reported the connection himself to his superiors, maintained that he had not talked with his sister-in-law and withdrawn from any contact with the accused, no further enquiry or measures had been necessary.

Where racial bias has arisen, the Convention organs have had regard to the steps taken by domestic courts to counteract its influence. Given the importance attached to the eradication of racism as a priority amongst Contracting States, courts are required to react in a firm manner, and if necessary it may appear, discharge the jury.

In *Remli v France*, where a juror was overheard outside the courtroom saying *"En plus je suis raciste"*, the applicant's lawyers brought it to the attention of the presiding judge who refused to take cognisance of it. Since domestic courts are under an obligation to verify their impartiality when a ground arises not manifestly without merit, the failure to take any steps disclosed a violation.

In *Gregory v United Kingdom* however, where a note was received from the jury "jury showing racial overtones 1 member to be excused" the judge consulted counsel and addressed the jury directing them as to their obligation to decide the case according to the evidence without prejudice. The Court admitted that there might be circumstances where a judge might have to discharge a jury but found that in this case a firmly-worded direction by an experienced judge who had observed the jury during the trial was sufficient to dispel doubts as to the impartiality of the tribunal. Conversely, in *Sander v United Kingdom*, where a note from a juror indicated that racist jokes were being made and that he or she feared a verdict based on the ethnic origin of the accused, the Court, by a narrow majority, considered that a firm redirection by the judge and the submission of a collective letter by the jury with an assurance that they would reach a verdict on the evidence alone was insufficient to take away a legitimate doubt as to the jury's impartiality. The majority distinguished *Gregory* as in this case the juror had, in a letter to the judge, admitted that he had made racist comments and they were not satisfied that the judge's direction however forceful could change racist views overnight. The minority placed more weight on the role of the judge, who was experienced and had observed the jury throughout and chosen to give a clear, detailed and forceful direction in place of discharging them.

The fact that jurors take oaths to acquit their duties impartially was not considered a sufficient guarantee to outweigh the doubt on their impartiality in *Holm* deriving from their political affiliations, yet was mentioned as a guarantee in *Gregory*, which concerned apparent racial bias and in *Pullar* and *Simsek*, concerning personal connections. It was not mentioned at all in *Sander*.

---

[10] 43471/98, (Dec.) July 9, 2002.

4. Secrecy of jury deliberations

The prohibition on publishing details of jury deliberations was found compatible   IIA–115
with Art.10 of the Convention, where a newspaper and two editors were fined for
contempt of court for revelations about a controversial trial.[11] The Commission
noted that secrecy was the basis of the jury system in the UK and that the absolute
nature of the offence could be regarded as necessary to protect jurors and prevent
undue influence on their decisions by factors outside the jury room. While research
into juries in fraud cases had been recommended by the Royal Commission on
Criminal Justice, the Commission observed that research was not in issue in the case,
which solely concerned revelations in a high profile trial.

[11] 24770/94, (Dec.) November 30, 1994.

Legal aid in civil cases

Key provision:

IIA–116   Article 6, para.1 (access to court).

Key case law:

Airey v Ireland, October 9, 1979, Series A, No.32; 2 E.H.R.R. 305; *Aerts v Belgium*, July 30, 1998, R.J.D. 1998–V, No.83; 29 E.H.R.R. 50; *Gnahoré v France*, September 9, 2000, 2000–IX; *McVicar v UK*, May 7, 2002, ECHR 2002–III; *Bertuzzi v France*, February 13, 2003.

1. General considerations

IIA–117   There is no right as such in the Convention to receive legal aid in cases concerning civil rights and obligations. Issues may arise where lack of legal aid has the effect of depriving an applicant of effective access to court. The right of access to court is not however unlimited. Limitations may be compatible where they do not restrict or reduce access to the extent that the very essence of the right is impaired, where they pursue a legitimate aim and disclose a reasonable relationship of proportionality between the means employed and the aim sought to be achieved.[1]

2. Lack of access to court

IIA–118   It appears that in principle legal aid may be required for effective access to court in two circumstances, where the complexity of the case requires it and where legal representation is compulsory.[2]

The leading case on the complexity point was, until recently, *Airey v Ireland*. A denial of access to court in violation of Art.6, para.1 was found where, in the absence of legal aid in relation to separation proceedings in the High Court, the applicant could not be expected to pursue proceedings herself. This was where the procedure was complex, raising complicated points of law and necessitating proof of adultery, unnatural practices or cruelty; it might have involved expert evidence, the examining of witnesses; and the subject-matter entailed an emotional involvement scarcely compatible with the degree of objectivity required by advocacy in court.

The elements identified in *Airey* are likely to arise in many civil disputes, few of which would not be complex from the point of view of the lay litigant. The Commission in practice confined the application of the *Airey* principles, giving weight to the reasons given by the authorities for refusal of legal aid. It considered that due to limited resources States could legitimately restrict the grant of legal aid, imposing contributions or requiring a case to be well-founded, not vexatious or frivolous. In such a case an applicant would bear the burden to bring the case some other way (by himself or obtaining assistance from another source), although the Commission would have regard to whether the assessment by the authorities was

[1] *e.g. Ashingdane v UK*, May 28, 1985, Series A, No.93; 7 E.H.R.R. 528, para.57.
[2] *Gnahoré*, para.38.

arbitrary.[3] The Commission generally found that unrepresented applicants still enjoyed reasonable access to court where they had the opportunity to be heard under the proper and effective control of the fairness and conduct of the proceedings by the court.[4] The Court has effectively adopted this approach since, finding for example no violation in *Gnahoré v France* for refusal of legal for an appeal due to lack of any arguable ground where the procedure offered substantial guarantees against arbitrariness in the decision-making procedure.[5]

Even where legal aid is granted however, the responsibility of the Government does not necessarily come to an end. In *Bertuzzi v France*, where the applicant fulfilled the conditions for legal aid which was accorded by the legal aid office of the first instance court, there was a violation where three lawyers in turn declined to act for him because of their personal connections with the lawyer that the applicant was suing. The Court considered that the authorities were under an obligation to ensure the appointment of replacement counsel. This can be contrasted with the situation where the applicant's own conduct is to blame for the withdrawal of the legal aid appointed lawyers.[6]

As regards circumstances where legal representation is rendered compulsory, the Court found a violation of Art.6, para.1 in *Aerts v Belgium* where the applicant was refused legal aid in proceedings concerning his right to liberty and compensation for unlawful detention before the Court of Cassation. Domestic law required representation by counsel and thus the Legal Aid Board's refusal of legal aid impaired the very essence of the right to a tribunal.[7] It was not relevant in that context that the Board had considered the appeal was not well-founded as the Court considered it was for the Court of Cassation to determine that issue.

Grounds for refusal linked to abuse of process may also be acceptable, as in a case where the Commission found that even though the applicant had prospects of success in suing for divorce it was compatible to refuse her legal aid in view of court findings that she had not intended to set up married life with her husband (marriage was to obtain him an entry permit) and that she had divorced before in similar circumstances. The Commission did not find unreasonable the court's view that she knew the position and did not require legal protection.[8]

The mere fact that the other side is legally aided does not render the refusal of legal aid incompatible with Art.6, para.1.[9]

---

[3] *e.g.* 8158/78, (Dec.) July 10, 1978, 21 D.R. 95, refusal of legal aid to a prisoner was not arbitrary, the Commission finding the allegations unsubstantiated.

[4] *e.g.* 9353/81, (Dec.) May 11, 1983, 33 D.R. 133.

[5] *e.g.* the Legal Aid Office was presided over by a judge of the Court of Cassation and an appeal lay to the President of the Court; similar reasoning in *Del Sol v France*, February 26, 2002, ECHR 2002–II; *Nicholas v Cyprus*, 37371/97, (Dec.) March 14, 2000, where the Court relied on Commission case law that refusal of legal aid was not a denial of access to court where the proceedings had no prospects of success and the costs of funding was disproportionate to any likely damages—it also noted that the applicant had had *"pro bono"* assistance for some time and he had not attempted to find similar assistance later.

[6] *Renda Martins v Portugal*, 50085/99, (Dec.) January 10, 2002—the applicant had gone through 7 counsel and it was his lack of co-operation that based the decision not to provide any further replacement and to suspend the proceedings generally.

[7] In *Gnahoré*, the Court commented that it was the requirement of legal representation that was decisive in *Aerts* (para.41).

[8] 11564/85, (Dec.) December 4, 1985, 45 D.R. 291.

[9] 9353/81, n.4 above.

3. Defamation

Even though defamation cannot, even in meritorious cases, be subject to a grant of legal aid in the UK, the Commission did not find the blanket prohibition to disclose any violation of Art.6, para.1, considering that it could be legitimate to exclude certain categories of legal proceedings altogether from legal aid and that it had not been shown to be arbitrary to do so in that case (having regard to the fact that the applicant secured a settlement and an apology by himself).[10] In *McVicar v United Kingdom*, the Court confirmed that defamation was not so complex as to require legal assistance and found in the circumstances that the applicant was well able to present his case effectively, obtaining some legal assistance by other means and that his emotional involvement was not incompatible with the degree of objectivity required by advocacy in court.

4. Prohibition orders

IIA–119 The Commission found it compatible for a prohibition order to be used to prevent applications for civil legal aid where an applicant had made numerous applications. This is comparable to regulation of access for bankrupts, persons of unsound mind and vexatious litigants, where the aim is to prevent abuse of legal aid authorities.[11]

Cross-reference

Part IIA: Access to court
Part IIA: Legal representation in criminal proceedings

[10] 10871/84, (Dec.) July 10, 1986, 48 D.R. 154; see also 10594/83, (Dec.) July 14, 1987, 52 D.R. 158; 27436/95, etc. (Dec.) July 2, 1997, 90–A D.R. 45.
[11] 27788/95, (Dec.), January 27, 1996: the applicant could apply for the 5 year ban to be lifted.

Legal representation in criminal proceedings

Key provision:

Article 6, para.3(c) (right to legal assistance of own choosing or where insufficient   IIA–120
means to be given free when the interests of justice require).

Key case law:

Artico v Italy, May 13, 1980, Series A, No.37; 3 E.H.R.R. 1; *Pakelli v Italy*, April 25,
1983, Series A, No.64; 6 E.H.R.R. 1; *Goddi v Italy*, April 9, 1984, Series A, No.76;
Kamasinski v Austria, December 19, 1989, Series A, No.168; 13 E.H.R.R. 36;
Monnell and Morris v UK, March 2, 1987, Series A, No.115; 10 E.H.R.R. 205;
Granger v UK, March 28, 1990, Series A, No.174; 12 E.H.R.R. 469; *Quaranta v
Switzerland*, May 24, 1991, Series A, No.205; *S v Switzerland*, November 28, 1991,
Series A, No.220; *Croissant v Germany*, September 25, 1992, Series A, No.237–B; 16
E.H.R.R. 135; *Imbroscia v Switzerland*, November 24, 1993, Series A, No.275;
Maxwell v UK, October 28, 1994, Series A, No.300–C; 19 E.H.R.R. 97; *Boner v UK*,
October 28, 1994, Series A, No.300–B; 19 E.H.R.R 246; *Poitrimol v France*,
November 23, 1993, Series A, No.277; 18 E.H.R.R. 295; *Tripodi v Italy*, April 22,
1994, Series A, No.281–B; 18 E.H.R.R. 130; *Lala v Netherlands*, September 22,
1994, Series A, No.297–A; 18 E.H.R.R. 587; *John Murray v UK*, February 8, 1996,
R.J.D. 1996–I, No.1; 22 E.H.R.R. 29; *Daud v Portugal*, April 21, 1998, R.J.D.
1998–II, No.69; 30 E.H.R.R. 400; *Twalib v Greece*, June 9, 1998, R.J.D. 1998–IV,
No.77; *Brennan v UK*, October 16, 2001, ECHR 2001–IX; *Meftah v France*, July 26,
2002, ECHR 2002–VII; *Czekalla v Portugal*, October 10, 2002, ECHR 2002–VIII;
Ocalan v Turkey, March 12, 2003.

1. General considerations

The provisions of Art.6, para.3 depend on a criminal charge having been brought.   IIA–121
The case-law indicates that they are aspects of the general principle of fairness
guaranteed in the first paragraph. As with the first paragraph, they are not to be
assessed on the basis of an isolated incident or element but having regard to the
proceedings as a whole.[1]

Article 6, para.3(c) guarantees three rights; the right to defend oneself; where one
does not wish to do so, the right to appoint a lawyer of own choosing; or where
certain conditions are met, the right to free legal assistance.[2]

2. Pre-trial representation

The right to legal representation applies not only to the trial, but to the pre-trial   IIA–122
stages.[3] It does not, however, confer unlimited access to legal representation.

[1] *e.g. Can v Austria*, (Rep.), July 12, 1984, Series A, No.96; 8 E.H.R.R. 121—their intrinsic aim is always
to ensure or contribute to ensuring the fairness of the proceedings as a whole—thus often the sub-
paragraphs are considered in conjunction with para.1.
[2] *Pakelli*, para.31.
[3] *Can*, n.1 above, citing ICCPR and r.93 of Standard Minimum Rules for the Treatment of Prisoners
(Council of Europe Res. CM(73)5).

The case law indicates that any restrictions on free contact with defence counsel must remain an exception and must be justified by special circumstances, the accused's right to communicate with his advocate out of hearing of a third person being a basic requirement of a fair trial in democratic society.[4] Where a lawyer is bound by professional obligations, the Court is unlikely to be persuaded in the absence of objective justification that restrictions are necessary to prevent the risk of collusion through or with the lawyer.[5]

Significant pre-trial restrictions are likely to raise issues. Restriction of three months on free unsupervised contact during the crucial investigation stage disclosed a violation in *Can*. Seven month surveillance of defence counsel visits in *S v Switzerland* disclosed a violation even though there was a two year period without restrictions before trial, indicating that it is not necessary to show damage to the presentation of the defence at trial from the restrictions and the right is to effective representation throughout the proceedings. In a highly complex and important criminal trial, provision of two one-hourly visits per week to lawyers was not considered sufficient to allow preparation for the trial.[6] Delay of more than one year in appointing counsel, during which a number of procedural acts were carried out, including questioning of the applicants and their medical examination, also disclosed a violation.[7]

Whether an applicant can claim a violation from a refusal to allow access to a solicitor immediately on arrest will depend on the circumstances. Short periods of several days have been found not to infringe defence rights.[8] Where, however, in *John Murray v United Kingdom*, the applicant, arrested for terrorist offences, was refused access to solicitor for 48 hours there was a violation having regard to the special features of the procedures in the early interrogation stage in Northern Ireland where inferences could be drawn from silence or responses to police questions. Since the accused was in a position where his defence could be irretrievably prejudiced, restriction on access to legal advice was incompatible with Art.6, para.3(c) without it being necessary to show the applicant would have acted differently if he had seen his solicitor.[9] In the absence of any features of oppression or consequent risk to the fairness of the later trial, lack of access in circumstances not at the fault of the authorities does not appear to raise issues, for

---

[4] *S v Switzerland*, para.48; *Ocalan*, paras 146–151—inability to confer with defence counsel out of hearing of security officers; *Brennan*, the Court found no compelling reason for the presence of a police officer during the important first interview of the applicant with his lawyer, where there was no allegation that the solicitor was likely to collaborate in passing information to other suspects.

[5] *e.g. Can*, n.1 above; *S v Switzerland*, where there were vague unsubstantiated doubts of collusion.

[6] *Ocalan*, para.154.

[7] *Berlinski v Poland*, June 26, 2002.

[8] 11526/84, (Dec.) September 5, 1988, 57 D.R. 47—where an applicant's inability to consult for three days prior to appearing before the investigating judge did not infringe defence rights, as there was free consultation afterwards and the applicant was able to make full use of procedures and remedies; 12391/86, (Dec.) April 13, 1989, 60 D.R. 182 concerning two and a half days without access to a lawyer, where the reason to deny access was potential prejudice to enquiries (the solicitor's premises were being searched), there was no indication that he had made any confessions or been unable to preparehis defence over following year or to apply for bail.

[9] See also *Magee v UK*, June 6, 2000, ECHR 2000-VI, where there was a 48 hour bar on access to a solicitor, during which period the applicant confessed, irretrievably prejudicing the defence, the Court found the restriction was incompatible with the rights of the accused; *Averill v UK*, June 6, 2000, ECHR 2000-VI, violation for 24 hour period where the applicant's silence was held against him.

example where the police tried to contact the solicitor who was unavailable before the interview took place or where the solicitor delayed a day in coming to see the applicant.[10]

Actual presence of a solicitor during police interviews has not as yet been held essential, where there are other sufficient guarantees concerning the reliability or use of statements recorded.[11]

3. Legal representation of own choosing

Generally, problems will arise where in proceedings, which determine a criminal charge, the applicant is denied the right to be legally represented.[12]   IIA–123

The right to legal assistance, free or otherwise, does not confer an absolute right to choose counsel. Domestic courts may override even the choice of a counsel paid for by the applicant, where there are relevant and sufficient grounds.[13] Potentially issues could arise where a court barred counsel for lack of qualifications but the Commission and Court would be likely to accept domestic rules on eligibility which were not totally unreasonable or arbitrary. In *Meftah v France*, the Court accepted the system whereby applicants could only use members of the Conseil d'Etat or Cassation bar and were prevented from using other lawyers or representing themselves. It noted the nature of the proceedings, which concerned points of law and were largely written and took account of European Union law providing that member States could lay down specific rules of access to supreme courts to ensure the smooth administration of justice.[14]

Courts may also appoint defence counsel which an accused considers unnecessary or objectionable. Where in *Croissant v Germany*, the applicant had appointed two counsel and objected to the third appointed by the courts, the Court found that the domestic court's reasons were relevant and sufficient, namely serving the interests of justice by avoiding interruptions or adjournments.

Where a court bars counsel from appearing on grounds that the accused has failed to surrender to custody, the Court has not been convinced that this is a proportionate response having regard to the importance of assuring an accused's defence.[15] It is for the domestic courts to ensure that an accused is properly defended and that counsel who appears is afforded the opportunity to act. In *Poitrimol*, where the applicant had appealed against his conviction for child kidnapping but did not appear, the appeal court refused to hear his counsel on the grounds of appeal as a convicted person who failed to surrender was not entitled to instruct counsel. While it is important for an accused to be present, it was more important for him to be adequately defended. Even if properly summoned, this does

---

[10] *Brennan*, paras 44–48: the applicant did not make any confessions during the period in which access was barred and no inferences were drawn from his silence during that period; *Harpur v UK*, 33222/96, (Dec.) September 14, 1999: the applicant's confessions were made after the 24 hour denial of access.

[11] *Brennan*, paras 51–55—reference to thorough examination of possible oppression at the trial: presence of a lawyer or tape recording were safeguards against misconduct but not indispensable preconditions of fairness.

[12] e.g. *Ezeh and Connors v UK* , October 9, 2003, ECHR 2003–X, paras 131 and 134.

[13] *Croissant*, para.29.

[14] para.45.

[15] e.g. *Poitrimol*, para.38; *Lala*, para.33.

not in absence of excuse for failure to appear justify depriving him of the right to be defended by counsel.[16]

Where, however, a lawyer appointed by an applicant failed to attend a hearing in cassation proceedings because he was ill, the Court in *Tripodi v Italy* appeared to find that the State could not be responsible for the shortcomings of a lawyer appointed by the accused, bearing in mind code provisions indicating that lawyers should provide replacements.[17] President Ryssdal, dissenting, noted that the lawyer was required to rest completely so could not be expected to act, while the Commission had found that courts are not allowed to remain passive but must take steps to ensure an accused is properly defended. There seems no reason why the obligation by a court to ensure a proper defence should depend on the method of appointment of the accused's lawyer (see Section 5 below).

4. Free legal assistance

IIA–124   Free legal assistance does not exclude liability to repay the fees later. It only has to be free at the time of trial, and while the applicant's insufficiency of means continues. In *Croissant v Germany*, the German system whereby convicted accused may be required to reimburse fees after trial was not found to be incompatible *per se* with Convention, where the lawyers appointed by the court could be regarded as necessary and the amounts charged not excessive. According to Commission case-law, a problem only arose if liability was enforced regardless of financial position.[18]

There are two conditions:

(a) *Financial eligibility*

IIA–125   This aspect has been rarely disputed. Generally, it is for the domestic authorities to evaluate the applicant's financial circumstances. The Court will however review their decisions for arbitrariness or lack of adequate foundation. In *Pakelli v Germany*, where the Government contested that the applicant was indigent at the time of the appeal, though the ground for refusal of legal aid concerned the class of offence, the Court was satisfied by the documentary materials put forward by applicant and the fact that he had been found to qualify for legal aid from the Commission. In *RD v Poland*, the Court, noting that the applicant had initially been found eligible for legal assistance and that the later refusal did not indicate that his financial situation

---

[16] See also *Van Geyseghem v Belgium*, January 21, 1999, ECHR 1999–I, paras 33–35—counsel would have raised a crucial statutory limitation and even if the appeal court had looked at the point of its own motion, counsel's assistance was still regarded as indispensable for resolving conflicts and for the exercise of the rights of the defence; *Van Pelt v France*, May 23, 2000: violation where the appeal court refused to hear the applicant's counsel when the applicant was absent in hospital; *Krombach v France*, February 13, 2001, ECHR 2001–II, violation where the applicant failed to appear at trial and his counsel were prevented from raising legal objections, *e.g.* estoppel.

[17] See also *Milone v Italy*, 37477/97, (Dec.) March 23, 1999: where the applicant's lawyer failed to appear due to participation in a strike and the Court of Cassation refused to adjourn, the Court found that the lawyer should have notified the court earlier of his absence and taken steps to obtain a replacement—the Government was not therefore responsible for the shortcomings of the applicant's chosen lawyer.

[18] *e.g.* 9365/81, (Dec.) May 6, 1982, 28 D.R. 229.

had in fact improved, found there were strong indications that he did not have sufficient means.[19]

(b) *Interests of justice*

This condition does not require it to be proved that legal assistance if provided **IIA–126** would have altered the course of the proceedings, as the Government argued in *Artico v Italy*, for example, by pleading a statutory limitation.[20] This was impossible to prove and would render the guarantee ineffective. However, this does not necessarily exclude the need to establish that the interests of justice require representation by pointing to reasons why in a particular stage in proceedings the accused required the assistance of a lawyer, namely that there was potentially something of material value which a lawyer could contribute.

Generally, the seriousness of the offence and the severity of the sentence at stake are the crucial issues in the assessment of whether the interests of justice require legal representation.[21] The Court has also had regard on occasion to additional factors such as the complexity of the court procedure and any difficulties of language or comprehension of the accused.[22]

(I) First instance

In deciding whether interests of justice require legal representation, the Court looks **IIA–127** at the seriousness of the offences and the potential sentence imposable; complexity of the case is an additional factor, lack of which is not decisive. In *Quaranta v Switzerland*, for example, where there were no special difficulties in establishing facts, the Court considered that issues arose concerning applicable measures as well as matters relating to the applicant's personal situation, foreign origin, underprivileged background and long criminal record, which appear more relevant to sentencing. It found his appearance before court on minor drugs charges facing up to eighteen months did not enable him to present his case in an adequate manner.

(II) Leave to appeal versus appeal proceedings

The Court rejected the argument that the guarantees of Art.6, para.3(c) ceased to **IIA–128** apply after the first instance proceedings or the stage at which domestic terms the applicant is regarded as "convicted".[23] Appeal, leave to appeal and continental cassation proceedings on conviction and/or sentence concern the determination of a criminal charge and the guarantees of Art.6, paras 1 and 3 continue to apply though the manner of that application will depend on the nature and significance of the proceedings, taking into account the powers of the court and the manner in which the applicant's interests were presented and protected.[24]

---

[19] December 18, 2001, para.46; see also *Twalib*, para.51, where the applicant had been assisted by legal aid counsel at first instance, and *pro bono* on appeal, the Government's claim was unsubstantiated that the applicant could have paid for counsel at the cassation level.

[20] para.35.

[21] *e.g. Twalib*, para.52.

[22] *e.g. Twalib*, para.53—difficulties of cassation procedure for which a lawyer is obligatory at any hearing and the fact the applicant, a foreigner, was unfamiliar with the Greek language or legal system.

[23] *Meftah*, para.40.

[24] *e.g. Monnell and Morris*, para.58; *Meftah*, paras 41–42.

Leave to appeal and appeal hearings may be distinguished. Leave to appeal proceedings where the prosecution are not present may not require free legal assistance. In *Monnell and Morris v United Kingdom* the applicants had representation at first instance and advice on the merits of an appeal with the possibility to put in written submissions. The Court found that they were able fairly and effectively to present their application and interests of justice were met in ability to make written submissions, taking into account the fact that counsel had advised there were no grounds of appeal.

Conversely, in the Scottish system where there was a general right to appeal, without leave, and applicants appeared in person in oral proceedings at which the prosecution was represented and could address the court, it was found that the nature of the proceedings would, where there was a serious matter at stake, require legal representation to be fair. This was found to be the case in *Granger v United Kingdom* where difficult legal issues were at stake on which there was oral argument before the court by the Solicitor General in which applicant was unable to play effective part.[25] But subsequent cases have showed that where substantial sentences are at stake, that alone will render matters sufficiently serious for the interests of justice to require legal representation at the appeal hearing.[26] In these cases, the applicants had presented arguments on their own behalf, perhaps not inexpertly in some instances, but there has been no question of considering that this rendered the provision of legal assistance unnecessary in the interests of justice. Where legal aid for an appeal was not available, the fact that the applicant made no effort to lodge his own grounds or ask for assistance did not prevent a violation being found.[27]

The Commission rejected some cases concerning minor offences with low sentences where it considered that the interests of justice did not require legal representation, for example, nine months' sentence for assault where the Commission considered that there were no complex legal issues requiring assistance;[28] 60 days for failure to give a breath specimen, taking car, etc.;[29] conviction for breach of peace, one year suspended sentence.[30] The Court has not confirmed this case law.

5. Scope of the obligation to provide legal assistance

IIA–129 The appointment of a legal aid lawyer does not exhaust the obligations of the State. Legal assistance provided must be practical and effective[31] and if the authorities are notified that a legal aid lawyer is unable to fulfil his duties the authorities are under

[25] See also *Pham Hoang*, where the applicant, fined several million francs for drugs offences, was refused legal aid counsel for cassation appeal—interests of justice required legal representation having regard to the serious consequences at stake, the complexity of issues and his inability to present and develop the appropriate arguments (*e.g.* only experienced counsel could seek to persuade the court to depart from its previous caselaw); *Pakelli*, where the applicant could not respond to the judge rapporteur or contribute to case law development.

[26] Violations in UK cases: *Maxwell* (5 years, no complex issues in the case); *Boner* (8 years); *Wotherspoon.*, 22112/93, (Rep.) October 16, 1996 (life imprisonment; relatively complex issues); *Murdoch*, 25523/94, (Rep.) October 16, 1996 (two years; relatively complex); *Robson*, 25648/94, (Rep.) October 16, 1996, (appeal against sentence only; concurrent sentences of over 12 years: still need lawyer even if sentencing issues less complex).

[27] *Biba v Greece*, September 26, 2000, para.30.

[28] 17120/90, (Dec.) December 3, 1990.

[29] 14001/88, (Dec.) January 19, 1989.

[30] 13098/87, (Dec.) May 6, 1988.

[31] *Daud*, para.39.

an obligation to replace him.[32] Once they are put on notice of a problem, they cannot remain passive.[33] Where appointment of a lawyer is made in circumstances that affect the effectiveness of his participation issues may arise, as in *Goddi v Italy*, where the court did not inform the applicant's lawyer of the hearing and the lawyer appointed in replacement knew neither the client or the file. Failure to ensure the effective defence of an accused was found by the Commission in *Biondi v Italy*, where a lawyer failed to appear at an appeal though notified and the interests of justice required the defence be represented to answer the prosecution and expand the grounds of appeal.

The State is not however liable for every shortcoming of a legal aid lawyer.[34] The conduct of the defence is essentially a matter between the lawyer and defendant.[35] The competent authorities are only required to intervene if failure by legal aid counsel to provide effective representation is manifest or sufficiently brought to their attention in some other way.[36] The Court will have regard to the proceedings in their entirety and the mere fact that counsel in some respects acted against what applicants consider to be their best interests will not be sufficient to render the representation below the required standard,[37] for example, where counsel refused to draft grounds of appeal as the file did not disclose any statutory grounds.[38] Where however an appeal is declared inadmissible as a result of the failure of official counsel to comply with a formal requirement, this may be distinguished from tactical error or shortcoming in argument. In *Czekalla v Portugal*, the failure of the legal aid lawyer to complete the grounds of appeal with the necessary formal conclusions, which led to the rejection of the appeal, was found to deprive the applicant, a foreigner ignorant of the language, of a practical and effective defence. Elsewhere the Court noted that generally litigants had to expect procedural rules to apply in the interests of legal certainty and where the applicant had the opportunity to lodge grounds in time himself no problem of access to court arose.[39] Leeway is given to the

---

[32] *e.g. Artico*, where legal aid lawyer refused the appointment because of other commitments and the authorities failed to appoint a substitute.

[33] *Daud*, para.42: where the applicant had applied to the court for an interview with his lawyer who had done nothing in eight months, the court should have enquired into the manner in which the lawyer was fulfilling his duty, possibly replacing him earlier and should have adjourned the proceedings when new counsel was appointed three days before the trial and needed time to prepare.

[34] *Artico; Kamasinski; Imbroscia*, where the applicant's counsel was absent during initial interrogations with prosecutor but the Court noted the short period, lack of complaint by the applicant and the provision of replacements by the authorities.

[35] *e.g. Czekalla*, para.60. See also *Alvarez Sanchez v Spain*, 50720/99, (Dec.) October 23, 2001, ECHR 2001–XI, where the Court observed that direct interference by a judge with a counsel's conduct of a case would be incompatible with the independence of the profession from the state.

[36] *Kamasinskii*, para.65; *Daud*, para.38; *Czekalla*, para.60.

[37] *e.g. Kamasinski*, where the applicant criticised the brevity of counsel's visits, counsel's failure to inform him of prosecution evidence etc; 9728/82 (Dec.) July 7, 1983, 6 D.R. 155: there was no problem where legal aid counsel limited unnecessary repeated consultations to save costs to the legal aid fund. Nor is an accused entitled to require counsel to adopt particular defence strategy: 9127/80, (Dec.) October 6, 1981, where the court-appointed counsel refused to maintain the applicant's not guilty plea, the Commission noted that the lawyer found the plea impossible to maintain and that the applicant could have addressed the court himself.

[38] *Rutkowski v Poland*, 45995/99, (Dec.) October 19, 2000, ECHR 2000–XI—counsel's opinion was shared by the Ministry of Justice and the Court did not consider in the circumstances that this rendered the applicant's defence ineffective; *Alvarez Sanchez*, n.35 above, the failure of the counsel to lodge an appeal in time to the Constitutional Court in an amparo appeal which did not involve a review of conviction or sentence was not so serious a shortcoming as to render his defence rights ineffective.

[39] *Freixas v Spain*, November 21, 2000, ECHR 2000–X.

domestic courts as regards their assessment of the appropriate qualifications of legal aid counsel.[40]

An applicant cannot claim a right to choose who is appointed as his legal aid counsel. The Court has stated that domestic courts must have regard to the applicant's wishes but these could be overridden where there were relevant and sufficient grounds for holding this necessary in the interests of justice.[41]

The Commission had little sympathy for accused who dismissed counsel during proceedings or failing to obtain an adjournment or fresh counsel continued the proceedings unrepresented.[42] Where the person has sacked numerous solicitors already, it is perhaps more obvious that the situation is of his own making and the domestic court may reasonably regard it as delaying tactics.[43] Where a person faces serious charges and loses confidence in inexperienced counsel, it would perhaps be harder to dismiss a complaint lightly. However it would require gross or obvious failure on the part of the defence counsel beyond mere exercise of tactical judgment that might be disagreed with, before the Court would be likely to find an obligation on the authorities to replace counsel.

Cross-reference

Part IIA: Legal aid in civil proceedings

---

[40] *Freixas,* n.39 above, where in the absence of concrete indications of incompetence, the fact counsel specialised in labour, not criminal, law was not a problem under Art.6, para.3(c).

[41] *Croissant,* para.29; *Lagerblom v Sweden,* January 14, 2003, para.54, where there was no violation in failing to appoint the applicant's preferred Finnish speaking lawyer, where he had sufficient knowledge of Swedish himself.

[42] *e.g* 8386/78, (Dec.) October 9, 1980, 21 D.R. 126: where counsel withdrew but the judge refused to adjourn for new counsel, the Commission considered that the judge's view that other counsel would be similarly embarassed was not unreasonable in light of the applicant's admissions in court and noted that he was given the opportunity to defend himself but chose not to; 13572/88, (Dec.) March 1, 1991, 69 D.R. 198: where a *Sami* was unrepresented on appeal, due to his rejection of the court-appointed lawyer whom the court found had not failed to fulfil his functions, the Commission held that Art.6 para.3(c) did not give a right to choose, or change, official counsel—regard was also had to the minor sentence imposed on conviction (1 month).

[43] 24667/94, (Dec.) May 20, 1996, 85–B D.R. 103 where the applicant dismissed the lawyer towards the end of the trial.

Legislative interference in judicial process

Key provision:

Article 6, para.1 (fair trial).

Key case law:

Stran Greek Refineries v Greece, December 9, 1994, Series A, No.301–B; 19 E.H.R.R. 293; *Pressos Compania Naviera v Belgium*, November 20, 1995, Series A, No.332; 21 E.H.R.R. 301; *Papageorgiou v Greece*, October 22, 1997, R.J.D. 1997–IV, No.54; *National & Provincial Building Society v UK*, October 23, 1997, R.J.D. 1997–VII, No.55; 25 E.H.R.R. 127; *Zielinski and Pradal & Gonzalez v France*, October 28, 1999, ECHR 2000–VII; 31 E.H.R.R. 532; *Kutic v Croatia*, March 1, 2002, ECHR 2002–II.

1. General considerations

Where the legislature passes a law which has direct and significant effect on the adjudication of pending civil claims, issues will generally arise under Art.6, para.1. In *Stran Greek Refineries v Greece*, the Court rejected the Government argument that the legislative action was outside the court proceedings, emphasising that fairness applied to the proceedings in their entirety. While there was no doubt that the appearances of justice before the courts was preserved, the principle of the rule of law and the notion of fair trial precluded any interference by the legislature with the administration of justice designed to influence the judicial determination of the dispute.[1] Such interference could only be justified on compelling grounds of general interest.[2] Where however the legislation is introduced after the conclusion of civil proceedings and therefore without influencing the outcome of the case, no problem may arise under Art.6 which does not go so far as to provide that the effects of final judgments in civil proceedings may not subsequently be overridden by the legislature.[3]

2. Effect on the proceedings

In *Stran Greek Refineries*, the law which was passed effectively excluded any meaningful examination since it took away any enforceability of the court's findings. The Court in finding a violation also referred to the case law on equality of arms. Where the State is a party in proceedings, use of its legislative powers may clearly place an opponent at a substantial disadvantage. Where the effect of a legislative measure, in conjunction with the method and timing of its enactment, is effectively

---

[1] *Stran Greek Refineries*, para.49: violations were found under Art.6, para.1 and Art.1 of Protocol No.1 (interference with property rights).

[2] *e.g. Zielinski*, para.57.

[3] *Preda and Dardari v Italy*, 28160/95 and 28382/95, (Dec.) February 23, 1999, ECHR 1999–II: the Court considered the statute was aimed not at interfering with the applicants' case but at ensuring equal treatment of all those in the applicants' position.

to extinguish a pending claim, a violation of Art.6, para.1, is likely to arise in that the applicant is thereby deprived of a fair hearing.[4]

The aspect of access to court, combined with lack of equality of arms, was the basis for violation of Art.6, para.1 in the Commission's report in *Pressos Compania Naviera*, where the applicant shipowners with claims pending before the courts, complained of legislation which was passed to exempt the State and its pilots from liability for negligent acts. The intervention was an interference in access to court, which was not proportionate and deprived the applicants of the right to obtain a decision on their civil rights following a fair trial before a tribunal. In *Zielinski and Pradal & Gonzalez v France*, the Court found a violation where a statute was passed endorsing the position taken by the public authorities in pending disputes and thereby determining the substance of the dispute in place of the courts. Though the case law often refers to the legislative intervention being decisive for the outcome of the proceedings in favour of State party,[5] it has also been considered sufficient where a court decision was based only subsidiarily on the statute concerned.[6] An intervening legislative measure which had the effect of staying indefinitely ongoing civil cases for compensation for war damage deprived the applicants of access to court.[7]

3. Justifiable interventions

IIA–133   Legislative interference may, even if retrospective, be compatible with Art.6. In *National & Provincial Building Society v United Kingdom*, where retrospective legislation intervened with the building societies' prospects of obtaining restitution of tax paid under invalid regulations, the Commission followed, by a narrow majority, the *Stran Greek Refineries* approach that intervention by the legislature influencing proceedings in the State's favour was *per se* objectionable. However, the Court held that Art.6, para.1 could not be interpreted as preventing any interference with pending legal proceedings to which the State was a party, though respect for the rule of law and a fair trial required the use of retrospective legislation to be regarded with great circumspection. While in *Stran Greek Refineries*, there was a nine-year old private law dispute with the Government as a party to a contract where an arbitration award had been given and there was an inconsistency in the State position since the Government had originally requested arbitration, in this case there were special circumstances, namely, a clear intention of Parliament to tax the money from the beginning, legislation swiftly introduced to prevent windfalls and the frustration of the legislative purpose by the fortuitious exploitation of technical defects in the original regulations.

Where domestic courts were reaching conflicting decisions on entitlements to special employee allowances, the Court rejected the Government's argument that intervention by the legislature was necessary to impose uniformity in pending proceedings, considering that divergences were an inherent consequence of any

---

[4] *Papageorgiou*, paras 34–40; see also *Anagnastopoulos v Greece*, November 7, 2000, ECHR 2000–XI, paras 19–20.
[5] *Stran Greek*, para.50; *Preda and Dardari*, n.3 above; *Agoudimos and Cefallonian Sky Shipping Co v Greece*, June 28, 2001, para.35.
[6] *Anagnostopoulos*, para.21.
[7] *Kutic*, paras 28–33, the Court rejected the Government argument that the measure was only temporary—it had lasted over 6 years.

judicial system based on a network of trial and appellate courts and that the role of the Court of Cassation was precisely to resolve such conflicts.[8]

Cross-reference

Part IIA: Access to court
Part IIA: Equality of arms
Part IIB: Property

[8] *Zielinski*, para.59.

Length of proceedings

Key provision:

IIA–134   Article 6, para.1.

1. General considerations

IIA–135   The requirement that proceedings do not exceed a "reasonable time" applies to both the determination of criminal charges and civil rights and obligations. The principles are well-established in a series of cases dominated by Italy. The reasonableness of the length of proceedings is to be assessed in the light of the particular circumstances of the case, regard being had in particular to three heads, the complexity of the case, the conduct of the applicant and the conduct of the authorities. On the latter point, what is at stake for the applicant is taken into account. Thus, criminal proceedings will generally be expected to be pursued more expeditiously than civil. Where time may play a role in determining the merits, such as child care and custody cases[1] or where time is pressing for other reasons, there may be special need for diligence on the part of the authorities.[2]

The Court has emphasised the importance of administration of justice without delays which might jeopardise its effectiveness and credibility. The accumulation of breaches, which show a continuing situation that has not been remedied, may, as in the case of Italy, lead to a finding of a practice incompatible with the Convention.[3]

2. Period to be taken into consideration

IIA–136   Civil proceedings generally commence from the institution of the relevant court procedure which concerns the determination of a dispute relating to civil rights and obligations.[4] The proceedings terminate on the date of giving judgment in the final

---

[1] The child may bond with new carers, *e.g. H v UK,* July 8, 1987, Series, A No.120–B; need for "exceptional diligence" in *Johansen v Norway,* August 7, 1996, R.J.D. 1996–III, No.13, para.88 and *Paulsen-Medalen and Svensson v Sweden,* February 19, 1998, R.J.D. 1998–I, No.63, para.42.See also *Schaal v Luxembourg,* February 18, 2003, where the six years of criminal proceedings for alleged child abuse had an effect on the applicant's applications for contact and residence in care proceedings—exceptional diligence was required (para.35); *Boca v Belgium,* November 15, 2002, ECHR 2002–IX, para.29, where one years and two months' delay in setting down custody appeal was excessive.

[2] *e.g.* claims by AIDS victims for compensation for contaminated blood banks in *X v France,* March 31, 1992, Series A, No.234–C; 14 E.H.R.R. 483 (a period over two years was excessive) and *Pailot v France,* April 22, R.J.D. 1998, 1998–II, No.69 (1 year, 10 months too long); where the applicant has suffered injuries, special, even exceptional diligence, has been required, *e.g. Silva Pontes v Portugal,* March 23, 1994, Series A, No.286–A; 18 E.H.R.R. 156, para.39 and *Martins Moreira v Portugal,* October 26, 1988, Series A, No.143; diligence has also been required in employment disputes, *e.g. Nibbio v Italy,* February 26, 1992, Series A, No.228–A; and in criminal cases, where the applicant is in detention, *e.g. Motsnik v Estonia,* April 29, 2003, para.40.

[3] *Botazzi v Italy,* July 28, 1999, ECHR 1999–V. Following a finding of administrative practice, subsequent violations of Art.6 in that respect disclose aggravating circumstances, *e.g. Rotondi v Italy,* April 27, 2000, para.15.

[4] *Darnell v UK,* (Rep.) October 26, 1993, Series A, No.272; 18 E.H.R.R.—despite lengthy internal disciplinary enquiries, until the applicant was dismissed, there was no "dispute" as to civil rights or obligations. See however *Selmouni v France,* July 28, 1999, ECHR 1999–V, para.111, taking the starting point for the applicant's compensation claim from the date of his express complaint about serious police ill-treatment rather than the formal lodging of proceedings before the investigating judge.

instance or, where later, the issuing of the written judgment to the applicant.[5] Where a court decision only became final after a year, the Court took that date.[6] Subsequent costs and enforcement proceedings may be taken into account, where related to substantive proceedings concerning civil rights and obligations.[7]

Criminal proceedings commence from the moment that a formal charge is brought against the applicant[8] or where the person has otherwise has been substantially affected by actions taken by the prosecuting authorities as a result of the suspicion against him.[9] The charge may be defined as the "official notification given to an individual by the competent authority of an allegation that he has committed a criminal offence" which also corresponds to the test whether the situation of the suspect has been affected.[10] This may be the date of arrest,[11] the date the applicant was officially notified that he was to be prosecuted, the date preliminary investigations were opened, the date of opening of a criminal investigation,[12] the request for an investigation following initial questioning of the applicant[13] or the date of police interrogation where the applicants became aware of the existence of an investigation concerning them.[14] Measures taken unknown to the applicant with no repercussions do not start time running.[15] Where specific separate counts are added later, the dates are taken from those occurrences as relevant.[16] The proceedings end when the charges are finally determined or the sentence imposed becomes final.[17] This may be the date of the conclusion of last appeal or the issuing of the judgment.

Length complaints may be examined where the proceedings have not terminated if it is alleged that there has already been unreasonable delay.[18] Where the Convention organs only became competent *ratione temporis* during the course of

---

[5] *e.g. Soares Fernandes v Portugal*, April 8, 2004, para.17.

[6] *Trevisan v Italy*, February 26, 1993, Series A, No.257–F.

[7] *Robins v U.K.*, September 23, 1997, R.J.D. 1997–V, No.49 (costs); *Di Pede* and *Zappia v Italy*, September 26, 1996, R.J.D. 1996–IV, No.17 (enforcement).

[8] *Pedersen and Baadsgaard v Denmark*, June 19, 2003, para.39—date taken from the charging of the applicants—the initial reporting of the applicants to the police was not enough without any enforcement measures of criminal procedure.

[9] *e.g.* 9132/80, (Rep.) December 12, 1983, 41 D.R. 13: where the applicant was implicated in proceedings against another person, the date was taken from the moment that the authorities searched his premises, when it became clear that a suspicion existed that he was an accomplice and this measure severely affected his position, becoming known to other people; *Ewing v UK*, 11224/84, (Rep.) October 6, 1987, 56 D.R. 71: date of arrest; *Hozee v Netherlands*, May 22, 1998, R.J.D. 1998–III, No.73, when the applicant was first questioned and informed officially that he was under suspicion of having committed a criminal offence.

[10] *e.g. Eckle v Germany*, July 15, 1982, Series A, No.51, para.73.

[11] 9559/81, (Dec.) May 9, 1983, 33 D.R. 158.

[12] *Mylnek v Austria*, 11688/85, (Rep.) March 10, 1988, 62 D.R. 120; see *Löffler v Austria*, October 3, 2000, para.19, where an applicant was convicted and the proceedings re-opened, the start date was the re-opening, not earlier procedures which had resulted in a final decision.

[13] 13017/87, (Rep.) July 4, 1989, 71 D.R. 52.

[14] *Martins and Garcia Alves v Portugal*, November 16, 2000—the Court rejected the Government argument that the date ran from the appearance before the investigating judge.

[15] *Guisset v France*, September 26, 2000, ECHR 2000–IX, para.519; *Echeveste and Bidart v France*, March 21, 2002, paras 77–78, where the applicants were not aware of the arrest warrants issued against them, the date taken was their notification, while in custody on other charges, of the court orders against them.

[16] *Jesso v Austria*, 9315/81, (Rep.) May 7, 1986, 50 D.R. 44.

[17] *Eckle*, n.10 above, para.77.

[18] *e.g. Mylnek v Austria*, (settled before the Court), (Rep.) December 9, 1991, Series A, No.242–C : period of 3 years 9 months and still pending.

proceedings, the time already elapsed was taken into account in assessing the reasonableness of length of proceedings after that date.[19] Where a violation has already been found by Convention organs in respect of pending proceedings, the delay already elapsed is also taken into account in assessing the reasonableness of time taken in the later part of the proceedings.[20] Also in cases where an applicant absconds during the proceedings (criminal) that period is deducted.[21]

3. Victim status

IIA–137   The fact that an applicant is acquitted does not deprive him of victim status for the purpose of a length complaint.[22] Where, however, national authorities have acknowledged the breach of the Convention expressly or in substance and afforded redress for the breach in circumstances where it would duplicate the domestic process to bring complaints to Strasbourg the applicant ceases to be a victim for purposes of an application.[23] This requires an acknowledgement in a sufficiently clear manner of the failure to observe the reasonable time requirement and redress is required, such as reducing the sentence in an express and measurable manner.[24]

The Commission found that where a court failed to find, or expressly denied, a violation of the Convention, the applicant still could claim to be a victim but any action taken by the court in reducing the sentence in view of the length was to be taken into account in the assessment of the reasonableness of the delay.[25] The Court has also taken reduction of sentence into account in finding no violation.[26] The logic of this approach is not readily apparent since the applicant had suffered the delay whatever the result and without an express acknowledgment of the breach.

4. Complexity of the case

IIA–138   All aspects of the case may be relevant to the assessment of complexity of the proceedings, including the subject-matter, whether there are disputed facts, number of accused, international elements, number of witnesses, volume of written evidence. The economic nature of offences will not render proceedings especially complex *per se*, the Court looking to the procedural aspects, factual and legal issues in each case.[27]

The complexity of the case, balanced with the general principle of securing the proper administration of justice may justify a not inconsiderable length of time. In

---

[19] *Mitap and Müftuoglu v Turkey*, March 25, 1996, R.J.D. 1996–II, No.6.

[20] *Rotondi v Italy*, cited n.3 above, para.14.

[21] *e.g. Girolami v Italy*, February 19, 1991, Series A, No.196–E.

[22] 13156/87, (Dec.) July 1, 1992, 76 D.R. 5.

[23] *Eckle*, n.10 above, para.66.

[24] *Eckle*, n.10 above; 9299/81, (Rep.) July 12, 1985, 46 D.R.5 where the Swiss authorities implicitly acknowledged the breach, finding that there had been considerable delays and reduced 2 and half years to 18 months and decided not to enforce expulsion order; 17669/91, (Dec.) March 31, 1993, 74 D.R. 156—reduction from 2 years 6 months to 8 months half suspended in light of excessive delay; *Neubeck v Germany*, 9132/80, (Rep.) December 12, 1983, 41 D.R. 13, where the applicant remained a victim as the courts only referred to part of the excessive delay without quantifying the reduction, the Commission finding a vague reference to fact that sentence would have been longer was insufficiently clear.

[25] *e.g. RB v Switzerland*, 18905/91, (Rep.) May 24, 1995, no violation in light of complexity of case and fact the domestic court reduced sentence from 24 to 16 months.

[26] *e.g. Hozee*, cited n.9 above, para.54.

[27] *Pelissier and Sassi*, March 25, 1999, ECHR 1999–II, para.71.

Boddaert v Belgium,[28] the Court found that six years almost three months was not unreasonable since the case concerned a difficult murder enquiry, and the parallel progression of two cases. Nor did seven years and ten months disclose a violation in *CP v France* where the criminal proceedings concerned complex company fraud investigations.[29] In a civil case, *Katte Klitsche v Italy*,[30] the Court found that eight years disclosed no violation, notwithstanding three identified periods of abnormal delay, since the case, a land developmental planning matter, was complex on facts and law and having regard to importance of environmental interests and importance for Italian case law.

However, even where a case is complex, there is a point where this ceases to suffice. In *Ferrantelli and Santangelo v Italy*, where the applicants were convicted finally after 16 years, the Court agreed that the case concerned a complex, difficult murder trial, acknowledged the sensitive problems of dealing with juveniles and that the proceedings were generally active but when the case was looked at as a whole, the only possible conclusion was unreasonable delay.[31]

5. Conduct of the applicant

Only delays attributable to the State may justify a finding of failure to comply with the "reasonable time" requirement.[32]   IIA–139

An applicant who stays outside the jurisdiction, for example failing to answer to an arrest warrant or who flees, cannot complain about length, even though the criminal proceedings remain pending indefinitely as a result.[33]

An applicant in principle cannot have it held against him that he has made full use of the procedures available to him under domestic law to pursue his defence.[34] An applicant is not required actively to co-operate with the judicial authorities but nonetheless his conduct may be taken into account as an objective factor for which the Government are not responsible.[35] The fact that an applicant has applied for expedition is often a factor in his favour but failure to do so is not necessarily crucial, particularly where the Government have not shown that the possibility of speeding

---

[28] October 12, 1992, Series A, No.235.
[29] August 1, 2000. See also *Debbasch v France*, December 3, 2002, no violation for almost eight years in a complex international art fraud case, with numerous letters rogatory; nor in *Hozee*, cited n.9 above, for more than eight years in complex fraudulent tax case concerning a network of interlocking companies.
[30] October 27, 1994, Series A, No.293–B.
[31] August 7, 1996, R.J.D. 1996–III, No.12; see also *Pafitis v Greece*, February 26, 1998, R.J.D. 1998–I, No.66, para.91.
[32] *e.g. Proszak v Poland*, December 16, 1997, R.J.D. 1997–VIII, No.59.
[33] *e.g. AP v Italy*, 27679/95, (Dec.) June 24, 1996; *Erdogan v Turkey*, 14723/89, (Dec.) July 9, 1992, 73 D.R. 81; *JA, RA, and PM v Italy*, 37658/97, (Dec.) October 27, 1998.
[34] *Eckle*, n.10 above, para.82; *CP v France*, n.29 above, para.31, applicants were not penalised for making use of procedures offered by domestic law.
[35] *e.g. Eckle*, n.10 above: there were allegations of deliberate obstruction but though the applicants slowed matters by numerous applications and appeals, the Court still found one of the main causes of the length of the proceedings to be the conduct of the judicial authorities; *Barfuss v Czech Republic*, July 31, 2000, para.74, the Court took into account the fact that the applicant changed his defence by submitting new facts deliberately not mentioned during the investigation; *Debbasch v France*, n.29 above, the applicant's excessive applications were regarded as significantly contributing to the overall length; *Humen v Poland*, October 15, 1999, para.66, the applicant's failure to submit to a brain scan, plus delaying effect of his inaccurate account of facts.

up the proceedings is a real one.[36] Some time-wasting or dilatory conduct will not prevent a violation where it does not contribute substantially to the overall length of proceedings.[37]

The factor of the applicant's conduct was significant in *Monnet v France*[38] (contested judicial separation lasting seven years one month) where the applicant contributed considerably to prolonging the proceedings by two requests for deferment, delay in submitting documents and in setting down for the hearing of the appeal. In *Ciricosta and Viola v Italy*,[39] concerning an application to suspend works likely to interfere with property rights and where the applicants had requested at least 17 adjournments and not objected to six others requested by other party, though 15 years on its face appeared unreasonable, the Court held that, while the courts were responsible for some delay, they did not bear the primary responsibility and did not accept that the judge was negligent in not putting an end to the applicants' dilatory conduct. However in *Beaumartin v France*[40] where the applicants contributed to delay by bringing the case in the wrong court and in submitting pleadings four months after lodging appeal, the authorities were more at fault, the court taking over five years to hold the first hearing and the respondent ministry taking 20 months to file its pleadings.[41]

6. Conduct of the judicial authorities

IIA–140   Even in legal systems applying the principle that the procedural initiative lies with the parties, the courts have an obligation to ensure trials progress with sufficient expedition and will not necessarily escape responsibility where the parties are themselves largely responsible for dragging out proceedings unnecessarily.[42] In extreme cases their passivity in allowing such conduct can call in doubt the credibility of the legal system.[43]

The Court also has regard to the principle of proper administration of justice, namely, that domestic courts are under a duty to deal properly with the cases before them.[44] Domestic court decisions concerning the taking of evidence, to join cases, adjourn for particular reasons, are therefore likely to be given some weight, at least

---

[36] *e.g. Ceteroni v Italy*, November 15, 1996, R.J.D. 1996–V, No.21, where the judge had never refused any adjournments by liquidator and the Court accepted that applications by the applicant would have had no effect; *Horvat v Croatia*, July 26, 2001, ECHR 2001–VIII, para.57. Contrast *M v UK*, 13228/87, (Dec.) February 13, 1990 where the Commission took into account that the applicant consented to the steps which delayed proceedings; *Ewing v UK*, 11224/84, (Rep.) where the Commission noted that the applicant could have applied for expedited hearing before House of Lords and found the overall period 3 years 10 months was not unreasonable overall; *Pedersen and Baadsgaard*, n.7 above, where the Court noted that the applicant had not objected to any adjournments.

[37] *e.g. Kudla v Poland*, October 26, 2000, ECHR 2000–XI, para.130.

[38] October 27, 1993, Series A, No.273–B.

[39] December 4, 1995, Series A, No.337.

[40] November 24, 1994, Series A, No.296–B.

[41] See also *Portington v Greece*, September 23, 1998, R.J.D. 1998–VI, No.90, where even if the applicant had been responsible for some adjournments, this did not account for the over eight years taken in the appeal proceedings.

[42] *e.g. Pafitis*, n.31 above, para.93.

[43] *Berlin v Luxembourg*, July 15, 2003, 17 years for disputed divorce proceedings; see also *Papageorgiou v Greece*, October 22, 1997, 1997–VI, No.54, para.48; *Van Vlimmeren v Netherlands*, September 26, 2000, para.35.

[44] *Boddaert*, n.28 above, para.39.

up to a certain point. For example in *Ewing v United Kingdom*,[45] the joining of three cases, which delayed the trial was not shown to be arbitrary or unreasonable, or as causing undue delay giving account to the due administration of justice. However the Commission in *Reilly v Ireland*[46] noted that the decision taken to separate murder and burglary proceedings meant that the responsibility to ensure a speedy determination of the charges was more onerous given the potential impact on length of the proceedings.

Excuses as regards backlog or administrative difficulties are not accepted since States are under an obligation to organise their judicial systems in such a way that their courts can meet the Convention's requirements.[47] A temporary backlog before a court will not entail liability provided the authorities take reasonably prompt remedial action to deal with the exceptional situation.[48] Where the state of affairs becomes prolonged or a matter of structural organisation, provisional methods, such as giving priorities, are no longer sufficient and the State cannot postpone further the adoption of effective measures.[49] However the obligation on States to organise judicial systems to comply with the requirements of Art.6 does not apply in same way to a Constitutional Court which has a role of guardian which may render it necessary to take other considerations into account, *e.g.* the importance of cases in political and social terms rather than chronological order.[50] Matters outside the authorities' control will not be held against them, where they do what is within their power to progress the proceedings, for example, delays arising from the execution of letters rogatory in another jurisdiction[51] or difficulties arising from a strike by the Bar.[52] The Court has not taken into account any delaying effect of a reference to Art.177 to the European Court of Justice, since this would adversely affect the system introduced by the EEC Treaty and offset its aim.[53]

Where specific periods of delay are attributable to courts, *e.g.* delay in the transmission of a file or documents from one instance to another or delay in issuing judgment, violations may be found where the rest of the proceedings were otherwise

---

[45] n.36 above.

[46] 21624/93, (Rep.) February 22, 1995.

[47] *e.g. Pelissier and Sassi v France*, n.27 above, para.74.

[48] *e.g. Bucholz v Germany*, May 6, 1981, Series A, No.42; 3 E.H.R.R. 597 (alleged economic recession causing backlog in labour courts: five years over three instances disclosed no violation, since the authorities showed consciousness of responsibilities and had made efforts); *Foti v Italy*, December 10, 1982, Series A, No.56 (troubles in Reggio causing unusual political and social climate taken into account but violation still disclosed).

[49] *Zimmerman and Steiner v Switzerland*, July 13, 1983, Series A, No.66; 6 E.H.R.R. 17, where there had been a steady increase in volume of administrative litigation since 1969, such that there was no temporary excess of work but a question of structural organisation to which the authorities had not given a satisfactory response. Since there were three and a half years during which the case was largely stationary, there was a violation.

[50] *Sussman v Germany*, September 16, 1996, R.J.D. 1996–IV, No.15. Given the unique circumstances of reunification and the serious social implications of the disputes, the Constitutional Court was entitled to give priority to 300,000 employment cases—no violation for proceedings lasting 3 years 4 months. Similar reasoning in *Gast and Popp v Germany*, February 25, 2000, ECHR 2000–II—grouping of cases to obtain comprehensive view of espionage and treason issues, no violation for 2 years, 9 months/2 years, 10 months; *Jankovic v Croatia*, 43440/98, (Dec.) October 12, 2000, ECHR 2000–X, reasonable for Constitutional Court to group cases to obtain comprehensive view of pension rights problems.

[51] *Wloch v Poland*, October 19, 2000, ECHR 2000–XI, paras 149–150: that, together with the complexity of the case, justified six years of criminal proceedings.

[52] *Pafitis*, n.31 above, para.96—the Athens Bar was regarded as independent professional association.

[53] *Pafitis*, n.31 above, para.95.

not lacking in diligence.[54] The Court has also referred to the failure of the Government to provide convincing explanations for periods of delay.[55] In some cases, the Court has found no violation on the basis that there has been steady and regular judicial activity in a case, without any substantial period of inactivity.[56] Some tardiness at a particular stage may also be acceptable where overall, taking into account the number of levels of jurisdiction, the time taken is not unreasonable.[57] Conversely, in cases of particularly excessive delay the time taken may *per se* appear too long and the burden will weigh particularly heavily on the Government to provide an explanation.[58]

UK length cases

Civil:
Bullerwell[59] (disablement benefit proceedings): under seven years: manifestly-ill founded.
Robins[60] (costs) over four years: violation.
Davies[61] (company director disqualification): four years, five months: violation
Somjee[62] (industrial tribunal/racial harassment): over eight years, nine months for longest of three sets of interlocking proceedings: violation
Foley[63] (contract) over 14 years: violation
Price and Lowe[64] (property) over 12 years: violation.

Criminal:
Howarth[65]: over two years for an Attorney General's reference on sentence: violation.
Mellors[66]: over three years, eight months.

---

[54] e.g. in *Reilly*, n.46 above, the Commission commented adversely on 12 months for the Supreme Court to render judgment and 14 months for the trial judge to approve the transcript of evidence; in *Bunkate v Netherlands*, May 26, 1993, Series A, No.248–B the Court singled out 15 and a half months for the court of appeal to send the casefile to the Supreme Court; *Kudla* , n.37 above, para.130, a delay of nearly one year and eight months in holding a retrial after the original conviction was quashed.

[55] e.g. *Barfuss*, cited n.35, paras 82–83: violation for criminal proceedings taking 3 years, 10 months and 7 days.

[56] e.g. *Humen*, n.35 above, para.69; *Punzelt v Czech Republic*, April 25, 2000, para.96.

[57] *Nuutinen v Finland*, June 27, 2000, ECHR 2000–VIII, para.110; *Motsnik*, n.2 above, para.42.

[58] e.g. *Schaal v Luxembourg*, n.1 above—6 years for one criminal instance; *Comingersoll SA v Portugal*, April 6, 2000, ECHR 2000–IV—17 years for enforcement of bills of exchange.

[59] 48013/99, (Dec.) December 12, 2002.

[60] n.7 above.

[61] July 16, 2002.

[62] October 15, 2002.

[63] October 22, 2002.

[64] July 29, 2003.

[65] September 21, 2000.

[66] July 17, 2003.

Presence in court

Key provision:

Article 6, para.1 (right to a fair trial) and para.3(c) (right to defend oneself in   IIA–141
person).

Key case law:

Goddi v Italy, April 9, 1984, Series A, No.76; 6 E.H.R.R. 457; *Colozza v Italy,*
February. 12, 1985, Series A, No.89; 7 E.H.R.R. 516; *Monnell and Morris v UK,*
March 2, 1987, Series A, No.115; 10 E.H.R.R. 205; *Kamasinki v Austria,* December
19, 1989, Series A, No.168; 13 E.H.R.R. 36; *FCB v Italy,* August 28, 1991, Series
A, No.208–B; 14 E.H.R.R. 909; *Kremsow v Austria,* September 21, 1993, Series A,
No.268; 17 E.H.R.R. 322; *Poitrimol v France,* November 23, 1993, Series A,
No.277; 18 E.H.R.R. 130; *Zana v Turkey,* November 25, 1997, R.J.D. 1997–VII,
No.57; 27 E.H.R.R. 667.

1. General considerations

The applicant, generally, has a right to be present during criminal proceedings. The   IIA–142
object and purpose of Art.6, para.1 and 3(c)–(e) presuppose the accused's presence.
It is considered to be of capital importance that a defendant appear, both because of
his right to a hearing and the need to verify the accuracy of his statements and
compare them with those of the witnesses.[1] This is not an absolute right, as in
special circumstances where witnesses have to be heard anonymously or where the
accused is unruly.[2] Nor will claimed ill-health necessarily require an adjournment.[3]
The Commission in *Colozza* stated however that the rights of the defence could not
be said to have been respected if the applicant had not been given the "possibility"
of attending. In this context, the authorities must show requisite diligence in
ensuring the accused's right to be present in an effective manner, having regard to
the prominent place which the right to a fair trial enjoys in a democratic society.[4]

The most difficult problems have arisen in conviction *in absentia* cases where States
retain the right to continue proceedings where an accused absconds or fails to appear.

2. Waiver

Waiver by an accused of his right to be present may be possible but must be   IIA–143
unequivocal and attended by the minimum safeguards commensurate to the
importance of the right.[5]

---

[1] *Poitrimol,* para.35; *Ninn-Hansen v Denmark,* 28972/95, (Dec.) May 18, 1999, ECHR 1999–V.
[2] *Colozza,* (Rep.) para.17. See also 31066/96, (Dec.) January 14, 1998, where the applicant through his
own deliberate conduct failed to appear at first instance and appeal and it was not unreasonable for the
courts to continue without him.
[3] See *Ninn-Hansen,* n.1 above, where the court held on the basis of medical evidence that after a stroke
the applicant's state of health did not preclude his presence at the remainder of the trial and continued
the final oral pleadings in his absence.
[4] *FCB v Italy,* para.35.
[5] *e.g. Poitrimol,* para.31.

In *Zana v Turkey*, where the applicant was not present before the National Security Court which convicted him, the Court found that the procedural objection raised by the applicant on previous appearance in the Assize Court and his refusal to speak Turkish did not give rise to any implicit waiver of his right to appear.

Mere failure to appear is insufficient. In *FCB*, where the applicant was detained in the Netherlands, the Milan Court of Appeal held a retrial in his absence although informed by his counsel that he was detained abroad. The Court considered that the applicant had not expressed the wish to waive attendance and was not impressed by the argument that he had used deliberate delaying tactics in not providing the Italian authorities with his address. The crucial consideration was that the Italian authorities were aware that the applicant was subject to proceedings and it was hardly compatible with the diligence required in ensuring defence rights were effectively exercised to continue the trial without taking further steps to clarify the position.[6]

Where there are difficulties in proving whether an applicant who knew of the date of trial was unable to attend, the Court has placed a certain burden on the applicant in substantiating his case. In *Goddi v Italy*, where the applicant, placed in detention on other charges claimed that he had told the prison authorities of a hearing, the Government contested this. In absence of substantiation from either side, the Court considered that it could not be established that the Government were at fault.[7]

3. Opportunity for rehearing on the merits

IIA–144   Proceedings *in absentia* may not be incompatible with the Convention if the person concerned can subsequently obtain a hearing complying with Art.6, namely which provide a fresh determination of the merits of the charge.[8] Remedies which put the burden on the applicant to show that he had not tried to evade justice, been prevented from attending by *force majeure*, or that the authorities had not complied with applicable rules of service have been found insufficient.[9] The Commission appeared to take the view that the guarantee to "everyone" of a fair trial included those who deliberately absconded[10] although the Court in *Poitrimol v France* expressed doubt as to whether the requirement for a rehearing would apply to an accused who unequivocally waived his right to appear.[11] However, where an applicant by his own deliberate conduct was unable to attend the trial, the Court found that his conviction *in absentia* and the refusal to grant him a retrial did not amount to a disproportionate penalty.[12]

---

[6] Also *Kremzow v Austria*: a failure by the applicant to apply to attend the appeal hearing did not constitute a waiver, particularly as domestic procedures provided that, even without a request, the accused should attend where necessary in the interests of justice and there was a positive duty on the State to ensure his attendance; *Jones v UK*, 30900/02, (Dec.) September 9, 2003, no waiver from failure of accused to attend trial where there was no established practice of trials *in absentia*.

[7] para.29.

[8] *Colozza*, para.29; *Poitrimol*, para.31; *Jones*, n.6 above, where the Court of Appeal's power to hear fresh evidence and opportunity for the applicant to seek fresh determination of his conviction, if there was any evidence to challenge it, was sufficient after his deliberate non-attendance at trial.

[9] *Colozza*, para.29; *Stamoulakatos v Greece*, (Rep.) May 20, 1992, Series A, No.271.

[10] e.g. *Stamoulakatos*, n.9 above.

[11] *Poitrimol*, para.31.

[12] *Medenica v Switzerland*, 20491/92, (Dec.) June 14, 2001, ECHR 2001–VI: reference to the margin of

4. Exclusion from the hearing

Where proceedings concern only points of law, no issue may arise from the refusal to allow an accused to attend in addition to his lawyer. The Court considers that personal attendance of an accused at the appeal hearing does not take on the same crucial significance as it does for trial. In *Kremzow v Austria*, where the applicant was excluded from a hearing on points of nullity (law), the Court found his presence was not required by Art.6, paras 1 or 3(c), his lawyer being able to attend and make points on his behalf.[13] There was a breach however where the applicant was excluded from the hearing of the appeal on sentence, which involved an increase in sentence to life imprisonment, committal to special prison and a ruling on the motive for the crime which the jury had been unable to establish. Since the assessment of the applicant's character, state of mind and motivation were significant to the proceedings, and there was much at stake for the applicant, fairness required that he be present and able to participate as well as his lawyer.[14] It is not decisive, apparently, that the accused fail to make a request to attend as the State is under a positive duty to enable him to attend to "defend himself in person."[15]

IIA–145

In leave to appeal proceedings, absence of the accused and lawyer may be compatible where the nature of the issues are not such as to require presence and having regard to the prior proceedings (in particular previous legal representation and legal advice as to the prospects of appeal). In these circumstances the interests of justice and fairness may be met by the possibility of presenting written submissions to the court.[16]

In *Kamasinski v Austria*, in rejecting a complaint of discrimination in that accused persons at liberty were not excluded from appeal hearings, the Court appeared to give weight to the difficulties that attach to the attendance of prisoners which do not apply to accused persons at liberty or civil parties.

Cross-reference

Part IIA: Legal representation in criminal proceedings
Part IIA: Public hearing and judgment

---

appreciation to be accorded to the State authorities—the Swiss court found that the applicant had made inaccurate and equivocal statements to the US court deliberately to secure a decision (a restraining order) rendering his attendance at trial impossible. This assessment was not found to be arbitrary or based on manifestly erroneous premises.

[13] See also *Kamasinski*, para.106; *Pobornikoff v Austria*, October 3, 2000, para.27; concerning the special nature of the proceedings before the Court of Cassation in France, see *Meftah v France*, July 26, 2002, ECHR 2002–VII, where the inability of the applicants to attend an oral hearing was not a problem in a system where only specialised counsel were allowed to appear.

[14] Similar violation in *Pobornikoff*, n.13 above, para.32.

[15] *Pobornikoff*, n.13 above, para.32, citing *Kremzow*, para.68, where in Austrian law a court should have an appellant brought before it if his personal presence appears necessary in the interest of justice.

[16] *Monnell and Morris*.

Presumption of innocence

Key provisions:

IIA–146   Article 6, para.2 (presumption of innocence).

Key case law:

Minelli v Switzerland, March 25, 1983, Series A, No.62; 5 E.H.R.R. 554; *Lutz v Germany*, August 25, 1987, Series A, No.123; *Schenk v Switzerland*, July 12, 1988, Series A, No.140; 13 E.H.R.R. 242; *Salabiaku v France*, October 7, 1988, Series A, No.141–A; 13 E.H.R.R. 379; *Sekanina v Austria*, August 25, 1993, Series A, No.266–A; 10 E.H.R.R. 182; *Allenet de Ribemont v France*, February 10, 1995, Series A, No.308; 20 E.H.R.R. 557; *John Murray v UK*, February 8, 1996, R.J.D. 1996–I, No.1; 22 E.H.R.R. 29; *Leutscher v Netherlands*, March 26, 1996, R.J.D., 1996–II, No.6; 24 E.H.R.R. 181; *Heaney and McGuinness v Ireland*, December 21, 2000, ECHR 2000–XII; *Daktaras v Lithuania*, October 10, 2000, ECHR 2000–X; *Phillips v United Kingdom*, July 5, 2001, ECHR 2001–VII; *Butkevicius v Lithuania*, March 26, 2002, ECHR 2002–II; *O v Norway, Ringvold v Norway, Y v Norway* and *Hammern v Norway*, February 11, 2003, ECHR 2003–II.

1. General considerations

IIA–147   The presumption of innocence applies to persons charged with criminal offences.[1] The principle has had relevance in regard to the different ways domestic systems deal with factual presumptions and the evidentiary burden of proof; the way in which courts penalise defendants in costs or issue qualified acquittals; and the prohibition of public statements of guilt by officials.

It is construed quite narrowly in its application. It does not cover the detention of remand prisoners in the same regime as convicted prisoners[2] or the obligation to surrender to detention prior to the hearing of an appeal.[3] The Court has commented that while it is not *per se* contrary to Art.6, para.2 for the authorities to enforce a monetary penalty before the decisions become final, such measures must be confined within reasonable limits, leaving it open as to whether issues could arise in a situation where an applicant suffered serious detriment disproportionate to the interests pursued.[4]

---

[1] However, in *Albert and Le Compte v Belgium*, February 10, 1983, Series A, No.58; 5 E.H.R.R. 533, the Court held that the presumption of innocence applied to disciplinary proceedings against doctors, whether they were civil or criminal, the principles set out Art.6, paras 2 and 3 being implicit in para.1.

[2] *Peers v Greece*, April 19, 2001, ECHR 2001–III, para.78.

[3] *Cuvillers and Da Luz v France*, 55052/00, (Dec.) September 16, 2003.

[4] *Janosevic v Sweden*, July 23, 2002, ECHR 2002–VII, paras 106–110, where the enforcement of substantial tax surcharges could have had serious implications notwithstanding the ability to obtain repayment on appeal, the Court noted that the State's financial interests weighed less heavily as it did not concern payment of due taxes but on the facts of the case no adverse enforcement had in fact taken place.

2. Burden of proof: evidential presumptions

Rules which impose presumptions of law and fact which act to place the burden on the defendant to rebut them are not *per se* contrary to Art.6, para.2. They must however be confined within reasonable limits which take into account the importance of what is at stake and the rights of the defence. In particular, the operation of presumptions must not strip a trial court of any effective power of assessment of the facts or guilt.

Thus, in *Salabiaku v France*, where the applicant was took delivery of a locked trunk which proved to contain drugs, he was subject to a presumption of responsibility. Since however the domestic courts maintained a freedom of assessment and gave attention to the facts of the case, quashing one conviction, the Court found no violation.[5] Where in *Pham Hoang v France* a presumption was applied to the driver of the car involved in a drugs deal who was convicted of possession, the Court found that it was not irrebuttable nor prevented the driver from raising a defence (*e.g. force majeure*, unavoidable mistake or necessity). Since the court refrained from any automatic reliance on the presumption, basing its finding of guilt on a cumulation of factors (the circumstances of the arrest and his earlier involvement in the gang's activities) the presumption was not applied in a matter incompatible with Art.6, para.2.

Similarly in a Maltese case, the Commission found that it was acceptable to impose liability on a company director for customs offences committed by the company unless he could show that the offence was committed without his knowledge and that he exercised all due diligence to prevent the commission of the offence. This was not an irrebuttable or self-contradictory presumption and the courts retained a genuine freedom of asessment in determining whether an offence had been committed by the applicant.[6] In cases where the owners of pit bull terriers and other specified breeds were faced with a presumption that the dog was dangerous unless proved otherwise the Commission found no violation since there was the opportunity to disprove the assumption and courts retained an area of assessment, albeit limited, where the matter was put in issue.[7]

However difficult presumptions are to rebut as long as the applicant is left with some means of defence it is likely that no violation will arise. The Court has talked of balancing the rights of the defence against the importance of what is at stake, indicating that context may also be of relevance, as in taxation, fundamental to State's financial interests, where sanctions to ensure submission of correct information may regarded as essential to the functioning of the system.[8]

Presumptions drawn as to the illicit source of income during proceedings after conviction for drugs offences for the purposes of imposing a confiscation order did not offend Art.6, para.2 as it was part of the sentencing process and assessment of the applicant's character and conduct after he had been found guilty of the charge.[9]

---

[5] There was a defence of "unavoidable error" and the court gave weight to the fact that he had been warned by an official not to take the trunk unless he was sure it was his and therefore he had been put on notice and could have checked the contents.
[6] 16641/90, (Dec.) December 10, 1991.
[7] *e.g. Bates v UK*, 26280/95; *Foster v UK*, 28846/95 and *Brock v UK*, 26279/95: (Decs.) January 16, 1996.
[8] *Janosevic*, n.4 above.
[9] *Phillips*, para.35. See however the dissenting opinion of Sir Nicolas Bratza finding that Art.6, para.2 clearly could extend beyond conviction into the confiscation proceedings but found that the operation of the statutory presumptions in the applicant's case did not exceed reasonable and fair limits.

If allegations were made of a nature or degree as to amount to the bringing of a new charge, Art.6, para.2 might become applicable however.[10]

Even without any formal presumptions of fact or law, the way in which the courts approach the evidence may raise issues. A breach of the presumption of innocence was found where an Austrian court proceeded to convict the owner of a car for causing injury by negligence on the basis of assumptions that it was mainly the applicant who drove the car, even though other family members drove the car on occasion and there was no evidence to identify him as the driver. The way in which the courts approached the evidence, asserting that it was for the applicant to put forward a contrary version of events to the prosecution case, was perceived as going too far and giving the impression of a preconceived view of the applicant's guilt.[11]

3. Statements made by judges or courts

(a) *Comments during the proceedings*

IIA–149 The principle of presumption of innocence requires that when carrying out their duties the members of a court should not have any preconceived idea that the applicant has committed the offence charged.[12] A distinction is drawn between statements made reflecting the opinion that the person is guilty and statements which merely describe a "state of suspicion", the latter being unobjectionable prior to the final determination by the court.[13] Where a judge made the comment at a press conference before the conclusion of the trial that she had not decided whether to convict or partially acquit, this disclosed a preconceived view of the applicant's partial guilt and infringed Art.6, para.2, as did her suggestion that the accused prove their innocence.[14]

Statements made by a judge in issuing provisional measures of seizure pending criminal proceedings thus did not fall foul of the presumption of innocence, where they referred to the existence of suspicion and not a finding of guilt.[15] The presumption of innocence excludes a finding of guilt outside the criminal proceedings before the competent trial court and it is irrelevant to a finding of breach that procedural safeguards apply in parallel proceedings which prejudge the matters at trial.[16]

---

[10] e.g. *Phillips*, para.35; *Bohmer v Germany*, para.55: a violation was found as the appeal court in revoking a suspended sentence assumed the role of the trial court and unequivocally declared that the applicant had committed an offence during probation.

[11] *Telfner v Austria*, March 20, 2001.

[12] e.g. *Barbera, Messegué and Jabardo v Spain*, December 6, 1988, Series A, No.146, para.77.

[13] e.g. *Lutz v Germany*, para.62; *Leutscher*, para.31. See also *Daktaras v Lithuania*, 42905/98, (Dec.) January 11, 2000, where a comment by the Regional Court to the accused as "one of the leaders of the underworld" reflected the witnesses' testimony so far and did not suggest that the applicant was guilty.

[14] *Lavents v Latvia*, November 28, 2002, paras 126–127.

[15] *Gokceli v Turkey*, March 4, 2003, para.46: the Court appeared to give weight to the legal context rather than the actual terms used by the judge which on their face appeared to refer to the offence having been committed.

[16] *Bohmer v Germany*, October 3, 2002, para.67: revocation of suspended sentence proceedings which found that an offence had been committed on probation before the actual trial of the charges had been concluded.

(b) *Orders on acquittal or termination of proceedings*

Article 6, para.2 applies to criminal proceedings in their entirety, not solely the part dealing with the merits. Thus comments made by judges on the termination of proceedings or following acquittal which reflect the opinion that the applicant is guilty will violate the presumption of innocence.[17] Thus in *Minelli v Switzerland* where a court in declining to follow the normal rule of awarding costs to the accused remarked that he "very probably" would have been convicted but for the termination of the proceedings because of rules of prescription, a violation was found. Where an applicant was acquitted by one court and refused costs by a different court, the presumption of innocence guarantee still applied to the second proceedings and was violated where the second court found that serious grounds for suspecting him still existed.[18] Some voicing of suspicion regarding an accused might be conceivable before the conclusion of the proceedings, as in *Lutz v Germany* but it was not permissible to rely on such suspicions after an acquittal became final.[19]

IIA–150

Where therefore a judge makes remarks which expressly or by clear implication attribute guilt to the acquitted defendant, there is likely to be a violation. In *Moody v United Kingdom*[20] and *Lochrie v United Kingdom*,[21] the judge's comments on disallowing the costs for a failed prosecution for sale of obscene material which were to the effect that material was obscene and that the applicants should nonetheless be penalised for dealing with it were incompatible with the presumption of innocence. Conversely, in *DF v United Kingdom*, where the judge refused a full costs order on acquittal commenting that the case stank of greed and that the applicant had brought the case upon himself by not saying anything to clear himself during the investigation, the Commission found that that the refusal of costs was not made on the basis of any continuing suspicion being harboured and that though the judge referred to greed his comments could not be interpreted as implying any finding of dishonesty which was an element of many criminal offences.[22]

(c) *Findings or comments in other proceedings*

Where issues related to criminal charges on which a person has been acquitted arise in civil cases, courts may deal with the aspect of civil responsibility arising from the same facts but must regard themselves bound by the finding of the criminal court with regard to criminal responsibility. Therefore no violation was found where labour courts dismissed a teacher who had been acquitted of the charge of supplying drugs to a boy who committed suicide under their influence. The domestic court referred to the surrounding circumstances in which the teacher failed to help the boy

IIA–151

---

[17] *e.g. Minelli*, para.37.

[18] *Sekanina*.

[19] *e.g. Baars v Netherlands*, October 28, 2003–in refusing costs for a prosecution terminated for delay before a verdict, the court's reasoning amounted in substance to a determination of the applicant's guilt, not a mere reference to the existence of a state of suspicion.

[20] 22613/93, (Rep.) January 16, 1996.

[21] 22614/93, (Rep.) January 18, 1996.

[22] 22401/93, (Dec.) October 24, 1995; see also, *e.g. Byrne v UK*, 37107/97, (Dec.) April 16, 1998; *Fashanu v UK*, 38440/97, (Dec.) July 1, 1998, where comments in refusing costs concerning a defendant's conduct bringing suspicion on himself and misleading the prosecution by giving no explanations etc have not posed a problem.

in appropriate ways rather than contradicting the finding of the criminal court in its acquittal.[23]

Refusal of damages for pre-trial detention of an acquitted accused based on findings that a necessary reasonable suspicion existed at the time before the acquittal did not infringe the presumption of innocence.[24] Statements made in refusing compensation which express or imply the continuing existence of suspicion, or otherwise call in doubt the correctness of the acquittal, have disclosed violations.[25] An acquittal in criminal proceedings does not as as such preclude the establishment of civil liability to pay compensation to the victims arising out of the same facts on the basis of a less strict burden of proof. However, breach of the presumption of innocence will arise if the decision on compensation acted in such a way or used such language in its reasoning as to create a clear link between the two sets of proceedings as could bring Art.6, para.2 into play.[26]

4. Statements implying guilt by other State authorities

IIA–152 The presumption of innocence is binding not only on the court before which a person charged is brought but on other State organs.[27] In *Allenet de Ribemont v France*, where the applicant, while in police custody, was described at a press conference by senior police officers as being the instigator of the murder under investigation, the Court rejected the Government argument that Art.6, para.2 only applied to the judicial authority in the context of criminal proceedings ending in a conviction but held that it applied to other public authorities where an applicant was "charged with a criminal offence". Since the declaration of guilt was made without

---

[23] 9295/81, (Dec.) October 6, 1982, 30 D.R. 227; also 11882/85, (Dec.) October 7, 1987, 54 D.R. 162 where a janitor of a school was acquitted of theft but his dismissal upheld by an industrial tribunal.

[24] *Hibbert v Netherlands*, 38087/97, (Dec.) January 26, 1999.

[25] *Asan Rushiti v Austria*, March 21, 2000; *Lamanna v Austria*, July 10, 2001. The Court commented in those cases that it was irrelevant whether it was the trial court or another later court which made the remarks or whether they were allegedly based on the terms of the jury's verdict; see the Norwegian cases, *O* and *Hammern*, where the proceedings for compensation brought by the acquitted accused were closely linked by time, legislation and practice to the criminal proceedings such as to attract the application of Art.6, para.2 and comments by the High Court refusing compensation on the basis that the applicants had probably committed sexual abuse were considered as voicing suspicion incompatible with the presumption of innocence.

[26] *Y v Norway* (violation where in the compensation decision the High Court made an express finding that the applicant had probably committed the offences charged; conversely, *Ringvold v Norway* (no violation where the findings were not considered by the court to state expressly or in substance that the conditions for criminal liability were fulfilled).

[27] 7986/77, (Dec.) October 3, 1978, 13 D.R. 73, where the applicant complained that the Minister of Justice had made a statement on television to the effect that she had committed criminal acts although she had not yet been convicted, the Commission rejected the complaint, as although the statement could have been more carefully worded, in context the words could be taken as information given to the public about the basis of suspicion against the applicant and the announcement of a trial; 20755/92, (Dec.) October 10, 1994, where the Commission found that the Parole Board as a public authority was bound by the applicant's acquittal on charges of rape and incest not to treat him guilty of these offences (allegedly committed while on release). It was not however precluded, in refusing release, from examining the circumstances leading up to the prosecution in its overall assessment of the applicant's risk to the public; similarly, *Murati v Switzerland*, 37285/97, (Dec.) July 1, 1998, where the authorities refused a residence permit on grounds of the risk of the applicant's future offending; *Daktaras*, where remarks by State officials aimed at describing the circumstances of the applicant's arrest and referring to his dangerous character were not found to be formal declarations of guilt which could encourage the public to believe him guilty.

any qualification or reservation and encouraged the public to believe the applicant guilty in prejudgment of the assessment of the facts by the competent judicial authority, there was a violation, which was not cured by the fact that the applicant was later released by a judge for lack of evidence. The Court emphasises however that statements must be taken in their context, giving some allowance for infelicitous phrasing In *Daktaras v Lithuania*, where it was "unfortunate" that the prosecutor referred to the applicant's guilt having been "proved' by the evidence, the Court noted that he was using the same term as the applicant in his application for a discontinuance and it was evident, in the context, that both were referring to the existence or not of sufficient evidence to justify the continuance of the proceedings.[28]

However, it appears that statements made implying involvement in criminal acts will not offend where no criminal proceedings are pending or anticipated. Where in the House of Commons a Minister named two Belgian applicants as involved in sanction busting in Namibia, the Court noted that there was no suspicion that the applicants had committed any offence within UK jurisdiction and no proceedings intended. In those circumstances the applicants could not be regarded as "charged with a criminal offence" for the purposes of Art.6, para.2.[29]

Where adverse comments appear in the press, this may adversely affect the fairness of the trial under Art.6, para.1, in particular through their effect on the jury. Issues might still arise under Art.6, para.2 where the press coverage could be regarded as inspired by, and thus under the responsibility of, the authorities.[30]

5. Penalties for failure to give information

In a number of contexts, liability involving fines or imprisonment may be imposed where a person fails to comply with a requirement to provide information. The Commission did not find a problem in traffic offences, where an owner of the car was liable if he did not give the name of the person driving at the time of the offence, such presumption considered acceptable.[31] The Court cast doubt on this case law as failing to take into account the right to silence but in *Weh v Austria* considered that the imposition of a fine on the owner of a car for giving inaccurate information about the driver at the time of a purported speeding incident was not sufficiently connected with a pending criminal charge against the owner as to offend against the privilege against self-incrimination.[32]

Imposition of penalties for failure to provide breath specimens or material independent of the will of the accused person, even if the material is likely to be

IIA–153

---

[28] See also *Butkevicius*, where certain comments by the Prosecutor General could be regarded, in context, as referring not to guilt but to the existence of sufficient evidence to justify proceedings but the comment by the Chairman of the *Seimas* (Parliament) amounted to a declaration of guilt, prejudging the assessment by the competent judicial authority.

[29] *Zollman v UK*, 62902/00, (Dec.) November 27, 2002. Cf. *Montera v Italy*, 64713/01, (Dec.) July 9, 2002—comments in a Parliamentary report concerning links between magistrates and the mafia did not offend Art.6, para.2 as they referred to a state of suspicion against the applicant and did not disclose a finding of guilt.

[30] *Wloch v Poland*, 27785/95, (Dec.) March 30, 2000—where the Court left it open whether the press were inspired by public authorities' remarks and found that the coverage was not such as affect the impartiality of the trial court and amount to a breach of the presumption of innocence. See Fair trial, Jury.

[31] 23681/94, (Dec.) May 17, 1995, car caught by radar for speeding, owner refused to say who drove and was fined 50,000 pesetas.

[32] April 8, 2004.

incriminating, has not been found either to infringe the presumption of innocence or the privilege against self-incrimination.[33]

Where the question of the right to silence or privilege against self-incrimination has been in serious issue however, the Convention organs have tended to treat the issue as one of fairness under Art.6, paragraph. 1 rather than the presumption of innocence.[34]

However, in *Heaney and McGuinness v Ireland*, the conviction and imprisonment for six months of the applicants for failure to account for the movements at the time of an attack on a security checkpoint was found to infringe both the privilege against self-incrimination and the presumption of innocence. The Court laid emphasis on the degree of compulsion imposed on the applicants to incriminate themselves in serious offences which extinguished the very essence of their right to silence and also contravened the basic principle that the prosecution have to prove their case without resort to evidence obtained by coercion or oppression in defiance of the will of the acused, which aspect was closely linked to the guarantee of presumption of innocence until proof of guilt according to law.

6. Cure on appeal

IIA–154   It may be possible for a breach of presumption of innocence to be cured by a superior court making the matter clear where the person was acquitted or the proceedings terminated.[35] This occurred in *Adolf v Austria*,[36] where in discontinuing the proceedings for triviality, the Austrian court made ambiguous Statements, which the applicant claimed were capable of suggesting that he had inflicted bodily harm on the complainant. However the Supreme Court on the applicant's application clearly stated that discontinuance was not to include anything in the nature of a verdict of guilt and it would have been preferable if the lower court had stated this more explicitly. The Court found that the lower court judgment had to be read in light of the Supreme Court ruling and therefore the applicant was cleared of any finding of guilt and the presumption of innocence no longer called into question.

It may always be possible therefore for breach of presumption of innocence to be cured by a superior court making the matter clear where the person was acquitted or proceedings terminated. Where the applicant was found guilty and the breach occurred during the proceedings, it might be more problematic to cure without acquitting or sending back for re-trial.

Cross-reference

Part IIA: General principles
Part IIA: Right to silence

---

[33] *e.g. Tirado Ortiz and Lozano v Spain*, 43486/98, (Dec.) June 15, 1999. See also Pt IIA, Right to silence.
[34] See Pt IIA: Right to silence *e.g. Condron v UK*, May 2, 2000, ECHR 2000–V: the direction by the judge concerning the drawing of inferences from the applicants' failure to answer police questions breached Art.6, para.1, with no separate issue arising under Art.6, para.2.
[35] *Austria v Italy* (1966) 788/60, 6 Ybk of the ECHR 740, where a breach is so gross as to distort the course of the proceedings, cure may not be possible.
[36] March 26, 1982, Series A, No.49.

Public hearing and judgment

Key provision:

Article 6, para.1 (right to public hearing and public pronouncement of judgment). **IIA–155**

Key case law:

Albert and Le Compte v Belgium, February 10, 1983, Series A, No.58; 5 E.H.R.R. 533; *Pretto v Italy*, December 8, 1983, Series A, No.71; 6 E.H.R.R. 182; *Axen v Germany*, December 8, 1983, Series A, No.72; 6 E.H.R.R. 195; *Sutter v Switzerland*, February 22, 1984, Series A, No.74; 6 E.H.R.R. 272; *Campbell and Fell v UK*, June 28, 1984, Series A, No.80; 7 E.H.R.R. 165; *H v Belgium*, November 30, 1987, Series A, No.127–B; 10 E.H.R.R. 339; *Ekbatani v Sweden*, May 26, 1988, Series A, No.134; 13 E.H.R.R. 504; *Hakansson and Sturesson v Sweden*, February 21, 1990, Series A, No.171–A; 13 E.H.R.R. 1; *Helmers v Sweden*, October 29, 1991, Series A, No.212–A; *Jan-Ake Andersson v Sweden*, October 29, 1991, Series A, No.212–B; 15 E.H.R.R. 218; *Fejde v Sweden*, October 29, 1991, Series A, No.212–C; 17 E.H.R.R. 4; *Schuler-Zgraggen v Switzerland*, June 24, 1993, Series A, No.263; 16 E.H.R.R. 405; *Fredin v Sweden (No.2)*, February 23, 1994, Series A, No.283–A; *Diennet v France*, September 26, 1995, Series A, No.325–A; 21 E.H.R.R. 554; *Botten v Norway*, February 19, 1996, R.J.D. 1996–I; *Bulut v Austria*, February 22, 1996, R.J.D., 1996–II, No.5; *Stallinger and Kuso v Austria*, April 23, 1997, R.J.D. 1997–II, No.35; *Werner v Austria and Szucs v Austria*, November 24, 1997, R.J.D. 1997–VII, No.56; *Eisenstecken v Austria*, October 3, 2000, ECHR 2000–X; *Riepan v Austria*, November 14, 2000, ECHR 2000–XII; *B and P v UK*, April 24, 2001, ECHR 2002–III; *Goç v Turkey*, July 11, 2002, ECHR 2002–V.

1. General considerations

There are two hearing aspects—whether the proceedings are open to public and **IIA–156**
whether there is an oral hearing at which applicant may address the court.

2. Public hearing

The public character of proceedings before judicial bodies protects litigants against **IIA–157**
the administration of justice in secret without public scrutiny. It maintains public
confidence in the courts and in rendering the administration of justice visible
contributes to the achievement of a fair trial, a fundamental guarantee in a
democratic society.[1] While practice varies in States as regards hearings and
pronouncement of judgments, the Court will look at the realities of the procedure,
the purpose underlying the guarantee rather than at the formalities which are of
lesser importance.[2]

Generally a public hearing is required before the court of first and only instance.[3]
Lack of public hearing will not be cured by a public hearing before an appeal or

---

[1] *Axen*, para.25, *Werner*, para.45; *B and P*, para.36.
[2] *Axen*, para.26.
[3] *e.g. Gautrin v France*, May 20, 1998, R.J.D. 1998–III, No.72, where no public hearing of medical disciplinary case.

cassation instance where that body does not consider the merits of the case or is not competent to deal with all aspects of the matter.[4] Where a public hearing has not been provided at first instance, exceptional reasons will be required to justify refusal of one at second instance.[5] Even in a relatively trivial civil case, a claimant cannot generally be denied a public hearing in court procedures aimed at simplifying or expediting cases.[6] In criminal cases, given the possible detrimental effects on fairness of a lack of public hearing at first instance, this could only be remedied by a complete re-hearing before the appeal court.[7]

In the context of court martials, a hearing may still be sufficiently public where access to the hearing room on a military base is conditional on members of the public signing in, such measure justified by reasonable security and safety concerns.[8] The fact that a hearing may be open to the public in formal sense may not however be enough where the proceedings are taking place outside normal court facilities. Thus in *Riepan v Austria*, where the criminal trial took place inside a prison, the Court found that practical obstacles to public attendance arose and that inadequate compensatory measures were taken to ensure that the public had notice that the hearing was taking place together with information about how to obtain access.

3. Absence of a hearing

IIA–158 Hearings may not take place at all where a domestic court decides on the basis of written submissions. It generally flows from the notion of a fair trial that an accused person is entitled to attend a trial hearing in criminal matters. Where in civil proceedings, there is no hearing before the first and only judicial instance, and the proceedings raise issues of fact and law, it is likely that a violation will arise.[9] However, in *Schuler-Zgraggen v Switzerland*, there was no oral hearing before the Federal Insurance Court in respect of a claim for invalidity insurance. While the Court found that the rules made provision for the possibility of hearing on application by a party or by the court's own motion and that there was unequivocal waiver from the applicant's failure to ask for a hearing, it also made reference to the nature of the proceedings, which were highly technical concerning private medical

---

[4] *e.g. Albert and Le Compte*, para.37, where a public hearing in the Court of Cassation did not cure the lack of publicity before the professional tribunal; *H v Belgium*, where in reinstatement proceedings by a lawyer struck from the roll the proceedings were not heard in public or decision pronounced in public—there were no circumstances such as to warrant the proceedings being held *in camera*, no indication of waiver and this was not cured by later hearings as there was no appeal; *Diennet v France*, no public hearing in disciplinary body, not cured by medical appeal body being in public since not judicial with full jurisdiction.

[5] *Stallinger and Kuso*, para.51; *Goç*, para.47; *mutatis mutandis, Malhous v Czech Republic*, July 12, 2001, where the applicant did not have a public hearing before a tribunal at first instance and the subsequent court reviews were conducted without any hearing.

[6] *Scarth v UK*, July 22, 1999—the applicant, suing for GBP 697, was refused a public hearing in arbitration procedure in the County Court.

[7] *Riepan*, para.41—where the appeal court had the power to review facts, law and sentence but did not re-hear witnesses and its review did not have the requisite scope.

[8] *Hood v UK*, (Rep.) May 28, 1998, ECHR 1999–II, para.120. Security and identity checks acceptable also in *Allen v UK*, 35580/97, (Dec.) October 22, 1998.

[9] *Fredin (No.2)*: where the Supreme Administrative Court was the only instance but refused a hearing—it had jurisdiction over facts and law and the submissions were capable of raising issues of fact and law as shown by a dissenting minority who considered that it was necessary to obtain clarifications at an oral hearing.

details and no issues of public importance, in which circumstances it considered domestic courts could have regard to reasons of expedition, efficiency and economy in avoiding holding hearings systematically. Similarly no oral hearing was shown to be necessary in a testamentary case concerning pure points of law[10] or in a social security benefits dispute where the medical reports were in agreement and no witnesses had been requested.[11]

The Government argument that the same approach should be taken to real property transaction disputes was, however, rejected by the Court in *Eisenstecken v Austria*, noting that matters of contract did not appear highly technical and the importance of what was at stake for the applicant (ownership of substantial parcels of land). Administration of justice and accountability of the State also outweighed considerations of speed and efficiency in a case for compensation for unlawful detention, where the issues could not be said to be technical in nature or could be dealt with properly on the basis of the case file alone.[12]

A hearing is not automatic for appeal or later proceedings, the Court allowing for factors of dealing expeditiously with court caseloads. The question must be settled with regard to the nature of the proceedings, the scope of examination and powers of the domestic court and the manner in which the applicant's interests are presented and protected.[13]

In leave to appeal proceedings, appeal or cassation proceedings involving only questions of law the lack of hearing may be justified by these special features.[14] Leave to appeal in a criminal case, where the applicants were not able to be present at leave to appeal against conviction and to present argument, did not raise issues of such a nature as to require their presence and since they had received free legal advice as to appeal (they had been advised no grounds arose) and were able to present written argument on all relevant issues, the interests of justice and fairness were satisfied.[15]

The fact that an appeal instance has jurisdiction over facts as well as law is not decisive, the nature of the issues to be decided in the particular case being more relevant.[16] In *Ekbatani v Sweden*, the Court found that the court of appeal could not fairly or properly determine the issues without hearing the complainant or applicant in person as the crucial question appeared to be their credibility. In *Helmers v Sweden* (a private prosecution in defamation by the applicant), the court of appeal had to examine questions of fact and law and make full assessment of the defendant's guilt

---

[10] *Varela Assalino v Portugal*, 64336/01, (Dec.) April 25, 2002; see also *Pursiheimo v Finland*, 57795/00, (Dec.) November 25, 2003, withdrawal of gun licence case (undisputed facts of alcohol abuse) where the evidence which the applicant wanted to present was not relevant to the outcome and the issues of fact and law could be adequately be dealt with on the basis of the written file.

[11] *Dory v Sweden*, November 12, 2002; in contrast, a violation arose in *Salomonsson v Sweden*, November 12, 2002, where the medical reports did differ and the applicant wished to give information on the points of difference.

[12] *Goç*: even if the unlawfulness and length of detention were not in doubt, elements of suffering relevant to moral damage and the level of compensation required that the applicant be heard.

[13] e.g. *Monnell and Morris*, para.56.

[14] *Monnell and Morris, Axen, Sutter*; see also *Bulut*, where no violation arose for lack of hearing when the Supreme Court rejected a plea of nullity in summary proceedings as manifestly lacking in merit, these being akin to leave to appeal proceedings and the nature of the grounds not such as to require a hearing.

[15] *Monnell and Morris, ibid.* Similarly, no problem arose in *Meftah v France*, July 26, 2002, ECHR 2002–VII, where the lay applicants were not allowed an oral hearing in the Court of Cassation, regard being had to the special nature of the proceedings.

[16] e.g. *Helmers*.

or innocence.[17] The Court also had regard to the seriousness of what was at stake for the applicant's professional reputation and career though it is not apparent why this would require an oral hearing which would otherwise was not warranted by the factual or legal isssues to be decided.[18] The minor importance of what is at stake appeared to play a decisive role in two other cases, *Jan-Ake Andersson v Sweden* (a road traffic offence and small fine) and *Fejde v Sweden* (illegal possession of firearm and small fine) where the Court referring to the minor nature of the penalties and the inability of the courts to increase them, found no violation for lack of oral hearing on appeal, since though the court had jurisdiction over facts and law, there were no issues which could not adequately be determined on the basis of the case-file.[19]

4. Waiver

IIA–159   A public hearing may be waived by the applicant if by his own free will and unequivocal.[20] Waiver must however not run counter to any important public interest, which appears to suggest that in serious cases the appearances of justice will require a public hearing regardless of the applicant's views.[21] Where in *Hakansson and Sturesson v Sweden*, the appeal court (the only judicial instance) had the power to hold an oral hearing but the applicants did not ask for one, this was found to constitute an unequivocal waiver of their right to a public hearing and there were no questions of public interest which would have rendered one necessary.[22] Where domestic law excludes the holding of hearings however, it is considered irrelevant whether or not the applicant asked for one. In *H v Belgium* there was no waiver although the applicant did not ask for public hearing, since there was no provision for it or practice in the procedures adopted, and little prospect of securing one.[23] In *Botten v Norway*, where the applicant made no request to be present or any

[17] See also similar reasoning in *Tierce v San Marino*, July 25, 2000, where the principal issue before the appeal judge concerned the guilt or innocence of the accused; also *Constantinescu v Romania*, June 27, 2000, paras 53–61; *Lundevall v Sweden*, November 12, 2002, para.39, concerning an assessment of the applicant's needs from a speech handicap, the Administrative Court of Appeal would have benefited from seeing him in person and a hearing could have provided relevant information for the determination of the issues.

[18] The lack of particularly convincing elements which might require a further hearing is indicated by the large dissenting minority (11 votes to 9 for violation). The importance of what was at stake for the applicants in *Monnell and Morris* was not apparently relevant in the leave to appeal proceedings. See also *Botten* where the Supreme Court had full jurisdiction, and overturned the acquittal on its assessment of "neglect" and dealing with sentencing (issues of personality and character) without hearing the applicant—reference to the effect on the applicant's professional career; *Arnarsson v Iceland*, July 15, 2003, violation where Supreme Court reversed acquittal without a hearing on the basis of its re-assessment of predominantly factual issues.

[19] The Commission found the cases indistinguishable from previous authorities, finding violations since the appeal court had jurisdiction over facts and law and had to reconsider guilt and innocence.

[20] *e.g. Albert and Le Compte*, para.35—the Court found that there was nothing in the letter or spirit of Art.6, para.1 to prevent waiver of this aspect in medical disciplinary proceedings.

[21] *Hakansson and Sturesson*, para.66.

[22] See also *Zumtobel v Austria*, September 21, 1993, Series A, No.268–A; 17 E.H.R.R. 116 unequivocal waiver found where the applicant was represented by a lawyer who did not request a hearing as was possible and the nature of the proceedings did not require a hearing (no issues of public interest); *Lundevall*, n.17 above, waiver where the applicant did not request a hearing at first instance.

[23] Also *Werner*, para.48, an applicant cannot be blamed for not making an application with no prospect of success; *Eisenstecken*, para.33.

objection, the Court found that the Supreme Court was under a positive duty to take positive measures to ensure his presence as necessary to a proper assessment.

5. Exclusion of public

There are specified exceptions to the requirement that proceedings be open to the public, *e.g.* morals, public order, national security, interest of juveniles, protection of private life of the parties or where strictly necessary in special circumstances where publicity would prejudice the interests of justice.[24]   **IIA–160**

The interests of protection of private life and the interests of justice were considered to justify the Belgian system of holding *"la procedure d'instruction"* in camera—full publicity becoming applicable after the investigation/preparatory stage when the trial of the issues began.[25]

In *B and P v United Kingdom*, where applicant fathers complained that applications for residence orders in respect of their children were heard place in chambers, the Court considered that such proceedings were prime examples of cases where the exclusion of press and public could be justified, namely, to protect the privacy of the child and parties and avoid prejudicing the interests of justice. In the latter context, it was essential, in order that the judge gain a full and accurate picture as possible of the child's situation, for parents and other witnesses to feel able to express themselves candidly on highly personal issues without fear of public curiosity or comment.[26]

Criminal trials with security problems must almost always be open to the public.[27] An escape history did not justify holding a trial in a prison, without proper access to the public, the Court noting that security concerns would only in very rare cases justify excluding the public.[28] However, as regarded disciplinary hearing in prisons, the Court considered in *Campbell and Fell* that practical difficulties in admitting the public to prison precincts or problems of transportation if the Board of Visitors met outside would render a requirement of public hearings disproportionate burden on the State.

6. Public pronouncement of judgment

The Court, faced with apparent absolute wording of this part of Art.6, noted in *Pretto v Italy*, *Axen v Germany* and *Sutter v Switzerland* that domestic courts had a variety of ways of rendering decisions public. Assuming that the drafters of the Convention could not have overlooked this, the Court refused a literal interpretation and held that the form of "publicity" to be given to the "judgment" in domestic law must be assessed in the light of the special features of the proceedings and by reference to the object and purpose of Art.6, para.1. It may be sufficient for higher   **IIA–161**

---

[24] *e.g. Guisset v France*, September 26, 2000, ECHR 2000–IX, para.73—no justification forthcoming for lack of public hearing in a disciplinary finances court. The converse, that a party or accused, could claim a right to *in camera* proceedings, has not been examined substantively as yet.

[25] *Ernst and others v Belgium*, July 15, 2003, paras 68–69.

[26] See also *AF v France*, 34596/97, (Dec.) October 21, 1998, hearing in private in medical disciplinary case justified by the evidence being given about the applicant's mental and physical state due to chronic alcholism.

[27] *Campbell and Fell*, para.87.

[28] *Riepan*, para.34.

instances with limited reviewing functions to dispense with pronouncement in open court where provision is made for some form of scrutiny by the public via publications or registries.[29]

At lower instances, the requirments are more stringent. Where there is no access to lower court judgments, there is likely to be a violation as in *Werner v Austria* and *Szucs v Austria*, in which the courts of first instance and courts of appeal did not give judgment in public nor were the full texts of their judgments openly available to the public in their registries, access limited to those with a "legitimate interest". However, in the special context of child care proceedings, the Court has found that the publication of judgments at first instance risked frustrating the aim of Art.6, para.1, which was to secure a fair hearing and that a literal interpretation should be avoided.[30] It was sufficient therefore in *B and P v United Kingdom* that anyone who could establish an interest could consult or obtain a copy and that the judgments of the first instance and appeal courts in cases of special interest were published allowing public scrutiny of their approach on such issues. It may also be sufficient where there is partial and delayed publication as in *Lamanna v Austria*, where first instance judgment on a compensation claim was summarised in the appeal court judgment which was only made public after the final decision by the Supreme Court.[31]

A violation was found in *Campbell and Fell*, since not only did the Board of Visitors not pronounce judgment publicly but also took no other steps to make their decisions public.

Cross-reference

Part IIA: Legal representation
Part IIA: Presence in court

---

[29] No violations in *Pretto*, *Axen* and *Sutter*, which concerned high instances of appeal or cassation, which had limited review powers, for example, being unable to alter the verdict but only to confirm or quash or render final. Regard was also had to whether there were public hearings and judgment at earlier stages. It was enough by way of publication in *Pretto* that the judgment of the Court of Cassation was deposited in the registry and available on demand. In *Sutter*, it was acceptable that the full text of the judgment of the military court of cassation was available from the court and this case was published in an official collection, although a dissenting minority noted the considerable delay in publication and that access was only to persons who established an interest.

[30] Particularly as it had been found justifiable to hold hearings in camera to protect the privacy of the children and parties and avoid prejudicing the interests of justice—to allow the publication of the judgment would defeat those aims.

[31] July 10, 2001.

Reasons for decisions

Key provisions:

Article 6, para.1 (fairness); para.3(b) (adequate time and facilities).   IIA–162

Key case law:

H v Belgium, November 30, 1987, Series A, No.127; 10 E.H.R.R. 339; *Van de Hurk v Netherlands*, April 19, 1994, Series A, No.288; 18 E.H.R.R. 481; *Ruiz Torija v Spain and Hiro Balani v Spain*, December 9, 1994, Series A, Nos 303–B and C; *De Moor v Belgium*, June 23, 1994, Series A, No.292; *Georgiadis v Greece*, May 29, 1997, R.J.D. 1997–III, No.38; *Higgins v France*, February 19, 1998, R.J.D. 1998–I, No.62; *Garcia Ruiz v Spain*, January 21, 1999, ECHR 1999–I.

1. General considerations

Article 6, para.1 has been interpreted as obliging courts to give reasons for their   IIA–163
decisions. This has been described as justifying their activities as a State authority, demonstrating to the parties that they have been heard and affording the possibility of having the decision reviewed on appeal.[1] A detailed answer to every argument is not required.[2] The Convention organs' resistance to constituting a fourth instance leaves in practice little scope for attacking the adequacy of the reasons given in judgments.[3] There has been no development under Art.6 as in the context of Arts 8, 9 and 10 that decisions must necessarily be supported by relevant and sufficient reasons, which requirement only comes into play where it is established that there has been an interference with a protected right. Art.6 confers primarily procedural protection based on the paramount consideration of fairness. It does not guarantee as such the "right" result and on the current approach by the Court reasoning of a decision is only likely to disclose a violation where there is clear arbitrary or grossly unreasonable failure on the part of the domestic court concerned.

2. Lack of reasons

Lack of reasons in a decision was taken as an aspect of procedural safeguards in *H v*   IIA–164
Belgium. In that case, the Bar Council's procedure was open to criticism in two respects: lack of public hearing and the lack of precision in rules or case law as to the meaning of the "exceptional circumstances" condition required for reinstatement to the Bar. The imprecise nature of the statutory concept rendered it all the more necessary for impugned decisions refusing reinstatement to give sufficient reasons. Since the decision in the case merely said that no such circumstances existed without explaining why those relied on by the applicant did not qualify, there was found to be a breach of Art.6, para.1, together with the aspect of lack of public hearing.

---

[1] *Suominen v Finland*, July 1, 2003, paras 36–37.
[2] *Van de Hurk.*
[3] e.g. *Garcia Ruiz v Spain*, para.28; *Papon v France (No.2)*, 54210/00, (Dec.) November 15, 2001, ECHR 2001–XII.

Juries in criminal cases rarely give reasoned verdicts. The relevance of this to fairness has been touched on in a few cases. Where in an Austrian case the jury in a criminal case gave no reasons for a verdict, the Commission found no unfairness since they were given detailed questions to answer on which counsel could apply to make modifications and this specificity made up for lack of reasons. In addition, the applicant could and did file grounds of nullity on basis that the judge wrongly explained the law.[4] The Court has stated that the requirement that reasons must be given must accommodate any unusual procedural features, such as the lack of requirement of jurors to give reasons. In *Papon v France (No.2)*, it was sufficient that a list of questions was put to the jurors and that the prosecution and accused could challenge any question or request additional questions be raised, the court giving a reasoned judgment in case of dispute.[5]

Lack of reasoning is likely to be more acceptable in the higher instances, in the same way that it may be compatible to dispense with oral or public hearings.[6] The Convention organs are unlikely to be demanding in the reasons given where the issues raised, from their nature or subject-matter, may legitimately receive short shrift. In a case dealing with the relatively trivial matter of a tax disc on a car,[7] the Commission found no violation where a fine was imposed by the *Cour de Cassation* without reasons when dismissing an appeal. It was enough for the Commission to note that the grounds of appeal appeared manifestly ill-founded and the *Cour de Cassation* rejected them after a thorough, amply reasoned examination.[8] In *Garcia Ruiz v Spain*, it was enough that the *Audiencia Provincial* endorsed the statement of facts and legal reasoning of the first instance court, although the Court commented that a more substantial statement of reasons might have been desirable.[9] Where there had been a detailed judgment on appeal, no problem arose where the Court of Appeal refused leave for further appeal to the House of Lords without reasons.[10]

3. Omissions and reliance on inadequate reasons

IIA–165 While a court has to give reasons, the Court has held that it is not required to answer all the points raised and that it was not its role to examine whether

---

[4] 25852/94, (Dec.) May 15, 1996. See also 15957/90, (Dec.) March 30, 1992, 72 D.R. 195, where the Commission noted that the extent to which reasons had to be given depended on the individual case, particularly its nature and complexity: although the applicant had been convicted of homicide on the simple "yes" response of the jury, the judge had put questions on the facts to the jury and the defence could contest the questions or request modifications, which compensated for the lack of reasoning and formed the framework of the decision; 20664/92, (Dec.) June 29, 1994, 78 D.R. 97.

[5] n.3 above.

[6] See Pt IIA: Public hearing.

[7] 15384/89, (Dec.) May 9, 1994, 77–A D.R. 5.

[8] *e.g.* 12275/86, (Dec.) July 2, 1991, 70 D.R. 47 where the *Conseil d'Etat* judgment dismissing an appeal and imposing a fine did not state exactly why it was vexatious, this was sufficiently shown by the fact that it rehearsed all the appeal grounds in detail finding them groundless.

[9] Also *Immeuble Group Kosser v France*, 38748/97, (Dec.) March 9, 1999 and *Bufferne v France*, 54367/00, February 26, 2002, ECHR 2002–III, where the *Conseil d'Etat* merely stated, without explanation, that no relevant points of law were made out; *Burg v France*, 34763/02, (Dec.) January 28, 2003, *Cour de Cassation* summary dismissal; *Kok v Netherlands*, 43149/98, (Dec.) July 4, 2000, ECHR 2000–VI, Supreme Court summary rejection of grounds of appeal.

[10] *Sawoniuk v UK*, (Dec.) May 29, 2001, ECHR 2001–VI; also *Nerva v UK*, 42295/98, (Dec.) July 11, 2000.

arguments are adequately met.[11] That said however, it appears that in appropriate circumstances a violation may arise however where domestic courts fail to answer relevant submissions which are not obviously ill-founded or where they make a manifest error of appreciation in the reasoning, which reflects on the fairness of the proceedings.

By way of guidance, the Court stated that the extent of the obligation to give reasons may vary according to the nature of the decision. It was necessary to take into account also the diversity of submissions that a litigant may bring into a court and the differences in Contracting States with regard to statutory provisions, customary rules, legal opinion, and the presentation and drafting of judgments -in other words, all the circumstances of the case.[12]

In *Ruiz Torija v Spain* (concerning an action against the applicant for breach in terms of lease of gaming machines) there was a total failure of the *Audencia Provincial* to address the applicant's clear and timely submission that the action was time-barred. The Court noted that it was not its role to rule if the objection was well-founded. It was enough that it was "relevant" in the sense that if the court had ruled in his favour the action would have been terminated. Conversely, the Court was not convinced that the objection was so ill-founded that it was unnecessary for the appeal court to refer to it. The first instance had allowed evidence on the point and in absence of mention in the judgment, it was not apparent whether it was impliedly rejected or whether the court had merely neglected to consider it. Since the point required an express reply not contained in a decision on the merits, there was a violation. A similar approach was adopted in *Hiro Balani v Spain*, a trademark dispute in which the applicant's claim that her trademark had priority would have been decisive if upheld. There was no answer in the Supreme Court's judgment to this "clearly relevant" submission, and the Court did not consider that it could be assumed that it was impliedly rejected. It was not so clearly ill-founded that no reply was necessary and there was a violation in the absence of that reply.[13]

Lack of detailed explanation of the finding of "gross negligence" in *Georgiadis v Greece* disclosed a violation since the lack of precision of the concept, which was decisive for the applicant's claim for compensation, required more detailed reasoning.

A clear mistake in reasoning or a failure to give reasons based on the applicable law may disclose a lack of fairness. In *Dulaurans v France*, the Court found a violation where the *Cour de Cassation* rejected the applicant's appeal on grounds that she failed to invoke a particular ground, which ignored, without explanation, the finding of the lower court and the applicant's written pleadings—the Court referred to the fact that the rejection of the appeal was based solely on a manifest error of

---

[11] *Van de Hurk*: on a general assessment of the judgment, the Court did not find it insufficiently reasoned. See also Commission's approach, *e.g.* 10153/82, (Dec.) October 13, 1986, 49 D.R.. 67: while the applicants had complained that the courts had distorted their presentation of their case, it was not the Commission's task to interfere with the legal assessment of claims made by national courts under domestic law, the application and interpretation of which was in principle reserved to them. A failure to discuss or referr explicitly to each submission was not unfair as long as the court heard the parties and their pleadings were considered. The fact that the court may have considered them as irrelevant or unfounded and implictly rejected them could not amount to a breach.

[12] *Ruiz Torija*, para.29; *Higgins*, para.26.

[13] See also *Higgins*, para.43, violation where the *Cour de Cassation* gave no reasons for not ordering a transfer of the third of three inter-connected cases from an appeal court on grounds of lack of impartiality, it being impossible to tell if this was oversight or a refusal and if so, on what grounds.

appreciation.[14] In *De Moor v Belgium*, the refusal of the Bar Council to admit the applicant as a pupil advocate disclosed a violation since it did not base itself on one of the grounds in the applicable code but held that it rejected the application in line with the practice not to admit persons who had fulfilled a full career outside Bar (which did not automatically disclose any unfitness or incompatibility under the Code). The Court phrased its finding to the effect that the bar council did not give the applicant a fair hearing since the reason which it gave was not a legally valid.[15]

Confused and contradictory reasoning which gave the applicant no clear idea of why the decision was reached disclosed a breach in *Hirvisaari v Finland*, where the Pension Board reduced the applicant's invalidity pension while at the same time referring to his deteriorating state of health and the appeal court merely upheld the decision without giving reasons of its own.[16]

4. Effective access to appeal procedures

IIA–166   Lack of reasons may raise problems under Art.6, para.3(b) or access to court, where it prevents effective use of appeal procedures. For example, issues may arise from lack of access to the judgment itself [17] or from insufficient detail as to the grounds of the first instance decision.[18] In the latter context, courts must indicate with sufficient clarity the grounds on which they base their decisions, since this is essential for the effective exercise of available rights of appeal.

[14] March 21, 2000.

[15] In addition to not providing a public hearing.

[16] September 27, 2001.

[17] *e.g.* where the appeal to Supreme Court was dismissed although the applicant had been unable to obtains copies of the judgments he was appealing against—15553/89, (Rep.) January 17, 1995, settled after admissibility.

[18] *Hadjianastassiou v Greece*, December 16, 1992, Series A, No.252: the judgment of the Court Martials Appeal Court gave only summary version of the answers to the points in issue and by the time the applicant received the full text he was barred from expanding his grounds of appeal. This restricted the defence to such an extent as to deprive him of the benefit of a fair trial.

Retrospectivity

Relevant provision:

Article 7 (prohibition of retrospective criminal offences or imposition of heavier penalties).

Relevant case law:

Sunday Times v UK (No.1), April 26, 1979, Series A, No.30; 2 E.H.R.R. 245; *Welch v UK*, February 9, 1995, Series A, No.307–A; 20 E.H.R.R. 247; *Kokkinakis v Greece*, May 25, 1993, Series A, No.260–A; 17 E.H.R.R. 397; *G v France*, September 27, 1995, Series A, No.325–B; 21 E.H.R.R. 288; *CR v UK*, November 22, 1995, Series A, No.335–B; 21 E.H.R.R. 363; *SW v UK*, November 22, 1995, Series A, No.335–C; *Cantoni v France*, November 15, 1996, R.J.D., 1996–V, No.20; *Baskaya and Okçuoglu v Turkey*, July 8, 1999, ECHR 1999–IV; 31 E.H.R.R. 292; *Coeme v Belgium*, June 22, 2000, ECHR 2000–VII; *Streletz, Kessler and Krenz v Germany*, March 22, 2001, ECHR 2001–II; *Veeber v Estonia (No.2)*, January 21, 2003, ECHR 2003–II.

1. General considerations

Article 7, an essential element of the rule of law, aims at the provision of effective safeguards against arbitrary prosecution, conviction and punishment.[1] Its importance is indicated by the fact that no derogation is possible under Art.15. It embodies the general principle that offences must be based in law, and that an individual should be able to know from the wording of the relevant provision, and if need be, with the assistance of the courts' interpretation of it, what acts and omissions will make him criminally liable.[2] That generally entails that the law must be adequately accessible—an individual must have an indication of the legal rules applicable in a given case—and he must be able to foresee the consequences of his actions, in particular, to be able to avoid incurring the sanction of the criminal law.[3]

In terms of the standard of legal certainty or foreseeability, absolute certainty cannot be required, and indeed may be undesirable, entailing the risk of excessive rigidity, since the law has to be able to keep pace with changing circumstances.[4] A

---

[1] *SW*, para.34.

[2] *e.g. Kokkinakis*, para.52; *SW*, para.35; *Baskaya and Okçuoglu*, paras 36–39, where "printed matter other than periodicals" covered books; *Schimanek v Austria*, 32307/96, (Dec.) February 1, 2000, "activities inspired by National Socialist ideas" was sufficiently precise.

[3] *e.g. G v France*, para.25, where notwithstanding changes in legislation leading to reclassification of the sexual offences of which the applicant was accused, these fell within the scope of the Criminal Code provisions, which were accessible and foreseeable.

[4] *e.g. Streletz, Kessler and Krenz*, concerning the trial of East German leaders, the fact that domestic courts had different interpretations of the old regime's legal provisions reflected the legal complexity of the case and as domestic law was largely for the interpretation of those courts, the Court did not find a problem under Art.7, particularly since in its view the conduct in question had been an offence at the relevant time; *Glassner v Germany*, 46363/99, (Dec.) June 28, 2001, ECHR 2001–VII, the conviction of a public prosecutor for deliberate perversion of justice in the trial of an opponent to the regime was similarly acceptable.

standard of "reasonable foreseeability" is sufficient.[5] The Court in *CR* and *SW v United Kingdom* noted that judicial interpretation of criminal law provisions was a widespread and even necessary feature. Article 7 could not be read as prohibiting the gradual clarification of the rules of criminal liability through judicial interpretation from case to case, but the resultant development must be within the bounds of reasonable foreseeability and not alter the "essence" of the offence.[6] Nor should the criminal law be extensively construed to an applicant's detriment, for example, by analogy.[7] Changes which are not to the accused's detriment escape the prohibition.[8]

Retrospective measures in other spheres are not expressly prohibited under the Convention and whether they offend will generally depend on the aims pursued and the proportionality of the effects.[9]

2. Retrospective criminal offences

IIA–169   The complaints brought tend to raise issues less of new statutes or laws being introduced or applied with retrospective effect but of the uncertainty or lack of precision of those unarguably in existence. In these cases, the issues depend on the analysis of whether or not in a particular jurisdiction at a particular time a legal provision complied with the requirement of reasonable foreseeability. In assessing this, the Commission considered that knowledge of specialised or technical provisions may be assumed amongst those persons who work in a particular field.[10]

The Convention organs have also qualified the reasonable certainty test with reference to the hypothetical person seeking appropriate legal advice.[11] In *Cantoni v France*, where there was allegedly inconsistent case law on the application of the term "medicinal product", the Court noted that a law may still satisfy the requirement of foreseeability, even if the individual has to take appropriate legal advice to assess the consequences of a given action. This was particularly so in respect of persons engaged in professional or commercial activities entailing a certain degree of risk.[12]

The borderline between reasonable and unreasonable development is an uneasy one. Clarification of an element of an offence will presumably not infrequently extend the criminal law to conduct previously thought to be excluded. For example, where the German courts interpreted an offence of coercion as extending to the applicant's participation in a sit-in in a public road, the Commission commented

---

[5] *Sunday Times*, para.49.

[6] *SW*, para.36; *CR*, para.34.

[7] *Baskaya and Okçuoglu*: violation where domestic courts by analogy extended the power of sentencing to imprisonment from another provision.

[8] *Kokkinakis*, para.52; *G v France*, para.26: to the extent the law applied retrospectively, it mitigated the seriousness of the offence.

[9] See: Fair trial guarantees, Legislative interference in proceedings; Tax.

[10] *e.g.* concerning a criminal prosecution of a butcher for failure to comply with food standards legislation—8141/78, (Dec.) December 4, 1978, 16 D.R.141.

[11] 8710/79, (Dec.) May 7, 1982, 28 D.R. 77 the applicants, convicted for blasphemous libel, alleged that the law lacked clarity, *e.g.* that the lack of intention to blaspheme was not established until their own case. The Commission found that courts could clarify existing elements and adapt to new circumstances. The findings in the applicants' case were an acceptable clarification and reasonably foreseeable with appropriate legal advice.

[12] See also *Chauvy v France*, 64915/01, (Dec.) September 23, 2003, where an editor and publishing house were to be presumed as having access to specialised legal advice and to be aware of the risks involved in publishing.

that extensive interpretation with a view to adapting an offence to the developments in society was acceptable if it could be reasonably brought under the concept of the offence and was foreseeable by the citizen. It concluded that this example of judicial creativity was compatible with Art.7.[13]

In marital rape cases from the UK which concerned the domestically controversial judicial abolition of an exemption from rape previously enjoyed by husbands, the Court had no difficulty accepting that the interpretation was reasonably foreseeable as part of a discernable trend of judicial interpretation.[14] It also had regard to the nature of the conduct, namely, rape which was essentially degrading, as showing that the development could not be said to be contrary to the purpose of Art.7 and was in fact in conformity with the fundamental objectives of the Convention, the essence of which was respect for human dignity and freedom. This would seem to indicate that judicial developments which are otherwise in conformity with the spirit of the Convention or relate to inherently objectionable conduct will be more readily found to be reasonably foreseeable.

In a similar vein, the Court commented that the ex-leaders of East German regime who had flagrantly disregarded the principles of legality could not plead the protection of Art.7 after German re-unification when they were tried concerning their responsibility for the deaths of persons shot while attempting to cross to the West.[15]

Changes in procedural rules which affect applicants' prospects of conviction detrimentally do not *per se* infringe Art.7, the Court recognising the general principle that procedural rules apply immediately to proceedings already under way. Thus, extension of a limitation period through the immediate application of a procedural law was not in violation of Art.7 in *Coeme v Belgium* where the relevant offences had never become subject to limitation. It was left open whether there would be a breach if a law restored the possibility of prosecuting acts which had become time-barred under the previous provisions.

For a Contracting State to rely on the argument that the applicant's conduct constituted a continuing offence committed after the entry into force of new or amended criminal provisions, the acts concerned must be clearly set out in the indictment and the decision of the courts make it clear that the ingredients of a continuing offence were made out by the prosecution.[16] Where offences related exclusively or even partly to acts which predated the amendment in the law, this did not form part of a "continuing offence."[17]

---

[13] 13079/87, (Dec.), March 6, 1989, 60 D.R. 256.

[14] There was a line of cases whittling away the application of the immunity. See however the substantial dissenting minority of the Commission who found that the abolition of a defence to husbands in circumstances in which it had previously been available went too far and should have been done by legislation, not retrospectively by the courts, a view shared by the Law Commission.

[15] *Streletz, Kessler and Krenz*, para.88. Nor in *KH v Germany*, March 22, 2001, ECHR 2001–I, could an individual soldier who shot unarmed people crossing the border rely on blind obedience to orders and the attitude of the regime where the acts nonetheless flagrantly infringed legal principles and internationally protected human rights.

[16] *Ecer and Zeyrek v Turkey*, February 27, 2001, ECHR 2001–III, para.33—in this case the terms of the indictment were inconsistent with the idea of a "continuing offence", not specifying any acts after the crucial date.

[17] *Veeber (No.2)*, paras 35–36; *Puhk v Estonia*, February 10, 2004, para.39.

3. Imposition of heavier penalties

IIA–170 Article 7, in its second sentence, prohibits the imposition of a heavier penalty than that applicable at the time of the offence. This may be contravened by a failure to apply the relevant sentencing rules[18] as well as by the retrospective application of new laws.[19]

However not all changes which have sentencing consequences to the detriment of persons awaiting trial or already convicted will fall foul of this provision. It does not apply where on appeal a sentence is increased within the statutory maximum which could have been imposed at first instance.[20] Where an offence is reclassified to allow it to be tried in a different court where the powers of sentencing are different, the applicant may be sentenced more heavily than he might otherwise anticipated but if the sentence is still within the statutory maximum applicable at the time of the offence the provision is not breached.[21] Nor was there any retroactivity where, due to delay in the trial, the applicant became fifteen and thus eligible for a custodial sentence.[22]

A significant impact on punishment was felt by life prisoners when the practice in parole changed to exclude the possibility of release before a minimum of 20 years for certain categories of murderers and other serious offenders. However since the harsh effect related rather to the execution of the penalty than to its imposition, the measure was compatible with Art.7.[23]

The notion of "penalty" has also been considered in a number of cases.[24] For the Court the starting point is whether the measure in question is imposed following conviction for a criminal offence.[25] Other relevant factors in identifying a "penalty" are the nature and purpose of the measure; its characterisation under domestic law; the procedures involved in its making and implementation and its severity. It was not found to cover the retrospective imposition on released sex offenders of an obligation to register with police.[26]

However, in *Welch v United Kingdom*, the retrospective imposition of a confiscation order on a suspect convicted of drugs offences concerned penalties having regard to its integral part of the conviction and sentencing process and the punitive nature of the measure.[27] Similarly, imposition of imprisonment ordered by a criminal court for non-payment of fines where intended to be a deterrent has also been found to

---

[18] *Gabarri Moreno v Spain*, July 22, 2003, paras 23–34.

[19] See *Ecer and Zeyrek*, n.16 above, where the applicants were tried for assisting the PKK by conduct carried out in 1988–1989, but sentenced according to a 1991 statute that increased by 50% the applicable sentence.

[20] *e.g.* 12002/86, (Dec.) March 8, 1988, 55 D.R. 218.

[21] 14099/88, (Dec.) April 14, 1989 where the sentencing powers of the Sheriff in Scotland in particular cases increased between the applicant's conviction and sentence—the Sheriff had always had powers to refer to a higher court if he considered his own powers inadequate.

[22] *Taylor v UK*, 48864/99, (Dec.) December 3, 2002.

[23] 11653/85, (Dec.) March 3, 1986, 46 D.R. 231; *Grava v Italy*, July 10, 2003, para.51: a Presidential decree on pardon concerned the execution of sentence not the penalty itself.

[24] See Pt IIA: Fair trial, Criminal Charge (penalties).

[25] *e.g. Jamil*, para.31.

[26] *Adamson v UK*, 42293/98, (Dec.) January 26, 1999: registration was seen as an administrative and preventive measure imposed separately from ordinary sentencing procedures.

[27] *e.g.* the sweeping statutory assumptions that all money in the possession of a convicted trafficker were proceeds of crime unless proved otherwise; that the judge could take into account culpability in allotting confiscation between various co-accused; and the possibility of imprisonment in default of payment.

involve a penalty and Art.7 was accordingly violated where a drug trafficker on conviction was subject to application of a retrospective law which increased the period of imprisonment in default of payment from a maximum of four months to two years.[28]

A distinction has also been drawn between preventive confiscation and punitive confiscatory measures, retrospectivity being prohibited only in respect of the latter. In *M v Italy*,[29] where a suspected participant in organised crime was subject to confiscation measures imposed retrospectively by an administrative tribunal separate from the criminal proceedings taken against him, the Commission distinguished between penal measures and measures with a preventive aim, such as the judicial investigation of the probable source of revenue of a person and its removal to prevent future use in a criminal organisation.

4. The exception: general principles of law of civilised nations

This exception in the second paragraph of Art.7 has so far been applied in several French cases, where the applicants had been convicted of crimes for acts committed during the Second World War. The Commission noted that the purpose of the second paragraph was to ensure that the rule against retrospectivity did not affect laws, which in the wholly exceptional circumstances at the end of Second World War were passed in order to punish war crimes, treason and collaboration. It applied equally to subsequent legislation on crimes against humanity.[30] Where the exception applies, it appears that the Court will not intervene to review the correctness of domestic courts' decisions or their interpretation of the applicable law.[31]

IIA–171

In *SW v United Kingdom*, the trial judge in the domestic proceedings had taken the view that the case fell within the exception in the second paragraph as concerning conduct (rape) which at the time it was committed was criminal according to the general principles of civilised nations. The Court and Commission's majority did not deal with the point. Mr Loucaides in his dissenting opinion in the Commission noted that the *travaux préparatoires* indicated that this provision was intended to cover prosecution of crimes against humanity in the context of the Nuremberg trials. While he did not exclude that other conduct might fall within the meaning of the phrase, a similar common law immunity for rape in the marital area existed or had existed until recently in a number of common law jurisdictions and he was not prepared to find sufficient international consensus as regarded marital rape. Rape as a systematic policy or inflicted by soldiers, however, is now expressly included within the definition of crimes against humanity and war crimes in the Statute of the International Criminal Court.

---

[28] *Jamil v France*, June 8, 1995, Series A, No.317; 21 E.H.R.R. 65: where the Court rejected the Government's argument that the measure was analagous to the seizure of property to compensate the damage suffered through the illegal import of prohibited goods.
[29] 12386/86, (Dec.) April 15, 1991, 70 D.R. 59.
[30] 29420/95, (Dec.) January 13, 1997, 88–B D.R. 148; *Papon v France*, 54210/00, (Dec.) November 15, 2001, ECHR 2001–XII.
[31] *Papon*, n.30 above.

Right to silence

Key provisions:

IIA–172 Article 6, para.1 (right to a fair trial); para.2 (presumption of innocence).

Key case law:

Funke v France, February 25, 1993, Series A, No.256–A; 16 E.H.R.R. 297; *John Murray v UK*, February 8, 1996, R.J.D. 1996–I, No.10; 22 E.H.R.R. 29; *Saunders v UK*, December 17, 1996, R.J.D. 1997–VII, No.53; 23 E.H.R.R. 313; *Condron v UK*, May 2, 2000, ECHR 2000–V; 31 E.H.R.R. 1; *Heaney and McGuinness v Ireland*, December 21, 2000, ECHR 2000–XII; *JB v Switzerland*, May 3, 2001, ECHR 2001–III; *Allan v UK*, November 5, 2002, ECHR 2002–IX.

1. General considerations

IIA–173 The right to silence has made a relatively recent appearance in the case-law dealing with procedural fairness in criminal trials. It appears to achieve more prominence in the Anglo-saxon systems, with the formalised system of cautions and the importance attached to oral evidence. There is however all over Europe an increase in the type of criminal/fiscal provisions which place defendants in the position whereby they are required to provide information on pain of a penalty.

In *Funke v France*, the Court laid down the general principle that Art.6, para.1 contains the right to anyone charged with a criminal offence to remain silent and not to incriminate himself. The right to remain silent under police questioning and the privilege against self-incrimination were found in *John Murray v United Kingdom* to be generally recognised international standards lying at the heart of the notion of a fair procedure and by providing an accused with protection against improper compulsion contributed to avoiding miscarriages of justice.

2. Coercion to provide incriminating documents or oral testimony

IIA–174 There are two situations which appear: firstly, where an individual is punished in some way for failing to provide information or material and, secondly, where information obtained by use of compulsory powers is used in a criminal prosecution. The approach taken by the Court in these cases is somewhat hard to reconcile analytically, and the leading case *Funke* has, as decided on its facts, attracted particular criticism.[1]

(a) *Penalties imposed for failure to provide information or documents*

IIA–175 In *Funke* itself, the Court found that the imposition of fines by the French customs on the applicant for failing to disclose documents concerning his financial trans-actions violated Art.6, para.1 as offending the principle against self-incrimination. The Commission had reached a different opinion, considering that the protection of

---

[1] *e.g.* SH Naismith, "Self-incrimination: Fairness or freedom"; [1997] 3 E.H.R.L.R.

a State's vital economic interests legitimately and reasonably required individuals to produce documents relating to matters within customs and fiscal control. It was to be viewed, not as a means of facilating prosecutions, but as essential for the implementation of the legislation in question and as a reasonable corollary of the trust reposed in citizens generally, allowing the State to forgo more restrictive measures of control and supervision. The Commission had in mind fiscal powers common everywhere in Europe which require disclosure of income which can be used as the basis of tax evasion proceedings. The Court found, without elucidating, that the special feature of customs law did not justify the coercion applied in this case.

Since then, it has been recognised that the requirement *per se* to provide information to the authorities under threat of penalty does not infringe the privilege against self-incrimination.

Although the cases are difficult to reconcile at times, the Court appears to be paying attention to whether the individual is subject to a criminal charge at the time, the nature and severity of the penalty and the type of material or information concerned.

Thus, in *Saunders v United Kingdom*, where the applicant gave oral testimony under compulsory powers in a company inquiry conducted by DTI inspectors, the procedure in the inquiry itself was not regarded as falling under the scope of Art.6. The applicant had not been charged at that time. It was the use of the transcripts in the subsequent criminal prosecution that offended Art.6. The Court also distinguished in that case material obtained through coercion or oppression against the will of the accused (*e.g.* confessions, incriminating statements) from the use of material obtained through compulsory powers, such as blood or other physical samples, documents obtained pursuant to a warrant, which have an existence independent of the will of the accused.

Following the approach of the Court in *Saunders* rather than *Funke*, the Commission subsequently found no infringement of Art.6, para.1 in the context of blood samples obtained under threat of prosecution;[2] and the requirement to provide information to the tax authorities.[3]

Unacceptable compulsion was imposed on the applicants in *Heaney and McGuinness v Ireland*, when they were convicted for failing to account for their movements to the police as required by s.52 of the Offences against the State Act 1939 and sentenced to six months' imprisonment. As they had been arrested on suspicion of involvement in a bombing and could be regarded as subject to a criminal charge at the time, the application of s.52 with a view to compelling them to provide information relating to charges against them destroyed the very essence of their privilege against self-incrimination and their right to remain silent. It would also appear that in *JB v Switzerland* it was the imposition of fines, which were not inconsiderable, on the applicant's failure to provide documents about his income at the time criminal tax evasion proceedings were pending that infringed the privilege against self-incrimination. However the finding of self-incrimination in that case concerning failure to provide documents would seem difficult to reconcile with the *Saunders* classification of documents as having an existence independent of the person concerned and outside the category of information obtained in defiance of the will of that person.

---

[2] 30551/96, (Dec.) April 9, 1997.

[3] *e.g.* 27943/95, (Dec.) February 26, 1997, 88–A D.R. 120 where the information was used in tax fraud and evasion proceedings.

In a later case, *Allen v United Kingdom*,[4] the Court emphasised that the right not to incriminate onself was primarily concerned with respecting the will of an accused person to remain silent in the context of criminal proceedings and the use of compulsorily obtained statements in criminal prosecutions: it did not *per se* prohibit the use of compulsory powers to require persons to provide information about their financial or company affairs. The Court noted that the obligation to disclose income and capital for the purpose of tax assessment was a common feature in Contracting States and it would be difficult to envisage taxation systems functioning effectively without it. It also pointed out that not every measure taken to encourage individuals to give information must be regarded as improper compulsion. The requirement therefore for an applicant to provide details of his assets under threat of a fine of up to £300 did not infringe Art.6. This appears to imply that measures imposing small fines will not be regarded as sufficiently coercive. The fact that the applicant was then prosecuted for giving inaccurate information could also be distinguished from cases involving convictions based on the incriminating content of the statements provided. Privilege against self-incrimination could not, the Court said, be regarded as giving a general immunity to actions (*e.g.* perjury) motived by the desire to evade investigation by the revenue authorities.

A distinction between a penalty imposed for giving inaccurate information and that for failing to provide incriminating information was also drawn in *Web v Austria*, in which the Court had to consider a speeding case. While the Commission had previously found it acceptable to fine owners when their cars were caught in speed traps, or illegally parked, and they did not name the driver at the time,[5] the Court noted that these decisions did not take into account the right to silence identified in *Funke*. However, as the owner in this case was penalised for giving inaccurate information about the driver of the car at the relevant time and no prosecution was pending against him in respect of the speeding charge, the majority considered there was insufficient connection with a "criminal charge" to cause a self-incrimination problem.[6]

Where a person is fined for failure to give evidence in proceedings in which he is a witness, the approach has been similarly unclear. In *K v Austria*,[7] the fine was treated as interference with freedom of expression, Art.6 not being applicable to proceedings in which the applicant was not subject to a criminal charge. In *Serves v France*, however, where the applicant refused to take the oath to appear as a witness before an investigating judge in a murder case, the Court found that the applicant could be considered subject to "criminal charge" for the purposes of Art.6. However, the fines imposed on him for his refusal did not constitute measures compelling himself to incriminate himself. Although the applicant had, on his account, refused since he did not wish to answer incriminating questions, the Court took the rather narrow view that the fines were imposed on him for refusing to take

---

[4] 76574/01, (Dec.) September 10, 2002, ECHR 2002–VIII.

[5] 23816/94, (Dec.) May 17, 1995 where a car owner was fined when his car was caught in a speed trap and he alleged coercion, either to be convicted himself or inform on another. The Commission saw no problem with the right to silence, since the car used to commit the offence was registered in the applicant's name and he had the overall responsibility for the use to which the car was put.

[6] The minority noted that if he had admitted that he was the driver a criminal prosecution would surely have followed, to which his defence possibilities would have been minimal. The situation where an applicant has been penalised for refusing to name the driver, or prosecuted following an admission, have yet to be considered by the Court.

[7] 16002/91, (Rep.) October 13, 1992, Series A, No.255–B (settled before the Court).

the oath, a requirement to ensure truthfulness which did not force witnesses to answer specific questions.[8]

(b) *Use of material obtained by compulsion in criminal prosecutions*

In *Saunders v United Kingdom*, where transcripts of evidence given by the applicant   **IIA–176** under compulsory powers of DTI inspectors were used in the later criminal prosecution, the Court identified the essence of the privilege against self-incrimination as requiring the prosecution to prove their case without resort to evidence obtained through coercion or oppression against the will of the accused and accordingly found a violation of Art.6. While the Government argued that the statements to the inspectors were in fact exculpatory, the Court found that use of admissions of knowledge, which were relevant to credibility or contradicted other evidence, could be used by the prosecution to incriminatory effect.

As to whether there may be legitimate restrictions on the privilege against self-incrimination, the Court in *Saunders* also rejected the Government's argument that the complexity of corporate fraud and the vital public interest justified the measures applied, even with alleged procedural safeguards. The right applied in criminal proceedings without distinction.

Indirect methods of coercion in obtaining incriminating statements may also fall foul of Art.6. In *Allan v United Kingdom,* the applicant's conviction rested to a significant degree on the evidence given by an informer who had been placed in his cell and coached by the police to "push him for what you can" while at the same time putting him under pressure in normal interviews. The Court noted that freedom to remain silent was effectively undermined where a suspect, who has remained silent during police questioning, is subject to subterfuge to elicit answers to the same questions. In this case it found that the applicant had been subject to psychological pressures while he was in a susceptible position and thus the information could be regarded as having been obtained involuntarily and in defiance of his will. Thus the use of the information at trial impinged on his right to silence.

3. Drawing of inferences from silence

In *John Murray*, the Court held that the right to silence was not absolute and while   **IIA–177** it might be incompatible to base a conviction solely or mainly on an accused's silence or on a refusal to answer questions, it was equally obvious that the privilege did not prevent an accused's silence being taken into account in situations which clearly called for an explanation. It had been alleged that the inferences which could be drawn from the failure of a suspect in Northern Ireland either to give explanations to the police for his presence at the scene of a crime or to give evidence at trial amounted to violations of both the right to fair trial and presumption of innocence. However, in this case, the applicant had not been subject to direct coercion of the type in *Funke* and *Saunders*, being neither fined nor threatened with imprisonment. Having regard to the position in other Contracting States where the conduct of the accused can be freely taken into account in the assessment of the

---

[8] The Court minority and the Commission majority found that the fines were penalties attracting the guarantees of Art.6 and that a violation arose from the imposition of the fine without taking the privilege against self-discrimination properly into account.

evidence, the Court found that the use of inferences was an expression of the common sense implication drawn where an accused fails to provide an innocent explanation for his actions or presence at the scene of a crime. In the particular case, where the applicant was found at a house where an IRA kidnap victim was being held and there was other evidence implicating him, there were sufficient safeguards to comply with fairness and the general burden of proof remained with the prosecution who had to establish a *prima facie* case before the inference could be brought into play by the judge, who sat without a jury.[9] The Court did however find a violation of Art.6, para.3(c) in that the applicant was denied access to legal advice as to his position at a stage of police questioning which might irretrievably prejudice the defence.

Where it is the jury, rather than the judge, which has the role of drawing any adverse inferences, the Court examines whether the judge's direction to the jury reflects the proper balance between the right to silence and the circumstances in which an adverse inference can be drawn from silence. Particular caution is required when weight is to be attached to silence to police questioning and where an accused has been advised by his lawyer to maintain silence this must be given appropriate weight.[10] In *Condron v United Kingdom*, there was a breach of fairness where the judge mentioned the applicants' reasons for not answering police questions (namely the advice of their solicitor who had doubts about their fitness to cope) but did so in terms that left the jury at liberty to draw inferences even if satisfied as to the plausibility of the explanation. As it was not possible to tell what significance inferences played in the jury's decision to convict and as it was their role to draw inferences, properly directed, the defective summing-up could not be cured on appeal.[11]

It is not however every shortcoming in a summing-up that will be incompatible with the exercise of an accused's right to silence, whether in a police station or in the witness box. Examining the essential gist of the judge's direction and whether the key elements regarding the exercise of the right to silence appear, the Court has in a number of cases found the alleged misdirections or omissions did not render the proceedings unfair and that the direction was nonetheless confined in a manner compatible with the applicant's exercise of his right to silence.[12]

Cross-reference

Part IIA: Fairness: general principles
Part IIA: Legal representation in criminal proceedings
Part IIA: Presumption of innocence

---

[9] See also *Averill v UK*, June 6, 2000, paras 44–52, where the presence of incriminating fibres on the applicant called for an explanation and no violation arose from the judge's drawing of very strong adverse inferences from his silence to police questioning.

[10] *Condron*, para.59.

[11] paras 63–66, distinguishing *Edwards v UK*, December 16, 1992, Series A, No.247–B, paras 34 and 39. See also *Beckles v UK*, October 8, 2002, paras 61–66, where the judge failed to direct the jury not to draw inferences if satisfied by the accused's explanation for silence and indeed his comments had undermined the explanation.

[12] The Court has also had regard to whether counsel objected at the time to the judge's direction and to other procedural safeguards, *e.g.* that the judge has verified whether the accused is aware of the possible consequences of not giving evidence. See *Marlow v UK*, 42015/98, (Dec.) December 5, 2000; *Smith v UK*, 64714/01, (Dec.) December 12, 2002.

Sentencing

Key provisions:

Article 6 (fair trial); Art.3 (inhuman and degrading punishment).

IIA–178

Key case law:

Weeks v UK, March 2, 1987, Series A, No.114; 10 E.H.R.R. 293; *Hussein v UK* and *Singh v UK*, February 21, 1996, R.J.D. 1996–I, No.4; *V v UK*, December 16, 1999, ECHR 1999–IX.

1. General considerations

Matters of sentencing generally fall outside the scope of the Convention.[1] It is irrelevant whether a burglar is sentenced to five years or ten or whether a suspended sentence is granted for mitigating circumstances. There have been a few hints that a sentence may be so disproportionate that it could disclose a violation. For example, in *Hussein v United Kingdom* and *Prem Singh v United Kingdom*, the Convention organs agreed with the applicants that a true life sentence imposed on children even for murder would raise problems under Art.3, while in *V v United Kingdom*, the Court referred to the ban on life imprisonment of children without possibility of release in Art.37 of the UN Convention on the Rights of the Child.[2] Indeterminate sentences for adults have been found compatible with the Convention where there is sufficient link between the original conviction and continuing detention,[3] although there are also indications that a life sentence for an adult without possibility of release could raise issues under Art.3.[4] Issues of arbitrariness could also arise under Art.5 where sentencing provisions make no allowance for the individual circumstances of the offender or the offence.[5]

IIA–179

2. Discrimination

However, a measure, which might not in itself offend, may do so if applied in a discriminatory manner. As regards sentencing policies or practices, this has been touched on in a number of cases but no findings of violation made as yet. In *P v*

IIA–180

---

[1] *e.g. Weeks*, para.72; *Sawoniuk v UK*, (Dec.) May 29, 2001, ECHR 2001–VI, concerning the imprisonment for life of a very elderly and infirm convict .

[2] While it accepted that children could be subject to punitive sentences and detained under an indeterminate sentence allowing for continued detention where necessary for the protection of the public, it commented that an unjustifiable and persistent failure to fix the tariff (the minimum period representing punishment and deterrence), leaving the applicant in uncertainty for many years over his future could raise issues under Art.3.

[3] *Weeks*, (Rep.) December 12, 1993, para.73.

[4] 7994/77, (Dec.) May 6, 1978, 14 D.R. 239; *Einhorn v France*, 71555/01, (Dec.) October 16, 2001, ECHR 2001–XI.

[5] *e.g. Partington v UK* 58853/00, (Dec.) June 26, 2003, concerning s.2 of the Crime (Sentences) Act 1997 which required the imposition of a life sentence on the commission of a third serious offence: since however the Court of Appeal had interpreted the legislation to allow a lesser sentence to be imposed in "exceptional circumstances", no arbitrariness arose under Art.5, para.1.

United Kingdom, complaints concerning different regimes applicable to boys and girls was settled.[6] In *Nelson v United Kingdom*, a juvenile offender in Scotland claimed that he was not able to benefit from remission in sentence unlike adults or children in England and Wales. The Commission commented that while complaints about length of sentence, passed after due process of law by a judge in possession of the facts of the case, would not fall within the scope of the Convention, a settled sentencing policy which affected individuals in a discriminatory fashion might raise issues of Art.14 in conjunction with Art.5. However in the actual case, any difference with adults was justified since different considerations applied in relation to children and any difference between the regime in Scotland and that in England and Wales was based on geographical grounds and not on personal status.[7]

In *Grice v United Kingdom*, the Commission also commented that discriminatory release procedures would be problematic but did not find that the applicant AIDS sufferer had substantiated his complaint that prisoners suffering from other illnesses were better treated than he was as regarded compassionate release.[8]

3. Fair trial

IIA–181 Procedural rights under Art.6 apply equally to criminal proceedings dealing with sentence. Thus failure to conform with fairness and guarantees of legal representation prior to the passing of sentence may lead to violation.[9]

The sentencing aspect of a trial cannot be usurped by the executive. The role of the Home Secretary in the fixing of tariff (the part of sentence representing punishment and deterrence) in various types of life sentences imposed by courts disclosed a violation of Art.6, in particular as he could not be said to be a tribunal independent of the executive.[10]

Cross-reference

Part IIA: General principles
Part IIA: Legal representation in criminal proceedings
Part IIA: Retrospectivity, Retrospective imposition of heavier penalties

---

[6] 15397/89, (Dec.) January 8, 1992.

[7] 11077/84, (Dec.), October 13, 1986, 49 D.R. 170.

[8] 22564/93, (Dec.) April 14, 1994, 77–A D.R. 90; see also 22761/93, (Dec.) April 4, 1994, 77–A D.R. 98 where an AIDS sufferer claimed that AIDS was not taken into account as a mitigating factor in sentence unlike other illnesses but specifically excluded. However no discrimination was made out on the facts of the case.

[9] *e.g.* lack of legal aid on sentencing appeal in *Murdoch v UK (No.2)*, 25523/94 (Rep.) October 16, 1996; independence and impartiality in *Findlay v UK*, February 25, 1997, R.J.D. 1997–I, No.30.

[10] *V v UK*, para.120, concerning children detained during Her Majesty's pleasure; *Easterbrook v UK*, June 12, 2003, paras 26–29 and *Stafford v UK*, May 28, 2002, ECHR 2002–IV, para.87, concerning adult mandatory life prisoners.

Tribunal established by law

Key provision:

Article 6, para.1 (fair trial before a tribunal established by law).   IIA–182

Key case law:

Le Compte v Belgium, June 23, 1981, Series A, No.43; 4 E.H.R.R 1; *Campbell and Fell v UK*, June 28, 1984, Series A, No.80; 7 E.H.R.R 1; *Sramek v Austria*, October 22, 1984, Series A, No.84; 7. E.H.R.R. 351; *H v Belgium*, November 30, 1987, Series A, No.127; 10 E.H.R.R. 339; *Belilos v Switzerland*, April 29, 1988, Series A, No.132; 10 E.H.R.R. 466; *Demicoli v Malta*, August 27, 1991, Series A, No.210; 14 E.H.R.R. 47; *Pfeiffer and Plankl v Austria*, February 25, 1992, Series A, No.227; 14 E.H.R.R. 692; *Van de Hurk v Netherlands*, April 19, 1994, Series A, No.288; 18 E.H.R.R. 481; *Beaumartin v France*, November 24, 1994, Series A, No.296–B; 19 E.H.R.R. 485; *Procola v Luxembourg*, September 28, 1995, Series A, No.326; 22 E.H.R.R. 193; *Bulut v Austria*, February 22, 1996, R.J.D. 1996–II, No.5; 24 E.H.R.R. 84; *Coeme v Belgium*, June 22, 2000, ECHR 2000–VII; *Posokhov v Russia*, March 4, 2003, ECHR 2003–IV.

1. General considerations

Civil rights and obligations or criminal charges must be determined by a "tribunal   IIA–183
established by law".

A tribunal does not have to be court of the "classic" kind integrated with the standard judicial machinery[1] but the fact that it carries out judicial functions is not enough.[2] Even a court, which generally fulfills the ordinary conception of a judicial organ, may in certain circumstances lose this classification. According to the case law it must be a body independent of the parties, in particular of the executive, and impartial, upon which national legislation confers a power of binding decision in a particular area.[3] This is sometimes expressed as involving substantive aspects, namely its judicial function in determining matters within its competence on the basis of rules of law and after proceedings conducted in a prescribed manner, and also procedural aspects, *inter alia*, independence, impartiality, duration of members' terms of office.[4] There is an obvious overlap with the separate requirements of independence and impartiality contained in Art.6, para.1.

2. Lack of legal basis

A court which acts in disregard of legal provisions governing its jurisdiction and   IIA–184
composition may cease to be regarded as "established by law."[5]

---

[1] *Campbell and Fell*, para.76.

[2] *Le Compte*, para.55.

[3] *Sramek*, para.36; *Lecompte*, para.55; Commission report, para.114, in *McMichael v UK*, February 24, 1995, Series A, No.307–B the Children's Panel was not a tribunal as *inter alia* it was intended not to be a court but to deal with children's cases in a non-contentious manner.

[4] *Belilos*, para.64.

[5] The phrase established by law covers not only the legal basis for the existence of the tribunal but its composition in each case—*Buscarini v San Marino*, 31657/96, (Dec.) May 4, 2000.

In *Coeme v Belgium*, there was not at the relevant time any basis in domestic law for the Court of Cassation to try anyone but a minister and therefore the Court of Cassation could not be considered a "tribunal established by law" in conducting the trial of four other applicants at the same time as the minister. Failure to conform with the rules regarding the listing of names of lay members of the District Court and their length of service disclosed a violation in *Posokhov v Russia*, where there was no legal basis for the participation of two jurors in the applicant's trial.[6]

Since however it is primarily for domestic courts to interpret national law, including the rules governing their own constitution and procedures, the Court has stated that its supervisory role will only come into play in cases of flagrant disregard of applicable laws.[7]

3. Plurality of roles

IIA–185   The mere fact that a body has a plurality of functions (administrative, regulatory, adjudicative, advisory or disciplinary) does not exclude it from being a tribunal. Thus, in *H v Belgium*, the Court considered that the *Conseil de l'ordre d'avocats* could be considered a tribunal as it was exercising a judicial function in deciding on the application for readmission and its impartiality and independence were beyond dispute.[8] However, in *Procola v Luxembourg*, in the context of structural impartiality, the Court found that the fact that four out of five members of the *Conseil d'Etat* acted in both advisory and judicial functions in the same case was capable of casting legitimate doubt on their impartiality.[9]

4. Disqualified judges

IIA–186   The Court has held that the right to be tried by a court whose composition is in accordance with law is a right of essential importance, whose exercise does not depend on the parties alone. There was a violation therefore in *Pfeiffer and Plankl v Austria*, where two disqualified judges sat in circumstances where domestic law did not permit waiver. Where however in *Bulut v Austria*, there was a disqualified judge who sat but counsel waived objection during the proceedings, the Court found that domestic law permitted waiver and that the matter was examined by higher courts which found the composition of the lower court complied with the law.[10]

5. Power to decide

IIA–187   The power to render a binding decision, which may not be altered by a non-judicial authority to the detriment of a party, is a basic attribute of a tribunal. In *Van de Hurk v Netherlands*, the tribunal deciding milk quota disputes was subject to a

---

[6] See also *Lavents v Latvia*, November 28, 2002, para.115, where the Regional Court which reheard an application sent back by the Senate of the Supreme Court was made up of the same composition as the original tribunal contrary to its ruling.

[7] *Coeme*, para.98; *Lavents*, n.6 above, para.114; *Buscarini*, n.5 above.

[8] It did find the fairness of the procedures contrary to Art.6, para.1 in two respects—no reasons for the decision and no public hearing—whereas the Commission had stated robustly that it was not a tribunal due to the nature of its functions, constitution and lack of procedures.

[9] It found it unnecessary to decide if it was an independent tribunal—paras 43–45. See *Kleyn v Netherlands*, May 6, 2003, ECHR 2003–VI—it was not fatal where the body was not dealing with the "same case" in its dual roles (Pt IIA: Independence and impartiality, Section 3(c) Dual roles).

[10] para.29.

legislative provision which gave the Government the power to deprive judgments of their effect. There was a violation therefore, notwithstanding the Government's argument that the power was never used. In *Beaumartin v France*, the character of "tribunal" was not satisfied where the *Conseil d'Etat* referred the question of interpretation of the treaty to the Foreign Minister and thus had neither full jurisdiction nor independence from the executive.[11]

6. Procedural guarantees

Lack of independence and impartiality may operate to deprive a body of the necessary character of a "tribunal" or disclose a violation *per se*. In *Belilos v Switzerland*, where a police officer sat in a judicial function deciding cases on a Police Board, the Court referred to its case law on the characteristics of a "tribunal" but its finding of a violation of Art.6 centred on the legitimate doubts as to the independence and organisational impartiality of a civil servant who would return to other departmental duties and would tend to be seen as a member of the police force subordinate to superiors and loyal to colleagues. Similarly, the Court in *Demicoli v Malta* found that the House of Representatives played a judicial function in determining the applicant journalist's guilt of breach of privilege but it was not impartial since two members impugned in the publictions participated throughout proceedings. The Commission had doubted whether part of the legislature could by its very nature be considered a court, having regard to its links with the executive.

IIA–188

Cross-reference

Part IIA: Access to court
Part II1: Independence and impartiality

---

[11] See also *Chevrol v France*, February 13, 2003, where the *Conseil d'Etat* deferred to the view of the Foreign Minister on the application of a bilateral agreement about recognition of medical qualifications.

Witnesses

Key provision:

IIA–189 Article 6, para.3(d) (right to examine and have cross-examined witnesses).

Key case law:

Unterpertinger v Austria, November 24, 1986, Series A, No.110; 13 E.H.R.R. 175; *Bricmont v Belgium*, July 7, 1989, Series A, No.158; *Kostovski v Netherlands*, November 20, 1989, Series A, No.166; 12 E.H.R.R. 434; *Brandstetter v Austria*, November 28, 1991, Series A, No.211; 15 E.H.R.R. 378; *Windisch v Austria*, September 27, 1990, Series A, No.186; 13 E.H.R.R. 281; *Isgro v Italy*, February 19, 1991, Series A, No.194; *Delta v France*, December 19, 1990, Series A, No.191; 16 E.H.R.R. 574; *Asch v Austria*, April 26, 1991, Series A, No.203; 15 E.H.R.R. 597; *Vidal v Belgium*, April 22, 1992, Series A, No.235–B; *Saidi v France*, September 20, 1993, Series A, No.261–C; 17 E.H.R.R. 251; *Ludi v Switzerland*, June 13, 1992, Series A, No.238; 15 E.H.R.R. 173; *Edwards v UK*, December 16, 1992, Series A, No.247–B; 15 E.H.R.R. 173; *Baegen v Netherlands*, October 27, 1995, Series A, No.327–B; *Doorson v Netherlands*, March 26, 1996, R.J.D. 1996–II, No.6; 22 E.H.R.R. 330; *Ferrantelli and Santangelo v Italy*, August 7, 1996, R.J.D. 1996–III, No.12; 23 E.H.R.R. 288; *Van Mechelen v Netherlands*, April 23, 1997, R.J.D. 1997–III, No.36; 25 E.H.R.R. 647; *Sadak v Turkey (No.1)*, July 17, 2001, ECHR 2001–VIII; *S.N. v Sweden*, July 2, 2002, ECHR 2002–V.

1. General considerations

IIA–190 Courts are allowed a fair measure of discretion in governing their proceedings. Judges may assess to what extent a requested witness may provide admissible or relevant testimony and intervene to prevent, for example, time-wasting or irrelevant questioning.[1] While the exercise of this discretion is subject to the overriding fairness principle, fairness is judged in relation to the proceedings as a whole and it will be rare that isolated, limited interventions by a judge will exceed that margin however annoying or frustrating to the defence. Since matters of the assessment of evidence are primarily for judges and courts, decisions that a proposed witness's testimony is irrelevant will not disclose a violation unless clearly arbitrary, unreasonable or it is substantiated that the witness was essential to the fair conduct of the proceedings or, in criminal proceedings, to secure the rights of the accused.[2]

"Witness" as used in the Convention is an autonomous term, not governed by domestic law classifications, and will cover situations where statements by a person

---

[1] *Vidal*, para.33 referring to "appropriate"; *Bricmont v Belgium*, "necessary" or "advisable". See *Perna v Italy*, July 25, 2001, finding that the applicant had not shown the relevance to the issues of evidence of two witnesses and the complainant whom the courts had refused to hear in defamation proceedings; *Kok v Netherlands*, 43149/98, (Dec.) July 4, 2000, ECHR 2000–VI, where the Court did not question the domestic courts' assessment of particular questions as irrelevant.

[2] See, *e.g. Bricmont*, para.89: "exceptional circumstances" required to find domestic courts' decisions in this area incompatible with fairness. Also *Barbera, Messegué and Jabardo v Spain*, December 6, 1988, Series A, No.146; 11 E.H.R.R. 360, para.68: it was not for the Convention organs to assess whether or not evidence was correctly admitted and assessed but to ascertain whether the proceedings as a whole, including the way in which evidence was taken, were fair; and *Wierzbicki v Poland*, June 18, 2002, where the courts gave detailed reasons for refusing to hear the applicant's witnesses, which were "not tainted by arbitrariness".

are used by a court or read out at trial.[3] Whatever the position in domestic law, it covers statements made by co-accused which may serve to a material degree as the basis for a conviction and thus constitute evidence for the prosecution.[4]

The most difficult problems arise where witnesses are not available for cross-examination even though their statements are admitted in evidence for the prosecution, whether by reason of vulnerability to threats (organised crime, terrorism) lack of compellability (wives etc) security of undercover policemen, or where the witness has died or disappeared. The Court is alert to the inherent dangers of anonymous witnesses. While it claims not to underestimate the importance of fighting organised crime, it considers that the right to fair administration of justice holds so prominent a place in democratic society that it cannot be sacrificed to expediency. A series of sometimes contradictory Court judgments deals with the problems arising in different situations.

2. Use of anonymous witnesses or written evidence from unexamined witnesses

A number of principles have been established[5]:   IIA–191

- in principle all evidence must be produced in the presence of the accused at a public hearing with a view to adversarial argument;
- use of statements in absence of oral testimony is not *per se* incompatible with Art.6, paras 1 and 3(d) but must be compatible with the rights of the defence;
- this rule generally means that accused must be given a proper and adequate opportunity to challenge and question a witness against him either when the witness makes the statement or later[6];
- it is generally not compatible, where there has been no opportunity to challenge the evidence given by witnesses, for a conviction to be based solely or to a decisive extent on their statements.[7]

Any measure restricting the defence should be strictly necessary and if a less restrictive measure can suffice then that measure should be applied.[8] The Court does not consider that genuine fear of reprisals or of revelation of the identity of undercover police officers can be decisive or overrule the interests of fairness to the defence.[9] Domestic courts also must make proper assessment of any alleged threat

---

[3] *e.g. Isgro*, para.33.

[4] *Luca v Italy*, February 27, 2001, para.41, ECHR 2001–III.

[5] *e.g. Kostovski; Unterpertinger*.

[6] *e.g. Isgro*, where the opportunity at trial to confront and question a witness, unavailable before the investigating judge, was sufficient to respect the rights of the defence; *Padin Gestoso v Spain*, 39519/98, (Dec.) December 8, 1998, ECHR 1999–II, no problem arose from the inability of the accused lawyer to question a co-accused during the investigation where there was an opportunity to do so during the public trial.

[7] *e.g. Unterpertinger*, a violation was found where the conviction for assault was mainly based on the complainants' written statements; *Windisch*: the conviction was based largely on anonymous witness statements; *Ludi*: a violation was found where the conviction was not based solely on the written statements of the undercover agent but these played a role in establishing the facts leading to conviction; *Doorson*, where the Court seemed to suggest that even in presence of counterbalancing features (*e.g.* possibility of counsel questioning the witnesses) a conviction should not be based solely or to decisive extent on anonymous witness evidence; *Asch*, where the alleged victim refused to testify, the Commission found the case indistinguishable from *Unterpertinger* but the Court found no violation, seeming to rely on the fact that the conviction was not solely based on her statement.

[8] *Van Mechelen*, para.58.

[9] *Kostovski; Saidi*, where the Government argued that the witness drug addicts were fragile pyschologically but the Court found that notwithstanding their state and the difficulties in obtaining evidence, such a restriction on rights of the defence was not justified (*i.e.* conviction decisively based on their anonymous statements).

to witnesses.[10] While in *Ludi v Switzerland*, there was a legitimate interest in maintaining the anonymity of the undercover policeman the Court was not persuaded that this rendered it impossible to arrange an opportunity for a confrontation or opportunity to question him in such a way as would preserve that anonymity. In *Van Mechelen v Netherlands*, where the undercover policemen gave evidence in a room separate from the defence but connected by a sound link, the Court was not convinced that these extreme limitations had been shown to be necessary in that case and they were not counterbalanced by the fact that the investigating judge who had ascertained the agents' identities had in a detailed report for the court stated his opinion as to their reliability and credibility.[11]

The Court has found it insufficient to respect the rights of the defence that an accused is only able to put written questions to an anonymous witness, since this deprives him of the opportunity to demonstrate the unreliability or prejudice of the witness.[12] Reference has been made to the importance that the trial court itself should hear the anonymous witness to be able to judge reliability[13] However the Court has acknowledged that it may prove necessary in certain circumstances for the judicial authorities to refer to depositions made during the investigative stage and as long as the accused has been given an adequate and proper opportunity to challenge those depositions, when made or at a later stage, their admission in evidence may not in themselves contravene Art.6, paras 1 and 3(d).[14]

Some allowances may also be made with respect to victims of sexual offences, particularly children. Due to the special features of such cases, the Court has said that Art.6, para.3(d) cannot be interpreted so as to require that questions be put directly by the accused or his counsel through cross-examination or other means.[15] In *Baegen v Netherlands*, the Commission narrowly found no violation where an accused was able to confront the alleged victim of sexual abuse but did not have the opportunity to question her. The Commission had regard to special features of rape and sexual offences trials and accepted that in criminal proceedings concerning sexual abuse measures may be taken to protect the victim provided such are reconcilable with an adequate and effective exercise of the rights of the defence. Since the accused had not used his opportunity to put written questions or applied to the court to hear her and he had the opportunity to contradict her evidence by submitting to blood or other tests, it was not established that he was unable to challenge the victim's credibility. Similarly in *SN v Sweden*, where the initial police

---

[10] *Van Mechelen*, para.61. See also *Visser v Netherlands*, February 14, 2002, where the courts did not carry out an examination of the well-foundedness of an anonymous' witness's fear of reprisals; *Kok*, n.1 above, where there were sufficient reasons to keep secret the identity of the informant.

[11] However, in *Kok*, n.1 above, the hearing of an anonymous witness by the investigating judge apart from counsel was attended by sufficient safeguards—the case appears to be distinguishable on the basis that the defence was handicapped to a lesser degree as the anonymous testimony was not decisive for the conviction and there were adequate reasons supporting the anonymity of the witness.

[12] *Kostovski*, para.42; *Van Mechelen*, para.62.

[13] *e.g. Isgro*, where the investigating judge saw the witness (no violation); *Delta*, where the court did not (violation).

[14] *Sadak v Turkey*, para.65—the accused had had no opportunity at any stage to examine witnesses on whose testimony the courts had largely based their decisions and *AM v Italy*, December 14, 1999, ECHR 1999–IX, where the applicant's lawyer was expressly banned from attending the examination of the alleged abuse victim and other witnesses under letters rogatory. Contrast *Solakov v FYROM*, October 31, 2001, ECHR 2001–X, where the applicant and his lawyer failed to take up any opportunity to participate in the examination of witnesses in the USA.

[15] *SN v Sweden*, para.52. See also *Oyston v UK*, 42011/98, (Dec.) January 22, 2002, where the Court found no unfairness arising from limitations put on the questioning victims of sexual offences about previous sexual experiences.

interview with the 10-year-old victim was videotaped and the applicant's counsel was able to arrange for questions to be put in a second taped interview, the Court noted that the applicant's counsel had consented to the form of the second interview, not insisting on postponement to allow him to be present and apparently satisfied that all his questions had been covered. As the courts had taken requisite care in assessing the child's statements and credibility, the Court found no violation arose from the failure to hear the child in court.[16]

In several cases, the Court seemed to accept that the applicant may claim a right to "confront" the witnesses against him, namely, to be physically present and question the persons who have identified him as a suspect.[17] But there may be circumstances where it is sufficient for counsel to confront and question a witness in the absence of the accused. In *Doorson v Netherlands*, where the Court found that there were relevant and sufficient reasons for the anonymity of the drug addict witnesses and the domestic court knew the identities of the witnesses and was able to assess their credibility.[18]

Where a witness is no longer available due to death or disappearance, the Court appears to give weight to whether the authorities are at fault in failing to produce him. In *Isgro v Italy*, the Court noted that the authorities had attempted to find the missing witness.[19] In *Ferrantelli and Santangelo v Italy*, where the applicants complained that there was no confrontation with a witness who died, the Court noted that the Government was not responsible for the death and that the statement was found by the domestic courts to be corroborated by other evidence.[20]

Failure to request explicitly the hearing of particular witnesses may not be fatal to an applicants' complaints. Any waiver of rights must be unequivocal and where the testimony is a significant part of the court's decision and the accused has complained, albeit in indirect terms, of his inability to challenge it, it is expected that the authorities take positive steps themselves to ensure the accused's rights are enjoyed in an effective manner.[21]

---

[16] See however *PS v Germany*, December 20, 2001, where a conviction for sexual offences was decisively based on the 8 year old victim's statement to the police and the victim had not been heard in the court itself for very vague reasons. While the second instance court ordered a psychological expert report on the victim's credibility, this occurred some eighteen months after the event and did not enable the defence to challenge her evidence effectively.

[17] *e.g. Saidi*, where the conviction was based solely on the statements of witnesses identifying him to police as drug dealer and he wished a "confrontation" with them.

[18] paras 70–73: however the conviction was not solely or decisively based on the statements; contrast *Saidi* above.

[19] Also *Doorson*, para.80, where despite the court's efforts it was impossible to secure the attendance of a witness, there was no unfairness in relying on his statement, especially since it was corroborated by other evidence; also *Kennedy v UK*, 36428/97, (Dec.) October 21, 1998, where a key witness had been unable to appear during a retrial due to mental illness, the Commission had regard to the fact that the defence had been able to examine him during the first trial and appeal and part of the retrial; *Calabro v Italy and Germany*, 59895/00, (Dec.) March 21, 2002, where the Italian authorities had done all that could be expected in tracing a witness in Germany; *Verdam v Netherlands*, 35253/97, (Dec.) August 31, 1999, where the victims could not be traced; *Wester v Sweden*, 31074/96, (Dec.) January 14, 1998, concerning illness of a former co-accused;

[20] The Commission found a violation since it was the Government's fault that they had not acted more speedily and the statement had, as in *Ludi*, played an important role in establishing the facts leading to conviction.

[21] *Sadak*, para.67; see also *Craxi v Italy (No.1)* December 5, 2002, no waiver of rights where any challenge to use of written statements, lawfully admitted, by witnesses whom the applicant had not had the chance to question, would have had little chance of success.

3. Refusal to call witnesses for the defence

IIA–192   Article 6, para.3(d) does not require the attendance and examination of every witness for the defence.[22] Nor will the domestic authorities be held responsible where it is impossible to obtain the attendance of a particular witness required by the defence.[23]

Its essential aim has been stated as ensuring equality of arms in examining witnesses, though considerations of equality do not exhaust the provision. A violation was found in *Vidal v Belgium* where the Court of Appeal heard no witnesses for the prosecution or defence, refusing to call the four witnesses requested by the defence. Since however it overturned the acquittal on basis of the co-accused's statement and case file and increased sentence without giving reasons for rejecting the defence's request, the Court found that this was inconsistent with the notion of fair trial and that the rights of the defence were restricted in breach of Art.6. Where, as in *Brandstetter v Austria*, a court appoints an expert, the fact that he issues a report unfavourable to the defence will not require the court to appoint another on request of the defence. Where there was no reason to challenge the objectivity of expert, there was no breach of equality of arms otherwise the procedure would continue *ad infinitum*. In *Doorson*, the Court found no problem where the domestic court refused to call a defence expert to give general evidence that drug addicts were not reliable witnesses, noting that it was a matter for the domestic court which could consider that the evidence did not as such elucidate the facts of the case and would not contribute much since similar evidence had already been given by other experts.

Nonetheless, the Court has found that the failure to call an expert witness may render proceedings unfair in breach of Art.6, para.1 where the questions of fact and law could not otherwise be adequately resolved. In *Elsholz v Germany*, a violation arose where the domestic courts in a child access proceedings failed to seek psychological expert evidence requested by the applicant father, supported by the youth office, as to the 5–6 year old child's views. However in a later case, concerning alleged failure of domestic courts to seek psychological reports on the child's views on access, the Grand Chamber re-iterated that as a general rule it was for domestic courts to assess the evidence before them, including the means to ascertain relevant facts and having regard in particular to the age and maturity of the child who was heard in the proceedings, found the courts well able to reach a reasoned decision on the issues without the expert evidence requested by the applicant.[24]

Cross-reference

Part IIA: Equality of arms
Part IIA: Evidence

---

[22] *Vidal*, para.33.
[23] *Ubach Mortes v Andorra*, 46253/99, (Dec.) May 4, 2000, ECHR 2000–V, where the witness was in Spain and also could not attend on health grounds.
[24] *Sommerfeld v Germany*, July 8, 2003, ECHR 2003–VIII, (concerning failure to order expert opinion on the negative views to contact expressed by a 13 year old), where the Court's reasoning was under the procedural aspect of Art.8, with no separate issue under Art.6. Similar reasoning regarding the failure of the court to hear a 5-year-old concerning contact, where there was expert evidence as to the undesirability of direct questioning—*Sahin v Germany*, July 8, 2003, ECHR 2003–VII.

Abortion

Key provisions:

Articles 2 (right to life), 3 (prohibition on torture and inhuman treatment), 8 (respect for family and private life), 9 (freedom of conscience and religion), 10 (freedom of expression) and 11 (freedom of assembly).

IIB–001

Key case law:

Open Door Counselling and Dublin Well Woman v Ireland, October 29, 1992, Series A, No.246; 15 E.H.R.R. 244; *Vo v France,* July 8, 2004, ECHR 2004.

1. General considerations

Abortion continues a controversial subject in Council of Europe States generally and reveals widely differing approaches, ranging between liberal freedom of choice to women in Norway and almost total prohibition in Ireland. Sensitive to the difficult moral and ethical issues involved and to the lack of consensus, the Commission was reluctant to intervene and condemn any particular State policy that has been adopted, with the result that no cases on the practice of abortion ever reached the Court until very recently. The Court has largely followed the Commission's approach and accorded a wide margin of appreciation to States.[1]

IIB–002

There have been peripheral issues arising around the abortion, in particular, the steps taken, publicly, to support or criticise the practice, which have given rise to case law in the context of Art.10.

2. Who can complain?

Only a person directly affected by the measure or legislation in question may bring a complaint. This includes any woman of child-bearing age (it is not required for a woman to be pregnant)[2]; the husband of a woman who intends to have an abortion[3]; the putative father of a foetus carried by an unmarried mother.[4] It does not include a minister who considers that domestic legislation permitting abortion is

IIB–003

---

[1] *Vo,* para.82, concerning the moment at which life begins.
[2] 6959/75 *Brüggeman and Scheuten v Germany,* (Dec.) May 19, 1976, 5 D.R. 103.
[3] 8416/79, (Dec.) May 13, 1980, 19 D.R. 244; *Boso v Italy,* 50490/99, (Dec.) September 5, 2002, ECHR 2002–VII.
[4] *H v Norway,* 17004/90, (Dec.) May 19, 1992, 73 D.R. 155.

wrong[5] or a man (husband and father of children) who objects to legislation on principle.[6]

3. Right to life of the unborn child

IIB–004   The Commission tended to the view, without deciding, that the foetus or unborn child was not protected by Art.2.[7] It referred to the terms of Art.2 as not appearing to apply to an unborn child. In *Boso v Italy*,[8] the Court left the question open and stated that, even assuming the foetus could attract the protection of Art.2, in the circumstances of the case, where abortions were only permitted on grounds of risk to the mother, the State had not exceeded the margin of appreciation accorded to it in this delicate area. It may be noted though that in a controversial French case dealing with adoption it has found that measures taken by the State with a view to avoiding the number of abortions carried out, in particular illegal abortions, pursued the legitimate aim of respecting life.[9]

This does not necessarily exclude the application of the Convention in other circumstances, perhaps outside the medical context of abortion.[10] In *Vo v France*, where the mother lost the foetus due to a mistake by a doctor, the Court considered, in the absence of any European consensus, that it was neither appropriate or desirable to decide whether the unborn child was a person for the purposes of Art.2. However, on the assumption that Art.2 was applicable, it considered that it was sufficient by way of procedural protection that a prosecution lay for any injury to the mother and damages were payable for negligence. It was not necessary that a charge of involuntary killing could be brought against the doctor.

4. Inhuman treatment

IIB–005   In *H v Norway*,[11] the potential father raised the issue of the pain possibly caused to the 14-week-old foetus by the abortion procedure. The Commission found this allegation to be unsubstantiated by the material before it.

5. Rights of a potential father

IIB–006   A potential father cannot derive a claim to be consulted in advance of any abortion. While his rights to potential family life may be interfered with by an abortion, they have to be weighed against the rights of the mother. Where the abortion is on

[5] 11045/84 (Dec.) March 8, 1985, 42 D.R. 47.

[6] 7045/75, (Dec.) December 10, 1975, 7 D.R.87.

[7] 6959/75 *Brüggeman and Scheuten v Germany,* (Rep.) July 12, 1977, 10 D.R.100. In *Open Door Counselling,* the Court left open whether the restriction on abortion could be considered as pursuing the aim of protecting the rights of others in the sense of the unborn child.

[8] n.4 above.

[9] *Odievre v France*, February 13, 2003, ECHR 2003–III, para.45.

[10] 23186/94, *Mentes v Turkey*, (Dec.) January 9, 1995 where the Commission declared admissible complaints alleging the security forces' expulsion of villagers from their homes, including a claim that in the resulting trauma a pregnant woman gave birth prematurely to twins who died. Her claims were rejected as unsubstantiated when she failed to give evidence before the Commission delegates: (Rep.) March 7, 1996, R.J.D 1998–IV.

[11] n.4 above.

grounds of the medical welfare of the mother, the rights of the mother have been found to outweigh those of the father.[12] Where the abortion was not on health grounds but social hardship in *H v Norway*, the Commission still found that the rights of the woman, as the person primarily concerned by the pregnancy and its termination, prevailed over the father, notwithstanding that the couple had planned to marry and had together planned the pregnancy. The Court reached the same conclusion in *Boso v Italy*, where the applicant complained that his wife had obtained an abortion without any possibility of intervention on his part.[13]

6. Rights of the woman

Availability of abortion

As indicated above, where domestic legislation allows abortion, whether on health or non-health related grounds, the woman's rights prevail over the putative father's. The position is different where the legislation restricts abortion and it is the woman who claims a wider right under domestic law. In a German case,[14] a law was struck down by the Constitutional Court as unconstitutional, which permitted abortion within 12 weeks without particular ground of necessity. Abortion was subsequently limited to particular grounds. The Commission found that this legislation did not constitute an interference with the applicant women's rights to respect for private life. It had regard to the fact that abortion was permissible, that the health and distress of the mother were taken into account (albeit in restricted scope) and that the criminal provisions did not penalise women excessively (*i.e.* a pregnant woman was exempt from punishment if the abortion was performed by a doctor within 22 weeks and had made use of counselling).

IIB–007

There has as yet been no case introduced by a woman alleging that she has been prevented from having an abortion because of either a blanket prohibition or because she fell outside restrictive conditions. The new Court's reaction would be likely to be cautious. In *H v Norway*, the Commission referred to the fact that laws on abortion differed considerably between the Contracting States and that "assuming that the Convention may be considered to have some bearing in this field" it found that in such "a delicate area" States must have a certain discretion. Varying restrictions are therefore acceptable. Even if the Commission was tentative about the Convention organs' competence to strike down any particular legal regime on abortion, the possibility is still there however.[15]

---

[12] 8416/79, n.3 above.

[13] n.3 above.

[14] *Brüggeman and Scheuten* (Rep.), n.8 above.

[15] The case of *Att-Gen v X* in Ireland in 1992 was an example of how a blanket prohibition could affect a teenage girl, pregnant from an alleged rape, who had been prevented by injunction from leaving Ireland to seek an abortion in the UK. The Irish Supreme Court on March 5, 1992 did accept that termination of pregnancy could be permissible under the Irish Constitution where it was established as a matter of probability that there was a real and substantial risk to the life of the mother if the termination was not effected, with the result that the case did not come to Strasbourg. There would conversely be the other end of the spectrum where, for example, in the case of a mentally ill woman, steps were taken to carry out an abortion dispensing with her consent.

7. Information about abortion

IIB–008
Even where abortion is not lawful however, women may claim the right to access to information from others relating to abortions performed lawfully in another Contracting State, at least where another person or body is willing to give the information. It is arguable whether the State or public authority could be obliged to make available such information themselves.

In *Open Door Counselling and Dublin Well Women v Ireland*, where two women's counselling organisations, two individual counsellors and two women of childbearing age complained about an Irish Supreme Court injunction which restrained the two organisations from providing certain information to pregnant women concerning abortion facilities outside Ireland in the context of non-directive counselling, the Court found a breach of Art.10. The Court considered that the State did not have an unfettered or unreviewable discretion in the field of morals and held that the restriction was unnecessary, giving weight to the sweeping nature of the injunction regardless of the age, health or circumstances of the woman concerned, the fact that it was not against the law for a woman to travel abroad and that it prevented the provision of information about abortion facilities which were available lawfully in other Contracting States. It noted that in any case the information was available in other forms (via magazines and telephone directories) and that the ban appeared to penalise women who were less resourceful or educated and created a risk that women, in the absence of proper counselling, might seek abortion at later stages and fail to take advantage of medical supervision after an abortion.

8. Expression of views in respect of abortion

IIB–009
The Commission found it justifiable under Art.10 for individuals to be penalised where they expressed their views on abortion in certain circumstances to which others might object. It held that it was an acceptable restriction on freedom of expression where a doctor employed by a Catholic hospital was sacked following expression of views favourable to abortion in a letter to a newspaper.[16] It had regard to the contractual link freely undertaken by the doctor with an organisation whose convictions on abortion were well-known. On the other hand the Commission also found it justified for the protection of the reputation of others under the second paragraph of Art.10 where a doctor was fined for expressing the opinion that abortion advice centres were embryo-killer syndicates and the trade union organisation advocating them was "Nazi".[17] The Commission had regard to the light penalty. Such restrictions might perhaps be found disproportionate if they went beyond relatively small fines or sanctioned persons for the expression of more moderate or considered views outside the context of special contractual relationships.

Where an applicant in Poland was convicted of aiding and abetting abortion and sentenced to one and a half years' imprisonment and fined, the Court found that Art.10 did not even apply as it was not the expression of views held by the applicant in respect of the legal status of abortion which was in issue nor had the applicant engaged in any kind of public debate.[18]

[16] 12242/86, (Dec.) September 6, 1989, 62 D.R. 151.
[17] 12230/86, (Dec.) December 12, 1987.
[18] *Tokarczyk v Poland*, 51792/99, (Dec.) January 31, 2002.

9. Position of medical staff

There has only been one case indirectly raising issues as to the participation of   IIB–010
medical staff in abortion procedures. In a Swedish case, three trainee midwives
objected to being required in their training to insert contraceptive coils which they
considered to have an abortive effect.[19] The case was however struck off when the
midwives were allowed to qualify with their certificate indicating that they had not
conducted such procedures.

10. Freedom to demonstrate

Where an association against abortion carried out a public demonstration which was   IIB–011
disrupted by others in favour of abortion, the Commission found that it had a right
to be protected by the State in the exercise of its freedom of assembly although in
the circumstances of the case the State had not failed in its obligations (*i.e.* it
accepted the argument, *inter alia*, that more intrusive police intervention would in
fact have escalated the violence that occurred).[20]

States may restrain the activities of protesters for or against abortion, in the
interests of preventing of crime or disorder and protecting the rights of others. Thus
it was a legitimate restriction to impose an injunction to prevent an applicant
handing out leaflets at the door to an abortion clinic and seeking to dissuade women
from entering. Under Art.9, the activities which primarily aimed at persuading
women not to have an abortion did not constitute the expression of a belief.[21]

---

[19] 12375/86, (Dec.) October 7, 1987.
[20] *Plattform Ärzte v Austria*, 10126/82, (Dec.) October 17, 1985, 44 D.R. 65.
[21] 22838/93, (Dec.), February 22, 1995, 80–A D.R. 187; 30936/96, (Dec.) September 10, 1997: the
applicants' conviction for breach of the peace for entering an abortion clinic to conduct a communal
praying session was considered justified for the protection of the rights and freedoms of others.

Aids

Key provisions:

IIB–012   Articles 3 (prohibition of inhuman treatment), 5 (liberty and security of person), 6 (fair trial within a reasonable time), 8 (respect for private life) and 14 (prohibition of discrimination).

Key case law:

X v France, March 31, 1992, Series A, No.234–C; 14 E.H.R.R. 483; *Vallée v France*, April 26, 1994, Series A, No.289; 18 E.H.R.R. 549; *A v Denmark*, February 8, 1996, R.J.D. 1996–I; 22 E.H.R.R. 458; *Z v Finland*, February 25, 1997, R.J.D. 1997–I; 25 E.H.R.R. 371; *D v UK*, May 2, 1997, R.J.D. 1997–III; 24 E.H.R.R. 423.

1. General considerations

IIB–013   No case has ever been brought alleging that a State has failed to protect an individual's right to respect for life or security of person through inadequate regulation of public bood bank facilities. It would appear that where State liability for contamination of blood transfusions may have been in question, Contracting States have taken the responsibility of providing a monetary fund of some kind to which there has been a possibility of applying for compensation. It has been in the context of such proceedings for compensation that many applications have arisen, involving allegations of delay in the outcome.

The stigma and social difficulties facing AIDS sufferers have not been subject to much exposure in applications, presumably since these are matters of pervasive effect rather than express Governmental policy. Issues have arisen concerning the disclosure of medical details of AIDS sufferers; the risk of inhuman treatment resulting from expulsion to a country where no drugs treatment or support care is available[1] and sentencing and release procedures applicable to convicted prisoners suffering from AIDS.[2]

2. Delay in compensation proceedings

IIB–014   Proceedings for compensation brought by those who developed HIV from contaminated blood supplies concern the determination of civil rights within the meaning of Art.6, para.1 as the outcome would be decisive for private rights to damages for injuries.[3] The Convention organs have emphasised the particular need for expedition in proceedings where the applicant is suffering from a disease such as HIV or full-blown AIDS where deterioration and death may ensue very rapidly. In *X v France*, the applicant, a haemophiliac who had received blood transfusions in a State

---

[1] *D v UK.*
[2] *Grice v UK*, 22564/93, (Dec.) April 14, 1994, 77–A D.R. 90; *RM v UK*, 22761/93, (Dec.) April 14, 1994, 77–A D.R. 98.
[3] In *X v France,* the Court dismissed the Government's argument that the proceedings raised public law issues of the State's exercise of its regulatory authority rather than civil rights.

hospital, discovered that he was HIV positive and filed for compensation to the relevant Government authority. When he died just over two years later, his appeal was still pending at the Administrative Court of Appeal. The Court found that the period of over two years was unreasonable. Though the matter of establishing the State's liability was complex, the Government should have been aware that proceedings were imminent and ought to have commissioned an objective report on liability immediately after the commencement of the cases against them. While two years might not have been dilatory for the average administrative court proceeedings, the Court considered that given the incurable nature of the infection and the applicant's reduced life expectancy, exceptional diligence was called for on the part of the domestic authorities, notwithstanding the number of similar pending cases.[4]

Even where the applicants had themselves contributed not inconsiderably to the delay, the Court found this did not dispense the courts from ensuring compliance with the requirement of reasonable time which in these cases involved the need for exceptional diligence. Furthermore, although in *Karakaya v France* and *Vallée v France*, the applicants had received compensation from a State fund during the administrative proceedings, the Court found that what was at stake in the proceedings continued to be of great importance, in both pecuniary and non-pecuniary terms. The requirement of exceptional diligence did not apply however to proceedings brought by relatives of a deceased AIDS victim.[5]

3. Discriminatory treatment

(a) *Sentencing and release procedures*

The only cases before the Convention organs raising allegations of prejudical treatment of HIV or AIDS sufferers have related to the approach taken by the courts in sentencing, and the policy adopted by the prison authorities in early release, of convicted applicants with the disease. While the Commission noted that questions of length of sentence generally fell outside the scope of Art.5 and that there was no right as such to early release, it did find that where procedures relating to the release or sentencing of prisoners appeared to operate in a discriminatory manner, an issue could arise under Art.14 in conjunction with Art.5. It rejected the cases on their facts, however, for perhaps less than convincing reasons.

In *Grice v United Kingdom*, where the applicant, suffering from full-blown AIDS and sentenced to four years, was refused early release from prison on compassionate grounds, he argued that the Home Office was discriminating against HIV/AIDS sufferers, none of whom had ever been released early on compassionate grounds, whereas prisoners suffering from other non-life threatening illnesses, such as senile dementia or treatable illnesses like cancer, were being released. The Commission noted that the applicant's life expectancy had been given by his doctor at trial as two years and then later as 6–12 months but while in prison he had not suffered any sudden deterioration and he had not been incapacitated in any way or threatened by the development of the opportunistic infections to which AIDS sufferers are prone. The Commission concluded that there was no indication that the

IIB–015

[4] See also *Vallée* and *Karakaya*, where proceedings for compensation had lasted four or more years; *A v Denmark*, periods of over 5 and 6 years disclosed violations.
[5] *A v Denmark*.

applicant had been treated differently by the Home Secretary in the exercise of his discretion as to early release on compassionate grounds.[6]

In *RM v United Kingdom*, in sentencing the applicant who had AIDS, the Court of Appeal expressly refused to take into account his medical condition. It took the approach that on appeals on sentence by AIDS sufferers it was not for the court to alter an otherwise proper sentence to achieve a desirable end, which was rather a matter for the royal prerogative of mercy. Before the Commission, the applicant argued that there was a general practice by the courts of accepting as a substantial mitigating factor in sentence an illness which would definitely shorten the offender's life and that Court of Appeal had singled out HIV/AIDS sufferers for less favourable treatment. The Commission noted the medical monitoring which even a year into his sentence still gave him a life expectancy of months and possibly up to two years and found that he had not suffered any serious deterioration or failed to receive proper care in prison. In these circumstances the Commisson found that it was not unreasonable or disproportionate for the Court of Appeal not to take his illness into account in mitigating the sentence to be imposed. There was also a reference to the margin of appreciation. The Commission did not address the applicant's arguments that, reasonable or not, other sufferers of illnesses which limited life expectancy in a less or as equally drastic way were benefitting from mitigation of sentence.[7] The Commission's reasoning is not persuasive. While there may indeed have been nothing wrong or unreasonable in the way the applicant was treated in prison where fortunately he did not become very ill, the Commission's approach ignored the point that Art.14 complaints are about the risk of particular vulnerable groups being singled out for different treatment and that such differences are not compatible under Convention principles if not objectively and reasonably justified.

(b) *Other areas*

IIB–016 There has as yet been no case where it has been alleged that information relating to a person's HIV status has been used to their detriment, for example, as a basis for dismissal from employment or as the basis for depriving them of some service or benefit. Whether that would raise a problem would depend very much on the facts of the case. There is no right to employment as such under the Convention and acts by private companies or bodies would not necessarily engage the responsibility of the State. The circumstances of the case would have to support the contention that the act or deprivation interfered with an aspect of private life and that the State owed an obligation to provide protection against such interference even by private bodies.

4. Disclosure of medical condition to others

IIB–017 Disclosure of medical details of an HIV/AIDS sufferer may be accepted as justified under Art.8 where there are legitimate interests in permitting disclosure and there are adequate safeguards. However, where general public disclosure is concerned

---

[6] It is to be noted that the Commission did not comment on the applicant's arguments disputing the Government's contention that death had to be imminent for a person to obtain early release (citing the sufferers of senile dementia or treatable cancer). It is difficult to assess, if it was correct that persons threatened with less urgent conditions were benefitting from early release, what objective or reasonable justification there could be for treating those with AIDS differently.

[7] There was the example of Ernest Saunders who had his sentence reduced by the Court of Appeal in the light of medical evidence of pre-senile dementia (May 16, 1991).

there is less likely to be a convincing justification. The Court has emphasised that the interest of the individual in confidentiality of medical records will weigh very heavily in the balance and measures compelling disclosure attract the most careful scrutiny.[8] Respect for confidentiality of health data is identified as being a vital principle in the legal systems of all the Contracting Parties, crucial not only to respect the privacy of the patient but also to maintain confidence in the medical profession and health services.[9]

In *TV v Finland*,[10] in respect of allegations concerning disclosure of a prisoner's HIV condition to persons within the prison, the Commission found that access by prison and medical staff to information concerning his HIV status *prima facie* constituted an interference with his right to respect for his private life guaranteed under Art.8 of the Convention. However, this was not unlawful, pursued the aim of protecting the rights of others with whom he came in contact and there was no evidence that the information was passed beyond the staff who dealt with him and who could justifiably expect to receive information relating to a disease carried by him which could be passed on through contact with blood. Impliedly, the case might have gone further if in fact it had appeared that the personal information relating to his condition had been circulated more widely than those immediately dealing with him or that the information had been stored in such a way as to make it accessible to others unconnected with him.

In *Z v Finland*, disclosure of the applicant's HIV status was made during a criminal trial where her ex-husband was facing charges of attempted manslaughter on the basis that he had had forced sexual intercourse with women when he knew that he was HIV positive. Four principal points were at issue: the court orders requiring the applicant's doctors to give evidence at the trial; the seizure of her medical records; the decision to make the material in the file accessible to the public from 2002; and the disclosure of her name and medical condition in the Court of Appeal's judgment. All four were undisputed as constituting interferences with private and family life and the principal argument concerned the justification of the measures. The Court found that the first three pursued legitimate aims—the prevention of crime in relation of measures of investigation and protection of the rights of others in maintaining the transparency of court proceedings through public access to files. However, the Court doubted that the publication of the applicant's full names as well as her medical condition following their disclosure in the Court of Appeal's judgment could be justified for any aim, including the prevention of crime.

As to whether the four measures could be justified as necessary under the second paragraph of Art.8, the questioning of the applicant's doctors was acceptable since it was carried out *in camera* and the proceedings bound by confidentiality enforceable under civil and criminal law: this furnished adequate and effective safeguards against abuse. The seizure of her medical records and inclusion in the file was also proportionate. The Court was uninterested in allegations that not all the material was relevant to the investigation and not prepared to question the domestic court assessment in that respect. However the order which would make the material

---

[8] *Z v Finland*, para.96.
[9] *ibid.*, the Court cited a recommendation of the Committee of Ministers (Council of Europe), which pointed out that lack of confidence might lead persons to avoid seeking assistance, endangering their own health and the general community—R(89) 14 on the ethical issues of HIV infection in health care and social settings adopted October 24, 1989, explanatory memorandum paras 166–168.
[10] 21780/93, (Dec.) March 2, 1994.

public by 2002 was disproportionate in its effects on the applicant, which outweighed any general interest in making files public. It also found that the publication of her identity and condition in the appeal judgment was disproportionate, in particular, since the lower court had felt able to issue an abridged version of its judgment excluding the name and part of the reasoning.

5. Inhuman and degrading treatment

IIB–018 Access to medical treatment or standards of medical care have not arisen directly but in connection with expulsion of persons from Contracting States to countries where the standard of care and treatment are deficient. The UK Government strenuously resisted the claims in *D v United Kingdom*, where an applicant suffering AIDS alleged that on expulsion to St. Kitts his life-expectancy would be shortened and his final days subject to lack of medical care and support. The Government argued that finding a violation would open the floodgates to claims from persons with AIDS who were refused entry to European States where inevitably higher standards of medical and support care were available. The Commission dismissed this on the basis that UK responsibility was engaged in this particular case because, rather than expelling the applicant on arrival, they prosecuted him for drugs possession and held him in jail, where he became dependent on the drugs treatment provided. The argument that he would suffer the natural consequences of a disease contracted outside the UK did not divert responsibility either, since the Commission considered that the lack of treatment and adequate support would lead in all probability to painful and degrading circumstances prior to his death. The Court found that Government responsibility could arise from expelling an AIDS sufferer but in finding a violation emphasised the exceptional facts, in particular the very severe deterioration in the applicant's health by the time of the hearing. Subsequent cases have distinguished the judgement on that basis. Where the applicant has not been in an advanced or terminal stage and there is some prospect of medical care and family support, expulsions have been found acceptable.[11]

[11] See, *e.g. SCC v Sweden*, 46553/99, (Dec.) February 15, 2000: no problem arose out of the deportation of the applicant, with HIV, to Zambia where some treatment and family support were available; *Henao v Netherlands*, 13669/03, (Dec.) June 24, 2003: expulsion of the applicant, HIV-positive, to Colombia was acceptable, as treatment was in principle available and he had family there; conversely, *BB v France*, 30930/96, (Rep.) March 9, 1998, R.J.D. 1998–VI, pp.2613–2614: the Commission found that expulsion would breach Art.3 where the applicant's infection was at an advanced stage necessitating repeated hospital stays and the care facilities in the Congo were precarious.

Armed forces

Key provisions:

Articles 5 (liberty), 6 (fair trial), 8 (private life) and 10 (freedom of expression).   IIB–019

Key case law:

Engel v Netherlands, June 8, 1976, Series A, No.22; 1 E.H.R.R. 647; *Hadjianastassiou v Greece*, December 16, 1992, Series A, No.252–A; 16 E.H.R.R. 219; *Vereinigung demokratischer Soldaten Osterreichs v Austria*; December 19, 1994, Series A, No.302; 20 E.H.R.R. 55; *Mitap and Müftüglü v Turkey*; (Rep.) December 8, 1994, annexed to the judgment of the Court, March 25, 1996, R.J.D. 1996–II, No.6; *Findlay v UK*, February 25, 1997, R.J.D. 1997–I, No.30; 24 E.H.R.R. 221; *Kalaç v Turkey*, July 1, 1997, R.J.D. 1997–IV, No.41; 27 E.H.R.R. 552; *Grigoriades v Greece*, November 25, 1997, R.J.D. 1997–VII, No.57; 27 E.H.R.R 464; *Larissis v Greece*, February 24, 1998, R.J.D. 1998–I, No.65; 27 E.H.R.R. 329; *Hood v UK*, February 18, 1999, ECHR 1999–I; 29 E.H.R.R. 365; *Smith and Grady v UK*, September 27, 1999, ECHR 1999–VI; *Cooper v UK*, December 16, 2003, 29 E.H.R.R. 493; *Grieves v UK*, December 16, 2003.

1. General considerations

Armed forces personnel continue to enjoy the rights guaranteed under the   IIB–020
Convention although the special disciplinary context may allow certain limitations on their exercise which could not be imposed on civilians.[1] Obvious and inevitable restrictions following on military service will not raise issues, *e.g.* rules on uniform and haircuts[2] but joining up does not waive fundamental rights to liberty and fair trial.

2. Military discipline

Matters purely of internal discipline are unlikely to raise issues where the sanctions   IIB–021
do not involve deprivation of liberty or other punishments serious enough to fall within the concept of a criminal penalty.[3] Any detention which involves a deprivation of liberty within the meaning of Art.5 will attract its procedural guarantees. Whether a restriction for a soldier, as opposed to a civilian, constitutes a deprivation of liberty depends on the extent to which it deviates from the normal conditions of life in the armed forces of Contracting States. The case law indicates that light arrest, involving restriction to quarters in off-duty hours, was not sufficient but that strict arrest, involving being locked in a cell day and night and exclusion from normal duties was.[4] The procedural guarantees will include the right to be brought promptly before an officer exercising judicial functions who has the

---

[1] *Engel*, para.57.
[2] 8209/78, (Dec.) March 1, 1979, 16 D.R. 166.
[3] See Pt IIA, Fair trial guarantees, General Principles: Criminal Charge.
[4] *Engel*, paras 59–63.

power to order release and the right to bring proceedings challenging the lawfulness of the detention.[5] In *Hood v United Kingdom*, the commanding officer of an arrested soldier was not regarded as sufficiently independent or impartial to fulfil the role of a judicial officer in deciding on pre-trial detention under Art.5, para.3, due in particular to his responsibilities for internal discipline and order in his command and his significant involvement in any subsequent prosecution.

Dismissal from the armed forces falls outside the scope of Art.6, para.1 as not concerning the determination of civil rights and obligations, due to the public service aspect.[6]

3. Military justice

IIB–022   Where a criminal charge is involved, Art.6 rights play a full role. A prisoner is entitled, *inter alia*, to fair hearing, before an independent and impartial tribunal, and within a reasonable time.[7] Potentially, this may mean legal representation and legal aid for such if he cannot afford it.[8]

The Convention organs appear to dislike in principle situations where civilians are subject to the jurisdiction of military courts. In *Mitap and Müftülu v Turkey*, the Commission considered that this *per se* raised doubts as to independence and impartiality and found that the presence on the court martial of an army officer and two military judges (who were linked with the military hierarchy for the purposes of their career and subordinate to the commander of the state of martial law whose security forces were carrying out the arrests) was not cured by the presence of two civilian judges and was sufficient to give objective reason to doubt the independence and impartiality of the tribunal.

There is however nothing in the provisions of Art.6 which in principle exclude the determination by service tribunals of criminal charges against service personnel.[9] Whether or not there are justifiable doubts as to the independence and impartiality of a particular court-martial will depend on the circumstances. Some weight has been given to the presence of irremovable civilian judges, the irremovability of military members during their mandate and as to whether the military members were not answerable to any authority.[10] Where military members remain subject to military discipline and assessment reports for promotion purposes or remain part of the hierarchical chain of command, problems of independence and impartiality have arisen.[11]

Serious structural problems were disclosed in *Findlay v United Kingdom*,[12] where there were hierarchical links between the officers on the District Court Martial and the convening officer, who acted as prosecutor. The fact that the decision of the

---

[5] Art.5, para.3, *e.g. De Jong, Baljet and Van den Brink v Netherlands*, May 22, 1984, Series A, No.77; Art.5 para.4, *e.g. Engel*.
[6] *e.g. Batur v Turkey*, 38604/97, (Dec.) July 4, 2000.
[7] *e.g. Jordan v UK (No.2)*, December 10, 2002—unreasonable length of court martial, over 4 years, 7 months.
[8] *Morris v UK*, February 26, 2002, ECHR 2002–I, para.89, it was not contrary to Art.6, para.3(c) to require the applicant to pay £240 contribution to legal aid.
[9] *Cooper*, para.110.
[10] *e.g.* 12717/87, (Dec.) September 8, 1988, 57 D.R. 196; 8209/78, (Dec.) March 1, 1979, 16 D.R. 166.
[11] *e.g. Sahiner v Turkey*, September 25, 2001, concerning Martial Law Courts.
[12] See also *Coyne v UK*, September 24, 1997, R.J.D. 1997–V, No.48 and *Cable v UK*, February 18, 1999, reaching similar findings concerning RAF courts martial.

court martial was not effective until confirmed by the convening officer was also contrary to the well-established principle that a "tribunal" had the power to give a binding decision, which may not be altered by an non-judicial authority. In *Grieves v United Kingdom*, concerning naval courts martial, there were insufficient guarantees where the judge advocate was a serving officer on whom reports were made to his hierarchical superiors and there was no permanent presiding officer who was irremovable and not subject to reports. The Court was not convinced by arguments that the unique nature of naval service required these roles to be filled by serving officers who had detailed knowledge of the naval way of life. In *Cooper v United Kingdom*, which concerned air force courts martial, the presence of a civilian judge advocate and a permanent president did however furnish sufficiently strong guarantees of independence taken in conjunction with detailed briefing notes to the two service members of the court martial, who were not assessed in conjunction with their judicial decision-making.[13] The "reviewing authority"'s power to alter verdicts and sentences was not however found to be a problem as in any event the final decision was always taken by a judicial body, the Court Martial Appeal Court.

4. Restrictions on private life

Members of the armed forces do not waive their rights under Art.8. While an old Commission case considered that a prohibition on homosexual acts between soldiers could be considered as necessary for the protection of morals and the prevention of disorder given the special conditions of army life,[14] the Court has since held that it was an unjustified interference with private life to hold investigations into soldiers' private lives, including detailed interviews with the soldiers and third parties and that their consequent administrative discharge on sole ground of sexual orientation also constituted a disproportionate interference with the right under Art.8.[15] It was unconvinced by the Government's arguments that the presence of homosexual personnel would have a negative effect on morale and risk diminishing operational effectiveness, noting that the applicants concerned had not been shown to pose disciplinary or other problems and that any untoward effects from inappropriate behaviour could be dealt with by a conduct code, rather than a blanket ban. The Court required particularly serious reasons for interference in this intimate part of an individual's life, even in the army context and although there was a reference to the State's margin of appreciation in matters of national security, it found a lack of any concrete evidence to support the Government's fears. To the extent that these were based on negative attitudes held by some service personnel, it emphasised that this prejudice could not justify interferences with rights any more than negative attitudes to race, origin or colour.

IIB–023

5. Restrictions on freedom of expression and freedom to receive information

Interferences with soldiers' access to outside sources of information have been treated with some robustness by the Commission and Court which have not been overly sympathetic to the protective attitude of State authorities, although acknowl-

IIB–024

[13] See also *Yavuz v Turkey*, 29870/96, (Dec.) May 25, 2000, where military officers on the Supreme Military Administrative Court offered sufficient independence, *e.g.* irremovability during term of office and no supervisory assessment by military authorities.

[14] 9237/81, *UK*, (Dec.) October 12, 1983, 34 D.R. 68.

[15] *Smith and Grady v UK*; *Lustig-Prean and Beckett*, September 27, 1999.

edging that the proper functioning of an army presupposes rules preventing the undermining of military discipline.[16] Soldiers still enjoy freedom of expression and to receive and impart information. An assertion by the Austrian authorities that a magazine was a threat to discipline and to service efficiency had to be substantiated by specific examples, of which none were given.[17] The magazine in question was not found by the Court to overstep what was permissible in the context of a mere discussion of ideas, including army reform, which must be tolerated in the army of a democratic State. There was thus a violation in respect of both the magazine producers, whose publication was not allowed to be distributed internally and in respect of the soldier who was fined for distributing it. Where an applicant was prosecuted for distributing leaflets to British soldiers, there was a distinction to be drawn, the Commission found, between publications aimed at inciting disaffection and those expressing opinions as to the policy of using the army in Northern Ireland. Since the applicant was expressly encouraging soldiers to go absent without leave as a means of protest and had not been dissuaded by other means from giving up her activities, the Commission found that her conviction and sentence to eight to nine months' imprisonment was not disproportionate to the aim pursued.[18]

Security considerations are given full weight where measures are applied in respect of the disclosure of information by army personnel. In *Hadjianasstiou v Greece*, where an officer was sentenced to five months for revealing military data in a study submitted to a private company, the Court referred to the special responsibilities incumbent on military life. Since the officer was involved in an experimental missile programme and bound by a duty of discretion, the Court agreed with Government that the disclosure was capable of revealing the State's progress in weapons development and thus damage security interests.

Where a soldier expresses criticism of the armed forces, the domestic authorities' reaction must be proportionate. In relation to an admiral who made critical statements on television, the Commission accepted that suspension was proportionate reaction given the nature of his comments which were found by the domestic courts to discredit Government information policy and, by condemning modern warfare and matters of defence policy, give rise to doubts that he would fulfil his obligations to the State.[19] Where however the criticism was conducted internally, by means of a letter to a senior officer, in terms which did not name any other officer critically but raised matters of public concern, the Commission found a disciplinary sanction of three months' imprisonment disproportionate.[20]

6. Freedom of religion

IIB–025 Where members of the armed services have been penalised or subject to measures resulting from religious affiliations or activities, issues have arisen under Art.9. These cases primarily relate to steps taken in the Greek army against proselytisers and in the Turkish army against Islamic fundamentalists.[21] The importance of respecting the inner spiritual convictions of a person is such that it is arguable that

[16] *Vereinigung demokratischer soldaten*, para.36; *Grigoriades*, para.45.
[17] *Vereinigung demokratischer soldaten*.
[18] *Arrowsmith v UK*, 7050/75, (Rep.), October 12, 1978, 19 D.R. 5.
[19] 23576/94, (Dec.) November 29, 1995.
[20] *Grigoriades*.
[21] See, *e.g. Kalaç v Turkey*; 18673/91; *Larissis v Greece*.

espousal of a particular religion should, without more, justify sanctions of dismissal. However, in contrast to the approach taken in the gays in the army cases under Art.8, the Court has found that disciplinary measures may be imposed in respect of Islamic fundamentalism without reference to any requirement to show demonstrable prejudice to discipline or the functioning of the service.

In *Kalaç v Turkey*, where a military judge was forced into early retirement allegedly as a result of his religious convictions, the Court found that in choosing to pursue a military career he accepted the restrictions implied by a system of military discipline, including regulations forbidding, *inter alia*, an attitude inimical to the established order reflecting the requirements of military service. Since the applicant was able to fulfil the normal forms through which a Muslim practised his religion and the reasoning for the order was based not on his religious opinions but his conduct and attitude,[22] it found that the compulsory retirement had not interfered with any right guaranteed under Art.9. Thus, since no interference was found, the Court had no need to examine the necessity or proportionality of any measures under the second paragraph. Since then the Court has stated in terms that disciplinary regulations may include a duty for military personnel to refrain from participating in the Islamic fundamentalist movement, whose aim and programme is to ensure the pre-eminence of religious rules.[23]

A distinction was drawn by the Convention organs in a Greek case where air force officers who were members of the Pentecostal church were tried for proselytism.[24] The interference with their rights to manifest their beliefs was found to be justified where the proselytism related to servicemen in the applicants' unit having regard to the special character of the relationship between a superior and subordinate in the army which rendered the subordinate more susceptible to influence. Conversely, where the offences related to proselytism of civilians, outside this special relationship, the interferences were not found to be justified.

Cross-reference

Part IIA: Fair trial, General considerations: Criminal Charge
Part IIB: Freedom of expression
Part IIB: Freedom of religion
Part IIB: Right to life (concerning Armed Forces' use of lethal force)

---

[22] A fine distinction—the conduct included the adoption of unlawful fundamentalist opinions. The Court has effectively accepted that disciplinary action based on military objection to particular alleged opinions does not interfere with rights under Art.9. This approach has been followed in numerous other dismissal cases, where grounds included the applicants' wives wearing of headscarves—this was still viewed as concerning conduct and activities in breach of military discipline and the principle of secularism rather than based on the applicants' religious beliefs of opinions or the observance of their religious duties, *e.g.* *Tepeli v Turkey*, (Dec.) 31876/96, June 12, 2001 and *Sen v Turkey*, (Dec.) July 8, 2003.

[23] *e.g. Sen*, n.22 above, citing *Yanasik v Turkey*, 14524/89, *Turkey*, (Dec.) January 6, 1993, 74 D.R. 14 where a military cadet was dismissed from an academy in Turkey. No interference with religious belief was found as the Commission accepted that the dismissal was for disciplinary reasons, although these included grounds that he had participated in fundamentalist activities.

[24] *Larissis*.

Arrest

Key provisions:

IIB–026   Article 5 para.1(c) (right to liberty exception of lawful arrest for the purpose of bringing before the competent legal authority on reasonable suspicion of committing an offence, or where reasonably necessary to prevent the commission of an offence or fleeing after commission of an offence.

Key case law:

Brogan v UK, November 29, 1988, Series A, No.145–B; 11 E.H.H.R 117; *Fox, Campbell and Hartley v UK*, August 30, 1990 Series A, No.182; 13 E.H.R.R. 157; *Murray v UK*, October 28, 1994, Series A, No.300–A; 19 E.H.R.R. 193; *Lukanov v Bulgaria*, March 20, 1997, R.J.D. 1997–II, No.34; *Erdagöz v Turkey*, October 22, 1997, R.J.D. 1997–VI, No.54; 32 E.H.R.R. 443; *K-F v Germany*, November 27, 1997, R.J.D. 1997–VII; *Wloch v Poland*, October 19, 2000, ECHR 2000–XI; *O'Hara v UK*, October 16, 2001, ECHR 2001–X.

1. General considerations

IIB–027   Arrest in this section refers to the use of power to detain to investigate or prevent crime. The key issues have arisen from the standard of suspicion justifying arrest and only to a lesser extent, the conditions and procedural safeguards surrounding the arrest. Requirements of lawfulness lay emphasis on conformity with domestic procedural safeguards and generally the Convention organs have not been overly rigorous in their scrutiny, assuming the *bona fides* of the police and requiring only the minimum indications of grounds for the arrest, sufficient to exclude clear arbitrariness or oppressiveness.

2. Existence of arrest or detention

IIB–028   In the ordinary course of events, there is no doubt as to whether a person has been held or detained by means of the exercise of a power of arrest. Occasionally, there is a question mark as to the nature and degree of the loss of liberty.[1]

3. Grounds of arrest

IIB–029   Three heads of arrest are included in Art.5, para.1(c). Most cases have concerned arrest on reasonable suspicion of having committed an offence, while the heads of reasonably necessary to prevent an offence[2] or "to prevent a person fleeing after an offence" have been seldom invoked.[3]

---

[1] See Pt IIB, Deprivation of liberty.
[2] Preventive detention outside the scope of criminal proceedings does not fall within Art.5 para.1(c)— *Jecius v Lithuania*, July 31, 2000, paras 50–52.
[3] See, however, *Lukanov*: the Commission found that where there is no reasonable suspicion of an offence

"Offence" in this context appears to enjoy a wide definition. In *Brogan v United Kingdom*, the applicants argued that arrest under prevention of terrorism legislation on suspicion that a person is or has been involved in acts of terrorism was not on suspicion of having committed a specific offence but of involvement in unspecified acts of terrorism which could not be regarded as an "offence" for the purposes of Art.5, para.1(c). The Court found that the definition of terrorism as the use of violence for political ends was well in keeping with the idea of an offence.[4]

4. Reasonable suspicion of having committed an offence

The standard is simply one of a reasonable suspicion. It is not required that the existence and nature of the offence be definitely proved since that is the purpose of the investigation.[5]

IIB–030

The fact that domestic law does not set the same standard of suspicion will not necessarily disclose a violation on arrest, since the Convention organs will examine whether on the facts of the individual case there nonetheless existed a reasonable suspicion.[6]

The Court found that "reasonable suspicion" presupposed the existence of facts or information that would satisfy an objective observer that the person concerned may have committed the offence. However, what is to be regarded as reasonable will depend on the circumstances.[7] Terrorist crime, it held, fell into a special category due to considerations of urgency and reliance on information which might be reliable but could not be revealed without risk to the source. Therefore the same standards could not always apply, subject to the rider that the criterion is not stretched to the point that the essence of the safeguard is impaired.[8]

That said, there is a fine line between those cases where the suspicion grounding an arrest is sufficiently founded on fact and those where it is not.[9] In *Fox, Campbell and Hartley v United Kingdom*, where the applicants were arrested on suspicion of being terrorists, the Court considered that some factual elements at least must be

---

having been committed the applicant's detention cannot be justified by an alleged danger of fleeing having committed an offence; the Court found it unnecessary to decide. See also *Eriksen v Norway*, May 27, 1997, R.J.D. 1997–III, para.86 concerning detention pending a decision whether to impose a further period of security detention of a person convicted of an offence and subject to a special preventative sentence.

[4] The Court cited its findings in *Ireland v UK* judgment, January 18, 1978, Series A, No.25, paras 196–197. Breach of the peace has also been regarded as an offence: *Steel v UK*, September 23, 1998, R.J.D 1998–VII, No.91, para.49.

[5] *e.g.* 8083/77, (Dec.) March 13, 1980, 19 D.R. 223 where a solicitor who failed to appear before the court when a case was relisted was arrested for contempt of court, the fact that the court of appeal found that there had been no contempt did not mean that a reasonable suspicion had not existed at the time; 9627/81, (Dec.) March 14, 1984, 37 D.R. 15. For a recent Court statement, *O'Hara*, para.36.

[6] *Fox, Campbell and Hartley*, para.31.

[7] *ibid.*, para.32; 27143/95, (Dec.) January 14, 1997, 88–A D.R. 94 where the Commission noted the risks attaching to basing reasonable suspicion on statements of Mafia *"pentitii"* and had regard to whether the domestic courts had assessed their credibility.

[8] *ibid.*, paras 31–32; *O'Hara*, para.35; *Cisse v France*, 51346/99, (Dec.) January 16, 2001, ECHR 2001–I; also 8098/77, (Dec.) December 13, 1978, 16 D.R. 11: concerning an arrest on espionage (ordered by a judge) where suspicions were based on a small number of elements which was nevertheless qualified as reasonable, the decision giving weight to the judge's knowledge and experience in assessing the basis of suspicion.

[9] *O'Hara*, para.41.

furnished by the Government capable of satisfying the Court that the applicants wre reasonably suspected, particularly since domestic law set a lower threshold of merely honest suspicion. The fact that the two suspects had had previous convictions for acts of terrorism connected with the IRA was not sufficient for an arrest some seven years later.[10]

Where however the Government is able to point to even indirect facts supporting their suspicion, as in *Murray v United Kingdom*, where the applicant was arrested under a similar provision as in *Fox, Campbell and Hartley*, there may be no violation.[11] In that case, where the applicant was arrested for involvement in IRA fund raising, the Court emphasised the special exigencies of investigating terrorism and recognised the need for use of confidential sources in fighting terrorism. It was also influenced by findings of domestic courts in the applicant's false imprisonment action where the judge had found the arresting officer transparently honest and that the applicant was genuinely suspected of having been involved in collecting funds for the purchase of arms for the IRA, the Court commenting that honesty and *bona fides* were an indispensable element of reasonableness. It added a new factor, the short period that the arrest lasted, four hours which strangely suggests the strength of the suspicion required alters with duration of the arrest.

Sufficient accountability in domestic proceedings, where the Convention test of reasonable suspicion is applicable, may meet the requisite standard and provide the necessary guarantee against arbitrary arrest, even where, as in the *O'Hara* case, there was in the domestic court's view "scanty evidence" of any connection between the applicant and the murder under investigation.[12]

There is a certain reluctance perhaps by the Court to find that authorities have acted in bad faith in carrying out arrests. In *Erdagöz v Turkey*, the applicant alleged that his arrest for allegedly producing false evidence that an attack had been committed on his shop was motivated by police resentment against him for complaints which he had made. No fact was apparently adverted to by the Government as justifying the arrest and the Commission noted that in fact a suspect was prosecuted for the attack on the shop which he had reported. However, the Court considered that suspicion was based on specific facts (*e.g.* the applicant's conduct) and saw no reason to disagree with the public prosecutor's finding that the 24 hours detention was for the purpose of confirming or dispelling the suspicion that he had falsely reported a criminal offence. The Court accordingly appears to require convincing evidence before it will find arbitrariness on the part of the police or other authorities.[13]

However where the allegations in proceedings against a suspect rely on matters which do not disclose an offence, the arrest and detention may fall outside the permitted exception, since the existence of reasonable suspicion requires that the facts relied on can be reasonably invoked as falling under prescribed criminal

[10] See also *Berktay v Turkey*, March 1, 2001, paras 199–201, finding a violation where the Government provided no basis justifying the arrest of the applicant during a house search.
[11] The Commission had found a violation seeing no real distinction with *Fox, Campbell and Hartley* the elements relied on by the Government being insufficient to found reasonable suspicion (*e.g.* her brother's conviction in the USA on arms buying charges).
[12] The applicant alleged that as prominent member of Sinn Fein he was targeted by the police as an automatic suspect.
[13] See *Smirnova v Russia*, July 24, 2003, ECHR 2003–IX, paras 65–71, where the repeated detaining of the applicants during an investigation on the basis of insufficiently reasoned decisions disclosed a violation of Art.5, para.1 as well as para.3.

behaviour. Thus, in *Lukanov v Bulgaria*, where the applicant, a minister of the previous regime, was arrested and detained allegedly for misappropriation of funds, the Commission observed that the grounds of the accusations referred solely to his transfers of monies in aid to the Third World which was not an offence. Thus the facts invoked against the applicant at the time of his arrest and during his continued detention could not in the eyes of an objective observer be construed as amounting to the criminal offence of misappropriation of funds and there was no reasonable suspicion of his having committed an offence to justify the detention.[14] In *Wloch v Poland*, the uncertainties surrounding the interpretation of the domestic law imposing an offence in trading in children caused the Court to doubt the legality of the applicant's detention on suspicion of such activities, though it relied on the domestic investigation into the factual aspects of the suspicion and the suspicion that he had also committed the offence of inciting persons to give false evidence as showing that there was nothing arbitrary or unreasonable in his detention.[15]

5. Purpose to bring before a competent legal authority

This is the purpose underlying Art.5, para.1(c) read in conjunction with Art.5, para.3. Applicants arrested under the three heads must all be brought before a judge, or released.[16]   **IIB–031**

It has sometimes been argued that the apparent purpose of an arrest was not to bring before a competent legal authority but to gather information without necessarily intending to charge the person with anything. In *Brogan*, where the applicants argued that they were neither charged nor brought before a court, the Court agreed with the Commission that the existence of the purpose (to bring before a court if sufficient and usable evidence had been obtained during the police investigation) had to be considered independently of the achievement of that purpose. Arrest under Art.5, para.1(c) did not presuppose that charges have to be brought but that the criminal investigation be furthered by way of confirming or dispelling the concrete suspicion. Evidence may prove unobtainable or impossible to produce in court. In the particular case, there was no indication that the police investigation was not in good faith and it could be assumed that, if they had been able, the police would have laid charges and brought the applicants before the competent legal authority. The fact that they were questioned about specific offences showed that their arrest was grounded in concrete suspicions.[17]

---

[14] The Court's reasoning took a different emphasis, namely, that as none of the criminal provisions relied on specified or implied criminal liability could be incurred by participating in collective decisions of this kind, the deprivation of liberty was not "lawful"—paras 42–45.

[15] paras 108–117.

[16] *Lawless v Ireland*, July 1, 1961, Series A, No.3, pp.51–52 para.14, where the Government unsuccessfully argued a construction excluding the second and third heads, *i.e.* suspicion that a person would commit an offence or flee having committed one. The arrest of persons suspected of IRA membership for the purposes of internment, without the prospect of bringing them before a judicial authority was found by the Court to be contrary to Art.5, para.1(c) and para.3, though covered by Ireland's derogation under Art.15.

[17] See also *K-F v Germany*, paras 57–62; *Perry v UK*, 63737/00, (Dec.), September 26, 2002, where the applicant suspect was brought to the police station ostensibly for questioning and was filmed, without his knowledge, for identification purposes, the Court considered that this covert purpose did not render the detention either unlawful or arbitrary.

6. Lawfulness and procedural safeguards

IIB–032   It is not required that arrest be ordered by a judge[18] but the individual must be brought promptly before a judge for the purposes of Art.5, para.3.[19] The arrest must be carried out in accordance with a procedure prescribed by law according to the second sentence of Art.5, para.1 and must also be "lawful" in terms of the various sub-paragraphs.[20] Reasons for the arrest must also be given promptly under Art.5, para.2.

Cross-reference

Part IIB: Deprivation of liberty
Part IIB: Pre-trial detention
Part IIB: Reasons for arrest and detention
Part IIB: Review of detention

---

[18] 7755/77, (Dec.) May 18, 1977, 9 D.R. 210.
[19] See Pt IIB: Pre-trial detention.
[20] See, *e.g. Steel*, n.4 above: the Court found that the conduct of three applicants handing out leaflets peacefully about arms sales did not justify any fear of a breach of the peace and their arrests were not lawful (paras 62–65); *Lucas v UK*, 39013/02, (Dec.), March 18, 2003: the arrest of the applicant for sitting in the road was regarded as lawful under Art.5, para.1; *Lukanov*, paras 42–45.

Childcare cases

Key provisions:

Articles 6 (fair hearing), 8 (respect for family life) and 14 (prohibition of   IIB–033
discrmination).

Key case law:

W, B and R v UK, July 8, 1987, Series A, No.121; 10 E.H.R.R. 29; *O and H v UK,*
July 8, 1987, Series A, No.120; 10 E.H.R.R. 82 and 95; *Olsson v Sweden,* March 24,
1988, Series A, No.130; 11 E.H.R.R. 259; *Eriksson v Sweden,* June 22, 1989, Series
A, No.156; 12 E.H.R.R. 183; *Margareta and Roger Andersson v Sweden,* February 25,
1992, Series A, No.226–A; 14 E.H.R.R. 615; *Rieme v Sweden,* April 22, 1992, Series
A, No.226–B; 16 E.H.R.R. 155; *Keegan v Ireland,* May 26, 1994, Series A, No.290;
18 E.H.R.R. 342; *Hokkanen v Finland,* September 23, 1994, Series A, No.299–A; 19
E.H.R.R. 139; *Kroon v Netherlands,* October 27, 1994, Series A, No.297–C; 19
E.H.R.R. 273; *McMichael v UK,* February 24, 1995, Series A, No.307–B; 20
E.H.R.R. 205; *Johansen v Norway,* August 7, 1996, R.J.D., 1996–III, No.13; 23
E.H.R.R. 33; *Bronda v Italy,* June 9, 1998, R.J.D. 1998–IV, No.77; *Soderback v
Sweden,* October 28, 1998, R.J.D., 1998–VIII, No.94; 29 E.H.R.R. 95; *Ignaccolo-
Zenide v Romania,* January 25, 2000, ECHR 2000–I; *Nuuttinen v Finland,* June 27,
2000, ECHR 2000–VIII; *Elsholz v Germany,* July 13, 2000, ECHR 2000–VIII;
Scozzari and Giunta v Italy, July 13, 2000, ECHR 2000–VIII; *TP and KM v UK,*
May 10, 2001, ECHR 2001–V; *K and T v Finland,* July 12, 2001, ECHR 2001–
VII; 31 E.H.R.R. 212; *Kutzner v Germany,* February 26, 2002, ECHR 2002–I; *P, C
and S v UK,* July 16, 2002, ECHR 2002–VI; *Sylvester v Austria,* April 24, 2003;
Covezzi and Morselli v Italy, May 9, 2003; *Sahin v Germany,* July 8, 2003, ECHR
2003–VII; *Sommerfeld v Germany,* July 8, 2003, ECHR 2003–VIII.

1. General considerations

This section concerns three situations where care, custody and contact with children   IIB–034
may raise issues under the Convention. The first category involves the most
common cause of complaint, namely, intervention by State authorities to remove
children from their families and subsequent decisions taken as to contact, custody
and adoption. The second category concerning regulation by the courts of custody
and contact disputes following divorce or separation of the parents has produced
fewer significant cases. Thirdly, there is a small group of cases dealing with issues of
parental rights arising in non-conventional family groupings.

Given the seriousness of the interferences in the first category, the Court gives
complaints careful scrutiny. It has generally confined its role in line with its
pronouncements on the nature of European supervision, in particular, that it is not
its function to substitute its view on the merits for that of the domestic authorities.
In this area, the domestic courts are particularly well placed to assess the
requirements of the welfare of the children and under the "margin of appreciation"
doctrine, a significant measure of discretion is accorded to domestic authorities in
the performance of their functions and in their evaluation of the factors which may

appear to them to be critical for the protection of the health or morals of a child.[1] Consequently, if, after judicial proceedings in which the parent's interests are fairly protected, a judgment is issued removing custody or contact on the basis that the measure is necessary for the welfare of the children, it is unlikely that an application would succeed on the basis of a complaint that the decision was wrong.[2] The cases have concentrated on procedural aspects: access to court, delay, legal representation, etc. The merits of a decision may however be challenged indirectly through the requirement, outlined below, that decisions must be supported by relevant and sufficient reasons.

2. Interferences by domestic authorities

IIB–035   Steps taken *vis-à-vis* parents regulating contact with their children, removing custody or parental responsibility, *prima facie* constitute interferences with family life which require justification under Art.8, para.2. Parents include natural fathers, where there has been cohabitation or other factors showing a relationship of sufficient constancy as to create *de facto* family ties.[3] The biological link does not however confer an absolute right to obtain parental rights, the interests of the child prevailing over the natural father's where any clash of Art.8 rights occur.[4]

The extent to which interferences may occur in respect of other family members or concerned persons depends on the nature of the relationship with the child. In grandparent cases,[5] the Commission took the view that links between grandparents and grandchildren varied from family to family and each case had to be examined on its facts to determine whether there were sufficient links to constitute "family life" and thereby bring the relationship within the protection of Art.8. In determining whether the decisions taken by the social services interfered with the rights guaranteed under this provision, the Commission considered that different standards would normally apply than where a parent was involved. For example, a grandparent's access to a child was normally at the discretion of the child's parents in any case and regulation of access by a local authority *per se* would not constitute an interference. There might however be an interference where a local authority

---

[1] *e.g. Bronda*, para.59, *TP and KM*, para.70. The Court also takes into account the fact that perceptions as to the appropriateness of intervention by public authorities vary between Contracting States, depending, *inter alia*, on traditions relating to the role of the family—*K and T v Finland*, para.154, *Kutzner*, para.66.

[2] The notion of "necessity" as applied by the courts however requires more pressing justification that the fact that a child could be placed in a more beneficial environment, *e.g. K and T v Finland*, para.173, *Kutzner*, para.69.

[3] See *Keegan*, para.44: a child born out of a relationship of two persons cohabiting outside marriage *ipso iure* is part of the "family unit" and a family bond exists even if at the time of birth the parents no longer co-habit or the relationship has ended; *Kroon*, para.56: the natural father did not cohabit but there was a longstanding relationship from which four children were born; *Elsholz*, para.43. However in 22920/93, (Dec.) April 6, 1994, 77–A D.R. 108, the Commission were not prepared to find family life existed where the applicant claimed to be the father of a child of a married woman or a right to prove the link through a blood test—it distinguished *Keegan* on the basis the mother disputed his claims, there was no element of planning or cohabitation and thus insufficient links in fact or law to bring the case within Art.8. Similar conclusion in *Nylund v Finland*, 27110/95, (Dec.) June 29, 1999 , ECHR 1999–VI.

[4] *e.g. Yousef v Netherlands*, November 5, 2002, where the mother had died and the child was living with her uncle, the courts' refusal to give legal recognition of paternity which the applicant intended to use to disrupt her current family situation struck the right balance.

[5] 12399/85, (Dec.) March 9, 1988; 12402/86, (Dec.) July 14, 1988, 55 D.R. 224; 12763/87, July 14, 1988, 57 D.R.216.

diminished the access necessary to preserve a normal grandparent-grandchild relationship. The Court has acknowledged that ties between near relatives such as grandparents and grandchildren falls within "family life" since such relatives may play a considerable part in family life.[6]

The Commission accepted that an uncle may have a relationship with a child of such a nature as to attract the protection of Art.8, where he had acted as a "father figure" and lived in close contact with the child, such that refusal of access by the social services when the child was taken into care disclosed an interference.[7] An older case also indicates that a foster-parent may have sufficient links with a child to attract the protection of Art.8 of the Convention.[8]

Children in care may themselves, through an appropriate representative, complain that their rights under the Convention have been infringed by measures taken by social services. Although in early cases the Commission had regard to whether the parent had any legal right to represent the child,[9] the Court has stated that the conditions concerning standing under the Convention are not necessarily the same as those in national law. In order to ensure that the child's interests are put forward and effectively protected, it has held that a natural parent may introduce an application on behalf of the child even if he or she no longer has parental rights under domestic law.[10]

The case law has established a number of key areas where violations may arise.

(a) *Procedural protection of rights*

The first UK cases before the Court established the important principle that the decision-making process in childcare matters afford sufficient procedural protection of parents' interests.[11] Where in *W v United Kingdom*, for example, the local authority passed a parental rights resolution in respect of the applicant's child S and proceeded to take a series of decisions—placement in long-term foster-care with a view to adoption, restriction and termination of access—without advance consultation or discussion with the applicant or his wife, the Court noted that it was crucial in an area where decisions may prove irreversible (*i.e.* a child may form new bonds

IIB–036

---

[6] See *Scozzari and Giunta*, para.221—no problem was found concerning the grandmother's complaints of denial of access due to her own inconsistent behaviour and lack of co-operation; *Bronda*, paras 59–63, where the child's interest in remaining with her foster parents outweighed that of her grandparents.

[7] *Boyle v UK*, (Rep.) February 9, 1993, Series A, No.282–B.

[8] 8257/78, (Dec.) July 10, 1978, 13 D.R. 248.

[9] In *Hokkanen*, since in the domestic proceedings the father no longer had legal custody and had no right in domestic terms to represent the child, the Commission found that he could not complain on behalf of the child in Strasbourg.

[10] *Scozzari and Giunta*, paras 138–9; *P, C and S v UK* (Dec.) December 11, 2001, where the child had been adopted and the natural parents were not considered safe guardians by the authorities, it was still considered essential that potential claims be put forward on her behalf. See also *SP, DP and AT v UK*, 23715/94, (Dec.) May 20, 1996) where the Commission allowed a case to be introduced on behalf of three children by the solicitor who had represented them in care proceedings and who complained of the unjustifiable delay as prejudicing their welfare. Although he no longer represented them in domestic terms, the Commission noted the importance that children's rights be practically and effectively protected and that in the absence of any conflict of interest or the existence of more appropriate representation, found the solicitor had sufficient links with the children and the subject-matter of the claim to represent them in Strasbourg.

[11] This does not automatically require access to court, lack of which would rather raise issues under Art.6 where civil rights were concerned, but covers the intervention by the social services, which may be crucial for the development of events.

with his alternative carers) that there is adequate protection for parents against arbitrary interferences. In the circumstances of this case, the Court found that the applicant had been insufficiently involved in critical stages of the decision-making which affected his relationship with S. Accordingly he had not been afforded the requisite consideration of his views or protection of his interests in violation of Art.8 of the Convention.

Since these decisions, particular attention has been paid to the procedural fairness of the decision-making process regarding parents and other members of the family, whose relationship with a child has been subject to interference.[12] Relevant factors, assessed on the particular facts of each case, include the opportunity to make submissions, in person or in writing, before decisions are reached[13]; access to the reports and documents relied on in the decision-making[14]; the provision of legal representation to parents[15]; the holding of public hearings and the obtaining of necessary independent psychiatric opinion.[16] Procedural requirements do not go so far as to require domestic courts always hear the child in court on the issue of access, this issue depending on specific facts of the case with due regard to the age and maturity of the child.[17]

Although the responsibility lies on the authorities to ensure that a parent is placed in a position where he or she can obtain access to information basing care measures, there is no absolute right of a parent to view materials. In *TP and KM v UK*, the applicant mother complained that she was prevented for a year from viewing a video of a disclosure interview crucial to the decision to remove her daughter into care as the doctor and social worker involved considered that this was not in the interests of the child. The Court emphasised, to the Government's argument that she had not applied to the court for disclosure, that it was not the sole responsibility of the parent nor lay at her initiative, to obtain the evidence on

---

[12] No explicit procedural requirements are contained in Art.8: the emphasis is on fairness and due respect to the interests to be safeguarded, *e.g. McMichael*, para.87; *Buscemi v Italy*, September 16, 1999, ECHR 1999–VI, para.58 (no violation concerning expert evidence procedure).

[13] *e.g. Boyle*, n.7 above, where the uncle was a *de facto* father to the child in care, the Commission found a violation in that there was no meaningful consultation with him by the social services, which took the decision to end access without prior invitation of his views; 17071/90, (Dec.) February 13, 1990, where a mother complained of the inclusion of her child's name on a child abuse register, her position was adequately safeguarded by the opportunity to submit her views in writing beforehand; *Covezzi and Morselli v Italy*, paras 134–139: violation arose from the applicants' inability to put forward effectively their objections to the care measures over significant periods.

[14] *e.g. McMichael*, where the Children's Hearing only summarised orally the reports concerning the applicant parents and their baby.

[15] *P, C and S v UK*, paras 92–100, 134–137: violations of both Arts 6 and 8 where the court continued the hearing of care order and freeing for adoption applications when the applicant parents were unrepresented. See also Pt IIA: Legal Aid in Civil Cases.

[16] *Elsholz*, paras 52–53: the courts did not obtain independent psychological evidence concerning the child's (aged 5–6) position on access with her father, where the child, questioned by the judge, knew of the mother's objections and had shown hostility to the father: violations of both Arts 8 and 6. However in *Sommerfeld*, paras 69–75, no violation arose from a failure to obtain a psychological report on the access possibilities between child and natural father:the distinction with *Elsholz* appears to be the age of the child—she was 13 and had been questioned several times by the judge who was recognised as being able, in the case of such a mature child, to evaluate her statements and assess whether she was capable of making up her own mind, without expert evidence.

[17] *Sahin*, paras 73–74, no violation for failure to hear a child aged 3–5 years during the access proceedings.

which the removal was based and that the local authority should have submitted the issue of disclosure to the court for it to determine the issues.[18]

The level of consultation or involvement in the decision-making process required may differ in respect of non-parental relatives.[19]

(b) Emergency measures

A wide margin of appreciation applies to the authorities' assessment of the necessity of taking a child into care.[20] The Court also accepts that when emergency care orders are made it may not be possible, due to the urgency of the situation, to involve the parents in the decision-making process and that it may deprive the measure of effectiveness to give prior warning of the measure to those seen as the source of possible harm to the child. However the Court will examine whether there exist circumstances justifying an abrupt removal without prior consultation or notification and whether the authorities have carried out a proper assessment of the impact of the measures and the existence of possible alternatives.[21] Extraordinarily compelling reasons must exist for a baby to be physically removed from the mother after birth.[22] In *K and T v Finland*, the Court found the removal of a baby from her mother at birth was not so justified, as the authorities were well aware of the mother's mental problems, both mother and child were in hospital care and no consideration was given to other less drastic ways of protecting the child from harm.[23] In *P, C and S v United Kingdom*, the Court found that there were sufficiently compelling reasons to issue an emergency protection order for a new born baby whose mother had a conviction for previously harming a child and was suspected of suffering from Munchhausen's Syndrome by proxy. It did however find a violation concerning the implementation of the protection order, namely, the removal of the baby from the hospital into care rather than a less drastic form of supervision of mother and baby within the hospital.[24]

IIB–037

[18] paras 80–83. See also *KA v Finland*, January 14, 2003, para.105, stating that as a general rule the authorities have an obligation to make available all case-materials even in the absence of a request by the parents.

[19] 12763/87, n.5 above: while the decision to end all contact with their grandchild constituted an interference with family life, the Commission did not expect that grandparents be involved in the procedures to the same extent as parents: it was sufficient that the local authority consulted the grandparents regularly, allowed them to make representations at case conferences and provided a procedure for review.

[20] e.g. *Johansen*, para.64.

[21] *K and T v Finland*, para.166.

[22] *K and T*, para.168.

[23] para.168: conversely, the emergency care order for the older child was justified as he was already in voluntary care and had showed signs of disturbance—para.169; *TP and KM*, para.74, where the emergency removal of a four year old, later found to be based on mistaken assumptions, was, at the time, justified by strong suspicions of abuse and inability of the mother to protect her; *Covezzi and Morselli*, para.104, where the removal of four children was justified by multi-generational sexual abuse and doubts about parental protection; *KA v Finland*, n.18 above, paras 98–102, removal into care justified even though investigation into incest allegations not completed.

[24] See also *Venema v Netherlands*, December 17, 2002, where the mother was also suspected of Munchhausen Syndrome by proxy, the Court found the issuing of an emergency care order violated Art.8, essentially because, in contrast to *P, C and S*, the authorities had not allowed the parents any input before the order was made.

(c) *Access to court*

IIB–038 A parent's rights to contact with, and custody of, a child constitute "civil rights" the determination of which requires a fair hearing before an independent and impartial tribunal pursuant to Art.6. In less technical terms, where an important issue concerning a parent's relationship with a child is at stake, a parent should be able to challenge the decision in a court. A violation was found, for example, in *R v United Kingdom*, where the mother of a child in care under a parental rights' resolution and to whom access had been refused by the local authority was unable to go to a court to challenge that refusal. Where a natural father had no standing in care proceedings concerning a child taken into care and no prospect of applying for contact, the case was settled after being declared admissible.[25] Inability of a natural father to challenge before a court the adoption of a child disclosed a violation in *Keegan v Ireland*.

Access to court for other relatives would not appear to be regarded an automatic requirement, having regard to the basic principle that Art.6, para.1 only applies to procedures concerning the recognition of a right which has a legal basis in domestic law. Thus, the Commission found that Art.6, para.1 could not be invoked by grandparents, since it did not consider that under English law grandparents enjoyed a right of custody of or access to their grandchildren.[26]

(d) *Delay in proceedings*

IIB–039 Child care proceedings must be managed with particular expedition, having regard to the importance of what is at stake and since the nature of the issues is such that the lapse of time may influence their outcome.[27] In *H v United Kingdom*, where an application for access was not decided for almost two years, the judge had refused access but criticised the delay as "quite deplorable" and commented that it had seriously prejudiced the position of the applicant, who by that point had not seen the child for three and a half years during which time she had been settled for 19 months with prospective adopters. Under Art.6, the Court found a violation since the applicant had not received a fair hearing within a reasonable time having regard to the importance of what was at stake for her.[28] Under Art.8, the violation lay in that delay had led to a *de facto* determination of the issue whereas an effective respect for the applicant's family life required that the question be determined solely in light of all the relevant considerations and not by the mere effluxion of time.

Whether the length of child care proceedings will disclose a violation under Art.8 will depend largely on the prejudicial effect on the outcome of the proceedings. Protracted criminal proceedings which have the direct consequence of seriously curtailing enjoyment of family life may also raise issues.[29] Under Art.6, the general

---

[25] 11468/85, (Dec.) October 15, 1986, 50 D.R. 199; 11240/84, (Rep.) May 13, 1988, 56 D.R. 108, where a natural father had no access to court to challenge a reduction in access.
[26] 12763/87, n.5 above.
[27] *e.g. Johansen*, para.88; *Hoppe v Germany*, December 5, 2002, para.54.
[28] Also *Nuutinen* , paras 109–120—violation for proceedings lasting over 5 years; *Paulsen-Medalen and Svensson v Sweden*, February 19, 1998, R.J.D., 1998–I, No.63.
[29] *Schaal v Luxembourg*, February 18, 2003: violations of Arts 6 and 8 due to the five year duration of the investigation into allegations of sexual assault of a child by the applicant father. Until his acquittal, his contact rights had been terminated to safeguard the child.

considerations applicable to length complaints are relevant, such as the complexity of the case and whether the applicant contributed to the delay.[30] A delay at one stage may be acceptable if the overall duration of the proceedings is not excessive.[31] (See Pt IIA: Fair Trial, Length of Proceedings.)

(e) *Relevant and sufficient reasons*

As stated above, the Court does not consider itself a court of appeal from domestic courts. Particularly in this area, it shies away from substituting its opinion on the merits. However it does not as result limit its review of a case solely to procedural matters. This was established in *Olsson v Sweden*, where the applicants' three children were taken into care, the social authorities considering that their development was in danger due, *inter alia*, to their parents' inability to satisfy their need for stimulation and supervision. In care, the children were separated and placed in foster-homes up to 600 km from their parents' home. In assessing whether this interference with the parents' rights was justified under the second paragraph of Art.8 as "necessary" in the children's interests, the Court repeated the principle that a margin of appreciation was left to the State in assessing the necessity of measures but held that it exercised a supervisory jurisdiction which was not confined to ascertaining whether the State had exercised its discretion reasonably, carefully and in good faith. It had also to consider whether the reasons adduced to justify an interference were "relevant and sufficient". On the facts of the case, it found that the decision to take the children into care initially was supported by such reasons (*e.g.* evidence that the children were retarded in their development, the fact that other measures had been tried without success). Regarding the implementation of the care order however, the Court found that, particularly since the measure was seen as temporary, the placing of the children in separate homes at such long distances was not supported by relevant or sufficient reasons. In this respect, there was a violation of Art.8.[32]

The Court will therefore review the decisions of domestic courts to determine whether they are supported by reasons which are both relevant and sufficient.[33]

IIB–040

---

[30] *e.g.* 13288/87, (Dec.) February 13, 1990 where a judge found no sensible explanation for 20 month delay in wardship proceeding, the Commission found that the time was not unreasonable under Art.6 nor had the case been determined solely by the effluxion of time contrary to Art.8: it had regard in particular to the complexity of the case, involving four children, and the failure of the applicant to take steps to expedite the matter (*e.g.* she agreed to the procedural steps which led to the longest periods of delay). Unlike *H v UK*, the applicant had had contact with the children during the proceedings and she had been partly successful, obtaining the return of 2 children.

[31] *MC v Finland*, 28460/95, (Dec.) January 25, 2001.

[32] Contrast *Covezzi and Morselli,* paras 128–130: the separate placement of four children was supported by psychological evidence.

[33] *e.g. Johansen*, where there were relevant reasons to support the permanent placement in the mother's conduct and the need for stability but these were not sufficient, *i.e.* the mother's lifestyle was improving and access was going well; *Margareta and Roger Andersson*, where there were relevant reasons in the child's difficulties and stress but that these were not sufficient to justify the almost complete deprivation of contact, by even letter and telephone, for over one and a half years; *EP v Italy*, November 16, 1999, where there were relevant and sufficient grounds for taking the child into care based on the mother's psychiatric disorders but no convincing explanation of why all contact was broken off; *Kutzner*, paras 77–82, where the removal into care, access restrictions and separate placements of the children which could only lead to "alienation" from the parents were not supported by sufficient reasons, *e.g.* although the applicants were lacking in intellectual capacity, expert reports indicated that the children's welfare was not in jeopardy and other measures of educational support were available; *Scozzari and Giunta*, para.171, where the authorities acted "irresponsibly" in suspending contact visits on the basis of an allegations of sexual assault in the absence of proper and prompt verification.

Where a court did not go into detail in its judgment, for example, expressly refraining from repeating evidence out of sympathy for the mother, the Commission took into account the evidence (medical and other reports) before the court in assessing whether the decision was adequately supported.[34] It is questionable whether, if a court failed to give any reasons at all for its decision, although there was material before it which might have furnished "relevant and sufficient reasons", the Court could or should embark on a reconstruction of what the court might have been thinking. In a more recent judgment, the Court has stated that the decision-making authorities and courts must give such detailed reasons as would allow the parent or custodian to appeal effectively and that vague descriptions or reference to "documentation on file" would be insufficient.[35]

(f) Rehabilitation

IIB–041 The taking into care of a child should normally be regarded as a temporary measure to be discontinued as soon as circumstances permit and any measures of implementation should be consistent with the ultimate aim of reuniting natural parent and child.[36] In *Hokkanen v Finland*, it was said that Art.8 confers a right for parents to have measures taken with a view to being reunited and that there is an obligation on the authorities to take such measures.[37] However, while there is a presumption of rehabilitation in favour of the parent, particular importance is attached to the best interests of the child, which may override those of the parent. A parent cannot claim a right to measures which would harm the child's health and development.[38]

Thus, measures taken with the aim of permanently depriving a parent of contact or custody, for example permanent placement with a view to adoption, must only be applied in exceptional circumstances and can only be justified if motivated by an overriding requirement pertaining to the child's best interests. While authorities enjoy a wide margin of appreciation in assessing the necessity of taking a child into care, a strict scrutiny will apply to any further restrictions which entail the danger of curtailing relations between parent and child.[39] Where, prior to termination of access, a mother's contact with her daughter in care was going well and there were signs of improvement in her life, the difficulties experienced by the social authorities in respect of measures concerning her son and the risk of disrupting the daughter's placement if access was given, did not disclose such overriding requirement.[40] In *K*

---

[34] *e.g.* 13288/87, n.30 above.

[35] *KA v Finland*, para.105.

[36] *Johansen*, para.78; in *Rieme*, the Court found that the gradual re-introduction of access between the applicant and his daughter did not disclose any hindrance of their reunion, having regard to the length of time she had lived in the foster-home.

[37] *e.g. Eriksson*, where the care order had been lifted but the social authorities continued to prohibit removal from the foster home, the Court noted that while difficulties might arise on the termination of care where children have spent long periods away from their parents, the unsatisfactory situation ensued in this case from a failure to ensure any meaningful access between mother and child with a view to reuniting them. See *Olsson*, para.81; *Margareta and Roger Andersson*, para.91; in *Kutzner*, para.76, the Court considered that the positive duty to take steps to facilitate re-unification took on progressive force as the separation continued.

[38] *Johansen*, para.78; *EP v Italy*, cited above, para.62.

[39] *e.g. Johansen*, para.64; *Gnahoré v France*, September 19, 2000, ECHR 2000–IX, para.54.

[40] *Johansen*, para.84; *EP v Italy*, n.33 above, where the suspension of parental responsibility was not based on accurate information or informed medical opinion and no apparent consideration given to supervision of contact.

and T v Finland, in finding a failure by the authorities to take sufficient steps towards reunification, the Court noted the exceptionally firm negative attitude shown by the authorities which only carried out enquiries once during seven years as to the possibility. The minimum that could have been expected was for the situation to be examined anew from time to time to see if there had been improvements, while the restrictions and prohibitions on access contributed to hindering any progress. It referred to a failure to make the serious or sustained effort to facilitate family reunification expected for the purposes of Art.8.[41]

The obligation to take measures to reunite parent and child is not absolute, however. The Court has acknowledged the need for preparatory steps and the requirement to balance the interests and rights and freedoms of all concerned. Nonetheless, there would appear to be an obligation that they take all necessary steps to facilitate reunion as can reasonably be demanded in the special circumstances of each case. Failure to give proper consideration to rehabilitation may therefore raise issues.[42] In *Gnahoré v France*, the Court considered that the failure of a parent to cooperate in preparatory measures could be a relevant, although a not "absolutely decisive" factor[43] and in light of the genuine efforts towards rehabilitation made by the authorities in that case and the fact that the applicant's behaviour caused the failure of the measures implemented, no lack of respect was shown by the omission of possible additional steps.[44]

(g) *Other issues*

It is not inconceivable that admissible complaints could arise under Art.3 concerning the alleged inhuman or degrading treatment of children subject to the perhaps over-zealous attentions of a local authority. The circumstances surrounding the removal of a child from its home by a local authority, the subsequent medical examination and interviews could inflict a level of distress and suffering on the child that brought the treatment within the scope of Art.3. In the context of compulsory medical treatment, the Court has found that as a general rule treatment which was a therapeutic necessity would not violate Art.3[45]; action by a local authority which had the *bona fide* intention of protecting that child might however still fall foul of Art.3 if it had departed from perceived ideas about desirable practices. On the other hand, it is now established that failure by the authorities authority to protect a child from abuse can disclose a violation of Art.3, where they did not take reasonable steps to prevent ill-treatment of which they knew or ought to have known.[46]

IIB–042

---

[41] paras 177–179; *KA v Finland*, paras 142–147, similar lack of "serious and sustained effort" and lack of genuine or regular reviews of the situation; *Scozzari and Giunta*, paras 174–183, where the social authorities altered the practical effect of contact orders by providing only sporadic visits and accentuating the rift between children and parents, the courts did not conduct thorough reviews of the situation and paras 210–216, concerning the negative influence of the placement in the "Il Forteto" community which was not sufficiently under the supervision of the relevant authorities.

[42] *e.g.* 18546/91 (Dec.) August 31, 1992 where the social services took an immediate decision to have a baby adopted where the mother after birth was admitted to a psychiatric unit—case was struck off after settlement.

[43] Obstruction and withdrawal from the proceedings by the parents were significant factors in finding no violation arising from prolonged interruption in contact in *Covezzi and Morselli*, para.122.

[44] Cited above, para.63.

[45] *Herczegfalvy v Austria*, September 24, 1992, Series A, No.244; 15 E.H.R.R. 437.

[46] *Z v UK*, May 10, 2001, ECHR 2001–V; *E v UK*, November 26, 2002.

Unjustified removal of a child from its home could also raise problems under Art.5 concerning arbitrary detention. A failure to respect the religious affiliations of a child in care could fall within the scope of Art.9 (freedom of religion) and a failure to ensure the proper education of a child in care could raise a problem under Art.2 of the First Protocol (right to education).

Although no right of access to court to obtain damages for the negligence of social services can be derived from Art.6 where domestic law does not provide a substantive right of action, issues may arise under Art.13 if the remedies available do not include the possibility of obtaining a determination of the allegations of breach of rights and an enforceable award of compensation.[47]

3. Regulation of disputes by the courts

IIB–043   Increasingly, the State is not directly involved in taking children into care but is called on to regulate the custody between different claimants, generally, in divorce and separation cases. Mostly these cases have been dismissed by the Convention organs since the decisions taken by the courts, having regard to the margin of appreciation, could be justified as being in the interests of the child, even where, for example, an adoption order in favour of the mother's new husband severed the applicant father's links with the child.[48]

The case of *Hoffman v Austria* indicated that reliance by the courts on discriminatory factors, not related to the welfare of the children, would disclose a violation of Art.8 in conjunction with Art.14. But the narrow margin in the Court (five to four) indicated that disapproval of a domestic court approach to the facts of a case may resemble an overruling of its assessment of the welfare of the children.[49] Prejudicial reliance by the Portugese court in awarding custody of a child to the mother on the homosexual orientation of the applicant father founded a similar violation in *Salguiero da Silva Mouta v Portugal*.[50] The decision by German courts refusing a natural father access to a child born out of wedlock on the basis that, where the mother was deeply opposed to contact, only special circumstances could

---

[47] See Z, n.46 above, where there was no possibility of obtaining determination of negligence claims or an enforceable award of damages for failure to protect the children from abuse and neglect by their parents; *TP and KM*: no possibility of negligence findings or an enforceable award for any damage caused to mother or child by the removal into care on the basis of mistaken assumptions.

[48] *Soderback*, paras 30–34: allowing the mother's partner to adopt was in the interests of the child, who had lived with adoptive father since she was eight months old and not disproportionate in its effects due to the relatively weak ties between the child and biological father, who had never had custody or care of the child.

[49] The applicant mother, a Jehovah's witness, while awarded custody by the two lower courts, lost to the father in the Supreme Court which overruled the lower courts' assessment of the children's welfare based on expert evidence and held that the children were at risk of being social outcasts and from the mother's refusal of blood transfusions. The Court majority found that the Supreme Court was clearly influenced, as shown by its tone and phrasing, by considerations regarding the applicant's religion. The minority considered that it was legitimate for the Supreme Court to look at the effect of the mother's religious affiliation on the children's welfare, that the decision could not be said to be based only on her religion and that it was not for the Convention organs to substitute their opinion concerning the children's welfare. Similar violation found in *Palau-Martinez v France*, December 16, 2003.

[50] December 21, 1999, ECHR 1999–IX, paras 35–36—the applicant's sexual orientation was the decisive factor in the custody decision, a distinction not acceptable under the Convention.

justify an assumption that access was in the child's best interests was found to be discriminatory in *Sahin v Germany*.[51]

Failure to enforce court orders as to custody and contact may also raise issues. The test appears to be whether the authorities have taken all necessary steps to enforce decisions as can be reasonably demanded in the special circumstances of each case. In *Hokkanen v Finland*, a violation of Art.8 arose from the authorities' inaction over several years in enforcing the court orders for access where the grandparents refused to return a child to the applicant father. While the Government argued that there were limited options open to the authorities in face of wilful intransigence of the persons with custody, the Court, without specifying what they could have done and noting that coercion was undesirable, found that the only steps taken by the social authorities had been to hold three meetings and that it could not be said that reasonable efforts to facilitate reunion had been made.[52] Where one party is in breach of a court order, the applicant cannot claim however that the authorities bear an absolute duty to enforce it and he or she must bear a certain share of the responsibility in making the appropriate applications and actively and constructively participating in the proceedings.[53]

Difficulties in enforcement may arise with particular complexity where one parent takes the children to another jurisdiction and seeks to thwart adverse custody decisions reached in the original country of residence. The Court has stated that the State's obligations under Art.8 to secure the reunification of the custodial parent and the children must be interpreted in light of the Hague Convention of October 25, 1980 on the Civil Aspects of International Child Abduction, in particular where the respondent State is a party.[54] It has emphasised that the adequacy of measures depends on the swiftness of their implementation, noting also the obligations under the Hague Convention to act expeditiously and account for any period of inaction of more than six weeks.[55] While the Court has generally stated that coercive measures involving children are not desirable, in this context it has stated that the use of sanctions must not be ruled out in the event of unlawful behaviour by the parent with whom the children live.[56] Violations of Art.8 have accordingly been found in a

---

[51] German law at the time gave married fathers a right of access whereas fathers of children born out of wedlock had to show it was in their best interests. Similar violation in *Sommerfeld*. Contrast *Elsholz*: no discrimination as the courts had based themselves on specific findings of detriment to the child from access which would have had the same result if present in cases of married fathers.

[52] See also *Hansen v Turkey*, September 23, 2003: the imposition of three small fines was not adequate and no steps were taken by the authorities to locate the children before scheduled access visits. Contrast *Glaser*, September 19, 2000, where the Court noted that significant difficulties flowed inevitably from the intransigence of the mother who went into hiding; *Nuutinnen*: no violation arising from lack of enforcement of the father's contact rights against a mother whom he had assaulted, as drastic measures of enforcing escorted visits would not have been in the child's best interests and overall the courts had acted reasonably in a very difficult conflict; *Kallo v Hungary*, 70558/01, (Dec.) October 14, 2003, where it was enough that warnings had been issued and maximum fines imposed on the obstructive mother, the applicant not himself wishing for or requesting more coercive measures to be applied.

[53] *Glaser*, cited at n.52, para.70; see also *Nuutinen*, para.135, where reference was made to the applicant's inappropriate and aggressive behaviour to officials involved in the procedures.

[54] *Ignaccolo-Zenide*, para.95—at para.113, it took into account that the authorities did not take the measures required in Art.7 of the Hague Convention; *Sylvester*, para.57; *Iglesias-Gil et AUI v Spain*, April 29, 2003, paras 56–57.

[55] The strict obligation of expedition is illustrated in *Sylvester*, where delays of 2 and 3 and a half months in the proceedings were regarded as important (paras 67–68).

[56] *Ignaccolo-Zenide*, para.107. See also, *Paradis v Germany*, 4783/03, (Dec.) May 15, 2003, where the applicant mother had breached a Canadian order by taking the children to Germany, the Court found that the German court's decision to order their return to Canada, if necessary, by force did not violate Art.8.

number of cases where State authorities failed to take measures with the requisite promptness or effectiveness in enforcing the return of children or to facilitate the preparatory contact with the children to prevent alienation from the custodial parent.[57] As the Government is under an obligation to equip itself with the effective means to comply with the Convention, it cannot rely on any gaps in domestic law allowing for measures or sanctions to be imposed[58] nor can it rely on any purported procedural omissions by applicants to absolve it of its obligations.[59] Furthermore, while a change in relevant facts, affecting the assessment of the child's best interests, may exceptionally justify the non-enforcement of a return order, the Court requires to be satisfied that the change in situation was not brought about by the State's failure to take the measures reasonably expected to enforce the return order.[60] As in ordinary domestic child care proceedings, effective respect of family life requires that the issues should not be decided by the mere effluxion of time.[61]

4. Parental rights in non-conventional families

IIB–044 Presumptions of paternity in favour of the married father have been found to pursue the legitimate aims of certainty and security in family relationships. However, there may be circumstances where the presumption clearly flies in the face of common sense and social and biological reality should prevail. In *Kroon v Netherlands*, an irrebuttable presumption of paternity in favour of the husband of the mother of the child was found to disclose a lack of respect, where the husband had long disappeared from the scene and the biological father was unable have his paternity recognised.[62]

Homosexual relationships do not fall within the scope of "family life" for the purposes of Art.8. In a case where two women lived together in a longterm lesbian relationship, sharing parental roles in respect of a child born to one of them by artificial insemination by donor (AID), the partner of the mother could not rely on Art.8 to claim a right to obtain parental authority over the child.[63] The Commission found that, despite the evolution of attitudes towards homosexuality, Art.8 did not import a positive obligation on a State to grant parental rights to a woman who was living with the mother of a child. While homosexual relationships could raise issues under the concept of "private life", the restriction complained of in this case did not

---

[57] *Ignaccolo-Zenide*, paras 107–113; *Sylvester*, paras 66–72. See also *Iglesias-Gil*, n.54 above, paras 58–62, violation due to the lack of adequate steps taken by Spain where the applicant mother resided to enforce decisions against a father who had absconded to the USA with the child; *Maire v Portugal*, June 26, 2003, violation where the authorities took over 4 years to locate the abducted child and mother.

[58] *Ignaccolo-Zenide*, para.108; *Sylvester*, para.68. See also *Iglesias-Gil*, n.54 above, para.61, where the authorities could not rely on the legislative *lacuna* which prevented the issue of an international arrest warrant for the absconded father.

[59] *Ignaccolo-Zenide*, para.111; *Sylvester*, para.71. Contrast however the references to applicants' responsibilities in non-Hague Convention cases, n.53 above.

[60] *Sylvester*, para.63.

[61] *Sylvester*, para.69.

[62] Contrast *Youssef v Netherlands* , n.4 above: 22920/93, n.3 above, where the applicant claimed to be the father of a child born in wedlock living with the mother and her husband, the Commission found no issues arising under Arts 6, 8 and 14 arising from the courts' refusal to order a bloodtest on the child, in particular, since this risked disrupting the stability and security of the child's home. Issues could also arise where a married father separated from the mother of a child was unable to rebut the presumption of paternity.

[63] 15666/89, (Dec.) May 19, 1992.

reveal any curtailment of the enjoyment of their private life. As regarded discrimination, homosexual couples could not, in the Commission's view, be equated with a heterosexual couple as regarded parental authority.

Where a domestic system did not provide for the recognition of the change of gender of a transsexual, the Court, referring to the controversial nature of the transsexual phenomenon and the use of AID, rejected the claim that Art.8 imposed a positive obligation to recognise in law the parental role of the transsexual father.[64] It did accept that the relationships of a transsexual, his partner and the partner's child fell within the scope of Art.8 as *de facto* family life but did not consider that they suffered any practical prejudice from the lack of formal legal recognition as would impose an obligation on the State to take any steps. The Commission, differing in its opinion, had given weight to the emotional or psychological needs of the family against which it found no overriding factor militating against recognition. Following the finding in *Christine Goodwin v United Kingdom* that the refusal of legal recognition to a post-operative transsexual violated her right to respect to private life and the right to marry, it would appear likely that the Court's view on the family life aspect of Art.8 will also be subject to modification.[65]

Cross-reference

Part IIA: Fair trial, Access to Court
Part IIB: Homosexuality
Part IIB: Transsexuals

---

[64] *X, Y and Z v UK*, April 22, 1997, R.J.D. 1997–II, No.35; 24 E.H.R.R. 133.
[65] July 11, 2002, ECHR 2002–VI.

Compensation for detention

Key provision:

IIB–045 Article 5, para.5 (enforceable right to compensation for arrest or detention contrary to the provisions of Art.5).

Key case law:

Wassink v Netherlands, September 27, 1990, Series A, No.185–A; *Brogan v UK*, November 29, 1988, Series A, No.145–B; 11 E.H.R.R. 117; *Fox, Campbell and Hartley v UK*, August 30, 1990, Series A, No.182; 13 E.H.R.R. 157; *Thynne, Gunnell and Wilson v UK*, October 25, 1990; 13 E.H.R.R. 666; *Sakik v Turkey*, November 26, 1997, R.J.D. 1997–VII; 26 E.H.R.R. 662; *NC v Italy*, December 18, 2002, ECHR 2002–X; 28 E.H.R.R. 82.

1. General considerations

IIB–046 The right to compensation for arrest or detention is conditioned on the existence of a breach of one of the other four paragraphs of Art.5. Such a breach must have been established directly or in substance. Where the Court has given a decision as to breach in a previous application or where a domestic court had found a breach of one of the paragraphs but rejected the claim for compensation, the Court can proceed directly to consider Art.5, para.5. If there is no finding by domestic courts, the Court must examine whether the applicant is a victim of arrest or detention in contravention of the provisions of Art.5 before proceeding to para.5.[1]

2. Availability of compensation

IIB–047 The right to compensation must be enforceable. An opportunity to apply for *ex gratia* payment would not be adequate. It presumably extends only to financial compensation. However, in *Bozano v France*,[2] the Commission stated that the right to compensation might be of broader scope than mere financial compensation but could not confer a right to secure release since that was covered by Art.5, para.4.

The existence of the right in domestic law to obtain compensation for the breach must be established with a sufficient degree of certainty. In *Sakik v Turkey*, where the Government argued that the applicants could have made various applications for compensation, the Court noted that there was no example of any person obtaining compensation by these methods and that the constitutional provisions relied on appeared to cover only detention which was unlawful in domestic terms. It accordingly found a violation.[3]

The availability of compensation for the deprivation of liberty concerned may suffice for the purposes of Art.5, para.5, even if it is not given expressly for an

[1] *e.g.* 6821/74, (Dec.) July 5, 1976, 6 D.R. 65; 7950/77, (Dec.), March 4, 1980, 19 D.R. 213.
[2] 9990/82, (Dec.) May 15, 1984, 39 D.R.119.
[3] *cf. AC v France*, 37547/97, (Dec.) December 14, 1999: the possibility of using art.L.781–1 of the Judicial Procedure Code to obtain damages had become sufficiently certain over time.

alleged breach of Art.5. In *NC v Italy*, the Court found no violation where the applicant could apply for compensation for pre-trial detention on the grounds of his acquittal without having to prove that his detention had been unlawful or too long. Such damages would have been "indissociable" from any compensation to which the applicant might have been entitled under Art.5, para.5 as a consequence of his deprivation of liberty being contrary to Art.5, para.1 or 3.

3. Existence of damage

The Commission and Court disagreed as to whether the existence of the right could in domestic law be made dependent on the existence of damage. In *Wassink v Netherlands*, there was a failure to comply with procedure prescribed by law[4] under Art.5, para.1 but the applicant could only apply for compensation under Dutch law if he could show damage. The Commission took the view, based its earlier case law,[5] that the Art.5 para.5 right to compensation was not conditional on damage. The Court found Art.5 para.5 was complied with, if it was possible to apply for compensation in respect of a deprivation of liberty effected in conditions contrary to the other paras 1–4 but that States were not prohibited from making the award dependent on the ability of the person to show damage resulting from the breach. It distinguished victim status which can exist even if there was no damage but held that there could be no question of compensation if there was no pecuniary or non-pecuniary damage to compensate. This was stated to be without prejudice to just satisfaction (Art.41) considerations.

IIB–048

4. Domestic lawfulness

Where there is no possibility of applying for compensation for a breach of Art.5 paras 1–4, there will be a violation. The Convention organs have rejected arguments by the UK Government that the right should only accrue where the arrest or detention was unlawful in domestic terms or arbitrary. Until the Convention was incorporated in domestic law it was only possible to challenge domestic unlawfulness in the courts in the UK and this led to automatic breaches of Art.5, para.5 where arrest or detention under the other provisions was lawful in domestic terms but failed to comply with Convention standards.

IIB–049

Violations of Art.5, para.5 were accordingly found in *Brogan v United Kingdom* (breach of Art.5, para.3 for delay in being brought before a judicial officer); in *Fox, Campbell and Hartley v United Kingdom* (a lack of conformity with Art.5, para.1(c) standard of reasonable suspicion on arrest) and in *Thynne, Gunnell and Wilson v United Kingdom* (breach of Art.5, para.4 for lack review of the lawfulness of the continued detention of discretionary lifers).

---

[4] No registrar was present at the hearing.
[5] *e.g.* 10313/83, (Dec.) July 12, 1984, 39 D.R. 225, citing *Artico v Italy*, May 13, 1980, Series A, No.37, para.35 in which the Court stated that for Art.6, para.3(c) an applicant need not show that lack of legal representation caused actual prejudice and the existence of a violation was conceivable even in the absence of prejudice: prejudice was only relevant in the context of Art.50 (now Art.41).

5. Adequacy of compensation under domestic law

IIB–050 Issues may arise if the amount of compensation is derisory. An applicant awarded £350 for four and a half hours unlawful detention by the police argued that it did not reflect the seriousness of the breach, would not discourage other infringements, was out of proportion to the costs of an action and would lead to the refusal of legal aid in future cases. The Commission agreed that since the Convention guaranteed rights that were practical and effective a right of compensation which set levels too low might no longer "enforceable" in practical terms. However, it considered that the amount awarded for the short detention period could not be said to be so low as to be negligible for the purposes of Art.5, para.5.[6]

---

[6] 28779/95, (Dec.) November 27, 1996. See *Attard v Malta*, 46750/99, (Dec.), September 28, 2000, where the Court rejected the applicant's arguments about the paucity of the compensation (MTL 100), plus legal costs, paid to him for an unlawful arrest of a few hours.

Corporal punishment

Key Articles:

Articles 3 (prohibition of inhuman and degrading treatment), 8 (respect for family and private life), and Art.2 of the First Protocol (right to education and respect for the right of parents to ensure education of children in conformity with their religious and philosophical convictions).

IIB–051

Key case law:

Campbell and Cosans v UK, February 25, 1982, Series A, No.48; 4 E.H.R.R. 293; *Tyrer v UK*, April 25, 1978, Series A, No.26; 2 E.H.R.R. 1; *Costello-Robberts v UK*, March 25, 1993, Series A, No.247–C; 19 E.H.R.R. 112; *A v UK*, September 23, 1998, R.J.D., 1998–VI.

1. General considerations

The Convention organs have taken a generally critical view of corporal punishment. This reflects the position that almost alone in Contracting States the UK considered, and still does to certain degree, that there may be legitimate physical punishment of children.

IIB–052

2. Judicial corporal punishment

There is only one case. It concerned the use of the birch in the Isle of Man as a punishment of the 15-year-old applicant *Tyrer*, for assault on another pupil of his school and to which he had pleaded guilty in the juvenile court. The punishment, three strokes, was inflicted in circumstances where he was required to take down his clothing and bend over a table, held by two policemen while a third administered the strokes. The skin was raised but not cut by the birch and the applicant was sore for a week and a half afterwards.

IIB–053

In finding this treatment was degrading punishment contrary to Art.3, the Court gave particular significance to the institutionalised nature of the violence, referring to the deliberate treatment of an individual as an object in the power of the authorities and inflicted with punishment which constituted an assault on personal dignity and physical integrity. It also had regard to the psychological effect—mental anguish—resulting from the delay of three weeks from sentencing and the way the applicant was kept waiting in the police station before the punishment. The fact that the applicant was required to strip aggravated the degrading nature but was not a determining factor.

It is clear that in finding the punishment degrading and rejecting the argument that local conditions justified the practice,[1] the Court was heavily influenced by the

---

[1] The Government argued under Art.63, para.3 that Art.3 had to be applied with due regard to local requirements in territories. However, the Court found that public opinion in favour of the punishment was not sufficient—there would have to be positive and conclusive proof of a requirement for the punishment imposed by the conditions on the island and there was no indication that criminal justice would falter without it.

fact that judicial corporal punishment was not found in the great majority of Contracting States. The risk of corporal punishment, such as flogging, on an applicant's threatened expulsion to another country, may disclose issues under Art.3 and provide grounds for interim measures under r.39.[2]

3. As a means of discipline in school

IIB–054 The UK has produced singlehandedly the leading cases in this area. The use of corporal punishment in its State schools was held to be incompatible with parental convictions and, where suspension resulted, could disclose a denial of education.[3] Whether or not it would constitute punishment contrary to Art.3 depends on the circumstances of each personal case.[4]

(a) Interference with education and parental convictions

IIB–055 Concerning State schools, the Court found that there was a breach of the right of parents to ensure their children's education in accordance with their religious and philosophical convictions where parents objected to the use of the belt ("tawse") in the schools attended by their children. The rejection of physical punishment was found of the necessary cogency and seriousness to constitute a "philosophical conviction" and a view worthy of respect in a democratic society. Where one child was suspended since the parents refused to accept his return to school subject to the condition of accepting physical punishment as a disciplinary sanction, there was an additional violation of the child's right to education.

(b) Inhuman and degrading treatment

IIB–056 In privately run schools, the Court has found that the State is responsible for regulating the conduct of those schools and it can examine whether disciplinary measures infringe the provisions of the Convention. However, in *Costello-Robberts v United Kingdom*, it found that the punishment complained of—the boy was slippered three times on the buttocks through his shorts with a rubbersoled gym shoe—was not of the level of severity required to fall within the scope of "degrading punishment". There was in particular no evidence of any severe, longlasting effects. It merely expressed reservations about the automatic imposition of this kind of punishment (after a reaching a certain number of demerit marks) and the way in which the boy had to wait for three days for the punishment to be inflicted.

However, in *Y v United Kingdom*,[5] the Commission had found a violation of Art.3. The circumstances were more severe, since the boy was caned four times through his trousers by the headmaster who took several steps back and ran before striking. The boy had complained of severe pain afterwards and had four weals across his buttocks

---

[2] e.g. *Razaghi v Sweden*, 64599/01, (Dec.) March 11, 2003 where the applicant faced the alleged risk of 99 lashes for immoral behaviour on return to Iran.

[3] *Campbell and Cosans.*

[4] *Y v UK*, October 8, 1991, Series A, No.247–1; *Warwick v UK*, 9471/81, (Rep.) July 18, 1986, 60 D.R. 5, the Commission observed that, as a general rule, moderate corporal punishment in schools would constitute institutionalised violence of the kind observed in *Tyrer*.

[5] n.4 above.

with heavy bruising and swelling. The Commission found this disclosed degrading treament and punishment having regard to the significant physical injury and humiliation which he suffered. The case was settled before the Court.

The Commission found that the humiliation aspect of corporal punishment was of particular significance in *Warwick v United Kingdom*,[6] concluding that there was a violation of Art.3 by way of degrading punishment where a 16-year-old girl, a female of marriageable age, was caned on her hand by a male headmaster in the presence of another male teacher.

(c) *Invasion of physical and moral integrity*

The argument that the infliction of minor corporal punishment discloses a violation of Art.8, respect for private life, as an invasion of moral and physical integrity is unlikely to be successful in light of the Court's judgment in *Costello-Robberts*. The Commission, rejecting a violation of Art.3, nonetheless had considered that the scope of Art.8 was wider and that a separate issue arose which disclosed a violation. Corporal punishment was in its view an invasion of physical and moral integrity, respect for which had not been consented to by reason of enrolment in a private school and there was no justification advanced for its necessity. The Court did not exclude the possibility that Art.8 might afford protection in the disciplinary field wider than Art.3. However it considered that sending a child to school inevitably involved some degree of interference with private life and the treatment in this case did not entail such adverse effects on physical or moral integrity sufficient to bring it within the scope of the prohibition of Art.8.

IIB–057

4. Parental chastisement

Conversely, there have been parents who have claimed the right to chastise their children. In cases introduced by Swedish parents objecting to the complete prohibition on physical punishment of children in the Code of Parenthood, the Commission held that the Swedish law, which imposed a normal measure for the control of violence extending to the chastisement of children by their parents, was intended to protect the potentially weak and vulnerable and did not interfere the parents' right to respect for private and family life.[7] The claim that philosophical views of parents should enable them to birch their children met with no sympathy.

Where the law permits physical chastisement, issues may arise where this level is set too high, or is too vague to apply effectively and allows inhuman and degrading treatment to be inflicted on a child. A Contracting State is under a positive obligation to ensure the children are effectively protected from treatment contrary to Art.3 through its laws. Thus where a step father was prosecuted for assault on a boy with a cane but acquitted, the Court found that the provision in English law for the defence of reasonable chastisement as applied in practice deprived children of adequate protection.[8]

IIB–058

---

[6] n.4 above.

[7] 8811/79 (Dec.) May 13, 1982, 29 D.R. 104 and 12154/86 (Dec.) October 23, 1987, unpublished.

[8] *A v UK*, paras 21–24: the 9-year-old applicant had been beaten with a garden cane applied with considerable force on several occasions leaving weals and bruises. The burden of proof had been on the prosecution to prove that the assault went beyond the limits of lawful punishment. Although the applicant had been subjected to treatment of a severity prohibited by Art.3, the jury acquitted the stepfather.

Cross-reference

Part IIB: Education
Part IIB: Torture and ill-treatment

Defamation and the right to reputation

Key provisions:

Articles 6 (access to court), 8 (respect for private life) and 10 (freedom of expression). **IIB–059**

Key case law:

Lingens v Austria, July 8, 1986, Series A, No.103; 8 E.H.R.R. 103; *Oberschlick v Austria*, May 23, 1991, Series A, No.204; 19 E.H.R.R. 389; *Castells v Spain*, April 23, 1992, Series A, No.236; 14 E.H.R.R. 445; *Prager and Oberschlick v Austria*, April 26, 1995, Series A, No.313; 21 E.H.R.R. 1; *Tolstoy v UK*, July 13, 1995, Series A, No.316–B; 20 E.H.R.R. 442; *De Haes and Gijsels v Belgium*, February 24, 1997, R.J.D. 1997–I; 25 E.H.R.R. 1 *Oberschlick v Austria (No.2)*, July 1, 1997, R.J.D. 1997–IV No.42; *Janowski v Poland*, January 21, 1999, ECHR 1999–I; *Bladet Tromso and Stensaas v Norway*, May 20, 1999, ECHR 1999–III; *Nilssen and Johnsen v Norway*, November 25, 1999, ECHR 1999–VIII; *Bergens Tidende v Norway*, May 2, 2000, ECHR 2000–IV; *Lopes Gomes da Silva v Portugal*, September 28, 2000, ECHR 2000–X; *Jerusalem v Austria*, February 27, 2001, ECHR 2001–II; *Feldek v Slovakia*, July 12, 2001, ECHR 2001–VIII; *Nikula v Finland*, March 21, 2002, ECHR 2002–II; *McVicar v UK*, May 7, 2002, ECHR 2002–III; *A v UK*, December 17, 2002, ECHR 2002–X; *Cordova v Italy (No.1)*, January 30, 2003, ECHR 2003–I; *Cordova v Italy (No.2)*, January 30, 2003, ECHR 2003–I; *Lesnik v Slovakia*, March 11, 2003, ECHR 2003–IV.

1. General considerations

The right to honour and good reputation as such is not guaranteed by Art.8, though matters relating to private life will fall within the scope of that provision.[1] Most complaints arise in the context of proceedings for defamation, or procedural problems connected with obtaining redress through the courts for slights to reputation. There are two categories of claimant: those claiming protection of private life and those who have an interest in publishing information free of court sanction. In a Swedish case, the Commission noted the conflict of interest, commenting that where a question arose of interference with private life by publication in the mass media the State had to find a proper balance between the Convention rights involved, the right to respect for private life and freedom of expression.[2] **IIB–060**

---

[1] 10733/84 (Dec.) March 11, 1985 41 D.R.211 where Spanish officers complained about a punishment imposed on them in relation to the civil war period as infringing their right to honour and reputation (*i.e.* loss of rank and privileges).

[2] 11366/85, (Dec.) October 16, 1986, 50 D.R.173 the fact the applicant was not successful in his defamation action did not show a lack of protection, the courts giving adequate consideration to the applicant's interests in striking the balance.

2. Access to court

IIB–061   The right to enjoy a good reputation is a civil right for the purposes of Art.6, para.1 and applicants may generally claim the right of access to court to pursue defamation proceedings,[3] to the extent such is provided in domestic law.[4]

The general principle is that, while access to court is not absolute, it may only be restricted for legitimate aims pursued in a proportionate manner and a restriction must not impair the essence of the right.[5] The procedural and substantive limitations on defamation actions must be assessed in light of those considerations.

(a) Lack of legal aid

IIB–062   Since in the UK there was an exclusion of legal aid for defamation actions, a number of cases have arisen alleging that this deprived applicants of effective access to court. While a blanket ban, allowing no discretion or regard to prospects of success, might appear *per se* disproportionate, the Commission had exclusive regard to the individual circumstances in each case, the merits of the claims and to what extent each applicant had managed to take proceedings relating to the substance of his case without legal aid. It considered that legal aid could legitimately be restricted with regard to financial criteria and certain categories of cases, referring to the inherent riskiness of such claims and found no arbitrariness arising from the lack of legal aid.[6] This approach has been essentially adopted by the Court in *McVicar v United Kingdom*, where it found that the applicant, defendant in defamation proceedings brought by a wealthy celebrity, was not prevented by lack of legal aid from presenting his defence effectively in the High Court. It did not consider that the law of defamation was sufficiently complex as to require a person in the applicant's position to have legal assistance.

(b) Privilege and immunities from actions for defamation

IIB–063   Where certain categories of persons are protected from actions for defamation, issues arise as to whether this constitutes restriction on access to court.

Parliamentary privilege is generally recognised as compatible with the Convention, pursuing the legitimate aim of free Parliamentary debate in the public interest.[7] Even where a M.P. named the applicant in a speech in Parliament about anti-social behaviour, making made extremely serious allegations which were clearly unnecessary in a debate on municipal housing policy, the Court essentially found

---

[3] *Helmers v Sweden*, October 29, 1991, Series A, No.212; 15 E.H.R.R. 285, citing *Golder v UK*, February 21, 1975 Series A, No.18; I E.H.R.R. 524.

[4] *e.g.* where domestic law limits excludes actions for group defamation, there is no civil right to attract the guarantees of Art.6—11862/85, (Dec.) July 10, 1986—the applicant could not sue as a member of the class of gypsies in regard to disparaging posters.

[5] *Ashingdane v UK*, May 28, 1985, Series A, No.93; 7 E.H.R.R. 528.

[6] 10871/84 (Dec.) July 10, 1986, 48 D.R. 154: the applicant pursued proceedings himself and obtained a settlement; 10594/83 (Dec.) July 14, 1987 52 D.R. 158, the applicant could bring the issues before the Industrial Tribunal in proceedings for unfair dismissal, where the reasonableness of the employer's belief in his dishonesty was considered.

[7] 3374/67 Collection of Decisions 29 p.29; *Golder v UK*, 4451/70 (Rep.) June 1, 1973 p.44 para.93; conversely a Parliamentarian cannnot claim a right to privilege where the legislature waives it—19890/92, (Dec.) May 3, 1993 74 D.R. 234.

that it was justified in light of the importance of protecting free speech in Parliament, similar immunities being a feature of most of the Contracting States of the Council of Europe and that the absolute privilege attaching to speeech inside Parliament was not disproportionate in the circumstances.[8] While the Court referred to the applicant's possibility of obtaining alternative redress through her own M.P. taking up the matter internally,[9] the importance of legislators' free speech was found to outweigh the lack of any remedy.[10]

Where, however, in *Cordova v Italy (No.1)* immunity attached to an ex-President enjoying the status of a senator for life, the Court found that the rejection of the applicant's claims for defamation disclosed a disproportionate bar on his access to court. It noted that the derisory letters sent to the applicant were not linked to the exercise of legislative or parliamentary functions but rather to a personal quarrel between individuals. The same conclusion was reached in *Cordova v Italy (No.2)* where immunity had applied to the statements of an M.P. outside the legislature during an electoral meeting and the Court again noted a lack of connection between the statements made and parliamentary function.

Privilege attaching to Department of Trade Inspectors' reports was found to respect the proportionality principle in *Fayed v United Kingdom*, as it was in the public interest in regulating public companies that the inspectors report freely and they were bound by rules of rationality, legality and procedural propriety. The Court also found that the limits of acceptable criticism were wider where businessmen in large companies were concerned, particularly, where they have knowingly laid themselves open to close scrutiny of their acts through their conduct.

3. Interference with freedom of expression

Convictions or damage awards imposed in respect of defamatory statements constitute interferences with the freedom of expression and the cases turn on issues of necessity and proportionality. Where the media is involved, journalist applicants tend to win. Great emphasis is laid on freedom of expression as one of the essential foundations of a democratic society and on the importance of the freedom of the press to impart infomation of ideas and information and act as a public watchdog.[11] In that role, journalists are allowed a certain leeway to exaggerate, and even to be provocative[12] or harsh,[13] as long as there is an issue of public interest[14] and an

IIB–064

---

[8] *A v UK.*

[9] 25646/94, (Dec.) January 17, 1996, 84–A D.R. 122; 29099/95, (Dec.) January 17, 1996: the Commission in finding found the privilege of Irish parliamentarians proportionate had regard to the fact that the complaints were reviewed by the Committee of Privileges.

[10] *Zollman v UK*, 62902/00, (Dec.) November 27, 2003, where the foreign applicants, "named and shamed" in Parliament did not have that option.

[11] e.g. *Lingens*, paras 41 and 44; *Bladet Tromso*, para.59; *Feldek*, para.78.

[12] *Prager and Oberschlick*, para.38.

[13] *Feldek*, para.84.

[14] This is given a wide interpretation, e.g. *Bergens Tidende*, where the Court rejected the Government's argument that the allegations made by women about a cosmetic surgeon's negligent treatment at a private clinic were private matters but considered that they concerned an important aspect of public health; *Maronek v Slovakia*, April 19, 2001: the applicant, involved in a housing dispute, addressed an open letter to the Prime Minister, which did not exclusively concern his individual problems but also issues of public interest (para.56).

underlying basis of fact[15] and they act in good faith in order to provide accurate and reliable information in accordance with the ethics of journalism.[16] Indeed a degree of exaggeration should be tolerated according to the Court in any public debate of general concern[17] though both journalists and others must not overstep certain bounds.[18] Private individuals and associations lay themselves open to scrutiny when they enter the arena of public debate.[19]

Where critical comment by journalists is made on matters of public interest and relating to the conduct of politicians, the importance of the freedom of political debate and the consideration that limits of critical comment are wider for politicians, who inevitably and knowingly open themselves to public scrutiny, are key factors. Very strong reasons are required to justify restrictions on political speech in particular.[20] In *Lingens v Austria*, where a journalist was convicted in a private prosecution for criticising the Chancellor of Austria for supporting an individual allegedly involved in war crimes and accusing him of immoral, undignified conduct, the Court found the articles relevant to current debate and that the position at domestic law, which required a journalist to prove not only facts but value judgments, imposed an impossible requirement.[21] In *Oberschlick v Austria*, where a journalist was fined for quoting a formal complaint lodged against a politician in criminal proceedings which accused him of making discriminatory statements concerning immigrant women's rights to family allowances, the Court found the article contributed to a debate of public importance on the treatment of foreigners and that it was undisputed that the publication was factually correct in reproducing the complaint. In these circumstances, the interference could not be justified as necessary, even if the applicant had been provocative and misleading in his form of presentation.[22] Where the applicant writer accused a Government minister of a fascist past in *Feldek v Slovakia*, the Court rejected the proposition that a value

---

[15] *e.g. Prager and Oberschlick*, para.38; see *Oberschlick (No.2)*, below; *Lopes Gomes da Silva v Portugal*, paras 34–35. See also *Bladet Tromso* where the Court considered that the impugned article which accused seal hunters of cruelty had to be taken in context of a series of articles putting forward different points of view and seen as part of an ongoing debate of national concern—the applicant journalist had also been entitled to rely on the contents of an official inspector's report without carrying out independent research; *Thoma v Luxemburg*, March 29, 2001, where the applicant had repeated controversial passages from another article and the Court commented that journalists could not generally be expected to distance themselves formally when quoting from other sources (para.64).

[16] *Bergens Tidende*, para.53.

[17] *Nilssen and Johnsen*, para.52—a heated public debate between the police, prosecution and researchers who had published findings on police brutality and where professional reputations on both sides were at stake.

[18] *e.g. Constantinescu v Romania*, June 27, 2000, ECHR 2000–VIII, where the applicant was convicted for calling three teachers *"delapidatori"*, the Court found that he could have contributed to the debate on trade union affairs without using this word.

[19] *Jerusalem*, paras 38–39.

[20] *Feldek*, para.83.

[21] See also violations in *Dalban v Romania*, September 28, 1999, ECHR 1999–VI, where the courts in convicting the applicant did not properly examine his evidence in support of his allegations and *Jerusalem*, where the Austrian courts had required the applicant to prove the truth of her value judgments about an alleged "sect" but refused to consider her evidence.

[22] The Commission had commented that where a politician's own statements had been provocative, others had a right to be provocative back. See also *Oberschlick (No.2)* where the journalist was fined for calling a politician a *"trottel"*—the Court found a violation noting that the article responded to deliberately provocative statements by the politician and had a factual basis; *Lopes Gomes da Silva*,: the Court noted that the applicant's comments had been "polemical" but supported by an objective explanation.

judgment could only be considered such if it was accompanied by the facts on which the judgment was based. It noted that in this case the value judgment was based on information already known to the wider public from earlier publications.

The important role played by politicians themselves in contributing to public debate and a free democratic process has also been recognised. Elected representatives represent their constituents, defending their concerns and interference in their role calls for the closest scrutiny. In *Castells v Spain*, a violation of Art.10 was found where a member of Parliament was convicted for an article attributing acts of violence to the Government, receiving a suspended sentence of one year and barred from public functions for one year. It was accepted that the purpose of the conviction was to protect order but the matter concerned issues of public interest and he was not allowed to rely on truth or good faith. The Court stated that limits of permissible criticism was wider in relation to governments than to private individuals or even politicians and that the dominant position of governments made it necessary for them to respond with restraint.[23]

On the other hand, where defamatory attacks are made on the judiciary, special regard is had to the need of the judiciary to enjoy public confidence and the limits of permissible criticism may be narrower. In *Prager and Oberschlick v Austria*, the Court by a narrow margin found the conviction of a journalist for alleging serious misconduct by certain judges justified for maintaining the authority of the judiciary and protecting judges' reputations. Referring to the "special role of the judiciary" as the guarantor of justice, it considered that the classification by the domestic courts of the impugned passages as unjustifiably defamatory fell within the margin of appreciation and that the applicant journalist could not invoke good faith or compliance with professional ethics since the research which he had undertaken did not appear adequate to substantiate such serious allegations and he had not given any judge an opportunity to comment on the accusations against him.[24]

While civil servants acting in an official capacity are, like politicians, subject to wider limits of acceptable criticism, the Court seems to give weight to the need to protect them in the performance of their functions from offensive and abusive remarks, particularly those who should enjoy public confidence. In *Janowski v Poland*, it was not disproportionate to fine the applicant for heated words in a "lively exchange" in which he called two municapal guards "oafs" and "dumb".[25] Nor was it disproportionate to protect public prosecutors in *Lesnik v Slovakia*, where the applicant was convicted of insulting conduct for writing letters to a public prosecutor and his superior alleging misconduct, including the taking of a bribe,

[23] See, concerning narrower limits applying to criticism of private individuals, *Tammer v Estonia*, February 6, 2001, ECHR 2001–I, paras 62–68; concerning the important role of municipal elected representatives, *Jerusalem*, para.36.

[24] Narrow majorities in Commission and Court. The minority considered that judges also had to act under public scrutiny. Contrast *De Haes and Gijsels*, where journalists were convicted for defaming judges in articles about a controversial custody case, the Court noted that though they might have been polemical and aggressive, their comments had a factual basis and were proportionate to ongoing public debate.

[25] The Court majority had regard to the fact that the applicant insulted them in front of bystanders and seemed to regard the dispute as akin to a personal quarrel rather than exercise of freedom of expression on a matter of public debate, though, as the minority noted, the applicant had been objecting to the guards moving on market stall holders when they had no legal authority to do so.

which allegations the Court majority were serious and unsubstantiated.[26] In *Nikula v Finland* however, the Court considered that the possible chilling effect on defence lawyers of penalising criticism did not justify the conviction of a defense lawyer for making remarks during a trial about the prosecutor's conduct of the case.

4. Injunctions and size of awards

IIB–065 Outside the sphere of journalistic and political debate, restraints on defamatory publications have been found more justifiable. An injunction imposed on Count Tolstoy, sued by Lord Aldington for passages on a book alleging involvement in sending prisoners of war and refugees to the Soviet Union where they were massacred, was found to be proportionate, not exceeding the purpose of preventing repetition of allegations found to be defamatory.

The size of the damages award imposed on Tolstoy by a jury, which exceeded one million pounds, was however disproportionate and in breach of Art.10. There was a lack of adequate safeguards in the procedure, since national law allowed the jury great latitude and awards could only be set aside on appeal on limited grounds. The unfettered and unpredictable power of juries to award damages in defamation was the subject of a complaint by *The Times*, which considered that this disclosed an unjustifiable restriction on their journalistic activities in general. The Commission found that a newspaper could claim to be a victim even if no defamation proceedings had been brought if the state of the law was too vague to allow the risk of proceedings to be predicted but that they had not established such vagueness by reference to any award or any specific article in which it had in any way been inhibited from imparting information.[27]

5. Right of reply

IIB–066 While it would be doubtful that a right of reply to defamatory comments would be implied under the Convention, the Commission found that where it existed in domestic law this did not impinge on the freedom of expression of the other party obliged to publish.[28] While it may be compatible with Art.10 to require a newspaper to publish a notice indicating the institution of proceedings for defamation, it was not necessary to impose fines for failure to publish a notice concerning the decision of the first instance court in favour of the complainant, where the appeal proceedings were still pending and undecided.[29]

---

[26] The minority considered that private citizens should be free to make complaints to public officials and their superiors without risking prosecution for defamation or insult, particularly where the allegations were not made in the media. Judges Bratza and Maruste thought that civil servants should tolerate criticism, even where expressed in abusive, strong or intemperate terms and the allegations serious and unfounded. See also *Perna v Italy*, May 6, 2003, conviction and fine justified for attack on a public prosecutor's alleged abusive conduct.

[27] 14631/89, (Dec.) March 5, 1990, 65 D.R. 307.

[28] 13010/87 (Dec.), July 12, 1989 62 D.R. 247: it was not necessary for courts to verify the content of the reply as it had to be prompt to be effective; *Societe Prisma Presse v France*, 66910/01, (Dec.) July 1, 2003, containing comments as to the appropriateness of a requirement on a magazine to publish the court's finding of a breach of privacy.

[29] *Krone Verlag GmbH v Austria (No.2)*, November 6, 2003.

Cross-reference

Part IIA : Access to court
Part IIB : Private life
Part IIB : Freedom of expression

Deprivation of liberty

Key provision:

IIB–067   Article 5, para.1 (right to liberty and security of person, subject to exceptions sub-paras (a)–(f).

Key case law:

Lawless v Ireland, July 1, 1961, Series A, No.3; 1 E.H.R.R. 15; *De Wilde, Ooms and Versyp v Belgium*, June 18, 1971, Series A, No.12; 1 E.H.R.R. 373; *Engel v Netherlands*, June 8, 1976, Series A, No.22, 1 E.H.R.R. 706; *Ireland v UK*, January 18, 1978, Series A, No.25; 2 E.H.R.R. 25; *Van Droogenbroeck v Belgium*, June 24, 1982, Series A, No.50; 4 E.H.R.R. 443; *Guzzardi v Italy*, November 6, 1980, Series A, No.39; 3 E.H.R.R. 333; *Bozano v France*, November 18, 1986, Series A, No.111; 10 E.H.R.R. 175; *Weeks v UK*, March 2, 1987, Series A, No.114; 10 E.H.R.R 293; *Nielsen v Denmark*, November 28, 1988, Series A. No.144; 11 E.H.R.R 175; *Ciulla v Italy*, February 22, 1989, Series A, No.148; 13 E.H.R.R 346; *Drozd and Janousek v France*, June 26, 1992, Series A, No.240; 14 E.H.R.R. 745; *Kemmache v France (No.3)*, November 24, 1994, Series A, No.296–C; 19 E.H.R.R. 349; *Benham v UK*, June 10, 1996, R.J.D. 1996–III, No.10; 22 E.H.R.R. 293; *Amuur v France*, June 25, 1996, R.J.D., 1996–III, No.11; *Bizzotto v Greece*, November 15, 1996, R.J.D., 1996–V, No.21; *Lukanov v Bulgaria*, March 20, 1997, R.J.D. 1997–II, No.34; 24 E.H.R.R. 121; *K-F v Germany*, November 27, 1997, R.J.D. 1997–VII, No.58; *Raninen v Finland*, December 16, 1997, R.J.D. 1997–VIII, No.60; 26 E.H.R.R. 563; *Riera Blume v Spain*, October 14, 1999, ECHR 1999–VII; *Witold Litwa v Poland*, April 4, 2000; *Jecius v Lithuania*, July 31, 2000, ECHR 2000–IX; *Mancini v Italy*, August 2, 2001, ECHR 2001–IX; *Conka v Belgium*, February 5, 2002, ECHR 2002–I; *Stafford v UK*, May 28, 2002, ECHR 2002–IV; *Ocalan v Turkey*, March 12, 2003, pending before the Grand Chamber; *Vasileva v Denmark*, September 25, 2003.

1. General considerations

IIB–068   The case law indicates the importance of physical freedom and emphasises that exceptions are exhaustively limited to those set out in the sub-paras of Art.5, para.1 (see sections below) and which are to be interpreted narrowly.[1] If the detention does not fall within any of these categories then it cannot be justified under Art.5, para.1 however "useful" the aim might be.[2]

The principal aim is to prevent arbitrary deprivation of liberty. The emphasis is on procedural rights and safeguards, with perhaps limited scope for challenging the merits of decisions of deprivation of liberty. However, in the context of detention of alcoholics, the Court has held the detention of an individual is such a serious

---

[1] *Winterwerp*, para.37.
[2] *e.g. Ciulla*, para.41: arrest and detention of a mafia suspect as a preventive measure based on suspicion could not be regarded as following conviction within sub-para.1(a) or for the purpose of bringing him before a court within sub-para.1(c) despite the acknowledged importance of the fight against the mafia. See also *Engel*, para.57: the claim of special exclusion for military discipline was not accepted.

measure that it can only be justified where other, less severe measures have been considered and found insufficient to protect the individual or public interest.[3]

2. Existence of deprivation of liberty

Whether some-one is deprived of their liberty depends on examination of the concrete situation, account being taken of a whole range of criteria, such as the type, duration, effects and manner of the implementation of the measure in question.[4] In ordinary circumstances, any element of compulsion restricting a person to custody or to attend a particular location falls within the scope of Art.5, para.1.[5] Even where a person has submitted voluntarily to a particular regime of detention, this does not exclude the operation of Art.5 with regard to challenging the lawfulness or seeking discharge. For example, in *De Wilde, Ooms and Versyp v Belgium*, where the Government argued that the applicants had given themselves up to the police voluntarily, the Court considered that liberty was too important for person to lose the benefit of protection under Art.5 merely because he might have surrendered himself. Scrupulous supervision was still required that measures were necessary for the purposes of Art.5, para.1.

IIB–069

The apparent ability of a person to leave the alleged place of detention may not be decisive, regard being had to the reality of the situation. In respect of asylum claimants restricted on arrival in airports to particular zones or holding areas, the Commission considered that since they were able to leave the airport, by taking a plane elsewhere, they were not in fact deprived of their liberty.[6] The Court in *Amuur v France* however found that the mere fact that an asylum seeker may leave the country does not exclude a deprivation of liberty, since this may be a theoretical possibility if no other country is offering the protection which they seek or is prepared to take them in. Thus an asylum seeker held in restricted conditions for an extended period of time may claim to be deprived of liberty.[7]

In certain contexts however, restrictions which might constitute deprivation of liberty if imposed on an adult civilian will not for other categories of person. In *Engel v Netherlands*, it was found that military life imposed a special disciplinary regime on persons stricter than in civilian life and it was necessary to examine whether a restriction clearly deviated from normal conditions of life in the armed forces in Contracting States, having regard to the nature, duration, effects and manner of execution of the penalty in question. Light arrest which meant confinement in off-

---

[3] *Witold Litwa*, para.78.

[4] *Guzzardi*, para.92; 8334/78, (Dec.) May 7, 1981, 24 D.R. 103: though a threat to detain in accordance with the law could not infringe Art.5, para.1, it was implied that threat of arbitrary or unjustified detention could infringe the right to security of person.

[5] Order to be taken by force to undergo a blood test fell under Art.5, para.1(b): 8278/78, (Dec.) December 13, 1979, 18 D.R. 154; 24722/94, (Dec.) April 10, 1995, 81–A D.R. 130: an applicant, suffering from a nervous disorder, was taken to the police station, the Commission found no deprivation of liberty, since he agreed to go, the police acted out of humanitarian reasons and in the station he was free to move around; conditional release or release on licence has not yet been found to affect liberty; nor the fact that an arrest warrant or order for detention was in force, where the person was still at liberty, *e.g.* 12778/87, (Dec.) December 9, 1988, 59 D.R. 158. House arrest qualified as detention in *Mancini* as did forcible deprogramming of cult members in a hotel in *Riera Blume*.

[6] 19066/91, (Dec.) April 5, 1993, 74 D.R. 179.

[7] The Court implied that short periods while practical matters were arranged, *e.g.* repatriation or granting of asylum would only constitute a restriction on movement. Twenty days in *Amuur* went beyond this; 14 days qualified in *Shamsa v Poland*, November 27, 2003.

duty hours to military premises, without being locked up, was not covered. Nor was aggravated arrest, where for 12 days an applicant was confined in offduty hours to a specially designated place and barred from recreation. However, strict arrest even for short periods where a person was locked in cell by day and night and no longer fulfilled duties was a deprivation of liberty, as was committal to a disciplinary unit, where persons were held in a particular establishment which they could not leave for periods of months and were locked in cells at night.

Special considerations also apply to children, since they are inevitably subject to restrictions in the home and school. The taking of a girl from school for questioning by the police about pilfering was not a deprivation of liberty, apparently since it was not intended to be and there were no irregularities.[8] In *Nielsen v Denmark*, measures taken by the parental rights holder involving admittance of boy of 11–12 years to a hospital psychiatric ward against his will, were not found by the Court to disclose a deprivation of liberty. It emphasised family and parental rights under Art.8 and the inevitable restrictions imposed on children who in school and elsewhere have to abide by certain rules and who may have to be hospitalised for medical treatment. Since the decision to place the child was taken, on the basis of medical advice, with the view to protect the child's health and the conditions in the ward and the treatment which he received were not inappropriate (though the door was locked this was to protect the children and avoid disturbance to other patients), the nature of the restrictions was not such as to be similar to the cases of deprivation specified in Art.5, para.1. The Court gave little weight to the view of the child, since at age 12 it must still be possible for him to be admitted to hospital at the request of the holder of parental rights. The Commission had found a deprivation of liberty which was not justified, since he was not mentally ill in any real sense and having regard to his understanding and views, it could not be regarded as a voluntary placement.[9]

It would therefore appear that as long as there is some medical or educational justification for the placement by parental rights holders, confinement of children to particular establishments will not constitute a deprivation of liberty.[10] Rather dubiously the Court relied on the *Nielsen* case in the context of the forcible removal of an 84 year old from her home to a care establishment and found that Art.5, para.1 did not apply, apparently as she was not placed in a closed ward and retained freedom of movement and the placement was in her own interests.[11]

Not surprisingly perhaps, prisoners who are already under detention cannot claim a deprivation of liberty as occurring when they are transferred elsewhere[12] or subject to more restrictive form of confinement.[13] This is regarded instead as a modification of the conditions of lawful detention or imprisonment.[14] Thus prisoners cannot

[8] 8819/79, (Dec.), March 19, 1981, 24 D.R. 158.
[9] There had been difficulties, since although the mother had won custody after divorce, the boy had repeatedly run away to live with his father.
[10] Where local authorities place children under their care in pure disciplinary or specialist facilities however, either under court orders or under statutory provisions providing for "secure" accommodation, there is likely to be a deprivation of liberty, e.g. *DG v Ireland*, May 16, 2002, ECHR 2002–III, *Koniarska v UK*, 33670/96, (Dec.) October 12, 2000.
[11] *HM v Switzerland*, (Dec.) January 29, 2002, ECHR 2002–IX, as Art.5 did not apply, the Court did not have to deal with the applicant's argument that "neglect" was not a ground for deprivation of liberty.
[12] e.g. *Perry v UK*, 63737/00, (Dec.) September 26, 2002, where the applicant, held on remand, was transferred to a police station where he was being covertly filmed for identification purposes. This raised issues under Arts 6 and 8, not 5.
[13] e.g. *Bollan v UK*, 42117/98, (Dec.) May 4, 2000, ECHR 2000–V.
[14] 7754/77, (Dec.) May 9, 1977, 11 D.R. 216.

invoke Art.5 in relation to the type of regime to which they are subjected, or in relation to the location of their prison.[15] Where there was a "deplorable delay" in transferring a prisoner from one regime to one far more suitable, he was still subject to the same lawful deprivation of liberty, although the difference in quality of life was of immense significance for him.[16] Issues could only arise if there was some failure to conform to lawful requirements with regard to the type of detention.[17]

3. Relationship with freedom of movement

The borderline between a deprivation of liberty and a restriction on freedom of movement, subject to separate protection under Art.2 of Protocol 4, is a difference of degree and intensity and not nature or substance.[18] In the UK context, exclusion orders which may restrict persons suspected of terrorism from entering mainland UK from Northern Ireland have not been found to impose restrictions of such a nature or degree as to constitute a deprivation of liberty (see Part IIB: Freedom of movement).

IIB–070

4. Relationship with "security of person"

While Art.5, para.1 guarantees not only the right to liberty but "security of person" this latter aspect has proved to have no real independent existence. It cannot be used to cover ideas of physical integrity which have been found to fall, where appropriate, within the scope of Art.8 and in more extreme cases, Art.3.[19] In *East African Asians v United Kingdom*,[20] the Commission found the use of the concept of "security of person" in juxtaposition to the right to liberty referred to the aspect of arbitrary interference with liberty. The application of entry regulations did not constitute an interference with this right notwithstanding the threat to the applicants' personal existence posed by the measures excluding them from the UK.

IIB–071

The Court in *Bozano v France* also appeared to equate the notion to the arbitrary aspect of interference with liberty. Where an applicant was removed from France by the police by way of a "disguised extradition", it stated that what was at stake was not only the right to liberty but the right to security of person and concluded that the measures taken to circumvent a court decision against extradition were neither "lawful" or compatible with the right to security of person. In *Ocalan v Turkey*, the Court also commented that an arrest made by the authorities of one State on the territory of another without the consent of the latter, would affect the person's individual rights to security under Art.5, para.1.[21]

In the case of disappearances in custody, where arbitrariness and lack of safeguards are acutely in issue, the Commission and Court found violation of the

---

[15] 11703/85, (Dec.) December 9, 1987, 54 D.R. 116; 11208/84, (Dec.) March 4, 1986, 46 D.R. 182.

[16] *Ashingdane v UK*, May 28, 1985, Series A, No.93; 7 E.H.R.R. 528.

[17] See below: Section 5. "In accordance with a procedure prescribed by law" and lawfulness.

[18] *Guzzardi*, para.93.

[19] *e.g.* 5573/72, (Dec.) July 16, 1976, 7 D.R. 8; 7050/75, (Dec.) October 12, 1978, 19 D.R. 5; 11208/84, n.15 above, where it did not apply to an integration policy of republican and unionist prisoners alleged to place them at physical risk; nor in *Akdivar v Turkey*, (Rep.) para.229, R.J.D. 1996–IV, No.15, concerning destruction of home, livelihood and personal security.

[20] 4403/70 *et al.* (Rep.) December 14, 1973, 78–A D.R. 5.

[21] para.88.

aspect of "security of person" together with the right to liberty. They noted that compliance with procedures and the existence of safeguards were essential to prevent the risk of extra-judicial execution and torture.[22] Indeed disappearances disclose a particularly grave violation of Art.5.[23]

5. "In accordance with a procedure prescribed by law" and lawfulness

IIB–072

Article 5, para.1 imposes two lawfulness criteria: firstly, in the first paragraph, that a deprivation of liberty must be in accordance with a procedure prescribed by law; and, secondly, in each sub-paragraph listing the exceptions, a requirement that the detention, arrest or order be lawful.[24] These overlap, since the Court considers that "lawful" covers procedural as well as substantive rules, and are regarded as underlining the importance of the aim of Art.5, para.1 to prevent arbitrary detention.[25]

Most cases appear to consider both requirements of "lawfulness" together.[26] It is regarded as referring essentially to domestic lawfulness, both substantive and procedural, which is for national authorities to interpret.[27] The Court has also stated that it is not its role to assess the facts which led a national court to adopt one decision rather than another, otherwise it would be acting as a court of third or fourth instance.[28] Nonetheless since compliance with domestic law is an integral part of the obligations of Contracting States, the Court is competent to satisfy itself of such compliance where relevant, subject to its inherent limits in the European system of protection.[29] The Convention organs have a certain jurisdiction to review whether domestic law has been complied with and the manner in which it is done, in particular that domestic law is not interpreted or applied in an arbitrary manner, since no arbitrary detention can ever be regarded as "lawful".[30] For example, the

---

[22] *Kurt v Turkey*, May 25, 1998, R.J.D. 1998–III, No.74, para.129; *Cakici v Turkey*, July 8, 1999, ECHR 1999–IV, para.105, concerning the importance of keeping accurate custody records.

[23] *Kurt*, n.22 above; *Cakici*, n.22 above, para.107; *Cyprus v Turkey*, (Rep.) October 4, 1983, 72 D.R. 5.

[24] No legal basis for arrest and detention, *e.g. Denizci v Cyprus*, May 23, 2001, ECHR 2001–V, para.392; *Baranowski v Poland*, March 28, 2000, ECHR 2000–III, paras 53–58 (pre-trial detention by executive order); *Shamsa*, n.7 above, paras 55–60, detention in transit zone not based on a judicial decision or specific legal provision.

[25] *Winterwerp v Netherlands*, October 24, 1979, Series A, No.33, para.4; 2. E.H.R.R. 387.

[26] *e.g. Raninen*, (unlawful arrest of conscientious objector).

[27] It can include measures based on custom, as in *Drozd and Janousek*, where applicants sentenced in Andorra but held in France alleged there was no statutory or legal basis for their detention there but the Court found that the practice was based on well-established custom .

[28] *Kemmache (No.3)*, para.44; 10689/83, (Dec.) July 1984, 37 D.R. 225, where Barbie claimed that his arrest was not lawful (*i.e.* disguised extradition), the Commission found that the decision of the Court of Cassation upholding the arrest as lawful was not arbitrary.

[29] *Lukanov*, para.41: on examination of the Criminal Code, the Court was not persuaded that the applicant's participation in a collective decision to send aid to the Third World constituted a criminal offence; conversely, see *Wloch v Poland*, October 19, 2000, ECHR 2000–XI, where the applicant's arrest and detention on child trafficking charges was found compatible with Art.5, as, notwithstanding difficulties of interpretation of the law, it was not shown that the domestic court's approach was arbitrary or unreasonable.

[30] *Winterwerp*, paras 40 and 45; *Tsirlis and Kouloumpas v Greece*, May 29, 1997, R.J.D. 1997–III, No.38; 25 E.H.R.R. 198, where Jehovah Witness ministers were detained for refusing national service, although under domestic law ministers of known religions were exempt, their detention had no basis in domestic law and was arbitrary; *PL v France*, 21503/93, (Rep.) April 11, 1996, R.J.D. 1997–II, No.34 where convicted prisoners had the right to deduction of pre-trial detention, the refusal to take into account the

measures applied by the domestic authorities in *Conka v Belgium* were incompatible with Art.5, para.1, where the applicant gypsies were lured under false pretences to the police station in order to facilitate their expulsion and in circumstances removing any realistic possiblity of challenging the measure.

As in references to lawfulness under other provisions of the Convention, it has been interpreted as referring in addition to the "quality of law", *i.e.* compatibility with the rule of law, that the rules be sufficiently accessible and precise,[31] sometimes also emphasised as the general principle of legal certainty, which is of particular importance where the exercise of powers to detain is involved.[32]

In practice, this gives much leeway to domestic systems but might also be said to avoid breaches which are technical and lacking, essentially, in merit.[33] The fact that a conviction is quashed on appeal does not render it unlawful[34] nor the fact that detention is found to be justified by the courts on an interpretation which is novel, although reasonably foreseeable.[35] Continued detention for two months pending examination of a prolongation request, regarded as lawful by the domestic courts, was not found arbitrary.[36] Lack of precision in the issuing by a court of a detention order was not regarded as fatal, where jurisdiction existed and the meaning was clear to all present.[37] The Court has sometimes referred to a finding that the domestic court did not act in bad faith.[38]

Where an order for detention is later quashed by a superior court it does not automatically affect the validity of the detention retrospectively.[39] In *Benham v United Kingdom*, where the applicant was committed for failure to pay his poll tax by magistrates who failed to comply with the requirement to verify if his failure was due to culpable neglect, the Court had regard to the position at domestic law concerning the review by higher courts of magistrates' decisions. Since it found that the Divisional Court's decision could not be said to indicate with any certainty that the magistrates' decision was in excess of jurisdiction as opposed to an error made within its jurisdiction it was not established that the order was invalid *ab initio* and the detention unlawful. Nor did it find any element of

---

period on remand which the courts had annulled as unlawful (thus ceasing to have legal existence) was arbitrary; *Erkalo v Netherlands*, September 2, 1998, R.J.D. 1998–VIII, No. 88, where the applicant's detention was not based on any judicial decision, although in Dutch law the failure of the prosecutor to lodge the extension request until after the expiry of the time-limit did not effect the lawfulness of the continued detention.

[31] *Amuur*, where the rules applying to the holding of asylum seekers in international airport zones did not have the quality of law, since they contained no guarantees against arbitary interferences, *e.g.* court review, access to legal or social assistance, time-limits, procedures.

[32] *e.g. Baranowski*, n.24 above, para.52; *Shamsa*, n.7 above, para.49.

[33] *e.g.* 9997/82, (Dec.) December 7, 1982, 31 D.R. 145: where the applicant complained that the appointment of an emergency duty judge was not valid, the Commission found that there was no reason to interfere with the Constitutional Court's appreciation of domestic lawfulness, no arbitrariness arising; 28574/95 (Dec.), November 25, 1996, 87–A D.R. 118, where the Court of Appeal did not find that procedural irregularities affected the lawfulness of detention, the Commission found the defect sufficiently remote from the procedural and substantive requirements for detention; *Douiyeb v Netherlands*, August 8, 1999, where the error in the order of detention was clerical.

[34] 7629/76, (Rep.) March 9, 1978, 13 D.R. 57.

[35] 9174/80, (Rep.) October 11, 1983, 40 D.R. 42.

[36] *Rutten v Netherlands*, July 24, 2001.

[37] *Jecius*, paras 68–70.

[38] *Jecius*, para.69.

[39] *e.g. Bozano*, para.55; *Douiyeb*, n.33 above, paras 44–45.

arbitrariness in the magistrates' decision to commit, referring to no apparent bad faith or failure to attempt to apply the legislation.[40] This appears, unsatisfactorily, to mean that if a superior domestic court, when quashing an order of detention, refrains from clearly specifying the nature or type of defect in the proceedings, the Court will not step in decide itself whether the detention was unlawful in domestic terms.

Where the way in which a prisoner is detained appears to contravene a requirement of domestic law, there may be scope for an issue to arise. There must be some relationship between the ground of permitted deprivation of liberty relied on and the place and conditions of detention.[41] In *Bizzotto v Greece*, where a judge convicted a drug addict and indicated that he should be detained in an appropriate clinic for treatment, the Commission found that his detention in an ordinary jail did not comply with the measures ordered against him in domestic law. The Court took the view that since the applicant had been convicted and sentenced for the purposes of punishment, the decision of the court at the same time to order his detention in a prison with medical facilities did not affect the main ground for his detention, which lay under Art.5, para.1(a). It considered that provisions merely laying down the arrangements for implementing sentences could not in principle have any bearing on the "lawfulness" of a deprivation of liberty.

If the failure to comply could concern something more fundamental than a manner of implementation of a sentence, for example, detention of a mental health patient in a prison, the result may perhaps be different. The Court has said that in principle the "detention" of a person as a mentally ill prisoner would only be "lawful" if effected in a hospital, clinic or other appropriate institution.[42] In *Mancini v Italy*, the three day delay in releasing the applicants from prison to house arrest violated Art.5, para.1, as although house arrest involved a form of deprivation of liberty, it was of a different nature from prison detention and could not be regarded as a continuation of the latter. It is unlikely though that a person convicted of offences in respect of whom a judge had made comments or recommendations on the need to treatment could claim successfully under Art.5 if the authorities failed to respond.

6. The permitted exceptions

IIB–073   These are not exclusive of each other. Detention may fall within more than one category.[43]

---

[40] The Commission had differed. See also the detailed separate opinion from Mr N. Bratza and the dissenting opinions in the Court. In the later cases, *Perks v UK*, October 12, 1999 no violation arose where the High Court quashed orders of detention which were regarded as falling within the jurisdiction of the magistrates.

[41] *Ashingdane*, para.44.

[42] *Aerts v Belgium*, July 30, 1998, R.J.D. 1998–V, No.83, para.46; *Hutchison Reid v UK*, February 20, 2003, ECHR 2003–IV, para.54.

[43] *e.g. Silva Rocha v Portugal*, November 15, 1996, R.J.D. 1996–V, No.23, where a prisoner was detained by a court after committing acts constituting an offence but without criminal responsibility due to his mental state: Art.5, paras 1(a) and (e) applied; *Eriksen v Norway*, May 27, 1997, R.J.D. 1997–III, No.37: detention on special security grounds was based on Art.5, paras 1(a) and (c).

(a) Article 5, para.1(a): conviction by a competent court

This sub-paragraph refers to lawful detention after conviction. It does not require IIB–074 the conviction itself to be lawful in the sense that it is maintained on appeal. The fact that the first instance court's ruling is overturned as disclosing an error does not take the detention pending the appeal outside the exception.[44] A violation was found however where an applicant ended up serving a longer sentence than that imposed by the relevant courts, taking into account the applicable reductions.[45]

"Court" for the purposes of this exception has been described as an organ which is judicial in that it is independent of the executive and the parties to the case and offers adequate procedural guarantees.[46]

Detention after conviction by a competent court requires not only that the detention follow the conviction in point of time but must result from, follow and depend upon or occur by virtue of the conviction.[47] The passage of time may break the causal link between a conviction and period of detention or continued detention, where the prolongation has no longer any connection with the objectives of the initial detention or was based on an assessment that was arbitrary or unreasonable in terms of those objectives.[48] Sufficient causal connection between the conviction and detention has been found where a discretionary life prisoner is recalled to prison on revocation of his licence[49]; where the Court of Appeal has ordered that time spent in custody pending the appeal not be counted towards sentence[50]; and when orders for the preventive detention of convicted recidivists have been renewed.[51] However, where a prisoner sentenced to a mandatory term of life imprisonment for murder was released on licence and then subject to recall due to the risk of his committing further non-violent offences (i.e. fraud), the Court found that no sufficient causal connection between his detention after recall and the original sentence for murder.[52]

Where a sentence of life imprisonment is imposed, even on a juvenile, by a competent court in accordance with domestic law, any issues as to disproportionality or appropriateness fall to be dealt with under Art.3, not Art.5.[53]

Enforcement by a Contracting State of a custodial sentence passed by the courts of another State falls within this exception, although the enforcing State should not provide assistance if the conviction is the result of a flagrant denial of justice.[54]

---

[44] e.g. 7629/76, (Rep.) March 9, 1978, 13 D.R. 57; 9132/80, (Dec.) December 16, 1982, 31 D.R. 154: Art.5, para.1(a) applies even where by domestic law detention after the first instance is classed as detention on remand pending the appeal.

[45] Grava v Italy, July 10, 2003.

[46] e.g. 7341/76, (Rep.) March 4, 1978, 15 D.R. 35: the chief military prosecutor did not qualify; 17571/90, (Dec.) September 2, 1993, 75 D.R. 139, the Military Court of Appeal did.

[47] Weeks, para.42.

[48] Van Droogenbroeck, para.40. See Weeks, para.51: recall to prison of a discretionary lifer due to his aggressive unstable behaviour was not arbitrary or unreasonable in terms of the objectives of the sentence imposed on him.

[49] Weeks.

[50] Monnell and Morris v UK, March 2, 1987, Series A, No.115; 10 E.H.R.R. 205.

[51] e.g. 9167/80, (Dec.) October 15, 1981, 26 D.R. 248.

[52] Stafford, paras 81–82—the Government could not claim an power to detain the applicant to prevent future indeterminate offending under the original sentence.

[53] V v UK, December 16, 1999, ECHR 1999–IX, para.104.

[54] e.g. Drozd and Janousek; 16462/90, (Dec.) January 19, 1994, 76 D.R. 18.

(b) *Article 5, para.1(b): obligation imposed by law or non-compliance with order of the court*

IIB–075 This head of detention requires that a measure is taken to secure the execution of specific and concrete obligations. The obligation does not have to arise from a court order but may also derive from the law *per se*, although it must be sufficiently specific and concrete.[55] This has included short term internment for psychiatric observation ordered by a court[56]; four day detention on order of a court for non-payment of a fine[57]; judicial order to undergo a blood test[58]; arrest for non-compliance with a compulsory residence order[59]; obligation to submit to a security check on entry to Great Britain[60]; committal by magistrates for failure to pay the community charge[61]; detention following refusal to agree to be bound over[62] and detention in order to establish a person's identity.[63]

The aim of the detention must be to secure the fulfillment of the obligation, not to punish.[64] In *McVeigh v United Kingdom*,[65] the Commission noted that as soon as the obligation had been fulfilled the basis for the detention under this leg ceased.[66] It was also of the view that while there was no express requirement to that effect, the provision was primarily intended to cover the situation where a person has wilfully or negligently failed to perform an obligation. Therefore while detention in the absence of a prior breach of duty was not excluded, it considered that in order to exclude arbitrary deprivation of liberty the circumstances had to warrant the use of detention to secure the obligation and generally it would be required to show that the person was given an opportunity to fulfil the obligation and had failed.[67]

Relying on *McVeigh*, the Court has stated that a balance must be drawn between the importance in a democratic society of securing the immediate fulfilment of the obligation and the importance of the right to liberty, in which balance duration is a significant factor. Thus, in *Nowicka v Poland*, the detention of the applicant for 83 days for the purpose of obtaining two psychiatric examinations in the context of a

[55] *Guzzardi*, para.101: where the warning of a police chief to a mafiosi suspect was not sufficient; *Lawless*, (Rep.) December 19, 1959—measures to secure public order and State security were not concerned with the execution of specific obligations.

[56] 6659/74, (Dec.) December 10, 1975, 3 D.R. 92.

[57] 6289/73, (Dec.) July 7, 1977, 8 D.R. 142.

[58] 8278/78, (Dec.) December 13, 1979, 18 D.R. 154.

[59] 8916/80, (Dec.) October 7, 1980, 21 D.R. 250; see, however, *Ciulla*, where the arrest and detention predated the compulsory residence order and so fell outside Art.5, para.1(b).

[60] *McVeigh v UK*, 8022/77, etc. (Rep.) March 18, 1981, 25 D.R. 15.

[61] *Benham*.

[62] *Steel v UK*, September 23, 1998, R.J.D. 1998-VII, No.91—where the applicant protesters were detained after refusing to be bound over to keep the peace, the Court rejected complaints that the magistrates' order was too general or unspecific or that there was any arbitrariness in the procedure.

[63] 16810/90, (Dec.) September 9, 1992, 73 D.R. 136; *Vasileva*, para.40.

[64] 7341/76, (Rep.) April 3, 1978, 15 D.R. 35 (punishment for breach of military discipline); 10600/83, (Dec.) October 14, 1985, 45 D.R. 155 (detention of conscientious objector to secure acceptance of military service).

[65] n.60 above.

[66] See also *Nowicka v Poland*, December 3, 2002, para.64: violation found where the applicant's detention continued after the psychiatric examination.

[67] Despite any prior failure by the applicant, their arrest and detention on entry to Great Britain was justified exceptionally by the exigencies of fighting terrorism and the short duration of the measures. The Commission talked of striking a balance between the need to ensure the fulfilment of the obligation and the right to liberty. See also 10719/84, (Dec.) May 13, 1987, 52 D.R. 111, where it was acceptable to hold a person for several hours at a police stations for an identity check.

private neighbour dispute disclosed a violation, particularly as she was held for weeks before each examination and also post-examination.[68] In *Vasileva v Denmark*, detention for more than 13 hours of a 67-year-old woman, who had refused to give the police information about her identity, was found to exceed the time proportionate to the cause of her detention.[69]

(c) *Article 5, para.1(c): suspicion of committing a criminal offence, etc.*

See Pt IIB: Arrest.   IIB–076

(d) *Article 5, para.1(d): detention of minors*

The purpose of the deprivation of liberty of a minor must be either for "educational   IIB–077
supervision" or the purpose of bringing the minor before the competent legal authority. Where in *Bouamar v Belgium* a 16-year-old juvenile was held in a remand prison without any purpose of bringing proceedings, the Court rejected the Government's claim that the measure was part of an educative programme in a general sense. The only reason for the placement was that no proper place was available and there were no staff or facilities available in the prison to carry out any educational aim.[70] However, more recently, the Court has commented that "educational supervision" is not to be equated rigidly with notions of classroom teaching and includes many aspects of the exercise by a local authority of parental rights for the benefit and protection of the person concerned. Thus, the detention of a teenager in a secure centre for seriously disturbed young people which had a multi-disciplinary approach was covered, even though the applicant attended few, if any, classes.[71]

Detention of a minor held for observation in specialist centre was found to be for the purpose of bringing him before the competent legal authority, since he was suspected of committing offences and was to be brought before the Juvenile Commission in due course. The length of time (eight months) was not so excessive or unjustifiable as to cast doubt on the genuine purpose of the detention, *i.e.* to obtain medical reports.[72]

(e) *Article 5, para.1(e): mental health patients, vagrants, alcoholics, prevention of infectious diseases, etc.*

The link between the categories under this sub-paragraph is that the persons   IIB–078
concerned may be deprived of their liberty either to be given medical treatment or because of considerations dictated by social policy, or on both medical and social

---

[68] n.66 above.

[69] The applicant had been in dispute with a bus ticket collector. The Court looked at the earlier Commission cases, noting the special context of terrorist checks in *McVeigh* and implying that more than 6 hours would not be acceptable in normal circumstances. No problem arose for one hour's detention while police checked the applicant's identity in *Novotka v Slovakia*, 47244/99, (Dec.) November 4, 2003.

[70] February 29, 1988, Series A, No.129.

[71] *Koniarska*, n.10 above. However, in *DG v Ireland*, n.10 above, there was a breach where a teenager was held for a month in a penal institution, where any educational or recreational facilities were entirely voluntary and optional.

[72] 8500/79, (Dec.) December 14, 1979, 18 D.R. 238.

grounds. The Court takes the view that the predominant reason why the Convention allows their deprivation of liberty is not only that they are dangerous for public safety but also that their own interests may necessitate their detention.[73]

For mentally ill persons, see Pt IIB, Mental health.

In respect of vagrants, the Court in *De Wilde* accepted the Belgian definition of persons without fixed abode or means of subsistence and no regular trade or profession. The detention applied to the applicants in the case was found to fall within that definition and disclosed no arbitrariness in the decision or procedure whereby they were placed at the disposal of the Government.[74]

The term "alcoholics" has been held to cover not only those in a clinical state of alcholism but also those whose conduct and behaviour under the influence of alcohol pose a threat to public order or to themselves.[75] In *Witold Litwa v Poland*, where the applicant, severely sight-impaired, was taken for over six hours to a sobering up centre, the Court found the detention arbitrary as it was based on a rather trivial factual basis and other less severe measures, provided for by law, such as being escorted home, had not apparently been considered.[76]

Even fewer cases have arisen concerning detention for quarantine purposes. A case is pending examination of the merits as to the justification of the detention of an applicant in hospital under an isolation order to prevent him spreading HIV infection.[77]

(f) *Article 5, para.1 (f): pending expulsion or extradition*

IIB–079   See Pt IIB: Detention pending extradition and expulsion.

7. Types of detention not covered by the exceptions

IIB–080   Where a court has ordered release, some delay in carrying out the decision may be inevitable although the authorities should keep this to a minimum. Where an applicant remained in custody for a further seven hours, while certain formalities were being carried out, the Court found no violation.[78] Where applicants have been deliberately retained in custody pending the authorities' intention to apply other measures, the detention has been found to fall outside the exceptions allowed by Art.5.[79] Detention on arrest which exceeded the statutory maximum of 12 hours by 45 minutes, was also found to disclose a violation in *KF v Germany*.[80] It distinguished

---

[73] *Witold Litwa*, para.60.

[74] In *Guzzardi*, the Government failed in their argument that mafia suspects were subject to restrictions as a type of vagrant.

[75] *Witold*, paras 61–62.

[76] Contrast *HD v Poland*, 33310/96, (Dec.) June 7, 2001, where the detention of the applicant was lawful—her conduct having been "rowdy", "aggressive", etc.

[77] *Enhorn v Sweden*, 56529/00, (Dec.) December 10, 2002.

[78] *Giulia Manzoni v Italy*, July 1, 1997, R.J.D. 1997–IV, No.41.

[79] *Quinn v France*, March 22, 1995, Series A, No.311; 21 E.H.R.R. 529; *Doran v Netherlands*, 15268/89, (Rep.) July 8, 1993. Also *Labita v Italy*, April 6, 2000, ECHR 2000–IV, paras 172–173, where 12 hours' detention after acquittal was not due to relevant administrative formalities but merely the absence of the registration officer.

[80] The Commission found that a delay of 45 minutes was not such as to deprive the applicant of his liberty in an arbitrary manner contrary to the spirit and purpose of Art.5, para.1: (Rep.) September 10, 1996.

the cases in which some delay in release had been accepted, since in those cases the period of detention was not laid down in advance by statute but ended as a result of a court order. Whereas in *KF v Germany* the maximum period was laid down in law as obligatory and the authorities were under a duty to comply with it.

Internment or detention without trial is excluded. In *Lawless v Ireland*, the ministerial power to detain persons suspected of being engaged in activities prejudicial to public order or State security could not be considered as detention for failure to comply with an order of court or to secure the fulfilment of an obligation prescribed by law nor for purpose of bringing the person before a court under Art.5, para.1(c). In *Ireland v United Kingdom*, the internment power in Northern Ireland fell outside Art.5, para.1(c) since whether or not persons were in fact suspected on reasonable grounds of involvement in terrorist offences their detention was not for the purpose of bringing them before a judicial authority which was the other essential element of para.1(c).[81]

Other examples of detention not permitted by Art.5, para.1 include deprivation of liberty of a person confined and placed under guardianship for extravagance and idleness[82]; possibly, collusion by State agents with private individuals to bring within State territory against his will a person living abroad[83]; preventive measures, including compulsory residence, based on a policy of general prevention against dangerous individuals such as *mafiosi* (without reference to the commission of any specific offence)[84]; detention of cult members for "deprogramming" purposes[85]; preventive detention in connection with unspecified banditism and criminal association where no criminal proceedings were pending[86]; and extra-territorial measures seizing the applicant outside the Contracting State where that State has beyond all reasonable doubt acted in a manner inconsistent with the sovereignty of the host State and contrary to international law.[87]

Cross-reference

Part IIB: Arrest
Part IIB: Detention pending extradition and expulsion
Part IIB: Extradition
Part IIB: Mental Health
Part IIB: Pre-trial detention
Part IIB: Review of detention

---

[81] However, in both *Lawless* and *Ireland v UK* valid derogations under Art.15 were found to be in place.

[82] 7397/76, (Dec.) December 13, 1977, 11 D.R. 58, settled (Rep.) March 8, 1979, 15 D.R. 105.

[83] *Stocké v Germany*, March 19, 1991, Series A, No.199 (Rep.): the Commission considered this, if proved, might render arrest and subsequent detention unlawful within the meaning of Art.5, para.1; see however *Reinette v France*, 14009/88, (Dec.) October 2, 1989, 63 D.R. 189: where a suspected terrorist on St. Vincent was dragged onto a runway near a French military plane where officers executed letters rogatory, the Commission found no reason why co-operation between St Vincent and French authorities could raise problems under Art.5.

[84] *Guzzardi*, para.102; see also *Ciulla*: the arrest and detention predated the court order of compulory residence and thus fell outside Art.5 para.1(b).

[85] *Riera Blume*.

[86] *Jecius*.

[87] *Ocalan*, para.92: the arrest of Ocalan by Turkish officials in Nairobi was however conducted in co-operation with the Kenyan authorities.

Derogation: states of emergency

Key provision:

IIB–081 Article 15.

Key case law:

Lawless v Ireland, July 1, 1961, Series A, No.3; 1 E.H.R.R. 15; *Ireland v UK*, January 18, 1978, Series A, No.25; 2 E.H.R.R. 25; *Brannigan and McBride v UK*, May 26, 1993, Series A, No.258–B; 17 E.H.R.R. 539; *Aksoy v Turkey*, December 18, 1996, R.J.D. 1996–VI, No.26; 23 E.H.R.R. 553; *Sakik v Turkey*, November 26, 1997, R.J.D. 1997–VII, No.58.

1. General considerations

IIB–082 Article 15 permits a Contracting State to derogate from its obligations under the Convention, excepting Arts 2 (save in respect of deaths resulting from lawful acts of war), 3, 4 and 7 in time of war or other public emergency threatening the life of the nation and to the extent strictly required by the exigencies of the situation.

In derogation cases, the Convention organs have adopted the approach of examining the substantive complaint first and then, if there is a violation, proceeding to examine whether it is covered by the derogation in question.[1] This leaves no uncertainty as to what measures are in breach of the Convention. While there is a requirement of strict limitation of derogations to the exigencies of the crisis, in practice the Convention organs have given States considerable leeway.

Currently, there is a derogation lodged in respect of UK (concerning the "war against terrorism" response to the September 11 attacks).[2]

2. Obligation to inform the Secretary General of the Council of Europe

IIB–083 The Secretary General should be informed without undue delay of the reasons for the derogation and the measures being taken. This appears to require identification of the laws concerned, and possibly also provision of the texts concerned.[3]

In *Aksoy*, where compliance was not adverted to before the Commission, the Court stated that it could raise the point of its own motion, though in view of its

---

[1] Violations of Art.5 were found in respect of internment without trial in *Lawless* (Arts 5, para.1(c) and 3); *Ireland v UK*, extra judicial detention imposed on terrorist suspects was not in compliance with Arts 5, paras 1(c), 2, 3 or 4; *Brannigan and McBride*, there the power to hold persons for up to 7 days without being brought before a judge infringed the requirement of promptness in Art.5 para.3, as did the 14-day period in *Aksoy*. In all but *Aksoy*, the derogation conformed with the requirements of Art.15.

[2] Previously the UK had a derogation in place in respect of the Northern Ireland conflict, which was lifted in February 2001, following the peace process. Turkey until recently had derogations concerning primarily the security situation in the south-east.

[3] In *Lawless*, the Irish Government had provided a copy of the relevant Proclamation and Act and the reasons were given as being "to prevent the commission of offences against the public peace and order and to prevent the maintaining of military or armed forces other than those authorised by the Constitution." No issue arose from notification of the UK derogations in *Ireland v UK* and *Brannigan and McBride*.

finding that the measure was not strictly required, it did not do so. There was a strong hint that the Turkish notification to the Secretary General was insufficient: no specific measures relating to Art.5 had been detailed beyond a reference to the power of the State of Emergency Governor irrelevant to the case.[4]

Where a derogation is expressed as applying to a particular part of a country, the State cannot rely on the derogation applying to events taking part elsewhere, even if it was part of a response to the general problem underlying the derogation.[5]

There is no requirement for the Contracting State to promulgate in its territory the notice of derogation.[6]

3. Time of war

No derogation concerning a state of war has yet been in issue.   IIB–084

4. State of emergency threatening the life of the nation

This refers to an exceptional situation of crisis or emergency which affects the whole   IIB–085
population and constitutes a threat to the organised life of the community.[7] The Court allows a wide margin of appreciation. It is primarily for the Contracting State with its responsibility for the life of the nation to determine whether that life is threatened by a public emergency and, if so, how far it is necessary to go to overcome it. By reason of their direct and continuous contact with the pressing needs of the moment, the national authorities are in a better position than international judges to decide both on the presence of such an emergency and the nature and extent of the derogations necessary to avert it. The margin of appreciation is not altogether unlimited, the Convention organs being empowered to rule on whether States have gone beyond the extent strictly required by the exigencies of the crisis.[8]

In *Brannigan and McBride*, the Court rejected the submissions of the applicants and intervenors arguing against a wide margin of appreciation particularly where the crisis was of a quasi-permanent nature as in Northern Ireland and the rights essential for the protection of detainees. It merely repeated its earlier view and stated that in exercising its supervision it would give appropriate weight to relevant factors such as the nature of the rights affected, the circumstances leading to and the duration of the emergency situation.[9]

The existence of an emergency claimed by a Government has not yet been rejected. In *Lawless*, the Court found that the existence of such an emergency was reasonably deduced by Irish Government having regard, *inter alia*, to the existence on their territory of a secret army engaged in unconstitutional activities and using violence to attain its aims, the operation of this army outside its territory seriously jeopardising its relations with its neighbour and the steady, alarming increase in terrorist activities from 1956–1957. The existence of such an emergency at the

---

[4] *Aksoy*, paras 31–32.
[5] *Sakik*, paras 36–39: the derogation, aimed at fighting terrorism, was framed as applying to the state of emergency region and the arrest of the applicants took place elsewhere.
[6] *Lawless*, para.47.
[7] *ibid.*, para.28.
[8] *Ireland v UK*, para.207; *Lawless*, para.28.
[9] *Brannigan and McBride*, paras 41–43.

relevant time (early 1970s) was not in issue in the *Ireland v United Kingdom* case. The issue was also not contested in the *Aksoy* case, in relation to the extent and impact of PKK activity in south east Turkey.

The nature of the situation arising from the attacks on September 11, 2001, which has been claimed by the UK Government to justify a derogation of Art.5 rights in respect of foreign nationals suspected of involvement in terrorism, has yet to be examined by the Court.[10]

5. "Strictly required by the exigencies of the situation"

IIB–086 The Court has accepted measures as justified by this high standard even where there was, arguably, considerable doubt as to their efficacy or necessity. It has paid considerable attention to the existence of safeguards mitigating against abuse and given weight to the willingness of the authorities to introduce additional safeguards as the situation evolves. Notably, in the only case *Aksoy*, where the derogation fell foul of this requirement, the Government failed to provide a convincing reason for the length of time of incommunicado detention and there was a manifest lack of safeguards against abuse.

In *Lawless* and *Ireland v United Kingdom*, the Court accepted the arguments that the ordinary law had proved unable to check terrorism and steps were necessary to counter the difficulties of obtaining evidence to convict persons involved with the IRA due to the secret and terrorist nature of the groups and the fear inspired by them. In *Ireland v United Kingdom*, the Court found that a power to detain some-one unsuspected of a crime or offence but for the purposes of obtaining information could only be justified in very exceptionable circumstances but that these existed in Northern Ireland at this time (*e.g.* the alleged need to question persons who were too scared to give evidence freely). The Court did not accept the argument that the use of extra judicial detention was ineffectual (the Irish Government stated it clearly did not brake terrorism and the UK had abandoned it gradually and then wholly). The Court stated that it was not its role to judge in the place of the UK Government what was the most prudent or most expedient policy to combat terrorism and it had to exercise its power of supervision, not in light of retrospective considerations but only having regard to the conditions and circumstances reigning at the time.

In contrast, in *Aksoy*, which concerned the power to detain for up to 30 days,[11] the Court acknowledged the difficulties of investigating terrorist crimes but found the period unacceptable, as being exceptionally long and leaving the applicant vulnerable to arbitrary interference with the right to liberty and to torture. It noted a lack of detailed reasons as to why judicial intervention was not practicable. The Government had referred solely to difficulties of investigations in a vast geographical area.

The factor of abuse of power may be relevant. In *Lawless*, the Court included in its reasoning that it had found no indication that the powers were used against the applicant for any other purpose than that for which they were granted (*e.g.* suspected involvement with the IRA).

---

[10] Declaration, dated December 18, 2001, setting out the extended power of arrest and detention provided in the Anti-terrorism, Crime and Security Act 2001 and derogating from Art.5 para.1(f).
[11] The applicant was held for 14 days.

In *Brannigan and McBride v United Kingdom*, it was argued that the derogations were not a genuine response to an emergency situation but to counter the Court's decision in *Brogan v United Kingdom*, where the power of detention of terrorist suspects for up to seven days was found in breach of Art.5, para.3. The Court observed that the power had been considered necessary under emergency measures since 1974 to deal with terrorism and found that the derogation was clearly linked to the persistence of the emergency situation. As regarded the apparent interim nature of the derogation, the Court found that, as this was expressed to be pending review of other possibilities of judicial control, this disclosed a process of continued reflection entirely in keeping with the spirit of Art.15. It found that absence of judicial control could be regarded as necessary having regard to the various reports on terrorism issued in relation to the difficulties of investigating and prosecuting terrorist crime. It noted, without rejecting, the Government's view that it was essential to prevent disclosure to the detainee and his legal advisers of the information on which the extension of detention was required and that the independence of the judiciary would be compromised if judges were involved in the granting of extensions, particularly as in Northern Ireland the judiciary was small and vulnerable to attack and the Government understandably attached importance to public confidence in their independence.

On the issue of safeguards, recourse to formal courts has not been required, but weight has been given to any participation by courts or the judiciary in a reviewing procedure of the measures as applied.[12] Reference has also been made to the constant supervision by Parliament or other independent bodies, though the practical effectiveness of this is not apparent.[13] In *Ireland v United Kingdom*, where the safeguards were less apparent or effective than in *Lawless*, the Court placed emphasis on the fact that the authorities responded to the situation by evolving towards protecting individual liberties in the measures as amended and commented that while the provision of satisfactory judicial, or at least administrative, remedies was desirable from the outset, it would be unrealistic not to distinguish the phases. It could not be expected of a State struggling against a public emergency to render itself defenceless by being required to provide complete safeguards from the outset. On this view, Art.15 allows, pragmatically, for progressive adaptations in providing human rights protection, without the apparent need to establish that the initial draconian response was in fact necessary.

Similarly, leeway is given as regards the timing of the complete removal of restrictions. Where in 1998 an applicant was held for seven days without being brought before a judge, it was argued that the security situation in Northern Ireland had been transformed due to the peace process and the power was no longer justified. The Court found that it could still be said that the measures were required by a state of emergency, noting that outbreaks of terrorist violence were still occurring and emphasising that the national authorities were best placed to decide both the presence of an emergency and the nature and scope of the derogation necessary to avoid it.[14]

---

[12] In *Lawless*, reference is made to a detention commission (two of the three members were judges); in *Ireland v UK* to a valuable if limited recourse to the courts and a certain measure of protection from an advisory committee, commissioners and appeal tribunal; and in *Brannigan and McBride* to regular independent review of the legislation.

[13] See *Marshall v UK*, 41571/98, (Dec.) July 10, 2001: the Court dismissed objections that the annual Parliamentary debate or executive review of the measures were meaningless exercises—it was enough that the authorities addressed the issues with sufficient frequency.

[14] *Marshall*, n.13 above.

In *Aksoy*, the Court found insufficient safeguards available to protect detainees. There was a denial of access to lawyers, doctor, relatives and friends which left the applicant completely at the mercy of those holding him. The Government's reliance on supervision by public prosecutor and the prohibition of torture in Turkish law was not enough.[15]

6. Consistency with other obligations under international law

IIB–087   The only case where other international obligations were identified was *Brannigan and McBride*, where the applicants referred to the UK's obligations under the International Covenant and Civil and Political Rights and claimed that it was essential for valid derogation from Art.4 of the Covenant that the derogation had been officially proclaimed. The Court noted that the Secretary of State had made a statement to the House of Commons detailing the reasons for the derogation, which was sufficiently formal and public in its view.

---

[15] In contrast to *Brannigan and McBride*, where the Court found important measures of protection against arbitrary detention, *e.g. habeus corpus*, the right to see a solicitor after 48 hours and to inform a relative or friend.

Detention pending extradition and expulsion

Key provisions:

Article 5, paras 1 and 1(f) (lawful detention pending extradition or expulsion and   **IIB–088**
para.4 (review of lawfulness of detention).

Key case law:

Bozano v France, December 18, 1986, Series A, No.111; 9 E.H.R.R. 297; *Soering v UK*, July 7, 1989, Series A, No.161; 11 E.H.R.R 439; *Kolompar v Belgium*, September 24, 1992, Series A, No.235–C; 16 E.H.R.R. 197; *Quinn v France*, March 22, 1995, Series A, No.311; 21 E.H.R.R. 529; *Chahal v UK*, November 15, 1996, R.J.D. 1996–V, No.22; 23 E.H.R.R. 413; *Dougoz v Greece*, March 6, 2001, ECHR 2001–II; *Slivenko v Latvia*, October 9, 2003, ECHR 2003–XI.

1. General considerations

A person may be detained pending extradition subject to the general safeguard   **IIB–089**
imposed by Art.5, para.1 and the specific context of Art.5 para.1(f) which provides
the exception to the right to liberty of "lawful arrest or detention" which is "with a
view" to extradition or expulsion. Undue length of detention may render it
incompatible with this provision. Conditions of the detention may also raise issues
under Art.3 as disclosing inhuman and degrading treatment.[1]

2. Lawfulness

The detention must "in accordance with a procedure prescribed by law" and also be   **IIB–090**
"lawful".[2] The dominant theme is the prevention of arbitrariness. (See section
Deprivation of liberty.)

In *Chinoy v United Kingdom,* where the applicant complained that in the
extradition proceedings in the UK the magistrate had regard to tapes allegedly
obtained in breach of French law, the Commission found no breach of the lawfulness
criteria of the detention since the use was not in breach of English law and not
arbitrary.[3] Where steps are taken by the authorities by way of "disguised
extradition", issues may however arise as to the lawfulness. In *Bozano v France*, the
French courts had refused an extradition request. The procedure whereby the police
proceeded to enforce a deportation order, which had the effect of delivering the
applicant to the requesting State, was found by the Court to disclose arbitrariness, in

---

[1] *e.g. Dougoz*, where the serious overcrowding and lack of sleeping facilities where the applicant was held
for several months pending his expulsion breached Art.3. See Prisoners, Conditions of confinement and
Torture and ill-treatment.
[2] *e.g.* 15268/89, *Doran v Netherlands*, (Rep.) July 8, 1993, where notwithstanding the order to release of
the applicant the public prosecutor told the prison to retain him pending an intended extradition, the
detention was not in accordance with a procedure prescribed by law; *Dougoz v Greece*, where the detention
of the applicant on the opinion of a public prosecutor as to the applicability by analogy of a ministerial
decision on administrative expulsion was not based on a "law" of sufficient "quality" within the meaning
of the Court's case law.
[3] 15199/89, (Dec.), September 4, 1991.

particular having regard to the way in which it was executed, suddenly and forcibly, depriving the applicant of making use of any remedies theoretically available to him and not giving him the choice of destination.

Flaws in a detention order will not necessarily render the period of detention unlawful within the meaning of Art.5, para.1, particularly where the putative error is immediately detected and redressed by the release of the persons concerned.[4]

3. With a view to extradition or expulsion

IIB–091   Only the existence of extradition proceedings justifies the detention. In *Quinn v France*, the failure to release for 11 hours pending the French authorities' instigation of extradition proceedings by the Swiss constituted detention outside the scope of the exceptions in Art.5, para.1.

In *Chahal v United Kingdom*, in the context of expulsion, the Court has said that all that is required is that action is being taken with a view to deportation and that it is immaterial for the purposes of Art.5, para.1(f) whether the underlying decision to expel can be justified under national or Convention law.[5] Nonetheless if is it apparent that the detention is for some other purpose resulting from some misuse of power it may cease to be justifiable.[6]

Where for a legal, practical or administrative reason, a person held for the purposes of extradition or expulsion cannot in fact be removed, issues may arise as to whether the detention can in those circumstances be considered as justified as being "with a view to extradition". In *Ali v Switzerland*, the Commission noted that the Swiss wanted to extradite the applicant to Somalia but could not as he had no travel document. Since the execution of the extradition was impossible, the detention could no longer be regarded as "with a view to extradition" within the exception of Art.5 para.1(f) and infringed Art.5 para.1.[7]

4. Effect of length

IIB–092   If insufficient diligence is shown in the extradition or expulsion proceedings, the detention may also cease to be justifiable for the purpose of Art.5, para.1(f).[8] Although in *Quinn v France*, a period of almost two years detention pending extradition was found to exceed a reasonable time, the Convention organs will accept considerable delays and the Court in *Chahal* has considered it relevant to have regard to lack of arbitrariness.[9]

Two years and eight months was found by the Court in *Kolompar v Belgium* to be not unreasonable since the extradition proceedings proper were completed less than

---

[4] *Slivenko*, para.149, citing *Benham v UK*, June 10, 1996, R.J.D. 1996–III, No.10, paras 42–47.

[5] See also *Slivenko*, para.146.

[6] 7317/75, (Dec.), October 6, 1976, 6 D.R. 141.

[7] 24881/94, (Rep.) February 26, 1997: later struck off by the Court due to the applicant's disappearance.

[8] *e.g.* 8081/77, (Dec.) December 12, 1977, 12 D.R. 207; 7317/75, n.6 above.

[9] *Chahal*, paras 117 and 123; 15933/89, (Dec.) October 14, 1991, the longest detained person without trial in the UK (almost 6 years at the time of his second application) facing extradition to Hong Kong— as regarded the length of proceedings, the Commission considered that an assessment of diligence depended on all the circumstances. It looked at the complexity of the case (several countries involved, voluminous documentation), the conduct of the applicant (his failure to ask for expedition and his repeated *habeas corpus* applications) and, since he appeared to be protracting the proceedings deliberately, found that he could not complain of delay.

one month after the decision to release in respect of other criminal charges and the detention was continued due to the applicant's successive applications for release, in which the courts gave their decisions within a normal time. He could not, the Court said, complain of a situation which he had largely created.[10]

In *Chahal v United Kingdom*, a period of over three years five months was acceptable to the Court due to the seriousness and difficulties of the issues (allegations of risk on return to India and national security aspects) and the procedural safeguards in place against arbitrary detention. This overruled the Commission which noted delays between procedural steps in the domestic proceedings and gave weight to the need for utmost expedition where the person was unconvicted and without charge.[11]

A period of detention prior to extradition where the applicant is serving a prison sentence following conviction by the sending State is not taken into account as it falls under Art.5, para.1(a) and not (f).[12]

5. Remedies

Where there is a breach of Art.5, para.(1)f, the applicable provisions with regard to effective redress are Art.5, para.4 which requires access to a review of the lawfulness of the detention by an appropriate judicial body[13] and Art.5, para.5 which requires an enforceable right in domestic law to receive compensation in domestic law.   IIB–093

The Commission found that *habeas corpus* complied with Art.5, para.4 in providing the means to challenge the lawfulness of the detention for the purposes of extradition.[14] Neither *habeas corpus* or judicial review however was found by the Court to furnish an adequate review of the lawfulness of the expulsion of the applicant in *Chahal v United Kingdom*, where the courts could not scrutinise the national security grounds relied on by the authorities.

A delay of two-and-a-half months in *habeas corpus* proceedings challenging lawfulness in a deportation case was found to comply with the requirement of promptness in Art.5 para.4—this is longer than has been found compatible in review of other types of detention but was with regard to the complexity of the issues and the significance the case had for all asylum-seekers at that time and may be regarded as an exceptional decision.[15] In *Kadem v Malta*, a cumbersome procedure which failed to obtain a hearing before the applicant's release 23 days after his arrest was not regarded as "speedy" for the purposes of Art.5 para.4.[16]

---

[10] The Commission considered that there must be a responsibility on States to prevent the undue prolongation of extradition proceedings in finding the correct balance between the restrictions on the right to liberty and international obligations. Belgium could not just adopt a passive attitude and was required to take positive steps to expedite the proceedings.

[11] More recently, one-and-a-half years' was acceptable in *Eid v Italy*, 53490/99, (Dec.) January 22, 2002.

[12] *Raf v Spain*, June 17, 2003, para.64.

[13] e.g. *Dougoz*, where appeals to the leniency of government ministers did not satisfy Art.5, para.4; *Conka v Belgium*, February 2002, ECHR 2002–I, where the applicant gypsies were tricked into coming to a police station, arrested and expelled without any effective possibility of challenging the measure in a court.

[14] 19319/91, (Dec.) September 2, 1992.

[15] 28201/95, (Dec.) November 27, 1996.

[16] January 9, 2003.

Cross-reference

Part IIB: Deprivation of liberty
Part IIB: Extradition
Part IIB: Reasons for detention
Part IIB: Review of detention

Discrimination

Key provision:

Article 14 (prohibition against discrimination).   IIB–094

Key case law:

Belgian Linguistic case, July 23, 1968, Series A, No.6; 1 E.H.R.R. 252; *Kjeldsen, Busk Madsen and Pedersen v Denmark*, December 7, 1976, Series A, No.23; 1 E.H.R.R. 711; *Marckx v Belgium*, June 13, 1979, Series A, No.31; 2 E.H.R.R. 330; *Van der Mussele v Belgium*, November 23, 1983, Series A, No.70; 6 E.H.R.R. 471; *Abdulaziz, Cabales and Balkandali v UK*, May 28, 1985, Series A, No.94; 7 E.H.R.R. 163; *Lithgow v UK*, July 8, 1986, Series A, No.102; 8 E.H.R.R. 329; *Johnston v Ireland*, December 18, 1986, Series A, No.112; 9 E.H.R.R. 203; *Darby v Sweden*, October 23, 1990, Series A, No.187; 13 E.H.R.R. 774; *Pine Valley Developments Ltd v Ireland*, November 29, 1991, Series A, No.222; *Hoffman v Austria*, June 23, 1993, Series A, No.255–C; 17 E.H.R.R. 293; *Schuler-Zraggen v Switzerland*, June 24, 1993, Series A, No.263; 16 E.H.R.R. 405; *McMichael v UK*, February 24, 1995, Series A, No.307– B; 20 E.H.R.R. 205; *Gayguzuz v Austria*, September 16, 1996, R.J.D. 1996–IV; 23 E.H.R.R. 364; *Stubbings v UK*, October 22, 1996, R.J.D. 1996–IV; 23 E.H.R.R. 213; *Van Raalte v Netherlands*, February 21, 1997, R.J.D. 1997–I; 24 E.H.R.R. 503; *Petrovic v Austria*, March 27, 1998, R.J.D. 1998–II; *Smith and Grady v UK*, September 27, 1999, ECHR 1999–VI; 29 E.H.R.R. 493; *Thlimmenos v Greece*, April 6, 2000, ECHR 2000–IV; *Ch'are Shalom Ve Tsedek v France*, June 27, 2000, ECHR 2000–VII; *Elsholz v Germany*, July 13, 2000, ECHR 2000–VIII; *Cyprus v Turkey*, May 10, 2001, ECHR 2001–IV; *Wessels-Bergervoet v Netherlands*, June 4, 2002, ECHR 2002–IV; *Willis v UK*, June 11, 2002, ECHR 2002–IV; *Sahin v Germany*, July 8, 2003, ECHR 2003–VII; *Sommerfeld v Germany*, July 8, 2003, ECHR 2003– VIII; *Nachova v Bulgaria*, February 26, 2004.

1. General considerations

Article 14 encapsulates a crucial human right. Discrimination, in its many insidious   IIB–095
forms, could be described as one of the fundamental evils afflicting society and is at
the heart of many tangible atrocities. However its role in the Convention system has
been limited both by its drafters and approach adopted by the Convention organs.
There has nonetheless been a recent emphasis on the condemnation of racism and
ethnic hatred with corresponding positive obligations on the State to maintain the
confidence of minorities in the ability of the authorities to protect them from racist
violence.[1] In this area, positive and procedural obligations are developing.

According to the case law, an applicant must establish that he is subject to a
difference in treatment from others in a comparable position in the enjoyment of
one of the rights guaranteed under the Convention, which difference cannot be
objectively and reasonably justified, having regard to the applicable margin of
appreciation.

---

[1] *Menson v UK*, 47916/99, ECHR 2003–V; *Nachova*, para.157.

2. Protection only of enjoyment of guaranteed rights and freedoms

IIB–096   By its formulation, the provision has been tied inexorably to the other substantive rights in the Convention. An applicant complaining of discrimination must allege it in respect of, for example, freedom of religion or fair trial. It is useless to invoke it the area of employment rights, housing provision, political office, pay, access to private leisure facilities or the media. The new Protocol No.12, which was opened for signature on November 4, 2000, contains a wider guarantee against discrimination. It has not yet obtained the ten ratifications necessary for it to come into force.[2]

In *Belgian Linguistics*, the Court noted that the provision had "no independent existence" and it was as though it was an integral part of each of the substantive articles.[3] Further, extreme discrimination has been held by the Convention organs to constitute degrading treatment contrary to Art.3.[4]

Where the alleged discrimination relates to a matter which falls within the scope of one of the substantive articles, the provision may become operable.[5] Thus special treatment of taxation under Art.1 of the First Protocol bestows on it an exclusion from the normal guarantee of protection for property but where taxation legislation appears to single out persons for unfavourable treatment, issues may arise under that provision in conjunction with Art.14.[6] Sentencing matters generally fall outside the scope of Art.5 but issues have been held as possibly arising if sentencing policy appears to effect individuals in a discriminatory manner.[7] In *Inze v Austria*, concerning a difference in land inheritance between children born in and out of wedlock, the Court emphasised that under Art.1 of the First Protocol it was not for the Court to say who should inherit. However Art.14 came into play where by operation of law a distinction operated based on birth in or out of wedlock as regarded the differences in inheritance rights.

3. Difference in treatment

IIB–097   Not all differences in treatment are relevant for the purposes of Art.14. The examination for discrimination is only meaningful if the applicant is seeking to

---

[2] The UK has neither signed nor ratified; Ireland has signed.

[3] At p.34, para.9; for a more recent statement, *Petrovic*, para.22.

[4] In relation to race discrimination: *East African Asians v UK* (Rep.) December 14, 1973 78 D.R.5; *Cyprus v Turkey*, para.303, concerning the severe discrimination against the Karpas Greek community in northern Cyprus. The same argument did not succeed in respect of sex discrimination in *Abdulaziz*: while the Commission found a degrading treatment finding inherent in a violation of Art.14, the Court found no separate issue under Art.3.

[5] *Petrovic*, para.28: the issue of parental leave allowances, granted to mothers but not fathers, was thus considered to fall within the scope of Art.8 as a means by which the State demonstrated respect for family life; *Willis v UK*, paras 35–36: right to receive widow's benefits was sufficiently pecuniary to come within the scope of Art.1 of Protocol No.1 without the Court needing to decide whether the benefit could constitute a "possession" under that provision; *Frette v France*, February 26, 2002, ECHR 2002–I— see the minority dissenting opinion at p.32–33, explaining at some length why, though there was no right to adopt under Art.8 and France had gone beyond what was required, it had a duty to implement the system so that there was no unwarranted discrimination on grounds listed in Art.14.

[6] 11089/84 (Dec.) November 11, 1986 49 D.R. 181.

[7] 11077/84 (Dec.), October 13, 1986 49 D.R. 170; 22761/93, (Dec.) April 14, 1994, 77–A D.R. 98.

compare himself to others in a comparable positions, or analogous situations or, in another formulation, is in a "relevantly similar" situation to those others.[8]

For example, married couples are not in analogous situations with unmarried couples since they have chosen a particular legal regime to govern their relations, marriage having a special status which continues to be characterised by a distinct corpus of rights and obligations[9]; IRA Category A prisoners could not seek to compare themselves with prisoners of no security risk[10]; advocates are not in analogous positions to other professions, even with those connected with the law like the judiciary or bailiffs, the professions in question being characterised by a corpus of rights and obligations of which it would be artificial to isolate one element[11]; companies subject to nationalisation are not in an analogous situation to property owners subject to compulsory purchase.[12]

This may appear at times to overlap with the objective and reasonable justification concept (see Section 5, below) since a finding that two situations are not comparable will generally rely on reasons, akin to objective and reasonable justification, disclosing material difference.[13]

While violations of Art.14 have generally concerned situations where the State has treated differently persons in analogous situations without providing a reasonable or objective explanation, the Court has extended the provision to situations where a State without an objective and reasonable justification fail to treat differently persons whose situations are significantly different. Thus, in *Thlimmenos v Greece*, the Court found a violation of Art.14 in conjunction with Art.9 where the applicant, a Jehovah's witness had been convicted for refusal to wear a military uniform on religious grounds. He was then excluded from exercising the profession of chartered accountant on the basis that he had a serious criminal conviction. Taking the view that the applicant's conviction on conscientious grounds differed from other criminal offences which might render a person unsuitable to enter the professsion, it found there was no objective and reasonable justification for not treating the applicant differently from other persons convicted of a felony. The discrimination therefore lay in failing to introduce appropriate exceptions to the bar on entry. This approach has yet to produce a violation in any other case however.[14]

4. On grounds of personal status

The Court has stated that Art.14 is only concerned with discriminatory treatment   IIB–098
having as its basis a personal characteristic or "status" by which persons or groups of persons are distinguishable from each other.[15] It thus aims to strike down the

[8] *Markx*, para.32; *Van der Mussele*, para.46; *Larkos v Cyprus*, February 18, 1999, ECHR 1999–I; 30 E.H.R.R. 597, para.30, where the applicant as a tenant renting State-owned property was in a relevantly similar situation to tenants renting from private landlords.
[9] 11089/84, n.6 above.
[10] 19085/91, (Dec.) December 9, 1992.
[11] *Van der Mussele*.
[12] *Lithgow*.
[13] See, *e.g. Stubbings*, where the Court effectively held that victims of deliberate and negligently inflicted injury were not in analogous positions since the prescription rules applicable to the two categories had developed separately with different characteristics and even if they were in analogous positions, there was reasonable and objective justification since they had different characteristics.
[14] See, *e.g. Chapman v UK*, January 18, 2001, ECHR 2001–I, para.129, where the applicant failed to persuade the Court that as a gypsy it was discriminatory to apply the same planning rules to her as to the sedentary majority.
[15] *Kjeldsen*, para.56.

offensive singling out of an individual or members of a particular group on their personal attributes. Art.14 lists the obvious ones: sex, race, colour, language, religion, political or other opinion, national or social origin, etc. The list is not exhaustive, Art.14 referring to "any ground" and concluding with "or other status".

The limits of the concept of personal status have not been much discussed. It does not extend to differences in treatment deriving from differing rules applicable between regional jurisdictions within a State, where, in other words, the difference results from the geographical location where the person finds himself and not any personal characteristic. Thus it is not a difference in treatment on grounds of personal status for people in Scotland to be subject to the poll tax before people living in England[16] or where a juvenile offender in Scotland did not enjoy an entitlement to remission accorded to such offenders sentenced in England and Wales[17] or where different practices allegedly applied between Northern Ireland and England and Wales concerning access of terrorist suspect to solicitors on arrest.[18] This reflects the fact that many Contracting States have regional jurisdictions, with differing rules and procedures and avoids interpreting Art.14 to require universally identical laws throughout each country. Geographical difference presumably could base a claim for discrimination where perhaps it was apparent that a particular area was subject to a law because its citizens were individuals sharing a common personal element, beyond their residence in the location.

5. Justification for difference in treatment

IIB–099   While Art.14 is not expressly subject to exceptions, it has been interpreted as incorporating the practical recognition that not every difference in treatment in the enjoyment of the protected rights and freedoms can be prohibited. The Court in the *Belgian Linguistics* case noted that a literal application of the French version "*sans aucune distinction*" would lead to "absurd results" and referred to the inherent differences existing in legal situations and problems which call for differing legal solutions. The test applied to assess which differences in treatment are objectionable or not is whether they are based on objective and reasonable justification. The existence of the justification has to be assessed in relation to the aims and effects of the measure under consideration, regard being had to the principles which normally prevail in democratic societies. It must not only pursue a legitimate aim but there must be reasonable relationship of proportionality between the means employed and the aim sought to realised. Therefore the concepts of legitimate aim, proportionality, are brought in and, inevitably, the margin of appreciation.[19]

Whether there is objective and reasonable justification will depend on the circumstances of each situation.

Administrative difficulties generally should not suffice, as in *Darby v Sweden* where this was the sole basis for barring non-residents who worked in Sweden from an exemption to church tax available to residents in Sweden. Nor can objective and reasonable justification for the interferences with rights be derived purely from negative attitudes, varying from hostility or unease, that a particular minority might arouse. In *Smith and Grady v United Kingdom*, the Court held that, insofar as the ban

---

[16] 13473/87 (Dec.) July 11, 1988.

[17] 11077/84, n.7 above.

[18] *Magee v UK*, June 6, 2000, ECHR 2000–VI, para.50.

[19] *Belgian Linguistics* case, p.35, para.10.

on homosexuals in the army represented a predisposed bias on the part of a heterosexual majority against a homosexual minority, this could not justify discriminatory treatment any more than similar negative attitudes towards those of a different race, origin or colour.

A certain allowance is, however, given to States as regards the timing of changes which reflect a shift in society's attitudes, as in *Petrovic v Austria*, where it noted that the grant of parental leave to fathers was a recent development and the Austrian legislature could not be criticised for extending measures to fathers as well as mothers in a gradual manner. This was where there was no common standard amongst Contracting States on the issue at the relevant time and Austria, whose legislation could be regarded in fact as progressive, could not be held to have exceeded its margin of appreciation. Furthermore, where a domestic court makes a finding of discrimination which requires legislative change, the Court found that the continued application of the discriminatory provisions for a short period of time pending legislative amendment may be regarded as proportionate.[20]

6. Relationship with substantive complaints

In many cases, an applicant subject to a particular measure will argue that the measure infringes a substantive right, without necessary justification and that he is, by the implementation of that measure, subject also to unjustifiable discrimination. Where a violation is found of the substantive article, it is often the case that the Court will find no separate issue to arise under Art.14. It is a practice which may not be based on unavoidable logic but may rather give proof of a certain judical economy. For example, in *Moustaquim v Belgium*, the Court found the proposed measure of expelling the applicant, a second generation immigrant, to a country in which he had no family, disclosed a violation of Art.8 , but found it unnecessary to examine the complaint under Art.14. However, his claim that this measure constituted discrimination since the measure was imposed on him due to his nationality was arguably a separate legal issue, the fact that the complaint concerned the same measure not logically precluding the existence of two separate grounds of violation.[21]

IIB–100

Conversely, a finding of no violation of a substantive article does not preclude the examination of the discrimination complaint, as in *Abdulaziz v United Kingdom* where the claims under Art.8 were rejected.[22] This is the type of case where the essence of the complaint is the discriminatory application of the measures, which otherwise disclose no fundamental incompatibility with the provisions of the Convention.

There are some cases where it is more difficult to analyse whether the case is primarily about the substantive provision or discrimination. There have accordingly been decisions, where the Convention organs have chosen to examine the complaints under Art.14 alone. In *Hoffman v Austria*, the applicant, who lost custody of her

---

[20] *Walden v Liechtenstein*, 33916/96, (Dec.) March 16, 2000—7-month period.

[21] Similarly, no separate issue arose under Art.14 in the gays in the army cases once a breach of Art.8 was found (*e.g. Smith and Grady v UK*, paras 115–116) or in the transsexual cases (*Christine Goodwin v UK*, July 11, 2002, ECHR 2002–VI, para.108).

[22] *Abdulaziz*—there was no interference with family life since the applicants and their spouses had no expectation of a grant of residence and could live together elsewhere; whereas discrimination arose as the rules applied differently to male and female spouses.

children to her divorced spouse in a decision which gave considerable weight to her beliefs as a Jehovah's witness, invoked Arts 8 and 14. Since the deprivation of her family rights was based on apparent discrimination on religious grounds, the Court found a violation of Art.14 and considered that it was not necessary in its view to look at Art.8 alone since it would involve the same arguments.[23]

To succeed in establishing violations of a substantive provision and a discrimination violation would require showing that separate arguments and considerations of some significance arose.

7. Particular discrimination areas

(a) Sex

IIB–101   The Court has emphasised that, advancement of equality of the sexes being a major goal in Contracting States, it would require very weighty reasons for a difference in treatment on grounds of sex to be compatible with the Convention. Such reasons have been lacking in a number of cases, which, interestingly, tend more to concern discrimination against men than against women.

No convincing justification was found for a court decision refusing a woman a disability pension which had as its only basis the assumption that women give up work on having children, a difference of treatment based on sex for which there was no objective and reasonable justification[24]; the inability of a man to add his surname before that of his wife's, while the law allowed a woman to add hers to her husband's name[25]; an obligation on a man to pay a fire service levy in lieu of actual service based on a local tradition of male participation in fire brigade where women, who did not serve, did not have to pay either[26]; rules allowing the entry of foreign wives of citizens but not foreign husbands, which might pursue the legitimate aim of protecting the labour market but that aim could not be justified by differentiating between men and women for impact on employment[27]; exemption of childless women over 45 from paying social security contributions towards child benefit, as whether or not it was a legitimate aim to spare the feelings of childless women, there were equally men who could not procreate[28]; the ineligibility of widowers to apply for benefits on the deaths of their spouses in circumstances where a woman could obtain a Widow's Payment or Widowed Mother's Allowance[29]; or for a 38 per cent difference in the old age pension which the applicant woman received compared with a man.[30]

---

[23] See also the Commission's approach in *Stubbings*: the complaint was analysed by the Commission as alleging that the hindrance on access to court from prescription rules was unreasonable and disproportionate since it did not apply to other catogories of litigant suffering from injuries—essentially discrimination and to be treated under Art.14.

[24] *Schuler-Zgraggen*.

[25] *Burghartz v Switzerland*, February 22, 1994, Series A, No.280–B; 18 E.H.R.R. 101.

[26] *Karlheinz Schmidt v Germany*, July 18, 1994, Series A, No.291–B; 18 E.H.R.R. 513: while it might have been once justified in imposing the service on men alone, there was no justification for a difference in financial obligations.

[27] *Abdulaziz*.

[28] *Van Raalte*, paras 42–43.

[29] *Willis*; see also *Matthews v UK* (friendly settlement), July 15, 2002, where the male applicant complained that unlike women who became eligible at age 60, he had to wait until 65 for a free London bus pass.

[30] *Wessels-Bergervoet*.

The Commission to some extent accepted positive discrimination in favour of women as objective and reasonable justification for difference in treatment in the context of tax.[31] This was where rules had developed with the aim of encouraging women to work and advance the equality of the sexes, which resulted in a situation that where the wife was the major breadwinner of a married couple the tax allowance proved more favourable than where the major breadwinner was the man. The Commission accepted the aim as legitimate, noting that the difference only applied in 3 per cent of cases. It considered the margin of appreciation must be wider in the realm of taxes and pragmatically accepted that systems of taxation inevitably differentiated between groups of taxpayers and marginal situations might arise. As the discrepancy in treatment was not particularly large or widespread, it is possible that the case would have proceeded differently if there had been a significant financial disparity.

(b) *Marital status*

Marriage consisting of a special legal regime, differences of treatment between non-married couples or parents and married couples have been found not to disclose discrimination. Differences in the parental rights or responsibility over children accruing to natural fathers and married fathers were accepted in particular due to the differences in the nature of relationships of fathers with children born out of wedlock.[32] Where concrete decisions however are taken in respect of contact rights however, the Court has examined the circumstances of the case. In *Elsholz v Germany*, notwithstanding apparent differing tests applying between natural and married fathers (a presumption of contact being beneficial for the child operating in favour of the latter), the Court examined the court decisions and found that on the facts of the case it had not been shown that a divorced father would have been treated more favourably. However, in two later cases, *Sahin v Germany* and *Sommerfeld v Germany*, the Court found that the procedures showed that the applicants as natural fathers were treated less favourably in that the mother's refusal of access to a child could only be overridden by a court where access had been shown to be in the interest of the child. This heavy burden of proof was apparently found to have played a role in the negative decisions reached.[33] A natural father also did not enjoy a right of appeal which was available to a divorced father.[34]

IIB–102

(c) *Race*

The Court has issued strong recent statements emphasising the importance of condemning racism and requiring positive steps to be taken to enforce criminal law against those who carry out racial violence.[35]

IIB–103

Discrimination based on race had already been recognised by the Commission in the *East African Asians* case as forming a special form of affront to human dignity

---

[31] 11089/84, n.5 above.

[32] *McMichael*, para.98; see also 29779/96, (Dec.) October 21, 1998, where the Commission found objective and reasonable justification for legislative provisions which permitted parental responsibility to be removed by a court from unmarried fathers, whereas no such possibility existed for married, divorced or separated fathers.

[33] *Sahin*, paras 89–95; *Sommerfeld*, paras 88–94.

[34] *Sommerfeld*, paras 95–98.

[35] *Menson*, n.1 above; *Nachova*, para.157.

which, in aggravating circumstances, can amount to degrading treatment in breach of Art.3. The passing of legislation targetting a particular racial group for exclusion from entry to the UK was found to reach this level, having regard to the serious difficulties in which this placed Asians from East Africa who were being expelled from their African homes and were at risk of being "shuttlecocked" from one place to another. The extreme restrictions imposed on the Karpas Greek community in Northern Cyprus based on their ethnic origin, race and religion, which controlled and isolated them to an extent found to be debasing and contrary to the very notion of respect for human dignity, also disclosed a violation of Art.3 in *Cyprus v Turkey*.

Where racist violence may be in issue, the authorities are under an obligation under Art.2 to pursue an official investigation with vigour and impartiality, *inter alia*, to maintain confidence of minorities in their ability to protect them. Failure thoroughly to investigate possible racist motives for a killing was found in *Nachova v Bulgaria* to disclose a procedural breach of Art.14. In the absence of a proper investigation into the shooting of two unarmed Roma conscripts by military police, the Court also held that the burden of proof shifted onto the Government and in the absence of an explanation for events with a racist colouring it found that there was also a substantive breach of Art.14 in conjunction with Art.2. It had regard in that finding to other international bodies' concerns about racist violence in Bulgaria and two previous cases against Bulgaria in which Roma had died in State custody in breach of Art.2.

Where the racism alleged is less overt, it is likely to be harder to substantiate or bring under Art.14. In *Abdulaziz*, where rules rendered it more difficult for spouses in arranged marriages from India and Pakistan to enter,[36] the Court found that these rules applied without differentiation between persons on grounds of race or ethnic origin and that it was legitimate for immigration purposes to favour persons having close links with the UK. Similarly, different treatment as to entry and residence applying to non-citizen aliens from in and outside the European Union has been found to be objectively and reasonably justified by the special legal regime concerned.[37]

(d) *Religion*

IIB–104 Reliance on a parent's membership of a religious community (Jehovah's Witnesses) in a court decision on the custody of the children constituted a difference in treatment in *Hoffman v Austria*. While it pursued a legitimate aim (protection of health and rights of the children) it was not reasonably proportionate to base the decision essentially on a difference in religion. This was a majority of five to four, the minority agreeing with the Austrian Supreme Court that account could be taken of blood transfusions and risk of social isolation concerning the children's welfare. The majority essentially relied on the tenor of the Supreme Court's judgment, finding that its tone and attitude were negative on the religious aspect without taking into account the evidence accepted in the lower courts of the emotional need of the children for their mother. Also the Supreme Court gave undue weight to its view that the mother had infringed domestic law in bringing the children up as Jehovah's Witnesses since this was not the religion of the parties at the time of their marriage,

---

[36] Concerning ancestry links with the UK and that the parties to a marriage must have met.
[37] *Moustaquim*, para.49, see n.17.

an objection based purely on disapproval of the mother unrelated to the children's welfare.[38]

The Court found no objective and reasonable justification in *Canea Catholic Church v Greece* for the situation whereby the applicant church could not take legal proceedings to protect its property rights due to a denial of its legal personality, whereas the Orthodox Church and Jewish Community could do so, without any formality or required procedure.[39]

The mere fact however that one religious body or group enjoys more favourable treatment than others will not always disclose discrimination contrary to Art.14.

With a narrow majority, the Court found in *Cha'are Shalom Ve Tsedek v France* that no discrimination arose from the authorities' decision to give exclusive rights for ritual slaughter to one mainstream Jewish body and to refuse permission to the applicant association whose Jewish members wished to observe stricter rules. The majority considered that it had not been shown that the applicants' members were seriously affected (as they could obtain *glatt* meat from other sources, *e.g.* Belgium) and allowed leeway to the authorities in the "delicate relations" between the State and religions.[40] In a Spanish case,[41] the Court also rejected complaints from Protestant bodies about the favourable position enjoyed by the Catholic Church due to provisions allowing taxpayers to allocate part of their income tax either to the Catholic Church or for other charitable purposes. It again referred to the margin of appreciation that had to apply to the "fragile relations that exist between the State and religions" and referred to the different financing arrangements of churches existing between Contracting States based on their individual history and traditions. Since Protestants could make other kinds of donations on fiscally advantageous terms to their own churches and the Catholic Church had entered into a specific agreement with the Government which imposed reciprocal obligations (the Catholic Church undertook to place at the service of Spanish society its historic, artistic and documentary heritage) any difference in treatment was not disproportionate.

(e) *Birth*

While it may be legitimate to protect and nurture traditional family relationships, **IIB–105** the Court considers, having regard to the importance of social integration, that there is no justification for subjecting children out of wedlock to different rules in relation to the possibility of inheriting property from parents. In *Marckx v Belgium*,[42] the Court found no objective or reasonable justification under Art.14 in conjunction with Art.8 in that a child born out of wedlock was subject to rules whereby the mother had to take special steps for the family link to obtain legal recognition and limiting the unmarried mother's ability to leave property to a child born out of wedlock. It was not enough, as the Government argued, that the mother could take

---

[38] Similar violation found in *Palau-Martinez v France*, December 16, 2003.

[39] December 16, 1997, R.J.D. 1997–VIII; 27 E.H.R.R. 521.

[40] The minority was not happy about substituting their own opinion as to the seriousness of an interference with a group's religious beliefs for that of the persons concerned, noting that the essential object of Art.9 was to protect individuals' most private convictions. They did not consider the monopoly had been shown to pursue a legitimate aim or to be proportionate, given the importance of ensuring religious pluralism.

[41] *Alujer Fernandez and Caballero Garcia v Spain*, 53072/99, (Dec.), June 14, 2001, ECHR 2001–VI.

[42] See also *Johnston*, a similar situation in Ireland, but with a finding of a violation of Art.8, no separate issue arose under Art.14.

other steps to protect the child's interests.[43] The Court also rejected the notion that unmarried mothers were less likely to wish to take the responsibility for caring for a child as unproved by the figures or that the risk of upsetting "legitimate" families by allowing "illegitimate" members to share family property was an acceptable motive for deriving a child of fundamental rights.

A variant in *Inze v Austria* concerned the precedence taken by a legitimate child over one born out of wedlock as regarded designation as the principal heir of a farm in case of intestacy. Examining the case under Art.14 in conjunction with Art.1 of the First Protocol, the Court found the justifications general and abstract. It rejected the Government's reference to the "convictions" of the local rural population as part of the "traditional outlook." Nor was it persuaded by the arguments of the Government in *Mazurek v France* that it was justified, for inheritance purposes, to penalise the applicant as an adulterine child, noting that such children could not be blamed for circumstances for which they were not responsible. Given the common European acceptance of the importance of equality between children born in and out of wedlock, very weighty reasons would now have to be advanced before a difference of treatment on that ground could be regarded as compatible with the Convention.[44]

(f) *National minorities*

IIB–106 National origin is not a permissible ground for excluding an applicant from employment or welfare benefits where he otherwise satisfies all the eligibility criteria.[45]

Arguments have been attempted that discrimination is revealed where members of a particular national minority appear to be more at risk of death or ill-treatment. However, as regards allegations in applications from the South-east of Turkey that forcible evacuation of villages, torture and death in custody discloses discrimination against people of Kurdish origin, the Court, relying on the Commission's findings, has found them unsubstantiated.[46] Where it was argued in cases from Northern Ireland that the vast majority of victims of security force killings were Catholics, the Court commented that statistics by themselves could not disclose discrimination.[47]

(g) *Sexual orientation*

IIB–107 See Pt IIB, Homosexuality.

---

[43] Referring to the recognition by the Committee of Ministers that the single mothers and children were a form of family no less than others (resolution of social protection) (*Marckx* p.14).

[44] February 1, 2000, ECHR 2000–II, paras 48–55; see also a finding of a violation of Art.14 in conjunction with Art.8 where the applicant, born out of wedlock, was treated differently from those children similarly born out of wedlock but recognised by their father, *Camp and Bourimi v the Netherlands*, October 3, 2000, ECHR 2000–X.

[45] *Gaygusuz*—the applicant had worked and paid contributions, the sole reason for exclusion being his alien status; *Koua Poirrez v France*, September 23, 2003: it was not relevant that the applicant's country of origin had not signed a reciprocity agreement with France on invalidity or other benefits.

[46] *Akdivar*, para.99.

[47] e.g. *Hugh Jordan v UK*, May 4, 2001, para.154.

Education

Key Articles:

Article 2 of Protocol No.1 (right to education) and Art.14 (prohibition of discrimination). IIB–108

Key case law:

Belgian Linguistics case, July 23, 1968, Series A, No.6; 1 E.H.R.R. 252; *Kjeldsen, Busk Madsen and Pedersen v Denmark*, December 7, 1976, Series A, No.23; 1 E.H.R.R. 711; *Campbell and Cosans v UK*, February 25, 1982, Series A, No.48; 4 E.H.R.R 293; *Costello-Roberts v UK*, March 25, 1993, Series A, No.247–C; 19 E.H.R.R. 112; *Valsamis v Greece*, December 18, 1996, R.J.D. 1996–VI; 24 E.H.R.R. 294; *Cyprus v Turkey*, May 10, 2001, ECHR 2001–V; 23 E.H.R.R 244.

1. General considerations

There have been few cases exploring the substance of this provision, "no person shall be denied the right to education". This possibly reflects the fact that in general the Contracting States cater adequately for perceived educational needs. IIB–109

The Court in an early case held that the provision enshrines the right of everyone to education.[1] But education is a wide concept. It is not just children who require education; there is a whole range of technical, vocational and professional training as well as undergraduate and postgraduate studies which may be pursued until the grave. And it would be an expensive exercise for a State to guarantee such further studies and training on an unlimited scale.[2]

There is Commission case law to the effect that the right to education is concerned primarily with elementary education and not necessarily advanced studies such as technology. This is derived from two cases: where the Commission rejected in very brief terms the complaint of the 27-year-old applicant that he was unable to continue specialised technological studies in prison[3] and where the Commission found that foreign students, who were claiming to follow various studies but were being expelled from the UK under applicable immigration measures, could not rely on Art.2 as granting them a right to stay in the country.[4] Since then the Court has found a violation of Art.2 in respect of a failure of the Turkish Cypriot authorities in northern Cyprus to make available appropriate secondary-school facilities to the Greek Cypriots.[5] A case is pending in which the Court will have to consider whether

---

[1] *Kjeldsen*, para.50.
[2] The only reservation made by the UK under the Convention relates to Art.2 of Protocol No.1, stating that the principle in the second sentence of Art.2 is accepted only so far as it is compatible with the provision of efficient instruction and training, and the avoidance of unreasonable public expenditure. The validity of the reservation is untested.
[3] 5962/72, (Dec.) March 13, 1975, 2 D.R. 50.
[4] 7671/76, (Dec.) May 19, 1977, 9 D.R. 185.
[5] *Cyprus v Turkey*, paras 278–280.

restrictions placed on university education fall within the scope of the education right.[6]

2. Access to education

IIB–110   Access to education cannot, practically, be without limitations, notwithstanding the absence of any express restrictions in Art.2 of the First Protocol.

The Commission found a complaint inadmissible where a 16 year old was suspended for bad behaviour: it was not found to be a denial of education for his return to school to be made conditional on his undertaking to be of good behaviour.[7] Where, in the *Campbell and Cosans* case, a boy was suspended as a result of a refusal by himself and his parents to accept the disciplinary use of the "tawse" in a Scottish school, which conflicted with the parents' right to ensure the teaching of their children in line with their philosophical convictions, there was however a finding by the Court of a denial of education to the boy.

Interruptions in education caused by lawful detention[8] or restrictions incidental to immigration measures[9] found compatible with Art.8 of the Convention have not been found to raise issues. Where local authorities issue enforcement notices to remove gypsy caravans stationed on land without planning permission, the Court has so far held that the applicant gypsies have failed to substantiate complaints that the children were effectively denied the right to education as a result of the legitimate planning measures.[10] Restriction on access to one particular aspect of the curriculum has also not been found to constitute a denial of education, where a girl in a wheelchair had no access to the science labs.[11]

While leaving open the question as to whether Art.2 of Protocol No.1 applied to university or higher education, the Court has held that it must in any event permit restrictions on access to those who apply for entrance in accordance with applicable formalities and pass any necessary examinations.[12] The Commission also rejected earlier complaints of expulsions on disciplinary grounds on the basis that it has not been shown to injure the substance of the right.[13] Where a State makes available advanced educational institutions, it would appear likely that the Court would, notwithstanding the rather old Commission precedents, consider itself competent to examine whether an applicant was being denied access to it on unreasonable and arbitrary grounds.[14] It would probably seek to avoid however being dragged into debates as to academic ability: presumably it would be more interested in fairness of procedures, and any element of discrimination on racial or other grounds to the extent that such could be proved (see below, Section 7. Discrimination).

[6] *Eren v Turkey*, 60856/00, (Dec.) June 6, 2002, where the applicant was denied entry to university despite obtaining one of the highest results on the basis of an apparently arbitrary decision that he must have obtained the results by cheating.

[7] 13477/87, (Dec.) October 4, 1989.

[8] *Slivenko v Latvia*, 48321/99, (Dec.) January 23, 2002, ECHR 2002–II: brief periods of detention pursuant to deportation measures did not to pose a significant obstacle to an applicant's secondary education; *Durmaz v Turkey*, 46506/99, etc. (Dec.) September 4, 2001: interruption in full-time education during lawful detention after conviction was not construed as deprivation of the right to education.

[9] *e.g.* 23938/94, (Dec.), October 23, 1995; 26922/95, (Dec.), November 11, 1995.

[10] *e.g. Lee v UK*, January 18, 2001.

[11] *Molly McIntyre v UK*, 29046/95, (Dec.) October 21, 1998.

[12] *Lukach v Russia*, 40841/99, (Dec.) November 16, 1999.

[13] 24515/94, (Dec.) January 17, 1996, 84–A D.R. 98.

[14] *e.g. Eren*, n.6 above.

Prisoners cannot rely on Art.2 of Protocol No.1 to impose an obligation on the State to organise any particular type of education or training in the prison.[15] Where educational courses are provided, it is undecided whether any issues could arise from any discriminatory or arbitrary denial of access to the facilities.

However while there may be a right to education for a child—so much is clear—there is no right of access to a particular State school of choice. Parents who complained of the closure of a local school had their application to the Commission rejected on the basis that the children were able to attend another school a mile further away.[16]

There is no obligation on the State to provide any specific educational system. The provision does however guarantee that persons subject to the jurisdiction of a State should have the right to avail themselves of the educational institutions existing at a given time.[17] At the same time the Court recognises that the right to education calls for regulation by the State "regulation which may vary in time and place according to the needs and resources of the community and individuals".[18]

While there is a right to start and run a private school, this must be subject to conditions, namely, regulation by the State to ensure fulfillment of its responsibility to provide a proper educational system, even in the private sector. The Commission found in *Ingrid Jordebo v Sweden*[19] that the State's refusal to allow a private school to run senior classes (above 16 years) was not incompatible, having particular regard to the reasons given, *i.e.* an absence of teachers with the requisite qualifications.

3. State schools and public schools

The Commission and Court both found that the State is responsible for both State   **IIB–111** schools and privately run or public schools.[20] The State cannot absolve itself from its responsibility of securing the right of education to everyone by delegating its obligations to private bodies or individuals.

On the other hand, States are not obliged to grant subsidies to private education, for the establishment or running of private education.[21] A right cannnot be derived to obtain from the authorities the creation of a particular kind of establishment.[22] Problems may however arise where they hand out money to some educational institutions but not others or permit discrimination in the entrance requirements (see below).

4. Education in accordance with philosophical convictions

There is in effect no absolute right for parents to have their children educated in   **IIB–112** accordance with their philosophical convictions, only a right to have such rights respected.[23] Setting and planning of school curricula fall in principle within the

---

[15] *Valasinas v Lithuania*, 44558/98, (Dec.) March 14, 2000.
[16] 11644/85 (Dec.) December 1, 1986.
[17] *Belgian Linguistics*, pp.31–32.
[18] *Belgian Linguistics*, p.42, where it was not incompatible for the State to refuse to subsidise in the Dutch unilingual region primary school education in French.
[19] 11533/85, (Dec.) March 6, 1987, 51 D.R. 125.
[20] *e.g. Kjeldsen; Costello-Roberts.*
[21] 6853/74 (Dec.), March 9, 1977, 9 D.R. 27; 23419/94, (Dec.) September 6, 1995, 82 D.R. 41.
[22] *i.e.* in the context of language teaching in the *Belgian Linguistics* case, para.9.
[23] 10233/83, (Dec.) March 6, 1984, 37 D.R. 105.

competence of the State, along with questions of expediency which may legitimately vary from country to country. It is not forbidden to impart through education information or knowledge of a directly or indirectly religious or philosphical kind. Nor can parents object to the integration of such teaching into the school curriculum or otherwise all institutionalised teaching would risk becoming impracticable. Many subjects cannot avoid having some philosophical complexion or even religious elements, bearing in mind that some religions have a very broad dogmatic base and offer answers to every question of a philosphical, cosmological or moral nature.[24]

The concept of "convictions" has been defined by the Court as denoting views that attain a certain level of cogency, seriousness, cohesion and importance. It had more difficulty with notion of "philosophical" which has varying meanings and connotations from the serious to the trivial but it has held that it denoted in this context such convictions as are "worthy of respect in a democratic society" and which do not conflict with the fundamental right of the child to education. In *Campbell and Cosans*, the Court found that the applicants' views as to the use of the "tawse" in the Scottish school attended by their sons related to a weighty and substantial aspect of human life and behaviour, namely, the integrity of the person and the propriety or otherwise of the infliction of corporal punishment. It found that the provision of education subject to this disciplinary condition failed to respect the applicants' philosophical convictions.

Where a disciplinary measure is mild, the Court has given less weight to parental convictions. In *Valsamis v Greece*, where a child Jehovah's Witnesss was suspended for one day for failing to participate in Greek National Day celebrations to which her parents had objected as a nationalistic event commemorating a war, the Court noted that the child was exempted from religious studies and found nothing in the purpose of the parade or its arrangements which could offend the applicants' pacifist convictions to an extent prohibited by Art.2 or deprive them of their right to guide their children in line with their convictions.[25]

On the issue of the substance of what is taught, the Court has held that the State in fulfilling its duties must take care that information is conveyed in an objective, critical and pluralistic manner and must not pursue the aims of indoctrination that might be considered as not respecting parents' philosphical convictions. What that might mean will vary according to one's own views. In *Kjeldsen v Denmark*, the parents objected to sex education. The Court, having examined the material in question, found that Denmark had not overstepped the limit in the conveying of necessary factual information to enable the children "to take care of themselves and show consideration for others in that respect" without in any way attempting to exalt sex or incite them in such practices. The Court also gave weight to the fact that those parents who nonetheless objected were free to send their children to private schools or even to educate them at home.[26]

Nor does Art.2 of Protocol No.1 as such guarantee education in a particular language in accordance with the parents' preferences.[27] A failure to provide

---

[24] *Valsamis*, (Comm. Rep.), para.38; *Kjeldsen*, para.53.

[25] A minority of the Commission and Court however thought compelling children to participate on a school holiday day could be seen as an indirect attempt to indoctrinate them with a patriotic value system which was difficult to reconcile with the parents' right freely to choose the manner in which their children are educated. There was no plausible reason why it was necessary for her education to attend, particularly where she was already excused religious education classes.

[26] See more recently a similar approach in *Jiminez and Jiminez Merino v Spain*, 51188/99, (Dec.) May 25, 2000, ECHR 2000–VI.

[27] *Belgian Linguistics* case, para.3; *Skender v FRYOM*, 62509/00, (Dec.) November 22, 2001.

education in a particular language may however disclose a violation where it in effect denies the substance of the right, as in *Cyprus v Turkey*, where the Turkish authorities in Northern Cyprus abolished secondary schools in Greek while continuing to assume responsibility for the provision of Greek-language primary schools and where the possibility of sending the children away from home to secondary schools in the south could not be regarded as practical or reasonable option given the impact on family life. Issues of discrimination may also arise where there is a difference in treatment in access based on residential criteria (see below, Discrimination).

5. State education and home education

The State may provide for a compulsory system of education. This is not without controversy, since, not infrequently, parents objecting to the State system prefer to educate their children at home. The Commission found that State regulation of home education was part of its responsibilities to enforce educational standards and where refusal of permission for home education was based on its inadequacy, the Commission has effectively found that the State's assessment of the children's right to education prevailed over the parents' particular convictions.[28]

IIB–113

6. Special educational needs cases

A series of UK cases raised the issue of conflict between parents and education authorities as to the educational needs of children with perceived problems. The Commission gave leeway to the educational authorities in assessing what a child might require, and as to the efficient use of educational resources, with only the weak rider that parental views be taken into account as far as might be consistent with the needs of the child. In *Graeme v United Kingdom*,[29] where the child was epileptic, with other associated problems, the parents considered that he should not be taken out of mainstream schooling, advocating that handicapped chldren should be catered for within the normal system. The education authority made the child a ward of court and placed him in a special school. The Commission found the child's right to effective education prevailed over the parents' view, to the extent that such could be regarded as a philosophical conviction. While it examined the complaints as to the standard of the education, including complaints of abuse and lack of access to christian teaching, it found them ill-founded. Impliedly therefore, the Convention organs still retain a supervisory role and in a grossly unreasonable or arbitrary case might find the the education authority were not in fact pursuing the effective education of the child.

IIB–114

[28] In 10233/83, n.23 above, the applicants, who were educating their dyslexic children at home, had been convicted for failing to comply with orders requiring their attendance at a State school. The Commission found that it was not its task to decide whether the parents' or the State's views on education were better for the children and that the State had a responsibility to verify and enforce educational standards. Thus obliging parents to co-operate in the assessment of their childrens' educational standards to ensure a certain level of literacy and numeracy while nevertheless allowing children to be educated at home could not be said to disclose a lack of respect. In a Swedish case 17678/91, (Dec.) June 30, 1993, the parents obtained permission to educate their children until a certain age, when permission was withdrawn on ground that their education required social contact and a specialisation which the parents were not qualified to give—the Commission found the State had acted within its margin of appreciation in assessing the parents' ability to provide a viable alternative to State schooling.
[29] 13387/87, (Dec.) February 5, 1990; 25212/94, (Dec.) July 4, 1995, 82 D.R. 129.

7. Discrimination

IIB–115   Where unequal treatment is apparent as regards access to education, violation may arise under Art.14. In the *Belgian Linguistics* case, a violation was found where French-speaking children resident in a particular Flemish area were denied access to French-speaking schools outside that area but compelled to attend local Dutch-speaking schools.[30]

While a State is not obliged to fund particular educational schemes, Art.14 requires that authorities do not discriminate in the provision of available financial subsidies. However it may be justifiable for the State to make lesser grants available to private educational institutions than to public ones[31] or give preference to organisations providing a particular need.[32] Leeway is also given to education authorities as regards the measures taken to accommodate handicapped children in school buildings.[33]

Cross-reference

Part IIB: Corporal punishment
Part IIB: Discrimination

---

[30] Though other complaints of unequal treatment were dismissed as not having been made out, the Court accepted the aim of promoting linguistic unity within regions and knowledge of the normal language of a region as being in the public interest and not disclosing any discrimination. See *Skender v FRYOM*, n.28 above above, where the applicants' complaints about refusal of access to a Turkish-speaking school on the basis of her father's residence in a different district have been declared admissible.

[31] 7782/77 (Dec.) May 1, 1978, 14 D.R. 179 where it was legitimate and not unreasonable for the State to require the private body to foot 15% of capital costs.

[32] 23419/94, n.21 above—State subsidies were provided to church schools which were a widespread feature of the educational system.

[33] *Molly McIntyre*, n.11 above, where the applicant, suffering from muscular dystrophy, could not negotiate the stairs to the science labs and complained that she did not have the same access to the curriculum as her able-bodied peers, the Commission found that the authorities had taken other steps to facilitate her use of the school and the decision, in a small school, not to build an expensive lift, was not disproportionate and struck a fair balance between the demands of the area's school and her needs.

Electoral rights

Key provisions:

Articles 10 (freedom of expression and to receive and impart information) and Art.3   IIB–116
of Protocol No.1 (free elections ensuring the free expression of the people in the
choice of the legislature).

Key case law:

Mathieu-Mohin and Clerfayt v Belgium, March 2, 1987, Series A, No.113, 10 E.H.H.R
1; *Gitonas v Greece*, July 1, 1997, R.J.D. 1997–IV, No.42; *Pierre-Bloch v France*,
October 21, 1997, R.J.D. 1997–VI, No.53; 26 E.H.H.R 202; *Bowman v UK*,
February 19, 1998, Reports 1998–I, No.63; *Ahmed v United Kingdom*, September 2,
1998, Reports 1998–VI, No.87; 29 E.H.R.R. 1; *Matthews v UK*, February 18, 1999,
ECHR 1999–I; 28 E.H.R.R. 361; *Rekvenyi v Hungary*, May 20, 1999, ECHR 1999–
III; 30 E.H.R.R. 519; *Labita v Italy*, April 6, 2000, ECHR 2000–IV; *Podkolzina v
Latvia*, April 9, 2002, ECHR 2002–II; *Hirst v UK (No.2)*, March 30, 2004; *Zdanoka
v Latvia*, June 17, 2004.

1. General considerations

The Convention ascribes much importance to the values of a democratic society. The   IIB–117
human rights guaranteed in it are seen as being best guaranteed by "an effective
political democracy" (preamble). The proper and fair functioning of the mechanisms
of electing proper democratic and representative law making bodies could therefore
be expected to assume key importance.

The sparse case law is perhaps an indication of healthy democratic systems.
However, also significant is the fact that Art.3 of the First Protocol is the only
provision which is phrased in collective and general terms, rather than as a specific
individual right. The provision does confer rights. In *Mathieu-Mothin and Clerfayt v
Belgium,* the Court explained that the impersonal phrasing is in fact intended to give
greater solemnity to the commitment and reflect the fact that it was not concerned
with abstention or non-interference but with a positive obligation to hold democratic
elections. There are, however, implied limitations and a wide margin of appreciation.
Such limitations must not impair the essence of the rights such as to deprive them of
their effectiveness and should pursue a legitimate aim in a proportionate manner.[1]
Nonetheless, as applied in practice, the individual may have some difficulty in
establishing that personal restrictions in fact thwart the "free expression of the
people" as a whole.

2. Legislature

(a) *National legislature*

The legislature is not necessarily restricted to the national parliament or assembly.   IIB–118
Having regard to the federal or cantonal structure of some Contracting States,
regard must also be had to the particular constitutional system. For example, the
diets of the German Länder are legislature for the purpose of Art.3.[2]

---

[1] *Mathieu-Mohin*, para.52; *Gitonas*, para.39; *Matthews*, para.63.
[2] 27311/95, (Dec.) September 11, 1995, 82–A D.R. 158.

Local authorities with purely delegated powers will not qualify. While the regional councils of Belgium could submit bills, this was not enough, as they did not become law until passed by the national Parliiament in which legislative powers were exclusively concentrated.[3] The abolition of the GLC in London did not raise a problem since it was a creature of statute, its powers purely derivative, subordinate and subsidiary to Parliament which held absolute constitutional authority. While the GLC had considerable power, it was of an administrative nature, often subject to approval from executive authority. In particular, it did not exercise any inherent rule-making power and those powers delegated to it by Parliament were exercised subject to its ultimate control.[4]

Referenda, however significant in national politics, do not generally form part of an election for the legislature.[5] Nor do presidential elections fall within the scope of Art.3.[6]

(b) European Parliament

IIB–119 Initially doubtful that the drafters intended to cover anything but national legislatures, the Commission considered in 1979 that the European Parliament was an advisory body with certain supervisory and budgetary powers but noted that developments in the structure of the EEC might make it necessary for the Contracting States to guarantee Art.3 rights if new representatives bodies assumed at least in part the powers and functions of the national legislative bodies.[7] Eight years later, when a "Green" challenged the voting system in France for the European Parliament,[8] the Commission noted that the European Parliament's role had increased following the Single European Act but that it still did not constitute a legislature within the ordinary meaning of the term. By the time of *Matthews v United Kingdom*, which came after the Maastricht Treaty, the European Parliament's powers were no longer only "advisory and supervisory". The Court found that it was sufficiently involved in specific legislative processes leading to the passage of legislation and in the general democratic activities of the European Community to constitute part of the legislature for Gibraltar.[9]

3. Right to vote

IIB–120 Article 3 does not expressly guarantee the individual right to vote but refers generally to "conditions" to ensure free expression of the "people". While early case law considered that Art.3 implied the principle of universal suffrage[10] and there is recent emphasis on individual electoral rights as central to democracy and the rule of

---

[3] 6745 and 6746/74 (Dec.) May 30, 1975, 2 D.R. 110.
[4] 11391/85, (Dec.) July 5, 1985, 43 D.R.236; also not qualifying local authorities in Northern Ireland (5155/71, (Dec.) July 12, 1976, 6 D.R. 13), municipal authorites in Vladivostok (*Cherepkov v Russia*, 51501/99, (Dec.) January 25, 2000); Provincial Councils (*Santoro v Italy*, 36681/97, (Dec.) January 16, 2003).
[5] *e.g.* 7096/75 (Dec.) October 3, 1975, 3 D.R. 165; *Hilbe v Liechtenstein*, 31981/96, (Dec.) September 7, 1999, ECHR 1999–VI.
[6] 15344/89, (Dec.) December 14, 1989, 64 D.R. 211; 41090/98, (Dec.) October 21, 1998.
[7] 8612/79, (Dec.) May 10, 1979 15 D.R. 259.
[8] 11123/84 (Dec.), December 9, 1987 54 D.R. 52.
[9] paras 48–54.
[10] 2728/66 Coll. 25 p.38.

law,[11] the case law also establishes that the right to vote is not absolute or without limitation.[12] Exclusions must however not be arbitrary, disproportionate or affect the expression of the free opinion of the people.[13]

While a wide margin of appreciation applies in this area, this could not be relied on by the Government in *Hirst v United Kingdom (No.2)* to justify a blanket ban on prisoners' voting where this derived from historic tradition and not from considered legislative debate. The Court expressed doubt on the legitimacy of the purported aims of that ban, namely punishment and social rehabilitation, noting *inter alia* that a prisoner by fact of his imprisonment did not lose the protection of the other guarantees under the Convention and that removal of the vote cut a prisoner off even further from the democratic society in which he lived. It appeared to leave open whether a ban limited to imprisonable offences of a certain severity or imposed expressly by a trial judge on the facts of particular case would be acceptable. A blanket ban on all convicted prisoners sentenced to imprisonment however was arbitrary in its effects and indiscriminate in its application.[14]

That said, the Convention organs have found acceptable limitations:

- on persons convicted of collaboration during the war[15];
- based on residence requirements[16] and citizenship[17];
- imposition by a court, at the same time as a three year prison sentence, of a two-year disqualification from exercising public functions, including voting, on a member of Parliament for fiscal fraud.[18]

The striking off the electoral roll of suspect Mafia members subject to special police supervision was found to pursue a legitimate aim, but it was disproportionate to continue the measure after a suspect's acquittal.[19]

Exclusion of geographical areas from voting for a particular part of the legislature may be justified by historical or constitutional considerations, as in the case where a citizen of Jersey could not claim the right to vote for the UK Parliament although it had legislative power over the Channel Islands. The Commission noted that Channel Islanders were not resident in the UK and that they had their own elected

---

[11] *Hirst (No.2)*, paras 36 and 41.

[12] e.g. *Matthews*, para.63.

[13] 27614/95, (Dec.) May 21, 1997, 89–B D.R.76; *Hirst (No.2)*, paras 48–51.

[14] The Court distinguished 24927/94, (Dec.) April 14, 1998, 93 D.R. 15, where the Commission found acceptable the inability of an Irish prisoner to vote during an 18 month sentence, noting that the Commission had not referred to the elements of legitimate aim and proportionality identified in *Mathieu-Mohin*.

[15] 6573/74, (Dec.) 1974 1 D.R. 87: concerning discrimination, the Commission found objective and reasonable justification in preventing persons who had grossly misused in wartime their right to participate in public life from misusing their political rights in the future; 8701/79 (Dec.), December 3, 1979, 18 D.R. 250 where permanent deprivation of the vote for a person convicted of collaboration offences was not found arbitrary or calculated to prejudice the free expression of the opinion of the people.

[16] 7566/76, (Dec.) December 11, 1976, 9 D.R. 124, where a British citizen living abroad could not vote in Parliamentary elections; nor was it discrimination that diplomats and servicemen overseas were allowed to vote since they were posted abroad because of their duties and remained closely linked with their country and under Government control—impliedly accepting as a valid consideration an alleged risk of electoral fraud in the use of postal votes by other persons; *Hilbe*, n.5 above.

[17] 27614/95, n.13 above.

[18] *MDU v Italy*, 58540/00, (Dec.) January 28, 2003, the Court found that the punishment pursued the legitimate aim of ensuring effective functioning of the democratic regime and given the short duration was not arbitrary or disproportionate.

[19] *Labita*, para.203.

legislature, making reference to the exceptional and particular historical relationship between the two areas.[20] However, in *Matthews v United Kingdom*, the exclusion of the applicant as a resident in Gibraltar in voting in the European Parliament elections was found to disclose a violation as the legislation which emanated from the European Community formed part of the legislation in Gibraltar and the applicant was directly affected by it.[21]

A wide margin of appreciation applies to the formalities or conditions which an individual must fulfil to claim the right to vote.[22]

4. Right to stand for election

IIB–121 While an individual right to stand for election has also been implied as contained in principle by Art.3, it is not absolute or without limitation either. States are allowed considerable latitude in their constitutional regulation of parliamentarians' eligibility.[23] Examination of complaints seem to focus on two criteria: whether there has been arbitrariness or lack of proportionality and whether the restriction interferes with the expression of the opinion of the people. The Court has also held, more recently, that, in order avoid arbitrary exclusion of candidates, the rules concerning eligibility must be expressed with sufficient precision and decisions concerning a particular candidate taken by a body presenting minimum guarantees of impartiality and not enjoying an unfettered discretion.[24]

Age-limits on candidates in Belgium (25 for House of Representatives and 40 for the Senate) were not arbitrary or unreasonable.[25] In *Podkolzina v Latvia*, the Court did not object to a requirement as such that a candidate show a certain mastery of the national language, but found fault in the procedure, lacking objectivity and legal certainty, whereby the applicant, already holding a certificate, was required for unspecified reasons to undergo a special test. While it also may be legitimate for States to defend the democratic order by preventing certain persons from standing, *e.g.* due to racist or treasonous history,[26] the Court found that it was disproportionate in *Zdanoka v Latvia* to bar a candidate for her past membership of a communist party where there was no evidence of personal involvement in an attempted coup and no assessment of her current dangerousness to the democratic order. The Court emphasised that it was necessary to tolerate candidates who opposed official government policy or whose ideas were unpopular with the majority of the country.[27]

Systems of subsidies to political parties according to the number of votes gained (which may penalise smaller parties) was not found by the Commission to be a condition which blocked the free expression of the people.[28] Nor was objection taken to the conditions imposed on any group putting itself forward in an election to

---

[20] 8873/80, (Dec.), May 13, 1982, 28 D.R. 99.

[21] para.64.

[22] *e.g. Benkaddour v France*, 51685/99, (Dec.) November 18, 2003, where the applicant was refused inclusion on the electoral list for one district as he had not applied to be struck off the list where he was previously registered.

[23] *Gitonas*, para.39; *Zdanoka*, para.83.

[24] *Podkolzina*, para.35.

[25] 6745 and 6746/74, n.3 above.

[26] 16692/90, (Dec.) April 12, 1991; 8348/78 and 8406/78, (Dec.) October 11, 1979, 18 D.R. 187.

[27] para.98.

[28] 6850/74, (Dec.) May 18, 1976, 5 D.R. 90.

obtain 100 or 500 signatures of support. This was considered to be justified as preventing the electorate from being confused by groups which could not assume political responsibility.[29] A requirement of 200 signatures or three members of the regional parliament on a list was compatible in an Austrian case, in light of the Constitutional Court's reasoning, namely, that the conditions were easily satisfied by a party with a reasonable chance of sucess and pursued a legitimate aim of preventing undue splitting of the vote in a proportional representation system.[30]

Obligations to pay deposits have been found acceptable, where the amount did not impose an unbearable burden and it was seen as pursuing a legitimate aim of promoting the emergence of sufficiently representative currents of thought.[31]

Authorities are apparently not under an obligation to assist candidates, even where such assistance may be indispensable. Where a German prisoner complained that the authorities refused to circulate in prisons his publications and official forms to collect the 500 signatures necessary for a candidate to stand for election, the Commission recalled that the right to stand was not absolute, noted that prisoners were not prohibited from standing or voting, that the circulation of materials might have an effect on internal order and security and that other parties were also not afforded the possibility of circulating material in prison or collecting signatures.[32]

Disqualifications may legitimately be imposed where an elected member is already a member of another legislature. This was challenged by a member elected for the Northern Ireland Assembly in 1982, who was disqualified since he was a member of legislature of the Republic of Ireland. The Commission found the restriction not irreconcilable with Art.3 without much discussion. Under Art.14, where complaint was made that this condition was not applied to Commonwealth countries, the Commission considered it sufficient to rely on the special historical tradition and special ties existing with Commonwealth countries as reasonable and objective justification.[33]

Whether persons should be disqualified because of service for local authorities was challenged in the context of Greece and the UK. In *Gitonas v Greece*, the rule disqualifying persons who had held particular public offices in the constituency over the previous three years was found to pursue the legitimate aim of preventing undue influence on the electorate or unfair advantage *vis-à-vis* other candidates and not to be arbitrary or disproportionate. Nor was it found disproportionate in *Ahmed v United Kingdom* that local authority officers were required to resign if standing in elections, the rules reflecting a legitimate concern to maintain the political impartiality of local government officers.[34] The aim of maintaining the independence and impartiality of judges justified the requirement in Latvia that judges resign before they stand as candidates in elections.[35]

[29] 6850/74, *ibid.*
[30] 7008/75 (Dec.), July 12, 1976, 6 D.R.120.
[31] 12897/87 (Dec.), December 3, 1990, 67 D.R. 67 166, where the "Greens" complained that the deposit was only reimbursed if 5% of the votes was attained.
[32] 11728/85, (Dec.) March 2, 1987.
[33] 10316/83, (Dec.) March 7, 1984, 37 D.R. 129.
[34] para.75.
[35] *Brike v Latvia*, 47135/99, (Dec.) June 29, 2000.

5. Conditions ensuring the free expression of the opinion of the people

IIB–122 Elections should not be under any form of pressure as to the choice of one or more candidates and an elector must not be induced unduly to vote for any party.[36] No constraint must be exercised in respect of parties or candidates, particularly where there are minorities involved, in which context particular aspects may take on significance. Thus there was careful scrutiny of allegations concerning the way language groupings were "juggled" in various Belgian regional and legislative bodies.[37]

Article 3 does not as such require any type of electoral system, *e.g.* proportional, or majority vote with one or two ballots (all of which are part of the common heritage of political traditions in Contracting States).[38] There is reference to a "wide margin of appreciation" and the necessity to assess any electoral system in light of the political evolution of the country concerned.[39] This margin also applies to the formalities attaching to the valid lodging of a vote with the aim of preventing electoral fraud.[40]

However, whatever the chosen system, a general principle of equality of treatment of all citizens has been identified.[41] This does not mean however that all votes must have the same weight as regards the outcome of the election or that all candidates have equal chances of success. There is an acceptance that wasted votes are inevitable in all systems. There is reference also by the Court to the conflicting objectives sought by electoral systems which are both to reflect fairly faithfully the opinion of the people and yet to channel currents of thought to promote the emergence of a sufficiently clear and coherent political will.[42] Systems which aim to restrict the number of candidates or parties have been acceptable in light of the latter factor.[43]

A proportional representation system which was favourable to minority groups was accepted as enabling the people to express their opinion freely and as such clearly in line with the requirements of Art.3 of the First Protocol. To the extent that this disclosed discrimination it was justified in pursuing the aim of protecting the minority.[44] In respect of the Liberal Party's complaints about the majority vote system in the UK, the mere fact that not all votes would have the same weight was

---

[36] 9267/81, (Dec.) July 12, 1983, 33 D.R. 97 at p.131.

[37] *Mathieu-Mohin.*

[38] 7140/75, (Dec.), October 6, 1975, 7 D.R. 95.

[39] *Mathieu-Mohin*, para.54: features existing in one perhaps might be unacceptable in another but could be justified by the context; see also strong statement on margin of appreciation in *Podkolzina*, para.34.

[40] *Tsimas v Greece*, 74287/01, (Dec.) September 26, 2002, where the applicant lost his seat when votes were assessed as null and void due to lack of appropriate signatures.

[41] *Mathieu-Mothin*, para.54.

[42] *Mathieu-Mothin*, para.54.

[43] 11123/84, n.8 above: the discounting of parties/lists with less than 5% of the vote in a proportional representation system was legitimate to foster the emergence of sufficiently representative currents of thought and the forfeiture of deposits and no repayment of publicity expenses incurred by such lists was compatible in pursuit of this aim; *Federacion Nacionalista Canaria v Spain*, 56618/00, (Dec.) June 7, 2001, the setting of thresholds of vote percentages for parliamentary representation pursued the aim of preventing the excessive and dysfunctional fragmentation of Parliament; *Gorizda v Moldova*, 53180/99, (Dec.), July 2, 2002.

[44] 8364/78 (Dec.), March 8, 1978, 15 D.R. 247: Unionists alleged that the proportional representation system with the single transferable vote in operation in Northern Ireland (a simple majority vote applied elsewhere in the UK) unduly favoured the republican community.

not sufficient to disclose a problem. It was left open whether there would be a problem if the system used resulted in a pattern whereby particular religious or ethnic groups or communities could never be represented.[45]

Rules in Belgium concerning the eligibility of candidates who took the parliamentary oath in either French or Flemish to sit in particular groupings in the legislature and with different powers was not incompatible with Art.3 given the intention to achieve an equilibrium between the country's various regions and communities and to defuse language disputes in the country. Regard was also had to the wide margin of appreciation, a margin which was even greater given the system was incomplete and provisional pending installation of a permanent system.[46] Restrictions placed on candidates who refuse to take a prescribed oath on taking up their seat have been found not to interfere with rights under Art.3, the Court finding the requirement of affirming loyalty to the constitutional principles underlying a representative democracy was a reasonable condition attaching to parliamentary office.[47]

Access of candidates to media coverage is an important aspect of campaigning. In a French case, the Commission appeared to accept that issues could arise from the way air time was distributed on radio and television between different groupings but given the wide margin of appreciation the regulations in question were not unjustified or disproportionate as regarded the disadvantage suffered by smaller parties.[48] Matters of party financing have not yet come under detailed scrutiny in this context though in one case the less favourable financial State support given to small parties was not found to disclose any problems.[49]

6. Free elections at reasonable intervals

The Commission found that an increase from four to five year intervals for elections to the diet of a German Länder was not incompatible. It commented that the purpose of Art.3 was to ensure that fundamental changes in public opinion are reflected in the opinions of the representatives of the people, which aim however had to be balanced by the consideration that a Parliament must be able to develop and execute legislative programmes and that too short an interval would act as an impediment to planning and lead to petrification of the politicial groupings in Parliament which might then cease to bear any resemblance to the will of the electorate.[50]

IIB–123

---

[45] 8765/79 (Dec.), December 18, 1980, 21 D.R. 211.
[46] *Mathieu-Mothin.*
[47] *Martin McGuinness v UK*, 39511/98, (Dec.), June 9, 1998; see *mutatis mutandis* where there was a violation of freedom of religion under Art.9 where three candidates elected to the General Grand Council were required to take the oath "on the Holy Gospels"—*Buscarini v San Marino*, February 18, 1999, ECHR 1999–I; 30 E.H.R.R. 208.
[48] 11123/84, n.8 above, 30 minutes to big parties, 5 minutes to small parties.; also 24744/94 (Dec.) June 28, 1995: an independent candidate at EP elections complained of not being allotted air time, which was confined to main political parties (at least 12.5% vote): no problem with this under Art.10 since air time was inevitably limited; *Antonopoulos v Greece*, 58333/00, (Dec.) March 29, 2001.
[49] *Antonopoulos, ibid.*
[50] 27311/95, n.2 above.

7. Article 10: freedom of expression

IIB–124 This provision cannot be interpreted as bestowing the right to vote on an individual.[51] However freedom of expression and to receive and impart information may be relevant in the electoral process where restrictions are placed on candidates' or others' ability to communicate their ideas and policies.

A concern to prevent groups which espouse terrorist causes and violence from achieving public exposure in the political arena generated controversial cases in Ireland and the UK.[52] However restrictions imposed on the broadcasting of interviews with members of Sinn Fein were accepted, even though it was a lawful political party and could present candidates who could take office locally and in the legislature. It was argued, *inter alia*, in support of these measures that terrorists drew sustenance and support from the media coverage. The Commission gave particular weight to the aims pursued by both Governments in respect of fighting terrorism and assessed the measures as proportionate, since the information itself could be broadcast in the UK (using actor voice overs) and other means existed in the media in Ireland.

Restriction on the activities of an applicant publicising a single issue during campaigns was however found to be disproportionate. In *Bowman v United Kingdom*, where the applicant had been prosecuted for distributing leaflets publicising the views and voting record of candidates on abortion, the Court found that the expenditure limit of GBP 5 operated as a total barrier to her publishing the information and it was not satisfied that this very low limit was necessary for achieving the stated aim of securing equality between the candidates. More leeway was accorded to the restrictions imposed on political canvassing by local government officials in *Ahmed v United Kingdom*, which were found to be justified by the importance of maintaining their impartiality and political neutrality towards both council members and the electorate who cast their votes to enable the political complexion of the council to reflect their views.[53] In *Rekvenyi v Hungary*, the Court also found that limitations on the political activities of police officers, in particular barring membership of a political party, did not disclose a disproportionate restriction on their freedom expression, having regard to the historical background in Hungary and the fact that not all political activities were barred.

8. Article 6: access to court

IIB–125 In general, electoral and political rights of a candidate, voter or elected representative fall outside the scope of Art.6 as not concerning "civil rights". Its guarantees have been held not to apply to proceedings reviewing the legality of an election,[54] the eligibility of a candidate for election,[55] the dissolution of a political party[56] or whereby an elected candidate was removed from office for expenses irregularities.[57]

---

[51] 27614/95, n.13 above.
[52] 15404/89, (Dec.) April 16, 1991, 70 D.R. 262; 18714/91, (Dec.), May 9, 1994, 77 D.R. 42.
[53] The Court did give weight to their perception that the restrictions were carefully aimed at visibly objectionable partisanship and did not prevent officers from all political activity or speech (para.63).
[54] 11068/84, (Dec.) May 6, 1985, 43 D.R. 195.
[55] *Brike*, n.35; also *Zdanoka v Latvia*, 58278/00, (Dec.) March 6, 2003.
[56] *Refah Partisi v Turkey*, 41340/98, 41342–44/98, (Dec.) October 3, 2000.
[57] *Pierre-Bloch*.

The latter case, *Pierre-Bloch v France*, relating to proceedings involving the disqualification of the applicant, elected to the National Assembly, for one year and the imposition of a payment order, confirmed that civil rights and obligations did not cover political ones, such as the right to stand for election or the obligation to limit campaign expenditure. The fact that there was an economic aspect to the disqualification proceedings did not render them civil.[58] Nor so far have the penalties imposed, such as disqualification and payment orders, been found to be of a nature or severity as to render Art.6 applicable in its criminal aspect.[59]

Cross-reference

Part IIA: Fair trial guarantees, Access to Court
Part IIB: Freedom of expression

---

[58] See also *Shirley Porter v UK*, (Dec.) April 8, 2003, where the Court noted that the surcharge imposed on the applicant for losses caused to Westminster Council arose from regulations governing the conduct of public officials and could be considered as pertaining to public law but as the domestic courts had treated the case as involving the applicant's civil rights and obligations had assumed Art.6 applied.

[59] 24359/94, (Dec.) June 30, 1995, 82–B D.R. 56; in *Pierre-Bloch*, while the applicant was liable to prosecution with heavy fines and the possibility of imprisonment, this, if it occurred, would be separate from the disqualification proceedings. See also *Shirley Porter*, n.58 above, where the imposition of a surcharge on the leader of Westminster Council for wilful misconduct in selling council housing was not criminal as it was repayment of losses to the local authority and applicable only to public official; the considerable size of the surcharge (millions of pounds) was not sufficient to render it criminal.

Environment

Key Articles:

IIB–126   Articles 8 (private life and home), 13 (right to an effective remedy) and Art.1 of the First Protocol (peaceful enjoyment of possessions).

Key case law:

Powell and Rayner v UK, February 21, 1990, Series A, No.172; 12 E.H.R.R. 355; *Lopez Ostra v Spain*, December 9, 1994, Series A, No.303–C; 20 E.H.R.R. 277; *Balmer-Schafroth v Switzerland*, August 26, 1997, R.J.D. 1997–IV; *Guerra v Italy*, February 19, 1998, R.J.D 1998–I; *Athanassoglou v Switzerland*, April 6, 2000, ECHR 2000–IV; *Hatton v UK*, July 8, 2003, ECHR 2003–VIII.

1. General considerations

IIB–127   There is no provision specifically geared for protection of any "environmental" rights. It is perhaps difficult to fit the traditional notion of individual human rights with the collective interest of protection of ecosystems, the atmosphere or other environmental concerns. An early unpromising case by the Commission stated unreservedly: "no right to nature preservation is as such included among the rights and freedoms guaranteed by the Convention" with the result that an organisation set up to protest military use of marshland was accordingly unable to claim infringement of any protected right.[1] The Court has most recently stated that there is no explicit right in the Convention to a clean and quiet environment.[2]

But it is a reflection of the growing recognition of the crucial importance of environmental issues that matters concerning the quality of the environment and assertions of the need for protection against, or information concerning, environmental threats are increasingly appearing in cases.

2. Indirect environmental interests

IIB–128   In numerous cases concerning complaints by persons of restriction on use of their own land, the Convention organs have held that measures of town planning, building restrictions and sometimes even confiscation have been justified, protection of the environment being necessary in the "general interest" or for the protection of the rights of others. Preservation of rural areas thus obtains recognition under the Convention where it comes to State action in controlling their citizens' use of property. For example, when an applicant was prosecuted for infringing regulations prohibiting her inhabiting an old bunker on land in Jersey, the Commission recognised that planning controls are necessary and desirable to preserve areas of natural beauty[3] Positive obligations placed on landowners, for example, to plant particular types of tree in their forest land have also been found in the general

---

[1] 7407/76, (Dec.) May 13, 1976, 5 D.R. 161.
[2] *Hatton*, para.96.
[3] 11185/84, (Dec.) March 11,1985, 42 D.R.275.

interest as part of protection of environmental interests.[4] Restrictions on landowners' use of land have, however, been found to fall foul of Art.1 of Protocol No.1, even though the aim was to preserve the environment, where there was insufficient procedural protection to the individual property owner's interests.[5]

3. State responsibility for infringing environmental concerns

Where an individual complains that the State is responsible for harming the environment, the Convention organs have been less ready to find infringement of Convention rights. Government responsibility may flow from the fact that a official decision or regulation directly provides for the contested environmental nuisance or from a failure to regulate private industry in a manner securing proper respect for individual rights.[6]

IIB–129

Since there is no general environmental right guaranteed, an application will generally only be feasible where there is a direct individual interest at stake which can be brought under expressly guaranteed rights, for example, the right to respect for home and private life, or peaceful enjoyment of property. The individual has to point to direct and strongly prejudicial effect[7] and even then for a violation to be found, there must be no strong public interest to outweigh his.[8] Proportionality is likely to be the key consideration.

In a Norwegian case, while accepting that the building of a dam, which would flood large areas of land traditionally used for reindeer herding, could constitute an interference with the private life or lifestyle of two Lapps, the Commission found the measure justified in view of the relatively small area concerned in the vast northern region and that the actual impact on the individual was outweighed by the general and economic interest.[9]

---

[4] 12570/86, (Dec.) January 18, 1989, 59 D.R.127; it is also legitimate, for example, to regulate car exhausts to prevent pollution, *Svidranova v Slovak Republic*, (Dec), July 1, 1998.

[5] e.g. *Papastavrou v Greece*, April 10, 2003, where the decision to re-afforest an area, thereby seriously restricting the use of the applicants' land,, was confirmed without proper consideration of individual rights or the possibility of compensation.

[6] *Hatton*, para.119—the same considerations broadly apply in either case; see also the Commission finding in *Powell and Rayner* (Rep.) that the State was responsible for noise nuisance at airports since it regulated air traffic and built airports.

[7] e.g. 12816/87, (Dec.) January 18, 1989, 59 D.R. 186: a complaint about a military shooting range was rejected where it was not used in such a way as to cause important noise nuisance and the applicants had not been exposed to an intolerable or exceptional level or frequency of noise as to amount to an interference with private life or their right to enjoyment of their property (while on some days the noise was alleged to be unbearable, no firing was carried out on weekends or public holidays and a limit was in place of during during other days); 28204/95, December 4, 1995, 83–B D.R. 112, where the applicants in the Pacific areas under French jurisdiction complained unsuccessfully that the overground tests at Muratoa placed their lives and health at risk from the radiation and contamination of the water and sealife: however, since they lived at considerable distances, the Commission found that the potential consequences were too remote to be considered as directly affecting their personal situation (no sufficiently established degree of probability that damage would occur to their health where they were or that tests would, for example, fracture the atoll); *Asselbourg v Luxembourg*, 29121/95, (Dec.) June 29, 1999, ECHR 1999–VI, mere suspicions and conjectures arising from pollution risks inherent in steel production were not sufficient.

[8] e.g. *Khatun v UK*, 38387/97, (Dec.), July 1, 1998, where the Commission weighed the importance of regeneration of the Docklands against the dust nuisance suffered by the applicants and found the former prevailed.

[9] 9278/81 and 9415/81, (Dec.) October 3, 1983 35 D.R. 30.

The case of *Lopez Ostra v Spain* showed the Convention organs were prepared to find a violation, where there was a combination of a clear and significant risk to health and serious impingement on private life and home and the lack of timely and effective steps to deal with the situation. It also confirmed that States bear responsibility for the activities of private companies, where such are subject to regulation from local authorities.[10] The applicant complained of pollution from a plant treating waste which began to operate without a licence and was situated 12 metres from her home. The Court noted that she had had to live with the plant for a number of years and considered the domestic findings of significant health effects were convincing.[11] It seemed to accept that actual damage to health was not required for Art.8, since "unnaturally severe environmental pollution may affect individuals' well-being and prevent them from enjoying their homes in such a way as to affect their private and family health adversely without however seriously endangering their health".[12] There was a violation of Art.8, but the conditions were not severe enough for Art.3 to bite. In a later case, the Court stated that successful claims concerning pollution would have to show, arguably and in a detailed manner, a sufficient degree of probability of damage to health or quality of life due to inadequate precautions by the authorities and that the consequences of the acts complained of must not be too remote.[13]

Where an individual is therefore directly or seriously affected by noise or other pollution, an issue may arise under Art.8.[14] Sensibility to noise of nightflying of certain applicants living in close proximity to Heathrow runways was not however considered by the majority of the Court in *Hatton v United Kingdom* to intrude into an aspect of private life in such a manner as to attract the narrow margin of appreciation applicable to intimate interests under Art.8. A wide margin was applied instead as the night flying regulations at an airport with key economic importance concerned general policy decisions on which the role of the domestic policy maker had to be given special weight. It also appeared significant that, unlike *Lopez Ostra*, the airport in question was not acting unlawfully or in breach of regulations. The Court found that the applicants' interests were sufficiently protected by the consultation and monitoring processes and the possibility of taking judicial review proceedings for procedural irregularities and was not prepared to find that the authorities' decisions could only be justified if comprehensive data and research had been carried out on every aspect of the situation. Given the perceived minimal impact on health and private life therefore and the consideration that their property could still be sold without difficulty allowing the applicants to move away,[15] the Court considered that the balance had been fairly struck.

---

[10] Although the plant was run by a private company, the State was responsible since it had given a subsidy and planning permission had been given. The local authority had done little to resolve the unlawfulness of the plant's activities and had even appealed against the closure.

[11] *e.g.* the applicant's child suffered from acute bronchopulmonary infections.

[12] para.51.

[13] *Asselbourg*, n.7 above: the conditions of operation imposed by the authorities on the steel plant were not shown to be so inadequate as to disclose a serious infringement of "the principle of precaution"

[14] *Hatton*, para.96.

[15] Contrast two old Heathrow cases before the Commission, involving very serious noise nuisance, settled after admissibility (7889/77 (Dec.) July 15, 1980, 19 D.R. 186, (Rep.) May 13, 1982, 26 D.R. 5 and 9310/81, (Dec.) October 16, 1985, 44 D.R. 13, (Rep.) July 8, 1987, 52 D.R. 29), where there were difficulties in selling property and moving away.

4. Access to information about environmental risks

Where there are risks to health from severe environmental pollution, it now appears   **IIB–130**
that persons who are affected may derive a right to obtain information about those
risks from the relevant authorities under Art.8 of the Convention. While Art.10
contains a freedom to obtain information, this relates basically to information which
others wish to impart. In *Guerra v Italy*, the applicants, who lived near a chemical
factory which had experienced a serious explosion in the past and had been found to
fall short of standards, claimed that they had not been given information about the
risks presented by the factory or the measures to be adopted in case of an accident.
The Court although holding that Art.10 could not in the circumstances of the case
impose an obligation on the State to collect and disseminate information, nonetheless found a violation of Art.8, considering that the State had not fulfilled its
obligation to secure the applicants' right to respect for private and family life
through its failure to provide the applicants with essential information about the
risks posed to them by severe environmental pollution.

5. Access to court and remedies

The protection of environmental interests at domestic level may also be problematic.   **IIB–131**
Where access to court under Art.6 is concerned, an applicant must be able to claim
a dispute concerning a civil right.[16]

In *Balmer-Schafroth v Switzerland*, the Court found Art.6, para.1 was not applicable
to the procedure before the Federal Council which granted the extension of an
operating licence to a nuclear plant near the applicants' villages, overruling the
objections raised by the applicants on grounds of health. The Court's reasoning,
perhaps less than convincing, appeared to focus on the lack of any proof from the
applicants that the grant of the licence would have any decisive effect on their
physical well-being. The new Court maintained this view however, though by a
majority of 12 to 5, in *Athanossoglou v Switzerland*, finding that the report relied on
by the applicants did not show that the power plant exposed the applicants
personally to a danger that was serious, specific and, above all, imminent. This
approach would seem to impose a high threshold, in effect requiring the applicants
to prove their case on the merits in Strasbourg in order to vindicate a right to access
to court on a domestic level.[17] The Court was not impressed by the argument of the
applicants that judicial examination of the risks of nuclear energy was the
appropriate way to examine deficiencies, considering that the question of how best
to regulate the use of nuclear power was a policy decision for each Contracting State
to take according to its democratic processes.

Similarly, if domestic law does not acknowledge an applicant's standing to bring a
particular claim against an alleged polluter, no issues of lack of access to court may
arise.[18]

---

[16] *e.g. Lam v UK*, 41671/98, (Dec.) July 5, 2001, where the domestic courts found no cause of action
arose from the applicants' negligence claims against the local authority for licensing industrial activity not
covered by planning regulations and failing to take steps to end the health risks from toxic fumes, no
right arose engaging Art.6.
[17] The minority commented that this reversed the subsidiarity principle, the Court reaching its own
judicial assessment of risk to the applicants whereas in their view it was for the domestic courts to assess
whether there was a sufficiently close link between the operation of the power plant and the applicants'
rights to life and physical integrity.
[18] *Asselbourg*, n.7 above.

Failure by Governments to take steps to enforce judgments successfully obtained by applicants against polluters may more clearly raise issues under Art.6.[19]

In two UK cases, houseowners complained of the serious interference with their lives caused by noise of aircraft. Two of them, which were settled after admissibility, involved very serious noise interference from extensions and increased flights to Heathrow airport and a lack of any redress, including an inability to sell the property with change of use to obtain a reasonable price.[20] Though the issues were never settled on the merits, the cases implied that where developments occur which seriously impinge on occupation of private homes, without counterbalancing compensation to enable sale and removal elsewhere, there will be potential problems of access to court or lack of remedies under Arts 6 and 13.[21] Subsequently, in *Hatton v United Kingdom*, the Court found that judicial review did not provide sufficient scope of review of complaints about the impact of an increase in night flying on on the applicants' private and family lives and homes and the applicants accordingly did not have an effective remedy as required by Art.13.

[19] *e.g. Okyay v Turkey*, 36220/97, (Dec.) January 17, 2002, complaints declared admissible under Art.6 that the Council of Ministers had failed to stop the activities of three power plants which the courts had ordered to be suspended due serious pollution from nitrogen and sulphur dioxide.

[20] 7889/77, n.15 above: admissible under Arts 6, 8, 13 and 14 of the Convention and Art.1 of the First Protocol—settled on payment of £7,500 by the Government; 9310/81, n.15 above, where the house, quarter of a mile from a runway, was overflown by day and night, resulting in "intolerable conditions"—admissible under Arts 8 and 13 of the Convention and Art.1 of the First Protocol and settled on payment of £24,000. The report referred to recent legislation enabling the airport authority to buy noise blighted property in future.

[21] The Commission found a violation in *Powell and Rayner* under Art.13 since there was no possibility of action in nuisance for increase in noise since entry to the property, no possibility of compensation and official noise control measures were ineffective. The Court, finding no arguable claim on the substantive provisions, did not consider the matter further (see Pt IIB, Remedies).

Euthanasia

Key Articles:

Articles 2 (right to life) and 8 (respect for private life).

Key case law:

Pretty v UK, April 29, 2002, ECHR 2002–III.

1. General considerations

The subject of euthanasia or assisted suicide has rarely been considered. It may be observed that the term "euthanasia" itself has no common or established meaning within Contracting States.[1] While it would be inaccurate to state that there was any common approach to the controversial question of when people, terminally ill or otherwise, should be allowed, either by their own hand or with active or passive assistance, to take their own lives, it would appear that the countries which permit, as opposed to condone where appropriate, assisted euthanasia are few.[2] The principal case is *Pretty v United Kingdom*. While no violation was found in that case where the applicant, suffering from motor neurone disease, wished her husband to assist her to commit suicide, the Court's decision was limited to the facts of that case, in which the authorities had refused, before her death, to issue a declaration that her husband would not be prosecuted for any assistance given to her. It may nonetheless be deduced from the reasoning that prohibition of euthanasia, where one person actively brings about the death of another, may be regarded as compatible with the Convention.

IIB–132

2. Victim status

No victim issue arose in the *Pretty* case, where the application was lodged by the individual suffering from a terminal illness. Attempts have been made by various Dutch applicants to claim that the state of law in the Netherlands infringed their right to life. In the absence of any real or immediate likelihood that these individuals, in good health, were at risk of being killed by enthusiastic medical euthanasia-supporters, these cases have been disposed of as inadmissible in committees. Difficulties of victim status are likely to arise even where relatives of terminally-ill persons claim violations of the Convention. In a Spanish case,[3] the applicant was sister-in-law, and heir, of a young man, tetraplegic, who had challenged in the courts the prohibition on assisted suicide. He had died with assistance before the conclusion of proceedings and the Spanish courts had refused to allow the applicant to continue the proceedings after his death,. The Court considered that his claims in the domestic proceedings under Arts 2, 3, 8, 9, 13 and 14, were personal, non-transferable rights and that she could not claim to be a

IIB–133

---

[1] *e.g.* Council of Europe report, Replies to questionnaires for Member States relating to euthanasia, CDB1 (220) II.

[2] Netherlands is the famous example, followed in 2002 by Belgium.

[3] *Sanles Sanles v Spain*, 48335/99, (Dec.) October 26, 2000.

victim, even if she was affected personally by the distressing circumstances in which her brother-in-law found himself. A close relative of a person who died due to a deliberate intervention would be more likely to be found to have standing to bring on the deceased's behalf a claim that the death had been in some way unlawful or contrary to the Convention.

3. Right to life

IIB–134   The Court rejected the arguments in the *Pretty* case that Art.2 included not only the right to life but the right to die.[4] It also left open the question of whether the practice of euthanasia would infringe the right to life, noting that issues of personal autonomy and public policy arose and that conflicting considerations might arise that could only be resolved on examination of the particular facts of the case.[5]

4. Inhuman treatment

IIB–135   The suffering caused by illness or injury that leads a person to wish to end their life may clearly reach the threshold of severity covered by Art.3 of the Convention. Where however the Government cannot be held responsible for the injury or illness and is providing the necessary medical care and support, no "treatment" arises for which the State can be held responsible and no positive obligation arises requiring the State to permit or facilitate assisted suicide.[6]

5. Self-determination

IIB–136   While the Court's judgment in the *Pretty* case largely followed the conclusions of the House of Lords in the domestic proceedings, the Court differed in finding that the right to respect for private life provided for in Art.8, para.1 arguably covered the right to self-determination in the sense of deciding how or when to end one's life. It laid emphasis on the notions of "human dignity" and "human freedom". The reference to the concerns about increasing medical sophistication keeping people alive in states of advanced physical or mental decrepitude would appear to hint at freedom of choice extending at least so far as bestowing on applicants a choice to refuse medical treatment that kept them alive.[7] The Court did not however find the refusal of the DPP to give Mr Pretty an advance guarantee against prosecution an unjustified interference with the right under Art.8. It appeared particularly influenced by the risk to the vulnerable and sick by allowing exceptions to the general ban but noted that there was flexibility in the system of prosecution and criminal justice to deal sympathetically with so-called mercy killings.[8]

6. Freedom of conscience and discrimination

IIB–137   The arguments raised in the *Pretty* case under Arts 9 and 14 received short treatment, the Court obviously not considering that a wish to commit euthanasia was the type of belief falling within the scope of Art.9 or that the law prohibiting

---

[4] *Pretty*, para.39.
[5] *Pretty*, para.41.
[6] *Pretty*, paras 53–55.
[7] *Pretty*, para.65; see *B v NHS hospital*, Court of Appeal judgment of March 22, 2002 cited at para.18.
[8] *Pretty*, paras 74–77.

assisted suicide could be considered as discriminatory of the physically disabled unable to act for themselves.

7. Criminal proceedings

No cases have yet been brought by persons prosecuted or otherwise sanctioned, **IIB–138** either as medical personnel or a relative, for assisting some-one to die. It is unlikely that a doctor could rely on any of the rights under Arts 2, 3 or 8 of the Convention. Even assuming that a doctor succeeded in claiming that a belief in the moral necessity of euthanasia fell within the scope of Art.9, or that a relative's actions came under Art.8 in its family life aspect, a measure applied in "accordance with the law" would be likely to be found justified in pursuit of the legitimate aim of protecting public order or health. Possibly if the punishment was grossly disproportionate a problem might arise—however, if the fact finding domestic bodies found the act was not in good faith or abusive, the Court would hesitate to overrule them. Nor would it be possible to rely on Art.6 concerning the proceedings other than on generally applicable aspects of fairness since that provision does not concern itself with the content of the criminal law being applied.

Cross-reference

Part IIB: Private life, General Considerations

Expropriation, confiscation and control of use

Key provisions:

IIB–139   Article 1 of Protocol No.1 (peaceful enjoyment of possessions); Art.6 (access to court/fair hearing).

Key case law:

Sporrong and Lonnroth v Sweden, September 23, 1982, Series A, No.52; 5 E.H.R.R. 35; *James v UK*, February 21, 1985, Series A, No.98; 8 E.H.R.R. 123; *Lithgow v UK*, July 8, 1986, Series A, No.102; 8 E.H.R.R. 329; *Agosi v UK*, October 24, 1986, Series A, No.108; *Erkner and Hofauer v Austria*, April 23, 1987, Series A, No.117; 9 E.H.R.R. 464; *Hakansson and Sturesson v Sweden*, February 21, 1990, Series A, No.171; 13 E.H.R.R. 1; *Papamichalopoulos v Greece*, June 24, 1993 Series A, No.260–B; 16 E.H.R.R. 440; *Hentrich v France*, September 22, 1994, Series A, No.296–A; 18 E.H.R.R. 440; *Holy Monasteries v Greece*, December 9, 1994, Series A, No.301–A; 20 E.H.R.R 1; *Air Canada v UK*, May 5, 1995, Series A, No.316; 20 E.H.R.R. 150; *Matos e Silva v Portugal*, September 16, 1996, R.J.D. 1996–IV, No.14; *Akkus v Turkey*, July 9, 1997, R.J.D. 1997–IV, No.43; *Beyeler v Italy*, January 5, 2000, ECHR 2000–I; *Former King of Greece v Greece*, November 23, 2000, ECHR 2000–XII.

1. General considerations

IIB–140   Considerable room for manoeuvre is accorded in respect of expropriations and confiscations. A wide margin of appreciation applies to planning, nationalisation or other legislative interventions due to the complex or policy nature of the issues.[1] Examination of these cases tends to focus on whether a fair balance has been struck between the public and private interest and whether the applicant has been left with a disproportionate burden.[2] Deprivations of property must also conform with requirements of lawfulness, both as regards the existence of a basis for the measure in domestic law and the requisite quality of the law.[3]

Since property rights fall within the scope of Art.6, para.1 as civil rights, procedural safeguards generally apply regarding access to court for determination of claims and regarding requirements, *inter alia*, of fairness, reasonable length of proceedings, independent and impartial tribunals (See Pt IIA: Fair Trial).

---

[1] *Sporrong*, para.26; *James*, para.46: the margin is applied both to the assessment of the existence of a problem of public concern and the remedial action necessary. Where the legislature has made a choice by enacting a law in the general interest, the possible existence of alternative solutions does not in itself render the contested legislation unjustified, *e.g. Mellacher v Austria*, December 19, 1989, Series A, No.169, para.53, 33091/96, (Dec.) March 23, 1999, concerning restitution of property measures after the fall of communism.

[2] *Lithgow*, para.120.

[3] *Iatridis v Greece*, March 25, 1999, ECHR 1999–II (expropriation measure unlawful); *Carbonara and Ventura v Italy* May 30, 2000, ECHR 2000–VI (arbitrary and unforeseeable application of a constructive-expropriation rule).

2. Expropriation

(a) De facto deprivation

Generally, where ownership of the property remains or some form of exploitation, by way of sale or receipt of rents for example, the measure is not regarded as a *de facto* expropriation or deprivation of property within the meaning of the second sentence of the first paragraph of Art.1 of Protocol No.1 but an interference with peaceful enjoyment of possessions within the meaning of the first sentence.[4] However in *Papamichalopoulos v Greece*, where the navy constructed a naval base and officers' resort on the applicants' land, the Court found that although there had been no formal expropriation, their land was occupied and being unable to sell, bequeath mortgage or even gain entry, they had lost all ability to dispose or make use of it. This, combined with the failure of attempts to remedy the situation, entailed sufficiently serious consequences for the situation to disclose a *de facto* expropriation incompatible with the general guarantee set out in the first sentence of Art.1.

Whatever the classification of the measure under Art.1 of Protocol No.1, the balancing exercise underlies the Court's examination.[5]

IIB–141

(b) Public interest

The Court has stated that it will respect the legislature's judgment as to what is in the public interest unless it is "manifestly without reasonable foundation"[6] and that the notion of "public interest" is necessarily extensive.[7]

Public interest has been accepted as being involved in almost all cases so far. It has included *de facto* expropriation for national defence policy in building a base and officers' resort[8]; transfer of monastery land for the purpose of ending illegal sales and encroachments and controlling development[9]; expropriation of estates of the former ruling royal house[10]; price control systems for land purchase and rights of pre-emption for the prevention of tax evasion.[11]

IIB–142

(c) Proportionality—striking a fair balance

In assessment of whether a fair balance has been struck, or the applicant required to bear an excessive and disproportionate burden, the Court looks at the circumstances as a whole, considering issues of lawfulness, the length of time involved, procedural

IIB–143

---

[4] e.g. *Sporrong*, para.65; *Matos e Silva*, para.85.
[5] *Sporrong*, para.69.
[6] *James*, para.46; *Lithgow*, para.122.
[7] *Hentrich*, para.39.
[8] *Papamichalopoulos*.
[9] *Holy Monasteries*: while the Court acknowledged doubts as to the reasons where the property was not given to needy farmers but to co-operatives and public bodies, this nonetheless did not deprive the measure of its overall objectives as being in the public interest.
[10] *Former King of Greece*, paras 87–88—interests of clarifying the status of the republic.
[11] *Hakansson and Sturesson*; *Hentrich*; also 12736/87, (Dec.) May 5, 1988, 56 D.R. 254 (compulsory purchase for motorway construction);13135/87, (Dec.) July 4, 1988, 56 D.R. 268 (compulsory purchase to enforce habitable standards of housing).

safeguards and the effect on the applicant, in particular, whether compensation is available.[12]

Arbitrariness and lack of procedural safeguards were found to render the preemption measure in *Hentrich v France* disproportionate. The use of the power was selective, unforeseeable and punitive, no reasons were given and the applicants were not afforded an adversarial procedure in which to counter the allegations of tax evasion.[13] In *Hakansson and Sturesson v Sweden*, however, there was no lack of proportionality where the applicants were aware of the risk of not obtaining a permit to retain the estate bought at auction and although they had paid more, they received a sum reasonably related to the market price plus the auction costs.[14]

The manner and effects of the *de facto* expropriation were incompatible in *Papamichalopoulos*, namely, the seizure of the land, the length of deprivation and lack of any remedial action by the State.

The length of the proceedings concerning the expropriation measures may disclose of a violation under Art.6, para.1 where there is an unreasonable delay in the determination of civil rights and obligations. It may also form a decisive or significant part in the finding of violation under Art.1 of Protocol No.1. Thus in *Erkner and Hofauer v Austria*, where land consolidation proceedings took more than 16 years, the Court said that the complaints about the unreasonable length of proceedings under Art.6 could be distinguished from the question as to whether the disputed transfer was compatible with right of property, in which context delay was one element. On the latter, the Court found a violation referring to the disproportionate burden imposed on the applicants resulting from the uncertainty and also the lack of flexibility of the system (*e.g.* no compensation for loss on the forced exchange where worse land was allotted and no means of altering the position of owners during that time).[15] In other cases, where the essence of the complaint has been the delay in the proceedings, with no separate effect on property rights, the Court has found it unnecessary to decide whether the delay in the proceedings also disclosed a violation of Art.1 of Protocol No.1. Any effect on value of property or pecuniary damage is in that context to be taken into account in assessing just satisfaction for the breach of Art.6.[16]

The right to compensation is not express. The reference to deprivation being subject to the conditions provided by principles of international law was found to be relevant only to the position as regards non-nationals and it does not therefore

---

[12] *e.g.* 12736/87, n.11 above: compulsory purchase by a local authority of premises below habitable standards was proportionate since warnings and time for repairs were given and the property was in substantial disrepair; 13135/87, n.10 above, expropriation of parts of a Highland estate for road widening was reasonably proportionate, having regard to the compensation fixed by a Land Tribunal after a hearing with representation for the applicants.

[13] Also *Zvolsky and Zvolska v Czech Republic*, November 12, 2002, ECHR 2002–IX, where in revoking a transfer of property, the courts took no account of evidence as to the voluntariness of transaction or the compensation paid at the time.

[14] In *Hentrich*, however, the risk of preemption was also known and the applicants received the purchase price plus 10% and costs. The Court found that this was not sufficient to compensate for the loss of a property acquired without fraudulent intent. The arbitrary, punitive nature of the measure seems to be the main distinguishing feature.

[15] Also *Matos e Silva*: violations of Art.6 and Art.1 of Protocol No.1 for 13-year expropriation proceedings since the prolonged uncertainty aggravated the detrimental effects of the measures; *Almeida Garrett v Portugal*, January 11, 2000, 24 years' delay in finalising the amount of compensation for the expropriation.

[16] *e.g. Brigandi v Italy*, February 19, 1991, Series A, No.194–B.

incorporate international law principles for nationals as regards compensation.[17] However, the existence and extent of compensation is a material factor in the balance of the general interest and private rights, otherwise the protection of Art.1 of Protocol No.1 against confiscations would be illusory and ineffective.[18]

On the issue of the standard of compensation, deprivation without compensation in an amount reasonably related to the value of the property would normally be disproportionate, exceptional circumstances being required to justify a lack of compensation.[19] However, full compensation is not necessarily required since measures of economic or social reform may call for less than full market value.[20] In *Lithgow v United Kingdom*, concerning nationalisation, to which other considerations might apply than to ordinary expropriation, the Court stated that it would respect the legislature's judgment unless manifestly without reasonable foundation, the test generally applied since. Where an applicant enters into an agreement with the authorities and there is no element of oppression or coercion, the Court is unlikely to find a violation of Art.1 of Protocol No.1 in respect of allegations that the settlement did not properly reflect the value of the property.[21]

Lack of any compensation is therefore a significant feature. In *Erkner and Hofauer v Austria*, the lack of compensation for forced transfer of good land for worse, combined with delay and the inflexibility of the procedure, rendered the measures in violation of Art.1 of Protocol No.1. In the *Holy Monasteries*, where there was no compensation for the transfer of ownership of large areas of monastery land, the Court found a violation, rejecting the Government's arguments as to the exceptional, historical circumstances in which the property was acquired and used.

Methods of calculation have generally been unsuccessfully attacked and indeed, having regard to the standard of "manifestly without reasonable foundation" an assessment procedure would have to be grossly unfair or arbitrary to offend. In *Lithgow v United Kingdom*, where the applicant companies made numerous criticisms of the unfairness of the calculation process, the Court, *inter alia*, found the fact that there was an international practice in some areas of calculation did not indicate that this was the only way, referring to the thorough Parliamentary process during which valuation issues had been thrashed out.

In other cases, failure to make payments inflation proofed or to discount certain heads of damage has not been enough to render the compensation unreasonable.[22] An assessment method therefore that is geared at least ostensibly to compensating

---

[17] *Lithgow*, paras 111–119.

[18] *e.g.* 7987/77, (Dec.) December 13, 1979, 18 D.R. 31 (expropriation of property for road construction: complaint about level of compensation): the Commission took the view that there was no right to any particular amount of compensation but there would be a problem if there was a substantial reduction in compensation such as could be regarded as affecting the very substance of the right to compensation.

[19] *e.g. Holy Monasteries*, para.71. See also *Former King of Greece*, para.98, no convincing explanation for absence of compensation for expropriation of royal estates; *Yagtzilar v Greece*, December 6, 2001, ECHR 2001–XII: no compensation paid for over 70 years; *Zvolsky and Zvolska*, n.13 above, where there was no possibility of indemnity on revocation of a donation of property.

[20] *Lithgow*, para.121.

[21] *Guerrera and Fusco v Italy*, April 3, 2000.

[22] *e.g.* 13135/87, n.11 above, where the Land Tribunal granted about a sixth of the claimed losses and future costs of upkeep, the Commission found the method of assessment reasonable and that the lack of inflation proofing did not bring it outside the margin of appreciation; 7987/77, (Dec.) December 13, 1979, 18 D.R. 31 where assessment of agricultural value without account being given to future mineral potential was not unreasonable; 14265/88, (Dec.) January 19, 1989, 59 D.R. 281, where the applicant who had never lived in the property only received site value on expropriation.

for the property will pass muster even if the method used or figure reached differs greatly from that preferred by the aggrieved owner. The approach that the valuation is "reasonably related" to the property in question is sometimes used.[23] There is no right as such to full compensation in all circumstances, the Court accepting that there may be legitimate public interest objectives in reimbursing less than full market value.[24] A gross disparity between market value and compensation, without public interest justification, may however disclose a violation.[25]

Delay by the State in paying compensation due on expropriation, which due to 70 per cent inflation, caused the applicant substantial loss, was found by the Court to render the compensation inadequate.[26] An inflexible presumption that adjoining owners of expropriated land used for roads benefitted from the development and could not claim compensation for damage was "manifestly without reasonable foundation", leaving the applicants to bear an individual and excessive burden.[27] Nor should the authorities require applicants to have recourse to multiple proceedings to recover different elements of loss from an expropriation, as this delays payment and puts too much of a burden on the individual.[28]

3. Forfeiture and confiscation measures

IIB–144   Draconian powers for the seizure of goods in the customs or criminal context which pursue lawful and legitimate purposes have proved acceptable, subject to minimum requirements of procedural safeguards.[29]

The approach of the Court has been to regard confiscations as a control of use of property rather than deprivation. This approach places an emphasis on the general purpose of the measure rather than the effect on the applicant's property rights of the applicant. In *Agosi v United Kingdom*, smuggled kruggerrands obtained from the applicants by fraud had been seized by Customs which refused to exercise its discretion to return them to the applicant. The Court considered that, while in one sense the seizure disclosed a deprivation, it formed a constituent part of the procedure for the control of use of gold in the UK. Similarly, in *Air Canada v United Kingdom*, where an airliner was seized on discovery of a large cannabis resin shipment on board but released on payment of £50,000, the Court did not accept,

---

[23] e.g. *Hakansson and Sturesson*, para.54; *Papachelas v Greece*, March 25, 1999, ECHR 1999–II, para.48.

[24] *Holy Monasteries*, paras 70–71; *Papelachas*, n.23 above, para.48.

[25] e.g. *Platakou v Greece*, January 11, 2001, ECHR 2001–I: property expropriated for a museum with compensation one quarter/one fifth of the market value and the reason given by the authorities (its ruinuous state) was contradicted by the experts' valuations; *Jokela v Finland*, May 21, 2002, ECHR 2002–IV, where the amount paid for compensation for expropriation was based on a purported value of the property grossly inconsistent with the tax valuation; *Pincova and Pinc v Czech Republic*, November 5, 2002, ECHR 2002–VIII, where compensation was set at the price thirty years earlier and bore no reasonable relation to current value, with no regard to costs of upkeep of the property.

[26] *Akkus v Turkey*; also *Malama v Greece*, March 1, 2001, ECHR 2002–II, where the courts did not take the delay (70 years) in paying compensation for expropriated land into account, nor award interest for delay.

[27] *Katikarides v Greece*, November 15, 1996, R.J.D. 1996–V, No.20; paras 49–50: the applicants had strong arguments that the flyover deprived their remaining land of value.

[28] *Efstathiou and Michaelidis v Greece*, July 10, 2003, paras 30–33.

[29] e.g. *Handyside v UK*, December 7, 1976, Series A, No.24, para.62, where there was seizure and destruction of copies of "The Little Red Schoolbook", the Court commented that the second paragraph on control of use set up the State as sole judges of the necessity of an interference. Later cases mitigated this extreme approach.

as argued by the applicant, that they had been deprived of both airplane and money but found that the measures were part of the system for the control of use of an aircraft used to carry drugs.

It is accepted that smuggled goods will generally be the object of confiscation, a practice existing in many Contracting States. While the Commission in *Agosi v United Kingdom* considered that there had to be a link between the behaviour of the owner of smuggled goods and the breach of the law, such that the innocent owner should be entitled to recovery, the Court observed that this was not a common practice in Member States, where the fault of owner might be only one element in the balancing exercise.

However the Court did hold in *Agosi v United Kingdom* that there were procedural requirements implicit in the protection of property rights, namely that there should be procedures which enabled reasonable account to be taken of the link between the conduct of owner and breach of law and to afford the owner to put his case to the responsible authorities. In both *Agosi* and *Air Canada*, the possibility of judicial review of the Customs Commissioners' decisions were found to furnish sufficient procedural protection although the decisions were essentially unreasoned, limiting the ability to challenge them.[30]

Forfeiture of £240,000 found by customs officers in the applicant's car was a control of use and the Court did not find the proceedings to be unfair since the applicant had the opportunity to show the money was not connected with drug trafficking. Nor did the domestic court rely automatically on any statutory presumptions.[31] However, confiscation of money assessed by a court to be drug trafficking proceeds following conviction was not a control of use but a measure to secure the payment of a penalty within the meaning of the second paragraph of Art.1 of Protocol No.1 and not disproportionate where the procedure was fair.[32]

Less leeway was perhaps shown to the authorities regarding the pre-emption of sales of works of art by the authorities to prevent masterpieces leaving the country. In *Beyeler v Italy*, the legitimacy of this aim was not put in doubt but the Court emphasised that when using powers in the general interest it was incumbent on the authorities to act in good time, in an appropriate manner and with utmost consistency. The delay and vacillation of the authorities, together with the lack of clarity in the law and unjust enrichment from their acquisition of the painting at well below market value, thus disclosed a violation.

---

[30] In *Air Canada*, although no reasons were given at the time of the confiscation beyond the presence of drugs, the Court considered that against the history of previous warnings about security laxness by Customs, the company could not realistically claim to be unaware of the reasons. Taken with the important aim of combatting drug trafficking the measures of seizure and return of the aircraft on payment of money were not disproportionate.

[31] *Butler v UK*, 41661/98, (Dec.) June 27, 2002. The forfeiture of cars, used to carry drugs, has also been found a legitimate control of use of property, even if belonging to innocent third parties, where there was a procedure whereby they could apply for the return of their property: *CM v France*, 28708/95, (Dec.) June 26, 2001, ECHR 2001–VII; similar approach to forfeiture of a coach used in smuggling of illegal immigrants—*Yildirim v Italy*, 38602/02, (Dec.) April 10, 2003. Concerning confiscation of money unlawfully obtained or from organised crime: *Riela v Italy*, 52439/99, (Dec.) September 4, 2001, *Honecker v Germany*, 53991/00, (Dec.) November 11, 2001, ECHR 2001–XII.

[32] *Phillips v UK*, July 5, 2001.

4. Bankruptcy measures

IIB–145   Imposition of bankrupcy on a person, with removal of the power of disposal of his possessions, is regarded as a control of use of property that pursues in general terms a legitimate aim and falls within the margin of appreciation. However, the interference with property rights can become disproportionate if it lasts too long due to judicial inactivity, as in *Luordo v Italy*.[33]

Cross-reference

Part IIA: Fair trial, Civil rights
Part IIA: Fair trial, Access to court
Part IIB: Planning and control of property
Part IIB: Property

---

[33] July 17, 2003—bankruptcy lasted over 14 years.

Extradition

Relevant provisions:

Articles 2 (right to life), 3 (prohibition on torture, inhuman and degrading   **IIB–146**
treatment), 13 (right to effective remedy), and 34 (obligation on States not to hinder
the effective exercise of the right of individual petition).

Relevant case law:

Soering v UK, July 7, 1989, Series A, No.161; 11 E.H.R.R. 439; *Chahal v UK*,
November 15, 1996, R.J.D. 1996–V, No.22; 23 E.H.R.R. 413; *Mamatkulov and
Askarov v Turkey*, February 6, 2003; *Ocalan v Turkey*, March 12, 2003.

1. General considerations

Extradition is accepted by the Convention organs as a legitimate and desirable   **IIB–147**
means of enforcing criminal justice between States.[1] There is no right not to be
extradited.[2] Principally issues arise under the Convention regarding the detention
pending extradition and regarding allegations of breaches of human rights which
will occur in the receiving State if the extradition is carried out.

2. Risk of violations in receiving country

(a) *Ill-treatment*

Where on proposed extradition an applicant faces a real risk of treatment contrary   **IIB–148**
to Art.3 in the receiving State, the responsibility of the expelling State is engaged
and a violation arises. This principle was established in *Soering v United Kingdom*,
where conditions on death row in Virginia were found to expose the applicant,
facing two charges of capital murder, to the real risk of inhuman and degrading
treatment.

The risk must relate to a treatment which reaches a certain minimum level of
severity, taking into account all the circumstances, including the physical and
mental effects and where relevant the age, sex and health of the victim.[3] It has been

---

[1] *Soering*, paras 86 and 89, noting the legitimate interests of the international community in facilitating
the bringing to justice of offenders who move easily about the globe and the dangers facing States which
were obliged to become safe havens for alleged criminals.
[2] *Soering*, para.85.
[3] In *Soering*, the death row disclosed inhuman treatment having regard to the average length of detention
pending execution (6–8 years) with the ever present and mounting anguish of awaiting an execution, the
stringency of the custodial regime in the Mecklenburg Correctional Centre over that time, the applicant's
personal circumstances, in particular his youth and some indications that he had suffered from an
impairment of mental responsibility for his acts; *cf.* 10479/83, (Dec.) March 12, 1984, 37 D.R. 58, the
Commission had not found that the death row would involve Art.3 treatment having regard to the fact
that the element of delay derived from procedural safeguards used by prisoners.

left open whether the extradition to face the imposition of life sentence without possibility of early release would infringe Art.3.[4]

The way in which the extradition is enforced, even if involving the use of tranquillizers, has not yet been found to go beyond the inevitable trauma involved in the legitimate enforcement of an extradition decision.[5]

The Court has emphasised that the prohibition contained in Art.3 is absolute.[6] Therefore, if there is a real risk of such prohibited treatment in the receiving State, no principle of international enforcement of justice would justify implementing the extradition.

The risk of the ill-treatment alleged must be real and account will be taken of the assurances given by the authorities of the State requesting extradition to those of the State requested. The fact that the requesting State has recognised the right of individual petition may also be relevant. Where IRA prisoners were to be extradited from the Netherlands to the UK and were alleging that they would be ill-treated in the Maze prison, the Commission, in dismissing the complaints as manifestly ill-founded, had regard to assurances given to the Dutch authorities by the Deputy Director of the Maze prison and the fact that the UK had recognised the right of individual petition.[7] However in *Soering* the undertaking by the US authorities to inform the trial court of the wish of the UK that the death penalty should not be applied was not enough to diminish the risk in view of the prosecution's intention to seek the death penalty as merited.

Failure to comply with a request by the Court to suspend an extradition pending its proceedings may lead to a finding of a violation of the State's obligation under Art.34 of the Convention not to hinder the effective exercise of the right of individual petition. In *Mamatkulov and Askarov v Turkey*, the applicants were sent, despite such a request, to Uzbekistan where they allegedly risked serious ill-treatment as terrorist suspects. The applicants had not been in contact with their representatives after the extradition, which hampered their ability to prove their substantive complaints. The Court found that, although no breach of Art.3 had been established, the Government had failed to abstain from measures that prejudiced the integrity and effectiveness of the Court's final judgment and were thus in breach of Art.34.

(b) *Death penalty*

IIB–149   Extradition to face the death penalty, if imposed judicially after a fair trial, did not previously raise an issue by itself under Art.3. In *Soering*, the Court rejected the argument of Amnesty International that while Art.2 allowed judicial execution it

---

[4] e.g. *Gonzalez v Spain*, 43544/98, (Dec.) June 29, 1999: the Court, assuming that the life imprisonment without release was contrary to Art.3, took into account the fact that the Spanish courts had imposed the condition that he should not be imprisoned for his whole life; *Nivette v France*, 44190/98, (Dec.) July 3, 2001, ECHR 2001–VII: the Court had regard to the undertaking on oath by the District Attorney that he would not apply for the death penalty or a whole life sentence; *Einhorn v France*, 71555/01, (Dec.) October 16, ECHR 2001–XI, where the Court did not exclude the possibility, referring to various Council of Europe texts on the treatment of long-term prisoners.

[5] 25342/94, (Dec.) September 4, 1995, 82–A D.R. 134 where the applicant, who had attempted to commit suicide under strain of the imminent extradition, had to be given sedatives in view of her resistance to departure.

[6] *Chahal*, paras 80–81.

[7] 12543/86, (Dec.) December 2, 1986, 51 D.R. 272. See also Immigration and Expulsion, on the Convention organs's increased readiness to find problems within Contracting States which are not cured by their acceptance of the right of individual petition.

was nonetheless contrary to Art.3 to impose it. The two provisions had to be read in harmony with each other and Art.3 could not have been intended to include a general prohibition of the death penalty. The Court did not exclude however that in certain circumstances an issue might arise under Art.3 concerning, for example, the disproportionality of the sentence to the crime committed and personal circumstances of the accused, as well as the conditions of detention awaiting executions such as the death row phenomenon.

Now, where a country has ratified Protocol No.6 (abolition of the death penalty save in time of war) or Protocol No.13 (abolition of the death penalty in all circumstances), it would appear to be in potential violation of those provisions and Art.3 to extradite or expel some-one to face a real risk of imposition of the death penalty.[8] In a case concerning extradition from Macao to China for repeated vehicle thefts for which the death penalty was an option, the Commission applied an interim measure of suspension to Portugal.[9] The case was struck off when the domestic courts revoked an order that extradition should proceed.[10] In *Ocalan v Turkey*, the Court, noting that almost all Contracting States has ratified Protocol 6, gave a strong indication that this almost universal abandonment of the death penalty in peace time constituted a *de facto* abrogation or modification of Art.2 and a rejection of capital punishment as an unacceptable, if not inhuman, form of punishment.[11]

Assurances from the requesting State will be relevant to the existence of any potential violation from the extradition. In *Einhorn v France*, where the applicant was to return to Pennsylvania to face a murder charge, the Court considered the Goverment had obtained sufficient assurances such as to remove the danger of the applicant being sentenced to death, namely, affidavits sworn by the District Attorney that she would not seek the death penalty and the court would have no power to impose it of its own motion.[12]

(c) *Other violations in receiving State*

There is no general principle that a State cannot surrender an individual unless satisfied that the conditions awaiting him in the receiving country are in full accord with each of the safeguards of the Convention.[13] Where in *Soering* the applicant invoked Art.6, claiming that if he was extradited he would face a breach of Art.6, para.3(c) because of lack of legal aid for certain appeal applications, the Court did not exclude that an issue might be raised under Art.6 where the fugitive to be extradited had suffered or risked suffering a "flagrant denial" of a fair trial in a requesting country,[14] particularly where there is a risk of execution.[15] That was

IIB–150

---

[8] 22742/93, (Dec.) January 20, 1994, 76–A D.R. 164; *Ismaili v Germany*, 58218/00, (Dec.) March 15, 2001, where Germany had ratified Protocol No.6 but it was not substantiated that the offences facing the applicant in Morocco attracted the death penalty.
[9] See Procedure, Interim Measures.
[10] 25862/94, (Dec.) November 27, 1995, 83–A D.R. 88.
[11] paras 189–198.
[12] n.4 above; also 22742/93, n.8 above.
[13] *Soering*, para.112.
[14] Also 10383/83, (Dec.), May 3, 1983, 36 D.R. 209, where the Commission stated thata violation could not be ruled out if there was a risk of prosecution for political reasons which could lead to an unjustified or disproportionate sentence.
[15] *Soering*, para.13; *Ocalan*, paras 119–213.

however not the case in *Soering* where flattering remarks had been made as to the democratic character of the legal system which respected the rule of law and afforded considerable procedural safeguards.[16]

The meaning in practice of a "flagrant denial" of a fair trial has not yet been made clear. Where an applicant complainted of extradition to Hong Kong, the Commission did not find his allegations that at his trial he would face contested evidence taken in his absence in Malaysia or that a co-accused might be offered immunity to testify against him disclosed such a risk.[17] Nor was the trial facing a Russian facing extradition from Finland to Russia found to disclose the exceptional circumstances adverted to by the Court.[18] Evidence of extremely hostile media coverage in Pennsylvania where the applicant faced jury trial for murder did not furnish substantial grounds for believing that his trial would not take place in conditions complying with Art.6.[19]

Since the imposition of the death penalty on an applicant after an unfair trial was found to disclose a breach of Art.3 in *Ocalan v Turkey*, it would appear open to argue that extradition to face trial in such circumstances was also incompatible with the Convention. In that case, the applicant had been tried before a court which was not "independent or impartial" due to the presence of a military judge, he had not been assisted by his lawyers when questioned in police custody, had been unable to communicate with them out of hearing of third parties and was unable to gain direct access to the case file until a very late stage in the proceedings.

3. Extradition proceedings: fairness

IIB–151 Extradition proceedings in the sending State do not fall within the scope of Art.6, para.1 since they do not involve the determination of the criminal charge.[20] Even where a limited examination of the merits is undertaken in committal proceedings by the magistrates this is not considered part of the determination of the charges on which the extradition is sought.[21]

4. Remedies

IIB–152 Where it is alleged that there is a risk of Art.3 treatment on return, the Court held in *Soering*, disagreeing with the Commission, that judicial review furnished an effective remedy against extradition. The Court found that the approach of the courts, giving the "most anxious scrutiny" to claims of risk of ill-treatment was sufficient, notwithstanding the formally limited scope of the examination in judicial

---

[16] See, *mutadis mutandis, Tomic v UK*, 17837/03, (Dec.) October 14, 2003, where the concerns about trials of war criminals in Croatia was not sufficient for the applicant's expulsion to raise issues under Art.6, particularly since Croatia was a Contracting State.

[17] 15933/89, (Dec.) October 14, 1991; 19319/91,(Dec.) September 2, 1992, his complaints that, although Hong Kong had given procedural assurances this would not protect him when China took over, were rejected on the basis that the complaints were largely hypothetical and the lack of responsibility of the UK for the future acts of China.

[18] 16832/90, (Dec.) May 28, 1991, 69 D.R. 321 (the applicant alleged that KGB cases were decided by the Supreme Court as the only instance, with minimal publicity); 22742/93, n.8, risk to fairness of trial from alleged media publicity too hypothetical.

[19] *Einhorn*, n.4 above.

[20] *Mamatkulov and Askarov*, para.80.

[21] 10479/83, n.3 above; also 24015/94, (Dec.) May 20, 1994, 77–A D.R. 144.

review. While in *Chahal v United Kingdom*, concerning expulsion, judicial review was inadequate, this was due at least in part to the inability of the courts to undertake any independent scrutiny of the national security considerations which were at the basis of the decision to expel. Despite criticism of the inability of the courts to decide the question solely on the question of risk without reference to security considerations, the Court did not appear to overule its previous case law and it remains to be seen whether it would maintain its general view of the effectiveness of judicial review in an extradition case, where risk was not the sole question but other elements irrelevant to Art.3 played a decisive role in the decision to uphold the extradition.

Cross reference

Part IIB: Detention pending extradition or expulsion
Part IIB: Hindrance in the exercise of the right of individual petition
Part IIB: Immigration and expulsion
Part IIB: Torture and ill-treatment

Freedom of assembly

Key provision:

IIB–153   Article 11 (freedom of peaceful assembly).

Key case law:

Platform "Ärzte für das leben" v Austria, June 21, 1988, Series A, No.139; 13 E.H.R.R. 204; *Ezelin v France*, April 26, 1991, Series A, No.202; 14 E.H.R.R. 362; *Stankov and the United Macedonian Organisation Linden v Bulgaria*, October 2, 2001, ECHR 2001–IX; *Cissé v France*, April 9, 2002, ECHR 2002–III; *Djavit An v Turkey*, February 20, 2003, ECHR 2003–III.

1. General considerations

IIB–154   Exercise of this freedom is often closely connected with other rights, such as freedom of expression and thought, conscience and religion. Art.11 is the *lex specialis* where an assembly is concerned but the other two rights, Arts 9 and 10, may be taken into account in examining the effect and proportionality of the interference.[1] As with freedom of expression, freedom of peaceful assembly is one of the foundations of a democratic society[2] and protects demonstrations that may annoy or give offence to persons opposed to the ideas or claims that are being promoted.[3] It covers not only public but private meetings,[4] static gatherings as well as public processions, and in *Cissé v France*, it covered the occupation of a church by protesting aliens without valid residence permits. The right is capable of being exercised by not only individuals but by those organising the assembly, such as associations.

The right does not extend to demonstrations where organisers and participants have violent intentions which result in public disorder.[5] Where a Government argued that an assembly was unlikely to be peaceful due to reactions of other groups, the Commission considered that it was the intention to hold a peaceful assembly which was significant and the possibility of violent counter demonstrations could not as such to remove the right from the scope of first paragraph. The Commission expressed the opinion that it did not guarantee a right to pass and re-pass in public places, such a shopping centres, or to assemble for purely social purposes.[6]

Article 11 is not to be interpreted restrictively. The fact that an assembly is illegal will not necessarily remove it from the scope of the right, at least where it is peaceful in nature. Thus where an applicant was convicted for participation in an

[1] 25522/94, (Dec.) April 6, 1995, 81–A D.R. 146; also *Ezelin*, para.35.
[2] *e.g.* 8191/78 (Dec.), October 10, 1979, 17 D.R. 93.
[3] *Platform "Ärzte für das Leben"*, para.32; *Stankov*, paras 86 and 107, emphasising that national authorities must be alert to ensure public opinion is not protected at the expense of the assertion of minority views however unpopular.
[4] 8191/78, n.2 above.
[5] 8440/78, (Dec.) July 16, 1980, 21 D.R. 138.
[6] 33689/96, (Dec.) October 27, 1997, where West Indian youths were banned from a shopping centre; see however *Appleby v UK*, May 6, 2003, where Art.10, and impliedly Art.11, applied to the applicants' campaigning in a shopping centre against a development of public playing fields.

organised sit-in in a road, the Commission found that though it was illegal it was not actively violent and that the interference had to be justified in terms of the second paragraph.[7]

2. Regulation of assemblies

The requirement to obtain authorisation for an assembly does not as such constitute an interference.[8]   **IIB–155**

Whether a ban on processions is justified will depend on whether other less restrictive measures, including the imposition of conditions on the assembly as to time or place, are practicable. Where there was a one month ban on processions in London imposed by the police, the Commission considered that a general ban could only be justified if there was a real danger of disorder which could not be avoided by less stringent measures. In that case, it accepted that there was a tense atmosphere; that the police presence at other processions had not stopped damage to persons and property; and that 2,400 officers were necessary to police a National Front march. It also noted as regarded proportionality that the meetings could still be held in London, as well as processions outside London.[9]

Once there is some connection with public order, the Commission tended to afford a broad margin of appreciation to authorities' measures.[10] Where a ban on rallies in Trafalgar Square concerning Northern Ireland was applied to "Peace Now", a non-partisan group advocating negotiations, the Commission accepted the necessity to prohibit the meeting even though there was no real expectation of violence. The policy, based on politically sensitive considerations, was perceived as following the aim of prevention of disorder in a general sense. Nor was it disproportionate since it appeared that in the past a meeting by an Ulster group had turned into a political rally and it was reasonable for the authorities to seek to avoid a recurrence. It again was noted that it was open to hold the rally in other locations.[11]

The Court continues to apply in this sphere a wide margin of appreciation.[12] Considerable leeway was given in *Cissé v France*, where, although the Court regretted the manner of police eviction of illegal aliens from the church in which they had taken refuge, it considered that the authorities had shown a sufficient amount of toleration in permitting the occupation for two months and that it was not unreasonable to end the occupation. The grounds of justification are somewhat vague, since the protest had been peaceful and there had been no breach of public order. Reference was made instead to the deterioration in the health of hunger

---

[7] 13079/87 (Dec.) March 6, 1989, 60 D.R. 256.

[8] 8191/78, n.2 above.

[9] 8440/78, n.5 above.

[10] *e.g.* 8191/78, n.2 above, where there was a ban on all political meetings following a controversy over cantonal reorganisation with local feeling running high; 9905/82 (Dec.) March 15, 1984 36 D.R.187, where there was a ban on a meeting of a pro-German unification group justified by Austria's constitutional and international obligations to safeguard its statehood; 31416/96, (Dec.) October 19, 1998, concerning restrictions on assemblies near Stonehenge.

[11] 25522/94, n.1 above; also the *Gypsy Council v UK*, 66336/01, (Dec.) May 14, 2002, where restrictions on the traditional gypsy fair at Horsmonden were not disproportionate having regard to the possibility to hold a larger event at another location and the perceived disruption to public order relied on by the police.

[12] *Cissé*, para.53.

strikers inside the church and the inadequate sanitary conditions. Applying the wide margin of appreciation to these circumstances, the Court concluded that the restriction was not disproportionate.

In contrast, in *Stankov and the United Macedonian Organisation Ilinden v Bulgaria*, which concerned prohibitions over many years on commemorative meetings by a Macedonian association perceived by the authorities to be a threat to the territorial integrity of Bulgaria, the Court emphasised the right of the inhabitants of a region to assert a minority consciousness and that the key issue was whether there had been any incitement to violence. In the absence of any espousal of violent aims or likelihood of violence arising at the meetings, the risk of separatist declarations being made was not sufficient to justify a systematic and sweeping ban. The authorities were found to have overstepped the margin of appreciation in this case.[13]

States must also refrain from applying unreasonable indirect restrictions upon the right to assemble peacefully. Thus in *Djavit An v Turkey* the refusal to grant permits to the applicant to cross into southern Cyprus which prevented him from attending bi-communal meetings for six years constituted an interference with the applicant's freedom of assembly and disclosed a violation of Art.11 in the absence of any adequate law in existence regulating such restrictions.

3. Penalties for participation in public demonstrations

IIB–156 Minor criminal sanctions following protests which breach public order or obstruct the highway have been not been found disproportionate.[14]

Where a penalty is imposed on a person for participation in a lawful assembly in which there is no indication that they behaved in an unlawful or unruly manner, issues of proportionality are likely to arise. In *Ezelin v France*, the applicant lawyer participated in demonstration during which some participants shouted insults and painted graffiti. Disciplinary proceedings were brought against him and he was reprimanded for breach of professional discretion. The argument that the applicant had been free to participate but sanctioned only afterwards was not successful. There was an interference resulting from the sanction imposed on him for failing to disassociate himself from the demonstrators' insulting acts by leaving the procession. While the Court accepted that it pursued the prevention of disorder and that the penalty was light, the importance of the right was such that no sanction was compatible with Art.11 where a participant was not guilty of any reprehensible act in taking part in a demonstration that had been lawful.

In *Steel v United Kingdom*,[15] where the five applicants had participated in various protest activities and been arrested and detained, the Court examined the circumstances of each incident. Where two applicants had acted in a way likely to cause a breach of the peace, by walking in front of a grouse shooter about to take aim or climbing into trees about to be felled, the measures were not considered disproportionate. Where however three applicants were involved in a peaceful

---

[13] paras 90 and 107: while States enjoyed a wider margin of appreciation where there has been incitement to violence, the Court rejected the Government argument that a wider margin applied to issues touching on national symbols or national identity.

[14] 9278 and 9415/81, (Dec.) October 3, 1983 35 D.R. 30, where Lapps were arrested for a public protest outside Parliament after 4 days in a tent in area open to public traffic; 13079/87, n.7 above, conviction for sit-in in road as a non-violent obstruction of traffic.

[15] September 23, 1998, R.J.D. 1998–VII, No.91.

protest, giving out leaflets against the sale of fighter helicopters at a conference centre, the Court was not satisfied that the police had reasonable grounds for apprehending that breach of the peace might arise and the interference with their rights was disproportionate. The issues were dealt with by the Court under Art.10 and it did not consider it necessary to give separate consideration to the complaints raised under Art.11.[16]

4. Protection of "peaceful assemblies"

Freedom of peaceful assembly, if it is to be effective, cannot be limited merely to an obligation on the State not to interfere. The Court has found that positive measures may be required to regulate conduct between individuals. Participants must be able to hold a demonstration without fear of physical violence from those who oppose their ideas otherwise they will be deterred from openly expressing their opinions. In a democracy the right to counter demonstrate cannot extend to inhibiting the exercise of the right to demonstrate.[17]

IIB–157

Positive measures appear to impose a duty to take reasonable and appropriate measures to enable lawful demonstrations to proceed peacefully. It does not involve an absolute guarantee and there is a wide discretion accorded to the authorities as to the means to be used. No violation was found in *Platform Ärzte v Austria*, where counter demonstrators disrupted the applicant association's open air service, interrupting with loudspeakers and throwing eggs. Although the applicant association claimed the authorities had failed to protect its freedom of peaceful assembly, the Commission found, and the Court agreed, that the authorities had not failed in their duty since the police had been present in large numbers and had interposed themselves between the opposing groups and no damage or serious clash had occurred.

There is however no positive obligation to require privately owned shopping centres to allow access to individuals for the purpose of campaigning on issues of public interest.[18]

Cross-reference

Part IIB: Freedom of association
Part IIB: Freedom of expression
Part IIB: Religion, thought and conscience

---

[16] Also *Caroline Lucas v UK*, 39013/02, (Dec.) March 18, 2003, where the Court rejected the applicant's complaints under Arts 10 and 11, finding that it was not disproportionate to arrest the applicant for sitting in the road during a protest, conduct reasonably regarded as falling within the concept of breach of the peace.

[17] *Platform Ärzte*, para.32.

[18] *Appleby.*, n.6 above. The case was examined principally under Art.10, but the Court found that largely identical considerations arose under Art.11 (para.52).

Freedom of association

Key provision:

IIB–158 Article 11 (freedom of association).

Key case law:

National Union of Belgian Police v Belgium, October 27, 1975, Series A, No.19; 1 E.H.R.R. 518; *Swedish Engine Drivers' Union v Sweden*, February 6, 1976, Series A, No.20; 1 E.H.R.R. 617; *Schmidt and Dahlstrom v Sweden*, February 6, 1976, Series A, No.21; 1 E.H.R.R. 632; *Le Compte, Van Leuven and de Meyere v Belgium*, June 23, 1981, Series A, No.43; 4 E.H.R.R. 1; *Young, James and Webster v UK*, August 13, 1981, Series A, No.44; 4. E.H.R.R. 38; *Sibson v UK*, April 20, 1993, Series A, No.258–A; 17 E.H.R.R. 193; *Sigurjonsson v Iceland*, June 30, 1993, Series A, No.264; 16 E.H.R.R. 462; *Gustafsson v Sweden*, April 25, 1996, R.J.D. 1996–II, No.9; 22 E.H.R.R. 409; *United Communist Party v Turkey*, January 30, 1998, R.J.D. 1998–I, No.62; 26 E.H.R.R. 121; *Sidiropoulos v Greece*, July 10, 1998, R.J.D. 1998–IV; 27 E.H.R.R. 633; *Chassagnou v France*, April 29, 1999, ECHR 1999–III; *Rekvenyi v Hungary*, May 20, 1999, ECHR 1999–III; 30 E.H.R.R. 519; *Grande Oriente d'Italia di Palazzo Guistiniani v Italy*, August 2, 2001, ECHR 2001–VIII; *Wilson, National Union of Journalists v UK*, July 2, 2002, ECHR 2002–IV; *Refah Partisi (the Welfare Party) v Turkey*, February 13, 2003, ECHR 2003–II; *Gorzelik v Poland*, February 17, 2004, ECHR 2004–I.

1. General considerations

IIB–159 The freedom of association is a general capacity for all persons to join with others without interference by the State to attain a particular end.[1] It does not imply a right to attain the end sought.[2] It implies a negative right, not to be compelled to join an association, an aspect which has relevance in the area of trade unions. Freedom of assembly is an associated right which is dealt with separately.

2. Formation and dissolution of associations

IIB–160 The Commission expressed doubt as to whether the refusal to give legal status to an association constituted an interference within the scope of Art.11, para.1, where registration could not be considered an obstacle to the association pursuing its objectives.[3] However in more recent cases, the refusal to register has been found to be an interference without discussion.[4]

---

[1] It does not guarantee a general ability to mix socially with others, *e.g.* a prisoner cannot derive right to associate with other prisoners—where applicants were in isolation punishment the Commission took view that the complaints were incompatible *ratione materiae* as Art.11 concerned freedom to form or be affiliated to group or organisation pursuing particular aims. Despite the Government's argument in *United Communist Party* , it applies to political parties.

[2] 6094/73, (Dec.) July 6, 1977, 9 D.R. 5.

[3] 14223/88, (Dec.) June 5, 1991, 70 D.R. 218.

[4] *Sidiropoulos*, para.31; *Gorzelik*, para.52.

Where decisions by the authorities relating to the formation and dissolution of associations are found to interfere with the rights under Art.11, assuming such measures are prescribed by law, a considerable margin of appreciation is left to the authorities as to the necessity of the regulation. Refusal of registration on grounds of objection to the proposed name was acceptable where there was no indication that the association could not be registered under another name.[5] In a French case, concerning refusal of registration of the applicant's association promoting surrogate motherhood as contrary to the criminal code (incitement of child abandonment), the Commission found the interference justified having regard in particular to the margin of appreciation applying to the controversial subject of surrogacy and considering that the applicant could still carry out activities.[6] Similar leeway was given where a Portugese association supporting the old royal house of Braganza was dissolved, the Commission finding that such a decision could be considered as necessary to promote public order.[7] A refusal to register an association which through its memorandum of association sought to achieve the status of a national minority and thereby electoral privileges not accorded by domestic law was found justified to protect the existing democratic order and not disproportionate as it was not aimed preventing its cultural activities or manifestations of Silesian identity.[8]

Nonetheless, there has been an increased recognition of the role associations play in political life and in expressing and promoting the identity and culture of national and ethnic minorities.[9] Where therefore measures are taken against associations alleged to pursue objectives contrary to the State, the Commission and Court have emphasised that democratic societies have to tolerate a wide range of opinions, including those opposed to officially-sanctioned positions and that interferences have to be convincingly justified. The refusal of Greek authorities to register a Macedonian cultural association was an undisputed interference with its members' freedom of association which was not justified by relevant and sufficient reasons or proportionate. It found that it was not established that the association harboured separatist intentions or violent intention, and the fact that it promoted the idea of a "Macedonian" minority did not justify the measure.[10]

In *United Communist Party v Turkey*, the Court found that the reference in the Party's constitution to the Kurdish problem, perceived by the Government as a threat to the State's territorial integrity, did not justify the dissolution of the party. The constitution was geared to the democratic process and the Party had not engaged in activities at variance with that. Given the essential role of political parties in particular in the proper functioning of democracy, the Court held that the exceptions set out in Art.11 were to be construed strictly in their regard and only convincing and compelling reasons could justify restrictions on such parties' freedom of association.[11] In subsequent cases about dissolution of political parties in Turkey, the Court emphasised that the essential factor was whether the programme of the

---

[5] *APEH v Hungary*, 32367/96, (Dec.) August 31, 1999: the name, using the title of the tax authority, was allegedly defamatory and a potential source of confusion.
[6] 14223/88, (Dec.) June 5, 1991, 70 D.R. 218.
[7] 23892/94, (Dec.), October 16, 1995, 83–A D.R. 57 though the activities of the association hardly seemed a real threat to undermine the State; also 8652/79, (Dec.) October 15, 1981, 26 D.R. 89: banning Moon sect associations; 6741/74, (Dec.) May 21, 1976, 5 D.R. 83.
[8] *Gorzelik*.
[9] *Gorzelik*, paras 89–93.
[10] *Sidiropoulos*, paras 40–47.
[11] *United Communist Party*, para.46; *Freedom and Democracy Party (Ozdep)*, para.44.

party in question contained anything which could be regarded as a call for violence, an uprising or any other form of rejection of democratic principles.[12] Though the Court noted the Government's arguments in these cases as to the real underlying intentions of the banned parties and accepted that it might be necessary to compare official documents with acts and declarations made in practice, none of the parties concerned had acted in a way justifying their dissolution.[13]

However, in *Refah Partisi v Turkey*, where the Constitutional Court dissolved a popular political party perceived as advocating Islamic fundamentalism, the Court found that the Party could be regarded as posing a risk to the democratic constitution of the State in that it intended to set up a plurality of legal systems based on religious differences which would infringe the principle of non-discrimination and to introduce *sharia* which was incompatible with the democratic ideals of pluralism or human rights. It also took into account, somewhat rigorously, that the Party did not exclude recourse to force to implement its policy. The dissolution therefore met a "pressing social need" and was proportionate.[14]

3. Public law institutions and compulsory membership

IIB–161 Article 11 does not cover public law institutions. An obligation on a person to join a professional or occupational institution which is of a public law nature, pursuing aims of public regulation, will not offend, although it is relevant whether the applicant is able to join other professional associations to protect his interests.[15]

The fact that an association fulfills some statutory functions will not be decisive as to "public" status where the principal object is to protect the professional interests of its members. In *Sigurjonsson v Iceland*, the Government argued that FRAMI (taxi association) was a professional organisation of public law character, carrying out a role in price-fixing of services under approval of the administration. The Court found notwithstanding these aspects that it was primarily a private law association which protected the professional interests of its members and promoted solidarity, for example, by negotiation and presenting demands relating to working hours. The domestic characterisation of the institution has only relative value as the term

---

[12] *Socialist Party v Turkey*, May 25, 1998, R.J.D. 1998–III, paras 46–47; *Freedom and Democracy Party (Ozdep) v Turkey*, December 8, 1999, ECHR 1999–VIII, para.40.

[13] *United Communist Party*, para.48; *Yazar (HEP Party) v Turkey*, April 9, 2002; ECHR 2002–II, para.60; *DEP Party v Turkey*, December 10, 2002, para.47—though the speech of an ex-leader of the party given in Iraq was identified as approving the use of force, this one incident did not justify the dissolution of the party. Nor did the Court take into account the conviction, subsequent to the dissolution, of several DEP M.P.s of terrorist offences, noting that the trial had violated Art.6 (*Sadak v Turkey*, July 17, 2001, ECHR 2001–VIII) and that in any event these matters had not played a role in the Constitutional Court's decision to dissolve the party.

[14] The Grand Chamber was unanimous. The earlier Chamber judgment of July 31, 2001 had found no violation by a narrow margin. The minority found no convincing evidence that the party used or encouraged the use of violence or undemocratic means to destroy the secular system or establish the supremacy of an Islamic regime, in particular since when it was in power it took no such steps. It considered the Constitutional Court's reasoning, concerned with the anti-secularism of the party, did not justify the extreme measure of dissolution under Art.11 of the Convention.

[15] *Le Compte*; 14331–2/88, (Dec.) September 8, 1989, 62 D.R. 309 (obligation to join the *ordre des architectes*); 13750/88, (Dec.), July 2, 1990, 66 D.R. 188 (bar association in Spain); 14596/89, (Dec.), July 10, 1991, 71 D.R.158 (Austrian chambers of trade); 44319/98, (Dec.) April 3, 2001 (compulsory membership of notary chambers).

"association" has an autonomous meaning under the Convention. The key question is whether the body is an association for the purposes of Art.11.[16]

Outside public law and professional institutions, the Court has looked less leniently on compulsory membership of associations. In *Chassagnou v France*, the Court found the imposition of membership of hunting associations on the applicant landowners violated their freedom of assocation, giving particular weight in that case to the fact that they were being forced to join an association fundamentally contrary to their ethical convictions.[17]

4. Trade union aspects

Trade union freedom is a special aspect of the freedom of association. But it does not guarantee any particular treatment of trade unions or their members by the State. The phrase "for the protection of his interests" indicates that the provision is intended to protect the occupational interests of members by trade union action. This will include the right for the trade union to be heard although the State is left with a free choice in the means to be used towards this end. Under national law, trade unions should be enabled in conditions not at variance with Art.11 to strive for the protection of their members' interests.[18]

IIB–162

(a) *State responsibility*

Even if a Government is not directly responsible for the actions of or agreements reached by unions and employers, where the domestic law renders lawful such measures, State responsibility under Art.1 is engaged. Contracting States must therefore maintain supervisory control over trade unions and the way they wield their powers[19] and ensure that domestic law secures the rights contained in Art.11.[20]

IIB–163

(b) *Right of consultation*

The right to be consulted by the executive before measures are adopted is not implied. In *National Union of Belgian Police v Belgium*, where only a restricted number of trade unions were officially consulted, the National Union was able to present claims and make representations nonetheless, and while its lack of formal consultative status may have made it less attractive to prospective members, this did not disclose an interference under Art.11.

IIB–164

(c) *Collective bargaining*

Article 11 does not secure any particular treatment of unions or their members by the State such as the right that the State enter into any collective agreement with them. It has been found that collective bargaining is not indispensable for the

IIB–165

---

[16] *Chassagnou*, paras 100–102, where hunting associations were not public law institutions, consisting of private individuals and not exercising any processes of a public authority—paras 100–102.
[17] See paras 103–117.
[18] *National Union of Belgian Police*, para.39.
[19] *Young, James and Webster*.
[20] *Wilson, NUJ*, para.41.

effective enjoyment of trade union freedom and in no way constitutes an element necessarily inherent in the right, even where this may damage the union through reducing its membership.[21] A requirement on a trade union to provide an employer with the list of members before voting on industrial action was not regarded as a significant or disproportionate restriction on the right to take collective action.[22] Nor does the freedom of a trade union to make its voice heard extend to imposing on an employer an obligation to recognise a trade union.[23]

(d) *Preferential treatment/ discrimination*

IIB–166   As implied above, the practice by State authorities in conferring special recognition or status on particular unions has been found to compatible with the Convention. The Belgian system of conferring consultation status on three unions of State officials and not on the applicant police union was found to pursue a legitimate aim of ensuring a coherent and balanced staff policy, avoiding "trade union anarchy". Nor were the means used disproportionate as the disadvantage to the applicant was not deemed to be excessive.[24] A similar policy in Sweden did not offend proportionality, where the State preferred to sign collective agreements only with widely representative unions, to avoid excessive numbers of negotiating parties. The Court found no ill-intentioned designs in that policy.[25]

(e) *Right NOT to join a trade union*

IIB–167   In the leading case of *Young, James and Webster v United Kingdom*, the Court found that the notion of a "freedom" implied some choice in its exercise. Thus a negative right could not be excluded from the ambit of Art.11.[26] The test it applied was to examine whether in the particular case before it the form of compulsion struck at the very substance of the right guaranteed. Since the three applicants had received notices terminating their employment for failure to join a union, this was found to be the case. The Court noted that even had the applicants joined another union, they would still have been dismissed and it considered that their freedom of action had been rendered non-existent or of no practical value. This individual right outweighed the alleged general desirability of closed shops in the public interest.

---

[21] *Schmidt and Dahlstrom,* para.34; see also *Swedish Engine Drivers' Union* where the State had entered into a collective agreement with three large federations but refused to accept the smaller union, the Court noted that it was not mentioned specifically as a right, nor accepted in all Contracting States. Since individuals were free to join any trade union and the applicant union was able to engage in various kinds of activity, the refusal of the executive to enter into a collective agreement did not disclose a breach even if the union membership was suffering as a result; *Wilson, NUJ,* paras 44; 18881/91, (Dec.) January 13, 1992, 72 D.R. 278.

[22] 28910/95, (Dec.) April 16, 1998, where the Commmission found nothing sinister or intimidatory in the requirement.

[23] *Wilson, NUJ,* para.44.

[24] *National Union of Belgian Police.*

[25] Also 6094/73, n.2 above, where one student association was chosen as the official body with compulsory membership and another association complained of discrimination, the Commission found nothing unreasonable in the authorities choosing one union for the purpose of concentrating students together to facilitate the proper adminstration of the university.

[26] Also *Sigurjonsson,* where the Court's views on the negative right were stronger, noting that few Contracting States imposed compulsory membership and referring to international materials, *i.e.* ILO, EU, Council of Europe.

The Court was not persuaded that unions could not pursue their interests without compulsory memberships.[27]

While in *Young, James and Webster*, the Court emphasised the element of exertion of pressure to compel some-one to join an association contrary to his conviction, which had to considered also in light of Arts 9 and 10, it is not necessary for an applicant to object to trade union membership on any particular point of principle.[28] In *Sigurjonsson v Iceland*, the Government argued that the taxi association was non-political and that membership was not a question of the applicant's beliefs since he had previously joined the association. The Court considered that Arts 9 and 10 could still be affected since the applicant held a belief in freedom of occupation. Since he now wished to leave and was subject to compulsion striking at the heart of the right, there was a violation. The nature and strength of the objection may however be of relevance in the balancing exercise in assessing the proportionality of any interference.[29]

The Court's approach is to consider whether a proper balance is struck between the interests of the individual and any general interest in maintaining the compulsory membership, but has stated its objections to what may be construed as abuse of a dominant position.[30]

Compulsion which falls short of dismissal or removal of livelihood[31] may not strike at the heart of the right. In *Sibson v United Kingdom*, where an employee was faced with being sacked or moved to another depot, on roughly equivalent terms and pursuant to the terms of his contract, there was no violation.

(f) *Trade union relationships with members*

The right to join a trade union does not include the right to join a union of one's choice regardless of the rules. Trade unions must remain free to decide in accordance with union rules questions relating to admission to and expulsion from the union. Protection is primarily against interference by the State, although the State has to protect the individual against abuse of a dominant position. Expulsion from a union which was in breach of union rules, pursuant to arbitrary rules or entailing exceptional hardship, could constitute such abuse.[32]   **IIB–168**

Other objections of members to internal union rules have not disclosed abuse, *e.g.* where a union subscribed to compulsory collective home insurance on behalf of members.[33]

(g) *Trade union pressure on employers*

The position of the employer who may be the subject of intense union pressure is perhaps less protected by the Convention. While Art.11 applies to an employer forced to sign a collective agreement by a trade union, it does not extend to   **IIB–169**

---

[27] Also *Sigurjonsson*, para.41.
[28] Two applicants had objected to trade union policies and one to its political affiliations.
[29] *e.g. Sibson*, para.29.
[30] *Young, James and Webster*, para.63.
[31] *Sigurjonsson*: removal of taxi licence.
[32] 10550/83, (Dec.), May 13, 1985, 42 D.R. 178: the expulsion of the applicant from APEX due to TUC pressure was the act of a private body not engaging State responsibility since he did not lose his job and the measure was not in breach of union rules.
[33] 13537/88, (Dec.) May 7, 1990, 65 D.R. 202.

granting a right not to join a collective agreement.[34] The Court has referred to a wide margin of appreciation, noting the sensitive character of the social and political issues involved and the wide divergence of practice in Contracting States. It also gives weight to the interests of trade unions in undertaking industrial action, observing that the individual right to join trade unions for the "protection of his interests" implies action can be taken to protect occupational interests of trade unions.[35]

Thus, in *Gustafsson v Sweden*, where a restaurant owner was placed under considerable pressure by lawful industrial action aimed at securing his participation in a collective bargaining agreement, the Court found no violation having regard in particular to the margin of appreciation, the special character of collective bargaining in Sweden[36] and the consideration that the applicant could have avoided membership of an employer's association by an alternative, substitute agreement.[37] The view of the Court majority seemed to discount the relevance of the applicant's political objection to joining a collective agreement and imply that the infliction of economic damage is not enough to strike at the heart of the right where an employer is concerned.

(h) *Prohibition on trade union membership*

IIB–170　A special exception is contained in the second paragraph of Art.11, namely, the lawful imposition of restrictions on the exercise of rights by police, armed forces and administration of the State, which is not qualified by reference to the necessity of the measure. When GCHQ staff were not permitted to join any existing trade union, the Commission found that their functions were similar to that of police and vital to national security and therefore to be considered as part of the administration of the State. While the applicants argued that "restrictions" could not mean extinction of the right, the Commission found that, having regard to the wide margin of appreciation accorded in the protection of national security and the previous disruption by industrial action, the measure was not arbitrary. [38]

(i) *Disincentives on trade union membership*

IIB–171　Where domestic law permitted employers to offer financial incentives to employees to enter into new contracts by which they relinquished the right to trade union representation and the right to certain forms of industrial action, the Court found in *Wilson, National Union of Journalists v United Kingdom* that this effectively undermined or frustrated the trade union's ability to strive for the protection of its interests. By

---

[34] *Gustafsson*, para.52.

[35] *Gustafsson*, para.45.

[36] The Government emphasised that the applicant was challenging an important element in the "Swedish model" of industrial relations which was important to their welfare state, *i.e.* control by collective agreements rather than legislation.

[37] See also the Commission's opinion that the harsh measures (resulting in the sale of the applicant's restaurant) were not counterbalanced by strong legitimate interests in forcing him to sign a collective agreement; and two dissenting judges who considered that compulsion to enter a collective bargaining system was equally an infringement on negative freedom of association incompatible with an element inherent in that freedom, *e.g.* freedom for the applicant to negotiate his own labour agreements.

[38] 11603/85, (Dec.) January 20, 1987, 50 D.R. 228.

thus permitting employers to induce employees to surrender important union rights, the State had failed in its positive obligation to secure the enjoyment of Art.11 rights.

(j) *Right to strike*

The right to strike is not expressly guaranteed.[39] Where a German teacher, a civil **IIB–172** servant, was fined for voting to go on strike, the Commission noted that Germany generally accepted the right to strike but that civil servants were excluded due to the special character of their functions. Since there were no other elements restricting rights under Art.11, para.1, the Commission considered the ban acceptable.[40] It was also proportionate to issue an order prohibiting the strike of oil rig workers and to impose mediation and collective bargaining, where the union had already exercised its right to strike for 36 hours to some effect and there was the prospect of serious consequences to State revenue and damage to the installations if matters dragged on. The Court did emphasise that this did not mean a system of compulsory arbitration for bringing lawful strikes to an end would be considered proportionate in all cases and referred to specific and exceptional circumstances existing in that case.[41] Nor was it disproportionate for a court to prohibit a strike intended to force a public employer into protecting hypothetical future employees by effecting agreements with private companies to which it might transfer its functions, the Court finding that this did not effectively prevent the trade union's current members from safeguarding their own interests.[42]

5. Prohibitions on, or penalties flowing from, membership of an association

Where a person is penalised due to membership or activities as member of an **IIB–173** association or party or barred from such, the Court has often examined the issues under Art.10 of the Convention and dealt with Art.11 complaints as subsidiary. For example in *Vogt v Germany*, where the applicant school teacher had been dismissed due to her membership of the Communist Party, the Court carried out its assessment of legitimate aim, necessity and proportionality under Art.10 and after finding a violation of Art.10 on the basis of a lack of convincing justification for the measure, even in light of historical considerations attaching to the independence of the civil service, concluded that there was a violation of Art.11 on the essentially the same grounds.[43] However, in *Rekvenyi v Hungary*, where the applicant police officer was barred from political activities, including membership of any party, the Court found no violation under Art.10, acknowledging the importance in newly post-Communist Hungary of de-politicising the police, and for the same reasons, no violation of Art.11.

In *Grande Oriente d'Italia di Palazzo Guistiniani v Italy*, a freemason association complained of a new law barring freemasons from regional public office. While

---

[39] *Schmidt and Dahlstrom*, para.36.
[40] 10365/83, (Dec.) July 5,1984, 39 D.R. 237.
[41] *Federation of Offshore Workers' Trade Unions v Norway*, 38190/97, June 27, 2002, ECHR 2002–VI.
[42] *UNISON v UK*, January 10, 2002, ECHR 2002–I.
[43] September 26, 1995, Series A, No.323; also *Ahmed v UK*, September 2, 1998, R.J.D. 1998–VI, where the restrictions on local authority officers' political activities was found proportionate under Art.10, no violation followed under Art.11.

accepting that the law had the legitimate aim of maintaining public order and national security in an atmosphere of suspicion by the public of the role played by freemasons, the Court found that the chilling effect on the freedom of assocation in circumstances where membership was not in itself a reprehensible act could not be regarded as necessary in a democratic society.[44]

Cross-reference

Part IIB: Freedom of assembly

---

[44] Also *NF v Italy*, August 2, 2001, ECHR 2001–IX, where a applicant magistrate was disciplined for joining a freemason lodge, the law was insufficiently precise to satisfy the criterion "prescribed by law."

Freedom of expression

Key provision:

Articles 10 (freedom of expression and to impart and receive information) and 17 **IIB–174**
(bar on interpreting Convention to confer rights to engage in any activity aimed at
the destruction or limitation on its rights and freedoms).

Key case law:

Handyside v UK, December 7, 1976, Series A, No.24; *The Sunday Times (No.1) v UK*,
April 26, 1979, Series A, No.30; 2 E.H.R.R. 245; *Barfod v Denmark*, February 22,
1989, Series A, No.149; 13 E.H.R.R. 493; *Oberschlick v Austria (No.1)*, May 23,
1991, Series A, No.204; *The Observer and The Guardian v UK*, November 26, 1991,
Series A, No.216; 14 E.H.R.R. 153; *The Sunday Times v UK (No.2)*, November 26,
1991, Series A, No.217; 14 E.H.R.R. 229; *Thorgeir Thorgeirson v Iceland*, June 25,
1992, Series A, No.239; 14 E.H.R.R. 843; *Chorherr v Austria*, August 25, 1993,
Series A, No.266–B; 17 E.H.R.R. 358; *Vereinigung Weekblad Bluf! v Netherlands*,
February 9, 1995, Series A, No.306–A; 20 E.H.R.R. 189; *Piermont v France*, April
27, 1995, Series A, No.314; *Prager and Oberschlick v Austria*, April 26, 1995, Series
A No.313; 21 E.H.R.R. 1; *Goodwin v UK*, March 27, 1996, R.J.D. 1996–II, No.7;
22 E.H.R.R. 123; *De Haes and Gijssels v Belgium*, February 24, 1997, R.J.D. 1997–I,
No.30; 25 E.H.R.R. 1; *Oberschlick v Austria (No.2)*, July 1, 1997, R.J.D., 1997–IV,
No.42; 25 E.H.R.R. 357; *Worm v Austria*, August 29, 1997, R.J.D. 1997–V,
No.45; *Lehideux and Isorni v France*, September 23, 1998, R.J.D., 1998–VII, No.92;
30 E.H.R.R. 665; *Fressoz and Roire v France*, January 21, 1999, ECHR 1999–I; 31
E.H.R.R. 28; *Bladet Tromso and Stensaas v Norway*, May 20, 1999, ECHR 1999–III;
29 E.H.R.R. 125; *Bergens Tidende v Norway*, May 2, 2000, ECHR 2000–IV; *Lopes
Gomes da Silva v Portugal*, September 28, 2000, ECHR 2000–X; *Roy and Malaurie v
France*, October 3, 2000, ECHR 2000–X; *Tammer v Estonia*, February 6, 2001,
ECHR 2001–I; *Jerusalem v Austria*, February 27, 2001, ECHR 2001–II; *Feldek v
Slovakia*, July 12, 2001, ECHR 2001–VIII; *Perna v Italy*, May 6, 2003, ECHR
2003–V; *Roemen and Schmit v Luxembourg*, February 25, 2003, ECHR 2003–IV;
Pedersen and Baadsgaard v Denmark, June 19, 2003, ECHR 2003.

1. General principles

Freedom of expression has provoked some of the most concentrated and emphatic **IIB–175**
case law from the Convention organs. It often involves the cleaner cases (fewer
terrorists, criminals, or other undesirables) and raises nice defined issues of principle
for practitioner, politician, academic, civil right activists alike.

Freedom of expression is, the Court has underlined, one of the key pillars on
which an effectively functioning democracy rests. This fundamental importance
underlies the cases. Since the media are the most public and identifiable manifestation of the passage of ideas, information and opinions and therefore the most likely
to feel the effect of any official interference or restriction, a large percentage of the
cases involve journalists. The Court has recognised the role of the media in the free
flow of information and ideas in a democratic society. They are the "watchdog" of
democracy and there is a very strong presumption in practice towards the necessity

of the media being able to operate unhindered. As the case law has developed, there is little scope for restrictions on political speech or on debate of questions of public interest.[1]

The restrictions allowed under the second paragraph of Art.10 must be narrowly interpreted and the necessity for restrictions convincingly established, in addition to being lawful and pursuing legitimate aims.

However the above must be read subject to the Court's view of the role of the Convention organs. The adjective "necessary" implies a "pressing social need" in respect of interferences. Contracting States have a certain margin of appreciation in assessing whether such a need exists though this is subject to a "European supervision" of both the law and decisions applying it. This involves examining whether in light of the case as a whole the measure was proportionate to the legitimate aim pursued and whether the reasons adduced by the national authorities were relevant and sufficient.[2] Factors of significance in balancing the interest in freedom of expression against other claimed interests include the nature and severity of the restriction, its duration,[3] the public interest for and against exercise of the right,[4] whether the reasons for the restriction continue to be valid in light of changing circumstances and the nature of the publication/expression in issue, in particular its tone and balance, its factual accuracy and the relevance to public debate of any comment or opinion. The Court will also take into account whether the national authorities applied standards in conformity with the principles of Art.10 and based themselves on an acceptable assessment of the relevant facts.[5]

2. Scope of the right

IIB–176   The freedom covers not only information and ideas of a popular, uncontroversial nature but also those which might offend, shock or disturb. It protects the substance of the ideas and information expressed and the form in which they are conveyed.[6] It covers artistic expression and commercial speech (see sections 6 and 10 below).

There has not been much discussion over what means of expression is included. In *Groppera* the Government argued that music and advertising on radio did not constitute information or ideas for the purposes of Art.10. The Court did not consider it necessary to decide since broadcasting was separately mentioned in Art.10 as a form of expression without specifying its content. In an early case, the Commission said that Art.10 did not protect the commercial interests of newspapers, save possibly where the State failed in its duty to protect against excessive press concentrations.

The right cannot be invoked where, as set out in Art.17, it would imply the right to engage in any activity or perform any act aimed at the destruction of any of the

---

[1] *e.g. Castells v Spain*, para.43, *Thorgeir Thorgeirson*, para.63; *Murphy v Ireland*, July 10, 2003, para.67; *Sürek v Turkey (No.1)*, July 8, 1999, ECHR 1999–IV, para.61.

[2] *e.g. Sunday Times (No.2)*, para.47.

[3] *Sunday Times (No.1)*: it was relevant that the Thalidomide case had been dormant pending settlement for many years, in a "legal cocoon" from public enquiry.

[4] Where measures are taken to protect public order against disturbance, as in *Chorherr* (a protester arrested at a military parade) or in 28979/95 and 30343/96, (Dec.) January 13, 1997, 88–A D.R. 137 (terrorist aspect—see below) the balance is more readily found to have been respected. See however *Piermont*, where measures against a MEP were not regarded justified by public order.

[5] *e.g. Petersen and Baadersgaard*, para.83; *Perna*, para.39(c).

[6] *e.g. Oberschlick (No.1)*, para.57, *Jersild*, para.31.

rights and freedoms in the Convention, or limit them to an extent greater than provided for therein. Art.17 is very rarely applied however and was unsuccessfully invoked by the French Government in *Lehideux and Isorni v France*, where the applicants complained of their convictions for statements allegedly implying support of collaboration with the Nazis during the war. The Court did not consider that issues about Petain's role, which were part of an ongoing debate amongst historians, belonged to the category of clearly established historical facts, such as the Holocaust, whose negation or revision would be removed from the protection of Art.10 by Art.17.[7] In *Garaudy v France*, where the applicant disputed the reality, breadth and severity of the persecution of the Jews during the Holocaust, the statements were found to conflict with fundamental values of the Convention and pursuant to Art.17 the applicant could not therefore rely on Art.10 in respect of his complaints about his conviction for disputing crimes against humanity.[8]

3. Who can invoke the right?

Legal persons who are editors and publishers of magazines may claim to be victims as well as individuals such a journalists.[9] Trade unions, such as the NUJ, cannot claim to be victim of restrictions affecting their members[10] but journalists and producers of programmes could claim to be affected by measures aimed at broadcasting companies where as employees they were bound to comply with them.[11]   **IIB–177**

4. Media

The Court scrutinises closely measures banning publication by the press. While it may accept that measures pursue legitimate aims, it has required convincing justification. Journalistic freedom is accepted as covering possible recourse to a degree of exaggeration, even provocation.[12] The defences of justification and fair comment should also be available.[13] There is not unlimited freedom however, even for press coverage of matters of serious public concern, with reference being made to the duties and responsibilities inherent in the exercise of the freedom of expression, particularly where the rights of others are involved, requiring journalists to act in   **IIB–178**

---

[7] para.47.

[8] 65831/01, (Dec.) June 24, 2003, ECHR 2003–IX: the Court doubted whether other passages of the book, found by the courts to incite racial hatred, could fall within the scope of Art.10 but in any event found the conviction justified under the second paragraph. In 8348/78 & 8406/78, (Dec.) October 11, 1979, 18 D.R. 187, the Commission found that Art.10, pursuant to Art.17, did not apply to a racially discriminatory publication.

[9] 9615/81, (Dec.), May 5, 1983, 32 D.R. 231.

[10] *e.g.* 11553/85 and 11658/85, (Dec.), March 9, 1987, 51 D.R. 136.

[11] *Purcell v Ireland*, 15404/89, (Dec.) April 16, 1991, 70 D.R. 262.

[12] *e.g. Prager and Oberschlick*, para.38, *De Haes and Gijsels*, para.46.

[13] *e.g. Lingens*; *Oberschlick (No.1)*; *Colombani v France*, June 25, 2002, ECHR 2002–V (where the defence of justification did not apply to *Le Monde*'s article which contained allegations damaging to the reputation of a head of State). Though even where a statement amounts to a value judgment, the proportionality of an interference may depend on whether there is a sufficient factual basis as even a value judgment without any factual basis may be excessive, *e.g. De Haes and Gijsels*, para.47; *Obeschlick (No.2)*, para.33.

good faith in order to provide accurate and reliable information in accordance with the ethics of journalism.[14]

(a) *Injunctions and preventive measures*

IIB–179   Where the matter to be reported is of public interest or importance, it is hard for a State to find justification for the restriction in the absence of established damage to an interest of at least equal importance. Prior restraints are not inherently incompatible with Art.10 but call for careful scrutiny.[15] The Court has noted that delay in publication in the press leads to staleness quickly depriving news of interest and value.[16] Refusals of registrations which are tantamount to the prohibition of publication must be scrutinised under the terms of the second paragraph.[17]

An injunction was not found to be "necessary" in *Sunday Times (No.1) v United Kingdom*, where articles on the Thalidomide drug scandal raised matters of undisputed public concern and were moderate and balanced in nature. Notwithstanding the domestic courts' concern to prevent "trial by newspaper" in pending civil proceedings, the Court commented that courts could not operate in a vacuum and the media had a role in reporting matters that came before the courts, the public having a right to receive such information. An injunction against one newspaper preventing repetition of certain accusations was found proportionate where the domestic courts found that the statements had a competitive aim, including untrue and disparaging statements of fact, beyond participation in a matter of public debate.[18]

Measures to prevent publication or distribution on the basis of the confidential nature of the subject-matter generally cease to be justifiable or proportionate once the material has been made public. Seizure of a weekly periodical publishing security classified material from the Dutch security service was found to be disproportionate since 2,500 copies had already been sold at night and the continued ban on the distribution of the copy no longer served any purpose, notwithstanding the Court's acknowledgment that the security services could claim a high level of protection.[19]

---

[14] *e.g. Fressoz and Roire*, para.48; *Bergens Tidende*, para.53; *Verdens gang and Mrs Aase v Norway*, 45710/99, (Dec.), October 16, 2001, where the Court noted that the newspaper did not take sufficient steps to verify the truth of the allegations against the cosmetic surgeon which they published; *Bladet Tromso*, where the majority found that the newspaper could reasonably rely on the official report in issuing its story without carrying out its own research into the accuracy of the facts reported (the minority considered that the newspaper was aware of the controversy surrounding the report and the risk involved); *Thoma*, where the imposition of a penalty on a journalist for repeating quotations from another source was disproportionate, the Court noting that there could be no general requirement on journalists to systematically and formally distance themselves form the contents of a quotation; *Harlanova v Latvia*, 57313/00, (Dec.) April 3, 2000, where the journalist did nothing to verify the basis of serious allegations or to identify sources of information.

[15] *Observer and Guardian*, para.60; *Gaweda v Poland*, 14 March 2002, ECHR 2002–II, para.35; *Association Ekin v France*, July 17, 2001, para.56, where a blanket executive power to ban foreign books was unjustified.

[16] *Sunday Times (No.2)*, para.51.

[17] *Gaweda*, n.15 above.

[18] *Krone Verlag GmbH & CoKG and Mediaprint v Austria*, 42429/98, (Dec.) March 20, 2003. See also *Andreas Wabl v Austria*, March 21, 2000, paras 40–45, where an injunction limited to preventing a politician repeating the specific term "Nazi-journalism" about a newspaper was justified and it was no excuse that the newspaper had defamed him first.

[19] *Vereniging Weekblad Bluf!*; see also 10038/82, (Dec.) May 11, 1984, 38 D.R. 53 (settled after admissibility). where a solicitor, who allowed a journalist to read documents produced by the Government and read out in open court, was found in contempt of court.

Similarly, although initially an interlocutory injunction on the Observer and Guardian preventing publication of material from the *Spycatcher* book by an ex-MI5 official could be justified as necessary to maintaining the authority of the judiciary and also the aim of national security, once the book was published in the US with no ban on importation into the UK, the Court found that the interest of the plaintiff litigant in maintaining confidentiality had ceased to exist for the purposes of the Convention.[20] The interest identified at that later stage of maintaining confidence in MI5 and preventing their agents publishing in an unauthorised fashion did not justify the injunctions against the newspapers (as opposed to steps against the author himself and accounts for profits for use of confidential material).[21]

(b) *Penal sanctions for publication*

Where an article has been published and the journalist, editor or publisher pursued **IIB–180** by way of criminal sanction, the sanction constitutes an interference that requires convincing justification under the second paragraph. Where an article is based on fact, addresses matters of public interest, the balance is in favour of freedom of expression, notwithstanding polemical, aggressive or even provocative aspects.[22]

In this area, a certain weight is given to the need to protect judges from disparaging attacks. Although the Court has stated that courts as with other public institutions cannot be immune from criticism and scrutiny, a clear distinction had to be drawn between criticism and insult. In the latter case, it has gone so far as to comment that an appropriate punishment would not violate Art.10.[23] Thus, the "special role of the judiciary" which as the guarantor of justice must enjoy public confidence to function successfully outweighed other consideration in *Barfod v Denmark*, where a journalist was convicted for defamation in respect of an article criticising lay judges[24] and in *Prager and Oberschlick v Austria*, where the applicants published a strongly worded critique of the Vienna criminal judges, stepping over the limit of permissible exaggeration.[25] Where however in civil proceedings

---

[20] The measure was initially proportionate and supported by relevant and sufficient reasons since the book was only in manuscript form at that time, it was unclear what damaging disclosures might be made and the substantive action would be prejudiced by the publication.

[21] There was a large Commission and Court minority, with a stricter view on the acceptability of prior restraints, which considered that there was violation from the beginning, having regard to the fact that many of the allegations had been aired in previous publications, that prior restraint was doomed to failure with multinational publishing and to the interest of public in receiving the information.

[22] *e.g. Oberschlick (No.2)*, where the journalist in calling a prominent politician an idiot ("*trottel*") was commenting, albeitly provocatively, on public statements of the politician which were themselves provocative; *Lehideux and Isorni*, paras 52–55, polemical advertisement on the sensitive topic of Petain's collaboration policy, where Court referred to the need for the authorities to debate their own history openly and dispassionately and the inappropriateness of reacting with the same severity as decades ago; *Fressoz and Roire*, paras 51–52 public right to receive information about finances of public figures; *Bladet Tromso*, para.73, the importance of the public interest in seal hunting outweighed the seal hunters' interest in protecting their reputation; *Scharsach and News Verlagsgesellschaft v Austria*, November 13, 2003, para.44, labelling a politician as a "closet Nazi" did not exceed what was acceptable.

[23] *Skalka v Poland*, May 27, 2003, para.34.

[24] The journalist criticising the composition of the court implied that they voted in favour of their local government employer in Greenland in relation to a controversial tax measure.

[25] Narrow majorities: Court 5–4, Commission 15–12. The majority were influenced by the serious nature of the allegations (including breach of law and professional obligations) and that the applicant journalist could not invoke good faith or compliance with professional ethics since his research did not appear

journalists were found to have defamed judges in *De Haes and Gijsels v Belgium*, there was a violation since despite certain provocative elements the articles had an undisputed factual basis.[26] Where an article could reasonably be assessed as prejudicing the outcome of a trial by stating an opinion of guilt, the interests in maintaining the authority and impartiality of the judiciary rendered the imposition of a relatively light penalty by way of fine a not disproportionate interference.[27]

Criticism of police officers and politicians has, in the past, been subject to a more robust approach and more concern to avoid the stifling of open debate.[28] In *Thorgeirson v Iceland*, the conviction of a journalist for defamation of the police ("beasts in uniform") was not found to be justified to protect the rights of police officers. The Court noted that the article was based on objective fact—a known case of ill-treatment—and though expressed in strong terms it concerned a matter of public interest, its main thrust to urge the setting up of an impartial enquiry. In *Lopes Gomes da Silva v Portugal*, in finding disproportionate the conviction of the applicant journalist for an article describing a political candidate as, *inter alia*, 'buffoonish" and "grotesque", the Court commented that political invective often spilled over into the personal sphere, such being the hazards of politics and the free debate of ideas. The article was not however a gratuitous personal attack but was based on facts, supported by an objective explanation on a matter of political debate. On the other hand, no violation was found in respect of the journalist's conviction in *Tammer v Estonia* for offensive remarks on a public figure, about her role as a mother and in breaking up another politician's marriage, which could have been expressed without resort to insult and could not be regarded as pursuing issues in the public interest.

The Court has also drawn a distinction between civil servants and politicians. The limits of acceptable criticism may be wider of civil servants than of private individuals, but it could not be said that they knowingly lay themselves open to close scrutiny of their words and deeds to the same extent as politicians. Indeed, as they had to enjoy public confidence in conditions free of perturbation to fulfill their duties, it may be necessary for the State to protect them from unfounded accusations, particular reference being made to public prosecutors and superior police officers.[29] In *Pedersen and Baadsgaard v Denmark*, the conviction of television journalists for a programmme "The Blind Eye of the Police" levelling accusations of suppression of evidence against a chief superintendent was found to be justified,

---

adequate to substantiate such serious allegations and he had not given any judge an opportunity to comment. The minority put less weight on need to protect judges. In the Commission, the minority considered that judges also to had to act under public scrutiny and should tolerate even exaggerated forms of criticism if based on irrefutable fact.

[26] The articles referred to a controversial child custody case, including allegations of abuse and criticising the court decision in favour of the father, with imputations of cowardice and bias. See also *Skalka*, n.23 above, where a journalist under investigation was convicted for derogatory remarks about regional court judges, the eight month prison sentence was disproportionately severe to the aim of maintaining the authority of the judiciary.

[27] *Worm*, paras 52–58.

[28] See, *e.g. Worm*, para.50; Also Part IIB: Defamation.

[29] *Pedersen and Baadsgaard*, para.66; See also *Lesnik v Slovakia*, March 11, 2003, no violation disclosed by conviction of a non-journalist for allegations of unlawful conduct against a public prosecutor who as part of the proper administration of justice the Court majority considered attracted protection from unfounded accusations.

given the seriousness and factual nature of the allegation of unlawful conduct and the lack of adequate or sufficient research to substantiate it.[30]

Criminal sanction of individuals who make racist or anti-Semitic statements were generally found generally justifiable by the Commission.[31] However there is a fine line between legitimate reporting of nasty social phenomenon and the unacceptable repetition of racist propaganda. In *Jersild v Denmark*, a television programmer was convicted in relation to a documentary on "greenjackets" during which they expressed rascist views. The case turned on the weight given to the freedom of the press to report versus the weight given to offensive nature of the views reported on and the possible risk of encouraging those views by exposure. For the majority of the Court[32] finding a violation, the key factors were that the applicant did not express the racist views himself but was participating in the current public discussion on racism in the country, intending to portray the mentality and background of those racist individuals. It was relevant that the film was part of a serious news programme aimed at an informed audience and that its presentation made it clear that its aim was not the propagation of racism. "Interviewing" was also noted to be an important means of TV journalism and punishment of a journalist for views of the person interviewed would seriously hamper the contribution of the press to discussion of matters of public interest and should not be envisaged without particularly strong reasons.[33]

The Court has generally not been impressed by Government arguments that the penalty resulting from a prosecution was minor, considering that what matters is that the journalist was convicted at all.[34] Regard is sometimes had to the existence of alternative means of intervention and rebuttal, particularly through civil remedies[35] or in *Du Roy and Malaurie*, to the existing protection provided to rights of the accused where the applicant journalists were convicted for disclosing details about criminal proceedings.

(c) *Other restrictions on reporting*

Awards of damages in civil defamation proceedings may disclose unjustified or disproportionate interference with freedom of expression, raising similar considerations as considered above in the context of penal sanctions (see further Pt IIB—Defamation).

IIB–181

---

[30] See also *Perna*, where emphasis was laid on the highly offensive and gratuitous nature of the criticisms against the chief public prosecutor, which the journalist had not sought to verify, in finding the conviction and fine justifiable. The Court made no reference to any public interest in the contents of the article, although the applicant had claimed it was part of a debate on current affairs and public figures.

[31] *e.g.* 9777/82, July 14, 1977, 34 D.R. 158 (conviction for denying the extermination of the Jews).

[32] 12–7: the minority put greater emphasis on the importance of fighting racism which endangered the rights of others,and this outweighed the "good intentions" of journalists who were expected actively criticise racial discrimination (the applicant had not expressly condemned the racist views): the idea of provoking a healthy reaction displayed an optimism belied by experience.

[33] See, *mutatis mutandis, Muslum Gunduz v Turkey*, December 4, 2003—the prosecution of an applicant for extreme religious views expressed during a television programme concerning his muslim sect was disproportionate, where it was part of an ongoing public debate.

[34] *Jersild*, para.35; *Lopes Gomes da Silva*, para.36. Yet in *Tammer*, para.69, the limited fine was taken into account in finding the conviction proportionate and in *Perna*, para.39(d), the Grand Chamber referred to the nature and severity of the sentence as relevant factors.

[35] *Lehideux and Isorni*, para.57.

The Commission found that the administration of justice could require the exclusion of the press from court[36] or that secrecy of jury deliberations be maintained.[37] It is also compatible to impose conditions of accreditation on journalists who attend courts in a privileged capacity.[38] Prohibitions on publishing a certain details may raise issues, if not shown to be necessary. In one case, settled before admissibility, the name of a witness was subject to prohibition even though she was named in open court to avoid prejudicing the defence.[39]

Regarding restrictions imposed on publications about pending proceedings, comment on criminal trials may not extend to statements likely to prejudice, whether intentionally or not, the fair trial of an accused.[40] The Commission found it legitimate to impose a postponement on a TV programme about the Birmingham Six, scheduled for the close of the appeal hearing with portrayal of judges, counsel and witnesses by actors. It considered the restriction proportionate, agreeing that this method differed from press reports on the proceedings which were unaffected and having regard to its duration of eight weeks until the judgment was given. Although objectively judges would not be influenced, the appellants had a right to be assured that they would not be affected by external matters.[41] Similarly, the banning of a Channel Four "Court Report" intending to report a controversial official secrets trial, by way of dramatic reconstruction with actors reading edited highlights of the proceedings, was justified having regard to the real risk of prejudice if watched by the jury and as the programme could be issued with the same information read by newsreaders.[42] Contracting States also have a wide margin of appreciation in regulating the freedom of the press to transmit court hearings live. Thus it was compatible with Art.10 to refuse a radio station permission to transmit a murder trial live on radio, where the restriction applied to the media as a whole and steps had been taken to give access to the press on a non-discriminatory basis.[43] However, the prohibition on the publication by an Austrian newspaper of the photograph of a suspect in pending proceedings had not been shown to be necessary either to protect him against defamation or against violation of the presumption of innocence.[44]

As indicated by the Birmingham Six and Channel Four examples above, television journalism has an impact and immediacy which sometimes attracts interference from State authorities anxious to protect from nefarious influences. The Commission accepted the necessity felt by both the Irish and UK Governments to prevent any

[36] 13366/87, (Dec.) December 3, 1990, 67 D.R. 244: exclusion of press during sentencing. The Commission assumed that there was an interference, given the important role played by media in the administration of justice but Art.6 was of particular weight in a trial context (it allowed for *in camera* proceedings) and the exclusion was at the request of the defendant whose interests outweighed the journalists.

[37] 24770/94, (Dec.) November 30, 1994, heavy fines for newspaper and editors for contempt of court for publication of jurors' opinions on a controversial trial were justifiable, *e.g.* protection for jurors to speak freely in jury room. The Commission left open the question whether for example the interests of justice at a particular trial might justify disclosure.

[38] 23869/94, December 24, 1995, 80–B D.R. 162.

[39] 11552/85, (Dec.) July 15, 1988, 56 D.R. 148.

[40] *e.g. Worm*, para.50; *Du Roy and Malaurie*, para.34; *News Verlags GmbH & CoKG v Austria*, January 11, 2000, ECHR 2000–I, para.56.

[41] 14132/88, (Dec.) April 13, 1989, 61 D.R. 285.

[42] 11553/85 and 11658/85, n.10 above.

[43] *P4 Radio Hele Norge ASA v Norway*, 76682/01, (Dec.) May 6, 2003.

[44] *News Verlags GmbH*, n.40 above.

television exposure of members of the Sinn Fein (and other groups) which might serve the ends of the violent terrorists with whom they were purportedly linked. In *Purcell v Ireland*,[45] the measure prevented coverage of, *inter alia*, Sinn Fein members by way of interviews or recordings on any subject. In finding the restriction proportionate, the Commission stated that the defeat of terrorism was a public interest of the utmost importance and referred to difficulty of striking a fair balance where advocates of this violence seek access to the media for publicity purposes. It was noted that TV and radio were media of considerable power and influence and that their opportunity to correct, qualify or comment was more limited compared to the press. It was also relevant that the ban, although inconvenient, did not in fact prevent them from producing news items on any subject. Regarding a similar ban in the UK which allowed coverage of live interviews on TV but with use of actors' voice-overs, the Commission observed that there was no restriction as to the words or images transmitted and while the logic of the voice-over might be open to dispute, it could be regarded as one aspect of a very important area of domestic policy, namely, combatting terrorism.[46]

Outside the area of publication, journalists may claim some protection in their role as public watchdogs, in particular as regard protection of their sources.[47] This does not extend to an immunity from providing information or film when ordered to do so by a court which considers the material relevant in criminal proceedings.[48] However in *Goodwin v United Kingdom*, where a journalist was fined for contempt of court for refusing to identify the source of his information about a private company's confidential financial report, the Court found that the £5000 fine for contempt of court was a restriction on his freedom of expression and that the coercion exerted on a journalist risked having a chilling effect on future work and the willingness of sources to give information. Safeguards to the press were seen as of particular importance in maintaining freedom of expression in the interests of democratic society. Thus, limitations on the confidentiality of journalistic sources called for the most careful scrutiny. Since an injunction had effectively stopped the leak through the press, the alleged need to uncover the source to obtain the missing plan and prevent other possible leaks was not sufficient in the balance against the vital public interest in the protection of journalistic sources. Searches targeting journalists are regarded as even more serious. In *Roemen and Schmidt v Luxembourg*, Art.10 was breached where the authorities conducted a search of a journalist's home and office seeking to discover sources of leaked information concerning a government minister.[49] It would seem therefore that only an overriding requirement in the public interest, perhaps to prevent a serious crime or unmask the perpetrator of a serious crime, would justify coercive measures taken to identify journalistic sources.

Where journalists deliberately breach confidentiality, sanctions may be found justified. Where a parliamentary journalist was convicted and fined for publishing a

---

[45] n.11 above.

[46] 18714/91, (Dec.) May 9, 1994, 77 D.R. 42.

[47] *e.g. Roemen and Schmidt*, para.46.

[48] Where the BBC were summonsed to produce film of a riot, the Commission found that it was a normal civic duty to give evidence and it was not satisfied that this would result in greater risk to camera crews beyond that already incurred in filming such episodes—25978/94, (Dec.) January 18, 1996, 84–A D.R. 129.

[49] The Court noted that there were other methods by which the authorities could have pursued the leaks, i.e. questioning the civil servants concerned. Similar violation also found in *Ernst v Belgium*, July 15, 2003, where sweeping search warrants were issued to uncover sources of leaks from judicial investigation files.

confidential parliamentary document, the Commission found the measure could be justified for preventing disclosure of material received in confidence and was not disproportionate since the applicant was an accredited journalist who had known the document was confidential and use of penalties was aimed at maintaining the credibility of the system.[50] However, convictions of journalists in *Fressoz and Roire* for breach of professional confidence in respect of their use of confidential tax documents but whose contents were in the public domain was not considered proportionate. Accounting for profits on publication of confidential material was also held justifiable in the *Spycatcher* case.[51] While *The Times* alleged a vital public interest in the information about Government misdeeds, the Commission found no problem as the interference with newspaper's freedom of expression was minor, there was no prior restraint and few profits to account for and the information was obtained from an employee bound by confidentiality, which *The Times* had deliberately and knowingly published.

5. Broadcast licensing and programming

Key case law:

IIB–182   *Groppera Radio v Switzerland*, March 28, 1990, Series A, No.173; 12 E.H.R.R. 321; *Autronic AG v Switzerland*, May 22, 1990, Series A, No.178; 12 E.H.R.R. 485; *Informatsverein Lentia v Austria*, November 24, 1993, Series A, No.276; 17 E.H.R.R. 93; *VgT Verein Gegen Tierfabriken v Switzerland*, June 28, 2001, ECHR 2001–VI; *Murphy v Ireland*, July 10, 2003.

Article 10 contains specific reference in the third sentence of the first paragraph to the provision not preventing States from requiring the licensing of broadcasting, television or cinema enterprises. Briefly, national licensing systems are accepted as necessary for the orderly regulation of broadcasting enterprises and to give effect to international rules. Licensing is for the purpose of organising the technical aspects primarily. However, even where the licensing fulfills that function, it must still satisfy the requirements of para.2.[52] According to the Commission, the third sentence only applied to broadcasting, not to receipt of broadcasts whereas the Court found no need to decide since even if it was applicable there still had to be compliance with the requirements of the second paragraph.[53]

There is a recognition that restrictions should be minimal, with a presumption in favour of free access to transmissions.[54] Where a monopoly is imposed, even if can be said to contribute to the quality and balance of programmes and be consistent with third sentence, it may not prove to be justified in terms of second paragraph, particularly since it requires a pressing need to justify such a severe restriction.

[50] 10343/83, (Dec.), October 6, 1983, 35 D.R. 224.
[51] 14644/89, (Rep.) October 8, 1991, 73 D.R. 41.
[52] *e.g. Tele 1 Privatsfernsehgesellschaft MBH v Austria*, September 21, 2000.
[53] In *Groppera*, a ban on cable re-transmission of radio programmes in Switzerland from an unlicensed Italian station fell within the third sentence and pursued the legitimate aim of protecting the international telecommunications order and the rights of others (those stations with licences).
[54] See *Autronic*, para.61, where the Court stated that rejections should not be manifestly arbitrary or discriminatory and the necessity for any restriction convincingly established. It found no necessity to refuse authorisation to receive uncoded Russian television programmes which concerned no confidential information was concerned and were aimed at the general public.

In *Informatsverein Lentia v Austria*, a violation arose in circumstances where it was impossible to set up a private radio or TV station. The argument that this would prevent private monopolies, was not in the Court's view, borne out by other European countries of comparable size. Quality and variety could be maintained by other means (licensing conditions, etc.); there was no technical need for restrictions as frequencies were available and the *raison d'etre* of rigid monopoly no longer held since transmissions entered from other countries. However, where a terrestrial television broadcasting monopoly was mitigated by the ability of private broadcasters to create and transmit programmes via the cable net, the refusal of a territorial licence was no longer disproportionate.[55] A ban on applications for national radio broadcasting licence by religious bodies was justified to prevent any one group predominating and proportionate in the circumstances as they could apply for local licences.[56]

Some preferential treatment may be acceptable. The Dutch system of offering regional frequencies on a priority basis to public TV broadcasting organisations was compatible with the third sentence, and pursued the legitimate aim of maintaining pluralism, diversity and non-commercialism for audiences in the area.[57]

Regarding restrictions on the broadcasting of particular programmes, the Court found objectionable a ban on political advertising that prevented the airing of the applicant association's commercial denouncing the industrial farming of pigs. Although it found that the ban pursued the legitimate aim of preventing financially powerful groups from obtaining a competitive advantage, it placed emphasis on the need for convincing reasons to restrict participation in an ongoing public debate. As the association in question was not a powerful body which could endanger independent broadcasting or unduly influence public opinion, no "relevant and sufficient" grounds had been shown to arise in the applicant's case.[58] However in *Murphy v Ireland*, concerning a ban on religious advertising, the Court found no violation arising from the refusal to air on radio an advertisement about a presentation on the Resurrection. It found a wider margin of appreciation was to be accorded to the authorities in the sphere of morals and religion than in political speech and had regard to the divisiveness of religion in the history of Ireland, the limitation of the ban to broadcast media and the distinctly partial objectives of advertising, in finding that the Irish State could pursue the policy of a "level playing field" for all religions in the medium with the most powerful impact.

6. Artistic and cinematic

Key case law:

Muller v Switzerland, May 24, 1988, Series A, No.133; 13 E.H.R.R. 212; *Otto Preminger Institute v Austria*, September 20, 1994, Series A, No.295; 19 E.H.R.R. 34; *Wingrove v UK*, November 25, 1996, R.J.D. 1996–V, No.23; 24 E.H.R.R. 1.　　IIB–183

There have been few cases, authorities perhaps feeling their interests less challenged by works of art. The nature of the form of artistic expression may mean that it has a

---

[55] *Tele 1 Privatfernsehgesellschaft MBH*, n.52 above, paras 36–41.
[56] 44802/98, (Dec.) November 7, 2000.
[57] 25987/94, (Dec.) November 29, 1995, 84–A D.R. 149.
[58] *VgT Verein Gegen Tierfabriken*.

very limited audience, without the impact of mass media and that may affect the seriousness of any alleged risk to public disorder flowing from it.[59]

Controversy tends to arise where the "work" provokes religious or moral outrage. Freedom to receive and impart information and ideas includes the opportunity to take part in the public exchange of cultural, political and social information and ideas of all kinds, including artistic expression.[60] Artists cannot claim an unlimited freedom however but are subject to duties and responsibilities under the second paragraph of Art.10. In *Otto Preminger v Austria*, the Court stated that these included an obligation to avoid gratuitously offending others and infringing their rights, since this could not contribute to any public debate capable of furthering progress in human affairs. This approach would appear to place a strict burden on artists to avoid offending, since what is or is not gratuitous may be rather subjective, as shown in the *Otto Preminger* case, where the Court appeared to agree with the authorities that the provocativeness of the film outweighed the artistic merits, while the Commission took the view that the satirical elements predominated.

A wide margin of appreciation is generally afforded by the Court to Contracting States when regulating freedom of expression in relation to matters liable to offend intimate personal convictions within the sphere of morals, or especially, religion.[61] The Court considers that there is no uniform concept of morals, or of the requirements of the protection of religious beliefs, which differ from place to place and time to time. Local State authorities which are in direct and continuous contact with the vital forces of their country are thus, in principle, in a better position to give an opinion on the exact contents of these requirements as well as the necessity of the measures designed to meet them.[62] It found in *Muller v Switzerland*, where a painter and exhibitors were convicted for displaying paintings depicting sexual acts, that the domestic court's view that the emphasis on sexuality in some of its cruder forms was "liable grossly to offend the sense of sexual propriety of persons of ordinary sensitivity" was not unreasonable. It was not persuaded by the applicant's arguments that there had been no public outcry[63] and that he had been able to exhibit abroad and other areas of Switzerland without trouble. The Court was also influenced by the factor that the paintings were open to the public at large without restriction.

There was arguably more public outrage in *Otto Preminger*,[64] where the Salzburg authorities, at the prompting of the Catholic diocese, ordered the seizure and forfeiture of a film about to be shown portraying God, Christ and the Virgin in a satirical manner. The Court emphasised the protection of religious beliefs and the responsibility of the State to ensure the peaceful enjoyment of those rights under Art.9. It accordingly found that the measure pursued the legitimate aim in

---

[59] *Karatas v Turkey*, July 8, 1999, ECHR 1999–IV, para.52, where a poet was given allowance for his colourful imagery that would have limited impact; *Arslan v Turkey*, July 8, 1999, para.48, similar approach to impact of a literary work.

[60] *Muller*, para.27.

[61] e.g. *Wingrove*, para.58.

[62] *Muller*, para.35; *Wingrove*, para.58; 17634/91, (Dec.) September 2, 1991: conviction of artist and gallery owner for outraging public decency by the display of freeze-dried foetus earrings as a sculpture was justified—given the wide margin of appreciation in the area of morals and the public element of the display: no issue arose from the lack of defence of artistic merit.

[63] There had been some complaints—one man had thrown a painting on the floor and stamped on it.

[64] The Court found no violation by 6–3, while the Commission majority voted for violation, noting that the film was based on a play freely available in shops and was only open to an interested, feepaying adult audience.

protecting others from being insulted in their religious feelings. The seizure was necessary since there was a high proportion of Catholics in Tyrol (87 per cent), and although the film was only open to adults, there had been sufficient publicity about the film for public to have an idea about its subject-matter and to render the proposed screening "public" enough to cause offence. The Court considered that the authorities had weighed up the artistic elements against offensiveness and it could not disagree with their view of provocativeness of film. Consequently, the measures taken to ensure religious peace in the region and protect persons who might feel under attack, were within the margin of appreciation of the authorities.

The element of risk to public outrage and religious peace was nevertheless absent from *Wingrove v United Kingdom,* where a short video did not pass the British Board of Film Classification on grounds that it was blasphemous in its portrayal of Christ in a sexual context. The Court however found that the decision pursued the legitimate aim of protecting the rights of others not to be offended in their religious beliefs. Having regard to the wide margin of appreciation and the particular contents of the film, the decision was not arbitrary or unreasonable. It did not accept that argument that such a video could be restricted in its distribution by its classification, since once videos were marketed they were commonly lent, copied and otherwise escaped any regulation.[65]

7. Pornography

Key case law:

Scherer v Switzerland, March 25, 1994, Series A, No.287; 18 E.H.R.R. 276.   IIB–184

Criminal measures taken in respect of sale, distribution or trade in pornographic materials were generally found by the Commission to conform with the requirements of Art.10 as being necessary for the prevention of crime or the protection of morals.[66]

A key factor is whether the pornographic material is on display to the general public or suitably restricted to those adults interested. In *Scherer v Switzerland,* the Commission found a violation arose from the conviction of a porn shop owner for showing obscene homosexual films in part of his premises that was not open to public and as there was no question of the protection of morals of adults generally as none were confronted unintentionally with the material.[67] There were no particularly compelling reasons for the prosecution given. This case distinguished an early application rejected as inadmissible where the measures related to a chain of video shops open to the general public.[68] Protective measures aimed at children will be easier for the authorities to justify. No violation was disclosed by the criminal

---

[65] See also the *Gay News* case 8710/79, (Dec.) May 7, 1982, 28 D.R. 77, where there was a conviction for blasphemy for a poem detailing homosexual acts by Christ, the Commission found it compatible for a State to prohibit attacks of a particular severity on others' beliefs, noting that the material was available to general public and that the judicial authorities found it blasphemous after a thorough investigation.

[66] 9615/81, (Dec.), March 5, 1983, 32 D.R. 231: seizure of magazines destined for overseas markets justified for protection of morals, not as safeguarding those outside the jurisdiction, butas legitimate concern to stop UK becoming centre of flourishing export trade.

[67] Case was struck off before the Court when the applicant died.

[68] 16564/90, (Dec.) April 8, 1991.

prosecution and seizures in respect of "The Little Red Schoolbook" in *Handyside*, which contained factual and useful information on sex education but also passages capable of being interpreted as encouragement to indulge in activities harmful for children or even to commit criminal offences.

8. Parliamentary and electoral context

Key case law:

IIB–185 *Castells v Spain*, April 23, 1992, Series A, No.236; 14 E.H.R.R. 445; *Piermont v France*, April 27, 1995, Series A, No.314; 20 E.H.R.R. 301; *Ahmet Sadik v Greece*, November 15, 1996, R.J.D. 1996–V, No.15; 24 E.H.R.R. 323; *Bowman v UK*, February 19, 1998, R.J.D. 1998–I, No.63; 26 E.H.R.R. 1; *Jerusalem v Austria*, February 27, 2001–II.

The importance of freedom of expression for those participating in the democratic process has been affirmed. The requirement for elected representatives to be able to participate freely in political debate received recognition in the *Castells v Spain*, where a conviction of a senator for an article on the Basque situation which "insulted" the Government disclosed a violation. The Court found that freedom of expression was "especially important" for an elected representative who represents his electorate and defends their interests. This applied to political debate inside and outside the legislature, any interferences calling for the closest scrutiny. The Court further considered that it was permissible to criticise governments more widely than in relation to private citizens and governments should show restraint in resorting to criminal proceedings. While it might be compatible to take action against defamatory accusations devoid of factual basis or formulated in bad faith, in the case itself, the senator had not been afforded the chance to prove the factual basis of the article was true.

Special privileges for Parliamentarians by way of immunity from suit have been found compatible with the Convention.[69] In *A v United Kingdom*, the absolute immunity from suit enjoyed by members of Parliament for statements made within Parliament was found to be justified under Arts 6 and 8 by the crucial importance of freedom of political debate by the elected representatives of the people. The Court stated that very weighty reasons were required to justify interference with freedom of expression within the legislative forum. In *Jerusalem v Austria*, where an elected politician was sued for alleged defamatory speech in a council meeting not covered by parliamentary immunity, the Court considered that the statements which were issued during a debate on a matter of public concern attracted the protection of Art.10. On the other hand, blanket immunity to statements made outside the parliamentary context or outside the scope of parliamentary activity went too far.[70]

Article 10 also extends to visiting European Union Parliamentarians. Measures to expel and prohibit the entry in French Polynesia of a German MEP invited by a political party to be present at elections were not justifiable, notwithstanding the tense political atmosphere at the time, since the meeting had been peaceful, no

---

[69] See Pt IIB: Defamation.
[70] *Cordova v Italy (No.1)* and *Cordova v Italy (No.2)*, January 30, 2003.

disorder had arisen from the visit and her views had been a contribution to the existing local democratic debate in Polynesia.[71]

Where it is considered that an elected MP is expressing views that are dangerously provocative, States must still react in a suitable and adequate manner, using the means usually available in a democratic State. While the Commission in *Sadik v Greece*[72] noted that moderation in political debate may be desirable to avoid, for example, exacerbating ethnic tensions, in the absence of clear elements of incitement to violence, the imposition of a prison sentence on a MP for words used in an election campaign could not be regarded as proportionate.[73]

In the context of election campaigns, the rules may legitimately limit expenditure to ensure equality between candidates. However in *Bowman v United Kingdom*, where an anti-abortion campaigner was prosecuted for distributing leaflets about particular electoral candidates' views on abortion and related issues, the Court found it disproportionate to impose through a £5 limit what was effectively a total barrier on her participation in the electoral debate, particularly where there was no limit on the press to support or oppose any particular candidate or on parties or their supporters to advertise on a national level.

9. Statements threatening national security and public safety

Key case law:

Zana v Turkey, November 25, 1997, R.J.D. 1997–VII, No.57; 27 E.H.R.R. 667;   **IIB–186**
Incal v Turkey, June 9, 1998, R.J.D. 1998–IV, No.78; 29 E.H.R.R. 449; *Sürek v Turkey (No.1)*, July 8, 1999, ECHR 1999–IV; *Karataş v Turkey*, July 8, 1999, ECHR 1999–IV; *Ceylan v Turkey*, July 8, 1999, ECHR 1999–IV; 30 E.H.R.R. 73; *Baskaya and Okçuoglu v Turkey*, July 8, 1999, ECHR 1999–IV; 31 E.H.R.R. 10; *Özgür Gündem v Turkey*, March 16, 2000, ECHR 2000–III; 31 E.H.R.R. 49; *Erdoğdu v Turkey*, June 15, 2000, ECHR 2000–VI.

Where measures are taken in response to perceived terrorist threats by way of suppressing publications, a certain leeway is accorded to Contracting States, in acknowledgment of the seriousness and complexity of the situations that are often involved.[74]

Thus, the Court has accepted, in the context, of South East Turkey, that steps taken to prosecute and convict a person for statements in support of the PKK, an illegal terrorist organisation, could be said to pursue the legitimate aims of maintaining national security and public safety. Whether the measures could be justified as necessary and proportionate under the second paragraph of Art.10 appear to turn on a consideration of the perceived impact of the statements concerned. In finding a conviction justified in *Zana v Turkey*, the Court noted that

---

[71] *cf.* 28979/95 and 30343/96, n.4 above,—the exclusion order preventing the Sinn Fein leader from attending a political meeting in London was justified in the context of the fight against terrorism and sensitivity of the peace process.
[72] The Court upheld the Government's preliminary objection on exhaustion.
[73] The words "Turks" or "Turkish" to identify Moslems of Western Thrace did not qualify.
[74] *e.g. Öztürk v Turkey*, September 29, 1999, ECHR 1999–VI, para.59, where the Court gave the authorities the benefit of the doubt that the applicant's prosecution for publishing a book pursued the legitimate aim of preventing crime and disorder.

there had been serious disturbances in the region at the time and gave weight to the fact that the applicant was a former mayor of Diyarbakir (the principal city of the region) and that his statement gave express support to the PKK as a "national liberation movement" and referred in ambiguous, contradictory terms to PKK massacres as "mistakes". While the applicant did not express approval as such of violence, his words were, in the Court's view, open to several interpretations, and in light of the tensions existing at the time, they could be viewed as likely to exacerbate an already explosive situation.

In following cases, the Court has continued to examine whether the statements subject to criminal proceedings can be regarded as capable of inciting violence or as advocating violence, giving a wide margin of appreciation to the authorities, even where the courts have been examining different issues such as whether the statements had a separatist content.[75] However, as long as the impugned statements could not be construed, by tone, content or context, as inciting violence,[76] the mere fact that interviews or statements contained strongly disparaging views of Government policy or the expression of support for the idea of a separate Kurdish entity, would not justify a conviction.[77] The public had a right to be informed of different perspectives of security problems, however unpalatable that might be to the authorities,[78] just as media professionals had to exercise particular caution in publishing the views of representatives of organisations which resorted to violence to prevent the media becoming a vehicle for hate speech and the promotion of violence.[79]

The Court has been less impressed with criminal measures taken against publications on the ground that they have named State officials engaged in fighting terrorism and rendered them targets of retaliation. Where the news articles concerned events of public interest and the information was already at least in part in the public domain, it has found insufficient justification.[80]

---

[75] e.g. Sürek (No.1), paras 61–63.

[76] e.g. Erdoğdu, para.71: "Where a publication cannot be categorised as inciting to violence, Contracting States cannot with reference to the prevention of disorder or crime restrict the right of the public to be informed by bringing the weight of the criminal law to bear on the media."

[77] Özgür Gündem, paras 63 and 70; Incal, para.50, the appeal to Kurdish citizens to oppose the government through "neighbourhood committees" was not incitement of violence or hatred; Ceylan, paras 33–35, the trade union leader's article was virulent in tone ("State terrorism" and "genocide") but did not encourage the use of armed resistance; Karataş, paras 49–50, the poems were aggressive with "colourful imagery" about self-sacrifice for "Kurdistan" but taking into account that poetry is an artistic means of expression addressed to a very small audience, they were more an expression of deep distress than a call to uprising; Baskaya and Okçuoglu, paras 64–65, the authorities had not had sufficient regard to freedom of academic expression in penalising a socio-economic essay on the Kurdish problem, which contained strong criticism of Government policy but did not incite to violence; Osmani v FRYOM, 50841/99, (Dec.) October 11, 2001, where the impugned statements had identifiable effects of incitement, justifying a significant prison sentence. cf. Sürek (No.1) where the statements were regarded as "hate speech" and the "glorification of violence"; Sürek (No.3), July 8, 1999, para.40, where the article expressed a call to armed force, the applicant newspaper owner had provided the writer with an outlet for the stirring up of violence, even if he had not associated himself personally with the views.

[78] e.g. Baskaya and Okçuoglu, para.65; Sürek and Özdemir v Turkey, July 8, 1999, para.61, concerning a conviction for publishing interviews with a leading member of a proscribed organisation, which nonetheless had newsworthy content.

[79] e.g. Erdoğdu and Ince, para.54.

[80] Sürek (No.2), para.40; Özgür Gündem, paras 67–68.

Prohibition of a newspaper without reasons given for the decision or any adequate judicial control of the administrative measure was not good enough, even with a certain weight being given to problems of terrorism in the region.[81]

However, less drastic measures imposed with a view to stopping the IRA or other groups using the media to express their views were not found, with due regard to a wide margin of appreciation, to fall foul of Art.10. In *Purcell v Ireland*, the Commission found that the exigencies of the situation justified the banning of the airing on television or radio of interviews with or statements by Sinn Fein members and the more bizarre measure of using actors' voice-overs for such interviews was accepted in the UK.[82]

10. Commercial advertising and unfair competition

Key case law:

Barthold v Germany, March 25, 1985, Series A, No.90; 7 E.H.R.R. 383; *Markt Intern Verlag GmbH v Germany*, November 20, 1989, Series A, No.165; 12 E.H.R.R. 161; *Casada Coca v Spain*, February 24, 1994, Series A, No.285–A; 18 E.H.R.R. 1; *Jacubowski v Germany*, June 23, 1994, Series A, No.291; 19 E.H.R.R. 64; *Hertel v Switzerland*, August 25, 1998, R.J.D.D 1998–VI, No.87; 28 E.H.R.R. 534.

IIB–187

Commercial speech is covered. Matters relating to professional practice are not removed from the sphere of Art.10 because of the financial element.[83] In *Markt Intern Verlag GmbH v Germany*, the Commission considered that democratic society was based on the articulation of a wide spectrum of views, including those relating to economic interests.[84] It rejected the Government view that Art.10 only covered artistic, religious, political and scientific matters and excluded purely competition-related promotional statements.[85]

Regarding professional rules against press exposure, these appear justifiable, where the penalties are slight and pure advertising involved. The Court noting the wide variety of rules in States has commented that the domestic authorities are in the best place to assess where to strike the balance, special considerations attaching to the role of lawyers in the administration of justice and to doctors with general obligations to health of the community.[86] In *Barthold v Germany*, the injunction on a vet for making statements in the press was based on a disproportionately wide prohibition since it covered his expression of views about the problems of emergency night service and might discourage vets from giving their views in public debate and hamper the press in its role as public watchdog.[87] A ban on pure commercial

---

[81] *Çetin and others v Turkey*, February 13, 2003, ECHR 2003–III concerning the banning of a newspaper critical of the Government policy in the region.
[82] nn.10 and 46 above.
[83] *Barthold*, (Rep.), para.61: the Court did not find it necessary to decide since the article included information and opinions on matters of public concern. The issue was undisputed by the parties in the recent case *Stambuk v Germany*, October 17, 2002.
[84] (Rep.) paras 202–3.
[85] See also *Casada Coca*, para.35: no distinction between profit-making forms.
[86] *Casada Coca*, paras 54–55; *Stambuk*, n.83 above, paras 40–41, which seems to imply stricter restrictions can apply to lawyers than to doctors however.
[87] See also *Stambuk*, n.83 above, where the applicant doctor was fined for an interview in the press about new techniques (accompanied by a photograph), the Court considered that that the publicity aspect was secondary and that it impinged on the ability of the press to report on the subject.

advertising by a lawyer who sent circulars to collection agencies was found justified in the interests of clients and the profession and not disproportionate given the lightness of the penalty.[88] A disciplinary warning given to a lawyer for breaching an advertising ban was not disproportionate in *Casada Coca v Spain*.[89]

Restrictions on publications found by domestic courts to damage commercial interests of others have not been found objectionable. Indeed the Court has stated that a margin of appreciation for the authorities is essential in an area as complex and fluctuating as that of unfair competition,[90] although it will be reduced where what is at stake is not purely "commercial" statements but participation in a debate concerning the public interest, such a public health.[91] In *Markt Intern*, where an injunction was issued against a magazine to prevent publication of critical information about trading practices of particular enterprises, the Court found that while large undertakings opened themselves to public scrutiny and specialised press served a legitimate purpose there were limits on criticism. It gave weight to the fact that the domestic courts had assessed the issues, and the fact that different views were possible did not permit substituting its opinion for that of the domestic courts.[92] An injunction however placing detailed restrictions on a newspaper's price-comparison adverts was found not to strike the correct balance, impairing the essence of that type of advertising.[93]

11. Obligations and restrictions in employment or professional sphere

Key case law:

IIB–188   *Glasenapp v Germany*, August 28, 1986, Series A, No.104; 9 E.H.R.R. 25; *Kosiek v Germany*, August 28, 1986, Series A, No.105; 9 E.H.R.R. 328; *Vogt v Germany*, September 26, 1995, Series A, No.323; 21 E.H.R.R. 205; *Schopfer v Switzerland*, May 20, 1998, R.J.D. 1998–III, No.72; *Rekvenyi v Hungary*, May 20, 1999, ECHR 1999–III; 30 E.H.R.R. 519; *Wille v Liechtenstein*, October 28, 1999, R.J.D. 1999–VII; 30 E.H.R.R. 558; *Nikula v Finland*, March 21, 2002, ECHR 2002–II.

Where contractually a person is bound by reasonable terms of confidentiality or loyalty, measures to suspend or dismiss for breach have generally been compatible, for example, where a doctor expressed views on abortion objectionable to his Catholic hospital employer[94] or civil servants have been penalised for revealing

---

[88] 14622/89, (Dec.) March 7, 1991, 69 D.R. 272; in *Stambuk*, n.83 above, paras 29–30, the ban on advertising by doctors pursued the legitimate aim of protecting the interests of other medical practitioners and the proper regulation of community health.

[89] See also *Colman v UK*, settled before the Court, 16632/90, (Rep.) October 19, 1992, Series A, No.258–D, where the Commission found no violation where a doctor was prevented from newspaper advertising for patients.

[90] *Krone Verlag GmbH & CoKG v Austria*, December 11, 2003, para.30.

[91] *e.g. Hertel*, the conviction of an academic for publication of research setting out alleged risks of microwaves to health was not justified, nor the injunction preventing repetition of these claims. Where in the subsequent case, more limited restriction *i.e.* a requirement to add a qualifying statement, was imposed on future publications, the Court found this could be justified under the second paragraph in pursuing the legitimate interests of maintaining fair competition—*Hertel v Switzerland*, 53440.99, (Dec), January 17, 2002.

[92] See also *Jacubowski*, where prohibition of a circular on grounds of unfair competition was not disproportionate.

[93] *Krone Verlag GmbH*, n.90 above, paras 34–35.

[94] 12242/86, (Dec.), September 6, 1989, 62 D.R. 151.

official secrets. General restrictions on participation in political debate and activity may also be acceptable in certain sectors as was found in respect of members of the police in *Rekvenyi v Hungary* where particular importance attached to the political neutrality of the police after forty years of communist rule.

In *Vogt v Germany*, however, where the applicant was an appointed civil servant, a teacher, the Court narrowly found violation where she was suspended from a post for communist party activities.[95] While it was open to a State to impose a duty of discretion on civil servants, freedom of expression still applied to them. Since she was member of a lawful party, there was no criticism of her work (as regarded the alleged risk of indoctrinating children), the majority found the interference disproportionate.[96] Dismissal on the basis of lack of appropriate professional qualification or proper professional conduct does not, without more, infringe Art.10.[97]

As regards judges, senior members of the judiciary may be expected to show restraint in situations where the authority and impartiality of the judiciary could be called into question but any interference with the freedom of expression of a judge of this position calls for close scrutiny. In *Wille v Liechtenstein,* where the President of the Administrative Court was informed by the ruling Prince that he would not be re-appointed due to a statement made at a lecture on a controversial constitutional issue, the Court, finding a violation of Art.10, noted that the judge had not commented on a pending case and that there was no suggestion that his view had any bearing on his conduct as a judge or the performance of his office.

Disciplinary sanctions imposed by professional bodies may be acceptable where pursuing legitimate aims in a suitably proportionate manner. In *Schopfer v Switzerland*, the Court found no violation arising from a CHF 500 fine imposed on a lawyer for serious criticisms of the courts issued at a press conference, reference being made to the key role of lawyers in contributing to the proper administration of justice and maintaining public confidence therein. Any measures interfering with counsel's freedom of expression during a trial, however, threatens to conflict with Art.6 guarantees and the Court has stated it could only be in exceptional cases that criminal sanction of even a lenient kind could be imposed on defence counsel's freedom of expression.[98] Even a simple admonition by a disciplinary council on defence counsel for alleging that his client had been put under pressure by an investigating officer was found to have an unjustified "chilling" effect.[99]

---

[95] In *Glasenapp* and *Kosiek*, where the applicants, probationary civil servants, were dismissed for expression of particular political views, the Court found no violation on the special consideration that there was no right of entry to the civil service.

[96] 10 votes to 9: the minority gave greater weight to German history, the State's commitment to democratic order and considered that since the civil service was vital to the proper functioning of the State it was within its margin of appreciation to insist on conformity to strict rules.

[97] *Petersen v Germany*, 39793/98, (Dec.) November 22, 2001, ECHR 2001–XII, where on re-unification of Germany, the applicant was dismissed as a civil servant after scrutiny of his qualifications, which included political, rather than research-based, theses; also *Volkmer v Germany*, 39799/98, (Dec.) November 22, 2001, where a teacher was dismissed not purely for his past political opinions but as he had abused his position by using a pupil as a spy; *Pitkevich v Russia*, 47936/99, where a judge was dismissed not for expression of religious opinion but because of specific activities incompatible with judicial office, *e.g.* promising a favourable outcome if parties joined her church.

[98] *Nikula*: breach of Art.10 where a defence lawyer was privately prosecuted by a public prosecutor for alleged defamation in court.

[99] *Steur v Netherlands*, October 28, 2003.

12. Freedom to receive information

Key case law:

IIB–189   *Open Door and Dublin Well Woman v Ireland*, October 29, 1992, Series A, No.246; 15 E.H.R.R. 244; *Guerra v Italy*, February 19, 1998, R.J.D. 1998–I, No.64; *Cyprus v Turkey*, May 10, 2001, ECHR 2001–IV.

Article 10 cannot be used to derive a general right of access to information. In *Guerra v Italy*, the Court stated unequivocally that the freedom to receive information essentially prohibited a government from restricting a person from receiving information that others wished to impart. It did not impose on the authorities in that case the obligation to collect and distribute information about the health risks to the local community from the nearby factory.

    In *Open Door and Dublin Well Woman v Ireland*, there was a violation where a court injunction prevented the provision of information services concerning abortion by the applicant counsellors. The Court found the ban disproportionate in the circumstances, since it was absolute, the counselling given was neutral and the information lawfully available elsewhere in Ireland or by contact outside in a less supervised manner, which imposed a risk to those women who sought abortion at later stage and who did not not receive counselling or proper after-care. The vetting by the TRNC authorites in northern Cyprus in respect of school-books destined for primary school Greek-Cypriot children, which resulted in the unilateral censorship or rejection of large numbers of school-books, no matter how innocuous their content, was a denial of freedom of information in *Cyprus v Turkey*.

13. Positive obligations to protect the exercise of freedom of expression

Key case law:

IIB–190   *Ozgur Gundem v Turkey*, March 16, 2000, ECHR 2000–III; 31 E.H.R.R. 49; *Fuentes Bobo v Spain*, February 29, 2000; *Appleby v UK*, May 6, 2003, ECHR 2003–VI.

Genuine and effective exercise of this key freedom does not depend merely on the authorities' duty not to interfere but may require positive measures of protection, even between individuals. Thus, the Court found the authorities were under a positive obligation in *Özgür Gündem v Turkey* to take investigative and protective measures where an allegedly pro-PKK newspaper had been victim of a campaign of violence. A general obligation on the State to protect freedom of expression has also been found to arise in the employment context.[100] As in other contexts, issues of striking a fair balance arise, with a margin of appreciation to the State as regards appropriate policies, priorities and use of resources nor will the Court interpret the provision in such a manner as to impose an impossible or disproportionate burden on the authorities. Thus, in *Appleby v United Kingdom* where the applicant

---

[100] *Fuentes Bobo v Spain*, para.38.

campaigners had other means available to them to circulate their views, the Court did not consider that a positive obligation arose requiring that the State should ensure access to privately-owned shopping centres for the exercise of their freedom of expression. Article 10 did not bestow freedom of forum, though the Court did not exclude that where the bar on access to private property effectively destroyed the essence of the right, such as in a company-owned town, a positive obligation might arise for the State to regulate property rights in favour of exercise of freedom of expression.

Cross-reference

Part IIB: Army (section, Freedom of expression)
Part IIB: Defamation and right to reputation
Part IIB: Environment (4. Access to information about environmental risks)
Part IIB: Freedom of assembly (3. Penalties for participation in public protests)
Part IIB: Prisoners' rights (10. Education, leisure facilities and expression)
Part IIB: Private life (5(b) Access to personal information)

Freedom of movement

Key provision:

IIB–191   Article 2 of Protocol No.4 (liberty of movement within a State and freedom to leave).

Key case law:

Guzzardi v Italy, November 6, 1980, Series A, No.39; 3 E.H.R.R. 333; *Raimondo v Italy*, February 22, 1994, Series A, No.281–A; 18 E.H.R.R. 237; *Piermont v France*, April 27, 1995 Series A, No.314; 20 E.H.R.R. 301; *Labita v Italy*, April 6, 2000, ECHR 2000–IV; *Bauman v France*, May 22, 2001, ECHR 2001–V; *Denizci v Cyprus*, May 23, 2001, ECHR 2001–V; *Olivieira v Netherlands*, June 4, 2002, ECHR 2002–IV; 28 E.H.R.R. 289; *Luordo v Italy*, July 17, 2003.

1. General considerations

IIB–192   Where restrictions on movement are concerned, Art.2 of Protocol No.4 is regarded as the *lex specialis*. Article 5 which concerns deprivation of liberty has not been extended by the Convention organs beyond the conventional context of physical detention.

2. Restriction on movement

IIB–193   Whether there has been a deprivation of liberty rather than a restriction on movement depends on examination of the concrete situation, but is a distinction of degree and intensity, not of nature or substance. Account is taken of a whole range of criteria: the type, duration, effects and manner of implementation of the measures restricting the individual's liberty. In *Guzzardi v Italy*, the confinement of an applicant to the island of Asinara was found to be cumulatively a deprivation of liberty within the meaning of Art.5. While the area of confinement was much larger than a cell, it covered a tiny fraction of an island, nine-tenths of which consisted of a prison. He had to remain in his dwelling between 22.00 and 07.00 hours, report twice per day to the authorities and could only leave the island under strict supervision—a state of affairs which lasted 16 months. Conversely, in *Raimondo v Italy*, special police supervision, where the applicant could not leave home without informing the police and was under an obligation to report on certain days and to remain at home between 21.00 and 07.00 hours, was considered only a restriction on movement. Also, exclusion orders restricting persons in Northern Ireland from entering mainland UK have not been considered to be of such a degree as to constitute a deprivation of liberty.[1]

Refusal of a passport which did not prevent the applicant in Sweden from moving to other Nordic countries was still an interference with freedom of movement since freedom to leave a country implies freedom to leave for any country to which he

---

[1] *e.g.* 13709/88 and 13944/88, (Dec.), October 11, 1989.

may be admitted.[2] Seizure of a passport or other similar identity document also constitutes an interference.[3]

Minor impediments or conditions imposed on the freedom of movement will not be seen as interfering, *e.g.* the obligation to carry an identity card and present it on request of the police.[4] However, in *Denizci v Cyprus*, the requirement to report to the police every time the applicants wished to move their place of residence or visit friends or family in the north was found to disclose an interference with freedom of movement.[5]

3. "Lawfully" within the territory

Freedom of movement applies only to persons lawfully within the territory. This refers to domestic law, which may lay down the conditions to be fulfilled. Thus aliens provisionally allowed to stay in a certain district can only be regarded as lawfully in the territory as long as they comply with the conditions of their admission.[6] Nor is the provision applicable to an alien who has had his residence permit revoked.[7]

IIB–194

An alien who has entered immigration control cannot claim necessarily to be "lawfully" in the territory, a claim made by the applicant MEP in *Piermont v France* who was only stopped after her passport had been checked at New Caledonia airport. The Court considered that at such an airport passengers remained liable to checks as long as they were in its perimeter. Since the applicant was served with the order preventing her entry while still in the airport she could not be considered as having been lawfully within the territory.

4. Legitimate restrictions

Considerations of lawfulness,[8] necessity, legitimate aim and proportionality apply.

IIB–195

Refusal by Finland to issue a passport to a Finnish citizen resident in Sweden was an interference with freedom of movement but justified as necessary in the interests of national security and the maintenance of the *ordre public* since the applicant had failed to report for his military service. The Commission noted that the applicant had not invoked any ground warranting a departure from the usual rule, *e.g.* special need for travel and that he was able to re-apply at any time. It considered also that Contracting States were entitled to a wide margin of appreciation in the organisation of their national defence.[9] An injunction prohibiting an anti-abortionist campaigner

---

[2] 19583/92 (Dec.) February 20, 1995, 80 D.R. 38.

[3] *Baumann*, paras 60–62, where the Court dismissed the Government's argument that no restriction had taken place in fact as the applicant had been arrested shortly after requesting the return of his passport; *Napijalo v Croatia*, November 13, 2003, para.69.

[4] 16810/90, (Dec.) September 9, 1992, 73 D.R. 136.

[5] In *Luordi v Italy*, the obligation on the applicant not to leave his district without permission was, without discussion, within the scope of the provision, even though it was not apparent that he had ever wished to or that permission had ever been refused.

[6] 14102/88, (Dec.) October 9, 1989, 63 D.R. 195; 12068/86, (Dec.) December 1, 1986, 51 D.R. 237.

[7] 21069/92, (Dec.) July 9, 1993, 75 D.R. 245.

[8] *Olivieira*, paras 47–59—the Court examined whether the 14 day order excluding the applicant from the centre of Amsterdam on grounds of drugs use had a basis in domestic law and the quality of law (*e.g.* foreseeable and accessible); also *Denizci*, paras 404–406, where the Government had advanced no legal basis for the restriction on the movements of Turkish Cypriots.

[9] 19583/92, n.2 above.

from entering within 250 metres of an abortion clinic for 6 months was justified for the protection of the rights of others having regard to limited area and duration of the measure.[10] A court order prohibiting a Spanish mother from leaving Italy with her children was regarded as necessary to protect the rights of the Italian father and to maintain the *ordre public* in the sense of the administration of justice,[11] while an order excluding a habitual drugs user from the centre of Amsterdam for 14 days was found a proportionate measure for the prevention of crime and maintaining public order.[12]

Where the authorities exceed the justification in domestic terms, issues may arise. In *Raimondo v Italy*, special supervision measures imposed against the applicant, suspected of mafia crimes, were considered as necessary and proportionate in view of the threat to democracy posed by the Mafia. The measures ceased to be necessary or lawful from the filing of the revocation decision by the court in the registry or at the latest when applicant was informed a week later. Continued retention of a passport of an applicant initially suspected of crime but who was not prosecuted or needed as a witness ceased to be justified in *Baumann v France*.[13]

In *Labita v Italy*, continuation of severely restrictive measures against an applicant on grounds of alleged mafia links were found unnecessary after his acquittal.[14] The Court considered that it was legitimate for special supervision measures, including restriction on movement, to be taken against persons suspected of mafia membership prior to conviction where they were intended to prevent crimes being committed. It did not rule out that special measures could continue after an acquittal, but only where there was concrete evidence, though insufficient to secure a conviction, to justify reasonable fears that the person might commit criminal offences in the future.

Duration of a measure may render it disproportionate, particularly where the necessity for the restriction weakens with the passage of time. Thus, in *Luordo v Italy* although the Court accepted that the requirement on the applicant not to leave his place of residence without permission during bankruptcy proceedings was not in itself objectionable, the duration of those proceedings over fourteen years was disproportionate to any legitimate aim, even if it was not apparent that the applicant had ever wished to leave the area or that permission had ever been refused.

5. Overlap with other provisions

IIB–196 While in *Piermont v France*, the applicant MEP, as an alien subject to lawful expulsion measures, did not succeed in claims based on freedom of movement in respect of measures taken by the authorities to prevent her attending meetings in French Polynesia and New Caledonia, breaches of Art.10 were found since the measures interfered with her freedom of expression.[15] There was no point taken that

---

[10] 22838/93, (Dec.) February 22, 1995, 80–A D.R. 147.
[11] *Roldan Texiero v Italy*, 40655/98, (Dec.) October 26, 2000.
[12] *Olivieira*, paras 64–65.
[13] See also *Napijalo v Croatia*, lack of justification for continued retention of passport by customs where they did not pursue any proceedings against him.
[14] The applicant's wife was from a mafia family. The restrictive measures included weekly reporting to the police, a curfew between 8pm and 6am, a prohibition on attending bars or public gatherings or on leaving home without informing the supervision authorities.
[15] See Pt IIB: Freedom of expression.

Art.2 of Protocol No.4 was the *lex specialis* or that no separate issues could arise where an alien was lawfully restricted in her movements. When Gerry Adams, Sinn Fein President, was stopped from attending a meeting in the House of Commons, by an exclusion order allegedly for that purpose, the Commission noted that Art.2 of Protocol No.4 had not been ratified by the UK. While it examined the case on the basis that there had been an interference with freedom of expression, it found the measure justified as necessary to protect national security and prevent disorder and crime.[16]

Cross-reference

Part IIB: Deprivation of liberty
Part IIB: Freedom of association

---

[16] 28979/95 and 30343/96, (Dec.) January 13, 1997, 88–A D.R. 137.

Gypsies and minorities

Relevant Articles:

IIB–197   Articles 8 (private life, family life and home), 14 discrimination), Art.1 of the First Protocol (peaceful enjoyment of property) and Art.2 of the First Protocol (right to education).

Relevant case law:

Bryan v UK, November 22, 1995, Series A, No.335–A; 21 E.H.R.R. 342; *Buckley v UK*, September 25, 1996, R.J.D. 1996–IV; 23 E.H.R.R. 101; *Chapman v UK*, January 18, 2002, ECHR 2001–I; *Conka v Belgium*, February 5, 2002, ECHR 2002–I; *Nachova v Bulgaria*, February 26, 2004, pending before the Grand Chamber; *Connors v UK*, May 28, 2004.

1. General considerations

IIB–198   The Convention guarantees rights in respect, primarily, of the individual. The Convention case law emphasises this in an insistence that an applicant must be able to claim to be a victim, with direct and continuous affect on his enjoyment of a protected right. It sits uneasily therefore for a person to complain because he is a member of a group which is prejudiced in a general, less direct or immediate way.

Complaints tended until recently to slip between the provisions.[1] Until the entry of Central and Eastern European States into the Convention system, which have large Roma and other minorities, the cases derived principally from the UK, relating to the siting of gypsy caravans. These highlighted the difficulties facing gypsies, whose ability to lead nomadic lives has been seriously hindered, *inter alia*, by legislative provisions rendering unauthorised stationing of caravans on the highway or other land a criminal offence; the shortfall of official sites throughout the country; and difficulties of obtaining local authority planning permission for their own sites. This is a global situation that could be described as undermining the viability of the gypsy way of life but which is difficult for the Court to examine as a whole, confined as it is to the individual circumstances of each case and being reluctant to embark on abstract investigations.

---

[1] *e.g.* 11862/85, (Dec.) July 18, 1986, where posters in shops opposed gypsy sites implying that gypsies were dirty and attracted vermin, the applicant gypsy could not take action for group defamation under English law and consent was not given for prosecution for incitement to racial hatred—the Commission held that Art.6 could not grant substantive rights of defamation or no issues arose under Art.8; 18401/91, (Dec.) May 6, 1993, where a gypsy on an official site was threatened with summary eviction, it was argued with some force that she was in an impossible situation, due to the general shortfall of sites and the designation system in the area making it a criminal offence for gypsies to station their caravans on public or private land without consent—however, when during the proceedings the applicant was granted permission by the local council to remain where she was, the Commission avoided looking at the effect of the general situation, since it found no real indication that she wanted to travel elsewhere and she was no longer a victim.

2. Right to respect for private life, family life and home

Planning controls on the use of land, a common feature in Contracting States, have IIB–199
generally been found by the Commission and Court to be justified in the public
interest, for example prohibiting development in green belt or areas of rural
amenity[2] or the rights of others, for example, the contractual rights of a site owner.[3]
An individual who has been refused permission to occupy land is not in a strong
position under the approach adopted in Convention case law, which holds that Art.8
does not contain an express right to living accommodation. The Court has stated
that individual preferences cannot outweigh the public interest.[4] The fact that
planning and site provision is an area of policy and discretion has also resulted in a
wide margin of appreciation being accorded to the authorities and a reluctance to
impose positive obligations on the State to provide accommodation in a particular
place.[5]

Where however a gypsy family was established on a particular site and faced with
expulsion, the Commission found that issues could arise. The lack of reasonable
alternatives for the *Buckley* family, who had been refused planning permission for the
caravan on their own land and were faced with enforcement measures, was the basis
for the Commission's finding of a violation. Both the Court and Commission
accepted that the family's settlement on their land, even though never authorised,
nonetheless fell within the scope of "home" under Art.8. The Commission also
relied on a Norwegian case concerning Lapps which held a minority could claim the
right to respect for its particular lifestyle as being "private life" "family life" and
home".[6] In its view a gypsy could therefore claim that her way of life which involved
living in a caravan attracted protection under Art.8.

Regarding the compliance with the requirements of Art.8, the Court took a
stricter line than the Commission. The Commission approached the balancing
exercise from the point of view that gypsies from their lifestyle had more limited
options open to them and that they had special requirements. It found that the
applicant' interest in security for herself and her children and the continuation of
their lifestyle outweighed the slender public interst in planning controls in that case.
The Court emphasised however that in the area of planning controls the authorities
enjoyed a wide margin of appreciation under Art.8. Although it noted the
importance of respect for home, in effect this was given little weight. It was
unimpressed by allegations of the unsuitability of the alternative site available
nearby, commenting only that it was not as satisfactory as her own land and
discounting matters of individual preference. The Court considered that it was not
its role to enter into the merits of planning decisions, and it was sufficient to verify,
as in this case before the planning inspectors, that the competing claims were given

[2] *e.g.* 11723/85, (Dec.) May 7, 1987, 52 D.R. 250; 11185/84, (Dec.) March 11, 1985, (Dec.) 42 D.R.
275.
[3] 14751/89, (Dec.) December 12, 1990, 67 D.R. 264.
[4] *Buckley*, para.81.
[5] *Buckley*, para.75; 14455/88 (Dec.) September 4, 1991, where the applicant gypsies had sought
unsuccessfully in the courts to enforce the statutory obligation on local authorities to provide sufficient
sites to prevent being continually moved on from place to place, the Commission, though noting the lack
of adequate provision, was not prepared to find that the respect for family and private life extended to
obliging the authorities to build sites. Art.8 was about respect for lawfully established homes already in
existence.
[6] 9278/81 and 9415/81, (Dec.), October 3, 1983, 35 D.R. 30.

due consideration in a fair procedure. This approach was confirmed in *Chapman v United Kingdom*, where, though reference was made to some special consideration being given to the needs of gypsies, the Court found that Art.8 could not be interpreted as imposing a far-reaching positive obligation on the State to make available to the gypsy community an adequate number of suitably equipped sites. It also stated that it would be slow to grant protection to those who in conscious defiance of the prohibition of the law established their home on an environmentally protected site.[7]

In light of the Court's judgments above, a finding of violation is unlikely where a gypsy is refused planning permission for their land. Issues might still arise perhaps where eviction measures are imposed arbitrarily or in circumstances of extreme hardship. It will however be difficult for any gypsy to establish that there is no viable alternative at all to remaining on their own land.[8]

However, where a gypsy family had long been lawfully resident on a local authority site, the Court found in *Connors v United Kingdom* that their summary eviction had not been attended by adequate procedural safeguards, in particular the requirement that the local authority establish proper justification for the serious interference with their home, private and family life. The Court was not convinced by Government arguments that the nature of such sites or the purported reluctance of the occupants to participate in official proceedings justified the lack of effective court scrutiny of evictions.

3. Ill-treatment, discrimination and expulsion

IIB–200   Allegations of serious physical ill-treatment and unlawful killing of Roma victims have led to findings of breaches of Arts 2 and 3 in a series of cases from Bulgaria.[9] Lack of effective investigation or remedy, with procedural breaches of Arts 2 and 13, is an accompanying feature of these incidents. Initially, the judgments laid no emphasis on the ethnic identity of the victims and the Court found that there was no material enabling it to conclude beyond reasonable doubt that the killings, ill-treatment and ineffective investigations were motivated by racial prejudice.[10]

---

[7] *Chapman*, paras 90–116; also similar findings of no violations in respect of enforcement measures against gypsy occupation of land *Beard; Coster; Jane Smith;* and *Lee*, judgments of January 18, 2001; it may be noted that the Government settled a sixth case, *Varey*, in which the planning inspector's decision to grant the gypsy family's appeal was overridden twice by the Secretary of State.

[8] This will be particularly hard where a gypsy has given up a nomadic way of life, through force of circumstance, and adopted conventional housing, as in 31600/96, (Dec.) September 10, 1996, where the applicant had lived in housing for 17 years and when dying of cancer tried to end her days in a caravan: the Commission found that the local authority had made not unnegligible attempts to find a place for her caravan but in the circumstances they could not be held in breach of Art.8 in failing to provide such a site.

[9] *Assenov*, October 28, 1998, R.J.D. 1998–VIII (violation of Art.3 for failure to investigate allegations of beatings by the police of the 14-year-old applicant, as well as violations of Arts 5, paras 3 and 4, 13 and former 25 of the Convention); *Velikova*, May 18, 2000, ECHR 2000–VI (violations of Art.2 for the beating to death of a Roma in police custody and Arts 2 and 13 for the lack of effective investigation or remedy); *Anguelova*, June 12, 2002, ECHR 2002–IV (violations of Art.2 for death from injuries in custody of a 17 year old Roma boy and for the failure to provide timely medical care, as well as violations of Art.5, para.1 and Arts 2 and 13 for lack of effective investigation or remedy; *Nachova and others* (breaches of Arts 2 and 14 for the killing of two conscripts of Roma origin).

[10] *Velikova*, para.94; *Anguelova*, para.168—see Judge Bonello's partly dissenting opinion where he criticises the Court's insistence on using such unrealistic and high burden of proof, inappropriate for its functions.

However in *Nachova v Bulgaria*, where the two unarmed absconding Roma conscripts were shot dead in a blatantly excessive use of force and the military policeman was reported as using racial insults, the Court emphasised the importance of the fight against racism and stated that the authorities were under an obligation into investigate with rigour and impartiality to unmask any racist motives. In the absence of such an investigation, the burden of proof shifted to the Government to provide a convincing explanation that events were not shaped by discriminatory attitudes of State agents. On the facts of the case, without adequate investigation or explanation, and taking into account the previous cases and other international reports on the situation in Bulgaria, a procedural and substantive violation of Art.14 accordingly arose.

Where a group is openly singled out for differential treatment on the basis of ethnic origin, race and religion, proof is less of a problem, as in *Cyprus v Turkey*, where the hardship and restrictions suffered by an enclave of Greek Cypriots in the northern part of the island had been so severe and longlasting as to violate the very notion of respect for their human dignity.[11] The Court found aggravated breaches of Art.8 and a breach of Art.3, with no separate issue under Art.14.

Allegations are not uncommonly made that gypsies are treated more unfavourably than others who make applications for planning permission. Difficulties however of establishing that a refusal to a gypsy was based on grounds of his ethnic origin to the exclusion of normal planning considerations or that permission was granted to an non-gypsy in comparable circumstances rendered, and continue to render, success before the Court problematic save in the most flagrant cases.[12] It would be required to show blatant reliance on irrelevant planning factors, or a planning policy based on a clearly discriminatory element for serious issues to arise.[13] In *Chapman v United Kingdom*, where the applicant complained that the legal system failed to accommodate the gypsies' traditional way of life by treating them in the same way as the majority population and in that way discriminated against them, the Court avoided looking at the general situation, finding no lack of objective or reasonable justification for the measures taken against this individual applicant.[14]

Steps taken to expel Roma from one country to another must also comply with certain procedural standards. Where in *Conka v Belgium* the authorities used a ruse to bring the families to the police station to be detained pending their expulsion, the Court had regard to the limited information made available in their own language and the speed of the removal, which rendered futile any possibility of applying to the courts, and found that the strategem contravened the principles implicit in the Convention. The measure also contravened the prohibition on collective expulsions set out in Art.4 of Protocol No.4, namely the decision to enforce the expulsion was taken without a procedure affording sufficient guarantees that the personal circumstances of each individual had been genuinely taken into account.[15]

---

[11] *e.g.* the absence of normal means of communication, unavailability of Greek-Cypriot press, lack of secondary education in Greek, effect on residence rights on children sent to school in the south, limitations and conditions imposed on freedom of movement, with effects on access to medical treatment and participation in communal or religious events; inability to preserve property rights on departure or death.

[12] *e.g. Cyprus v Turkey* above.

[13] In 31006/96, (Dec.) July 2, 1997, where the applicant gypsies claimed that special allowance was required in the application of planning laws to them, the Commission found no such disregard of their position as to disclose discrimination.

[14] para.129.

[15] Also pending, *Sulejmanovic and Sultanovic v Italy*, 57574/00 (Dec.) March 14, 2002, where the complaints about the collective expulsion of Romany applicants were declared admissible.

4. Culture and education

IIB–201 Where planning measures concerning occupation of land by gypsies have been found to be in conformity with Arts 8 and 14, the Court has given short shrift to complaints that the restrictions disclosed any breach of Art.2 of Protocol No.1. Ignoring any difficulties resulting to attendance at school or continuity of school education, the Court found that the applicants had not substantiated that there had been in the circumstances any denial of education to the children of the families concerned.[16]

Nor can gypsies or other minorities claim any overriding right to continue traditional cultural activities, or even reside, in a particular location. Cases so far have found have found measures to be proportionate where alternative solutions have been provided.[17]

5. Access to court

IIB–202 Regarding the adequacy of court review of planning decisions, the Court's judgment in *Bryan v United Kingdom* indicates that special considerations apply in the planning sphere. The applicant, facing enforcement measures in respect of his barn conversion, had argued that the inspector in planning enquiries was not sufficiently independent of the Executive and the High Court's scope of review on points of law insufficient to address his complaints on the merits. The Court found that while the inspector did not provide guarantees of independence, the procedures were basically fair and the possibility of appeal on points of law to the High Court was sufficient review in a special area of administrative discretion. As a result, it would appear that gypsies who generally have problems on the merits of cases (for example, whether the planning considerations outweigh the compassionate circumstances) will effectively be deprived of any independent scrutiny of their cases and the planning authorities given an almost exclusive decision-making power if they keep within domestic law.

Cross-reference

Part IIA: Access to court
Part IIB: Discrimination

---

[16] *Coster*, para.137; *Jane Smith*, para.129; *Lee*, para.125: judgments cited above.
[17] *Gypsy Council v UK*, 66336/01, (Dec.), May 14, 2002, where a prohibition order was issued severely restricting the traditional horse fair at Horsemonden (a limited procession was allowed in the village and an alternative venue provided some 20 miles away): *Noack v Germany*, 46346/99, (Dec.) May 25, 2000, ECHR 2000–VI, where a community of Sorbs were required to transfer to another village to make room for lignite mining with accompanying measures aimed to protect their language and culture.

Hindrance in the exercise of the right of individual petition

Key provision:

Article 34, *in fine* (undertaking not to hinder the effective exercise of the right of individual petition) formerly Art.25, para.1, *in fine*.　　　　　IIB–203

Key case law:

Cruz Varas v Sweden, March 20, 1991, Series A, No.201; 14 E.H.R.R. 1; *Akdivar v Turkey*, September 16, 1996, R.J.D., 1996–IV, No.15; 23 E.H.R.R. 143; *Aksoy v Turkey*, December 18, 1996, R.J.D., 1996–VI, No.26; 23 E.H.R.R. 553; *Aydin v Turkey*, September 25, 1997, R.J.D. 1997–VI, No.50; 25 E.H.R.R. 251; *Petra v Romania*, September 23, 1998, R.J.D., 1997–VII, No.92; *Kurt v Turkey*, May 25, 1998, R.J.D., 1998–III, No.74; 27 E.H.R.R. 373; *Tanrikulu v Turkey*, July 9, 1999, ECHR 1999–IV; *McShane v UK*, May 28, 2002, *Mahmatkulov and Askarov v Turkey*, February 6, 2003, pending before the Grand Chamber; *Ocalan v Turkey*, March 12, 2003, pending before the Grand Chamber.

1. General considerations

The right of individual petition is the keystone of the supervision process, since it is　IIB–204
individuals and private organisations who provide the vast bulk of the cases under Art.34. The final sentence intends to safeguard the open and unimpeded access of the individual to Strasbourg by imposing the obligation on Contracting States not to hinder the exercise of the right of individual petition. In examining issues arising under former Art.25 (now Art.34), the Commission and Court had regard to the fundamental principle of interpretation of the Convention, that it must guarantee rights which are practical and effective as opposed to theoretical and illusory.[1] As an indication of its importance, the Commission used to raise any apparent problems of hindrance *ex officio*, such being a matter pertinent to its own functioning.[2]

Express obligations are imposed on States which sign the European Agreement relating to persons participating in proceedings of the European Court of Human Rights. This covers for example interference with prisoners' correspondence with the Convention organs (Art.3) and co-operation in allowing applicants to enter or leave territory for the purpose of attending hearings (Art.4).

It is a healthy sign that relatively few complaints are made that a Contracting State has either failed to co-operate with the Convention organs in the examination process or that it has interfered with the applicant in some way. Where allegations do arise of deliberate interference by a Government with an applicant during pending proceedings, which the Government denies, the Court is in a difficult position and may be faced by factual problems which it is ill-equipped to resolve.[3]

---

[1] *e.g. Cruz Varas*, para.99; *Aydin*, (Rep.) March 7, 1996, para.212.

[2] 13590/88, (Rep.) July 12, 1990, Series A, No.233–A, p.33. The Court would be likely to adopt the same view, now that it has taken over sole responsibility for applications.

[3] *e.g. Kurt*, para.161 where the applicant produced contradictory statements about her intentions, her lawyers claimed Government pressure while the Government alleged the PKK coercion to produce anti-

2. Substantive or procedural right

IIB–205 Former Art.25 was described in *Cruz Varas v Sweden* as a procedural right which could be invoked by individuals. The Commission followed a practice of making findings as to whether a Government had failed to comply with its obligations, until in *Akdivar v Turkey* the Court made a finding of a violation of Art.25, although stating in terms that it was of a procedural nature distinguishable from the substantive rights. The terminology used by the new Court tends to use the previous Commission formulation, though references to violation or non-violation of Art.34 also appear. No matters of relevance appear to flow from the varying usage.

Having regard to the procedural character of the right, the admissibility criteria appear to have no role, as regards at least the exhaustion of domestic remedies. Whether the Court would consider it appropriate to apply the six month time-limit to prevent stale issues is unlikely but an allegation dating back a considerable period without any convincing reason for failure to raise it earlier would presumably be a factor against the matter being taken up.

3. Hindrance

IIB–206 Hindrance in its normal meaning is not synonymous with complete obstruction but would appear to cover any step which renders the application process more difficult. Indeed, though it was initially questioned whether there could be hindrance where an applicant pursued his petition, it would have meant that no successful allegations of interference could be made since the applicants who were most effectively intimidated would have ceased to pursue their cases at all.[4] The Court made this position clear in *Akdivar* where indeed one applicant had withdrawn his application entirely before the Commission Delegates and the remaining applicants had continued notwithstanding the alleged intimidation.

4. Types of hindrance

(a) *Prisoners' correspondence and solitary confinement*

IIB–207 The occasional stopping of a letter to the Commission was not considered sufficient to raise an issue[5] and in *Campbell v United Kingdom*, the opening of letters to the Commission, without tampering or delaying, was insufficient to disclose any

State propaganda. Some allegations may prove impossible to clarify, as in *Aksoy*, where the applicant was tortured by palestinian hanging while in custody and then killed by unknown gunmen shortly after his case was communicated to the Government. His lawyer stated that two days before the shooting, the applicant had claimed that he was being followed and that his life was in danger. The Commission was "deeply concerned" by the death of the applicant but unable to resolve the matter. It therefore did not find any failure to comply with Art.25, a conclusion shared by the Court.

[4] In *Kapan v Turkey*, (Dec.) January 14, 1997, 88–A D.R. 17, the applicant failed to appear at a hearing in Strasbourg and in Turkey, his lawyers claiming that he feared for his life. However, following his continued silence, including a failure to provide written confirmation of his intention to continue the application, the Commission struck the case off. To give up these cases is perhaps unsatisfactory. But it underlines the reality that the system relies on applicants with the courage to complain and to maintain their complaints actively.

[5] 18264/91, (Dec.), September 8, 1993.

prejudice in the presentation of his application to the Commission.[6] No violation of Art.34 arose from delays of some weeks in transmitting the applicant's letters to the Court as they were not regarded as significant or hindering the exercise of his right of petition.[7] Where the main complaint concerns the opening or censorship of letters and the Court finds a breach of Art.8, no separate issue under Art.34 is likely to arise.[8]

Where the same *Campbell* alleged that he was being punished in solitary confinement for his applications to Strasbourg, the Commission took the complaint seriously enough to pursue the matter with the Government. It transpired however that he was held in segregation because he wanted to spend time on his various litigations and had refused to go on normal routine which would have involved working instead of spending time in his cell with his books and papers. Thus, there was no clear punitive intent and no indication that it hampered his right of petition.[9] In *Petra v Romania* however, the Court found a violation of former Art.25 where the applicant had been twice threatened by the prison authorities when he had asked to write to the Commission.[10] Refusal to provide writing materials for pursuing an application may also disclose a hindrance.[11]

As regards prisoners' access to lawyers for the Convention purposes, in *Ocalan v Turkey*, the refusal to grant two of the applicant's lawyers permission to enter the territory and alleged difficulties in the applicant communicating with his lawyers did not in fact prevent them from submitting an application to the Court on his behalf and thus there was no indication that his exercise of his right of individual petition had been impeded to any significant extent.[12]

(b) *Intimidation of applicants*

Contact by State authorities with applicants concerning their applications to Strasbourg is likely, save in exceptional and convincingly innocuous circumstances, to raise serious issues. The Court's approach in *Aydin v Turkey* however indicates that applicants must provide some concrete and independent proof of any harassment alleged.[13]

IIB–208

---

[6] The Commission did find a violation of the Art.8 correspondence right, as did the Court. Art.25 was not pursued before the Court.

[7] *Valasinas v Lithuania*, July 24, 2001, ECHR 2001–VIII, para.136—the Court had however found a breach of Art.8 in respect of censorship of the correspondence; in contrast, see *Slavgorodski v Estonia*, 37043/97, (Dec.) March 9, 1999, ECHR 1999–II, in which the Government acknowledged that the opening by the prison authorities of letters from the Commission to the applicant was a breach of former Art.25, later struck off on September 12, 2000, when the parties settled.

[8] *e.g. Klamecki v Poland (No.2)*, April 3, 2003, para.158.

[9] *Campbell v UK*, 12323/86 (Dec.) July 13, 1988, 57 D.R. 148.

[10] para.44; mere questioning for clarification did not disclose improper pressure in *Manoussos v Czech Republic and Germany*, 46468/99, (Dec.) July 9, 2002.

[11] *Cotlet v Romania*, June 3, 2000, where there were also delays in the mail which was sent and systematic opening of Strasbourg correspondence.

[12] para.240.

[13] paras 116–117: it disagreed with the Commission's more liberal approach requiring the Government to make a proper response to allegations. Also, *Demiray v Turkey*, November 21, 2000, ECHR 2000–XII, where the Court found insufficient facts to conclude that the applicant's family had been questioned about the application or otherwise harassed by the authorities; *Denizci v Cyprus*, May 23, 2001, ECHR 2001–V, paras 419–421, insufficient evidence to show that improper pressure had been placed on the applicants to retract their allegations; *Berktay v Turkey*, March 1, 2001, para.208.

Questioning of applicants about their applications will generally amount to an illicit and unacceptable form of pressure on applicants to withdraw their applications.[14] Even if contact by the authorities with applicants with a view to investigation of their complaints on a domestic level was compatible, the Commission considered that applicants' lawyers should be present and that it was never legitimate to question applicants about the circumstances in which they made their application, their motivation or what they intended to say in the application with a view to testing the accuracy of submissions made on their behalf.[15] In *Tanrikulu v Turkey*, the questioning of the applicant by the Chief Public Prosecutor as to the authenticity of the letter of authority provided by her lawyers to the Commission was, with other actions, interpreted as a deliberate attempt to cast doubt on the validity of the application and the applicant's credibility and a bid to frustrate the applicant's successful pursuit of her application. The Court agreed with the Commission that if a Government were concerned about forged documents they should bring their misgivings before the Convention organs.[16]

Unacceptable pressure includes direct coercion and flagrant acts of intimidation of applicants or potential applicants or their families or legal representatives and also other improper indirect acts or contacts designed to dissuade or discourage them from pursuing a Convention remedy. The vulnerability of the complainant is taken into account in assessing the propriety of any such contacts.[17]

(c) *Intimidation of lawyers*

IIB–209　Attempts to institute criminal and even disciplinary proceedings against the lawyers in connection with their participation in applications to Strasbourg will disclose a failure by the State to comply with obligations under Art.34, since this may have the effect of dissuading an applicant or his or her lawyer from pursuing a case, place obstacles in the path of pursuing an application and deter future applications. A

---

[14] *Akdivar*: violations of former Art.25 found where the Government produced a videotape of an applicant, and a villager with the same name as another applicant, denying the introduction of any application and stereotyped statements signed by several applicants to the same effect; see however *Manoussos*, n.10 above, where the questioning of the prisoner did not disclose any improper pressure on the facts; *Matyar v Turkey*, February 21, 2002, where the majority found insufficient evidence to support allegations of intimidation when an applicant was summoned for questioning by gendarmes, the minority considered that the presumption that this amounted to illicit pressure had not been rebutted in the absence of a convincing explanation about why it was necessary.

[15] Also *Kurt*, (Rep.) December 6, 1996, para.247, where the Commission found that contacts with an applicant to verify whether the application was genuine were inacceptable, since where such doubts existed it was for the Commission to verify the existence of a valid application; *Ergi v Turkey*, July 28, 1998, R.J.D., 1998–IV, No.81, the Convention organs found no plausible reason for the authorities, particularly the anti-terror police, to question the applicant about his application, even to verify his legal aid claim; *Akdeniz v Turkey*, May 31, 2000, paras 119–120, where applicants were questioned about their applications and in two cases detained over night.

[16] Also *Salman v Turkey*, June 27, 2000, ECHR 2000–VII, paras 131–132, where the applicant was questioned about her legal aid declaration of means from the Commission and blindfolded while at the Anti-Terror Department.

[17] *e.g. Kurt*, para.60; *Assenov v Bulgaria*, October 28, 1998, R.J.D., 1998–VIII, No.96, para.170— violation of Art.25 where the applicants were questioned about the application leading them to make a sworn declaration denying that they had; *Bilgin v Turkey*, November 16, 2000, para.135, where the applicant was questioned about his application by the gendarme authorities against whom he had made serious complaint; *Akkoç v Turkey*, October 10, 2000, ECHR 2000–X, para.126, where the applicant was questioned about her application during an interrogation involving torture.

failure to comply was found in *Kurt v Turkey* where a Government representative after a Commission hearing took the initiative in contacting the prosecution authorities with a view to taking action against the applicant's lawyer for making allegations which the applicant had not maintained in her oral evidence.[18] Even where the lawyer is later acquitted or the proceedings dropped, the institution of the proceedings is regarded as having a potential chilling effect.[19] There was on that basis a sufficient connection with an application to the Court for an adverse finding under Art.34 in *McShane v United Kingdom* where the police lodged a disciplinary complaint, later dropped, against the applicant's lawyer in inquest proceedings for allegedly infringing an undertaking in passing on documents to the applicant for use in her Convention application.

5. Failure of the Government to comply with procedural requests

(a) *Failure to comply with interim measures*

The refusal of a Government to comply with a Commission request for suspensive measures under its Rules of Procedure was not *per se* a failure to comply with its Art.25 obligations. In *Cruz Varas v Sweden*, where the authorities expelled the applicant to Chile despite the Commission's request to suspend the measure pending examination of allegations that he risked torture and ill-treatment on return, the Court found that no power to impose binding interim measures could be derived from former Art.25 or the Commission's Rules.[20] However it did accept that an individual could complain if steps were taken which interfered with the right effectively to pursue an application. On the facts of this case, finding no substantiated risk of ill-treatment, the Court noted that while compliance with the request would have facilitated the applicant's presentation of his case, in fact he remained at liberty in Chile and his counsel was able fully to present his views in his absence, without being hindered to any significant degree. However the Court commented that failure to comply with a request where a violation of Art.3 was later found would aggravate the breach.[21]

IIB–210

Nonetheless, when the new Court came to consider the status of its own interim measures in *Mamatkulov and Askarov v Turkey*, it emphasised the need to make the system effective and the status of the Convention as a living instrument, concluding that Contracting States were under an obligation to comply with requests for interim measures and to refrain from any act or omission which might impinge on the integrity and effectiveness of a future binding judgment under Art.46. In the particular case, it found that the failure of the Government to suspend the extradition of two applicants to Uzbekistan disclosed a violation of Art.34,

---

[18] See also *Sarli v Turkey*, May 22, 2001, paras 85–85, where criminal proceedings were commenced against a Turkish lawyer for submitting an application for the purpose, *inter alia*, of anti-state propaganda. It was irrelevant that the lawyer was not one of the applicant's named representatives in Strasbourg, as he had nonetheless been assisting them and was instrumental in introducing the application.

[19] *Sarli*, para.85.

[20] Now r.39 of the Rules of Court. See Procedure Notes, Interim Measures.

[21] An approach which it confirmed regarding its own rules of procedure until as recently as *Conka v Belgium*, 51564/99, (Dec.) March 13, 2001—where the Belgian authorities failed to suspend the expulsion measures against the gypsy applicants without explanation, the Court rejected the Art.34 complaint as manifestly ill-founded.

essentially as, since the applicants' extradition, their lawyers had been unable to communicate with them and it was for lack of substantiation that their complaints under Art.3 were rejected.

Not all failures to comply with interim measures however will breach Art.34. The Court reserved its position in *Ocalan v Turkey*[22] stating that in the exceptional circumstances of that case the refusal of the Government under a r.39 request to make available certain information did not prevent the applicant proving his case and that the information had been linked to the proceedings which placed the applicant at risk of the death penalty, which risk had meanwhile disappeared

(b) *Documents and other facilities*

IIB–211 A failure by a Government to provide documents or information, or to facilitate the taking of evidence before Delegates might also potentially raise issues under Art.34 where this substantially hindered the Strasbourg examination of the case. In cases of this kind however the Court tends instead to make a finding that the State has failed to comply with Art.38, (former Art.28 para.1(a)) which provides that States "shall furnish all necessary facilities" in the investigation of a case,[23] emphasising the importance of the Government's co-operation in Convention proceedings.[24] Alternatively, the Court may draw inferences from the failure of a Government to respond to questions or requests and proceed to find substantive violations.[25] The Commission referred in a number of cases involving the taking of evidence to the Court's statement in *Ireland v United Kingdom* that the conduct of the parties when evidence is being taken may be taken into account in the assessment of evidence.[26]

---

[22] paras 241–242.
[23] *e.g. Cakici v Turkey*, July 8, 1999, ECHR 1999–IV, para.76, where the Government gave no satisfactory explanations for failure to provide custody records or the non-attendance of witnesses at a fact-finding hearing; *Aktas v Turkey*, April 24, 2003, where the Government refused on short notice to make 11 witnesses available to the Commission without special security conditions barring the applicant's lawyers from participation; *Tas v Turkey*, November 14, 2000, where the Government delayed in providing information. *Cf. Timurtas v Turkey*, June 13, 2000, paras 72 and 123, no issues under Arts 34 or 38 where, impliedly, a Government witness had lied on oath before delegates.
[24] *e.g. Tepe v Turkey*, May 9, 2003, para.135.
[25] *e.g. Ergi*, n.15 above, failure to provide requested gendarme witnesses was taken into account in assessing the evidence.
[26] January 18, 1978, Series A, No.25 para.161; *Ergi*, n.15 above.

Home

Key provision:

Article 8 (respect for home).   IIB–212

Key case law:

Gillow v UK, November 24, 1986, Series A, No.109; 11 E.H.R.R. 335; *Chappell v UK*, March 30, 1989, Series A, No.152–A; 12 E.H.R.R. 1; *Niemietz v Germany*, December 16, 1992, Series A, No.251–B; 16 E.H.R.R. 97; *Funke v France*, February 25, 1993 Series A, No.256–A; 16 E.H.R.R. 287; *Murray v UK*, October 28, 1994, Series A, No.300–A; 19 E.H.R.R. 193; *Buckley v UK*, September 25, 1996, R.J.D. 1996–IV; 23 E.H.R.R. 101; *Mentes v Turkey*, November 28, 1997, R.J.D. 1997–VIII; 26 E.H.R.R. 1; *Camenzind v Switzerland*, December 16, 1997, R.J.D. 1997–VIII; 28 E.H.R.R. 458; *McLeod v UK*, September 23, 1998, R.J.D. 1998–VII; 27 E.H.R.R. 493; *Chapman v UK*, January 18, 2001, ECHR 2001–I; *Cyprus v Turkey*, May 10, 2001, ECHR 2001–IV; *Société Colas Est v France*, April 16, 2002, ECHR 2002–III; *Roemen and Schmit v Luxembourg*, February 25, 2003, ECHR 2003–IV; *Ernst v Belgium*, July 15, 2003.

1. General considerations

Home has been given a wide definition by the Convention organs. It is not   IIB–213
necessary that a home be lawfully established, significance attaching rather to the
nature of the occupation.[1] Further, since "home" and "private life" may overlap
with business and professional activities, the scope of Art.8 has been found to extend
to offices. This is seen as consonant with the essential purpose of Art.8 to protect
the individual against arbitrary interferences by public authorities.[2] Since companies
may claim rights as applicants under the Convention, it has also been interpreted as
covering company premises.[3] As in other aspects of Art.8, while it is primarily
interferences by public authorities which are concerned, there may in certain

---

[1] *Buckley*, paras 52–54, where the applicant gypsy established her home on land without planning permission—also *Buckley*, (Rep.) para.63, where the Commission found that "home" is an autonomous concept which does not depend on classification under domestic law but on the factual circumstances, namely, the existence of sufficient and continuous links, citing, 7456/76, (Dec.) February 8, 1978, 13 D.R. 40; *Gillow*, para.46, where, though the applicants were absent from their house for almost 19 years for professional reasons, they intended it to be their home, keeping furniture there and having no home established elsewhere.

[2] *Niemietz*, paras 30–31, where a search of a lawyer's office and seizure of documents by the police interfered with private life, home and correspondence; *Chappell*, search of premises used for residential and business purposes; *Roemen and Schmidt*, search of a lawyer's office; *Keslassy v France*, 51578/99, (Dec.) January 8, 2002, ECHR 2002–I, where the person's domicile was also head office of a company. Not all business activities will qualify—23953/94, (Dec.) September 6, 1995 82 D.R. 51 where a bar open to the public, which showed pornographic videos, was searched and videos seized, the Commission found that nature of the premises and and the business activities had to be taken into account—no interference with home or private life was found; 44568/98, (Dec.) September 18, 2003, police entry of a restaurant impliedly not covered.

[3] *Société Colas Est*, para.41, referring to the role of the Convention as a living instrument reflecting current conditions.

circumstances be positive obligations imposed on a State to protect the right to respect for home from others.[4] There is no right as such to be provided with a home however.[5]

2. Regulation of occupation

IIB–214   Any interferences with "home" must comply with the requirements of the second paragraph of Art.8. The Court has stated that the importance of the right to respect for home, which is pertinent to personal security and well-being, must be taken into account in the determining the scope of the margin of appreciation allowed to Governments.[6] However, in the balancing exercise of private against the general interest, certain features such as the perceived nature of planning controls have taken on significance. A wide margin of appreciation has been held to apply to the implementation of town and country planning schemes.[7]

In *Gillow v United Kingdom*, where the applicants were refused permission to reside in their house in Guernsey, the Court's emphasis was on the lack of any pressing social need for the restriction, with a failure on the part of the authorities to give sufficient weight to the applicants' personal circumstances notwithstanding the legitimate interest in controlling population on the island. In contrast, in *Buckley v United Kingdom*, the applicant gypsy's right to respect for the home established on her land was not of manifest weight against the Court's consideration that in the area of planning controls national authorities are in principle better placed to evaluate local needs and conditions and in the exercise of discretion involving a multitude of factors the authorities enjoy a wide margin of appreciation. In *Buckley*, the emphasis was accordingly on whether there was a procedure whereby the local authorities assessed the competing interests. Since the planning inspectors reached their decisions on the basis of relevant and sufficient reasons, the refusal of planning permission was not found to exceed the margin of appreciation. Although the applicant had argued that no practical alternative was open to her and that her personal circumstances were pressing, the Court, with less sympathy than in *Gillow*, stated that Art.8 did not allow individual's preferences as to their place of residence to override the general interest. In a later gypsy case, *Chapman v United Kingdom*, the Court has stated, as regards measures taken against occupation of land without proper planning permission, that it would be slow to grant protection to those who in conscious defiance of the law established a home on an environmentally protected site.[8]

Exclusion of displaced persons from returning to their homes in northern Cyprus was found in *Cyprus v Turkey* to infringe Art.8 as having no basis in law. Nor was the Court sympathetic to claims by Turkey that the policy should be regarded as

---

[4] 20357/92, (Dec.) March 7, 1994 76 D.R. 80 see "Private life, 3. State obligations". Positive obligations are only likely to arise fromf serious infringements in the personal sphere such as deliberate, health-threatening persecution. Unsolicited mail is insufficient: 24967/94, (Dec.) February 20, 1995, 80 D.R. 175.

[5] *Chapman*, para.99.

[6] *Gillow*, para.56.

[7] *Buckley*, para.75; also *Noack v Germany*, No.46346/99, (Dec.) May 25, 2000, ECHR 2000–VI, where the Sorbian minority in a village were resettled elsewhere to permit extension to mining activities.

[8] *Chapman*, para.102: while a Grand Chamber majority found no violation of Art.8, considering that the authorities had struck a proper balance, the dissenters gave greater weight to the interests of the individual gypsy in maintaining her caravan on her land.

justified pending the outcome of inter-communal talks on a whole range of issues. It further found aggravated breaches of Art.8 in its aspects of private and family life and home arising out of the surveillance, monitoring of movements and other restrictions imposed on the enclaved Greek Cypriot community remaining in the northern part of the island.[9]

3. Entry and search of property

Where the authorities enter property, to search, the interference may well cross the boundaries of most, or all, the separate protected interests under Art.8.[10] Requirements of customs control, investigation of terrorism or other crime, protection of the rights of others in the area of copyright and investigations into anti-competition agreements between companies have been accepted as legitimate aims for searches.[11] **IIB–215**

The case law has concentrated on the requirements that searches be "lawful" and attended by adequate procedural safeguards against arbitrariness and abuse.[12] Where orders are issued by courts, with an element of judicial supervision built in, there is likely to be sufficient safeguard, as in *Chappell v United Kingdom* where the applicant attacked unsuccessfully the draconian nature of Anton Pillar orders.[13] However, even where a court makes the order, it is necessary for its scope to be contained within identifiable limits. In *Niemietz v Germany*, the Court found the order for search and seizure of documents without any limitation to be disproportionate, particularly in the context of the confidentiality attaching to correspondence and documents of a lawyer.[14] The minor nature of the offence which led to the search was also of relevance in that case.[15] In *Roemen and Schmidt v Luxembourg*, where a lawyer's office was searched with a view to discovering a confidential source of her client journalist, a judicial officer was present but the Court found that the terms of the search were framed too widely and indiscriminately.[16] In finding the search

---

[9] See paras 281–301. These highly intrusive and invasive measures included the physical presence of State agents in Greek Cypriot homes during social events or visits by third parties.

[10] *e.g. Niemietz* (search of lawyer's office); *Mentes v Turkey*, where soldiers searched and burned houses, there was grave interference with private and family life and home.

[11] *Funke; Murray; Chappell; Société Colas Est*: also *Camenzind*, aim of maintaining telecom regulations.

[12] *Funke*, paras 54–57, where the Customs had exclusive competence to assess the expediency, number, length, and scale of investigation and the procedural safeguards were too lax and full of loopholes, the Court was not impressed by the supervision of a senior customs official or the presence of a police officer; *Camenzind*, search of house by a PTT official verifying conformity of telephones with regulations had adequate safeguards (including attendance of local public official on request), given the limited nature of the search; *Société Colas Est*, where there was no pre-judicial approval of the "visits" of investigators and insufficient safeguards governing the very wide powers of the administrative authority.

[13] It was sufficient that the plaintiff's solicitor rather than a court official carried out the order, since he would be subject to heavy sanctions for breach of undertakings to the court; also the order was only granted *ex parte* if certain conditions fulfilled and was subject to limitation. Also *Tamosius v UK* 62002/00, (Dec.) September 19, 2002, where sufficient supervision was provided by counsel independent of the search team; *Funke*, where the Court commented on lack of judicial supervision of wide Customs powers.

[14] The possibility of an independent observer was referred to as a special procedural safeguard that might be required in that context. See 15882/89, March 29, 1993, 74 D.R. 48 where search of a lawyer's office was accepted as attended by necessary safeguards, including a representative from a lawyers' association.

[15] Also *Funke*, para.58, where the lack of any criminal complaint against the applicant whose home was searched was relevant.

[16] para.70—the search warrant covered any item useful, or harmful, to the investigation. See similar breach in *Ernst*, where the applicant journalists were not charged with any offence and the warrant was without any limitation.

disproportionate, it also took into account the speed with which the search was carried out (the same day as the court order was issued) and its link with a breach of the Art.10 rights of the journalist.

The manner in which the entry or search is conducted must also be compatible with the requirements of Art.8, in particular the means employed should be proportionate to the legitimate aim pursued. In *McLeod*, while a power for the police to enter a house to prevent a breach of the peace was generally acceptable, the entry was not in fact justified in the circumstances of the case, in particular as the applicant was not present in the house at the relevant time and it should have been clear to the officers that there was little or no risk of disorder or crime arising. However, the circumstances existing in Northern Ireland were found to necessitate the precautions used by the army on entering houses.[17]

Cross-reference

Part IIB: Environment
Part IIB: Gypsies and minorities
Part IIB: Housing and tenancy
Part IIB: Private life

---

[17] *Murray*, where the occupants were briefly confined in one room.

Homosexuality

Key provision:

Articles 8 (private and family life) and 14 (discrimination).   IIB–216

Key case law:

Dudgeon v UK, October 22, 1981, Series A, No.45; 4 E.H.R.R. 149; *Norris v Ireland*, October 26, 1988, Series A, No.142; 13 E.H.R.R. 186; *Modinos v Cyprus*, April 22, 1993, Series A, No.259; 16 E.H.R.R. 485; *Laskey, Jaggard and Brown v UK*, February 19, 1997, R.J.D. 1997–I; 24 E.H.R.R. 39; *Smith and Grady v UK*, September 27, 1999, ECHR 1999–VI; 29 E.H.R.R. 493; *Lustig-Prean and Beckett v UK*, September 27, 1999; 29 E.H.R.R. 548; *Salguiero da Silva Mouta v Portugal*, December 21, 1999, ECHR 1999; 31 E.H.R.R. 1055; *ADT v UK*, July 31, 2000; *Sutherland v UK (striking out)*, March 27, 2001; *Fretté v France*, February 26, 2002, ECHR 2002–I; *L and V v Austria*, January 9, 2003, ECHR 2003–I; *Karner v Austria*, July 24, 2003.

1. General considerations

The Convention organs have made a limited contribution to tackling the problems   IIB–217
of stigmatisation and discrimination facing persons who are homosexual. While they made an early and important step in rejecting the criminalisation of adult homosexual acts, there have been somewhat slow and conservative responses to claims in the realm of family life, differing ages of consent and discrimination generally. There has been more readiness in the last few years to scrutinise the justifications for treating individuals in a less favourable manner merely on account of their sexual orientation, most notably in the gays in the army cases.

2. Right to private life

Dudgeon v United Kingdom established the important principle that private sexual   IIB–218
conduct, which is a vital element of an individual's personal sphere, cannot be prohibited merely because it may shock or offend others. In such an intimate aspect of private life, there must exist particularly serious reasons before interferences can be justified. The Court underlined in this context two of the hallmarks of a democratic society, tolerance and broadmindedness. In *Norris v Ireland*, it rejected the claim that States should enjoy extensive leeway as to what morals should require. The prohibition by criminal law of consensual sexual activities between adult homosexuals in private constitutes therefore an unjustified interference with the right to respect for private life. A homosexual applicant can claim to be a victim of such a violation through the mere existence of the criminal offence since this has a direct and continuous effect on his life. The Convention organs have not been persuaded by arguments that an individual applicant had not been prosecuted or threatened with prosecution or that there was no real incidence of prosecutions[1] or that there was a claimed policy of no prosecutions.[2]

---

[1] *Dudgeon* and *Norris*. It was noted in *Dudgeon* that private prosecutions were possible.
[2] *Modinos*, where the Att-Gen could not bind his successors.

As to what activities fall within the scope of "private life", the Court doubted that it covered group sado-masochistic activities.[3] In any event it found that the prosecution of such acts as assault and wounding, notwithstanding the consent of the adult victims, was justified for the aim of the protection of health, having regard to the extreme nature of the acts concerned. In the later case, *ADT v United Kingdom*, the new Court noted the *obiter* nature of the expressed doubts and found without reservation that the arrest and conviction of the applicant for engaging in acts, mainly of oral sex, with up to four other adult men in his own home disclosed an interference with his private life. It was not convinced that the mere videotaping of the activities, in the absence of any actual likelihood of the tapes being rendered public, was sufficient to take the acts outside the scope of "private life". In the absence of public health considerations in this case and given the purely private nature of the behaviour, the Court found the prosecution and conviction were not justified.

The way in which gays in the army were investigated in respect of their sexual orientation and sexual relationships and then discharged was found in the cases of *Lustig-Prean and Beckett v United Kingdom* and *Smith and Grady v United Kingdom* to disclose a violation of the right to respect private life.[4] The Court scrutinised in some detail the reasons put forward for the policy pursued by the Ministry of Defence and found them unconvincing, in particular as there was a lack of concrete evidence to substantiate alleged damage to morale or fighting power from the presence of homosexuals in the armed forces. It observed that negative attitudes expressed in an internal survey, to the extent that these reflected a predisposed bias of a heterosexual majority against a homosexual minority, could not by themselves amount to sufficient justification for the interferences with the applicants' rights, any more than similar negative attitudes towards those of a different race, origin or colour. Accordingly, it had not been shown that conduct codes or disciplinary rules could not adequately deal with any behavioural issues arising on the part of either homosexuals or heterosexuals. Regard was also had to the small number of Contracting States that maintained a blanket legal ban on gays in the armed forces and the widespread, if relatively recent, developments in the domestic law of Contracting States on this issue.

3. Age of consent

IIB–219   Measures prohibiting acts with minors under 21 were found justified in *Dudgeon v United Kingdom*, the Court finding that a margin of appreciation was left to Contracting States as to appropriate safeguards, including the age of consent, required for the protection of the young. The Commission noted that 21 might seem high but considered that the Government could rely on the report of the Wolfenden Committee, which had investigated comprehensively the area of sexual offence legislation and recommended the age of 21 as necessary to protect young men from influences of an undesirable kind.[5]

---

[3] *Laskey, Brown and Jaggard*, where the group was large, organised and circulated videos.
[4] This departs robustly from the early Commission decision which accepted the alleged need in the context of the armed forces to prevent blackmail and coercion and maintain trust and confidence: 9237/81, (Dec.) October 12, 1983, 34 D.R. 68.
[5] 7215/75, (Rep.) October 12, 1978, 19 D.R. 66, referring to a German case citing studies indicating a specific social danger in masculine homosexuality (*e.g.* male homosexuals often constituted a distinct socio-cultural group with a clear proselytising tendency towards adolescents and a resulting social isolation)—5935/72(Dec.) September 30, 1975, 3 D.R.45.

By the 1990s when the UK age limit had been reduced to 18,[6] the Commission found a violation of Art.14 in conjunction with Art.8 concluding that there was no objective and reasonable justification for the difference in age of consent of 18 for male homosexuals and 16 for heterosexuals.[7] It dismissed the argument that society was entitled to indicate disapproval of homosexual conduct and its preference for a heterosexual lifestyle, finding that this could not furnish objective and reasonable justification for inequality under the criminal law. The Court struck the case out after the Sexual Offences (Amendment) Act 2000 equalising the age of consent at 16 was brought into force on January 8, 2001.

Differing ages of consent were also rejected in *L and V v Austria*, where both applicants were convicted for homosexual acts with consenting adolescent males between 14 and 18 years, which criminal prohibition did not apply to girls of the same age for either heterosexual or lesbian relations. The Court effectively followed the Commission's approach in *Sutherland* and found a violation of Art.14 in conjunction with Art.8, noting the ever growing European consensus to apply equal ages of consent for heterosexual, lesbian and homosexual relations and finding that insofar as the impugned legislative provision embodied prejudice on the part of a heterosexual majority against a homosexual minority such negative attitudes could not amount to sufficient justification for differential treatment.

4. Right to family life

Despite the modern evolution of attitudes, the relationship of gays and lesbians did   IIB–220
not, according to the Commission, fall within the scope of the right to family life. Consequently, where the UK refused the homosexual partner of a British citizen leave to enter to live with his partner, the Commission found the refusal could not interfere with any family right. While it could raise issues as regarded private life, the Commission found that it had not been shown that the applicants were not able to live somewhere else or that their link to the UK was an essential element of their relationship.[8] Similarly, where the lesbian partner of the applicant died, her eviction from the partner's home (the partner was a secure tenant in public housing) did not concern any family life rights.[9] The Court left open the question in *Karner v Austria* as in that case the threatened eviction of a homosexual after his partner's death fell within the "home" aspect of Art.8.[10]

This approach, continued by the new Court, maintains an emphasis on the traditional married heterosexual couple as the core of the notion of family, which is becoming increasingly less the norm.[11] The Convention organs have been slowly

---

[6] The Criminal Justice and Public Order Act 1994 which pre-empted a pending case introduced by two applicants aged 20 in *Wilde, Greenhalgh and Parry v UK*, 22382/93, (Dec.) January 19, 1995, 80–A D.R. 132, struck off as matter resolved.

[7] *Sutherland*: the Commission noted that reports now gave a very different picture as to the desirability of introducing an equal age of consent, in particular, that the sexual pattern in young males was fixed by 16 and that the existing law might inhibit efforts to improve the health of young homosexual and bisexual men.

[8] 9369/81 (Dec.) May 3, 1983, 32 D.R. 220.

[9] 11716/85, (Dec.) May 14, 1986, 47 D.R. 274; also 28318/95, (Dec.) May 15, 1996.

[10] para.33.

[11] *Mata Estevez v Spain*, 56501/00, (Dec.), May 10, 2001, ECHR 2001–VI, where the rules allowing a surviving spouse to claim social security allowances did not apply to a homosexual partner, the Court found the difference in treatment pursued the legitimate aim of the protection of the family based on marriage bonds.

extending family life to situations where there is *de facto* family life between heterosexuals outside marriage. However, this has not extended to gays and lesbians with longstanding stable relationships, even where there have been children in the household. In *Kerkhoven v Netherlands*,[12] where two lesbians lived in a long-term relationship and shared parenting roles in respect of the child born by artificial insemination by donor, the courts refused an application by the mother's partner for parental authority. The Commission found that Art.8 did not import a positive obligation on a State to grant parental rights to a woman who was living with the mother of a child. While homosexual relationships could fall within the scope of private life, the Commission considered that the refusal of parental authority did not infringe on the private lives of the applicants. This approach seems to overlook or discount the problems which might arise on the death of the child's mother, where in the absence of any legal recognition of a parenting role of the partner, the partner may be at a disadvantage in upholding claims for continued custody of the child. Even where an effect on private or family life was assumed by the Court in the case of *Helen Craig v United Kingdom*, it found that the court orders in a child custody case which forbade any contact between the lesbian partner of a divorced mother and her children did not disclose any unjustified interference.[13]

Where the homosexual applicant is the parent of a child, an interference with family life would be likely to arise from any decisions on custody or contact requiring justification under the second paragraph of Art.8. In *Salguiero da Silva Mouta v Portugal*, where the Court of Appeal had reversed an order giving custody to the applicant father on the grounds that his homosexuality gave rise to an "abnormal situation", the Court avoided ruling on the Art.8 complaint however and instead found a violation of Art.14 in conjunction with Art.8 on the basis that the court's decision was based decisively on considerations of the applicant's sexual orientation, a discriminatory distinction which it stated was not acceptable under the Convention.

A homosexual is unable to claim a right to adopt a child however. In *Frette v France*, where the applicant, a homosexual, complained that, unlike single heterosexuals, he was unable to adopt a child, the Court found that, though there was no right as such to adopt a child guaranteed under Art.8, the fact that domestic law authorised single persons to apply for adoption and the decisive reason for refusing the applicant permission was his "choice of lifestyle" issues arose under Art.14 in conjunction with Art.8. However, it concluded, albeit by a very narrow majority, that the difference in treatment pursued the legitimate aim of protecting the health and rights of children. Given the lack of common ground in Contracting States and the divided opinion in the scientific community as to the possible consequences of a child being adopted by one or more homosexual parents, there was a broad margin of appreciation which the Government had not exceeded. The majority, as with the claim of a transsexual to recognition of family rights in *X, Y and Z v the United Kingdom*, appeared to take the cautious approach of finding that exclusion of rights could be justified where it had not been proved that having a "unconventional" parent was not harmful to a child. In contrast, the minority pointed out that the

---

[12] 15666/89 (Dec.) May 19, 1992.

[13] 45396/99, (Dec.) March 21, 2000 : the Court put weight on the fact that the mother of the children had in fact agreed to the limitations on contact. The children were in the custody of the father, who strenuously opposed any contact with his former wife's lesbian partner and there is no indication that the partner had ever enjoyed any meaningful contact with them.

decision of the French authorities was based solely on the fact that he was a homosexual without any reference to any specific conduct or traits that might be detrimental to a child's upbringing.

5. Right to marry

In view of the express wording of Art.12 "Men and women" and the reference to applicable national laws, the Court is perhaps unlikely to find that a right to marry could exist for homosexuals where the Contracting State forbids it. As with transsexuals and marriage though, the Court may be nudged in that direction by sufficient evolution in attitudes within Contracting States.[14] In those countries where gay marriages are allowed, the Court may have to accept that "family" relationships could be formed and then any inequalities would become harder to justify.

IIB–221

6. Discrimination

Where differences of treatment are concerned, it will depend very much on the area of right concerned whether the Court will accept that the homosexual can claim to be in an analogous position for the purpose of comparison. Even if he or she could, there would still remain the obstacle of establishing that the difference concerns a substantive right under the Convention and that there is no objective or reasonable justification for the difference.

IIB–222

In the context of family life, for example, the Commission found in *Kerkhoven* that a lesbian couple could not claim to be in a relevantly similar position as a heterosexual one as regarded parental authority, while the Court in *Mata Estevez v Spain* considered that it was within the State's margin to pursue the aim of protecting traditional married couples in providing them with social security allowances in the event of the death of one partner.[15]

Regarding justifications for differences of treatment, the alleged need to protect young men has at last been found not to be sustainable in *Sutherland v United Kingdom* and *L and V v Austria*, which refer to studies indicating that sexual proclivities are fixed by early adolescence and young males are not in any special need of protection from being "perverted" away from heterosexuality.

Though clear statements were made in the gays in the army cases and in *Salgueiro de Silva Mouta* as to the inacceptability of making distinctions based on considerations of sexual orientation, the majority in *Fretté* has found that a broad margin of appreciation applies in the context of adoption by homosexuals due to the lack of "common ground" or "uniform principles" in Contracting States, an approach which the minority considered as liable to take the protection of fundamental rights backwards.[16]

In other contexts, the Court has stated that just like differences in sex, differences based on sexual orientation require particularly serious reasons by way of justification. Thus in the absence of any convincing or weighty reasons for excluding persons in a homosexual relationship from protection under Rent Acts, the Court found a violation of Art.14 in conjunction with Art.8.[17]

---

[14] See *Christine Goodwin v UK*, July 11, 2002, ECHR 2002–VI, paras 84–85.
[15] n.11 above.
[16] *Smith and Grady*, para.97; *Salguiero da Silva Mouta*, para.36; *Frette*, paras 41–42 and opinion of Judges Bratza, Fuhrmann and Tulkens.
[17] *Karner*, para.37, citing *Smith and Grady*, para.90.

Cross-reference

Part IIB: Armed Forces
Part IIB: Discrimination
Part IIB: Private life

Housing and tenancy

Key provisions:

Article 1 of Protocol No.1 (peaceful enjoyment of possessions) and Art.6 (access to court/fair hearing).

IIB–223

Key case law

Sporrong and Llonroth v Sweden, September 9, 1982, Series A, No.52; *James v UK,* February 21, 1986, Series A, No.98; 8 E.H.R.R. 123; *Gillow v UK,* November 24, 1986, Series A, No.109; 11 E.H.R.R. 335; *Mellacher v Austria,* December 19, 1989, Series A, No.169; 12 E.H.R.R. 391; *Spadea and Scalabrino v Italy,* September 28, 1995, Series A, No.315–B; 21 E.H.R.R. 482; *Scollo v Italy,* September 28, 1995, Series A, No.315–C; 22 E.H.R.R. 524; *Velosa Barreto v Portugal,* November 21, 1995, Series A, No.334; *Larkos v Cyprus,* February 18, 1999, ECHR 1999–I; 30 E.H.R.R. 597; *Immobiliare Saffi v Italy,* July 28, 1999, ECHR 1999–V; 30 E.H.R.R. 756.

1. General considerations

There is no right to housing or accommodation in the Convention.[1] Generally, for issues to arise, an applicant must have an already existing property right or occupy the property. The cases have related principally to Government regulation of leases and rents. Such measures generally constitute a control of use and, if severe enough, *de facto* expropriation or outright deprivation as in *James v United Kingdom* where statute conferred a right to long leaseholders to acquire the freehold of the Duke of Westminster's property in London. Where a person enjoys a property right to the housing, an interference will raise issues under Art.1 of Protocol No.1[2] while Art.8 may become applicable, if the circumstances are such that his occupation of the property render it his home (see Pt IIB, Home). Once property or contractual rights are in issue, an applicant may generally also claim access to court and procedural safeguards of Art.6.

In these cases, the Convention organs carry out a balancing exercise in which effect on the applicant's rights is weighed against the wider interests.[3] Measures pursuing social or economic policies tend to attract a wide margin of appreciation.[4]

IIB–224

---

[1] *e.g. Marzari v Italy,* 36448/97, (Dec.) May 4, 1999, where the applicant, suffering from a serious illness, was evicted from local authority housing—the Court stated that although Art.8 did not guarantee the right to have one's housing problems solved by the authorities, a refusal to provide assistance to someone seriously ill might raise an issue because of the impact on his/her private life. In this case, however, the authorities had provided an alternative flat and the Court refused to enter into dispute about its adequacy.

[2] See, however, 19217/91, (Dec.) January 12, 1994, 76–A D.R. 76, where the Commission held that the right to live in a property of which one was not the owner was not a possession right (dispute about inheritance rights over a chateau); *JLS v Spain,* 41917/98, (Dec.) April 27, 1999, ECHR 1999–V, where a serviceman could not claim a property right when ordered to leave his military quarters.

[3] *Sporrong,* para.69.

[4] *James,* para.46.

2. Regulation of ownership

IIB–225   The transfer of property from one private person to another is not *per se* contrary to the Convention.[5] Transfers may pursue legitimate social and economic policies and implement social justice, as in *James*, where the transfer of long leases could be reasonably considered to remedy a social injustice. The margin of appreciation, where expropriation is concerned, is wide due to the nature of the political, economic and social issues involved. The Court in this area has stated that it will respect the legislature's judgment as to what is in the public interest unless it "manifestly without reasonable foundation".[6] Measures involving loss of the property altogether will generally require an element of compensation to satisfy the requirement of proportionality.[7]

3. Rent and tenancy control

IIB–226   A wide margin of appreciation applies also to rent control measures. Measures intervening in existing contracts may be acceptable, where there are legitimate social and economic aims to make accommodation more accessible to the less affluent. Thus in *Mellacher v Austria*, the striking reductions, up to 79 per cent in some cases, did not disclose a violation. The Court did not consider that it violated the principle of freedom of contract in that parties had entered into the agreement as to rents on freely determined market principles. The burden on the landlords was not found to be disproportionate and it was not for the Court to decide whether this was the best solution.[8]

Restrictions on landlords' ability to recover their property and evict tend to satisfy the requirements of the Convention, where they pursue social policies without disproportionate hardship to the individual property owners. Where an applicant complained that legislation was discriminatory in that it protected tenants to the detriment of landlord, the Court considered that due to the fundamental differences between landlords and tenants the two situations could not be considered as analogous or raise any issue of discrimination.[9]

In Italy, where there was a shortage of rented accommodation, owners of rented flats were obtaining eviction orders but were unable to have them enforced, due to emergency laws suspending the enforcement of evictions. Since the owners in *Spadea and Scalabrino v Italy* and *Scollo v Italy* could still sell the property and receive rents this was a control of use not a deprivation of property. The Court found that the suspension was a legitimate measure aimed at managing the effects of expiry of many leases, and the resulting hardship and social tensions. As regarded proportionality, while the applicants attacked the government policy which led to the

---

[5] *James*, para.46.

[6] *James*, para.46; *Immobiliare Saffi*, para.49: the Court is not keen to enter into assessments of policy and the margin is applied both to the assessment of the existence of a problem of public concern and the remedial action necessary.

[7] See Pt IIB: Expropriation and confiscation.

[8] Also, *e.g.* 15434/89, (Dec.) February 15, 1990, 64 D.R. 232, where the applicant who let property by license to avoid application of Rent Acts was affected by a House of Lords judgment requiring courts to look at the true legal nature of transactions and not give to effect to sham devices. The Commission referred to the wide margin of appreciation enjoyed by States in determining and remedying social problems and found that it was not a disproportionate effect to reduce rent.

[9] *Palumbo v Italy*, November 30, 2000 para.52.

situation of many leases expiring together without taking steps to make sure other accommodation was available, the Court noted that shortage of housing was a universal problem in modern society and that the law provided exceptions for landlords who urgently required their property. Where in *Spadea*, the tenants were very old and infirm and the period involved was not overly excessive apparently, the measure was not disproportionate. However in *Scollo*, where the applicant claimed priority, since he was disabled and the tenant had stopped paying rent, there was a violation since the authorities failed to implement their own provisions to give him priority. Some years later however, when restrictions on landlords obtaining possession continued, the Court commented in *Immobiliare Saffi v Italy* that, while the staggering of enforcement of court orders to reinstate landlords was not itself incompatible with the Convention, the risk of imposing an excessive burden on landlords required the provision of procedural safeguards. As the system showed inflexibility and in practice non-priority cases remained outstanding, without any deadline for recovery of possession, and the applicant in the particular case had waited some eleven years without the possibility of compensation, the Court found that a fair balance had not been achieved and that there was accordingly a violation of Art.1 of Protocol No.1.

A fair balance was struck in *Velosa Barreto v Portugal*, where the applicant was prevented from taking possession of an inherited house to live in himself. The measure aimed at the social protection of tenants and the domestic courts had found that he had no urgent need for the property, as he lived with other members of his family.

Conversely, the removal of protection to tenancies may not disclose any interference with respect for home, where there is no immediate danger of eviction.[10] However, there was discrimination contrary to Art.14 together with Art.8 in *Larkos v Cyprus* where the tenants of State properties enjoyed less protection from eviction than private tenants. The Court considered that the Government when acting as landlord was in an analogous situation to other landlords and found no public interest grounds for treating their tenants differently.

4. Housing restrictions

The Channel Island's strict residential housing control was found in *Gillow v United Kingdom* to pursue the legitimate aim of regulating population to prevent over-development and maintaining the economy. However, refusal of both temporary and permanent licenses to the applicants, who returned to live in their house on Guernsey, which they had built 20 years before, was found disproportionate. In the balancing exercise, the Court emphasised the importance of "home" as pertinent to personal security and well-being and that special circumstances weighed in favour of the applicants, namely, that they had been in lawful occupation, had rented out the house as part of the available housing stock on the island, the house now needed repairs and no-one else could have lived there in the meantime. In contrast, an applicant, who lost resident status on divorce and was refused a licence, was not subject to a disproportionate interference since he was offered the possibility of part occupation if he carried out certain alterations.[11]

IIB–227

---

[10] *Strunjak v Croatia*, 46934/00, (Dec.) October 5, 2000, ECHR 2000–X.
[11] 7456/76, (Dec.) February 8, 1978, 13 D.R. 40.

Cross-reference

Part IIB: Expropriation and confiscation
Part IIB: Home
Part IIB: Planning and control of use of property
Part IIB: Property rights

Immigration and expulsion

Key provisions:

Articles 3 (inhuman and degrading treatment), 8 (respect for private and family life), 13 (effective remedy before national authority), 14 (prohibition against discrimination) and Art.2 of the First Protocol (right to education). Article 3 of Protocol No.4 (specific prohibition on expulsion of nationals) has not been ratified by the UK.

IIB–228

A. Introduction

1. General considerations

Immigration, and the arrival of people seeking asylum, if once tolerated or encouraged by Western European States for economic reasons or by virtue of political and philosophical conviction, are now subject to increasing restrictions. This has an effect not only on those outsiders seeking entry but also on people belonging to long-established communities in Contracting States, who do not enjoy full citizenship status and find the host authorities depressingly keen to resort to deportation as a measure of control. A not insignificant number of countries have changed their laws of nationality and citizenship placing the possibility of obtaining security of residence for non-nationals and their families even further out of reach.

IIB–229

The Convention organs have not been immune to the general atmosphere of "Fortress Europe". They have recognised the legitimate concerns of immigration control, without questioning too deeply the motivation behind it.[1] It is an area where, given the current political sensitivity of the issues, the Convention organs are unlikely to give vent to much creative interpretation. Their record may, to some, be disappointing. Immigrant communities and refugees are particularly vulnerable and, it might be thought, in special need of protection. The Commission was responsive to the hardship disclosed in some cases and there were a number of settlements, which left the issues on the merits unresolved. Both Commission and Court have found violations where the exercise of the power to expel exceeded what they found acceptable. However overall, the case law is negative, disclosed disagreement between the Commission and Court and can be criticised as logically inconsistent.

There are two important groups of cases. The first concerns situations where applicants claim that the expulsion will expose them to torture or ill-treatment—this will often be a refugee case, where the applicant has applied unsuccessfully for asylum under the Geneva Convention[2] or where refugee status has been revoked. The second concerns decisions by immigration authorities to expel, or refuse entry to, persons seeking to remain with or join other family members. There are also associated issues, of private life; denial of education where children are obliged to

---

[1] *e.g. Moustaquim*, para.43: "The Court does not in anyway underestimate the Contracting States' concern to maintain law and order, in particular in exercising their right, as a matter of well-established international law and subject to their treaty obligations, to control the entry, residence and expulsion of aliens." Also *Abdulaziz*, para.67: " the Court cannot ignore that this present case is concerned not only with family life, but also with immigration. . .".

[2] United Nations 1951 Convention on the Status of Refugees.

accompany a parent who is being expelled; discrimination, where the immigration rules appear to treat some groups less favourably than others; and the problem of effective remedies before national authorities for applicants claiming to be at risk of torture and ill-treatment or interference with their family lives.

Before dealing with the substantive issues, the problem of exhaustion of domestic remedies deserves individual mention.

2. Exhaustion of domestic remedies

Key case law:

Bahaddar v Netherlands, February 19, 1998, R.J.D. 1998–I, No.64; 26 E.H.R.R. 278; *Jabari v Turkey*, July 11, 2000, ECHR 2000–VIII.

IIB–230   The requirement for exhaustion of domestic remedies applies in the normal way. Special considerations arise as to the "effectiveness" of remedies as regards the scope of the review of immigration decisions and having regard to the potential irreversibility of expulsions where individuals may face death or torture on their return.

The Commission's case law established that a remedy without suspensive effect was not effective for expulsion complaints for the purposes of Art.35 (former Art.26) where there was a risk of persecution.[3] Where a person, if successful in the application, could later return from the country to which they had been sent and where there were no allegations of ill-treatment, lack of suspensive effect did not render an available remedy ineffective.[4]

Where a person alleges risk of death or ill-treatment if expelled, the Court, differing from the Commission (see below: Access to Court and Remedies) has found in the context of Art.13 that judicial review furnishes an effective remedy for refusal of asylum. Consequently, judicial review or its equivalent must be considered in light of current case law as potentially an effective remedy which must be exhausted if the case is to be declared admissible.

An application can be rejected as premature, as in a French case concerning Tamils, where the request for asylum had been refused but no expulsion order had been made and it was still possible once the order issued to appeal to the administrative courts which would have suspensive effect. This avenue of appeal was rigorous since it required a written application to be made within 24 hours of service of the expulsion order (though an applicant had the right to ask for an interpreter and legal counsel). The applicants' arguments that this rendered the appeal nugatory as a safeguard in practice were unsuccessful before the Comission, and ultimately the Court, indicating a somewhat strict approach.[5]

However, in special circumstances, a failure to pursue remedies through non-compliance with procedural formalities may not disclose a basis for rejecting an application for non-exhaustion. In *Bahaddar v Netherlands*, where the asylum appeal of an Bangladeshi applicant was rejected as his lawyer failed to submit grounds

---

[3] *e.g.* 7465/76 (Dec.) September 29, 1976 7 D.R. 153; 14312/88, (Dec.) March 8, 1989, 60 D.R. 284.
[4] *e.g.* 12097/86 (Dec.) July 13, 1987, 53 D.R. 210 where a Swiss, Austrian and Algerian, complaining under, *inter alia*, Arts. 8 and 9 were to be returned from Denmark to their countries of origin.
[5] *Vijayanathan and Pusparajah v France*, August 27, 1992, Series A, No.241–B, the Court upheld the Government's preliminary objection that the applicants could not yet claim to be victims.

within the time-limit, the Commission considered that, where there was a serious allegation that an applicant would be ill-treated if expelled, the domestic authorities should examine the case on the merits.[6] The Court upheld the Government's non-exhaustion objection though, as it was still possible for the applicant to lodge a fresh application in the courts. However, in *Jabari v Turkey*, where the applicant had failed to apply for asylum within the five day time-limit after her arrival, the Court found a breach of Arts 3 and 13, considering that the authorities had not provided a proper scrutiny of the factual basis of her claims. The Government's argument that the applicant had failed to comply with procedural requirements of a domestic remedy was rejected. Though the Court emphasised that applicants in Art.3 expulsion cases were not dispensed from exhausting available and effective domestic remedies, the rigid application of the five-day rule to the applicant took no account of her language difficulties and lack of a lawyer or other support and denied her any effective possibility of submitting an asylum request for consideration on the merits.[7]

B. Expulsion: risk of ill-treatment

Key case law:

Soering v UK, July 7, 1989, Series A, No.161; 11 E.H.R.R. 439; *Vilvarajah v UK*, October 30, 1991, Series A, No.215; 14 E.H.R.R. 248; *Nasri v France*, July 13, 1995, Series A, No.320; 21 E.H.R.R 458; *Chahal v UK*, November 15, 1996, R.J.D. 1996–V; 23 E.H.R.R. 413; *Nsona v Netherlands*, November 28, 1996, R.J.D. 1996–VI, No.23; 32 E.H.R.R. 170; *Ahmed v Austria*, December 17, 1996, R.J.D. 1996–VI, No.26; 24 E.H.R.R. 423; *HLR v France*, April 29, 1997, R.J.D. 1997–III, No.36; 26 E.H.R.R 29; *D v UK*, May 2, 1997, R.J.D. 1997–III, No.37; 24 E.H.R.R. 423; *Jabari v Turkey*, July 11, 2000, ECHR 2000–VIII; *Bensaid v UK*, February 6, 2001, ECHR 2001–I; *Hilal v UK*, March 6, 2001, ECHR 2001–II.

IIB–231

1. Responsibility of the expelling Government

While there is no right to asylum as such guaranteed under the Convention, where an applicant faces a real risk of torture or ill-treatment, including extra-judicial or arbitrary execution[8] on expulsion to a particular country, issues arise under Art.3 of the Convention. This is also where the Court may apply its discretion under r.39 to request interim measures pending the determination of the case in Strasbourg. (See Pt 1A3: Interim Relief). Where there is a real risk of a "flagrant denial" of Arts 5 and 6 rights on return to a country, issues may arise engaging the responsibility of the expelling State.[9] However, the scope of this responsibility has yet to be explored in any substantive way.

IIB–232

---

[6] 25894/94, (Dec.) May 22, 1995, (Rep.) September 13, 1996.

[7] (Dec.) October 28, 1999. See, *mutatis mutandis*, *Conka v Belgium*, February 5, 2002, ECHR 2001–I, where the manner of expulsion of the Roma applicants made it practically impossible for them to apply to the courts (breach of Art.5, para.4).

[8] See further Pt IIB, Extradition, section on Death penalty.

[9] See *Soering*, para.113; *Drozd and Janousek v France and Spain*, June 26, 1992, Series A, No.240, para.110; *Tomic v UK*, 17837/03, (Dec.) October 14, 2003: no risk of flagrant breach of Arts 5 or 6 where a former Serb paramilitary was returning to Croatia. Nor in *F v UK*, 17341/03, (Dec.) June 22, 2004, did any responsibility attach to the UK under Art.8 in expelling a homosexual to Iran where homosexual acts were prohibited.

Under Art.3, the obligation of the State extends in respect of everyone within their jurisdiction to a duty not to expose them to an irremediable situation of objective danger even outside their jurisdiction.[10] The argument of the UK Government in *Soering v United Kingdom* that a State should not be held accountable for acts committed outside its jurisdiction was rejected by the Court which found that Art.3 enshrined one of the fundamental values of the democratic societies making up the Council of Europe and considered that the provision should be interpreted so as to make its safeguards practical and effective. A State cannot therefore deport any persons with callous and convenient disregard for their likely fate once they have left its soil. In *TI v United Kingdom*, the Court considered that State responsibility could potentially arise in sending an asylum applicant to a safe third country if, in the circumstances, there was a real risk that the applicant would be sent on to a country where he faced treatment contrary to Art.3.[11]

Responsibility arises whether the source of the risk is the Government or authorities in the receiving State or other groups, such as rival warring or political factions[12] or organised crime groups,[13] where there is no indication of the authorities being able to provide protection.[14] The Commission seemed also prepared to accept risk to a Lebanese woman from her husband's family of being confined to a rigorous form of "house arrest" for refusal to comply with her husband's wishes.[15]

Threat to life may also arise from impact of an expulsion on a person's health apart from deliberately inflicted injury by others, although a high threshold has been held to apply particularly where a case does not concern the direct responsibility of the Contracting State for the infliction of harm.[16] For example, former r.36 was applied by the Commission where the removal of a pregnant woman with a history of premature labour posed a significant risk to the life of the unborn child, though the application was later rejected once after the birth there was no apparent risk to health to mother or child from an expulsion.[17] The psychological impact of the

---

[10] 10479/83 (Dec.) March 12, 1984 37 D.R. 158 : where the applicant alleged the risk of the death penalty on extradition to the US.

[11] 43844/98, (Dec.) March 7, 2000, where, without examing his asylum claims, the UK were expelling the applicant Tamil to Germany, which had already rejected his claims, under the Dublin Convention. On the facts, the Court was satisfied that he was not at risk of being expelled directly to Sri Lanka but could make a fresh application to the German authorities, which could take into account his complaints under Art.3. It was not concerned as such with whether or not Germany was unduly restrictive in its approach to non-State sources of risk but rather with the existence of any effective procedural safeguards protecting the applicant from removal.

[12] 23985–87–88/94 (Dec.) November 28, 1994: concerning deportation of Lebanese applicants who alleged that the Hezbollah would target them as collaborators, the Commission cited an Amnesty report describing the Hezbollah as an important political force with semi-governmental services and the largest faction in the Parliament.

[13] *HLR v France*, where the applicant alleged that on return to Colombia he would be at risk from the drug trafficking circles on whom he had given information to the police. The Court, unlike the Commission, found that the risk was not substantiated.

[14] e.g. *Ahmed*, where a violation arose from the proposed expulsion of the applicant to Somalia in a state of civil war where he risked treatment contrary to Art.3 with no indication of any public authority able to protect him.

[15] 25849/94, (Dec.) November 16, 1994. Former Rule 36 was applied, though the case was later rejected for lack of substantiation.

[16] *Bensaid*, para.40.

[17] 26985/95, (Dec.) June 15, 1996; also 27949/95, May 13, 1996 : where a woman had a history of psychiatric illness, with medical evidence indicating that the stress of removal to an environment where little treatment was available would lead to a risk of suicide, the case was communicated but declared inadmissible when she moved to Ireland and the risk of expulsion disappeared.

threatened expulsion to Algeria of the applicant *Nasri*, born deaf and dumb, was found by the Commission to constitute treatment of such severity as to breach Art.3. It had regard to his upbringing since the age of four in France where all his family lived and to his extremely limited communication and perception skills. The expulsion threatened him with prolonged sensory deprivation in an unfamiliar environment and to inflict on him such fear and anguish as might humiliate him and crush his personality.[18]

Lack of medical care and support in the receiving State may, in exceptional circumstances attracting compelling humanitarian considerations, disclose a breach, as in *D v United Kingdom* where the applicant, extremely ill in the advanced stages of AIDS, was threatened with expulsion to St. Kitts where no treatment or family care would be available. In cases where some medical and family assistance have been available for applicants suffering from mental or physical illness, the Court has not found a sufficiently real risk that removal would be contrary to Art.3.[19]

2. Type of ill-treatment alleged

The type of ill-treatment to be established is, in line with Art.3 case law,[20] severe. **IIB–233** Generally, a significant risk to health, physical or psychological, from deliberate ill-treatment or conditions has to be alleged. However even alleged risk to life is generally still considered in the context of Art.3. The Commission stated that Art.2 would only be in issue where the loss of life was a "near certainty" as a consequence of the expulsion.[21]

The following are generally not covered: risk of criminal trial and imprisonment following a criminal conviction or for desertion[22]; economic hardship[23]; risk of difficulties in travelling through military checkpoints from lack of identity cards[24]; refusal of a passport on return[25]; threat of prosecution and heavy sentence (*e.g.* ten years) for conscientious objection to service in the army.[26]

However, threat of prosecution for political offences may constitute Art.3 treatment, though the Commission considered that there must be a definite and serious risk of being prosecuted on such a basis and of receiving a long and severe sentence if convicted.[27]

3. Absolute right

The right under Art.3 is absolute. Once a risk of Art.3 treatment is established, the **IIB–234** threat posed by the applicant cannot reduce the level of protection afforded by the Convention. Thus in *Chahal v United Kingdom*, the Court rejected the Government

[18] *Nasri*: the Court, finding a breach of Art.8, strangely found it unnecessary to look at the Art.3 allegations.

[19] See Pt IIB: AIDS.

[20] See Pt IIB: Torture, Inhuman and Degrading Treatment.

[21] *Bahaddar*, n.6.

[22] 28152–3/95 (Dec.) September 11, 1995 : existence of criminal proceedings in Romania not raise issues on expulsion from France; 7334/76, (Dec.) March 8, 1976 5 D.R. 154—deserter from Jordanian army; also cases of persons evading military service in the Serbian army, *e.g.* 22508/93, (Dec.) October 21, 1993; 25129/94, (Dec.) January 11, 1995 (concerning a Muslim Albanian being returned to Serbia).

[23] *Tomic*, n.9 above.

[24] *Vilvarajah*.

[25] *Beldjoudi*, (Rep.) para.74.

[26] *e.g.* 11017/84 (Dec.) March 13, 1986, 46 D.R. 176.

[27] 11933/86, (Dec.) April 14, 1986 46 D.R. 257.

argument that the risk to the Sikh applicant, an alleged terrorist, on return to India had to be weighed against the threat to UK security if he remained. The Convention guarantee is thus wider than the Geneva Convention pursuant to which a refugee can forfeit his status. A Contracting State has to make do (not unreasonably perhaps) with using its criminal law to deal with any threat posed by a person on its territory.[28]

Similarly, where refugee status has beeen granted, a State will be required to have proper reasons for revoking that status and expelling the individual. In *Ahmed v Austria*, a conviction of an applicant for robbery did not justify the threatened expulsion, in the absence of any circumstances rebutting the risk of persecution.

4. Existence and assessment of risk

IIB–235   An applicant has to substantiate that he faces a real risk of torture or ill-treatment.[29]

(a) *Imminence and safeguards*

IIB–236   Expulsion must be imminent and not subject to safeguards diminishing the risk.[30]

Where the applicant to be expelled suffers from problems of health or disability, assurances by the expelling State that steps will be taken to ensure appropriate treatment have proved relevant.[31] Adverse comment was made by the Commission in finding violations in *Nasri v France* and *D v United Kingdom* of the absence of any steps taken by the expelling Government as regards verifying the available facilities or treatment.[32]

Available safeguards have also been of crucial relevance where the expulsion is of children, with the ill-treatment alleged deriving from the circumstances of their removal. Safeguards such as ensuring reception by welfare authorities and the existence of a care structure in the receiving State can be identified as reducing any alleged risk of psychological or physical harm. The failure of the Netherlands Government to investigate the personal situation of a nine year old girl who was being returned to Zaire or to take adequate steps themselves to ensure that she was properly met on her return received critical comment in the *Nsona v Netherlands*, but since Swissair had taken their own initiatives the Government escaped a finding of violation.

---

[28] *Chahal*, paras 79–81, (Rep.) para.104.

[29] *e.g. Vilvarajah*, paras 103 and 111.

[30] *e.g. Vijayanathan*, (Rep.) September 5, 1991 paras 118–121; 27249/95, (Dec.) September 15, 1995, 83–A D.R. 91, where 2 teenage Ugandan brothers were held in Sweden in psychiatric care *inter alia* for suicidal tendencies, their complaints under Art.3 regarding an expulsion order were rejected since no enforcement would be possible while compulsory medical care was necessary and the order would only be enforced if the applicants were met in Uganda by a child welfare official and a Swedish consulate officer; *Kalantari v Germany*, October 11, 2001, ECHR 2001–X: the case was struck off as with the annulment of the decision to expel the applicant to Iran there was no risk of a breach of Art.3, distinguishing *Ahmed*, where the measure had been suspended and the decision to expel remained in force.

[31] 29244/95, (Dec.) April 18, 1996, the applicant's complaints of expulsion to Senegal on the basis of mental illness were rejected since *inter alia* the French Government had ensured that appropriate care would be available on his return; 31362/96, (Dec.) January 23, 1997, the French Government's statement that the expulsion to Morocco would only occur if the applicant's treatment in an appropriate establishment for his mental condition was guaranteed was sufficient even if the level of care differed from that available in France; 37384/97, (Dec.), October 30, 1998, where the Swiss Government undertook to pay for the applicant's diabetic treatment on return to Angola.

[32] *Nasri*, (Rep.), para.61; *D v UK*, (Rep.) para.59.

Assurances made by the Governments of receiving States may be relevant but are scrutinised carefully. In *Chahal*,[33] an assurance of the Indian Government given to the UK authorities that the applicant, a Sikh militant, would receive the same legal protection as any other Indian citizen on his return did not satisfy the Convention organs as providing an effective guarantee.[34] It is perhaps conceivable that in a particular case a Government could provide sufficient guarantees to offset an alleged risk of ill-treatment but the quality of the guarantees would presumably have to increase in persuasiveness where the evidence of risk was strong or the nature of the risk particularly grave.

Where a person claims ill-treatment likely if expelled to a Contracting State, some weight has been given to the possibility of an applicant exercising the right of individual petition, presumably on the basis that a State's adherence to the Convention renders risk of ill-treatment less likely to materialise, taking into account the mechanisms which should be in place to safeguard the guaranteed fundamental rights.[35] That problems may however arise in Contracting States is illustrated by reports by the CPT (the European Committee for the Prevention of Torture) on conditions in places of detention which have revealed serious problems in a number of countries. While a violation based on a proposed expulsion from one Contracting State to another has yet to be found, interim measures have been applied on occasion, *e.g.* to an expulsion from France to Spain of an ETA member, possibly motivated by severe criticisms of the methods of the *guardia civil* by the CPT[36] and to expulsion of Kurds to Turkey.[37]

Internal flight has been rejected as offering a reliable guarantee against the risk of ill-treatment where human rights problems have not been confined to one part of the country and there are institutional links between the police authorities in the different regions.[38]

(b) *Substantiating the level of risk*

The Court holds that, given the absolute character of the provision and the fact it   **IIB–237** enshrines one of the fundamental values of the democratic societies making up the Council of Europe, its examination of the existence of a risk of ill-treatment in breach of Art.3 must be rigorous. It will, if necessary, assess the risk in light of material obtained *proprio motu*.[39]

That said, the mere possibility of ill-treatment is not enough.[40] Thus it may not be sufficient for an applicant to point to the general unsettled situation in a country or his membership in a group which occasionally faces problems.[41] It seems that the

---

[33] para.105; also (Rep.) para.113.

[34] *i.e.* there was insufficient judicial control of police activities targeting Sikhs.

[35] *e.g.* 12543/86, (Dec.) December 2, 1986, 51 D.R. 272; 28152–3/95, n.22 above; *Tomic*, n.9 above.

[36] 31113/96, (Dec.) December 5, 1996.

[37] *e.g. Incedursun v Netherlands*, June 22, 1999.

[38] See *Chahal*, para.104; *Hilal*, paras 67–68, where there was also the possibility of extradition from mainland Tanzania to Zanzibar where the situation was particularly precarious.

[39] *Vilvarajah*, paras 107–108.

[40] *ibid.*, para.111.

[41] *e.g.* 25129/94, n.22 above, where the Commission found no problem under Art.3 to send back to Serbia a Muslim Albanian; 22508/93 (Dec.) October 21, 1993 where a Muslim family complained of being sent back to an area in Serbia where Muslims were subject to harassment; *Katani v Germany*,

applicant has to establish that he faces a specific, personal risk of treatment contrary to Art.3. In *Vilvarajah v United Kingdom* concerning the expulsion of five Tamil applicants to Sri Lanka, the Court did not consider that it was enough that the situation was unsettled or that some Tamils might possibly be detained or ill-treated. This threat was apparently not specific enough to these five applicants, even in light of the fact that during the Convention proceedings three of the applicants were subjected to ill-treatment in Sri Lanka. The Court found that there was no special distinguishing feature which would have enabled the Secretary of State to foresee that they would be treated in this way.

Presumably however where there are indications of a high level of risk attaching to membership of a particular group it should be possible to establish the requisite substantiation of risk to the individual applicant, where at least the person is known to be implicated or wanted in connection with that group's activities. The difficulties of reaching an assessment of risk to a particular person are demonstrated in *Paez v Sweden*[42] where the Commission by 15 votes to 14 found no violation if applicant was returned to Peru. He was a supporter of the Sendero Luminoso, a terrorist group, and other family members had been arrested and one had disappeared. However, the majority noted that he was not a leading figure, had not participated in any terrorist atrocities and in particular he could not point to any warrant of arrest or similar evidence which would show that he would be of particular interest to the authorities. The minority noted, *inter alia*, that his mother and sisters had been granted asylum; that the refusal to the applicant seemed to rely on his terrorist affiliations, a ground not relevant under Art.3; and that the interest shown by the Peruvian press in the asylum seekers in Sweden was a significant factor increasing the risk.[43]

Risk must exist at the time when the person is expelled, or if the person has not been expelled, it is assessed at the time the Court considers the case.[44] Previous conditions only remain relevant to the extent that they cast light on the present situation. There was evidence supporting the allegations of the applicant *Cruz Varas* that he had suffered torture in the past but his complaints concerning his expulsion to Chile failed since at the time when he was returned democratic developments and voluntary return of refugees had begun. Conversely in *Chahal*,[45] the Convention organs found that, despite apparent improvements in treatment of Sikhs by members of the Indian security forces and a change in Government attitude, including the creation of a National Human Rights Commission, they were still not satisfied that the police in the Punjab in particular and security forces elsewhere in the country were under effective democratic control. Thus, there was a real risk that the applicant, a high profile and leading Sikh militant, would be a target of special

---

67679/01, (Dec.), May 31, 2001,where the Court appeared to reject the applicants' complaints on the basis that they had not shown that they were treated particularly worse than any other members of the Yezidi minority or other Georgian citizens and that the police lack of response to attacks by third parties was rather a sign of a general structural weakness in the country.

[42] 28942/95, (Rep.) December 6, 1996; settled before the Court, October 30, 1997, R.J.D. 1997–VIII, No.56.

[43] Contrast *Hilal*, the applicant's claims of previous torture in Tanzania were medically supported, his brother had died in custody and ordinary members of the oppositon group, such as he, were also at risk of police brutality.

[44] At the time the Court considers the case if the person has not been expelled, *e.g. Chahal*, para.97.

[45] paras 99–107, (Rep.) paras 108–114.

interest on his return and there were substantial grounds for believing that he would be exposed to a real risk of ill-treatment.

(c) Factors and materials taken into account

Existence of a real risk may be supported by previous incidences of ill-treatment on   IIB–238
arrest and detention, in respect of which medical and psychiatric reports are very useful, if not essential. Also relevant are considerations whether an applicant's involvement in opposition has been publicised and likely to be known to the authorities or other groups in the receiving State. The Court will also refer to Amnesty Reports and the UNHCR as well as reports by the UN Committee against Torture and country reports of the US State Department, and these sources may regarded as highly relevant but are at most persuasive.[46] The reports of the CPT are treated as particularly relevant when concerned with Contracting States, see, for example, its Public Statements on Turkey.[47] In *Jabari v Turkey*, where the applicant claimed to be at risk of stoning for adultery if expelled to Iran, the Court gave weight to the UNHCR's assessment of her credibility and its finding that she had a well-founded fear of persecution.

Factors which cast doubt on an applicant's case include inconsistencies in accounts to national authorities and serious doubts as to the authenticity of the documents.[48] Weight, often decisive, is given to domestic authorities' experience in dealing with applications.[49] Applicants must therefore be able to point to flaws or shortcomings in any assessment by the domestic authorities of the merits of their case.[50]

(d) Shuttlecocking

State immigration policies sometimes give rise to the risk of asylum seekers or   IIB–239
stateless persons being shunted from country to country. "Shuttlecocking" was an element in the Commission's finding of a violation of Art.3 in the *East African Asians* case,[51] where applicants holding British citizenship were refused entry to the UK and in some cases, forced to and fro unable to obtain entry to the UK or elsewhere.

---

[46] *e.g. Vilvarajah* (UNHCR reports on Sri Lanka and Amnesty International's position on return; *Ahmed v Austria* (Rep.) (information requested from the UNHCR on the situation in Somalia); *Paez v Sweden*,(Rep.) (the UN Committee against Torture, Peru's report to ECOSOC, US State Department Report, the HRC report on Peru, Human Rights Watch and Amnesty International); *TI v UK*, n.11 above (UNHCR intervention concerning the effect of the return, under the Dublin Convention, of an asylum seeker to Germany).

[47] *e.g.* its First Public Statement on Turkey was cited in *Aydin v Turkey*, 23178/94, (Rep.) March 7, 1996, para.159.

[48] *e.g. Nsangu v Austria*, 25661/94, (Rep.) May 22, 1995: the Commission noted inconsistencies in the story, delay in mentioning relevant grounds and doubts about the documents; 31026/96, (Dec.) October 24, 1996 where the alleged arrest warrant was undated and contained outdated wording. See also the strong weight given by the Court in *Nsona* to the fact that the aunt lied trying to bring her niece in, presenting a forged document: the authorities could not be blamed for refusing, once this was discovered, to accept claims unsupported by evidence.

[49] *Cruz Varas*, para.81; many cases before the Commission where the findings of the domestic authorities are quoted.

[50] *Jabari*, para.40, where the domestic authorities had not carried out any meaningful examination of the applicant's claims of being at risk of stoning; *Hilal*, para.62, where new evidence was not scrutinised by the Special Adjudicator and in reaching their decisions, the Secretary of State and courts relied not any any assessment of its credibility but on an "internal flight" argument.

[51] 4403/70 and others, (Rep.) December 14, 1973, 78–A D.R. 5.

The Commission also stated that the repeated expulsion of an individual to a country where his admission is not guaranteed, may raise an issue, particularly where it occurs over a long period of time without any country taking measures to regularise his position.[52] Deliberate steps to render oneself stateless are however likely to prejudice a case.[53]

(e) Expulsion of children

IIB–240   Issues have arisen as to whether the manner of implementation of expulsion or its effects are so traumatic for children as to constitute treatment contrary to Art.3.

Proposed expulsions of children where it has been alleged that there is no one to care for them on arrival in the receiving State have been declared admissible under Art.3. Two such cases settled, *Taspinar v the Netherlands*[54] where the applicant, resident in the Netherlands, brought his son to the Netherlands but was refused a residence permit for him with the result that the seven-eight year old boy was to be sent back to Turkey where allegedly no one remained to take care of him and *Bulus v Sweden* where a Syrian boy lived on the run for two years avoiding expulsion to Syria where he would have allegedly had to fend for himself.[55] In *Nsona*, where a nine year old girl was sent back to Zaire, the Court made critical comment of the failure of the Dutch authorities properly to investigate her personal situation and to take adequate measures in respect of her arrival. However, the circumstances did not reach the minimum level of severity prohibited by Art.3, in particular since the girl was not left unattended at the airport due to the initiative of the airline and she was brought back to the people previously taking care of her.

In exceptional circumstances, the conditions facing children on expulsion to another country may disclose treatment of such a severe nature as to inflict on them inhuman and degrading treatment contrary to Art.3. A high threshold is set for treatment from mere change of environment and living standards to fall within the scope of Art.3 and allegations require specific and concrete substantiation.

In *Fadele v United Kingdom*, children, with British citizenship living in the UK, lost their mother in an accident and the Nigerian father was refused leave to join the children in the UK, with the consequence that the children were forced to join him in Nigeria. The case was declared admissible, reflecting the extreme hardship which the children faced, but not resolved on the merits since the case settled when the Government granted the father a residence permit and the family returned.[56] However, where the level of hardship is low, hypothetical or unsubstantiated,

---

[52] 7612/76 (Rep.) July 17, 1980, 21 D.R. 73: the applicant was of African origin with no identity papers, subject to a series of arrests and moving to and fro from one country to another—settled when he left for Senegal with a travel document from the Belgian Government; *c.f.* 10798/84 (Dec.), March 5, 1986, 46 D.R. 112: the applicant of Algerian origin claiming to be stateless was repeatedly expelled from the Netherlands (over 20 times) but was found primarily responsible for his plight, *e.g.* he had not taken steps to seek Algerian citizenship nor substantiated that he was ever expelled back to the Netherlands rather than going back of his own free will.

[53] 28152–3/95, n.22 above, where the applicants renounced their Romanian citizenship in an apparent effort to render themselves stateless and avoid expulsion from France.

[54] 11026/84, (Rep.) October 9, 1985, 44 D.R. 262: leave to remain given.

[55] 9330/81, (Dec.) January 19, 1984, 35 D.R. 35 and (Rep.) 39 D.R. 75.

[56] The family lived in a compound which was filthy, with open sewers. The children attended no school and spoke no Nigerian language. The youngest suffered bouts of malaria including convulsions requiring blood transfusions and hospitalisation and all three suffered from typhoid, respiratory infections and gastro-entiritis—13078/87, (Rep.) July 4, 1991, 70 D.R.159.

complaints have been rejected, for example claim of a three year old British child was threatened with removal to Kenya with her mother who was being expelled, that she would have difficulties in obtaining treatment for problems with her hands and risk isolation from the Asian and African communities;[57] complaints from children, were obliged to accompany their mother to Jamaica, about the alleged risk to their psychological health and physical well-being from the change in environment;[58] and complaints about the alleged risk to a four year old child if sent to Colombia where his father was involved in drug trafficking circles.[59]

The situation where a child has the right to stay in a Contracting State but the custodial parent is being expelled also did not in the Commission's view constitute Art.3 treatment, even though it places the parent in the dilemma of taking the child, who will then lose educational and other advantages, or of leaving it in the UK in care. The Commission appeared to find it compatible with the requirements of Art.3 that the parent has the opportunity to bring the child and they are not forced to be separated.[60] The mere loss of benefits to which the children are entitled by their citizenship are not enough.[61]

C. Effect on family life

Key case law:

Abdulaziz, Cabales and Balkandali v UK, May 28, 1985, Series A, No.94; 7 E.H.R.R. 471; *Moustaquim v Belgium*, February 18, 1991, Series A, No.193; 13 E.H.R.R. 802; *Berrehab v Netherlands*, June 21, 1988, Series A, No.138; 11 E.H.R.R. 322; *Beldjoudi v France*, March 26, 1992, Series A, No.234–A; 14 E.H.R.R. 801; *Gul v Switzerland*, February 19, 1996, R.J.D. 1996–I, No.3; 22 E.H.R.R. 93; *Boughanemi v France*, April 24, 1996, R.J.D. 1996–II, No.8; *C v Belgium*, August 7, 1996, R.J.D. 1996–III; 32 E.H..R.R 19; *Nsona v Netherlands*, November 28, 1996, R.J.D. 1996–VI, No.23; *Ahmut v Netherlands*, November 28, 1996, R.J.D. 1996–VI, No.24; *Bouchelkia v France*, January 29, 1997, R.J.D. 1997–I, No.28; 25 E.H.R.R. 686; *Mehemi v France*, September 26, 1997, R.J.D. 1997–VI, No.51; *El Boujaïdi v France*, September 26, 1997, R.J.D. 1997–VI, No.51; 30 E.H.R.R. 223; *Boujlifa v France*, October 21, 1997, R.J.D. 1997–VI, No.54; 30 E.H.R.R. 419; *Baghli v France*, November 30, 1999, ECHR 1999–VIII; *Ciliz v Netherlands*, July 11, 2000, ECHR 2000–VIII; *Ezzouhdi v France*, February 13, 2001; *Boultif v Switzerland*, August 2, 2001, ECHR 2001–IX; *Sen v Netherlands*, December 21, 2001; 24 E.H.R.R.93; *Amrollahi v Denmark*, July 11, 2002; *Jakupovic v Austria*, February 6, 2003; *Slivenko v Latvia*, October 9, 2003, ECHR 2003–XI.

Apart from Art.3 ill-treatment issues, the principal ground on which expulsion measures have been contested has been Art.8 in respect of its disruption of "family life".

IIB–241

---

[57] 23938/93, (Dec.) October 23, 1995.
[58] 25297/94, (Dec.), January 16, 1996.
[59] 24865/94, (Dec.) October 23, 1995.
[60] *e.g.* 22471/93 (Dec.) September 6, 1994: the mother was expelled while the children remained in the UK as wards of court. However there was evidence that the mother consented to wardship, *i.e.* there was no forcible separation.
[61] Cases cited at nn.57–59 above.

Approach to the cases is a balancing exercise whether viewed as an interference where a decision is taken to expel a person previously lawfully resident or an allegation of failure to comply with a positive obligation to respect family life by granting entry. In weighing the individual's interest against the general policy concerns, a restrictive approach is taken to almost every factor: from the weight given to the nature of family life concerned, the importance of immigration concerns and public order, the high threshold of acceptable hardships to individuals and the wide margin of appreciation accorded to the State.

1. Existence of "family" links

(a) *"Family life"*

IIB–242   For the Court, where a child is born of a marriage, there is *ipso iure* family life between the parent and child, which only exceptional circumstances can break. This has been extended to parent-child relationships where there has been no cohabitation or marriage.[62] The fact in *C v Belgium* that the father was imprisoned, then deported or that son went to live with an aunt did not constitute exceptional circumstances. The Court did not comment on the aunt-niece relationship in *Nsona*.

The Commission in older cases excluded the mere existence of blood ties as being sufficient save between married parents and their minor children. It held that adult children and other relatives must show elements of dependency going beyond normal emotional ties *e.g.* monetary and practical links, evidence of regular contact.[63] This does not make allowance for the extended families found in some cultures,[64] or where families are poor, unable to contribute to each others support financially and are separated over time, with no opportunity to make contact and develop demonstrable relationships. *In Slivenko v Latvia*, the Court stated that "family life" is normally limited to the core family, without however specifying what that meant, beyond excluding one of the applicant's elderly parents who had been shown to have no links of dependency.[65]

(b) *Verification procedures*

IIB–243   Applicants seeking leave to enter often find themselves required to prove the claimed relationships with persons resident in the country. This has not been found to raise problems as long as fair opportunity has been given to present family claims.

Where an applicant complained about the procedures whereby his purported wife and son were refused entry, the Commission found that a country was entitled to set up domestic verification procedures for family claims and that it could not intervene as a supervisory body to decide if a decision was wrong but only whether the authorities had acted outside what might reasonably be required of them in ensuring the right to respect for family life.[66] Refusal of entry to a child when the

---

[62] *Gul*, para.32; *Boughanemi*, para.35; *Boultif*, para.28; *Al Nashif*, paras 112–113.

[63] *e.g.* 9492/81 (Dec.) July 14, 1982, 30 D.R. 232.

[64] 26373/95, (Dec.) October 16, 1995, whether the applicant's mother, 2 sisters, 7 brothers, etc. qualified as "family" in a refugee family re-unification case where the applicant had become head of the family in Somali terms was left open.

[65] para.94.

[66] 8378/78, (Dec.) May 14, 1980, 20 D.R. 168.

immigration authorities were not satisfied that he was the son of the putative father in the UK was not a problem, even though a DNA test later revealed a biological link and entry was refused since the son was no longer a minor. The Commission found no bad faith on the part of the immigration authorities at the time of the initial refusal and there had been a fair opportunity to present the claims.[67]

2. Spouses

The principles governing the extent of the State's obligation to admit spouses is laid down by the Court in *Abdulaziz, Cabales and Balkandali v United Kingdom*: **IIB–244**

- there is no general obligation on a Contracting State to respect the choice of married couples as to the country of matrimonial residence;
- States enjoy a wide margin of appreciation;
- it is relevant whether there are obstacles to establishing the marital home elsewhere, in the country of the spouse or the applicant's own origin or whether there are any special reasons why they should not be expected to do so;
- it is relevant whether, when marrying, they were aware of the problems of entry and limited leave situation.

Since in *Abdulaziz* there were no obstacles or special reasons and the couples were aware of their problematic immigration status at the time of marriage, no violation of Art.8 was found. It remains to be seen what relevance would or should be given to a situation where an applicant married in circumstances where neither spouse knew the problems of immigration status. Arguably, they would have to give a convincing explanation for ignorance of a potential problem. It is not obvious however that expectations at the time of marriage could ever play a significant role in finding a violation.

Many cases are rejected using the above criteria, with reference to the lack of obstacles to the spouses living elsewhere and their knowledge of the precarious immigration status beforehand. Occasionally, reasons have been put forward that an applicant cannot be expected to join a spouse elsewhere, for example, health, or the fact that the spouse would leave a business or employment[68] but the Convention organs have rarely accepted any as constituting a sufficient obstacle or special circumstances. The fact that an applicant suffered illness on a previous visit to Pakistan was not enough[69]; where a wife submitted that she was unable to live in Bangladesh as she was constantly ill there, the Commission found "no serious obstacles" existed and noted that she had lived there herself for 12 years previously.[70] A successful claim would require require strong substantiation and a high level of danger to health. However even where it was argued that no appropriate treatment was available in Sierra Leone for a particular intestinal disorder and epilepsy, supported by the only qualified neurologist in Sierra Leone, this argument was outweighed by the fact the illness was of long standing, known

---

[67] 19546/92, (Dec.) March 13, 1992; also 36287/97, (Dec.) July 10, 1998, where the Commission held that the procedural guarantee in Art.8 did not require decision-making authorities to afford the opportunity to lodge further submissions if the evidence of family relationship was not considered sufficient.

[68] *e.g.* 25073/94, (Dec.) February 28, 1996.

[69] 17229/90, (Dec.) February 12, 1992.

[70] 18713/91, (Dec.) April 1, 1992.

before the spouses married and that the deportation order on the husband was issued before the marriage.[71]

It may be noted that in most of these unsuccessful cases the spouse with residence rights or citizenship is nonetheless of a similar background to the spouse to be expelled, for example, having originated from the same part of the world, which will render, for the Covention organs' purposes, the possibility of the couple being able to set up the family unit elsewhere a practical option. Where the spouse has no such prior or family connections elswhere, the hardship involved in setting up married life in an African or Asian country is conceivably more significant. In *Beldjoudi v France*, part of the reasoning for finding a violation in expelling the applicant to Algeria, was that his wife was French, with French parents, had always lived there and to be uprooted to go to Algeria, where she did not speak the language, would cause her real practical or even legal obstacles and the interference might therefore imperil the unity or even existence of the marriage.[72] In *Amrollahi v Denmark*, the Court, in finding it would breach Art.8 to expel the Iranian applicant, found that it would cause the applicant's Danish wife and Danish children 'obvious and serious difficulties' to live in Iran. This appears to put an unfortunate emphasis on the ethnic or racial origins of the spouse but would still appear to be only one factor in the balancing exercise against legitimate immigration interests.[73]

The Commission accepted that a country may limit the number of wives as a matter of policy entering to live with a man settled in the UK. Excluding surplus wives was pursued the legitimate aim of preserving the Christian-based monogamous culture dominant in that society (as pursuing the protection of morals and of rights and freedoms of others) and a Contracting State could not be required to give full recognition to polygamous marriages in conflict with their own legal order or bigamy laws.[74]

3. Children

(a) *Entry to join family*

IIB–245   Where a child previously living apart from a parent outside a Contracting State is refused entry to join the family, violations may conceivably arise where the child has no practical alternative. However, there must be shown to be substantial existing family ties, which may be difficult where the individual has lived at a distance for some time. For example in *Ahmut v Netherlands*, the fifteen year old son left Morocco, where he had been brought up by relatives, to join his father in the Netherlands. The Court noted that the boy had lived most of his life in Morocco with which he had strong linguistic and cultural links, there were other family members in Morocco, the separation was the result of the conscious decision of the father to move to the Netherlands and there was nothing to stop them continuing the degree of family life they had before. While the father might prefer to intensify

---

[71] 24831/94, (Dec.) August 31, 1994.

[72] *Beldjoudi*, para.78.

[73] Also *Ciftci v Austria*, 24375/94 (Rep.) April 15, 1998, where the Commission found a violation of Art.8 where the applicant, to be expelled to Turkey, was married to an Austrian wife, with three children who were Austrian citizens; *Boultif v Switzerland*, August 2, 2001, ECHR 2001–IX where the applicant's Swiss wife could not be expected to follow him to Algeria.

[74] 19628/92, (Dec.) June 29, 1992.

his family links with his son in the Netherlands, Art.8, the Court said, did not guarantee a right to choose the most suitable place to develop family life.

The fact that the family is able to return to join the child may also be a decisive consideration. In *Gul v Switzerland* where the Turkish father lived in Switzerland and had applied unsuccessfully for his 12-year-old son to join him, the Court observed that the parents had caused the separation by moving to Switzerland and while it was admittedly difficult from a humanitarian point of view, there were no obstacles preventing them from living in Turkey, in particular since they could continue to receive their invalidity pension and benefits and it was not proved that the mother could not receive appropriate medical treatment in Turkey.[75]

The situation could conceivably change if the parent had succeeded in obtaining refugee status, in which case the argument that the family could return would be weaker. It may also be decisive if the parents can show a greater degree of integration into the society of the country. It was on this basis, in the case of *Sen v Netherlands*, that the Court distinguished the *Ahmut* case in finding that that the refusal to allow entry to the eldest daughter breached Art.8. The parents had both obtained longstanding and lawful resident status and two children had been born in the country. The Court gave weight to the consideration that these two children had no links with Turkey and commented, in contradiction of the approach in *Ahmut*, that the free choice of the parents to leave their eldest child in Turkey could not be regarded as an irrevocable decision that she should remain outside the family group. The *Gül* case was distinguished on the basis that the parents in that case did not have a permanent right of abode in the host country. Consequently, placing the parents in the situation of having to choose between their established life in the Netherlands or giving up the company of their daughter, the State was found, in this case, not to have struck a proper balance.

(b) *Expulsion of custodial parent(s)*

Whether removal or exclusion of a parent from a Contracting State is incompatible with the requirements of Art.8 as regards a child with residence will depend on a number of factors: the extent to which family life is effectively ruptured, whether there are insurmountable obstacles in the way of the family living in the country of origin of one or more of them, whether there are factors of immigration control (*e.g.* history of breaches of immigration law) or considerations of public order (*e.g.* serious or persistent offences) weighing in favour of exclusion.[76] The "age" and "adaptability" of the children are regarded as particularly significant.[77]

While applicants argued that weight should be given to the British citizenship of children, the Commission found the factor to be of no material weight, whether obtained *ius sanguine* through a parent rather than the accident of *ius soli*.[78] The

IIB–246

---

[75] Also *PR v Netherlands*, 39391/98, (Dec.) November 7, 2000, where the applicant had been refused entry for children left behind in the Cape Verde islands six years earlier, the Court noted that the separation had been her choice, there was no obstacle to the family living together in the islands and that Art.8 did not guarantee a right to choose the most suitable place to develop family life.

[76] *e.g.* 9285/81, (Dec.) July 6, 1982, 29 D.R. 205; 11970/86, (Dec.), July 13, 1987.

[77] See cases cited nn.57–59 above.

[78] *e.g.* 11970/86, (Dec.) July 13, 1987, where the Commission found it compatible with Art.8 to expect children of unlawful overstayers to follow their parents even if they had acquired theoretical rights of abode; cases cited at nn.57–59.

Commission was also unpersuaded by arguments as to "constructive expulsion" where a child British citizen forced by circumstances to accompany a non-national parent would be deprived of the benefits of the country of nationality and face long years of "exile" until able to return as an adult and face the difficulties adapting to life there again. Although this might constitute hardship, it would nonetheless not appear to disclose any effective bars to enjoying family life elsewhere.

Save for the case of *Fadele v United Kingdom*,[79] no case concerning the expulsion of custodial parent has yet been declared admissible, indicating that where young children are concerned, there are generally no obstacles to them accompanying the parent abroad.

(c) Expulsion of divorced or separated parent

IIB–247   Where a non-national parent is being expelled and the children are in the custody of the other parent (with citizenship or residence rights), after separation or divorce, family links may arguably be ruptured betweeen parent and child since there is no possibility of the child accompanying the parent.[80]

Whether the expulsion will in this situation disclose a violation will depend on a number of factors, in particular, the nature and strength of the parent's links with the child.[81] In *Berrehab v Netherlands*, the application was brought by father, ex-wife and child in respect of the proposed expulsion of the father from the Netherlands, after divorce, which threatened to break the ties between father and child. The fact the parents no longer cohabited was not decisive for the existence or otherwise of family life where the relationships arose out of a lawful and genuine marriage and the father saw the child four times a week, regular and frequent contact proving the strength of his ties.[82] The Court also had regard to the fact the father had been lawfully resident in the Netherlands for many years, had a home and job and that the Government had no real cause for complaint against him: therefore a balance had not been achieved between the interest of immigration control and the applicants' mutual interests in continuing their family ties. The illegal nature of the parent's presence in the country has been a decisive factor in rejecting other cases.[83] In *Ciliz v Netherlands*, the decision-making procedure concerning the father's expulsion disclosed a violation of Art.8, where the authorities prejudged the outcome

---

[79] n.56 above.

[80] Paradoxically, an applicant who has been divorced may therefore derive a right to stay to enjoy access to a child whereas those who enjoy an ongoing married relationship may be expected to uproot every family member and leave.

[81] Mere allegations of interest or links are not enough: there must be strong indications of an ongoing relationship, *e.g.* 26985/95, n.16 above, where the links of a boy with his father in the UK would be affected by removal to Ghana, the Commission noted the irregular nature of the contacts and that it had diminished to telephone contact such that the effect on "family life" would be minimal; 28627/95, (Dec.) January 17, 1997 where the child's father had not shown any commitment beyond a statement that he would like to see her.

[82] Also *Ciliz*, where the father, who was to be expelled to Turkey, had kept up contact, on a frequent, if not, regular basis.

[83] 26285/95, (Dec.) April 9, 1997, expulsion of a mother, entailing separation of a child from the father with whom she enjoyed frequent contact, was not disproportionate since the mother had been unlawfully in the country and started the relationship, bearing the child when her immigration status was irregular. Whereas in *Berrehab*, the relationship had developed while the father was lawfully resident and the residence was not revoked for any misconduct or breach of condition but only due to end of a marriage to a Dutch citizen.

of contact proceedings by expelling him during a period of trial contact sessions and he had not been convicted of any criminal offences warranting his removal.

(d) *Expulsion order against a minor*

In *Jakupovic v Austria*, the Court stated that very weighty reasons had to be put forward to justify the expulsion of a young person (16 years old in that case), particularly given the history of conflict in the country of origin and no evidence of close relatives remaining there. It gave close scrutiny to the boy's criminal record and giving weight to the absence of any elements of violence, found the expulsion would be a disproportionate interference with his right to respect for family and private life.

IIB–248

4. "Second-generation" immigrant expulsions

Where a State seeks to expel persons who have been legally settled in their territory but who have committed offences, the Convention organs look particularly at the extent of the links of the individual with the host State and receiving State: the length of residence; knowledge/ignorance of the language or culture; existence and strength of family links or friends in the respective countries; dependency on the family which remains behind in the Contracting State; and personal circumstances such as health or psychological state which might render removal of potentially drastic effect. These have to be balanced against the reasons for the removal and the assessment made whether the interests of the prevention of crime or disorder outweigh the effect of the removal on the applicant. This case-by-case approach has been criticised as a "lottery" for national authorities, lacking legal certainty and the opposing view has been put forward that there should be at least a very strong presumption that aliens who have lived most, or all their lives in a country should no more be expelled than nationals.[84]

IIB–249

Disproportionate effects were found in a number of cases, where in effect an applicant had lived most of his life in the expelling State, his family lived there and he had no real links or knowledge with the receiving State.[85] Legal ties of nationality are not in themselves decisive.[86] However where applicants have some links with the country of origin, they have been less successful. In *Boughanemi*, the Court found it

---

[84] *e.g.* Judge Morenilla dissenting in *Nasri* considering that the expulsion of non-nationals for misconduct was discriminatory, cruel and inhuman; Judge Martens, dissenting in *Boughanemi*, considering that expulsion might be exceptionally justified where very serious crime (terrorism or lead drug trafficker) was involved and Judges Costa and Tulkens, dissenting in *Baghli*, with comments as to the unnecessarily punitive nature of such orders on persons who had lived practically their entire lives in the expelling country.

[85] *Moustaquim* had arrived in Belgium aged two, all his close relatives were there and had acquired Belgian nationality, he had received all his schooling in French and visited Morocco only twice on holiday. *Beldjoudi* had been born and educated in France, knew no Arabic, had no links with Algeria apart from nationality and was married to French woman who has always lived in France. In *Mehemi*, the applicant had been born and schooled in France, most of his family lived there, including his wife and three children who had French nationality and who could not reasonably be expected to live elsewhere. See also *Lamguindaz v UK*, 16152/90,(Rep.) October 13, 1992, Series A No.258–C, settled before the Court, where the Commission found a violation of Art.8 for expelling the applicant who had lived in the UK from age 7–8, was educated there, his close relatives lived there and no real links with Morocco.

[86] *e.g. Ezzoudhi*, para.34.

probable that the applicant retained links with Tunisia, noting that he did not claim that he could not speak Arabic, or that he had cut off all ties. It gave particular weight to his offences and none to the fact that he lived as man and wife with a Frenchwoman and had a child, since this had occurred after the deportation order.[87] In *C v Belgium*, the applicant also had only moved to Belgium at the later age of 11 and still had links with Morocco.[88]

While in earlier cases, the Court found that the personal interests of the applicant outweighed quite significant criminal records,[89] there has been an apparent hardening in attitude and greater sympathy given to the public order policies of Contracting States, with particular reference to understanding the firmness with which the authorities treat offenders who contribute to the 'scourge' of drug trafficking.[90] In *Boughanemi* (four convictions, theft and aggravated proxenetism attracting prison sentences) the Commission found a violation but the Court did not. While it found the applicant's actual links to France weak, it "above all" attached importance to the fact the deportation was decided after he had been sentenced to almost four years imprisonment, for, *inter alia*, living on the earnings of prostitution in aggravating circumstances.[91] Although the applicant in *Bouchelkia* had lived in France since the age of two, the factor of his conviction of rape tipped the balance towards the interests of the State in expelling him.[92] The Court has also referred negatively to applicants' lack of desire to acquire nationality of the expelling country.[93]

Where however there are effectively no links with the receiving country and the applicant's record is not regarded as serious or shows mitigating factors, the balance may still tip against expulsion. In *Ezzouhdi v France*, where the applicant had lived in France since the age of five and had no apparent links but nationality with Morocco, his conviction for minor drugs possession charges was not sufficient for him to be regarded a threat to public order necessitating his expulsion. While in *Boultif v Switzerland*, where the applicant had committed a serious offence of robbery, albeit one attracting the relatively light sentence of two years, the expulsion order was found to be disproportionate, when balanced against the fact that the applicant's wife, a Swiss national with no connections with Algeria or knowledge of Arabic, could not be expected to follow him. Since it was practically impossible for him to live his family life outside Switzerland, and, with recent good behaviour, he presented only a comparatively limited danger to the public order, there was a violation of Art.8.

---

[87] Also *Bouchelkia*, where the marriage to a French national and birth of a child after the deportation order were discounted.

[88] *e.g.* he had married a woman there (later divorced).

[89] *e.g. Moustaquim* (an alleged 147 offences, mainly petty theft, carried out as an adolescent), *Beldjoudi* (seven custodial sentences, the last eight years for aggravated theft), *Nasri* (over ten convictions, one for gang rape).

[90] *Baghli*, para.48.

[91] Also *C v Belgium*, where the Court attached great importance to a drugs offence attracting 5 years; *Boujlifa*, armed robbery, etc.

[92] Also *Benrachid v France*, 39518/98, (Dec.) December 8, 1998, ECHR 1999–II, where the applicant arrived from Algeria aged 7 and all his family were in France, the Court rejected his complaint on the basis of a serious conviction (armed robbery) and an assumption that he had not cut all links with Algeria; *Djaid v France*, 38687/97, (Dec.) March 9, 1999, where the applicant had arrived in France aged 5 months and had 2 French children born out of wedlock (his links with the children were apparently strong)—the Court gave weight to his drug convictions and his knowledge at the time of the conception of the first child that he was liable to expulsion: *Baghli*, where the applicant arrived in France aged 2, his family and social ties were in France, this was outweighed by the drug conviction (3-year sentence).

[93] *Boulifa*, para.44, *El Boujaidi*, para.41, *Djaid*, cited above, *Baghli*, para.48—though it is not apparent whether in any of the cases the applicant would have had any prospect of obtaining citizenship.

D. Effect on private life

Expulsion of a person settled in a country may disclose an interference with private life, as well as family life.[94] Though most cases have turned on the aspects of family life, the Court has found expulsion measures to have violated both family and private life aspects in a few cases.[95] Where in *Slivenko v Latvia*, the whole family was to be deported together, the Court examined the case primarily as regarded the disruption to their private life and home. Although the Court found nothing incompatible *per se* with the arrangements for the withdrawal of Russian troops and their families, it found that in the particular case it was disproportionate to apply the measure to the descendants of a long retired officer who had been integrated into Latvia and had no equivalent ties in Russia. Applicants present in a country on a short-term or provisional basis may not be able to claim an interference with any established private life.[96]

IIB–250

Expulsions which threaten to have significant adverse effects on an applicant's mental health and sanity may raise issues under Art.8 in its aspect of physical and moral integrity.[97]

Arguments by child applicants that their forced departure to accompany their foreign mothers would deprive them of growing and developing in their country of birth and nationality have been rejected.[98] Presumably, if there are no effective obstacles to a small child living family life with its mother elsewhere there is no interference with private life either. "Private life" doubtfully applies to future benefits of living in a particular environment: there must be at least something specific to existing private life or elements relating to past private life.[99] Whereas "family" life has been held to extend to the development of potential relationships by the Commission in the case of natural fathers and their children,[100] it remains to be seen whether such an approach could be accommodated under the Art.8 private life aspect.

E. Effect on education

Expulsion of a child of school age will inevitably entail disruption of education and claims have been made, so far unsuccessfully, under Art.2 of the First Protocol.[101] Education will, arguably, be available at least at elementary level if not higher in most countries. It may be difficult to argue that deportation will deny "education"

IIB–251

---

[94] *e.g. C v Belgium*, para.25; *Boujlifa*, para.36; *El Boujaidi*, para.33; *Baghli*, para.37: where the applicants had lived most of their lives in the expelling State.

[95] *e.g. Ezzoudhi*, paras 26 and 33; *Mehemi*, paras 35–37; *Jakupovic*, paras 22–26. Cf. *Beldjoudi*, Judge Marten's concurring opinion finding a violation of the aspect of private life instead of family life, considering that this covered external relations with others and the right to establish and develop relationships with others.

[96] *e.g.* 9478/81, (Dec.) December 8, 1981, 27 D.R. 243, where the applicant was to be deported from Germany to Indonesia, the Commission said that to the extent that the circle of acquaintances established during her stay in Germany disclosed relationships recognised as 'private life' there could be no interference since the applicant knew at all times that her presence, and hence her ability to establish relationships with others, was temporary and subject to revocation.

[97] *Bensaid*, paras 46–48: sufficient risk not made out.

[98] n.57 and 59 above.

[99] See *Gaskin v UK*, July 7, 1989, Series A, No.160 where information about past childhood was in issue.

[100] *Keegan v Ireland*, (Rep.) February 17, 1993, para.48, Series A, No.290, para.48.

[101] Nor does disruption to schooling interfere with family life under Art.8: 9492/81, (Dec.) July 14, 1982, 30 D.R. 232.

as such, though it may diminish the choice or quality of the education. Also if a deportation measure is justifiable for the aim of legitimate immigration control where there is interference with family life it would be strange if Art.2 of the First Protocol granted residence rights for the purpose of education. The Commission has on that basis dismissed in very brief terms Art.2 of the First Protocol complaints where the expulsion has been found compatible with Art.8.[102] In *Ebibomi v United Kingdom*,[103] the two sons (aged 21 and 20) in full-time education claimed that they were supported by their mother financially and emotionally and if she was expelled their education would be prevented. The Commission found that the practical difficulties which might arise from the removal of their mother, which was compatible with Art.8 as a legitimate measure of immigration control, could not be construed as a deprivation of their right to education.

F. Access to Court and Remedies

Key case law:

IIB–252   *Soering v UK*, July 7, 1989, Series A, No.161; 11 E.H.R.R. 439; *Vilvarajah v UK*, October 30, 1991, Series A, No.215; 14 E.H.R.R. 248; *Chahal v UK*, November 15, 1996, R.J.D. 1996–V; 23 E.H.R.R. 413; *Jabari v Turkey*, July 11, 2000, ECHR 2000–VIII; *Maaouia v France*, October 5, 2000, ECHR 2000–X; *Bensaid v UK*, February 6, 2001, ECHR 2001–I; *Hilal v UK*, March 6, 2001, ECHR 2001–II; *Al-Nashif v Bulgaria*, June 20, 2002.

The Commission considered that there was no "civil right" to nationality or to a right of residence and that Art.6 had no application to asylum, expulsion, deportation proceedings or the like.[104] In *Maaouia v France*, the Court confirmed this approach, holding that decisions regarding the entry, stay and deportation of aliens did not concern either the determination of an applicant's civil rights or obligations or of a criminal charge against him within the meaning of Art.6, para.1.[105]

This is a restrictive approach, based at least partly on the view that questions of entry or residence of aliens involve discretionary acts of public authorities or are governed by public law.[106] An alien may therefore reside lawfully in a country with his family for decades and be expelled, with drastic effects on family life, private life, employment, livelihood and health, without recourse to a court, with the full procedural guaranteees, to challenge the decision. In other areas (see, *e.g.* social security, pensions, tax) the Commission and Court have seen less clear distinctions between public and private law areas and have had regard to effect on private life with analogies to matters such as contract.[107]

---

[102] n.57 and 59 above.

[103] 26922/95, (Dec.) November 29, 1995.

[104] 8118/77, (Dec.) March 19, 1981, 25 D.R. 105; 9990/82, (Dec.) May 15, 1984, 39 D.R. 119.

[105] para.123. The need for appropriate limitations on use of classified information was acknowledged. The Court also found violations of Arts 5, 4 and 13.

[106] See, *e.g.* the Commission's approach in 7729/76, (Dec.) December 17, 1976, 7 D.R. 164—the expulsion of a US citizen from the UK on security grounds was considered an act of state falling within the public sphere. In *Maaouia*, the majority interpreted an exclusion of alien' rights in Art.6 from the specific provision for procedural guarantees in Art.1 of Protocol No.7.

[107] Pt IIA: Fair Trial Guarantees, General Principles: Civil Rights and Obligations.

Though an applicant expelled or refused entry cannot claim a right as such to a court procedure to challenge the merits or lawfulness of the decision, there may be scope under Art.8 to lay claim at least to some procedural protections.[108] In *Al Nashif v Bulgaria*, the Court found a violation of Art.8 where the applicant's expulsion was ordered pursuant to a legal regime that did not provide the necessary safeguards. In that case, where the applicant was to be expelled as an alleged threat to public order due to his religious activities, the Court held that even where national security was at stake, the concepts of lawfulness and the rule of law required that such measures be subject to some form of adversarial procedure before an independent body competent to review them.

Lack of access to court aside, applicants may invoke Art.13 of the Convention, a right to an effective remedy. This is subject to the precondition of Art.13—that there is an "arguable claim" of a violation of another provision of the Convention (see section "Remedies") and in practice will generally only become operative once a substantive complaint has been declared admissible.

Article 13 does not automatically require a court remedy. However bodies which fail to provide sufficient procedural safeguards or who function by way discretionary powers will be unlikely to qualify. In *Chahal*, the Court found that the hearing before an advisory panel gave a restricted review to the case and also insufficient procedural safeguards, namely, no entitlement to legal representation, provision of few details to the applicant and only a power of recommendation, not decision. The Court made positive note of the system in Canada adverted to by intervenors.[109] Failure to provide an appeal against the proposed expulsion of the applicant in *Al-Nashif v Bulgaria* breached Art.13. There the Court stated that even in national security cases, as a minimum there should be an independent appeals authority, which is informed of the reasons grounding the decision (even if such reasons are not publicly available), competent to reject the executive's assertions of the existence of a threat to national security, with some form of adversarial proceedings and capable of examining whether a fair balance has been struck between the public interest and the individual's rights. The independent authority should also have the power to suspend the implementation of the measure.[110] Whatever the body however, it must also give an independent and 'rigorous scrutiny' of claims of a risk of ill-treatment contrary to Art.3 and be able to suspend the implementation of the measure.[111]

In the UK, the limited scope of judicial review was previously insufficient in cases concerning family and private life issues. It remains to be seen whether the Human Rights Act 1998 provides effective court scrutiny. Where however an applicant was alleging risk to life or ill-treatment falling within the scope of Art.3, the Court accepted that the "reasonableness" test of judicial review would furnish the domestic courts with the possibility of reviewing the extradition in light of allegations of serious risk of inhuman and degrading treatment and that where a decision put a life at risk the courts, according to Lord Bridge, would give the case the "most anxious scrutiny". Judicial review therefore furnished an effective remedy in respect of an extradition in *Soering v United Kingdom*, in respect of refusal of asylum to Tamils in

---

[108] See *Ciliz* (section 'Expulsion of divorced or separated parent' and (b) Verification procedures.
[109] This provided a court review, with the confidentiality of national security material maintained by hearings *in camera* and the appointment of security cleared counsel to examine any witnesses in the absence of the applicant and his representative.
[110] *Jabari*, para.49.
[111] *Jabari*, paras 49–50.

Vilvarajah and an application to prevent expulsion after release from prison for an AIDS sufferer in *D v United Kingdom*.[112] In *Chahal v United Kingdom*, however, concerning a Sikh militant who was threatened with deportation to India for reasons of national security, domestic courts could not examine the evidence as to the threat to national security on which the Secretary of State claimed to rely. The Court found that the domestic courts were unable to to review the decision of the Home Secretary with reference solely to the question of risk but could only satisfy themselves that the Home Secretary had balanced the risk against the danger to national security. This was ineffective in the circumstances.

The Secretary of State's ability to exercise his discretion in favour of an applicant on compassionate grounds or otherwise is unlikely to be regarded as an effective remedy. In *Youssef v United Kingdom*, where the applicant was applying for entry to enjoy access to his son in the UK, such leave could only be granted on an exceptional basis as being outside immigration provisions, and it was within the discretion of the Adjudicator whether to make a recommendation for leave and then within the discretion of the Secretary of State as to whether he followed the recommendation. For the Commission, this provided insufficient guarantees of efficacy for the purposes of Art.13 of the Convention.[113]

G. Discrimination

IIB–253 Discrimination has been found in immigration practices which differentiate between persons on ground of sex. In *Abdulaziz*, the Court found no objective or reasonable justification in applying different and restrictive rules to the entry of male spouses. It rejected the Government's argument that it could be assumed that women would live in the country of their husband or that entry of male spouses as opposed to female spouses had a distorting and adverse effect on the employment market.

On the other hand, arguments relating to less conventional marriage practices have failed. It is not discrimination to refuse entry to more than one wife of a man settled in the UK,[114] any difference in treatment flowing essentially from the practice of polygamy for which the respondent Government was not responsible under the Convention.[115]

Immigration policies frequently are accused as being of racist in application. It is however difficult for an applicant of Asian or African ancestry to prove that he was refused entry whereas a white immigrant from a European or North American origin did or would have obtained entry in the same circumstances. Discrimination was established in the East Africans Asians case where statutory rules were introduced which could be shown to target persons of a particular origin. A case is pending regarding claims that the rules applying to the entry of adopted children treat those from India differently on grounds of their origin, without any objective and reasonable justification.[116]

The favourable treatment applying to EEC citizens as regards entry and residence has been found to be based on objective and reasonable justification, namely, the distinct Community legal regime involved.[117]

---

[112] The scope of judicial review also satisfied Art.13 in *TI v UK*, n.11 above, *Bensaid*, paras 56–58 and *Hilal*, paras 77–78.
[113] 14830/89, (Rep.) June 30, 1992, Resolution DH(95) 246.
[114] 19628/92, n.74 above.
[115] 23860/94, (Dec.) November 29, 1995.
[116] *Singh v UK*, 60418/00 (admissible).
[117] *Moustaquim*, para.49.

Cross-reference

Part IIB: Extradition
Part IIB: Deprivation of liberty
Part IIB: Detention pending expulsion or extradition
Part IIB: Discrimination
Part IIB: Remedies
Part IIB: Torture and ill-treatment

Interception of communications

Key provision:

IIB–254   Article 8 (respect for private life, home and correspondence).

Key case law:

Klass v Germany, September 6, 1978, Series A, No.28; 2 E.H.R.R. 214; *Malone v UK*, August 2, 1984, Series A, No.82; 7 E.H.R.R. 14; *Schenk v Switzerland*, July 12, 1988, Series A, No.140; 13 E.H.R.R. 242; *Huvig v France*, April 24, 1990 Series A, No.176–A; 12 E.H.R.R. 528; *Kruslin v France*, April 24, 1990, Series A, No.176–B; 12 E.H.R.R. 547; *A v France*, November 23, 1993, Series A, No.277–B; 17 E.H.R.R. 462; *Halford v UK*, June 25, 1997, R.J.D. 1997–III, No.39; 24 E.H.R.R. 523; *Kopp v Switzerland*, March 25, 1998, R.J.D. 1998–II; *Amann v Switzerland*, February 16, 2000, ECHR 2000–II; 27 E.H.R.R. 91; *Khan v UK*, May 12, 2000, ECHR 2000–V; 31 E.H.R.R. 1016; *MM v Netherlands*, April 8, 2003; *Craxi v Italy (No.1)*, July 17, 2003.

1. General considerations

IIB–255   Interception of communications, telephone tapping in its most well-known form, has generally been found, where it exists, to constitute an interference with one or more of the interests protected under Art.8, para.1. In *Klass v Germany*, the Court found that interception of communications (telephone and post) was an interference with private and family life, correspondence and, potentially, home.[1] Correspondence covers not just materials which cross by post but also telephone communications[2] and telexes.[3]

The bulk of the Convention organs' examination of interceptions has concentrated on the lawfulness of the measures in the broad sense of conformity with the rule of law—that the powers are grounded in accessible and foreseeable legal rules and verifying the existence of safeguards against abuse. There have been not inconsiderable findings of violations on this ground. It might therefore be claimed that the Convention has been a useful tool in subjecting the use of covert technological techniques by the State to proper regulation.

2. Telephone tapping

(a) *Content of communication*

IIB–256   Article 8 applies regardless of the content of the telephone conversation. In *A v France*, the Government argued that conversations taped relating to the commission of murder did not relate to private life. The Commission held that the mere fact that a conversation concerned the public interest did not deprive it of its private

---

[1] para.41.
[2] *A v France*, para.37.
[3] 21482/93, (Dec.) June 27, 1994, 78–A D.R. 119.

character, while the Court did not specify why it did not accept this argument. In *Halford v United Kingdom*, conversations by telephone were covered, whether business or private, as was use of office telephones.

However, where an applicant utilised an open air channel, the interception did not constitute interference with "private life" since the conversation, on a wavelength accessible to other users, could hardly be classified as "private" communications.[4]

(b) *Establishing an interference*

As intended, many of the subjects of telephone tapping are oblivious to the interference. Others may suspect without any concrete proof. It may be only when the interception leads to a trial that the telephone tapping is disclosed in the interests of the prosecution. An interference however is disclosed by the process of interception, even where no use is made of the recorded material.[5]

IIB–257

In *Klass v Germany*, however, the applicants attacked the legislation known as G10 on the basis, *inter alia*, that while the State had the right to have recourse to interception measures, there should be provision for informing the subject after the measures had been lifted and for court control of the imposition and execution of such measures. They had no proof or indication that they were subject to any measures in fact. The Court stated in very broad terms that, "under certain conditions", an applicant may claim to be the victim of a violation occasioned by the mere existence of secret measures or of legislation permitting secret measures.[6]

This was repeated as a basis for finding interferences in *Malone v United Kingdom* "apart from any measures actually taken against him".[7] However the existence of victim status and interference was admitted by the UK Government who, without furnishing any details, accepted that as a suspected receiver of stolen goods he was member of a class of persons against whom such measures were liable to be employed. Regarding metering, although the Government stated that it had not been employed in his case, the Court still found that he was in a class of persons potentially liable to be directly affected by the practice and could on the basis of the *Klass* case claim to be a victim quite apart from any concrete measure taken against him.

However, the Commission which dealt at the admissibility level with many unsubstantiated, often delusional complaints, developed a more restrictive filter approach, unwilling to embark on a detailed examination of the state of domestic law and practice every time a complainant alleged that the CIA or the freemasons were tapping his telephone. A test, namely whether there was a reasonable likelihood that the applicant had been subject to such measures or was in a category of persons likely to be targetted, was taken from *Hilton v United Kingdom*,[8] which dealt with secret files.

The reasonable likelihood test was then used where a applicant trade union leader discovered from a television documentary that the telexes addressed to him from overseas were being routinely intercepted[9] and led to rejection of complaints about

---

[4] 21353/93 (Dec.) February 27, 1995, 80–A D.R. 101.
[5] *Kopp*, para.53.
[6] para.34.
[7] para.64.
[8] 12015/86, (Dec.) July 6, 1988, 57 D.R. 108.
[9] 21482/93, n.3 above. The Government accepted that there was a reasonable likelihood of interception.

telephone tapping by nuclear test veterans who had not adduced sufficient evidence to demonstrate a reasonable likelihood that they would be subject to interception measures as a result of their campaigning.[10] A fine distinction was drawn in *Halford* where the Government accepted that there was a reasonable likelihood that calls on the applicant's office phone were intercepted, which was not unlawful in domestic law. In respect of allegations of bugging her home phone on the public lines however, the Court, adopting the Commission's approach, found no reasonable likelihood on the evidence presented, namely, the applicant had no specific information that her home phones were bugged and it would have been unlawful for the police to have taken this step.

Where police assist private individuals in taping telephone conversations to obtain evidence of criminal activities, State responsibility has been found to be engaged. In *MM v Netherlands*, the Court rejected the Government's argument that it was the ultimately a Mrs S who was in control of events, in circumstances where it was the police who had suggested that she tape the applicant's conversations and connected the recorder to her telephone.[11]

3. "In accordance with the law"[12]

IIB–258   The notion refers, firstly, to the interference having some basis in domestic law and, secondly, to the quality of law, *i.e.* those aspects which render it compatible with the notion of the rule of law, including accessibility, foreseeability as to the circumstances in which and conditions under which authorities are empowered to interfere, which should be such as to provide protection against arbitrary interferences.

Insufficient basis in domestic law was the basis for violations in *Malone*, where the powers relating to the interception of post and telephone communications, including metering, were not clearly incorporated in legal rules. An absence of a prohibition against measures was not sufficient. Similarly, the Court found in *Halford* that there was no basis in domestic law for interception of "private" telecommunications systems, since the Interception of Communications Act 1985 did not apply to it nor was there any general law of privacy.

When applicants allege that the authorities fail to comply with the domestic law provisions, the Commission accorded domestic authorities a wide margin of appreciation in their assessment. Where, in an Italian case, the Court of Cassation found that the regulations were followed and conditions fulfilled as regarded the existence of adequate suspicion existed, the Commission did not find that the lawfulness criterion was breached.[13] The Court has also emphasised that it is primarily for the national authorities to interpret and apply domestic law and expressed reluctance to contradict the views of such authorities as to the legal basis of measures.[14]

As to the quality of law, interceptions are regarded as serious interferences which render it essential to have clear detailed rules on the subject particularly since

---

[10] 23413/94, (Dec.) November 28, 1995, 83–A D.R. 31; 21825/93, (Dec.) November 11, 1995.

[11] Also *A v France*, para.36.

[12] See Pt 1, "Convention approach".

[13] ". . .its power to review national authorities' compliance with domestic law is limited": 13274/87 (Dec.) September 6, 1990, 66 D.R. 164.

[14] *e.g. Kruslin*, para.29; *Huvig*, para.28; *Kopp*, paras 59–60.

technology continually becomes more sophisticated.[15] Relevant factors are the existence of a definition of the categories of person or offences which may attract measures, limits on duration, regulation of the circumstances in which records are destroyed, whether the originals are available for inspection by the judiciary.[16] The Commission recognised that flexibility was required by the subject-matter and that the concept of foreseeability did not require definition of terms like "national security" or "economic well-being" when used as pre-conditions for the application of measures. It rejected the argument that the discretion afforded by these terms was too wide and undefined and that it should be subject to judicial input through adversarial argument in courts to establish full meaning of the terms. It considered that it was acceptable for the terms to be elaborated by administrative and executive statements and instructions.[17]

4. Necessity

Interception is acknowledged as potentially pursuing the aim of preventing crime and disorder in the police investigation context[18] and in the sphere of national security, in which latter context the Court has acknowledged a wide margin of appreciation.[19] There has been no real scrutiny of the purposes of the systems as such in the absence of obvious abuses. The key point has been whether there exist adequate and effective guarantees against abuse.[20] This provides some overlap with "in accordance in law" but where the latter looks at whether the way the law as formulated provides sufficient safeguards by way of accessibility and foreseeability, this looks rather at the concrete procedural protections.

IIB–259

Relevant features include the existence of any independent scrutiny in the implementation process, significance attaching to judicial input or parliamentary supervision of the executive.[21] Though judicial control is regarded as ensuring the most effective supervision offering the best guarantees of independence, impartiality and procedure, the lack of it is not necessarily fatal where other independent bodies exist with sufficient powers and competence to exercise continuous and effective control.[22] Where an applicant argued that there was no court and parliamentary control in the UK, the Commission found that an independent tribunal with limited review powers and an independent commissioner of high judicial rank, whose

---

[15] *Kruslin*, para.33; *Huvig*, para.32; also *Kopp*, where a lawyer's phone was tapped, the law did not clearly state how legally privileged material was to be distinguished from other matters and the Court remarked on the 'astonishing' practice of entrusting the task to an official of the executive, without supervision by a judge; and *Amann*, where the law did not regulate in detail the case of persons, such as the applicant, who were fortuitously monitored during interception measures taken against other targets.

[16] *e.g. Kruslin*, para.35; *Huvig*, para.34; *Valenzuala Contreras v Spain*, July 30, 1998, R.J.D. 1998–V, No.83, para.59; *Prado Bugallo v Spain*, February 18, 2003, para.30.

[17] 21482/93, n.3 above.

[18] *Malone*; also 29839/96, (Dec.) May 18, 1998.

[19] *Klass*, para.49; *Leander*, para.59.

[20] *Klass*, para.50; 29839/96, n.18 above, where the Dutch courts provided adequate and sufficient, if indirect, control as regarded alleged negligence in taping privileged conversations.

[21] *e.g. Klass*, where an officer qualified for judicial office carried out scrutiny and there was supervision by a parliamentary body of the executive minister. Also 10439/83, (Dec.) May 10, 1985, 43 D.R. 34 where a senior judge was involved in review; 11811/85, (Dec.) March 8, 1988, 55 D.R. 182, where safeguards included judicial supervision within 24 hours.

[22] *Klass*, paras 55–56.

thorough and critical approach to his functions was disclosed in his reports, were acceptable.[23]

Limitations as to duration of warrants and requirement for prior authorisation have also been considered as safeguards.[24]

There is no requirement that a person subject to measures be informed afterwards, the Convention organs allowing that the secrecy and efficacy of the system would be undermined by such notifications.[25] Nor is it necessary that a tribunal ruling on complaint by applicant give reasons for a negative ruling, instead of confirming only whether or not there has been a contravention of the statutory provisions.[26]

The Commission and Court have shown a pragmatic attitude in assessing the efficacy of procedural safeguards. No system, it is said, can rule out abuse by over-zealous officials but where a procedure is in place designed to reduce measures to the necessary minimum and ensure their conformity with the necessary provisions, unless there is evidence to the contrary the Court will assume that the authorities are properly applying the legislation.[27] In the area of security checks, the Commission took a stance of setting a minimum necessary standard, rejecting arguments based on the existence of better protection systems elsewhere. Since the aim is to balance the needs of the State against the protection of individual' rights a system of effective, not foolproof, checks against abuses is required. For an issue to arise where there is a system of checks in place, it requires a fundamental inadequacy, evidence of abuse or failure to control or a clear gap in the protection, as in *Halford*, where the legislation omitted private telecommunication systems.

5. Postal interferences

IIB–260   The above considerations apply equally to interception of mail, though there are fewer cases dealing expressly with such allegations. While numerous complaints are made by persons suspicious of receiving envelopes or parcels which are torn and taped back together by the postal authorities, the Commission tended to apply a robust approach, requiring some form of substantiation of "interference" and applied the "reasonable likelihood" test to reject them.[28] As regards mishandling by the Post, an old Commission case states that Art.8 does not guarantee the perfect functioning of the postal service.[29]

There are some contexts where interference with mail is in fact routine or not unexpected, *e.g.* prisons, bankrupty. There are also criminal law provisions regulat-

---

[23] 21482/93, n.3 above.

[24] 10439/83, n.21; 13564/88, (Dec.) June 8, 1999.

[25] *Klass*; 21482/93, n.3 above; 10439/83, n.21 above, 11811/85 n.24 above.

[26] 21482/93, n.3 above.

[27] *Klass*, para.59; 21482/93, n.3 above, the Commission found this evidence was not furnished by the fact that the Interception of Communications Tribunal had never made a determination in favour of an applicant nor was it impressed by unsubstantiated rumours in the media that there was routine interception of businessmen's communications.

[28] 20591/92, (Dec.) December 2, 1992, where the applicant (involved with groups which attempt to visit Stonehenge at the solstice) alleged opening of his parcels, the Commission found that there was insufficient evidence that he was a person or in a category of persons in respect of whom the police would consider clandestine surveillance measures were necessary. No reasonable likelihood that his mail was interfered with by the police rather than merely damaged in transit (as claimed by the parcel service).

[29] 8383/75, (Dec.) October 3, 1979, 17 D.R. 227: reference to the volume of mail, statistical likelihood of some miscarriage which is generally known and special means provided to ensure safe delivery of particular letters on demand.

ing what may be sent by post, in particular, pornography.[30] Interferences based on enforcement of criminal law provisions are likely to be found justifiable, when in compliance with domestic law.

6. Use of material in court proceedings

The use in evidence at trial of material obtained by the police using interceptions has been examined under Art.6 "fairness" considerations. It seems to be an accepted source of evidence in domestic courts where lawfully obtained subject to a warrant and procedural safeguards.

However, the lawfulness is not decisive to fairness under Art.6 as shown in *Schenk v Switzerland*, where the taping by a hired assassin of a phone call with the applicant handed over to the police was unlawful as not ordered by the investigating judge. The Court considered this did not not render a trial automatically unfair or a disclose a ground of violation *per se*. It had regard to the circumstances, namely, the applicant had knowledge of the tape and how it was taken and was able to challenge its use and contents by calling the assassin or police inspector as witnesses. The Court found that the rights of defence were not disregarded. Though it attached weight to the fact that it was not the only evidence on which the conviction was based,[31] the case of *Khan v United Kingdom*, where the only evidence against the applicant had been obtained by covert surveillance conducted without proper legal basis, has since established that there will be no breach of Art.6 in basing a conviction solely on such evidence as long as there are adequate procedural safeguards by which the applicant can challenge the authenticity of, or unfairness of using the material. Subsequent cases have underlined that use of material at trial obtained without a proper legal basis will not generally offend the standard of fairness imposed by Art.6, para.1 where proper procedural safeguards are in place and the nature and source of the material is not tainted, for example, by any oppression, coercion or entrapment which would render reliance on it unfair. The way in which the material was obtained raises issues rather under Art.8 regarding the State's responsibility to secure the right to respect for private life in due form.[32]

Issues will therefore arise under Art.8 if interception material used at trial is obtained or used without regard to domestic lawfulness or is made public in circumstances which infringe private life without any corresponding relevance to the interests of preventing crime.[33] In *Craxi v Italy (No.1)*, the Court objected to the lack of safeguards surrounding the transcripts of the accused's private telephone

---

[30] *e.g.* 7308/75, (Dec.) October 12, 1978, 16 D.R. 32: stoppage of packages containing obscene materials.

[31] Also 15199/89, (Dec.) September 4, 1991, where the applicant was held pending extradition in London and during magistrates proceedings taped conversations obtained by US agents in Paris were used, complaints under Art.8 were rejected. There was no indication that the UK authorities had been involved in taking the recording, even assuming it had been unlawful in France and it was subject to limited use in court (no indication that it was read out or made known to public). Given the purpose of fulfilling extradition obligations and fighting drugtrafficking, there was no lack of respect under Art.8 and as regarded detention under Art.5, para.1(f) this was not arbitrary, or procedurally or substantively unlawful.

[32] *e.g. Chalkley v UK*, 63831/00, (Dec.) September 26, 2002; *Perry v UK*, 63737/00, (Dec.) September 26, 2002.

[33] *Mutatis mutandis*, *Z v Finland*, February 25, 1997, R.J.D. 1997–I, where medical material concerning a witness was made public.

conversations, not used in court by the prosecution but which found their way out of the court registry file into the hands of the press and were duly published.[34] The use of other parts of the transcript at the trial was not in accordance with law either as the prosecution failed to comply with domestic procedural safeguards requiring the material to be lodged with the registry prior to being read in court which would have allowed the defence to present their comments.

Cross-reference

Part IIA: Fair trial, Evidence
Part IIB: Surveillance and the secret files

---

[34] Even if the leak had come from one of the parties rather than a public official, the Government's responsibility was engaged as there was an obligation of safe custody and it had not taken effective steps to investigate the incident and sanction any breach of confidentiality.

Marriage and founding a family

Key provisions:

IIB–262 Articles 12 (right to marry and found a family) and 14 (prohibition against discrmination).

Key case law:

Airey v Ireland, October 9, 1979, Series A, No.32; 2 E.H.H.H. 305; *Rees v UK,* October 17, 1986, Series A, No.106; 9 E.H.R.R. 56; *Johnston v Ireland,* December 18, 1986, Series A, No.112; 9 E.H.R.R. 56; *F v Switzerland,* December 18, 1987, Series A, No.128; 10 E.H.R.R. 411; *Cossey v UK,* September 27, 1990, Series A, No.184; 13 E.H.R.R. 622; *Christine Goodwin v UK,* July 11, 2002, ECHR 2002–VI.

1. General considerations

IIB–263 The traditional marriage enjoys a favoured position in the Convention with Art.12 singled out for separate treatment and perhaps resulting in special status, for example, where married relationships are considered in the context of of family life and discrimination.[1] The Commission organs have interfered in practice little in how States choose to regulate this area. For the Court the right to marry guaranteed by Art.12 refers to the traditional marriage between persons of opposite biological sex, which interpretation is supported by the reference to the founding of a family.[2]

2. The right to marry

IIB–264 Article 12 is dominated by the reference to "according to the national laws governing the exercise of this right". Persons are expected, for example, to comply with the procedural formalities imposed by the State. A German could not therefore claim a violation when the registrar refused to register his marriage which had not involved the completion of the necessary administrative forms but only a religious ceremony.[3]

The principle is that the national laws may govern the exercise of the right but not injure its substance.[4] Generally recognised limitations such as capacity, consent, consanguinity or prevention of bigamy are likely to be compatible. For example, the Commission rejected a complaint from a muslim who complained that he could not marry a girl of 14 who had no legal capacity despite his assertion that his religion permitted marriage to a girl over 12. The Commission commented that it would not

---

[1] 11089/84, (Dec.) November 11, 1986, 49 D.R. 181: married and unmarried couples are not in analogous positions for tax purposes since marriage relates to a special regime of rights and obigations— *McMichael v UK,* February 24, 1995, Series A, No.307–B; 20 E.H.R.R. 205, automatic parental rights for married fathers as opposed to unmarried fathers were objectively and reasonably justified.
[2] *Rees;* see however the Commission's opinions in 7114/75, (Rep.) December 13, 1979, 24 D.R. 5 and 8186/78, (Rep.) July 10, 1980, 24 D.R. 72.
[3] 6167/73, (Dec.) December 18, 1974, 1 D.R. 64.
[4] 7114/75 and 8186/78, n.2 above.

be compatible to deprive a person or a category of persons of the full legal capacity to marry.[5]

Other legal bars which prevent marriage of consenting and legally capable adults may be expected therefore to raise issues[6] and it may be that traditional or historical limitations that have become anomalous could be challenged successfully.[7]

Where domestic law permits, and the authorities even facilitate, gender re-assignment, the inability of a transsexual to marry some-one of opposite gender to their re-assigned gender has been found to violate Art.12. Referring to findings in earlier UK cases, *Rees*, *Cossey* and *Sheffield and Horsham*, that this did not impair the essence of the right as the transsexual continued to enjoy the right to marry a person of the opposite birth gender, the Court in *Christine Goodwin v United Kingdom* rejected this argument as artificial and found that the UK could no longer restrict marriage to a union between a man and woman both of biological origin as defined at birth without reference to intervening phenomena. It noted that the corresponding and more recently drafted provision in the European Charter of Human Rights, Art.9, referred to the right to marry without framing it in terms of "men and women" and found no justification for preventing transsexuals from marrying. It is probably too early for changing attitudes and evolving practices in Contracting States with regard to homosexual marriages to lead the Court to find that Art.12 extends beyond marriage for opposite sexes (however defined).

Practical prohibitions have disclosed problems in other contexts. The Commission held that prison authorities could not legitimately refuse a prisoner permission to get married while serving his sentence. It was irrelevant to the Commission that the respective couples would not have been able to consummate the marriage or cohabit. Marriage to the Commission was the formation of a legally binding association between a man and a woman. The delay imposed on them before they could exercise their right to marry on their release was found to injure the substance of their right to marry.[8]

The imposition of time-limits has also been found incompatible in *F v Switzerland* where the Swiss attempted to regulate the frequency of divorces. A three year prohibition on re-marriage was imposed on an applicant after having been granted his third divorce. The Government argued that such temporary prohibitions were not arbitrary or disproportionate, pursuing the aim of preserving the stability of marriage, the protection of the rights of the future spouse and compelling proper reflection (impliedly no bad thing in this applicant's case). The Court disagreed, finding the restriction unreasonable, disproportionate and affecting the very essence of the right. A paternalistic attitude to regulate the entering into marriage of legally capable adults was therefore rejected as constituting an acceptable public policy interest.

---

[5] 11579/85, (Dec.) July 7, 1986 48 D.R. 253.
[6] *Selim v Cyprus*, July 16, 2002: the applicant's complaints under Art.12 that he was unable marry in Cyprus as there was no provision in domestic law for a Turkish Cypriot of the Muslim faith to contract a civil marriage, were settled after admissibility.
[7] *B and L v UK*, 35636/02, where a father-in-law and daughter-in-law wish to marry and are unable to do so, without obtaining a private act of Parliament. The case is pending.
[8] 7114/75 and 8186/75, n.2 above: the prisoners were serving 5 year and life sentences respectively.

3. Divorce

The Convention organs consider that the ordinary meaning of the provision is the formation of marital relationships and not their dissolution. The Court held that a restriction on divorce in a country adhering to the principle of monogamy cannot be regarded as injuring the substance of the right guaranteed by Art.12. Developments in society with regard to the availability of divorce were irrelevant having regard to the clear meaning of the text and to intent of the drafters, as shown from the *travaux préparatoires*, who deliberately omitted reference to dissolution of marrriage. In *Johnston v Ireland* therefore, the applicant's inability to obtain the dissolution of the marriage with his first wife to allow him to marry the woman with whom he had lived for over eight years and with whom he had founded a family, did not disclose a violation of Art.12.

    Conversely, where divorce was permitted in domestic law, this has not been considered as infringing the right to marry.[9]

IIB–265

4. Founding a family

There is no right to adoption as such to be derived from Art.12 or any of the other provisions of the Convention.[10] Where procedures for applying for adoption exist, any rights are subject under Art.12 to the requirements of "national laws". In a Dutch case the applicant and her husband who wished to adopt a Polish boy were refused permission as the proposed adoption did not fulfil the conditions set down in domestic law with regard, *inter alia*, to the difference in ages between themselves and the child. Their complaints were rejected as the measure was in accordance with national laws.[11] In the absence of blatant arbitrariness, it would be unlikely that matters of eligibility or procedural requirements for adoption under domestic law would raise issues. In *Fretté v France*, where there was a right to adopt under domestic law, the Court considered that complaints about discriminatory application of the law could fall within the scope of Art.14, though in the circumstances of that case, a narrow majority found that no violation arose from refusal to allow the applicant to adopt due to his homosexuality.[12]

    Regarding practical obstacles, prisoners have unsuccessfully claimed the right to conjugal visits, the Commission finding that no such right could be derived from Art.12.[13] With increasing concessions being made in prison regimes particularly in

IIB–266

---

[9] See *F v Switzerland*, para.38.

[10] 31924/96, (Dec.), July 10, 1997, 90 D.R. 134; *Fretté v France*, February 26, 2002, ECHR 2002–I, para.32 and (Dec.), June 12, 2001, rejecting as incompatible *ratione materiae* the complaints under Art.12 about a refusal of permission to adopt based on the applicant's homosexuality.

[11] 8896/80, (Dec.) March 10, 1981, 24 D.R. 177; also 7229/75, (Dec.) December 15, 1977, 12 D.R. 32.

[12] Three dissenting judges thought that the bar was not based on any individual consideration of the applicant's suitability or identified grounds of detriment to any adopted child; one of the majority judges found that Art.14 was not applicable, while the remaining three judges held that the refusal was based on the welfare of the children to be adopted and within the broad margin of appreciation, where the scientific community were divided on the possible consequences of such adoptions and bearing in mind the limited number of studies on the subject.

[13] 8166/78, (Dec.) December 3, 1978, 13 D.R. 241—where husband and wife were detained in the same prison, lack of conjugal visits was justifiable in the interests of security and good order under Art.8, with no separate issue under Art.12. Also 6564/74, (Dec.) May 21, 1975, 2 D.R. 105, no infringement in locking some-one up as no right to be given the actual possibility at all times to procreate!

the Nordic countries, the Commission hinted that the situation might be reviewable in the future. The issue was subject to two communications to the UK in combination with a complaint about a refusal to allow artificial insemination treatment of prisoners' wives, who due to factors of the age or health could not await their husbands' release. Where it was a matter of allowing a brief procedure for a prisoner to provide the necessary sample for his wife's doctor, there appeared to be little justification to put in the balance against the enjoyment of the right under Art.12. However, the cases were struck off when permission was granted.[14]

Abortion measures which are compatible with Art.8 cannot raise any separate issues under Art.12.[15] Where a couple is infertile the extent to which they could derive a right of access to new medical technologies is unexplored. There are aspects of resource allocation and costs which would make it unlikely that a couple could require a State to furnish treatment but where treatment is available, the decision-making procedure might perhaps be amenable to challenge on grounds of arbitrariness or discriminatory treatment.

Cross-reference

Part IIB: Homosexuality
Part IIB: Transsexuals

---

[14] 10822/84, (Dec.) May 7, 1987 and 17142/90, (Dec.) July 10, 1991.
[15] *Boso v Italy*, 50490/99, (Dec.), September 5, 2002, ECHR 2002–VII.

Mental health

Key provisions:

Article 5, para.1(e) (lawful detention of persons of unsound mind); 5, para.4 (review of detention); 8 (private life) and 3 (prohibition of ill-treatment).   **IIB–267**

Key case law:

Winterwerp v Netherlands, October 24, 1979, Series A, No.33; 2 E.H.R.R. 387; *X v UK*, November 5, 1981 Series A, No.46; 4 E.H.R.R. 188; *Luberti v Italy*, February 23, 1984, Series A, No.75; 6 E.H.R.R. 440; *Van der Leer v Netherlands*, February 21, 1990, Series A, No.170; 12 E.H.R.R. 567; *Wassink v Netherlands*, September 27, 1990, Series A, No.185–A; *Koendjbiharie v Netherlands*, October 25, 1990, Series A, No.185–B; 13 E.H.R.R. 820; *Keus v Netherlands*, October 25, 1990, Series A, No.185–C; 13 E.H.R.R. 700; *Megyeri v Germany*, May 12, 1992, Series A, No.237; 15 E.H.R.R. 584; *Herczegfalvy v Austria*, September 24, 1992, Series A, No.244; 15 E.H.R.R. 437; *Johnson v UK*, October 24, 1997, R.J.D. 1997–VII, No.55; 27 E.H.R.R. 296; *Aerts v Belgium*, July 30, 1998, R.J.D. 1998–V, No.83; 29 E.H.R.R. 58; *Musial v Poland*, March 25, 1999, ECHR 1999–II; 31 E.H.R.R. 720; *Matter v Slovakia*, 5 July 1999; 31 E.H.R.R. 783; *Varbanov v Bulgaria*, October 5, 2000, ECHR 2000–X; *Hutchison Reid v UK*, February 20, 2003, ECHR 2003–IV; *Rakevich v Russia*, October 28, 2003.

1. General considerations

The principal cases concern the procedures and safeguards relating to detention of persons on grounds of mental illness. Surprisingly few cases relate to the other disabilities imposed on mentally ill persons in the enjoyment of basic rights and freedoms, or to any allegations of ill-treatment within institutions. This presumably is a sad reflection that this vulnerable group of people face grave problems in putting forward or establishing claims.[1]   **IIB–268**

2. Admissibility points

The admissibility criteria apply in the ordinary way. A mental health patient is required to exhaust effective domestic remedies and to comply with the six month period. (See Pt IB—Admissibility Checklist).   **IIB–269**

3. Grounds for detention

Article 5, para.1(e) refers to persons of "unsound mind". The Court in *Winterwerp v Netherlands* noted that this was not a term which leant itself to precise definition since psychiatry was a progressing field, both medically and in social attitudes. It is   **IIB–270**

---

[1] In *Aerts*, where the applicant complained that the deficiencies on the psychiatric wing violated Art.3, the Court commented that it would be unreasonable to expect a severely mentally disturbed person to give a detailed or coherent description of what he had suffered but even allowing for that difficulty found it had not been established that the applicant had suffered inhuman or degrading treatment (para.66).

not sufficient that a person's views or behaviour deviates from the established norms. The concept is to be narrowly interpreted given the importance of the right to liberty.

The Convention organs will examine whether domestic law is compatible with the Convention.[2]

There are three basic requirements to establish that detention of a person of "unsound mind" falls within sub-para.1(e)[3]:

- "a true mental disorder" has to be established by objective medical expertise before the competent domestic authority except where it is an emergency procedure;
- it has to be a kind or degree to warrant compulsory confinement, and
- the validity of the continued detention depends on the persistence of the disorder.

In the assessment of whether the person should be detained as of "unsound mind", the authorities have a certain discretion or margin of appreciation with regard to the evaluation of the evidence subject to Convention supervision.[4] This will usually involve an examination of whether there was psychiatric evidence to support the assessment. No deprivation of liberty will be compatible with Art.5, para.1(e) if it has been ordered without seeking the opinion of a medical expert (save in emergency cases).[5] There has as yet been no case where the official medical view of the existence of mental illness has been negatived by the Court. The requirement that the applicant be suffering from a mental disorder warranting compulsory confinement does not import any condition that the condition is amenable to medical treatment, the so-called treatability criteria found in some domestic laws.[6] Confinement may be necessary not only where a person requires treatment or therapy but also where the person needs control and supervision to prevent harm to himself or others.[7] The medical opinion relied on should however reflect the applicant's condition at the time of the decision, a delay between the medical examination and the presentation of the opinion in court being capable of disclosing arbitrariness contrary to the principle underlying Art.5.[8]

As to the moment when detention ceases to be justified, the Court had found that the authorities may legitimately proceed with caution and a certain time may lapse while the applicant's condition is considered.[9] The authorities also enjoy a certain discretion as to the timing and conditions under which a person is released. Thus, in

---

[2] *e.g. Winterwerp*: the law which covered persons with a mental disorder rendering them a danger to themselves or others was compatible.

[3] *Winterwerp*, para.39.

[4] *e.g. Rakevich*, para.30, where the authorities received the benefit of the doubt as to the necessity of detaining the applicant after "a night long emotional study of the Bible".

[5] *e.g. Varbanov*, paras 47–48: the applicant was detained for psychiatric examination by a prosecutor without consulting a medical expert and no emergency was claimed- by not requiring a medical opinion prior to detention, domestic law failed to protect against arbitrariness.

[6] *Koniarska v UK*, 33670/96, (Dec.) October 12, 2000.

[7] *Hutchison Reid*, para.51: where the applicant's psychopathic disorder was not appropriate for hospital treatment, the Court found that it was not contrary to Art.5, para.1(e) to detain him in hospital as it was not disputed that his mental disorder made him a risk to the public.

[8] *Musial*, para.50, where the court decision ordering continued detention was based on an examination which took place some 11 months earlier; see also *Varbanov*, para.47; *Magalhaes Pereira v Portugal*, February 26, 2002, ECHR 2002–I, para.49.

[9] *Luberti*, para.29 where the applicant's detention reasonably continued pending court examination of the file and reports.

Johnson v United Kingdom, the Court did not consider that it automatically followed from a diagnosis that an applicant's mental disorder no longer persisted that he should be immediately or unconditionally released. However, any deferral of release had to be compatible with the purpose of Art.5, para.1 and not be unduly delayed. Over three years elapsing from a tribunal finding that the applicant was not mentally ill until his release did not fall with the authorities' discretion in managing his release into society in that case.[10]

Concerning emergency procedures, the Court will examine the facts leading to the emergency detention and the available medical reports or evidence at the time.[11] In *Winterwerp,* it considered the applicant's bizarre behaviour justified the steps taken (he was stealing, stripped off his clothes, etc.).[12] The Commission in *O'Reilly v Ireland* found admissible issues arising as to the justification of the extreme step of emergency detention, based on the complaint of the applicant's spouse and a visual examination by a general practitioner from the end of a garden.[13] In *Kay v United Kingdom,* where the Secretary of State ordered the recall to hospital of a prisoner whose prison sentence expired without first obtaining an up-to-date medical report of his state of mental health, the Commission found a violation since there was no emergency to justify this omission.[14] The time which should elapse before a full evaluation of the applicant's state occurs should be brief on any view of matters. The Court in *Winterwerp* found that a six-week delay was rather long but not so excessive as to render the detention unlawful.[15]

Since there must be some relationship between the ground of permitted deprivation of liberty and the place and conditions of detention, the detention of a person as a mental health patient will only be lawful for the purposes of Art.5, para.1(e) if effected in a hospital, clinic or other appropriate institution.[16] Thus in *Aerts v Belgium,* where the applicant suffering from a severe mental disturbance was held, while waiting trial, in the psychiatric wing of Lantin prison, the Court found a violation of Art.5, para.1 as the lack of appropriate medical supervision and treatment showed that the wing was not an institution appropriate for the detention of persons of unsound mind.

4. Procedure prescribed by law

The authorities must conform to requirements imposed by domestic law in the proceedings concerning detention.[17] Violations may result even from technical breaches, as in *Wassink v Netherlands,* where the registrar of the court was not

IIB–271

---

[10] The Court commented critically that the Mental Health Review Tribunal and the authorities did not have the necessary powers to ensure that the conditions attached to his release (namely placement in a supervised hostel) could be implemented within a reasonable time.

[11] *e.g.* in *Wassink,* the judge had four medical reports (two doctors had appeared and two had spoken on the telephone), statements from applicant's wife and a police report about an assault: there were thus no grounds for questioning the weight of the evidence on which the judge extended the emergency confinement by three weeks.

[12] Also *X v UK,* on recall of a person under conditional release, complaints by his wife of threats and fears for safety supported by her doctor were sufficient.

[13] 24196/94, (Dec.) January 22, 1996, 84–A D.R. 72; settled (Rep.) December 3, 1996.

[14] 17821/91, (Rep.) March 1, 1994. Contrast *Herz v Germany,* June 12, 2003, where the existing medical reports were over a year old but the applicant's violent conduct the day before provided sufficient basis for an emergency order.

[15] para.42.

[16] *Aerts,* para.46; *Hutchison Reid,* para.54.

[17] *e.g. Rakevich,* para.35, failure to grant or refuse the hospital order within five days of application (39 days).

present at the hearing as required by law. In *Van der Leer v Netherlands*, the applicant was confined without being heard though pursuant to the relevant law the judge should have heard her where the psychiatrist had no objection to such a procedure. The Court commented that at the very least the judge should have given reasons for departing from the pyschiatrist's opinion and there was a violation since an essential procedural requirement was not satisfied. The latter seemed to hint that a non-essential infringement of domestic procedure might not fall foul of the Convention.

5. Review of the lawfulness of the continued detention

IIB–272
A person of unsound mind who is compulsorily confined is entitled under Art.5, para.4 to take proceedings to challenge the lawfulness of their detention at reasonable intervals and to obtain a speedy judicial decision.[18] The applicant should enjoy a direct right of appeal or application and not have to rely on the intermediary of the detaining authority.[19]

Since the validity of detention under Art.5, para.1(e) depends on the persistence of the disorder, the review required by Art.5, para.4 includes verification of the applicant's mental state as necessitating detention.

Habeas corpus was not adequate in *X v United Kingdom*, where the applicant was recalled after his conditional release from a restriction order, since the court did not examine whether in fact the applicant's disorder persisted or whether the continuation of the compulsory confinement was necessary in the interests of public safety.

The Court previously held in *Ashingdane v United Kingdom* that there was no right to obtain a review of the location or conditions of detention, where the applicant disputed the justification of his continued detention at Broadmoor. Judicial control was not guaranteed of the legality of all aspects or details of the detention and it was not considered that the question of entitlement to a more appropriate regime concerned "lawfulness" for the purpose of Art.5, para.4.[20] Since *Aerts v Belgium*, however, where the Court held that issues of lawfulness would arise from placement of a mental patient outside a suitable therapeutic institution, it would appear issues could arise from lack of effective review of the suitability of the placement.[21]

(a) "Court"

IIB–273
The review must be conducted by "court", which must have a power to decide. In *X v United Kingdom*, the Mental Health Review Tribunal only had advisory powers and no binding power to release. A specialised body of this kind may be a "court" provided that it enjoys the necessary independence and offers sufficient procedural safeguards. A public prosecutor did not qualify in *Winterwerp v Netherlands*.

---

[18] *Musial*, para.43.
[19] *Rakevich*, paras 43–46.
[20] May 28, Series A, No.93, para.52—the applicant had been recommended as fit for transfer to an ordinary hospital.
[21] *Aerts*, paras 54–56—the opportunity for the applicant to apply for an injunction satisfied Art.5, para.4 in that case.

(b) *Procedural requirements*

The review must provide the requisite procedural safeguards. In the context of **IIB–274** mental illness, special safeguards may be required to protect persons who are not fully capable of acting for themselves.[22] While mental illness may justify restricting or modifying the exercise of their right of review, it cannot however justify impairing the very essence of that right.[23]

There was a violation in *Winterwerp*, where neither the applicant nor his representative were present before the courts which issued the orders of detention. The Court considered that the applicant must be heard either in person or through a representative. Further, answering the Government's point that the applicant had failed to instruct a lawyer, it was not for the person with unsound mind to take the initiative to obtain legal representation before applying to a court. The necessity for legal assistance was underlined in *Megyeri v Germany*, where the applicant challenged his detention in psychiatric hospital but was not represented before the court conducting the review. The Court found that where a person was confined in psychiatric institution on the basis of acts which would have been criminal offences for those criminally responsible, he should, unless there are special circumstances, receive legal assistance in subsequent proceeedings concerning that detention. It was doubtful that the applicant could address the medical and legal points arising and the Court emphasised the importance of what was at stake for him.[24]

What is required by way of procedure at the hearing may be minimal where emergency considerations apply. In *Wassink*, the Court found it compatible with Art.5, para.4 that the President of the court consulted experts and witnesses by phone, although failing to read his notes to the applicant or his counsellor and in the absence of the registrar who was required by law. The Court was influenced by the fact that the power exercised was an emergency one limited in duration to three weeks and considered that the President nonetheless had established the medical basis for continued detention.

Having regard to Art.5, para.4 cases dealing with other forms of detention, it is likely that access to documents and reports may be required, tempered however by the consideration whether an applicant should on health grounds be allowed to see particular documents.[25]

It is for the authorities to prove that he satisfies the conditions for compulsory detention, not the applicant, the converse. A violation of Art.5, para.4 arose in *Hutchison Reid v United Kingdom* where the applicant had to show that his mental disorder was not of a nature or degree making it appropriate for him to receive treatment in hospital and thus the burden of proof was on him to establish that his detention was not lawful.

---

[22] *Megyeri*, para.22; *Magalhaes Pereira*, n.8 above, para.56.
[23] *Wassink*, para.60.
[24] Also *Magalhaes Pereira*, n.8 above, paras 58–62—a breach of Art.5, para.4, for lack of effective legal assistance to the mentally disturbed applicant at the hearings concerning his detention. The Court rejected the Government's argument that an officially assigned lawyer was not required due to an alleged lack of legal issues—it was self-evident that such issues could arise.
[25] See Pt IIB: "Review of detention".

6. Timing of reviews

IIB–275   A person detained as being of unsound mind is entitled both to a speedy decision and to take proceedings at reasonable intervals.[26] The latter applies where there is no automatic periodic judicial review, the Court commenting in *X v United Kingdom* that it was not its task to specify which system of judicial review was appropropriate.

However, no initial review is required where detention is ordered by a court at the end of judical proceedings. In these circumstances, the review of lawfulness is regarded as incorporated. An initial review by a court is only required for the purposes of Art.5, para.4 where the decision to detain is taken by an administrative authority.[27]

A distinction may be made between the speed at which an applicant taken into detention or recalled should obtain a review and the time which should be taken in reaching decisions on release or continuance at later stages.

The first review should take place very rapidly. In *Wassink*, the Commission found that the applicant's discharge after three-weeks emergency confinement did not follow so speedily that it made a review of detention superfluous. A five-month delay on a hearing after recall was, not surprisingly, excessive in *Kay v United Kingdom*.

Concerning later reviews, four months for a court to issue a decision on an application for release was not speedy in *Koendjbiharie v Netherlands*. Where in another case it took almost three months to decide an application for release, the Commission, rejecting the case as inadmissible, commented that while on first sight this seemed excessive and required factors to justify it, it was not excessive in light of the applicant's conduct in challenging the impartiality of the expert and the conducting of thorough medical examinations.[28]

Where an applicant's conduct contributes to the length of proceedings, rendering it impossible to obtain an examination, this will be a relevant factor in assessing whether the court has acted reasonably.[29] However, the fact that an applicant applies for adjournments or shows disinterest does not absolve the court from acting speedily. In *Kay v United Kingdom*,[30] the Commission found the system of review on recall inherently slow, since it frequently took six months for cases to come before the Mental Health Review Tribunal. In this case there was a two year delay, the applicant's own requests for adjournments and later disinterest not being relevant, since anyway the first hearing had been set for five months after recall. Similarly, in *Musial v Poland*, the fact that the applicant requested that examination by particular doctors did not discharge the domestic court from its obligation to rule speedily on his request for release. In that case, the Court also did not find the medical complexity of the file sufficient to constitute exceptional grounds justifying a delay of over one year and eight months. Where the system provides appeals, these must also be taken in to account in assessing the speed and cannot provide an excuse for lack of proper expedition.[31]

Regarding reviews at reasonable intervals, an automatic review once per year was considered reasonable in *Megyeri*. In *Herczegfalvy v Austria*, the Court found intervals

---

[26] A court must decide speedily and at reasonable intervals—*Herczegfalvy*, para.75.

[27] *Luberti*, para.31.

[28] *Boucheras v France*, 14438/88, (Dec.) April 11, 1991, 69 D.R. 236.

[29] e.g. *Keus*; *Luberti*. However, in *Van der Leer*, para.35, the fact that the applicant absconded while the application was pending did not absolve the court from reaching a speedy decision since she could have been brought back against her will at any moment.

[30] Cited above.

[31] *Hutchison Reid*, paras 77–80, where the applicant's proceedings for release were heard by 4 instances lasting 3 years and 9 months and there were no exceptional grounds justifying the delay.

of 15 months and two years were not speedy but in not remarking on the period of nine months seemed to find that was compatible. It referred to the fact that the Austrian system recommended a yearly interval.

7. Access to court

The factor of mental illness may justify restrictions on access to court. In *Ashingdane* where leave was required to bring actions in relation to acts done in pursuance of the Mental Health Act 1959 the Court found that this pursued the legitimate aim of preventing those responsible for the care of mental patients being unfairly harassed by litigation and that the essence of the right was not impaired, since it was only a partial exclusion.[32]   **IIB–276**

However, the proceedings to detain a person *per se* do not involve the determination of a person's civil rights and obligations under Art.6, para.1. A different kind of court control is applicable to these cases under the special provisions of Art.5.[33]

8. Ill-treatment

In the context of force feeding, constraints, compulsory administration of drugs, the Court's view appears to be that such will not breach Art.3 if required for therapeutic reasons. In *Herczegfalvy*, the Commission doubted that it was necessary to apply massive force to administer medication and found that the fettering to bed for several weeks when the applicant was in a very bad physical state, combined with isolation, was excessive and disclosed inhuman and degrading treatment. The Court restricted itself to the medical necessity, holding that a measure which was a therapeutic necessity cannot be inhuman or degrading. While the duration of the period of handcuffing and restriction in a security bed was "worrying", there was nothing to disprove the Government's argument that, according to the psychiatric principles accepted at the time, medical necessity required it.[34]   **IIB–277**

For an Art.3 case to have any chance of success, it would appear necessary to show that the authorities applied treatment clearly injustifiable by any established medical norm.[35]

9. Right to treatment

The Court has stated in old cases that no right to a specific treatment appropriate to the applicant's condition can derived from Art.5, para.1(e).[36] However, the more recent case of *Aerts* discloses the possibility of challenging under Art.5 the holding of   **IIB–278**

---

[32] See above, *i.e.* if there was bad faith or negligence the case could proceed with leave of the court.

[33] *Neumeister v Austria*, June 27, 1968, Series A, No.8, para.23.

[34] Also *Frommelt v Liechtenstein*, 49158/99, (Dec.) May 15, 2003, necessity for neuroleptic drug treatment, constant surveillance and threat to force feed the applicant did not offend Art.3.

[35] *Buckley v UK*, 28323/95, (Dec.) February 26, 1997 where the administration of drugs in circumstances which led to the death of a patient did not disclose ground for negligence in domestic law, there was no basis for the Commission to find a violation.

[36] See *Ashingdane*, n.20 above; *Winterwerp*, where the applicant unsuccessfully claimed the right to have treatment to enable detention to be as short as possible and claimed that his meetings with psychiatrists were too short, too many tranquillisers, etc.

mentally ill prisoners in a regime where no adequate treatment or supervision is available.

10. Respect for private life

IIB–279 Forcible examination for psychiatric purposes is an interference with private life within the scope of Art.8. Although it may generally be found to pursue the aim of protecting the applicant's own health, it must also be necessary and proportionate within the meaning of the second paragraph of Art.8. In *Matter v Slovakia*, it was not found to be disproportionate to impose compulsory examination in a hospital where the applicant had refused a voluntary procedure and it was a necessary part of their supervision that the authorities verify whether the applicant continued to lack legal capacity.

Where other measures of control are applied to persons under mental health supervision, issues will arise if these do not, *inter alia*, comply with lawfulness criteria,[37] pursue legitimate aims or are disproportionate.[38] For example, the repeated summonsing of the applicant for psychiatric examination over a short period was not justified in *Worwa v Poland*.[39]

11. Limitation of capacity to act

IIB–280 The loss of capacity to administer property concerns "civil rights and obligation" under Art.6, para.1. In this context, lack of proper access to a court with requisite guarantees may constitute a breach.[40] Indeed the Court has considered that deprivation of legal capacity was a very serious interference with Art.8 rights itself and that the authorities were under an obligation to verify whether the measure continued to be justified.[41]

Cross-reference

Part IIA: Fair trial guarantees, Access to court
Part IIB: Compensation for arrest or detention
Part IIB: Deprivation of liberty
Part IIB: Review of detention
Part IIB: Torture, inhuman and degrading treatment

---

[37] *e.g.* 18969/91 (Rep.) June 30, 1993: complaints by person under guardianship of mail censorship: violation of Art.8 due to a total absence in law as to the permissibility of an interference with a ward's correspondence, the purpose and duration of such an interference etc.

[38] *e.g.* 26494/95, (Dec.) February 27, 1997, admissible under Art.8 concerning complaints from an involuntary patient that medical and other reports automatically went to a relative to whom she objected. Settled before the Court on March 30, 2000, on amending legislation permitting a patient to apply to court to change the designated "nearest relative".

[39] November 27, 2003—caused effectively by lack of proper co-ordination, the interference was not necessary under Art.8, para.2.

[40] See *Winterwerp*, where the applicant automatically lost capacity by law when committed to hospital in a process not affording the requisite guarantees; also *Matter*, paras 51–61: breach of Art.6 for unreasonable length of proceedings concerning the applicant's capacity.

[41] *Matter*, para.68.

Pensions

Key provisions:

Article 6, para.1 (fair hearing guarantees); Art.1 of Protocol 1 (right to property),   IIB–281
and Art.14 (prohibition of discrimination).

Key case law:

Schuler-Zgraggen v Switzerland, June 24, 1993, Series A, No.263; 16 E.H.R.R. 405;
Massa v Italy, August 24, 1993, Series A, No.265–B; 18 E.H.R.R. 266; *Gaygusuz v
Austria*, September 16, 1996, R.J.D. 1996–IV, No.14; 23 E.H.R.R. 364; *Süssman v
Germany*, September 16, 1996, R.J.D. 1997–VII, No.58; 25 E.H.R.R. 64;
Stamoulakatos v Greece (No.2), November 26, 1997, R.J.D. 1997–VII; *Wessels-
Bergervoet v Netherlands*, June 4, 2002, ECHR 2002–IV.

1. General considerations

Where a pension is based on private contract with private institutions, it will be   IIB–282
considered as both a "civil right" for the purposes of attracting the procedural
guarantees to determine disputes in proceedings and the right to a court and as a
pecuniary right classifying as property within the meaning of Art.1 of Protocol
No.1. Where the pension concerned is derived from a public or State context, the
issues overlap to some extent with those arising in the area of social security or
welfare benefits and it is less automatic that these two provisions apply.

The Convention organs have stated that there is no right as such to receive a
pension guaranteed in the Convention.[1] Where no basis for entitlement exists it is
unlikely that the Convention provisions can offer any ground of complaint.

2. Civil rights: applicability of Art.6, para.1

Where a pension is linked to contract or akin to a private contractual relationship,   IIB–283
Art.6, para.1 in its civil context is likely to be applicable and the normal guarantees
apply.[2]

Following the approach of the Court in *Schuler-Zraggen v Switzerland*, where Art.6
applied to a benefits claim since it concerned an interference with the applicant's
means of subsistence and related to an individual economic right, it appears that
pension claims of a similar character attract the same treatment. Where civil servant
pensions disputes have arisen, Art.6 has been held to apply notwithstanding the
public law context, on the basis of similarity with private law employment contract
or the pecuniary nature of the pension entitlement.[3] In recent cases, the Court has

---

[1] *UK*, 9776/82, (Dec.) October 3, 1983, 34 D.R. 153; *Hadzic v Croatia*, 48788/99, (Dec.) September 13,
2001.
[2] *e.g.* 9630/81, (Dec.) October 13, 1986, 49 D.R. 59, where a pension was awarded after an industrial
accident on the basis of contributions paid by the employer on behalf of his employees, such insurance
was considered as grafted onto the employment contract, governed by private law and similar to
insurance in private law; 10659/83, (Rep. July 3, 1989, 69 D.R. 7).
[3] *Massa*; para.26; *Sussman*, para.42.

stated, without qualification, that it found no reason to depart from its case-law that the right to a pension is a civil right.[4] Special diligence may attach to proceedings where the applicant's means of support is at stake, although due account has to be taken of the proper administration of justice in complex cases with importance for the system as a whole.[5]

3. Property rights

IIB–284   Where a person has contributed to a pension fund, this could, according to the Commission, in certain circumstances create a property right in a portion of such a fund and a modification of the pension rights under such a system could in principle raise an issue under Art.1 of Protocol No.1.

Where the payments are to a social security system, even assuming that this gives rise to a right to derive a benefit from the system, it cannot be interpreted as entitling that person to a pension of a particular amount.[6] A right to a pension based on employment can in certain circumstances be assimilated to a property right, where special contributions were paid or the employer has given a more general undertaking to pay a pension on conditions which can be considered part of the employment contract.[7] In *Walden v Liechtenstein*, where the Government argued that the payments made to the general pension system were on the basis of social solidarity and did not create a specific entitlement to a share in the fund, the Court considered that the applicant had a pecuniary right to a common married couples' pension which fell within the scope of Art.1 of Protocol No.1.[8]

An applicant must however satisfy domestic legal requirements governing the right before Art.1 of the First Protocol can apply.[9] Thus where by moving to Australia, the applicants ceased to qualify for future pension increases this did not amount to a deprivation of possessions.[10] The requirement to pay contributions for a minimum period to accrue a right must also be satisfied, where applicable.[11] Rules providing for the co-ordination of a pension with other State benefits or pensions have also been found compatible with Art.1 of Protocol No.1.[12]

Since the operation of a social security system is essentially different from the management of a private life insurance company, having to take account of political

---

[4] *e.g. Stamoulakatos v Greece (No.2)*, para.31. More recently, *Domalewski v Poland*, 34610/97, (Dec.) June 15, 1999, ECHR 1999–V—decision revoking an entitlement to a veterans' pension was decisive for pecuniary rights; *Trickovic v Slovenia*, June 12, 2001, para.40.

[5] *e.g. Sussman*, paras 55–57; *Trickovic*, paras 64–67, 69, where proceedings of over 2 years, 7 months was not excessive in the transition period to a democratic legal order.

[6] *e.g.* 5849/72, (Rep.) October 1, 1975, 3 D.R. 25, para.30; 10671/83, (Dec.) March 4, 1985, 42 D.R. 229; 25044/94 (Dec.) May 15, 1996, where the Commission held the applicant was entitled to benefit from the social insurance system to which he had contributed but not to any particular amount; *Domalewski*, n.4 above; *Jankovic v Croatia*, 43440/98, (Dec.) October 12, 2000, ECHR 2000–X.

[7] 10671/83, n.6 above; 12264/86, (Dec.) July 13, 1988, 57 D.R. 131.

[8] 33916/96, (Dec.) March 16, 2000. Also *Wessels-Bergervoet*, paras 39–43; *Srabjer and Clarke v UK*, 27004/95 and 27011/95 (Decs.), where the pension fund (SERPS) contained a social solidarity element but the right to a pension was still dependent on some contribution and therefore was a pecuniary right for the purposes of Art.1 of Protocol No.1.

[9] *Bellet v France*, 40832/98, (Dec.) April 27, 1999; *Hadzic*, n.1 above, (where the applicant did not fulfil the condition of having made himself available for service in the army prior to December 31, 1999).

[10] 9776/82, n.1 above.

[11] 7459/76, October 5, 1977, 11 D.R. 114 where the applicant, dismissed from his job after conviction, also lost his pension as he had not secured the necessary seniority.

[12] 10671/83, March 4, 1985, 42 D.R. 229; also *Bellet*, n.9 above, where the ex-civil servants were not allowed by law to collect pensions from both France and Monaco.

considerations particularly those of financial policy, it is conceivable that, due to a deflationary trend, a State may be obliged to reduce the amount of pension payable, as in the case of German re-unification. This kind of fluctuation was not seen by the Commission as having anything to do with the guarantee of ownership as a human right.[13] Thus the fact that an applicant's pension was less than he could have received under former East German system was not a problem. But the Commission did add that his level of pension was sufficient and did not deprive him of basic means of existence.[14] Proportionality issues (*i.e.* effect and hardship) could conceivably arise where a substantial reduction, affecting the substance of the right, is concerned.[15] Where an ex-public security officer was deprived of his veteran status and the special pension that went with it, the Court found that the essence of his pension rights was not impaired as he retained all the rights attaching to his ordinary pension under the general system.[16]

Forfeiture or termination of pension could conceivably disclose a deprivation of property where disproportionate or failing to strike the right balance between public and private interests.[17] In *Azinas v Cyprus*, although the Grand Chamber later upheld the Government's preliminary objection, the Chamber found that the forfeiture of a civil servant's pension on his dismissal interfered with his property right under the first sentence of Art.1 of Protocol No.1. Although the dismissal might pursue the aim of protecting the public and safeguarding the integrity of the administration, the retrospective forfeiture of pension rights did not serve any commensurate purpose. Given the drastic impact on him and his family of removal of their means of subsistence, a fair balance had not been struck.[18] On the other hand, suspension of payments while an applicant was in prison justifiably prevented him from deriving financial enrichment from his detention when he was being supported at the State's expense.[19]

4. Discrimination

Article 14 can only be invoked in respect of complaints falling within the scope of another substantive provision. In light of *Schuler-Zgraggen v Switzerland, Gaygusuz v Austria*[20] and *Van Raalte v Netherlands*[21] it is apparent that issues could arise from differences on entitlements or contribution obligations based, *inter alia*, on sex or race where a pension was sufficiently linked to employment or established pecuniary

IIB–285

---

[13] 5849/72, n.6 above.

[14] 24077/94, (Dec.) May 15, 1996.

[15] 25044/94, n.6 above, where the Commission found that the calculation had not been carried out in an arbitrary manner.

[16] *Domalewski*, n.4 above; also *Jankovic*, n.6 above.

[17] *e.g. Asmundsson v Iceland*, 60669/00, (Dec.) January 28, 2003, declared admissible, where under legislation that only affected a tiny minority, the applicant lost a disability pension (received for the previous 20 years) which was a major part of his means of subsistence.

[18] June 20, 2002.

[19] *Szrabjer and Clarke*, n.8 above.

[20] Where in the context of emergency subsistence, there were sufficient links with payments made from salary to bring the applicant's claim within the scope of Art.1 of Protocol No.1.

[21] February 21, 1997, R.J.D. 1997–I, No.39 where differences in social security contributions paid by men and women fell within the scope of Art.1 of Protocol No.1 and disclosed discrimination contrary to Art.14.

rights to fall within the scope of Art.1 of Protocol No.1 (see section Welfare Benefits).[22]

To disclose discrimination, differences in eligibility or quantification also have to be in respect of persons in relevantly similar situations and without reasonable and objective justification for difference in treatment.[23] Very strong reasons have to be put forward to justify differences based solely on ground of sex and marital status, as appears from *Wessels-Bergervoet*, where the Government argument that excluding the female applicant from a full pension was to prevent the undesirable accumulation of pension rights (she also received a pension from abroad), the Court noted that a man in her position could have benefitted from two pensions and found a violation.[24] A wide margin applies however to States in regulating their social policy.[25] This can include measures reducing pensions in pursuit of social justice or re-integration into the general system of previously privileged groups. In *Domalewski v Poland*, for example, the Court found that there was objective and reasonable justification in removing special veterans' pensions from ex-security officers who had assisted in preserving the previous totalitarian regime.[26] Some leeway in time is also given to Contracting States in redressing discriminatory differences in pensions, a gap of some seven months in changing the law being compatible with Art.14 in *Walden v Liechtenstein*[27] as not imposing a disproportionate burden on the applicant. It remains to be seen whether the Government legislation harmonising the ages in entitlement to State pensions for men (age 65) and women (60) in the UK over some decades will satisfy Art.14 in the absence of any apparent justification for the ongoing difference.[28]

Cross-reference

Part IIA: Fair Trial, General Principles, Civil Rights
Part IIB: Discrimination
Part IIB: Welfare benefits

---

[22] *Schwengel v Germany*, 552422/99, (Dec.) March 2, 2000: rights flowing from payments to a social insurance fund were considered property rights; *Wessels-Bergervoet*, para.43, rights to a pension from general insurance scheme.

[23] *Buchen v Czech Republic*, November 26, 2002, where there was no apparent objective or reasonable justification for removing pension rights from some categories of ex-military judges but not others. See conversely, 9776/82, n.1 above, when, by moving to Australia, the applicants ceased to be eligible for future pension increases, there was reasonable and objective justification since they had left the UK and there was a relevant social security scheme in Australia; 24077/94, n.14 above, even assuming that Art.14 applied, an applicant in East Germany was not in a comparable position to persons living in the West or to those in East Germany who paid supplementary contributions and anyway it was objective and reasonable to make pension rights conditional on the payment of contributions.

[24] Whether or not widowers can claim discrimination in respect of non-eligibility for pensions previously payable only to women is pending in *Runkee v UK*, 42949/98 and *White v UK*, 53134/99.

[25] *e.g. Jankovic*, n.6 above, where it was within this margin to reduce former Yugoslav army officers' pension to the lower level applicable in the ordinary system, while pensions for Croatian officers remained slightly higher.

[26] n.8 above. See also *Schwengel*, n.22 above, where the reduction in certain East German officials' special pensions to the average in East Germany was justified for reasons of social justice and not disproportionate; *Jankovic*, n.6 above, where reduction in former Yugoslav army officers' pensions was part of the policy of integration of pensions into the general system.

[27] n.8 above, reference to the complexity of social security law and legal certainty.

[28] *Pearson*, 8374/03, (Dec.) April 27, 2004: equalisation at 65 not complete until 2020.

Planning and use of property

Key provisions:

Article 1 of Protocol No.1 (peaceful enjoyment of possessions) and Art.6 (access to court/fair hearing).

IIB–286

Key case law:

Sporrong and Lonnroth v Sweden, September 23, 1982, Series A, No.52; 5 E.H.R.R. 35; *Allan Jacobsson v Sweden*, October 25, 1989, Series A, No.163; 12 E.H.R.R 56; *Tre Traktorer v Sweden*, July 7, 1989, Series A, No.159; 13 E.H.R.R. 309; *Fredin v Sweden*, February 18, 1990, Series A, No.192; 14 E.H.R.R 319; *Pine Valley Developments v Ireland*, November 29, 1991, Series A, No.222; 14 E.H.R.R 319; *Raimondo v Italy*, February 22, 1994, Series A, No.281–A; 18 E.H.R.R. 237; *Bryan v UK*, November 22, 1995, Series A, No.335–A; 21 E.H.R.R 342; *Phocas v France*, April 2, 1996, R.J.D. 1996–II, No.7; 32 E.H.R.R. 221; *Buckley v UK*, September 25, 1996, R.J.D. 1996–V, No.16; 23 E.H.R.R. 101; *Chassagnou v France*, April 29, 1999, ECHR 1999–III; 29 E.H.R.R. 615; *Chapman v UK*, January 18, 2001, ECHR 2000–I.

1. General considerations

Control of use of property, the "third rule" of Art.1 of Protocol No.1, is compatible where necessary in accordance with general interest. A wide margin of appreciation is accorded to the authorities. Where planning considerations are involved, the Court has emphasised the complex issues[1] and that this is an area where the authorities exercise discretionary powers.[2] As with use of expropriation powers, weight is given to the exercise by the legislature of its role to implement measures in the general interest.[3]

IIB–287

In older cases, the approach was taken that States were the sole judges of the necessity of a control of use and that the Convention organs were restricted to supervising the lawfulness and purpose (if legitimate) of the restriction.[4] More recently however, in line with the general development of case law, there is some examination of the proportionality of the measures applied. Whether a planning restriction is regarded as an interference with peaceful enjoyment of possessions or a control of use appears to depend on the intended primary purpose of the measure but the same considerations appear to apply in this area whichever classification is used.[5] Even where property is seized and ownership is lost in the area of confiscation this is regarded not as a deprivation of property but as a control of use due to the

---

[1] *e.g. Allan Jacobsson.*

[2] *e.g. Chapman*, para.92.

[3] *e.g.* 11763/85, (Dec.) March 9, 1989, 60 D.R. 128: legislation ending exclusive fishing rights for landowners: weight given to decision of democratic institutions that measure was necessary in the general interest.

[4] *e.g. Handyside v UK*, December 7, 1976, Series A, No.24, para.62; 10378/83, (Dec.) December 7, 1983, 35 D.R. 235.

[5] *Sporrong*, para.69, striking a balance between the general and individual interest underlies the whole of Art.1 of Protocol No.1.

purpose of the measure in, for example, controlling the importation of gold or fighting drug-trafficking (See Pt IIB: Expropriation and confiscation). This section deals with planning type restrictions and preventive measures.

2. Planning restrictions

(a) General interest

IIB–288   The Convention organs accept without particular scrutiny planning restrictions which affect development of property or occupation rights. Environmental concerns provide grounds of justification in the most general terms.[6]

(b) Proportionality

IIB–289   Consideration is given to whether the applicant knew or was subject to the restriction when he took over the property,[7] the existence of legitimate expectations or acceptance of the risk on purchase,[8] the extent to which the restriction prevents use of the land[9] and the availability of procedures importing flexibility and fairness[10] and the possibility of challenging the restriction.[11] Where measures are enforced against use of property for a home for planning reasons related to protection of the environment, the lawfulness of the initial occupation is highly relevant, if not decisive. In *Chapman v United Kingdom*, where a gypsy family had taken up unauthorised residence on their land in a Green Belt, the Court stated that it would be slow to grant protection to those in conscious defiance of the law. Nor did it consider that humanitarian considerations could be relied on to exempt even applicants in difficult personal circumstances from planning laws.

Indeed, few situations have arisen where control of use has been found disproportionate to the general interest being pursued.[12]

For example, where in *Tre Traktrorer v Sweden*, a restaurant lost its licence to sell alcohol, there was a control of use of the business and premises but no violation. There had been a progression of measures having regard to the company's discrepancies in its bookkeeping on alcoholic beverages and although there was a heavy burden on the company to justify itself (it alleged the shortfall was from

---

[6] *e.g. Pine Valley*, development refused in green belt; *Fredin*, refusal of exploitation of a gravel pit; 20490/92, (Dec.) March 8, 1994 76–A D.R. 90: enforcement procedures against intensified use of house as Buddhist pilgrimage centre, where planning controls were found necessary to preserve and improve landscapes.

[7] *Allan Jacobsson*; 11723/85, (Dec.) May 7, 1987, 52 D.R. 250, where enforcement proceedings against applicant for use of property for vehicle repair and haulage which had always been unlawful.

[8] *e.g. Fredin*, the Court found no legitimate expectation to continue the exploitation of the gravel pit; *Pine Valley*, where the applicants were involved in commercial development which entailed risk.

[9] *e.g. Allan Jacobsson*, where the applicant had one house on the property in which he could live but could not build a second.

[10] *e.g. Allan Jacobsson* where prohibitions were reviewed every few years and applications for exceptions were possible.

[11] *Papastavrou v Greece*, April 10, 2003, para.37—inability to challenge merits of decision to zone land for reafforestation.

[12] Interference with enjoyment of possessions under the first sentence of the first paragraph has been found more frequently where measures have been severe in their effects, *e.g. Sporrong* (long term restrictions imposed by expropriation permits).

thefts) there was a wide margin of appreciation and the measure not disproportionate.[13] In *Phocas v France*, where the restriction imposed on the applicant's ability to develop his property by an urban development plan was treated as an interference with enjoyment of possessions, the measure was found not disproportionate since there were procedures by which the applicant could require the State to buy his property. A disproportionate control of use under the second paragraph of Art.1 was exceptionally found in *Chassagnou v France*, where a law imposed the compulsory transfer of hunting rights over the applicants' land to hunting associations. While it was in the general interest to avoid unregulated hunting and foster the rational management of game, the Court noted the unequal way in which the law affected landowners throughout France and found that the balance was struck unfairly in compelling the applicants, opposed themselves to hunting, to allow others to make use of their land contrary to their personal convictions.[14]

3. Article 6 rights and planning cases

Proceedings relating to property rights, including disputes as to permitted use of the land, concern civil rights and obligations. However, following *Bryan v United Kingdom* it appears that limited court review of points of law in planning cases may suffice insofar as access to court is concerned. In *Bryan*, where the applicant alleged that the procedures before planning inspectors from which limited appeal lay to the High Court were insufficient to comply with the requirements of Art.6, para.1 the Court commented that limited review was a frequent feature of systems of judicial control of administrative decisions throughout Member States and this case illustrated the typical exercise of discretionary judgment in the regulation of citizens' conduct in the sphere of town and country planning. It found that the limited review by the High Court of factual questions was reasonably to be expected in specialised areas of law where the facts were already established in a quasi-judicial procedure conforming with many of the safeguards of Art.6, para.1. Thus the Court found that the planning inspector was bound to decide fairly and impartially and gave a fair hearing, notwithstanding a lack of independence or decision-making power, and that the High Court's review powers were sufficient.

IIB–290

4. Preventive measures

Measures aimed at preventing persons suspected of involvement in organised crime from using their property constitute a control of use and have generally been found to pursue the general interest and to be proportionate, in which context adequate

IIB–291

---

[13] Also 33298/96, (Dec.) October 21, 1998, where the measures prohibiting companies from deboning cattleheads were not regarded as disproportionate, notwithstanding the impact on their business, including closure (some compensation was paid and their capital assets remained); *Andrews v UK*, 37657/97, (Dec.) September 26, 2000, where legislation prohibiting gun shop owners from selling handguns did not impose an excessive individual burden, even though compensation was paid only for guns in stock not the reduction in value of the business; *Gallego Zafra v Spain*, 58229/00, (Dec.) January 14, 2003 (removal of authorisation for pharmacy)

[14] See conversely *Aschan v Finland*, 37858/97, (Dec.) February 15, 2001, where the granting of fishing rights to the public, without payment of the loss of value to the landowners, was not disproportionate: there were only economic, not moral, objections to the measures; *Posti and Rahko v Finland*, September 24, 2002, where the restriction on fishing in coastal waters under the applicants' leases was a legitimate control of use, for which some compensation was paid.

procedural safeguards against arbitrariness are required.[15] In *Raimondo v Italy*, where the seizure was a temporary measure, the Court found that it aimed at preventing the use of property in organised crime, which purpose appeared to be decisive in light of the Court's emphasis on the importance of fighting mafia crime, in which context confiscation of this kind was a real and effective weapon. While the initial measures were not disproportionate however, the Court did find a violation when, after the domestic court ordered the property restored, there was a delay in removing the entries of the measures from the public register.[16] Since the court had ordered rectification, the continuation of the measure was neither provided for by law or necessary in public interest.

Cross-reference

Part IIB: Expropriation and confiscation
Part IIB: Gypsies
Part IIB: Home
Part IIB: Housing and tenancy
Part IIB: Property

---

[15] 12386/86, (Dec.), April 15, 1991, 70 D.R. 59 where there was confiscation of property from a person suspected of mafia membership, the Commission found it was clearly in the general interest as designed to prevent the illicit use of possessions the lawful origin of which was not established, the State enjoying wide scope in preventive measures in face of a disturbing level of organised crime. It gave attention to whether there were effective judicial guarantees allowing the applicant a reasonable opportunity to put his case. Since a court established the facts in adversarial proceedings and there was no indication of arbitrary assessment of evidence, the measures were not disproportionate.

[16] A blot had remained on the title and caused practical difficulties in use.

Pre-trial detention

Key provision:

Article 5, para.3.   IIB–292

Key case law:

Neumeister v Austria, June 27, 1968, Series A, No.8; 1 E.H.R.R. 91; *Matznetter v Austria*, November 10, 1979, Series A, No.10; 1 E.H.R.R. 198; *De Jong, Baljet and Van Den Brink v Netherlands*, May 22, 1984, Series A, No.77; 13 E.H.R.R. 433; *Brogan v United Kingdom*, November 29, 1988, Series A, No.145–B; 11 E.H.R.R. 117; *B v Austria*, March 28, 1990, Series A, No.175; 13 E.H.R.R. 20; *Huber v Switzerland*, October 23, 1990, Series A, No.188; *Letellier v France*, June 26, 1991, Series A, No.207; 14 E.H.R.R. 83; *Kemmache v France (No.1)*, November 27, 1991, Series A, No.218; 14 E.H.R.R. 520; *Toth v Austria*, December 12, 1991, Series A, No.224; 14 E.H.R.R. 551; *Clooth v Austria*, December 12, 1991, Series A, No.225; 14 E.H.R.R. 717; *Tomasi v France*, August 27, 1992, Series A, No.241–A; 15 E.H.R.R. 1; *Brincat v Italy*, November 26, 1992, Series A, No.249–A; 17 E.H.R.R. 60; *W v Switzerland*, January 26, 1993, Series A, No.254–A; 16 E.H.R.R. 591; *Yagci and Sargin v Turkey*, June 8, 1995, Series A, No.319; 20 E.H.R.R. 505; *Mansur v Turkey*, June 8, 1995, Series A, No.319–B; 20 E.H.R.R. 535; *Van der Tang v Spain*, July 13, 1995, Series A, No.321; *Aksoy v Turkey*, December 18, 1996, R.J.D. 1996–VI, No.26; 23 E.H.R.R. 553; *Scott v Spain*, December 18, 1996, R.J.D. 1996–VI, No.27; 24 E.H.R.R. 391; *Muller v France*, March 17, 1997, R.J.D. 1997–II, No.32; *Sakik v Turkey*, November 26, 1997, R.J.D. 1997–VII, No.58; 26 E.H.R.R. 662; *Assenov v Bulgaria*, October 28, 1998, R.J.D. 1998–VIII, No.96; 31 E.H.R.R. 372; *Hood v UK*, February 18, 1999, ECHR 1999–I; 29 E.H.R.R. 365, *Aquilina v Malta*, April 29, 1999, ECHR 1999–III; *Caballero v UK*, February 8, 2000, ECHR 2000–II; 30 E.H.R.R. 643; *Labita v Italy*, April 6, 2000, ECHR 2000–IV; *Jecius v Lithuania*, July 31, 2000, ECHR 2000–IX; *Kudla v Poland*, October 26, 2000, ECHR 2000–XI; *Kalashnikov v Russia*, July 15, 2002, ECHR 2002–VI.

1. General considerations

There are two principal aspects under Art.5, para.3—first, concerning the time   IIB–293
permissible for a person arrested on reasonable suspicion of committing an offence
(or the other two grounds under Art.5, para.1(c)) to be held before being brought
before a judicial officer; secondly, limiting the time on which a person should be
held pending trial.

While there is no right to bail as such, Art.5, para.3 does not give the judicial
authorities the choice between bringing the accused to trial within a reasonable time
or granting him provisional release, as the purpose of the provision is essentially to
require release once continuing detention ceases to be reasonable.[1]

---

[1] *Neumeister*, para.4; *Jablonski v Poland*, December 21, 2000, para.83.

2. Initial arrest period

IIB–294 It is a fundamental safeguard against abuse of power by the police or any equivalent officer with the power of arrest or detention that the person is brought "promptly" before a judicial authority. It prevents oppression, coercion, arbitrary arrest and ill-treatment, giving less opportunity for marks to fade or for a person's will to be broken by pressure and isolation.[2] The Convention organs have emphasised the importance of judicial control against arbitrary deprivation of liberty as fundamental ingredient of the rule of law.[3]

Two principal issues have arisen in the case law: exactly what qualifies as "promptly" and as a judicial officer.

(a) Promptly

IIB–295 The Court has held that the degree of flexibility attaching to the notion is very limited. While individual circumstances must be taken into account in assessing promptness, their significance can never be taken to the point of impairing the very essence of the right.[4]

Brogan v United Kingdom indicates that four days may in exceptional circumstances, such as the difficulties attaching to terrorist investigations, be acceptable but beyond four days was unacceptable, exceeding the plain meaning of the word "promptly" and allowing a serious weakening of the guarantee to the extent of impairing its essence.[5] In later cases, where the Government have relied on the exigencies of terrorist crime, the Court has refused to allow this to be used as a *carte blanche* by investigating authorities and has not accepted any period in excess of four days.[6] For ordinary crimes, it would seem that the Court would set a shorter maximum but the point is as yet not expressly decided. Practical excuses are unlikely to be successful. Delay of five days for an applicant to be brought before a military court was not found to be justified on the basis of an intervening weekend and the involvement of personnel in manoeuvres, since this eventuality was foreseeable and steps could have been taken, such as sitting over the weekend.[7] However, in the special circumstances, where an applicant was arrested by customs at sea some 3,000 nautical miles from port, the Court found that the 16 days which it took to bring him before a judge did not breach the requirement of promptness as it had not been materially possible to bring him any sooner.[8]

Extension of the period to seven days for terrorist suspects was found to be compatible with the power to derogate under Art.15, where this was limited by the

---

[2] *Aksoy*, para.76; the importance of this safeguard re-iterated recently in *Dikme v Turkey*, July 11, 2000, ECHR 2000–VIII, para.66.

[3] *Brogan*, para.58; re-emphasised, *inter alia*, in *Sakik and Others*, para.44.

[4] *Brogan*, para.59.

[5] Violations found for periods of 4 days 6 hours, 4 days 11 hours; 5 days 11 hours and 6 days and 16-and-a-half hours. See also breach found in *O'Hara v UK*, October 16, 2001, ECHR 2001–X, 6 days 13 hours.

[6] *Sakik*, para.44 (12–14 days); also, *Gunay v Turkey*, September 27, 2001 (5 to 11 days); *Dikme*, n.2 above, para.66: the Court rejected the Goverment's argument that the investigation required a longer period as the evidence had to be gathered from the suspects themselves.

[7] *Koster v Netherlands*, November 28, 1991, Series A, No.221.

[8] *Rigopoulos v Spain*, 37388/97, (Dec.) January 12, 1999, ECHR 1999–II.

exigencies of a state of emergency and attended by safeguards against abuse.[9] Extension of the period to 14 days in Turkey was considered *prima facie* to be too long, impliedly with or without attendant safeguards.[10] (See Pt IIB—Derogation).

The review of the merits of police or administrative detention should be automatic. It is insufficient that an applicant can apply for review.[11] Article 5, para.3 however does not include a right to be brought repeatedly before a judge.[12]

(b) *Judge or other officer authorised by law to exercise judicial power*

The judicial officer does not have to hold the status of a judge but he must have some of a judge's attributes or guarantees. This includes independence of the executive and of the parties; the procedural requirement of hearing the individual himself; the substantive requirement of reviewing the continuation of the detention by reference to legal criteria; and the power to order release.[13]

IIB–296

Appearance before a court is not by itself a sufficient guarantee, where the question of justification for the continued detention is not to be dealt with until later.[14] Where the officer or tribunal has no power to release, they lack the requisite judicial power.[15] A breach will therefore arise where the judicial officer has no power to release by operation of law, as for example, where a statutory provision removes the judge's discretion to release in certain categories of cases.[16] A magistrate's power of review must also be sufficiently wide to to encompass the various circumstances militating for or against detention.[17]

An officer who combines functions of investigation and prosecution is likely to be lacking in independence and impartiality. There was a breach where the *auditeur militaire*, though independent from the military authorities, could be called upon to perform prosecution functions once a case was referred to the military court and was therefore not independent of the parties to the potential criminal proceedings.[18] Similarly, in *Huber v Switzerland*, where a district attorney took decisions relating to detention and also conducted the investigation and drew up the indictment, there was a violation.[19] Although the district attorney did not in fact act as prosecutor in the final proceedings as was possible under the applicable procedure, he could not be

---

[9] *Brannigan and McBride v UK*, May 26, 1993, Series A, No.258–B: a breach was found for 6 days and 14 hours and 6 days and 6 hours respectively but covered by the UK derogation in respect of the threats to the nation from terrorism.

[10] *Aksoy*, paras 82–84.

[11] e.g. *De Jong*, para.51; *Aquilina*, para.49; *Sabeur Ben Ali v Malta*, June 29, 2000, para.31.

[12] *Grauzinas v Lithuania*, October 10, 2000, para.25. Although Art.5, para.4 may in certain cases require a person be brought before a judge for the purpose of contesting the lawfulness of his detention when it lasts a long time: *Jecius*, para.84.

[13] *Scheisser v Switzerland*, December 4, 1979, Series A, No.34, para.31.

[14] *Van der Sluijs, Suiderveld and Klappe v Netherlands*, May 22, 1984, Series A No.78, para.46.

[15] e.g. *De Jong*, where the *auditeur militaire* made non-binding recommendations albeit accepted in practice; *Assenov*, para.148, where the applicant was brought before an investigator whose decisions as to release, not legally binding, could be overturned by a prosecutor.

[16] e.g. *Caballero*: the Government conceded that s.25 of the Criminal Justice Act 1994, in removing the power to grant bail for serious offences breached Art.5, para.3; *SBC v UK*, June 19, 2001: the Court made an express finding of breach as regards the automatic denial of bail.

[17] e.g. *Aquilina*, para.52, where the magistrate could only examine one ground of lawfulness of his own motion.

[18] *De Jong*, para.49.

[19] paras 42–43, which reversed *Scheisser*, n.13 above, para.34, which appeared to indicate that it was the effective concurrent exercise of dual functions which was problematic.

regarded as independent of the parties and his impartiality was capable of appearing open to doubt. Though the Court has not ruled out that a judicial officer may carry out other functions, he must do so without calling his impartiality and independence into doubt. It is the objective appearances at the time of decision of detention on remand which are material.[20]

(c) *Other procedural safeguards*

IIB–297 Representation by a lawyer has not been found to be required for the purposes of Art.5, para.3[21] though issues may arise under Art.6 para.3(c) (see Section: Legal Representation). The Court has also referred to Art.5, para.3 requiring the judicial officer to set out in the decision on detention the facts upon which that decision is based[22] and stressed the importance of "formal visible requirements stated in the 'law'" as opposed to standard practices.[23] In *Hood v United Kingdom*, it commented on the lack of any written record or opportunity for the applicant to make submissions but made no ruling on this aspect.[24]

(d) *Relationship with Art.5, para.4: review of lawfulness of detention*

IIB–298 Article 5, para.4 is a guarantee of a different order to, and additional to, that provided by Art.5 para.3. They can be applied concurrently, though obviously the procedure for bringing a person before a judge may have a certain incidence on compliance with para.4.[25] Conversely, compliance with Art.5, para.3 cannot be ensured by making an Art.5, para.4 remedy available as the review must be automatic.[26]

3. Length of detention on remand

IIB–299 As concerns the continuation of detention on remand, the role of the domestic authorities is seen as ensuring that the pre-trial detention of an accused person does not exceed a reasonable period. They must examine all the circumstances arguing for or against the existence of a genuine public interest justifying, with due regard to the presumption of innocence, a departure from the rule of respect for individual liberty and set them out in decisions on the applications for release. It is essentially on the basis of the reasons given in these domestic decisions and of the true facts mentioned by the applicant in his appeals that the Court considers it is called upon to decide whether or not there has been a violation of Art.5, para.3.[27]

---

[20] Also *Brincat*, para.41; *Hood*, paras 57–58, where the applicant's commanding officer took decisions on pre-trial detention and was also liable to intervene in subsequent proceedings on behalf of the prosecuting authority; cases concerning decisions on pre-trial detention taken by Polish prosecutors, *e.g. Niedbala v Poland*, July 4, 2000, para.53, where the Court dismissed the Government argument that the prosecutors had a judicial status as guardians of the public interest.

[21] *Scheisser*, n.13 above, para.36.

[22] *Scheisser*, n.13 above, para.31, *Letellier*, para.35.

[23] *Duinhof and Duijf v Netherlands*, May 22, 1984, Series A, No.79, para.34.

[24] para.60.

[25] *e.g. De Jong*, where there was both a breach of Art.5, para.3 for delays of 7, 11 and 6 days before the applicants were brought before a court and a breach of Art.5, para.4 for an inability to obtain review of the lawfulness of their detention over the same period.

[26] *Aquilina*, para.53.

[27] *e.g. Letellier*, para.35, *Mansur*, para.52.

Continuation of a reasonable suspicion that the applicant has committed an offence (the principal ground under Art.5, para.1(c)) is a *sine qua non* for the validity of the detention but with the lapse of time this no longer suffices and the Court must then establish whether the other grounds given by the judicial authorities continued to justify the deprivation of liberty. Such grounds must be relevant and sufficient and the competent national authorities must display "special diligence" in the conduct of the proceedings.[28] A period of detention may not be justified on the basis of the alleged shortness of time alone.[29] In the absence of reasons, or where an uninformative stereotyped form of decision is given by the courts, it would be unnecessary to consider whether they acted with particular diligence since there would be no sufficient grounds for the continued detention.[30]

The period of detention is calculated from the date of arrest/commencement of detention on Art.5, para.1(c) grounds until the judgment/conviction at first instance.[31]

Assessment of reasonableness can take into account a period of detention which is itself outside the Convention' organs competence *ratione temporis*, since whether continued detention in the later period is justified may depend on how much time has already been spent in custody.[32]

Article 5, para.3 does not place an obligation on authorities to release a detainee due to ill-health. Whether his condition is compatible with detention is largely a matter for the national courts and though issues could potentially arise under Art.3 that provision has not been interpreted as requiring release on health grounds or placement in a civil hospital to receive particular treatment.[33]

(a) *Relevant and sufficient grounds*

(I) Seriousness of the alleged offences and strength of suspicion

Existence and persistence of serious indications of guilt are relevant but cannot alone justify a long period of pre-trial detention and cannot be used to anticipate a custodial sentence.[34] After a certain period of time, persistence of reasonable suspicion no longer suffices and the Court examines whether the other grounds relied on by the judicial authorities justify the deprivation of liberty.[35] It is not apparent up to what moment, or lapse of time that suspicion alone will continue to justify detention but it is likely to be a matter of months. The Commission found a violation in the period of 14 months in *Can v Austria*[36] while in *Jecius v Lithuania* the

IIB–300

---

[28] See, *e.g. Yagci and Sargin*, para.50; *Letellier*, para.35.

[29] *Yagci and Sargin*, para.54.

[30] *e.g.* in *Mansur*, where the court gave stereotyped identical form of orders renewing detention and on three occasions no reasons were given; *Yagci and Sargin*, where the courts looked at the case four times in a three month period, but gave stereotyped refusal, with no explanation of why there was a danger of absconding.

[31] *B v Austria*, para.39: even where domestic law classifies detention pending appeal as detention on remand; *Kudla*, para.104.

[32] *e.g. Mansur*: 1 year 28 days after recognition of the Court's compulsory jurisdiction but 5 years 3 months before; *Kalashnikov*: 1 year 2 months and 29 days after the Convention entered into force for Russia, but 2 years, 10 months and 6 days before.

[33] *Jablonski*, n.1 above, para.82, citing *Kudla*, para.93.

[34] *e.g.* a period of 5 years 7 months in *Tomasi*, para.89.

[35] *Letellier*, para.35.

[36] 9300/81, (Rep.) July 12, 1984, Series A, No.96 (settled before the Court).

Court considered that suspicion against the applicant of having committed murder may initially have justified his detention but it could not constitute a "relevant and sufficient" ground for his being held in custody for almost fifteen months.[37]

For reasonable suspicion to persist there must be facts or information satisfying an objective observer that the person concerned may have committed an offence. In *Labita v Italy*, the Court considered that while a suspect might be validly detained at the beginning of proceedings on the basis of *pentiti* statements (informant evidence raising issues of reliability) they necessarily became less relevant with the passage of time, particularly when no further evidence was uncovered. Where in this case the statements were uncorroborated and in fact contradicted, very compelling reasons were required to justify the applicant's detention for two years seven months. The longer the pre-trial period of detention the stronger the reasons would have to be.[38]

It is not compatible with Art.5, para.3 for the burden to be placed on the applicant to establish grounds for his release, as this would be tantamount to overturning the purpose of the provision which makes detention an exceptional departure from the right to liberty. Thus, where the law provides for a presumption in respect of factors relevant to continued detention, the concrete facts outweighing the rule of respect for individual liberty must still be convincingly demonstrated.[39]

(II) Protection of public order

IIB–301   Some offences by their gravity and the public reaction to them may give rise to public disquiet capable of justifying pre-trial detention at least for a time. However, the Court has rejected Government claims on this ground in a number of cases, considering that this can only be justified in exceptional circumstances and must be based on sufficient evidence of facts indicating that the accused's release would actually disturb public order. There was insufficient evidence in *Letellier v France* where the Government referred to the "profound and lasting" disturbance to public order resulting from a premeditated murder.[40] While in *Tomasi v France*, where an officer was involved in an armed terrorist attack which resulted in death and serious injuries, some risk of disorder might have existed at the beginning but it must have disappeared after a certain time.[41]

(III) Risk of pressure on witnesses or collusion with co-accused

IIB–302   This is a relevant and unexceptional ground but as soon as the risk diminishes the ground will no longer be valid. With the passage of time, risk to the gathering of evidence has often been found to disappear, as in *Kemmache v France (No.1)* when the witnesses were questioned, the file closed and sent to court. Where, as in *W v*

---

[37] para.94, particularly as the suspicion was proved unsubstantiated by the trial court which acquitted him.

[38] *PB v France*, August 1, 2000, para.30, particularly strong reasons required to justify a period of 4 years 8 months.

[39] *Ilijkov v Bulgaria*, July 26, 2001, para.85—violation where the courts relied on the presumption that the person should be detained unless he showed exceptional circumstances and made no mention of any concrete facts that might justify continued detention.

[40] *Kemmache (No.1)*, para.52: counterfeiting did not qualify.

[41] e.g. *Olstowski v Poland*, November 15, 2001, para.78, where the courts' reliance on the "heavy load of social harmfulness" of the offence could not by itself justify lengthy detention (almost 3 years, 3 months).

Switzerland, findings of risk of collusion and interference are maintained on the basis of scrupulous examination of the evolving circumstances, the Court is unlikely to disagree but if, as in *Clooth v Austria*, decisions continuing detention are stereotyped and refer to the needs of investigation in a general and abstract fashion, it may be found that the detention ceases to be justified on this basis.[42]

(IV) RISK OF REPETITION OF OFFENCES

The Court and Commission have accepted the view of domestic courts that the existence of previous convictions for similar offences gives grounds for reasonable fears that the applicant might commit new offences.[43] But where domestic authorities relied on an alleged precarious psychological state of the suspect shown by previous offences of a different kind, this was found only to furnish a ground for extending confinement if accompanied by therapeutic measures.[44] A reference to the person's antecedents is not sufficient to justify refusing release.[45]

IIB–303

(V) DANGER OF ABSCONDING

The risk of absconding has to be assessed in light of the factors relating to the person's character, his morals, home, occupation, assets, family ties and all kinds of links with the country in which he is prosecuted. The expectation of heavy sentence and the weight of evidence may be relevant but not as such decisive and the possibility of obtaining guarantees (*e.g.* payment of security, other forms of judicial supervision) may have to be used to offset any risk.[46]

IIB–304

The Convention organs have criticised domestic courts which rely on this ground without indicating any factual basis, repeat stereotyped decisions or fail to consider the possibility of obtaining guarantees from applicants to ensure their appearance, *e.g.* financial conditions. In *Tomasi v France*, the Court considered that the domestic courts gave no proper consideration to this aspect, their decisions unreasoned as to why the risk of absconding was decisive despite the applicant's clean record and status as shopkeeper. The fact that he faced a serious prison sentence if convicted could not be the sole basis for finding such a risk.[47] On the other hand, where the likely sentence can be anticipated and the period in detention deductible, the lessening incentive to abscond should be taken into account.[48]

There must be continued grounds for believing the risk to subsist. In *Kemmache v France (No.1)*, there was some basis for suspicions since the applicant had previously failed to appear before the court on spurious grounds of car "mechanical" failure. Since however the courts did not rely on this reason after a particular date and added no fresh grounds, it could not be used to justify further detention.[49] However,

---

[42] Also *Debboub alias Husseini Ali v France*, November 9, 1999, para.44, where the courts did not explain the basis of the alleged risk; *Szeloch v Poland*, February 22, 2001, para.91, where the decisions were succinct, absent concrete facts and repetitive.

[43] *Toth*, para.70.

[44] *Clooth*, para.40.

[45] *Muller*, para.44.

[46] *e.g. Letellier, Matzenetter, Hauschildt v Denmark*, 10486/83, (Dec.) October 9, 1986, 49 D.R. 86.

[47] *e.g. Letellier*, para.43, concerning a mother of two children who ran her own business.

[48] *Can*, n.36 above.

[49] See also *Kudla v Poland*, paras 111–115, where the applicant's initial failure to give an address for service and a medical certificate could not justify detention for 2 years 4 months, no other element being adduced to support the alleged risk of absconding during that time.

findings of links with foreign countries, including funds or family, have provided sufficient grounds.[50] Although even where there are sufficient grounds for fear of flight, as in *Erdem v Germany* where the alleged PKK terrorist suspects had no links with Germany, this could not justified prolonged detention up to 5 years and 11 months.[51]

Regarding the type or level of guarantees that may be legitimately required by domestic authorities, these are not limited to money but can include residence and movement restrictions.[52] The level of bail set should not be set too high and should not be aimed at reparation of loss but to ensure the presence of the accused.[53] But where the applicant is implicated in large scale financial dealings of a fraudulent nature larger sums may not be unreasonable.[54] Continued detention of an applicant while the authorities sorted out the size and modalities of the bail payment led to a breach, where the court had already found that his release would not jeopardise the proceedings.[55]

(b) *Conduct of the proceedings: special diligence*

IIB–305   Courts must show "special diligence" in bringing cases of detained persons to trial, notwithstanding the existence of strong suspicion or other relevant grounds for the detention.[56] However, the requirement of special diligence had been held not to stand in the way of the proper administration of justice and there is an obligation on judges to clarify the facts and collect evidence prior to trial.[57] Even where a case was not particularly complex but was delayed when it was joined to another, the joinder was made in the interests of the proper administration of justice and the inevitable slowing down of the case was not incompatible with the speed requirement.[58] A finding of a domestic court of lack of due expedition or an extension of detention beyond the period normally acceptable in domestic law will not necessarily disclose a breach, since domestic and Convention standards may differ and the Court will examine the circumstances as a whole.[59]

---

[50] e.g. *W v Switzerland; Van der Tang.* See also *Czesky v Czech Republic*, June 6, 2000, para.79, where the applicant had left the country and obtained a false passport.

[51] July 5, 2001, ECHR 2001–VII, para.44.

[52] e.g. *Schmid v Austria*, 10670/83 (Dec.) July 9, 1985, 44 D.R. 195.

[53] e.g. *Can*, n.36 above, where the Commission criticised the sum set at the value of property subject to the arson attack rather than assessed *vis-à-vis* the applicant, his assets and his relation to the persons to provide the security; *Neumeister*, paras 13–14.

[54] e.g. *W v Switzerland*: the rejection of the applicant's offer of a CHF 30,000 guarantee was not unreasonable since the provenance of money unknown and the sum derisory in light of the size of the case (large scale fraud).

[55] *Iwanczuk v Poland*, November 15, 2001, paras 68–70—4 months, 14-day delay.

[56] e.g. *Letellier*, para.35.

[57] e.g. *Matznetter*, para.12; *B v Austria*, para.45.

[58] *Van der Tang; Can v Austria*, cited above. See also 9627/81, *Ferrari-Bravo v Italy*, (Dec.) March 14, 1984, 37 D.R. 15: 4 years 11 months was justified by the complexity of affair and the exceptional difficulties from the nature of the case (subversive terrorist aspects) and the fact the case joined other accused was reasonable for the administration of justice, and it was not required for the cases to be severed.

[59] *Wardle v UK*, 72219/01, (Dec.) March 27, 2003, where judge commented adversely on the extension obtained by the prosecution lodging of new charges on the expiry of the initial period, the Court noted relevant and sufficient reasons for the detention (previous absconding and offending on release), the complexity of the case and ongoing investigative measure: no lack of necessary despatch overall.

Consideration is had to the complexity of the investigation, the number of defendants, the nature of the legal issues and the international elements by way of letters rogatory.[60] A substantial gap in proceedings may be fatal as in *Vallon v Italy* where, although the Commission refused to question the merits of the decision to issue letters rogatory, an eight month delay between the reply and the setting down for trial founded a violation.[61] Also relevant are errors made by the authorities[62]; unnecessarily cumbersome procedures[63]; frequent adjournments and delays in issuing decisions[64]; the complexity of the case[65]; and the conduct of the applicant.[66] In respect of the latter, applicants are not required to co-operate actively with the judicial authorities and cannot be blamed for taking full advantage of the resources afforded by national law in their defence. Where conduct of an applicant goes beyond this, revealing an obstructive attitude, or contributing substantially to delaying proceedings, is perhaps a fine line.[67] Delay caused by the applicant will not rule out a breach where the dilatoriness of the authorities is still responsible for significant lapse of time.[68]

Table of lengths of detention

Previous Convention organs   IIB–306

Matznetter v Austria	—2 years, almost 2 months: no violation
Letellier v France	—2 years, 9 months: violation
Kemmache v France (No.1)	—2 years, 10 months: violation
Toth v France	—2 years, 1 month, 2 days: violation
Tomasi v France	—5 years, 7 months: violation
Clooth v Austria	—3 years, 2 months 4 days: violation
B v Austria	—2 years, 4 months 15 days: no violation

[60] *e.g. Matzenetter*, para.12; *B v Austria*, para.45.
[61] (Rep.), Series A, No.95. Also *Woukam Moudefo v France*, (Rep.) October 11, 1988, Series A, No.141–B, where there was 4-and-a-half months delay before the applicant was interrogated and a delay of 1 year in taking action on failure of certain witnesses to appear for a "confrontation."
[62] In *Tomasi*, there were numerous errors and omissions by the judicial authorities, *e.g.* proceedings instituted in court without jurisdiction.
[63] *e.g. Toth*, where on each new application for release or for extension in detention, the file was transferred (rather than copies) causing suspension of investigation.
[64] *Punzelt v Czech Republic*, April 25, 2000, paras 78–80; also *Vaccaro v Italy*, November 16, 2000, where no explanation was given, *inter alia*, for the 10 months to transfer from one court jurisdiction to another.
[65] *W v Switzerland*: exceptional complexity of large economic crime was a significant factor in finding no violation (by a narrow majority) for over 4 years.Conversely, in *Scott v Spain*, after 4 years 16 days of investigation the alleged difficulties in serving letters rogatory abroad did not justify the delay and the duty of "special diligence" was not observed; *Erdem*, n.51 above, para.46, the difficulties attaching to trial of PKK suspects did not justify detention of 5 years and 11 months.
[66] *e.g. Kalashnikov*, where the protacted proceedings were not attributable either to the complexity of the case or the applicant's conduct.
[67] *Yagci and Sargin*, where the Government attacked the applicants' tactics (*e.g.* filing of evidence and leaving the court in protest at security arrangements) but there was no indication that they were obstructive.
[68] *Trzaska v Poland*, July 11, 2000, where the applicant refused to attend 3 hearings but the case came to a stand still for over 8 months (*e.g.* change in compostion of court), the period of 4 years, 1 month and 18 days disclosed a breach overall; *Jablonski*, n.1 above, where the applicant's hunger strikes and self-mutilation did not prevent a breach for pre-trial detention of 3 years and nearly 10 months.

Woukam Moudefo v France	—3 years, 2 months, 25 days—Commission violation (settled before the Court)
Can v Austria	—14 months, 26 days—Commission violation (settled before the Court)
Van der Tang v Spain	—3 years, 1 month, 27 days: no violation
W v Switzerland	—4 years, 3 days: no violation (narrow decision —5:4)
Quinn v France	—1 year: no violation
Scott v Spain	—4 years, 16 days: violation
Muller v France	—almost 4 years: violation
Ferrari-Bravo v Italy[69]	—4 years, 11 months: manifestly ill-founded
Hauschildt v Denmark[70]	—2 years, 9 months: manifestly ill-founded
Di Stefano v UK [71]	—19 months: manifestly ill-founded
Deschamps v Belgium[72]	—23 months: manifestly ill-founded

New Court

Punzelt v the Czech Republic	—2 years, 6 months, 18 days: violation.
Labita v Italy	—2 years, 7 months: violation
Jecius v Lithuania	—14 months, 16 days: violation
Vaccaro v Italy	—more than 4 years, 8 months: violation
Kudla v Poland	—2 years, 4 months 3 days: violation
Jablonski v Poland	—3 years, nearly 10 months: violation
Ilijkov v Bulgaria	—3 years, 3 months, 27 days: violation
Erdem v Germany	—5 years, 11 months: violation
Iliowiecki v Poland	—1 year, 9 months, 19 days: violation
Kalashnikov v Russia	—1 year, 2 months, 29 days (after pre-Convention period of 2 years 10 months and 6 days): violation
Jasinski v Poland[73]	—1 year, 3 months, 6 days: manifestly ill-founded
Pantano v Italy[74]	—2 years, 8 months, 14 days: no violation

---

[69] 9627/81, (Dec.) March 14, 1984, 37 D.R. 15.

[70] Cited above: not excessive due, *inter alia*, to the substantial activity of the courts (136 court sessions in 18 months).

[71] 12391/86, (Dec.) April 13, 1989, 60 D.R. 182. Complex fraud with 100 witnesses and 3,000 pages of documents and though the applicant had strong ties with UK for 20 years he was still an Italian citizen and also had alleged links with organised crime abroad.

[72] Dangerous personality, death threats to witness, not unduly prolonged.

[73] 39865/96, (Dec.) January 21, 2003—no failure of diligence on part of authorities who were gathering evidence and laying new charges.

[74] June 3, 2003.

Prisoners' rights

Key provisions:

Articles 3 (prohibition of inhuman and degrading treatment), 5, para.4 (review of   **IIB–307**
lawfulness of detention), 8 (respect for family life, private life and correspondence),
13 (effective remedy for Convention breaches), and 14 (discrimination).

Key case law:

Golder v UK, February 21, 1975, Series A, No.18; 1 E.H.R.R. 524; *Silver v UK*,
March 25, 1983, Series A, No.61; 5 E.H.R.R. 347; *Campbell and Fell v UK*, June 28,
1984, Series A, No.80; 7 E.H.R.R. 165; *Schonenberger and Durmaz v Switzerland*, June
20, 1988, Series A, No.137; 11 E.H.R.R. 202; *McCallum v UK*, August 30, 1990,
Series A, No.183; 13 E.H.R.R. 597; *Campbell v UK*, March 25, 1992, Series A,
No.233; 15 E.H.R.R. 137; *Hercezegfalvy v Austria*, September 24, 1992, Series A,
No.244; 15 E.H.R.R. 437; *Keenan v UK*, April 3, 2001, ECHR 2001–III; *Valasinas v
Lithuania*, July 21, 2001, ECHR 2001–VIII; *Kalashnikov v Russia*, July 15, 2002,
ECHR 2002–VI; *Van der Ven v Netherlands*, February 4, 2003, ECHR 2003–II;
McGlinchey v UK, April 29, 2003, ECHR 2003–V; *Poltoratskiy v Ukraine*, April 29,
2003, ECHR 2003–V; *Ezeh and Connors v UK*, October 9, 2003, ECHR 2003–X.

1. General considerations

A convicted prisoner's deprivation of liberty does not mean that he loses protection   **IIB–308**
of the other fundamental rights in the Convention. The enjoyment of these must
however inevitably be tempered by the exigencies of his situation and the
requirements of security will weigh in any balancing exercise of justification. Where
ill-treatment is concerned, Contracting States are under an obligation not only to
refrain from inflicting treatment contrary to Art.3 but to take the steps necessary to
protect the safety and health of prisoners under their responsibility.[1]

A large proportion of the cases before the Commission and Court have been
introduced by prisoners, who are perhaps in a particularly vulnerable position,
almost, if not all, aspects of their lives being subject to regulation by authority. The
potential for interference and restriction in fundamental rights and freedoms is
considerable and reflected by the wide number of issues raised in prisoner cases.
These are examined below, following brief comment on non-exhaustion of domestic
remedies.

2. Exhaustion and remedies issues

A prisoner, notwithstanding the difficulties of his position, financial and practical, is   **IIB–309**
generally required to exhaust domestic remedies available in the UK. If a remedy is
available, he is expected to find a lawyer, apply for legal aid and pursue proceedings
in courts, including available appeals.

---

[1] *e.g.* positive obligation to protect from the violence of other prisoners as in *Pantea v Romania*, June 3,
2003, paras 192–196.

The principle that only effective remedies need to be exhausted applies. The Board of Visitors, which could not enforce its conclusions, was not effective nor the Parliamentary Commissioner who has no power of rendering a binding judgment. The Secretary of State has been found to constitute an effective remedy where a prisoner is complaining about the misapplication of one of the prison rules in his case but not where the prisoner challenges the rule itself.[2] The Commission hinted a doubt at the former assumption in a case where the prisoner's complaint about interference with correspondence was summarily discounted as groundless by the Home Office though his allegations were later proved correct.[3] Notwithstanding suspicion that the prison authorities did not always give detailed consideration to prisoners' grievances, the basic approach was that they must be given an opportunity to remedy mistakes before the Strasbourg organs embark on examining State responsibility for alleged violations. Accordingly, the Commission, in the context of Art.13, gave the authorities the benefit of the doubt "in the absence of any indication or evidence that as a matter of practice petitions to the Secretary of State are not properly or adequately examined."

Whether the courts may furnish an effective remedy will depend on the subject-matter of the complaint. Mere doubts about prospects of success does not exempt from exhaustion.[4] Civil claims for assault, negligence, trespass to goods would be required by Art.35, para.1, in appropriate cases.[5]

Where an applicant challenged the content of a prison rule, *e.g.* concerning censorship of correspondence, the position in *Silver* was that judicial review, limited to examining whether the measure was arbitrary, in bad faith, for an improper motive or *ultra vires* was not sufficient. However, where the prison rule is arguably *ultra vires* or there has been a misuse of power or failure to apply the rules, judicial review may furnish the possibility of an effective remedy: for example, where a prison rule allowed the the reading and stopping of confidential letters with a solicitor on wider grounds than merely to ascertain if they were in truth *bona fides* communications[6]; where orthodox Jewish prisoners complained of the Secretary of State's rejection of the proposal of a Jewish welfare association to provide kosher food where it could be argued that the special dietary requirements had to be taken into account in providing sufficient food of the necessary quality[7]; and where complaints were made that conditions of confinement in a special detention unit (the Inverness cages) were contrary to Art.3.[8]

The scope for effective judicial examination of prisoners' complaints may be presumed to have been extended by the Human Rights Act 1998 which allows the provisions of the Convention to be invoked expressly. The remedy of obtaining a certificate of incompatibility where the violation arises from the content of a statutory provision has however not been held to furnish an effective remedy for the purposes of Art.35, para.1 of the Convention.[9]

---

[2] *Silver*, para.116.

[3] 16244/90 (Rep.) May 4, 1993.

[4] See Pt IB Admissibility Checklist, 2. Exhaustion of domestic remedies.

[5] *e.g.* 14462/88, (Dec.) April 12, 1991.

[6] 20075/92, (Dec.) August 31, 1994; (Dec.) 20946/92, (Dec.) August 31, 1994; 37471/97, (Dec.) September 2001.

[7] 13669/88, (Dec.) March 7, 1990, 65 D.R. 245.

[8] 9511/81, (Rep.) May 4, 1989: the applicant acceded to the Government's submissions under Art.13 that where conditions were so severe as to be inhuman or degrading judicial review issues could arise concerning the proper exercise of power.

[9] *Hobbs v UK*, 63684/00, (Dec.) June 18, 2002.

3. Conditions of confinement

Minor unpleasantnesses, however unnecessary, petty or deliberately provoking, will not raise any issues under Art.3. More extreme treatment may receive examination by the Court but the case-law indicates that the threshold is high and in fact, until recently, no prisoners held in prison after conviction had secured a finding of a violation before the Court. In *Selmouni v France* in 1999, some 21 years after the leading judgment in *Ireland v United Kingdom* set the standard for Art.3 cases, the Court found that an increasingly high standard was required in the area of protection of fundamental rights and that acts previously classified as "inhuman and degrading treatment" as opposed to "torture" could be categorised differently in future.[10] Since then, there have been a number of violations based on conditions of imprisonment, showing more stringent standards are perhaps being applied, though the Court continues to emphasise that the distress or hardship complained of must be shown to go beyond the unavoidable level of suffering inherent in detention and to take into account the practical demands of imprisonment.[11]

IIB–310

The Court has stated that it applies in these cases a cumulative approach, as well as examining specific allegations.[12] Where it does find a violation, it has tended to categorise the treatment as "degrading" rather than "inhuman treatment".

(a) *Solitary confinement*

Segregation *per se*, or detention in a special high security regime, is not inhuman or degrading.[13] The Court, following the previous approach of the Commission, has acknowledged that prolonged removal form association is undesirable and that complete sensory deprivation coupled with complete social isolation can ultimately undermine the personality and could in certain circumstances amount to inhuman treatment which could not be justified by the requirements of security. Pursuant to the general Art.3 approach, the Court will examine the particular circumstances, for example, the duration, stringency, objective of the measures and the effects on the person.[14]

IIB–311

The Commission found acceptable quite rigorous regimes. Where there were reports of marked physical and mental deterioration in prisoners in segregation, the Commission found that there was no sensory deprivation, having regard, *inter alia*, to the provision of radio, TV and exercise and no complete social isolation, since they had contacts with their lawyers and each other, save for limited periods. It was also satisfied that there was no deliberate attempt to punish or break resistence.[15] When, after a fourteen months' lockdown, the applicant was suffering from lack of sleep, was highly agitated and anxious, having developed an obsessive compulsion to cope, the Commission found that conditions nonetheless did not constitute such complete sensory deprivation as would undermine his personality. In particular, he

---

[10] July 28, 1999, ECHR 1999–V, para.101 (a case of assault in police custody).

[11] *e.g. Kalashnikov*, para.95.

[12] *e.g. Dougoz v Greece*, March 6, 2001, ECHR 2001–II, para.46, *Kalashnikov*, paras 95 and 102.

[13] *e.g. Van der Ven v Netherlands*, para.50.

[14] See *Van der Ven*, para.51, citing *inter alia* to 8317/78, (Dec.) May 15, 1980, 20 D.R. 44.; 10263/83, (Dec.) March 11, 1985, 41 D.R. 149.

[15] 7572/76, 7586/76 and 7587/76, (Dec.) July 8, 1978, 14 D.R. 64.

received visits and was not deprived of association or exercise for excessively long periods.[16]

On the matter of duration of solitary confinement, 15 months in a cell of six square metres was not contrary to Art.3, even though the length was commented on as undesirable.[17] 23 months cellular confinement (23 and half hours in cell per day) for refusal to wear prison uniform was "severe" isolation but mitigated by daily visits from various persons and not sufficiently serious.[18] Where an IRA prisoner complained of 760 days of solitary confinement, the Commission found that he did not suffer from either sensory or social deprivation, with no physical symptoms besides loss of weight and that though this length of time was "undesirable" it fell short of treatment contrary to Art.3.[19]

Where Republican prisoners on a "dirty protest" complained of severe disciplinary sanctions and oppressive conditions,[20] the Commission, noting the elements of self-imposition and security, found that the circumstances were not severe enough to disclose prohibited treatment, nowithstanding its criticism of the inflexible attitude of the authorities, who were more concerned to punish the offenders than to resolve the deadlock. Dealing separately with the complaint about the restricted diet imposed in combination with cellular confinement, for which there was no security or other justification, the Commission considered that this was a stringent and wholly undesirable form of punishment but though harsh, it was still not severe enough to infringe Art.3.[21] However, even where a prisoner may have brought punishment or harsh restrictions on himself by revolt or fundamental non-co-operation the Government is not excused from its obligations and must constantly monitor conditions with a view to ensuring the health and well-being of all prisoners.[22]

The new Court has not questioned the necessity for special security regimes for particular prisoners[23] and in *Messina v Italy* was prepared to accept quite rigorous restrictions on Mafia prisoners as compatible with Art.3, in light of the security justifications for coping with their alleged dangerousness.[24] The special security

---

[16] 18942/91, (Dec.) April 6, 1991; the applicant had alleged that prisoners had gone for periods of several days without food. In this kind of case, the ability of the Government to provide convincing records of conditions is significant.

[17] 10263/83, n.14 above, where the applicant had two half hour periods of exercise and contact with prison staff, visits, medical examinations. The reason for the confinement—the complexity and seriousness of the ongoing investigation—was taken into account.

[18] 8231/78, (Dec.) March 6, 1982, 28 D.R.5.

[19] 8158/78 (Dec.) July 10, 1980, 21 D.R. 95: the applicant received visits and exercise, and regard was had to his security classification, attempts to escape and influence on other prisoners.

[20] e.g. loss of remission, cellular confinement, loss of privileges, i.e. visits, letters, exercise), removal of most cell furniture, no clothing, cold temperatures; alleged 24 hour denial of toilet access, hosing down of cells and occupants with cold water; slopping out, strip searches, restricted diet and cold food. But there was no sensory or social deprivation in the Commission's terms.

[21] 8317/78, n.14 above.

[22] 8231/78, n.18 above; 9511/81 (Dec.) July 9, 1984 where confinement in cages was under constant review; 7572/76, etc., n.15 above; 18942/91, n.16 above, the entire prison was locked down in extreme conditions—the Commission found a progressive relaxation and return to a normal routine; 8317/78, n.14 above.

[23] *Van der Ven*, para.55.

[24] 25498/94, (Dec.) June 8, 1999, ECHR 1999–V, where there was no access to telephone, or participation in communal sports, recreation or handicrafts (tools were forbidden), limits on family visits (one per month) and limited exercise, the Court found that this only imposed relative social isolation, noting that he did have some contact with other prisoners and some exercise and recreation.

regime "EBI" in the Netherlands however was found to inflict degrading treatment on two applicants, *Van der Ven* and *Lorse*. Though in some respects the regime was less restrictive on contact with others than in the Italian case, the Court appears to have placed particular significance on the aspect of automatic strip searches, each week and whenever the prisoner made visits, for example, to the clinic or dentist, which were not convincingly justified on security grounds. The length of time over which this, and other stringent security measures, were imposed was also given weight, and there is some reference to both applicants showing signs of psychological damage.[25]

(b) *Prison uniform, work and hair shaving*

There is nothing inherently degrading about the requirement to wear a prison uniform or to work.[26] Where however a prisoner had his head shaved for punishment reasons, unrelated to considerations of hygiene, the Court found the measure to be degrading contrary to Art.3.[27]

IIB–312

(c) *Cell conditions*

Applying a cumulative approach, the Court has found conditions degrading in a number of cases, with various factors such as serious overcrowding, excessive temperatures, lack of natural light, open toilets, lack of adequately hygienic or sanitary facilities.[28] The length of time over which the conditions have been suffered has generally received a reference and in one case lack of private toilet facilities did not disclose a problem due to its temporary nature.[29]

IIB–313

In the Ukrainian death row cases, where the applicants were locked up 24 hours a day in very restricted cell space, without natural light, little or no provision for exercise or activities and no water tap or sink in the cell, the Court found breaches of Art.3, commenting that though it bore in mind the difficult socio-economic conditions in Ukraine, lack of resources could not in principle justify prison conditions which were so poor as to reach the threshold of treatment contrary to Art.3.[30]

(d) *Nature of place of detention*

It has occasionally been argued that a prisoner, by the nature of his health or sentence, requires a particular regime of detention. However both in *Ashingdane* (mental health) and *Bizzotto* (drug addict), the Court dismissed the contention that

IIB–314

---

[25] *Van der Ven*, 3 and a half years, signs of depression; *Lorse v Netherlands*, February 4, 2003, 6 years, depressive and panic disorders.

[26] e.g. 8317/78, n.14 above; 8231/78, (Dec.) March 6, 1982, 28 D.R. 5; *Nazarenko v Ukraine*, April 29, 2003, para.139 (on uniforms).

[27] *Yankov v Bulgaria*, December 11, 2003, paras 112–121.

[28] *Dougoz* (serious overcrowding, absence of sleeping facilities); *Peers v Greece*, April 19, 2001, (no ventilation in high temperatures, unscreened toilet in shared cell); *Kalashnikov* (severely crowded cell, three to each bed, open toilets and insanitary conditions contributing to fungal infections and skin diseases).

[29] *Valasinas*, para.108.

[30] *Poltoratskiy*; also Ukrainian judgments of the same date: *Aliev, Kuznetzov, Dankevich, Nazarenko* and *Khokhlich*.

location of detention impinged on the lawfulness of the detention for the purposes of Art.5, para.1.[31] However, the Court in *Aerts v Belgium* held that in principle the detention of a person as a mental health patient would only be lawful for the purposes of Art.5, para.1(c) where effected in a hospital, clinic or other appropriate institution. As the Lantin psychiatric wing, due to lack of regular medical attention or a therapeutic environment was not an institution appropriate for the detention of persons of unsound mind, the proper relationship between the aim of the detention and the conditions in which it took place was deficient and there was a breach of Art.5, para.1.[32] No issues would appear to arise under Art.3 in the absence of severe inhuman and degrading circumstances resulting from the inappropriate regime.[33]

4. Medical treatment

IIB–315 States are under an obligation to secure the health and well-being of prisoners, *inter alia*, by providing the requisite medical assistance.[34] Complaints about the adequacy of medical treatment offered and received are not uncommon from prisoners however and a significant defect or failing is required to reach the threshold of Art.3.[35] It is not strictly necessary to show that the shortcoming had long term effects on health or was causative of any deterioration.[36] Thus prison authorities failed to comply with the standards imposed by Art.3 in *Keenan v United Kingdom*, where the applicant, mentally ill with suicidal tendencies, was not properly monitored and subjected, without informed psychiatric imput, to a disciplinary punishment of segregation during which he hung himself, even though it was not established that the authorities could have foreseen that he was likely to kill himself at that time. Similarly, in *McGlinchey v United Kingdom*, where a prisoner had died following complications from drug withdrawal symptoms, her family had dropped allegations under Art.2 as there was insufficient medical evidence to establish the lack of treatment caused the death. The Court nonetheless found a violation of Art.3 due to the lack of proper medical supervision of her deteriorating state and the delay in admitting her to hospital where more adequate treatment would have been available.

As regards complaints that ill-health or advanced age render an applicant unfit for detention, the Court has held that these elements do not *per se* render detention incompatible with Art.3, adopting a case-by-case approach. The Commission previously adopted a robust attitude and appeared to require convincing medical evidence that the prisoner was unfit for detention or that the facilities were

---

[31] *Ashingdane v UK*, May 28, 1985, Series A, No.93; *Bizzotto v Greece*, November 15, 1996, R.J.D. 1996–V, No.21. See Pt IIB: Deprivation of Liberty (5. In accordance with law and lawfulness) and Mental Health (8. Right to Treatment).

[32] Also *Hutchison Reid v UK*, February 20, 2003, ECHR 2003–IV, para.54 (sufficient link between the applicant's detention under a hospital order and the conditions of his detention in the State Hospital); *Brand v the Netherlands*, May 11, 2004, paras 61–66 (6 months' delay in transfer from prison to custodial clinic).

[33] *Aerts*, paras 65–66, no breach of Art.3 despite unsatisfactory conditions, largely as no evidence of serious effects on the applicant.

[34] *Kudla v Poland*, October 26, 2000, ECHR 2000–IX, para.94.

[35] *Kudla*, paras 95–100, no discernible shortcoming in the treatment of the applicant, with psychiatric problems, *e.g.* suicidal tendencies.

[36] See however, *Aerts*, para.66, where the applicant, mentally ill, was unable to show that the unsatisfactory conditions in the psychiatric wing had such serious effects on his mental health as would bring them within the scope of Art.3.

inadequate.[37] Even where prisoners were suffering from potentially fatal illnesses such as HIV with limited life expectancy, it was sufficient that they were receiving proper monitoring and care and that serious complications had not yet developed.[38] While the Court has yet to find that the factor of old age has subjected a prisoner to distress or hardship of an intensity exceeding the unavoidable level of suffering inherent in detention,[39] it reached findings of treatment contrary to Art.3 in *Price v United Kingdom*,[40] where the prison did not have the facilities to look after the severely disabled applicant and in *Mouisel v France*[41] where the applicant suffered from cancer. There were significant degrading elements in both cases, in *Price*, where the female applicant had to be manhandled on and off the toilet by male prison officers and in *Mouisel*, where the authorities insisted on handcuffing the applicant throughout his external hospital visits and treatment.[42]

Conversely, where there are complaints about treatment imposed on a prisoner against his will, complaints under Art.3 are unlikely to succeed where the measures are based on "therapeutic necessity". In *Herczegfalvy v Austria*, which concerned a person detained as mentally ill, the Commission found that the compulsory sedation, being fettered to a bed for several weeks and forced artificial feeding reached levels of inhuman and degrading. The Commission was impressed by the applicant's description of the "brutal" manner in which these measures were applied and found that notwithstanding the authorities' view that his state of health required treatment it was imposed in a disproportionate manner. The Court, less emotive, conceded that the length of time the coercive measures were applied was "worrying" but accepted that there was a therapeutic necessity according to the psychiatric principles accepted at the time. For the Court established medical principles were decisive and a measure which was therapeutic cannot at the same time be inhuman and degrading. This appears to imply that forced feeding of a person on hunger strike might not fall within the scope of Art.3 and to deny the possibility that a person could choose from motives of his own dignity or self-determination to refuse painful or humiliating, albeit life-saving, treatment. The Commission's view that treatment had to be not only to be medically necessary but carried out in conformity with humane standards is perhaps preferable.

---

[37] 13407/87, (Dec.) March 10, 1988, 55 D.R. 271 where a concentration camp survivor's claims of unfitness for detention were not substantiated by his own doctors, thus despite the special hardship that detention might cause him, manifestly ill-founded; 8244/78, (Rep.) December 5, 1979, 18 D.R. 148, where the applicant (74), suffered diabetes and other disorders, the Commission did not exclude that detention of a man of such age and ill-health could raise a problem under Art.3 but not in this case where the prison had a medical service with considerable expertise; 7994/77, (Dec.) May 6, 1978 14 D.R. 238; 9044/80, (Rep.) December 8, 1982, 33 D.R. 41.

[38] 22564/93, (Dec.) April 14, 1994 77–1 D.R. 90; 22761/93, (Dec.) April 14, 1994, 77–A D.R. 98.

[39] *Papon v France (No.1)*, 64666/01, (Dec.) June 6, 2001, ECHR 2001–VI (applicant over 90); *Sawoniuk v UK*, 63716/00, (Dec.) May 29, 2001 (applicant almost 80)—no evidence in either case that the applicants were not receiving any necessary treatment or supervision.

[40] July 10, 2001, ECHR 2001–VII—Judge Bratza expressed a separate opinion that the court should not have committed such a person (four-limb deficient thalidomide victim, with *inter alia* defective kidneys) without verifying that the prison could cope with her needs.

[41] November 14, 2002, ECHR 2002–IX.

[42] The manner of providing treatment caused suffering beyond what was inevitably entailed by detention or cancer therapy. Also *Henaf v France*, November 27, 2003—handcuffing of 75-year-old prisoner in hospital bed disclosed inhuman treatment.

5. Strip searches

IIB–316 Strip searches, including rectal examinations, have not been found a problem under Arts 3 or 8, where carried out for plausible security or crime prevention reasons[43] and in a manner avoiding unnecessary humiliation. Where a prisoner was required to urinate before a prison officer to provide a sample for testing for use of illegal drugs, the Commission accepted that it was desirable to control the use of drugs in prisons.[44] The circumstances were not severe enough for Art.3 and while there was an interference with private life, regard was had to the reasonable and ordinary requirements of imprisonment in which wider measures of interference might be justified than for persons at liberty. The measure was accordingly necessary for the prevention of crime and disorder. Frequent strip searches were found to be necessitated by the exceptional security requirements of the Maze Prison, where smuggling of dangerous items had occurred. The Commission found that while the circumstances were humiliating they were not deliberately degrading, referring to the lack of physical contact and the presence of a senior officer to prevent abuse.[45]

However, in *Valasinas v Lithuania*, the performance of a strip seach of a male prisoner in the presence of a female prison officer and without the use of gloves disclosed degrading treatment contrary to Art.3,[46] as did the weekly and systematic strip searching over long periods of prisoners in a high security facility in the cases of *Van der Ven v Netherlands* and *Lorse v Netherlands*, where the Court was not persuaded of the security justification.[47]

6. Visiting rights and access to family

IIB–317 The Commission considered that continued contact by a prisoner with his family and friends took on added importance in the context of Art.8 since normal means of continuing relationships had been removed. It had noted the European Prison Rules which emphasise the need to encourage links. Consequently, the Commission found that Art.8 requires the State to assist prisoners as far as possible to create and sustain ties with people outside prison in order to facilitate their social rehabilitation.[48] The Court has since endorsed this approach.[49]

There is no right to unlimited visiting.[50] In theory there should be good reasons for obstacles placed in the way of contacts and an absolute ban could only be

---

[43] *Valasinas*, para.117, *Van der Ven*, para.60.

[44] 21132/93, (Dec.) April 6, 1994, 77–A D.R. 75.

[45] n.14 above.

[46] Also *Iwanczuk v Poland*, November 15, 2001, para.59, where the strip search was accompanied by verbal abuse and derision.

[47] *Van der Ven*, paras 60–62; *Lorse*, n.25 above, paras 70–74: the Court disapproved of the automatic nature of the search on visits which deterred one prisoner from using facilities such as the hairdressers and the lack of any concrete need for searches every week. Also *Iwanczuk*, n.46 above, para.59, where no compelling justification was put forward for requiring the prisoner to strip to exercise his right to vote in the prison voting facilities.

[48] *e.g.* 9054/80,(Dec) October 8, 1982, 30 D.R. 113, refusal of visit by campaign group to a prisoner did not disclose an interference under Art.8 however; 13756/88, (Dec.) March 12, 1990, 65 D.R. 265.

[49] *Messina v Italy (No.2)*, September 28, 2000, ECHR 2000–X, para.61.

[50] 9054/80, n.48, reference to the burden placed on prisons by visits precluding unlimited visiting facilities.

justified in exceptional circumstances.[51] Obstructiveness deriving from a policy of moving a prisoner around at short notice for "cooling off" with the result that relatives arrived at a prison only to find he had been moved was the basis an admissible complaint which settled.[52] Arbitrarily limited numbers of visits from family members may not pursue or be proportionate to any legitimate aim, as in *Nowicka v Poland*, where the applicant detained for psychiatric examination was restricted to one visit per month for no particular reason.[53] However in *Messina v Italy (No.2)*, restrictions for long periods of only one visit or phone call per month were found justified due to the special security considerations attaching to the applicant as a mafia prisoner convicted of very serious offences.[54]

Prisoners held in special security categories are unable to derive from Art.8 the right to unsupervised visits or to visits unencumbered by partitions or screens, in particular where IRA prisoners and their families were concerned. The Commission found that though such restrictions were *prima facie* an interference they were justified in the interests of public safety and the prevention of crime and disorder.[55]

Visits by families are often rendered difficult and practically discouraged where a prisoner is held in a prison far from the district where his close relatives live. The Commission always started from the premise that a prisoner could not derive from Art.8 a right to choose the place of confinement and that separation from family and the hardship that caused inevitably flowed from imprisonment. It would only be in exceptional circumstances that the location of a prison long way from a prisoner's home or family might infringe the requirements of Art.8.[56]

No exceptional circumstances arose from the separation of IRA prisoners, held in mainland UK, from their families, based entirely in Northern Ireland or the Republic of Ireland.[57] In some cases, parents were elderly, in ill-health and unable to make the long journey, or other relatives not in receipt of State assistance could not afford the trip with the result that some prisoners received very few visits at all over long periods. The Commission commented on the fact that their place of imprisonment resulted from from the prisoners' arrest and trial for serious offences committed in England and Wales and noted the serious security considerations attaching to this category of prisoner. Where it was argued that there was no real security risk on transfer or the prisoner was not due to health or classification a security threat, this was still insufficient to raise issues. Even if other prisoners of

---

[51] *Lavents v Latvia*, November 28, 2002, para.141—long periods during which the applicant was barred from family visits (up to 1 year and 7 months) breached Art.8, as unnecessary to prevent collusion or interference in the ongoing investigation.

[52] 9466/81,(Rep.) May 15, 1986, 36 D.R. 41.

[53] December 3, 2002, paras 75–77; also *Poltoratskiy*, where limits of one visit per month (and a limit of one outgoing letter per month); *Khokhlich*, n.30 above (strict limits on parcels from relatives) was not based in law as required by Art.8, para.2.

[54] n.49 above, paras 72–74, where the Court appeared to give weight to the periodic mitigation of the restrictions as showing the authorities taking the pains to assist the applicant in maintaining contacts with family; *Kalashnikov v Russia*, 47905/99, (Dec.) September 18, 2001, where the restrictions on and supervision of family visits to a prisoner on remand was justified by the gravity of the charges against him and the risk of collusion or obstruction in the investigation.

[55] 8065/77, (Dec.) May 3, 1978, 14 D.R. 246.

[56] 5229/71, (Dec.) October 5, 1972, Coll. 42 p.14; 5712/72, (Dec.) July 15, 1974, Coll. 46: reference to thousands of miles overseas.; 15817/89, October 1, 1990, 66 D.R. 251, the interference from a refusal to transfer a Scot from an English to a Scottish prison so he could see his fiancé was a proportionate interference, provision being made for temporary visits under strict security conditions.

[57] 18632/91, 19085/91, 21596/93, (Decs.) December 9, 1992.

high security classification had been transferred, any difference in treatment was justified by the special and sensitive considerations arising out of the disposal of IRA prisoners within the prison system against the background of the political situation which remained subject to complex pressures.[58]

It would therefore appear that where transfers are concerned, there is a reluctance to impose positive obligations on Contracting States and an applicant would have to establish circumstances of extreme hardship and arbitrariness by the authorities.

As regards external visits, Art.8 does not guarantee a detained person an unconditional right for leave to attend the funeral of a relative. However, in *Ploski v Poland* where the applicant had lost both parents in the space of a month the Court considered that taking into account the seriousness of what was at stake for the applicant the authorities should only have refused him leave if there had been compelling reasons and in the absence of practicable solutions. As it did not appear that he has been held on charges concerning violent crime and there was the possibility, unconsidered, of escorted leave, the refusal was found disproportionate to the legitimate aims of public safety or the prevention of crime or disorder.[59]

7. Correspondence

IIB–318   Article 8 expressly guarantees the right to respect for correspondence and the Commission emphasised that this applied to prisoners, subject to the ordinary and reasonable reqirements of imprisonment. There should in principle be a free flow of correspondence and any stopping of a letter to a prisoner requires justification in rules which are accessible and public. In *Silver v United Kingdom*, the stopping of letters to outside bodies or letters complaining about prisoners' convictions or treatment in prison was not "in accordance with law" as the measures were unforeseeable, the relevant orders not having been published.[60] Numerous similar findings have followed in other jurisdictions, where prison authorities have placed restrictions on correspondence which have not had sufficient basis in law or the requisite quality of law.[61]

Regarding justifiable restrictions, the Commission referred in *Silver* to the perhaps understandable desire to support prison staff by preventing floods of outside criticism but it gave much greater weight to the need of prisoners to make outside contacts and express feelings to those outside contacts. In *Silver*, many restrictions were found unnecessary, *e.g.* the restrictions on letters to family and friends, complaints about public authorities and the requirement of prior ventilation of complaints before letters could be sent to legal advisers or members of Parliament. Later cases found that it was unnecessary to stop letters to the press[62]; letters of

---

[58] 23956/94, (Dec.) November 28, 1994; 23958/94, (Dec.) November 28, 1994.

[59] November 12, 2002, paras 37–39. Contrast however: *Marincola and Sestito v Italy*, 42662/98, (Dec.) November 25, 1999, where a Mafia prisoner was refused permission to attend his brother's funeral; *Georgiou v Greece*, 45138/98, (Dec.) January 13, 2000, where the Court brusquely dismissed complaints about refusal to attend a grandfather's funeral and a sick mother.

[60] Also 16244/90, (Rep.) May 4, 1993 where an unofficial agreement with police whereby letters of complaint were held back while the governor investigated was not "in accordance with the law".

[61] *Calegoro Diana v Italy*, November 15, 1996, R.J.D. 1996–V, No.21, where the power to censor mail was undefined; *Labita v Italy*, para.182–3, where the Minister of Justice had acted *ultra vires* in imposing restrictions and the restrictions continued though the court order had been rescinded; *Lavents*, n.51 above, para.136, too wide discretion left to the authorities; *Niedbala v Poland*, July 4, 2000, paras 81–82.

[62] *e.g.* 9511/81, n.8 above.

complaint to lawyers which have not been put to prison authorities; letters from lawyers to a prisoner instructed by his wife on his behalf[63]; matters intended for publication; letters to persons unknown to prisoners before their imprisonment[64]; letters seeking penfriends[65]; complaints to the police about ill-treatment to others[66]; letters concerning the institution of private criminal prosecutions; letters to unoffical organisations.[67]

The following measures may be necessary, *e.g.* restrictions on correspondence of a business nature (which may involve the proceeds of crime)[68]; the naming of other prisoners in the prison, which may raise security considerations[69]; the naming of prison officers in a context which raises a threat[70]; threats of violence[71]; letter naming a prison officer with imputations made against him intended for publication.[72]

Opening without stopping or delay may also be acceptable, as mere screening outside special categories of correspondence with courts or legal advisers is not by itself incompatible with Art.8.[73] Delay in sending a letter may disclose a violation though this is subject to the practical acceptance that where instructions are required as to whether a letter should be stopped, some time will elapse. Three weeks for a letter, not urgent in nature, was found to be acceptable.[74]

Regarding other restrictions on correspondence, the imposition of letter quotas may be justifiable, having regard to the vast quantity of mail the authorities have to deal with, at least where the level set is not unduly restrictive and the effect minimal.[75] There is no interference from the obligation to use prison notepaper assuming it is readily available[76] or from the insistence that the prisoner uses an official form.[77] A denial of notepaper altogether may disclose a violation.[78] As for the cost of correspondence, the State is not obliged as a general principle to pay postage for prisoners but depending on particular circumstances a failure to do so might severely restrict their ability to communicate by post. The provision of one paid letter a week was found sufficient by the Commission.[79] The prohibition on writing in a language not known to the prison censors was not disproportionate where translation facilities had been made available.[80]

Errors and mistakes are no justification for a failure to send a letter or for not notifying that the Post Office has returned a letter as the address was incomplete[81]

---

[63] *Schonenburger and Durmaz.*

[64] 8575/79 (Rep.) July 2, 1979.

[65] 11523/85 (Rep.) December 15, 1985.

[66] 9511/81, n.8 above.

[67] 7291/75, (Rep.) October 18, 1985, 50 D.R. 5.

[68] *Silver.*

[69] *ibid.*

[70] 16244/90, (Dec.) December 12, 1991.

[71] *Silver*, (Rep.) paras 413–415;11523/85, n.65 above.

[72] 16244/90, n.70 above.

[73] *William Faulkner v UK*, 37471/97, (Dec.) September 18, 2001.

[74] *Silver*; 9511/81, n.8 above, a delay of almost a month was compatible while the authorities contacted the addressee with a query.

[75] 12395/86 (Rep.) May 17, 1990, applicant had sent 600 letters, eight to thirty per week during the course of his application, some weeks 30, and it was not unreasonable to limit him to 24 Christmas cards.

[76] 7291/75, n.67 above.

[77] *William Faulkner*, n.73 above.

[78] 8231/78, (Rep.) October 12, 1983, 49 D.R. 5.

[79] 9659/82, (Dec.) May 5, 1983.

[80] *Chishti v Portugal*, 57248/00, (Dec.) October 2, 2003.

[81] 11523/85, n.65 above.

or for mistaken opening of letters on a regular basis.[82] On the other hand, accidental opening due to an administrative oversight (*e.g.* novice censor, failure to notice a marking) when accompanied by an apology, may not disclose a problem where there is no indication of a deliberate flouting or disregard of the applicable rules.[83] A Government is expected to maintain proper records relating to the handling of mail and where a dispute arises as to whether letters have been received by prisoners, it cannot discharge its obligations by merely supplying a record of incoming mail.[84]

Although prison regimes are showing increasing flexibility as regards access to telephone facilities, the Convention organs' approach has been to hold that there is no right to communications by telephone where adequate provision by way of mail is made.[85] Where telephone use is allowed, restrictions on the number of calls or authorised recipients is unlikely to raise problems in the current climate.[86]

8. Access to lawyer and to a court

IIB–319   A prisoner cannot be barred from taking action in the courts or be required to obtain prior consent by the Home Secretary to contact a lawyer for the purpose of taking possible action. Such a restriction is a breach of the principle of access to court, access for everyone being a crucial guarantee of the respect of the rule of law on a domestic level.[87]

Further, even a Category A prisoner is entitled under Art.6 to out of hearing visits with his legal adviser, as he can claim a legitimate and vital interest in keeping the subject-matter of such consultations confidential.[88] Other conditions imposed on access of a solicitor, including search and continual close presence of prison officers may be justified by security considerations.[89] Refusal of consultation with a doctor for an independent medical examination concerning alleged injuries may raise an issue under Art.6, para.1 where it concerns possible litigation for assault by prison officers, though there is as such no automatic right to such facilities.[90]

Regarding letters, imposing a delay on consultation by letter with a solicitor regarding possible claims pending internal enquiries—"prior ventilation rule"— was

---

[82] *Demirtepe v France*, December 21, 1999, ECHR 1999–IX, paras 9 and 27,where mistakes were made due to volume of mail and use of a machine, the Court found this was not "in accordance with the law" and therefore in breach of Art.8.

[83] 14176/88, (Dec.) January 19, 1989; 18264/91, (Dec.) September 8, 1993 struck off when the Government admitted two letters had have been wrongly stopped and no further hindrance followed; *William Faulkner*, n.73 above, the applicant ceased to be a victim under Art.34 in respect of a legal letter which the authorities accepted should not have been opened and gave an apology and assurance for the future; *Touroude v France*, 35502/97, (Dec.) October 3, 2000, no interference where only one letter out of many was opened in error and no indication of deliberate intention or system breakdown; *Armstrong v UK*, 48521/99, (Dec.) September 25, 2001, "incidental errors" where apologies and an assurance given during ombudsman procedures concerning opening of letters with the Court and solicitors.

[84] *Messina v Italy*, February 26, 1993, Series A No.257–H : the list contained the letters received at the prison and sent to the investigating judge to be censored, without trace of what happened afterwards.

[85] 9658–9/82, n.79 above; *AB v Netherlands*, January 29, 2002, para.92.

[86] 32783/96, (Dec.) September 11, 1997; 33742/96, (Dec.) September 11, 1997; *AB v Netherlands*, n.85 above, para.93.

[87] *Golder*, paras 35–36.

[88] *Campbell and Fell*; also *Ocalan v Turkey*, March 12, 2003, paras 146–151, where it was considered essential, despite security considerations, for the defence that the PKK leader have conferences with his lawyers out of hearing of security officers. The restriction on the number and length of the visits disclosed an additional grounds for violation of Art.6, paras 1 and 3(b) and (c).

[89] 12323/86, (Dec.) July 13, 1988, 57 D.R. 48; *Ocalan*, n.88 above, para.149.

[90] *Campbell and Fell*, (Rep.) paras 153–156.

found to disclose violations of both Art.6 (access to court) and Art.8 (respect for correspondence).[91] *Campbell v United Kingdom* settled that it was unjustified to open any correspondence with a lawyer outside the presence of the applicant and in the absence of a good reason. A blanket opening rule was incompatible and where there was reasons to suspect abuse or illicit enclosures, opening might be justified if guarantees against abuse were offered by allowing the prisoner to be present.[92] The opening of the applicant's letters with his defence lawyer was found to be disclose a justified interference where special considerations attached to the suspected terrorist status of the applicant and the implementation was supervised by a magistrate unconnected with the criminal trial.[93]

In *Campbell*, the same strong presumption against opening was found to apply to correspondence with the Commission, which were likely to contain complaints about the prison and lead to risk of reprisals by staff, and in later cases to correspondence with the Court.[94] Restrictive measures concerning correpondence with the Convention organs may also disclose interference with the right of individual petition contrary to Art.34,[95] including the failure to provide the necessary writing materials.[96]

A prisoner without funds is in a difficult position as regards pursuing his civil rights in a court. The Commission found that refusal of legal aid on the basis that there were no prospects of success was not incompatible with requirements of access to court, given that there was no specific right to legal aid in respect of civil matters in the Convention. There was the rider that the refusal had not been shown to be arbitrary. However the Commission accepted the refusal of legal aid even where counsel had stated there was *prima facie* case supported by medical evidence.[97]

9. Practice of religion and beliefs

Occasional complaints have been made concerning interference with religious beliefs or matters of conscience by prison regimes. Few serious issues have yet been found to arise. Claims by Orthodox prisoners that prison food failed to respect dietary requirements was contested strongly by the UK Government and failed for non-exhaustion.[98] The inability to obtain a particular item or lack of provision of a preferred item is insufficient. Short of compulsion to breach a strict religious dietary requirement or failure to provide sufficient food compatible with that diet, complaints are likely to fail.

IIB–320

---

[91] *ibid.*, paras 105–111; *McComb v UK*, 10621/83, (Dec.) March 11, 1985: screening of legal correspondence concerning pending court proceedings disclosed an admissible issue of interference with access to court. Settled.

[92] A complete ban on correspondence with the applicant's representative in Strasbourg proceedings was also found unjustifiable in *AB v Netherlands*, n.85 above, paras 86–88 although the representative, not a lawyer, was a former inmate of the same prison.

[93] *Erdem v Germany*, July 21, 2001, ECHR 2001–VII.

[94] Also *Rehbock v Slovenia*, paras 96–101, where there were no compelling reasons justifying the opening of letters from the Commission or Court; *Peers* , n.28 above, para.84, discounting the risk of Commission envelopes being forged to smuggle prohibited material into the prison as negligible; *Valasinas*, para.129.

[95] *e.g Petra v Romania*, September 23, 1998, R.J.D. 1998–VII, No.90, para.44. See section Hindrance in the exercise of the right of individual petition.

[96] *Cotlet v Romania*, June 3, 2003, para.71.

[97] 8158/78, (Dec.) July 10, 1980, 21 D.R. 95. The Commission commented that it was open to the prisoner to initiate proceedings by other means and referred to the fact that he had been able to find a lawyer to bring the case to Strasbourg.

[98] 13669/88, n.7 above.

What constitutes a religious commitment is perhaps a sensitive area. There has been no success as yet in claiming that working is against a religious belief.[99] Where a prisoner claimed that it infringed his vegan beliefs to work in a prison workshop which entailed contact with dyes, the Commission, which considered that vegan convictions in relation to animal products could fall within the scope of Art.9, appeared sceptical noting the Government's point that the applicant first refused the work on the basis that he preferred work outdoors and rejected the case, referring to the dubious substantiation of any link between the dyes and animals and the minor nature of the penalties which he suffered for refusing to work.[100] Where a life prisoner, converted after conviction to Islam, complained that while he had changed his name by deed poll the prison refused to use this name for some internal prison purposes, the question of whether this interfered with any religious belief was left undecided when the case settled.[101]

A personal belief that one is a political prisoner is not sufficent to constitute a right to wear personal clothing.[102]

The provision of facilities or the opportunity to worship or contact with religious ministers is probably required by Art.9. In *Chester v United Kingdom*,[103] a prisoner complained that he had been deprived of the possibility of attending religious services in the chapel which the Government stated had been closed down as being insecure. The case was communicated but later struck off, after it appeared that the applicant had received visits from the chaplain in his cell, services were conducted in the segregation unit and the applicant lost interest in pursuing the complaint. In *Kuznetzov v Ukraine*,[104] where a prisoner on death row was unable to attend the weekly religious services with other prisoners and was not visited by a priest for a number of years, the Court found a breach of Art.9 as the interference had no basis in law (not "in accordance with law") and thus did not need to consider the necessity of the restrictions.

10. Education, leisure facilities and expression

IIB–321 Limitation on educational and leisure activities may be justified by security or associated considerations as in *Boyle v United Kingdom* where a complaint concerning prohibition of pursuit of sculpting activities in his cell was found justified from the risk posed by the sculpting tools.[105] The refusal to Boyle, a prolific writer, of a typewriter was also rejected on the basis that that there was no indication that the lack of one hindered his freedom to communicate or impart ideas in manuscript.[106] Where there were drastic restrictions on access to library, TV and radio facilities, the Commission had regard to the prisoners' own responsibility for the protest campaign being waged.[107] Similarly, restriction on access to the library to a prisoner who

---

[99] 8231/78, (Dec.) March 6, 1982, 28 D.R.5.

[100] 18187/91, (Dec.) February 10, 1993.

[101] 26651/95, (Dec.) May 13, 1996. In 11046/84, December 10, 1985, 45 D.R. 236, where a murderer wished to lose his infamous name, it was compatible with Art.8 in the interests of prison administration to retain the name for internal purposes.

[102] 8231/78, n.99 above.

[103] 14747/89 (Dec.) October 1, 1990.

[104] n.30 above, paras 148–151.

[105] Also *Messina*, n.24 above, where the applicant was barred from craft activities requiring the use of dangerous tools and there was no indication that he was excluded from work altogether.

[106] 9659/82, n.79 above.

[107] 8317/80, n.14 above.

refused clothes was acceptable in light of his own difficult behaviour and the fact that he received books via the education officer.[108] However, severe, long term restrictions on exercise and other activities played a role in the finding of Art.3 violations in the Ukrainian death row cases.[109]

Violation of freedom of expression was found where there was a restriction on access to newpapers and periodicals to a difficult prisoner, which reduced his contact with the outside world and was not, unlike other restrictions, justified by considerations of security or order.[110] In the same case a general prohibition on sending out academic or scientific writings fell foul of Art.10. Imposition of seven days' solitary confinement as punishment for a prisoner writing allegedly defamatory statements against police and prison officers in his private diary disclosed a violation, the Court commenting that the authorities should have shown more restraint and provide particularly solid justification where the statements were written in the context of criticism of conditions of detention.[111]

Access to outside publications may be legitimately restricted to prevent crime and disorder or the protection of the rights of others, as in a case of a prisoner who complained that the authorities confiscated the anti-semitic "Gothic Ripples" literature.[112]

11. Internal prison discipline

Whether internal prison disciplinary proceedings attract the procedural guarantees of Art.6, para.1 depends on whether they fall within the *Engel* criteria (see Part IIA: Criminal Charge). Loss of remission was found to constitute a penalty akin to a deprivation of liberty in *Campbell and Fell*, as was the addition of extra days to a sentence in *Ezeh and Connors v United Kingdom*, where the Court stated that there would be a presumption that Art.6 applied to the imposition of extra days unless the deprivations of liberty involved were not "appreciably detrimental" given their nature, duration or manner of execution.[113]   **IIB–322**

Where Art.6 applies to prison disciplinary proceedings, the tribunal concerned must be impartial and independent of the executive and even where there are good reasons to exclude the public from the proceedings, some steps must be taken to give public scrutiny to the proceedings.[114]

Lack of legal assistance of a prisoner's own choosing for consultation before or at the hearing also disclosed a violation of Art.6, paras 3(b) and (c) in *Campbell and Fell*.[115] It was however compatible with Art.6, para.3(b) that the prisoner was only informed of charges five days before the hearing and that he received notices relevant to the proceedings only the day before, it being noted that he did not make a request for an adjournment. It is perhaps unlikely in the context of prison detention that liberal facilities will be considered necessary for the purposes of Art.6.

---

[108] 8231/86, n.78 above.

[109] *Poltoratskiy, et al.*, cited n.30 above.

[110] 8231/78, n.78 above.

[111] *Yankov*, n.27 above, paras 134–145.

[112] 13214/87, (Dec.) December 9, 1988, 59 D.R. 244.

[113] paras 120–129—40 and 7 day penalties qualified. See *Engel*, where 2 days did not.

[114] *Campbell and Fell*, where there were no steps to make the decision public. See also, *mutatis mutandis*, a violation in *Riepan v Austria*, November 14, 2000, ECHR 2000–XII, where a criminal trial took place in a prison without sufficient public access.

[115] Breach of Art.6, para.3(c) for lack of legal representation in *Ezeh and Connors*, paras 131–134.

The requirement for free legal representation under Art.6, para.3(c) is however conditional on the interests of justice. Whether a person could claim such legal aid is likely to depend on the nature and complexity of the issues and the importance of what is at stake for the applicant.

Cross-reference

Part IIA: Fair Trial Guarantees, General Principles, Criminal charge
Part IIB: Education
Part IIB: Marriage and founding a family
Part IIB: Private life
Part IIB: Review of detention
Part IIB: Torture and inhuman and degrading treatment or punishment

Private life

Key provision:

Article 8 (respect for private life).

Key case law:

Klass v Germany, September 6, 1978, Series A, No.28; 2 E.H.R.R. 214; *Dudgeon v UK*, October 22, 1981, Series A, No.45; 4 E.H.R.R. 149; *Rasmussen v Denmark*, November 28, 1984, Series A, No.87; 7 E.H.R.R. 371; *X and Y v Netherlands*, March 26, 1985, Series A, No.91; 8 E.H.R.R. 235; *Gaskin v UK*, July 7, 1989, Series A, No.160; 12 E.H.R.R. 36; *Niemietz v Germany*, December 16, 1992, Series A, No.251–B; 16 E.H.R.R. 97; *Funke v France*, February 25, 1993, Series A, No.256–A; 16 E.H.R.R. 297; *Costello-Robberts v UK*, March 25, 1993, Series A, No.247–C; 19 E.H.R.R. 112; *Burghartz v Switzerland*, February 22, 1994, Series A, No.280–B; 18 E.H.R.R.36; *Murray v UK*, October 28, 1994, Series A, No.300–A; 19 E.H.R.R. 193; *Stjerna v Finland*, November 25, 1994, Series A, No.299–B; 24 E.H.R.R. 195; *Laskey, Jaggard and Brown v UK*, February 19, 1997, R.J.D., 1997–I, No.29; 24 E.H.R.R. 392; *Z v Finland*, February 25, 1997, R.J.D., 1997–IV, No.44; 25 E.H.R.R. 371; *Amann v Switzerland*, February 16, 2000, ECHR 2000–II; 30 E.H.R.R. 843; *Rotaru v Romania*, May 4, 2000, ECHR 2000–V; *PG and JH v UK*, September 25, 2001, ECHR 2001–IX; *Mikulic v Croatia*, February 7, 2002, ECHR 2002–I; *Pretty v UK*, April 29, 2002, ECHR 2002–III; *Christine Goodwin v UK*, July 11, 2002, ECHR 2002–VI; *Peck v UK*, January 28, 2003, ECHR 2003–I; *Odievre v France*, February 13, 2003, ECHR 2003–III; *Hatton v UK*, July 8, 2003, ECHR 2003–VIII; *Perry v UK*, July 17, 2003; ECHR 2003–IX; *Smirnova v Russia*, July 24, 2003, ECHR 2003–IX; *MC v Bulgaria*, December 4, 2003, ECHR 2003–XII; *Glass v UK*, 9 March 2004, ECHR 2004–II; *Von Hannover v Germany*, June 24, 2004, ECHR 2004.

1. General considerations

Private life is not a concept which has received any exhaustive definition by the Convention organs, who have generally preferred as in most areas to restrict themselves to the particular problem in hand. Considering the potential width of the term, the number of cases which deal with "private life" has been relatively few. It is a notion which also tends to overlap with the other interests protected under Art.8—family life, home and correspondence, as in *Klass v Germany*[1] where interception of communications (mail and phone) was potentially an interference with family and private life, correspondence and home while, in *Mentes v Turkey*,[2] the Commission found that the deliberate destruction of the applicants' homes and possessions by the State security forces cut across the entire personal sphere protected by Art.8, family life, private life and home and it was not necessary to distinguish them.

[1] para.41.
[2] November 28, 1997, R.J.D. 1997–VIII, No.59: the Court adopted the Commission's reasoning, para.73.

The concept stands for the sphere of immediate personal autonomy. This covers aspects of physical and moral integrity.[3] It is wider than the right to privacy. According to the Commission, it ensures a sphere within which everyone can freely pursue the development and fulfillment of his personality.[4] This necessarily comprises the right to an identity[5] and includes the right to develop relationships with other persons, in particular in the emotional field and including sexual ones with other persons.[6] Thus for the Commission the notion of private life was not limited to "an inner circle" in which the individual might live his own personal life as he chose and exclude therefrom the outside world but extended further, comprising to a certain degree the right to establish and develop relationships with other human beings and the outside world.[7] The Court has been more hesistant in making broad statements[8] but was clear in its approach to intimate aspects of sexual life in the adult homosexual cases.[9]

An emphasis on human dignity has recently emerged,[10] with reference to the notion of "self-determination" and "quality of life" in *Pretty v United Kingdom*, where the Court found that the complaints of the applicant, suffering from a painful degenerative disease, about the inability to end her life with the assistance of her husband fell within the scope of Art.8 although the prohibition on assisted suicide was found justified as necessary to protect the vulnerable.[11] There is a strong hint that the Court would consider seriously complaints from a person who was prevented from exercising a choice to decline medical treatment that prolonged suffering or would continue life in a state of advanced mental or physical decrepitude.[12]

2. Extent of the "private" sphere

IIB–325   There are limits on the personal sphere or inner circle. While many measures by the State will affect an individual's possibility of developing his personality by doing what he wants, not all can be considered an interference with private life under Art.8. The Convention organs tended to find that the claim to respect for private life was automatically reduced to the extent that an individual brought his private life into contact with public life or other protected interests.[13] Thus no interference with private life arose where photographs were taken of a person participating in a

---

[3] *X and Y v Netherlands*, para.22. See also *Bensaid v UK*, February 6, 2001, ECHR 2001–I, para.47, where mental health was regarded as a crucial part of moral integrity and the preservation of mental health a vital precondition to the effective enjoyment of private life.

[4] 6825/75, (Dec.) May 18, 1976, 5 D.R. 86.

[5] *Burghartz*, (Rep.) para.47; *Mikulic*, para.54, finding an entitlement to establish details of identity as a human being and to obtain information with important formative implications (*i.e.* in paternity proceedings); *Odievre*, para.29, the adopted applicant's claims to discover the identity of her natural parents/family/circumstances of her birth concerned her private life.

[6] 6959/75, (Rep.) July 12, 1977, 10 D.R. 100.

[7] *Friedl v Austria*, (Rep.) May 19, 1994, Series A, No.305–B para.45.

[8] See *Stjerna*, para.37; *Burghartz*, para.24.

[9] *Dudgeon*, para.41. See Pt IIB: Homosexuality.

[10] *Pretty*, para.65, *Christine Goodwin*, para.90.

[11] *Pretty*, paras 61–78.

[12] *ibid.*, para.64.

[13] Also *Ludi v Switzerland*, July 15, 1992, Series A, No.238, para.40 where the Court excluded criminal activities from "private life"; Mr Geus, dissenting in *Burghartz* (Rep.) considered that the applicant's surname was a manifestly public feature.

public incident[14] nor in respect of communication of statements made during public proceedings.[15] In *Friedl v Austria*, the Commission considered it highly relevant, as regarded the taking of photographs by the police and their retention in files, to what extent the taking of the photographs amounted to an intrusion in the individual's privacy, whether it related to private matters or public incidents.

In the *Icelandic dog* case,[16] the Commission stated that protection of Art.8 did not extend to relationships of the individual with his entire immediate surroundings insofar as they did not involve human relationships (see below: Pets) In the context of abortion, the Commission took the view that pregnancy could not be said to pertain uniquely to the sphere of private life.[17] The life of the pregnant woman was seen as closely connected with the developing foetus and not every regulation of the termination of unwanted pregnancies would constitute an interference with the right to respect for private life.

However, the mere fact that the individual is in a public area or the personal information about an individual is accessible to others or in the public domain will not always exclude the application of Art.8. The Court has stated that a number of elements are relevant to the consideration of whether a person's private life is concerned in measures effected outside a person's home or private premises. A person's reasonable expectations as to privacy may be a significant, though not necessarily decisive, factor[18] as well as whether the individual voluntarily supplied the information or there was reasonable anticipation of the later use made of the material.[19] For example, publication of photographs taken of Caroline of Hannover's daily life, showing her, *inter alia*, shopping, riding, in a restaurant and at a beach club, were considered as clearly falling within the scope of her private life.[20]

Also a systematic or permanent recording of material taken in the public domain, or any processing of such data will generally bring the measure within the scope of Art.8.[21] The seriousness of the intrusion and the degree of public exposure resulting from the measure may also be relevant, as in *Peck v United Kingdom*, where the CCTV footage of the applicant's attempted suicide in a public place was shown on national television without adequate masking of his identity.

[14] 5877/72, 45 Coll. 90; *Steel and Morris v UK*, 68416/01, (Dec.) October 22, 2002, where McDonalds' use of inquiry agents to attend Greenpeace events did not fall within "private life", which was inapplicable to places freely accessible to the public; *Verliere v Switzerland*, 41953/98, (Dec.) June 28, 2001, ECHR 2001–VIII, finding interference, albeit compatible with Art.8, where insurance investigators monitored the applicant's movements, taking photographs and video footage in public places.

[15] 3868/68, 34 Coll. 10.

[16] n.4 above.

[17] 6959/75, n.6 above. See Pt IIB: Abortion.

[18] *PG and JH v UK*, para.57; *Peck v UK*, paras 58–63: the applicant could not have foreseen that the CCTV recording of his suicide attempt would be broadcast on national television.

[19] e.g. *Lupker v Netherlands*, 18385/91, (Dec.) December 7, 1992, where the photographs in the police album had not been obtained through any invasion of privacy but submitted in passport applications or taken on earlier arrests. Conversely, in *Perry*, para.41, the applicant, who had refused an identification parade, had no expectation that footage from a visible CCTV camera was being taken for video identification use: the ploy went beyond normal or expected use of the camera.

[20] *Von Hannover*, para.53.

[21] e.g. *Amann*, paras 65–66, concerning creation and storage of a card containing professional and business details; *Rotaru*, paras 43–44, where public information was systematically collected; *PG and JH*, para.59, concerning covert taping of the applicants' voices in the police station for voice analysis; *Perry*, paras 41–42, concerning covert videotaping of the applicant in the custody area for an identification video; *Verliere*, n.14 above. Conversely, viewing a person in the street or over CCTV cameras, where no recording is made, is not be covered: *PG and JH*, para.57; 32200/96–32201/96 (Dec.) January 14, 1998, 92–A D.R. 92.

Once Art.8 is applicable, the second paragraph imposes requirements of lawfulness and proportionality, including sufficient safeguards against abuse or disclosure inconsistent with private life rights. Lack of statutory regulation or provision of adequate protection for the individual has thus in a number of cases disclosed violation of Art.8.[22]

Difficulties imposed on the way on which a person can interract with the outside world and live their daily lives as a whole may, if sufficiently serious, fall within the scope of Art.8, as in *Smirnova v Russia*, where the applicant's internal passport, which was crucial to everyday life, from buying train tickets to obtaining medical treatment, had been withheld for over four years.[23] Although there is no right to nationality or to citizenship as such, it is not excluded that arbitrary denial of such could raise an issue under Art.8 where impacting on the private life of the individual.[24] Constraints on a person's choice of mode of dress also constitute an interference with private life, although the requirements to wear prison uniform or to adhere to a workplace dress code have been found proportionate and justifiable restrictions.[25] The Court found no direct link between the State's failure to ensure proper access for handicapped persons to a beach and the applicant's private life.[26]

3. State obligations: non-interference and positive protection

IIB–326 A Contracting State must not only restrict its own interferences to what is compatible with Art.8, which provides a primarily negative undertaking, but may also be required to take steps to secure respect for its rights, whether through the protection of domestic law or more specific measures.[27] The extent to which a State may be under such a positive obligation will vary with the differing situations obtaining in Contracting States which enjoy in this respect a wide margin of appreciation in determining the steps to be taken to ensure compliance with the Convention having regard to the needs and resources of the community and individuals.[28]

Insofar as positive obligations are concerned, the Court has helpfully indicated that the notion of "respect" is not clear cut. It has stated that a fair balance must be struck between the interests of the individual and those of the community and in striking that balance, the aims referred to in the second paragraph may be relevant.[29]

The cases illustrate that the impact on the applicant's rights must be serious and significant as in *X and Y v Netherlands* (which concerned a serious infringement of

---

[22] *e.g.* findings of lack of "lawfulness" or proper legal regulation in *Amann, Rotaru, PG and JH* and *Perry*; insufficient protection of the applicant's position in *Peck*, paras 80–87: no effort to obtain his consent to the TV transmission and inadequate masking of his identity.

[23] Also *B v France*, where daily aggravation arose from the anomalous gender identification on a transsexual's identity documents.

[24] *e.g. Karassev and family v Finland*, 31414/96, (Dec.) January 12, 1999, ECHR 1999–II.

[25] 8317/78, (Dec.) May 15, 1980, 20 D.R. 91; 36528/97, (Dec.) October 22, 1998.

[26] *Botta v Italy*, (Rep.) R.J.D. 1998–I, No.66, para.35—the Commission referred to a wide discretion in the area of recreational activities. Also *Zehnalova and Zehnal v Czech Republic*, 38621/97, (Dec.) May 14, 2002, concerning lack of disabled access to public buildings, there was insufficient concrete proof of serious detriment to personal development or ability to enter into relations with others.

[27] *Costello-Roberts*, para.26.

[28] *e.g. Abdulaziz v UK*, May 28, 1985, Series A, No.94, para.67.

[29] *Rees v UK*, October 17, 1986, Series A, No.106, para.37.

physical and moral integrity, *i.e.* rape) *Gaskin* (where fundamental values and essential aspects of private life or identity were concerned) or *B v France* (where the interference was daily and acute).[30] No positive obligation was found in *Costello-Robberts* (where the chastisement was minor).[31]

Whether an important State interest is involved may also be significant as in *Abdulaziz v United Kingdom* (where vital State interests in immigration were concerned), *Hatton v United Kingdom* (economic interests in maintaining Heathrow's competitiveness) and *Rees* and *Cossey* (claimed State interest in maintaining a historical birth record). In the latter cases, concerning claims of transsexuals to legal recognition of their change of gender, the Court was also swayed by the perceived controversial nature of the phenomenon and the lack of consensus within Contracting States on the approach to be adopted. The Court has since changed its view in *Christine Goodwin v United Kingdom*, its judgment indicating that the issues were perceived as less controversial, the consensus in Contracting States was clear and that there were no significant factors of public interest to weigh against the individual right to personal development. In *Odievre v France*, the interests of the natural mother and her family together with the potential impact on the general interest in avoiding illegal abortions rendered the matter of allowing an adopted applicant to obtain information about her birth origins both complex and sensitive and no failure to respect the applicant's private life was thereby disclosed.[32]

4. Privacy

The extent to which an issue might arise under private life for press intrusion or the disclosure of intimate, non-defamatory details of private life will be influenced, *inter alia*, by the extent to which the person concerned courted attention, the nature and degree of the intrusion into the private sphere and the ability of diverse domestic remedies to provide effective and adequate redress.[33] The press cannot rely on any notion of celebrity as justifying intrusive photography or coverage, the Court drawing a decisive distinction between the reporting of matters capable of contributing towards debate in a democratic society and the reporting of details of private life unlinked to official functions. Thus, in *Von Hannover v Germany*, a breach was disclosed by the publication of photographs of the daily life of the applicant, who though "a figure of contemporary society *'par excellence'*" did not exercise any official State functions and had a legitimate expectation of protection of her private life.

Where an applicant complained not only of difficulties in suing for defamation but of the lack of redress for revelations in a book of his love affairs, the Commission

IIB–327

---

[30] Also 20357/92 (Dec.), March 7, 1994, 76–A D.R. 80 where the harassment was extreme and frequent.
[31] Also 24967/94, (Dec.) February 20, 1995, 80–A D.R. 175: no positive obligation to protect from unsolicited mail, having regard to freedom of expression, a link with funding costs of student facilities: also the commercial information could be easily ignored.
[32] See however the persuasive dissent of 7 judges who found emerging consensus for the "right to know" and no significant prejudice arising from a procedure by which the competing interests, including the natural mother's desire for anonymity, could be balanced.
[33] 28851/95 and 28852/95, (Dec.) January 16, 1998, 92 D.R. 56, introduced by Earl and Countess Spencer concerning press coverage—rejected for non-exhaustion as in their case an action for breach of confidence was available; 36908/97, (Dec.) October 21, 1998, where an indistinct photograph was shot through a window, the Commission noted that there had been no intrusion, harassment or exploitation and it was attached to an article in the public interest.

noted the need for domestic law to balance the conflicting rights of freedom of expression and right to private life but on the facts of that case (he was relatively successful in his defamation action and settled the case) it was not established that the balance was unfairly struck.[34] Other cases concerning the taking of photographs[35] and a campaign of harassment by an ex-boyfriend which stopped short of actionable torts or crimes[36] were rejected for non-exhaustion, indicating that problems of exhaustion may arise where the domestic law situation leaves a doubt as to the existence of a remedy or appears to be subject to progressive interpretation. The criteria applied by domestic courts should however ensure effective protection of private life, not being too vague as to allow the person concerned to determine in advance when they must expect interference.[37]

5. Personal information

IIB–328   Protection of personal data falls within the scope of private life.

(a) *Content of "personal data"*

IIB–329   Public information can fall within the scope of private life where it is systematically collected and stored in files held by the authorities, particularly were such information concerns a person's distant past or where it is false and likely to injure reputation.[38] The Court has also stated that Art.8 corresponds with the Council of Europe's Data Protection Convention whose purpose is to secure for every individual his right to privacy with regards to the automatic processing of personal data relating to him and such personal data being defined as "any information relating to an identified or identifiable individual."[39]

Thus it is arguable that the fact of recording and using any personal data is an interference. While in one old case the obligation to carry identity cards and show them to police was considered not to constitute an interference if the cards did not disclose information relating to private life (the card included name, address, sex, date and place of birth and could exclude mention of personal identification number on request)[40] in *Friedl*[41] the personal data relating to establishing of identity by the police was enough to fall within Art.8. Where in *Zdanoka v Latvia* the courts reached a decision imposing restrictions on the applicant's political activities based on her past conduct, the Court found that there had been no interference with her private life as the information had been contained in public official archives or was common knowledge due to her notoriety in recent events and related essentially to

---

[34] 10871/84, (Dec.) July 10, 1986, 48 D.R. 154.

[35] 18760/91, (Dec.) December 1, 1993 where an insurance company had taken photographs of the applicant through a window in order to verify her state of health, the Commission found that she had failed to take an action to test the extent of constitutional protection.

[36] 20357/91, n.9 above, where it was claimed that the piecemeal protection by domestic law was inadequate: as there were case law developments extending injunctive relief to "harassment" threatening health the applicant was expected to test the matter in the courts.

[37] *Von Hannover*, paras 73–75.

[38] *Rotaru*, paras 43–44.

[39] Convention for the Protection of Individuals with regard to the Automatic Processing of Personal Data, January 28, 1981, in force on October 1, 1985: *Amann*, para.65; *Rotaru*, para.43.

[40] 16810/90, (Dec.) September 9, 1992 73 D.R. 136.

[41] n.7 above.

her public life.[42] It may be that the gathering of publicly accessible information or information relating to matters or records in the public domain (*e.g.* press cutting files or criminal records) would fall outside the scope of Art.8, where not obtained by specific or intrusive measures targeting a specific individual or stored long term in a secret file.

(b) *Access to personal data*

Where information is stored by public bodies which relates to the private life of a person, issues may arise from a refusal to grant access. The principal case so far is *Gaskin v United Kingdom,* which falls short of conferring any general right of access to data. The applicant, in local authority care for most of his childhood, was refused access to his files, which were described as forming the only coherent record of the applicant's early childhood and formative years. A person's entitlement to information of that kind was derived from its relation to his identity and formation of his personality. The Commission held that persons should not be obstructed by the authorities from obtaining such information without specific justification.[43] The Court commented that the finding of violation in the case was without prejudice as to whether general rights of access to personal data and information could be derived from Art.8. Notwithstanding that confidentiality of the records protected the children and rights of the contributors and was important for the receiving of objective and reliable information, it concluded that the applicant had a vital interest in receiving the information and that there was a failure to strike the appropriate balance as there was no independent procedure whereby access could be allowed when a contributor gave an improper reason for refusing, failed to reply, gave consent or could not be traced.[44]

IIB–330

Where an applicant's access to personal information held by social services was made subject to certain conditions, the Commission examined the reasonableness of the conditions. It was not arbitrary or unreasonable, in respect of a person with a history of mental illness and where the records related to a brief period, to provide for access to be given to the applicant's doctor who was to judge whether or not the applicant should receive them.[45] On the matter of security files, the Convention organs have not found a requirement of access of disclosure. Interferences, assessed against a wider margin of appreciation, may be justified where there are sufficient safeguards against the arbitrary use of powers.[46]

(c) *Collection and retention*

The recording of personal information for purposes of criminal investigation generally will concern private life but may be justified. This includes records of past offences, but also information obtained by the police in investigations where no

IIB–331

---

[42] 58278/00, (Dec.) March 6, 2003—there was apparently no official or secret file compiled on the applicant.
[43] (Rep.) para.89.
[44] See *MG v UK*, September 24, 2002, paras 27–32—no breach for period after entry of force of new appeal procedure which the applicant had not utilised.
[45] 27533/95, (Dec.) February 28, 1996, 84–A D.R. 169; also 30039/96, (Dec.) May 20, 1998—access to a deceased mother's medical file by the applicant's doctor was sufficient.
[46] 25099/94 (Dec.) April 5, 1995, 81–A D.R. 136, where the applicant had partial access. Applicants in other surveillance cases have had no access possibilities but the Convention organs have not pursued these issues. See Pt IIB, Surveillance.

criminal proceedings are brought and even where there is no reasonable suspicion in relation to a specific offence, where special considerations such as fighting terrorism can justify retention. In *McVeigh v United Kingdom*,[47] questioning, searching, fingerprinting and photographing of the applicants and subsequent retention of the relevant records constituted an interference but was justified in the interests of public safety and prevention of crime. This was where the applicants were arrested and detained under prevention of terrorism legislation when they arrived in England from Ireland. Even though no criminal charge was brought against them, the Commission accepted that the information was relevant for intelligence purposes and found that there was a pressing social need to fight terrorism which outweighed what it considered as minor infringements of the applicants' rights. Similarly in *Murray v United Kingdom*, on the arrest of the applicant, the recording of personal details and photographing were within the legitimate bounds of an investigation of terrorist crime. None of the details were found to be irrelevant to the arrest and interrogation procedures, which seems to imply that the Court would at least impose a check on the nature and extent of the information which the police and security forces recorded, albeit subject to a wide margin of appreciation.

The mere taking and storing of photographs by the police of a public demonstration was not found even to constitute an interference in *Friedl v Austria*. There was no identification of the persons on the photographs apparently and the photographs remained in a general administrative file and were not put in a data processing system. The Commission emphasised that the photographs were not taken in any operation invading the applicant's home. The taking of personal data establishing identity and recording that data was an interference but justified since taken for the purpose of pursuing a prosecution even though that did not ensue due to the trivial nature of the offences. Also the data was kept only for a general administrative file about the event and not entered into any data-processing system. This was only a "relatively slight interference" with the applicant's right to respect for his private life.[48] The retention of files destined purely for archivage for period of 50 years did not constitute an interference since there was no effect on private life.[49]

Another major area of personal records is the medical. The taking and storing of such records associated with treatment will generally be justified under the second paragraph, unless there is some failure or shortcoming as regards its use or disclosure to others.[50]

The compulsory requirement to provide information to a census (including sex, marital status, place of birth) was found to be an interference with private and family life but the Commission was satisfied that the interests of the individual were sufficiently safeguarded (replies were strictly confidential, names not used in the computer analysis and original forms not to be released in the Public Records Office for 100 years) and that the aim of economic well-being of the country was pursued.[51]

Compulsion by tax authorities to reveal details of personal expenditure was an interference but justified where the applicant had recently sold properties and the

---

[47] 8022/77, (Rep.) March 18, 1981, 25 D.R. 15.

[48] n.7 above.

[49] n.46 above.

[50] 14461/88, (Dec.) July 9, 1991, 71 D.R. 141: the retention of information in hospital records about psychiatric confinement after the applicant's release was an interference but justified where strict confidentiality was observed and the records served legitimate aims in running the hospital and safeguarding patients' rights, even though the applicant's detention had been unlawful.

[51] 9702/82, (Dec.) October 6, 1982, 30 D.R. 239; also 9804/82, (Dec.) December 7, 1982, 31 D.R. 231.

issue arose as to how he had disposed of large sums. It was accepted as necessary in the interests of the economic well-being of the country that he establish these matters though there was a hint that such powers wielded more indiscriminately would be disproportionate.[52]

(d) *Disclosure of personal records*

Disclosure to the public or third parties of personal information constitutes   IIB–332
interference less easily justified having regard to the recognition that the protection of personal data is of fundamental importance to a person's enjoyment of his private and family life.[53] The public interest in disclosure must outweigh the individual's right to privacy, having regard to the aim pursued and the safeguards surrounding its use.

The showing of a photograph of an applicant from police files to third persons constituted an interference but was justified for prevention of crime and proportionate since the photograph was used solely for investigation, was not generally available to public and had not been taken in way which intruded on his privacy, *i.e.* lawfully by police during earlier arrest.[54] Use by a court of an old police report in order to assess the criminal responsibility of the accused was found to be necessary for the prevention of crime.[55] Disclosure of details of arrest by the police to the press was, assuming this to be an interference, justified as being factual, summary and pursuing the legitimate aim of informing the public on matters of general interest.[56] While in *Z v Finland* it was found necessary to order the disclosure of a witness's medical records for the purposes of a trial, the publication of the witness's name and HIV status in the appeal judgment was not justified as necessary for any legitimate aim. The vital principle of confidentiality of medical data was emphasised in *Z v Finland* and *MS v Sweden*. However in the latter, the Court found that it was legitimate for State medical institutions to pass on to social insurance authorities details of the medical history of a claimant for benefits. The measure was proportionate since the details disclosed were relevant to the claim, there was a duty of confidentiality and staff incurred civil and/or criminal liability for abuse.

Provisions for general disclosure of categories of records to the public in the future may disclose issues where containing highly personal information. In *Z v Finland*, a further breach was disclosed from the fact that criminal files including the applicant's medical records (HIV status) would be made public within 10 years, while she might be still alive.[57]

A system of personal identity numbers (*e.g.* in civic registration and tax, health, social services, etc.) may not interfere as such but use of the system will be covered if it affects private life. Thus the Commission found an interference where the applicant's name appeared in a register of defaulting tax debtors to which the public

[52] 9804/82, (Dec.) December 7, 1982, 31 D.R. 231.
[53] *Z v Finland*, para.95; *MS v Sweden*, para.41.
[54] 20524/92, (Dec.) November 29, 1993, 75 D.R. 231.
[55] 8334/78 (Dec.) May 7, 1981, 24 D.R. 103; 7940/77 (Dec.) May 9, 1978, 14 D.R. 224 which hinted that the public disclosure of a criminal record would constitute an interference in defamation proceedings—this applicant however could apply for *in camera* procedure.
[56] 24744/94, (Dec.) April 6, 1995, where details appeared in the press following the applicant's arrest on suspicion of indecent assault on a boy, referring to confiscation at his home of large quantities of child pornography.
[57] *cf.* 25099/94, n.46 above, concerning a 50 year period.

451

had access, including credit companies.[58] However, the interference, of a minor nature, was accepted as necessary in the interests of the economic well-being of the country. The applicant had not shown that he was in fact refused credit because of the register and regard was had to the fundamental Swedish principle of public access to official documents. The Commission appeared to lend weight to the general desirability of public access to official data registers.

6. Reputation and defamation

IIB–333   The right to honour and good reputation as such is not guaranteed by Art.8, where there is no interference with private life involved.[59] The right to enjoy a good reputation is however a civil right for the purposes of Art.6, which guarantees access to court and fair determination of the issues. See Pt IIB, Defamation and the right to reputation.

7. Names

IIB–334   Names are not only a form of personal identification but also constitute a link to family and involve to a certain degree the right to establish relationships with others.[60] Since there is little common ground in Contracting States, the Court affords a wide margin of appreciation as to the restrictions on permissible changes. There are accepted public interest considerations such as the importance of given to the stability of family names, accurate population registration, safeguards to the means of personal identification and of linking the bearers of a particular name to a given family.

     Restrictions have, ultimately, been found compatible with respect for private life.[61] In *Stjerna v Finland*, where the applicant claimed his Swedish surname caused problems since it was liable to be mispronounced by Finnish speakers, caused delays in mail and gave rise to the pejorative nickname "churn", the Court was not persuaded that there was any particular inconvenience or singularity in his name, noting that many names gave rise to nicknames.[62]

     In France, where strict rules apply to first names, the Court found that it was also compatible with Art.8 to prohibit the registration of a baby as "Fleur de Marie". The Court, noting that the child could use the name in daily life, if not for official documents, found the "certain complications" which might arise were insufficient to raise issues of interference with family or private life. The Commission, noting that the naming of a child was undeniably an intimate part of the emotional life of its parents, had found no violation by a narrow margin.[63]

---

[58] 10473/83, (Dec.) December 11, 1985, 45 D.R. 121.

[59] 10733/84, (Dec.) March 11, 1985, 41 D.R. 211.

[60] *Stjerna*, para.37, citing *Burghartz*, para.24.

[61] Although discriminatory differences applied to men and women on marriage breached Art.14 in conjunction with Art.8—*Burghartz*.

[62] The Commission majority commented that there could in principle be no right to change one's surname under Art.8 but did not exclude exceptional cases might arise where a name caused suffering or serious difficulties.

[63] *Guillot v France*, October 24, 1996, R.J.D. 1996–V, No.19: the large Commission minority, and 2 judges, considered that first names were well inside the private sphere and that there should be rigorous control of interferences in their choice. While the name was unusual, it was not any more ridiculous than anachronistic names (*e.g Scholastique, Poppon, Polycarpe*) allowed as saints' names.

Other restrictions found acceptable include the refusal of the prison authorities for administrative purposes to use the name obtained by deed poll after an applicant's sentence began[64]; inability of a woman to use her maiden name for election (candidate or voter)[65]; inability of woman to take a name used by her ancestors 200 years before[66]; the prohibition of a woman 's continued use of her ex-husband's name as her legal name.[67]

8. Sexual and gender matters

The Commission established very early that a person's sexual life was an important aspect of private life. Thus the choice of affirming and assuming one's sexual identity comes within protection of Art.8.[68] The Court has, in the context of consensual sado-masochistic acts, commented that it is not however every sexual activity carried on behind closed doors which will necessarily fall within the scope of Art.8. It doubted in that case, where the activities were organised, involving numerous people and the making and distribution of video-tapes, whether the conduct fell entirely within the notion of private life, although in the absence of dispute by the Government or Commission it assumed an interference in that case.[69]

IIB–335

Matters relating to individual sexual life are of a particularly intimate nature within the scope of private life and require particularly sound reasons to justify interference. The hallmarks of a democratic society, tolerance and broadmindedness, have to be borne in mind and it is not enough that a particular activity might shock, disturb or offend.[70] Criminal law prohibition of consensual adult homosexual activity in private has accordingly found to be unjustified (see Pt IIB: Homosexuality).

Some aspects may be subject to State interference if in accordance with para.2, particularly where the protection of children is concerned.[71] Article 8 does not protect sex for remuneration professionally or activities amounting to prostitution.[72] While the disciplinary sanction of police officer for cohabiting with a homosexual engaged in prostitution was an interference, it did not go beyond what was necessary for the purpose of prevention of disorder (*i.e.* to protect the good reputation of the police force).[73]

---

[64] 11046/84 (Dec.) December 10, 1985: since it only concerned some internal prison documents and official prison contexts, it was considered as relating to the public administration and outside the scope of Art.8.

[65] 8042/77, (Dec.) December 15, 1977, 12 D.R. 202: the applicant could add the name to her married one.

[66] 16878/90, (Dec.) June 29, 1962: no particular inconvenience, only a wish by the applicant to manifest a closer link with ancestors.

[67] *Taieb dit Halimi v France*, 50614/99, (Dec.) March 20, 2001—the applicant could keep the name for professional and media use and the Court doubted that any inconvenience arose from the bar on use for administrative purposes capable of interfering with private life.

[68] *e.g.* 9369/81 (Dec.) May 3, 1983, 32 D.R. 220; 6959/75, (Dec.) May 19, 1976, 3 D.R. 103.

[69] *ADT v UK*, July 31, 2000, ECHR 2000–IX: the court accepted that group sex in the privacy of the home fell within the scope of Art.8. and found no likelihood of the videotape of the activities being made public.

[70] *Dudgeon*, para.60.

[71] 5935/72, (Dec.) September 30, 1975, 3 D.R. 46: justified to convict homosexual of acts with children under 16.

[72] 11680/85, (Dec.) March 10, 1988, 55 D.R. 178—conviction for unnatural debauchery (paid homosexual relations).

[73] 12545/86, (Dec.) December 12, 1988, 58 D.R. 126.

In *Laskey, Jaggard and Brown v United Kingdom*, the Court found criminal sanctions on sado-masochistic behaviour, even conducted between consenting adults in private for sexual gratification, to be justified for the protection of health, taking the view that the State was entitled to regulate conduct involving physical harm which was not of a trifling or transient nature but in fact extreme. This infliction of injury was sufficient to distinguish the case from the homosexual cases. It also commented, rather censoriously, that its finding on the grounds of health should not be interpreted as negativing the right of the State to deter acts of this kind on moral grounds.[74]

The daily aggravation of a humiliating nature facing a transsexual who was unable to obtain a change of name and official papers to reflect gender re-assignment was sufficient to disclose a breach of Art.8.[75] Inability to obtain legal recognition, which placed the transsexual in an anomalous position at risk of humiliation, vulnerability and embarrassment was also found to disclose a lack of respect for private life in *Christine Goodwin v United Kingdom*, weight being placed on the right of the transexual to personal development and physical and moral security in the full sense[76] (See Part IIB: Transsexuals).

9. Other personal relationships

IIB–336 The determination of an applicant's legal relations with a putative child concerns private life, even where what is at issue is a father's attempt to disprove paternity.[77] The delayed and ineffective procedure adopted by the courts in the paternity proceedings brought by the applicant against her putative father failed to secure her right to respect for private life in *Mikulic v Croatia*. However, where an applicant claimed that respect for private life in the sense of establishing relationships was infringed by the refusal of a court to order a blood test to prove whether he, rather than the husband, was the biological father of a child of a married woman, the Commission found that the decision was taken in interests of the child, who was remaining with the mother and her husband and required the stability and security of that home.[78]

Close relationships short of family life will generally fall within the scope of private life, for example the links between a foster mother and foster child[79]; relationships between fiancés[80]; relationships between homosexuals and their part-ners[81]; as may the links formed by a person who has lived for many years in a

---

[74] The argument that the law prohibited commonly practised types of masochism, heterosexual or otherwise was rejected in 22170/93, (Dec.) January 18, 1995. The applicants were not victims, unable to show any direct effect on their private lives, *i.e.* no threat of prosecution; the conduct was milder than in *Laskey* and there was no indication that such types of sado-masochism were being pursued.

[75] *B v France*.

[76] See also *Van Kuck v Germany*, June 12, 2003, paras 73–86, where the Court found the decision of the court rejecting the transsexual applicant's claims for payment of her gender re-assignment surgery against her insurance company failed to respect her private life.

[77] *Rasmussen*, para.33: though the procedural inequality whereby only husbands faced a time bar in paternity matters had objective and reasonable justification.

[78] 22920/93 (Dec.) April 6, 1994, 77 D.R.. 108; also *Nylund v Finland*, 27110/95, (Dec.) June 29, 1999, ECHR 1999–VI, where the Court similarly rejected the applicant's complaints about the courts' refusal to investigate paternity of a child born to a married couple.

[79] 8257/78, (Dec.) July 10, 1978, 13 D.R. 248.

[80] 15817/89, (Dec.) October 1, 1990, 66 D.R. 251.

[81] *e.g.* 9369/81, (Dec.) May 3, 1983, 32 D.R. 220. See Pt IIB: Homosexuality.

particular country, *i.e.* "the network of personal, social and economic relations that make up the private life of every human being".[82]

The means by which a person pursues relationships may attract the protection of Art.8 also. Penalties for use of a citizen's radio was an interference although justified by the need to regulate such use.[83]

10. Pets

Many would argue that the nature and strength of links between an owner and his pet should bring the relationship within the scope of "private life". However, in the *Icelandic dog* case[84] where the applicant was refused permission to have a dog in the city of Reykjavik, the Commission did not consider that private life extended to relationships with dogs. It considered that the keeping of dogs overlapped into the public sphere, necessarily involving interferences with the life of others.

IIB–337

In *Artingstoll v United Kingdom*,[85] an elderly man enlisted arguments that it was good for his health to have a dog to persuade that the refusal to allow a dog in his council communal sheltered housing was an unjustified interference with his private life. The Commission avoided categorically rejecting the idea of private life as encompassing the companionship of of pets. Instead it relied on the fact that when the applicant took up the lease it should have been known by him that dogs were not allowed. Later cases, more drastically, had owners of allegedly dangerous breed dogs complaining that the destruction of their pets was in violation of their right to private life. The Commission returned to its view in the *Icelandic dog* case.[86]

11. Health and safety measures

The Commission found that numerous measures which States take to protect the public against various dangers cannot be considered as infringing private life, referring *inter alia* to safety appliances in industry, obligation to use pedestrian crossings or subways, and compulsory seatbelts.[87]

IIB–338

A compulsory medical intervention, even of a minor nature, interferes with private life, although, in practice, physical interventions on the grounds of health have been found justified under the second paragraph of Art.8.[88] Compulsory vaccination, TB tests or X rays for children have been found to pursue the aim of protecting health while the disadvantages adverted to were not comparable to the former ravages of disease.[89] Where severe damage and death occurred in some cases as the result of a State-provided vaccination scheme, the Commission found that there was no lack of proper consent, there being a general knowledge of potential risks and the State had taken reasonable precautions.[90] If there is a dispute between

---

[82] *e.g. Slivenko v Latvia*, October 9, 2003, ECHR 2003–XI, para.96.

[83] 8962/80, (Dec.) May 13, 1982, 28 D.R. 112.

[84] 6825/75, n.4 above.

[85] 25517/97, (Dec.) April 3, 1995.

[86] *e.g.* 26280/95; 28846/95; 26279/95: (Decs.) January 16, 1996.

[87] 8707/79, (Dec.) December 13, 1979, 18 D.R. 255.

[88] *e.g. Matter v Slovakia*, July 5, 1999, paras 67–72, where the applicant was forced by court order to undergo psychiatric examination.

[89] 10435/83, (Dec.) December 10, 1984, 40 D.R. 251.

[90] 7154/75, (Dec.) July 12, 1978, 14 D.R. 31.

a parent and the doctors about the appropriate treatment for a seriously ill child, the Court has held that, in a non-emergency context, the doctors cannot ignore the lack of parental consent and should seek a ruling of the court.[91]

Compulsory testing has also been found justified in the context of prisons, where urine tests are imposed on prisoners to check for drugs. This is generally regarded as necessary to prevent crime and disorder in prisons.[92] The Court also found it justifiable, for the protection of public safety and the rights of others that crew members on Danish shipping undergo random urine testing.[93] Compulsory blood testing of a drunken driver was justified as necessary for the protection of the rights and freedoms of others[94] while compulsory psychiatric examination of a person facing criminal charges was justified for the prevention of crime even though the enquiries into private life was not relevant to the crime but criminal responsibility.[95] Court-ordered blood tests to resolve paternity have also been found justified for the protection of the rights and freedoms of others.[96] Where in *YF v Turkey*, the applicant's wife had been forced in police custody to undergo a gynaecological examination for which the Court noted that there had not been shown any medical or investigation necessity, it emphasised that such interference with physical integrity had to be prescribed by law and generally required the consent of the detainee.[97]

12. Measures of administrative control

IIB–339   Appointment of guardians for mentally ill persons has been found justified for the prevention of crime and disorder where, for example, the guardian had the power to consent to treatment without which the applicant was a risk to his warders.[98] The requirement of sex offenders to register with the police and give details of name and address interfered with private life but was justified for the prevention of crime and protection of the rights of others.[99]

13. Physical and moral integrity

IIB–340   Even where the State does not infringe itself on the private sphere of a person, it may be under a positive obligation to protect persons from incursions on their physical and moral integrity. The case establishing the principle was *X and Y v Netherlands*, where Y, mentally handicapped, was raped but had no legal capacity to appeal against the decision of the prosecution not to pursue criminal charges and her father had no standing to do so on her behalf. The Court found that positive obligations could arise requiring a State to adopt measures even in the sphere of the

---

[91] *Glass v UK*, paras 78–83.
[92] 21132/93, (Dec.) April 6, 1994, 77—A D.R. 75—it was hinted that testing might not be acceptable if applied to persons not detained.
[93] *Madsen v Denmark*, 58341/00, (Dec.) November 7, 2002, one test per year was not disproportionate.
[94] 8239/78, (Dec.) December 4, 1978, 16 D.R. 184.
[95] 8344/78, May 7, 1981, 24 D.R. 103.
[96] 8278/78, (Dec.) December 13, 1979, 18 D.R. 154.
[97] July 23, 2003.
[98] 8518/79, (Dec.) March 14, 1980, 20 D.R. 193.
[99] *Adamson v UK*, (Dec.) January 26, 1999, where there was no evidence that this placed him at risk of public humiliation or attack.

relations of individuals between themselves.[100] It found civil law remedies offered insufficient protection in cases of wrongdoing of this kind and that the criminal law suffered from a deficiency regarding Y which disclosed a lack of respect for her private life. It has been since confirmed in *MC v Bulgaria* that there is a positive obligation in Art.8, as well as Art.3, to enact criminal laws effectively punishing rape and to apply them in practice through effective investigation and prosecution. The lack of proper investigation of the "date rape" in that case resulting from undue emphasis on direct proof of lack of consent through signs of resistance by the victim failed to provide the requisite effective protection.

Positive obligations also arise in respect of children and the protection which they should receive from assaults. The Commission in *Costello-Roberts v United Kingdom* considered that Art.8 might afford wider protection that Art.3. Thus even though there was no violation of Art.3 (the slippering did not constitute degrading treatment), the same punishment could infringe the right to respect for private life.[101] However, the Court agreeing the slippering three times on the buttocks though his shorts by a rubber-soled gym shoe was not sufficiently severe for Art.3, was not persuaded that Art.8 would provide wider protection in the area of physical integrity. While it did not rule out that disciplinary measures at school might in certain circumstances affect the right to respect for private life, not every act or measure which might affect adversely physical or moral integrity necessarily gave rise to interference. It had regard to the fact that the sending a child to school necessarily involved some degree of interference with private life. More relevantly perhaps, the Court reasoned that the treatment in this case did not have sufficently adverse effects for his physical or moral integrity to bring it within the scope of the prohibition contained in Art.8.

Respect for private life also extends, to a certain degree, after death. In *Pannullo and Forte v France*, the delay in releasing the body of applicants' child for funeral after an investigation infringed Art.8 in both its private and family life aspects,[102] as did the refusal of the prison authorities to allow a detainee to attend his parents' funerals.[103]

14. Environment

Although there is no explicit right to a clean and quiet environment, considerable noise or other nuisance and pollution can undoubtedly affect physical well-being and interfere with private life and the amenities of home. This may also give rise to a pressing personal interest in having access to information relating to the extent and risk involved. A wide margin of appreciation will be accorded to Government's where the case concerns matters of general policy however.[104] (See Pt IIB: Environment).

IIB–341

[100] See also 20357/91, n.30 above: the Commission implied that. failure to provide adequate protection in criminal and civil law to persons suffering from harassment by another could give rise to a positive obligation.

[101] It considered that the sending of a child to a school did not amount to consent by the parents to corporal punishment and that there was no necessity for such punishment in a democratic society.

[102] October 30, 2002, ECHR 2001–X; the treatment of bodies during investigations or post mortems may also raise issues, *e.g. Dennis v UK*, 76573/01, concerning the removal of the victims' hands without informing the relatives.

[103] *Ploski v Poland*, November 12, 2002.

[104] *Hatton v UK*, para.122. See also the summary of previous case law on environmental issues at paras 96–104.

Cross-reference

Property

Key provisions:

Article 1 of Protocol No.1 (peaceful enjoyment of possessions) and Art.6 (access to court/fair hearing). **IIB–342**

Key case law:

Marckx v Belgium, June 12, 1979, Series A, No.31; 2 E.H.R.R. 330; *Sporrong and Lonnroth v Sweden*, September 23, 1982, Series A, No.52; 5 E.H.R.R. 35; *James v UK*, February 21, 1985, Series A, No.98; 8 E.H.R.R. 123; *Van Marle v Netherlands*, June 26, 1986, Series A, No.101; 8 E.H.R.R. 483; *Erkner and Hofauer v Austria*, April 23, 1987, Series A, No.117; 9 E.H.R.R. 464; *Inze v Austria*, October 28, 1987, Series A, No.126; 10 E.H.R.R. 394; *Tre Traktorer v Sweden*, July 7, 1989, Series A, No.159; 13 E.H.R.R. 309; *Fredin v Sweden*, February 18, 1991, Series A, No.192; 13 E.H.R.R. 784; *The Holy Monasteries v Greece*, December 9, 1994, Series A, No.301–A; 25 E.H.R.R. 640; *Stran Greek Refineries v Greece*, December 9, 1994, Series A, No.301–B; 19 E.H.R.R. 293; *Gasus Dosier v Netherlands*, February 23, 1995, Series A, No.306–B; 20 E.H.R.R. 360; *Pressos Compania Naviera v Belgium*, November 20, 1995, Series A, No.332; 21 E.H.R.R. 301; *Agrotexim v Greece*, October 24, 1995, Series A, No.330–A; 21 E.H.R.R. 250; *Phocas v France*, April 23, 1996, R.J.D. 1996–II, No.7; *Matos e Silva v Portugal*, September 16, 1996, R.J.D. 1996–IV, No.14; 24 E.H.R.R. 573; *National & Provincial Building Society v UK*, October 23, 1997, R.J.D. 1997–VII, No.55; 25 E.H.R.R. 127; *Brumarescu v Romania*, October 28, 1999, ECHR 1999–VII; *Former King of Greece v Greece*, November 23, 2000, ECHR 2000–XII; *Prince Hans-Adam II of Liechtenstein*, July 12, 2001, ECHR 2001–VIII; *Elia Srl v Italy*, August 2, 2001, ECHR 2001–IX; *SA Dangeville v France*, April 16, 2002, ECHR 2002–III; *Nerva v UK*, September 24, 2002, ECHR 2002–VIII; *Allard v Sweden*, June 24, 2003, ECHR 2003–VII.

1. General principles

Three limbs or distinct rules to the protection of property rights are contained in Art.1 of Protocol No.1—in the first sentence of the first paragraph which generally sets out the principle of non-interference with property; in the second sentence relating to deprivation (expropriation) subject to conditions; and in the second paragraph relating to control of use, also subject to specific conditions.[1] Before determining whether the first general rule has been complied with, the Court examines whether the second two are applicable. The three rules not however unconnected. The second and third are concerned with particular instances of interference with the general right and to be construed in light of the general principle of the first rule.[2] **IIB–343**

Interference with property, whether expropriation or control of use, will generally be justified if it respects the requirement of lawfulness and can be regarded as

---

[1] *Sporrong and Llonroth*, para.61.
[2] *James*, para.37.

pursuing the general or public interest. The Convention organs have imported a requirement of proportionality and the necessity to strike a fair balance between the demands of the community and the protection of the individual's interests.[3] The possibility of obtaining compensation is an important element in assessing whether individual bears excessive burden.[4] General and public interest is given a wide meaning and where the legislature intervenes in an area of economic or social policy, the Court will respect the State's assessment unless manifestly without reasonable foundation.[5] Adequate procedural protection of the applicant's interests in proceedings decisive for property rights is also a relevant factor in assessing whether a fair balance has been struck.[6]

Where ownership remains and some ability to exploit the property, a finding of *de facto* expropriation in the sense of deprivation of property is unlikely. Such cases falling short of expropriation are rather dealt with as an interference in the peaceful enjoyment of possessions.[7] Where the purpose of the measure is not intended as such to control the use of the property but to achieve other goals it will also tend to fall under the first sentence. For example, provisional land transfer in *Erkner and Hofauer v Austria* was dealt with under the first sentence of the first paragraph as there was no actual deprivation of property until the consolidation plan issued and there was no aim to control use but to restructure and improve farming.[8] Public interest declarations (pre-expropriation measures) in *Matos e Silva v Portugal* were also dealt with under the first sentence of the first paragraph. There was no *de facto* deprivation since ownership remained and the applicants could still use the land in a restricted manner and were able to sell. In *Phocas v France*, restriction on use of property, together with uncertainty as to future expropriation, resulting from an urban development plan was dealt with as an interference under the first sentence of the first paragraph.[9]

2. Property

IIB–344 Property or possessions for the purposes of attracting the protection of Art.1 of Protocol No.1 covers a wide range of interests. Possession has an autonomous meaning independent of formal classification in domestic law.[10] It is not limited to

---

[3] *Sporrong*, para.69.

[4] *e.g.* in *Sporrong*, a violation disclosed by long term expropriation permits on property which affected ability to sell and was not counterbalanced by the possibility of compensation or shortening the duration; *Former King of Greece;* no compensation provided for expropriation of royal family's estates; *Elia Srl v Italy*, long term uncertainty and no possibility of compensation. See Section: Expropriation, (c) Proportionality.

[5] *e.g. Lithgow* (nationalisation); *James* (sweeping leasehold reform); *Pressos Compania* (legislative intervention in pending tort claims). For rare examples of the Court finding no general interest in a measure, see *SA Dangeville v France*, where it perceived no general interest in not enforcing a community directive to allow the repayment of overpaid VAT; *Zwierzynski v Poland*, July 2, 2002, where police headquarters were squatting effectively in the applicant's property and refusing to leave.

[6] *e.g. Allard*, where the applicant's house was demolished before the conclusion of proceedings concerning her claims; *Tsironis v Greece*, December 6, 2001, where insufficient procedural protection of applicant's rights to property which was seized and sold at auction by a creditor; *Papastavrou v Greece*, April 10, 2003, no adequate protection against executive decision to zone land for reafforestation.

[7] *e.g. Sporrong*, where the applicant still owned the land and could dispose of it; *Fredin* where though the licence to exploit the gravel pit was removed the applicant did not thereby lose all meaningful use of the land, which also included a farm.

[8] See, similarly, *Elia Srl v Italy*, effect of building restrictions short of final expropriation.

[9] Despite a serious effect on his ownership rights however, the applicant was procedurally protected since he could apply for State to purchase his property within 3 years of his application.

[10] *e.g. Former King of Greece*, para.60—royal estates were regarded as owned by the applicants as private persons and could not be regarded as *sui generis* or as State property.

ownership of physical goods: other rights and interests constituting assets can also be regarded as property rights.[11] An interest in property, even if revocable in certain circumstances, can constitute a possession for the purposes of Art.1 of Protocol No.1, as in *Beyeler v Italy*, where the applicant had bought a work of art subject to the State's right of pre-emption.[12]

Where in *Matos e Silva v Portugal* the Government disputed that the applicants owned part of the old royal lands subject to the expropriation measures, the Court found that the applicants had occupied them undisputed for almost a century and the revenue which they derived from working it could qualify as possessions. In *Holy Monasteries v Greece*, where the Government also disputed that the applicants were owners, the Commission considered that, even if they held no registered title, they had "patrimony" rights *in personam*, which could be "possessions" without being property rights protected in Greek law. The Court held that the transfer of possession and control of the properties affected ownership and could not be regarded as a mere procedural exercise.

Article 1 of Protocol No.1 only applies to existing possessions and does not confer a right to obtain property.[13] An applicant must generally fulfil the conditions set by domestic law for ownership.[14] No legitimate expectation arises where there is a dispute as to the correct interpretation of and application of domestic law and the applicant's submissions are rejected by the domestic courts.[15] However, case law recognises in certain cases that "existing possessions" includes claims in respect of which an individual can claim to have at least a "legitimate expectation" of obtaining effective enjoyment of a property right[16]: (see further below: Claims and debts).

Driving licences are not items of property for purposes of Art.1 of Protocol 1.[17]

Where property rights cease or are altered pursuant to requirements or conditions fulfilled by law there is no interference with property.[18] There is some authority for the view that a trivial effect on property rights will not constitute an interference.[19] Inflation does not impose an obligation on the State under Art.1 of Protocol No.1 to maintain the purchasing power of sums deposited with financial institutions.[20]

---

[11] *Gasus Dosier*, where it was immaterial if the applicant's claim to the concrete mixer was a right of ownership or a security right *in rem* (ownership had passed to purchaser under contract subject to retention of title until full price paid which had not occurred at the time of seizure by tax authorities). Also, right by way from a restrictive covenant and receipt of annual rent are possessions—10741/84, (Dec.) December 13, 1984, 41 D.R. 226—as are patents: 12633/87, (Dec.) October 4, 1992, 66 D.R. 70.

[12] He had also possession of the painting for some years and the authorities had treated him as the owner.

[13] *Marckx*, para.50; 11628/85, (Dec.) May 9, 1986, 43 D.R. 270.

[14] e.g. *Hadzic v Croatia*, 48788/99, (Dec.) September 13, 2001, where the applicant did not fulfil the conditions for a pension.

[15] *Kopecky v Slovakia*, September 28, 2004, para.50.

[16] e.g. *Prince Hans-Adam II of Liechtenstein*, para.83; *Jantner v Slovakia*, March 4, 2003, where the applicant was not owner of land, but a claimant with no legitimate expectation that matter would be determined in his favour.

[17] 9177/80, (Dec.) October 6, 1981, 26 D.R. 255.

[18] 10443/83, Dec.) July 15, 1988, 56 D.R. 20: disciplinary suspension of civil servant's pension did not constitute and interference with property rights where suspension fulfilled legal requirements; 10426/83, (Dec.) December 12, 1984, 40 D.R. 234.

[19] *Langborger v Austria*, June 22, 1989, Series A, No.155: the Commission said the requirement in lease to pay small 0.3% of rent to tenants' association for rent negotiations was so small it was not interference.

[20] e.g. *Gayduck v Ukraine*, 45526/99, (Dec.) July 2, 2002, ECHR 2002–VI; *Ryabykh v Russia*, July 24, 2003, ECHR 2003–IX, para.63.

(a) *Business and professional interests*

IIB–345 Possessions were concerned in the revocation of a licence to serve alcoholic beverages in a restaurant, since it formed part of the economic interests of the restaurant and loss of it affected good will and value of the restaurant.[21] Where accountants were refused registration as chartered accountants when the profession was regulated by new legislation, the Court found that they had built up a clientele over years, which had in many respects the nature of a private right and constituted an asset and hence a possession.[22]

While the vested interests of a doctor in his private practice were "possessions", which could be interfered with by removal of a social security affiliation decisive to the running of his practice,[23] the withdrawal of doctors' licence to dispense medicine was not an interference with property, where the conditions for its exercise no longer existed.[24] Goodwill of a professional practice was an element in its valuation but did not constitute a possession to the extent not necessarily linked to the profession in question. The Commission found that dispensing was not automatically connected with their practice. There could be no reasonable expectation as to the lasting nature of benefits which could be withdrawn in accordance with pre-existing lawful conditions, so there was no property right affected in the licence. Future income would only constitute a possession if the money was earned or an enforceable claim to it existed.

Mere expectations of notaries that existing rates of fees would not be reduced by law did not constitute a property right.[25] Customs officers' income affected by change of custom levying on the Greek entry to the EU did not fall within "possessions".[26] Their licences were not revoked and it was not accepted that they had any vested economic interests or legitimate expectations of deriving future advantages. Nor had the income had not been earned or an enforceable claim to it in existence. Where exclusive rights of audience were removed from certain German courts, the lawyers' claims for loss of future income fell outside the scope of Art.1 of Protocol No.1, although their law practices and clientele could be regarded as assets and possessions.[27] Any interference however was not disproportionate given the transitional period to allow those affected to adjust to the changes. A tax consultant's clientele were also assets and the revocation of his appointment was a control of use of that property which was however justified given the applicant's lack of qualifications.[28]

---

[21] *Tre Traktorer.*

[22] *Van Marle*: the interference was not disproportionate since it was a legitimate aim to regulate a profession vital to the economic sector and provision for registration was made by way of proving competence by diploma or before a board.

[23] 11540/85, (Dec.) March 8, 1988, 55 D.R. 157—this was found a control of use in the general interest and not disproportionate, since the applicant did not meet the condition of being recommended by the appropriate authority, as part of comprehensive health care reform.

[24] 10438/83, (Dec.) October 3, 1984: the applicants' licence was dependent on there being no chemist in the area and was withdrawn when a chemist began operating.

[25] 8410/78, (Dec.) December 13, 1979, 18 D.R. 216: where notaries were obliged to reduce fees for certain public bodies, *e.g.* universities—the claim for fees would only to be considered as a possession when it came into existence on grounds of services rendered and on basis of existing regulations for the fees.

[26] 24581/94, (Dec.) April 6, 1995, 81–B D.R. 123.

[27] *Wendenburg v Germany*, 71360/01, (Dec.) February 6, 2003, ECHR 2003–II.

[28] *Olbertz v Germany*, 37592/97, (Dec.) May 25, 1999, ECHR 1999–V.

(b) *Inheritance and succession rights*

Article 1 of Protocol No.1 does not guarantee the right to obtain possessions by way   **IIB–346**
of intestacy or involuntary dispositions, although difference in treatment in matters
of inheritance may fall foul of Art.14 in conjunction with Art.1 of Protocol No.1.[29]
In *Inze v Austria* where the applicant, born out of wedlock, had acquired a right of
inheritance with other heirs, but was precluded by his birth from being a principal
heir, there was a property right in issue, as in *Mazurek v France*, where under
domestic law, the applicant had automatically acquired hereditary rights over his
mother's estate.[30]

(c) *Debts and claims*

Debts or claims in respect of property have to be sufficiently established to be   **IIB–347**
enforceable.[31] The applicant must be at least able to argue that he has a legitimate
expectation of obtaining effective enjoyment of a property right.[32] Hope of
recognition of an old property right that it has been impossible to exercise effectively
is not sufficient,[33] nor hope of a change of law to remove a condition for restitution[34]
or a conditional claim which lapses as result of non-fulfilment of the condition.[35] A
statement of intention to pay compensation did not confer a right sufficient for the
purposes of Art.1 of Protocol No.1.[36]

In *Stran Greek Refineries v Greece*, an arbitration award in favour of a company
pursuing damages against the State for breach of contract to build an oil refinery
constituted "possessions", since it was immediately enforceable, final and with no
right of appeal on the merits. There was an interference when, due to a legislative
measure, the award ceased to be enforceable. Although it might have not been in
the State interest to pursue the contract, the State had intervened to alter the
machinery set up under the agreement, after the judiciary had ruled on its validity
and no provision for compensation had been made by way of counterbalance.

In *Pressos Compania Naviera v Belgium*, the claims of applicants for negligence in
pending proceedings against pilots alleged to have caused damage to their vessels

---

[29] *Marckx*: limitation on an unmarried mother's ability to make gifts/legacies to her child disclosed
discrimination contrary to Art.14 in conjunction with Art.1 of Protocol No.1 but no violation under
Art.1 of Protocol No.1 in relation to the child's inability to inherit.

[30] February 1, 2000, ECHR 2000–II.

[31] *Stran Greek*.

[32] *e.g. Stretch v UK*, June 24, 2003, where the applicant had entered into a building lease with an option
for renewal for 21 years, he had a legitimate expectation to exercise the option even though it was found
later to be invalid due to a techicality (the local authority had acted *ultra vires* at the time in granting the
option). See *Kopecky* in n.15 above, for recent analysis of "legitimate expectation".

[33] *e.g. Prince Hans-Adam II of Liechtenstein*, concerning the Prince's claim in the German courts for
restitution of a painting expropriated from his father in 1946 by the former Czech authorities.

[34] *Gratzinger and Gratzeringova v Czech Republic*, 39794/98, (Dec.) July 10, 2002, ECHR 2002–VII, where
the applicants did not fulfil the condition of Czech nationality and had no legitimate expectation, only a
hope, that this condition would be set aside as unconstitutional.

[35] *e.g. Malhous v Czech Republic*, 33071/96, (Dec.) December 13, 2000, ECHR 2000–XII, where the
applicant brought proceedings to claim restitution of land which failed, under the statutory conditions, as
it was no longer was owned by the State.

[36] *Teytaud v France*, (Dec.) January 25, 2001, ECHR 2001–I, where the applicants had no legal right to
the compensation paid to the French State by Algeria for expropriated property notwithstanding
statements of intention by the authorities.

were assets as claims for compensation coming into existence under the rules of tort at the moment damage occurred. The Court noted that the applicants had a legitimate expectation that their claims would be dealt with in accordance with the law of torts and found that the 1988 Act which exempted the State and its pilots from liability for negligent acts, amounted to a deprivation of possessions. While the Court accepted the Government's arguments that the Act pursued the public interest, *e.g.* to protect the State's financial interests, harmonise laws with the Netherlands, it found the measure disproportionate since there was no measure of compensation. The Court also accepted the applicants' view that legal certainty did not require retrospective extinguishing of claims.

In *National & Provincial Building Society v United Kingdom*,[37] where the applicants had pending claims for the recovery of tax paid under invalid regulations, the Court expressed doubts that these claims constituted possessions, since they had not obtained an enforceable final judgment and it was questionable that they had a legitimate expectation that they would given the Government's clear intention to rectify the defects in the regulations. However, assuming that there was a control of use to secure payment of taxes, the Court found that the measure was remedial legislation to give effect to the original intention of the legislators and there was an obvious and compelling public interest in achieving that intention. As to balance, it considered that the Government had always made it clear that the sums should be liable to tax noting that the invalidity worked by way of giving a windfall for building societies to exploit and accepting the Government view that liability imposed for the gap period when assessment periods changed was fair.[38] A claim for overpaid VAT did however constitute an asset in *SA Dangeville v France*, where the claim was based on a Community norm that was perfectly clear, precise and directly applicable and created a substantive right.

Judicial application of procedural law in a particular case may also interfere disproportionately with claims to possessions as in *SA Dangeville v France* where the Conseil d'Etat refused to give effect to a directly applicable provision of Community law on a technical ground which estopped repayment of overpaid VAT. In *Brumarescu v Romania*, intervention by the Supreme Court in overturning a final and irrevocable judgment ordering the return of the applicant's property unlawfully expropriated during the communist regime was not found to be supported by any public interest and to impose an excessive burden on the individual owner.

Where there were undue to delays in repaying tax advances (some five to ten years) which were uncontested, the Court found the claims were property rights and that the uncertainty caused by the delays failed to strike a fair balance.[39] Failure by the authorities to execute claims that have been upheld in final court judgments will also raise issues of interference with property rights.[40] Lack of funds cannot justify such omission.[41]

---

[37] *National & Provincial Building Society v UK*, 21319/93, etc. (Rep.) June 25, 1996—as regarded "possessions", the Commission pointed out a divergence between the Court judgments in *Stran Greek* and *Pressos*—the Court having found that the domestic court judgment acknowledging *Stran*'s claim was not sufficiently established to be enforceable though the arbitration award was, while in *Pressos*, tort claims qualified though no judgments had issued.

[38] On Art.6, see Pt 11A, Fair trial guarantees, Legislative interference in pending cases.

[39] *Buffalo SRL in liquidation v Italy*, July 3, 2003.

[40] *e.g. Antonakopoulos v Greece,* December 14, 1999; *Dimitrios Georgiadis v Greece*, March 28, 2000: failure to pay pensions to which courts had found that the applicants were entitled.

[41] *Burdov v Russia*, May 7, 2002, para.41.

Claims for legal fees were possessions, where the client was liable for the fees for acts already carried out. The law which prevented the lawyer from recuperating those fees from directly from the State which was party in the proceedings imposed an excessive burden on the lawyer, whose choice not to seek payment from her impoverished clients was not arbitrary or unreasonable.[42]

(d) Shareholders' interests

A share in a company with an economic value is a possession, such that the loss of shares can constitute an interference with possessions or deprivation of property.[43] Issue of new shares which reduced an applicant's majority shareholding, depriving it of the ability to wield influence or control over the company was regarded as interference with "possessions".[44]

    IIB–348

Shareholders in a company cannot claim *per se* that their property rights are affected by the expropriation of property of that company.[45] Despite the Commission's finding in *Agrotexim v Greece* that the shareholders' rights were affected by the interference with the company's property and its capacity to enter into developments projects, the Court upheld a preliminary objection of no victim status since in fact it was not the property of the shareholders which was affected by the expropriation but the company which could have acted through its liquidator. Thus the shareholders were not entitled to act on behalf of the company. It was not enough to allege a fall in the value of their shares. The corporate veil was maintained.

3. Domestic court regulation of private law disputes

Domestic court regulation of property disputes according to pre-existing law does not as such engage the responsibility of the State under Art.1 of Protocol No.1. The fact that one party is inevitably unsuccessful is generally not sufficient, without some supervening act of administration or legislation affecting the applicant's position.[46] Where in *Nerva v United Kingdom*, the domestic courts ruled that the tips paid to the applicant waiters were the property of their employers and could be regarded as paid to them as part of their "remuneration", the Court considered that this was essentially a matter of interpretation of domestic law insufficient to engage the responsibility of the State under Art.1 of Protocol No.1.

    IIB–349

[42] *Ambruosi v Italy*, October 19, 2000.

[43] 8588–9/79, (Dec.) December 12, 1982, 29 D.R. 64; *Olczak v Poland*, 30417/96, (Dec.) November 7, 2002, ECHR 2002–X measures which devalued the applicant's shareholding in a bank were justified by its maladministration and the need to prevent its bankruptcy.

[44] *Sovtransavto Holding v Ukraine*, July 25, 2002, ECHR 2002–VII.

[45] *Agrotexim v Greece*; also 11189/86, (Dec.) December 11, 1986, 50 D.R. 121: minority shareholder in a company could not claim to be victim of levying of tax or charges on company but was a victim where a new shareholder was introduced free of charge which diminished relative value of his own rights as shareholder.

[46] *e.g.* 10082/82, (Dec.) July 4, 1983, 33 D.R. 247: order by House of Lords to pay £40 million to BP following frustration of contract for exploitation of Libyan oil concession; 11949/86, (Dec.) December 1, 1986, 51 D.R. 195: eviction of tenant following annulment of lease by landlord; 8588–9/79, n.42 above: redistribution of company shares. Though where State does intervene in legal relations of private individuals as regards property, the Commission stated that it must ensure the law does not create such inequality that a person is arbitrarily and unjustly deprived of property in favour of another, *i.e.* 13021/87, (Dec.) September 8, 1988, 57 D.R. 268.

Whether or not an applicant's property rights were determined fairly would generally fall to be examined under Art.6, para.1's procedural guarantees. Rights of property have long been been classified as falling "without doubt" within the scope of "civil rights" under Art.6, para.1.[47]

However, as the State is under a positive obligation to provide a judicial mechanism for settling effectively property disputes between private individuals and organisations, serious defects in the handling of such a dispute may raise issues under Art.1 of Protocol No.1 as well as Art.6.[48]

Cross-reference

Part IIA: Fair Trial, General Principles, Civil rights
Part IIA: Access to Court
Part IIB: Expropriation and confiscation
Part IIB: Housing and tenancy
Part IIB: Planning and use of property

---

[47] *Sporrong and Lonroth*, para.79, where the Court overruled the Commission's approach that there had been no determination since expropriation did not take place nor had there been any change in ownership.

[48] See *Sovtransavto Holding*, n.43 above, where the repeated annulation of decisions by the courts and varying interventions by the executive authorities in the proceedings concerning the lawfulness of share re-valuations disclosed violations of both provisions.

Reason for arrest and detention

Key provision:

Article 5, para.2 (right to be informed promptly in language understood of the   IIB–350
reasons for the arrest or detention).

Key case law:

X v UK, November 5, 1981, Series A, No.46; 4 E.H.R.R. 188; *Fox, Campbell and Hartley v UK*, August 30, 1990, Series A, No.182; *Van der Leer v Netherlands*, September 27, 1990, Series A, No.170, 12 E.H.R.R. 567; *Murray v UK*, October 28, 1994, Series A, No.300–A; 19 E.H.R.R. 193; *Conka v Belgium*, February 5, 2002, ECHR 2002–I.

1. General considerations

This is a safeguard against arbitrary arrest, requiring the person to be informed of   IIB–351
the grounds of arrest. This also provides an opportunity to challenge the
reasonableness of the suspicion and to use the remedy provided by Art.5, para.4 to
challenge the lawfulness of the detention.[1]

2. Scope of the guarantee

Article 5, para.2 applies not only to persons arrested under Art.5, para.1(c) despite the   IIB–352
apparent criminal law connotation of the words used although it may be subsumed, as
in *X v United Kingdom*, by a finding of a violation of Art.5, para.4.[2] In *Van der Leer v
Netherlands*, concerning the recall of of a mental health patient, the Court held that the
provision was to be interpreted autonomously as regards "arrested" and that it went
beyond criminal law measures.[3] It was closely linked to Art.5, para.4 which was not
limited in scope to arrest. Thus a failure to inform the applicant of the measures
against her disclosed a violation. It was not subsumed by a finding of a violation under
Art.5, para.4 for in this case the applicant, in voluntary residence at the hospital, was
not informed at all that she had been deprived of her liberty by a compulsory measure
and she should have been informed of this important change in her status, not merely
to enable her to challenge the lawfulness.

3. Nature and form of the information

The Court has not been rigorous as to what form the information should take,   IIB–353
though it should, at least, be in a language which the applicant understands.[4] The

---

[1] 8098/77, (Dec.) December 13, 1978, 16 D.R.1 11 and 34 D.R. 119. Art.5, para.2 is a weaker
guarantee than Art.6, para.3(a) which applies to preparation of the criminal trial.
[2] The Court found that it followed necessarily from the breach of Art.5, para.4 that to make effective use
of his right to challenge recall the applicant had to be promptly and adequately informed of the facts on
which the authorities relied: the issue was thus absorbed.
[3] paras 27–28.
[4] 11539/85, (Dec.) July 12, 1986, 48 D.R. 237, 242–243; 34573/97, (Dec.) May 21, 1998, where the

necessary information does not have to be given in writing or consist of a complete list of all the charges or disclose to the suspect all the information which might be available to the investigating judge.[5] It is not necessary for a person to be expressly informed since the Court has indicated that the surrounding circumstances of the arrest or its aftermath may be sufficient for the person to deduce the reasons.[6] As to how indirect the notification can be, the Commission and Court differed.

In *Fox, Campbell and Hartley v United Kingdom*, the Commission found a violation, since the applicants were not directly informed at the time of arrest that they were suspected, *inter alia*, of information gathering and courier work for IRA although they were questioned about particular activities. It considered that the elementary nature of the safeguard was such that it placed an obligation on the arresting authorities to provide a detainee with adequate information as to the reasons for the arrest as soon as was practicable. The Court did comment that being told on arrest that they were held as terrorists was not enough but found no violation since there was no ground to suppose that the reasons for the applicants' arrest were not brought to their attention during their interrogation within a matter of a few hours.

In *Murray v United Kingdom*, the Commission found a breach where the applicant on arrest was questioned about money and the USA which gave her only a vague indication, not sufficiently precise to enable her to understand why she had been arrested. The Court again differed, noting that from the reference to her brother it must have been apparent that she was being questioned about involvement in the purchase of arms for which her brother had been convicted and thus the reasons for arrest were sufficiently brought to her attention.

The degree of information will also depend on the kind of arrest or detention. In mere arrest for security check purposes unrelated to the existence of particular suspicions (*i.e.* an obligation under under Art.5, para.1(b)) it was sufficient if information was provided promptly as to the legal basis of the arrest and the nature of the check, namely, that they were to be fingerprinted, photographed, questioned and otherwise checked up on. Suspicion was not required under the relevant domestic order nor under Art.5, para.(1)(b) so it was compatible with Art.5 that the applicants were not told what suspicions were being held against them during the 45-hour period of detention.[7]

A lesser standard also applies to arrest with a view to extradition where the information given need not be so complete as in the case of arrest for the purpose of bringing someone to trial.[8]

English-speaking applicant should have been nonetheless aware from certain Italian phrases that extradition was being sought on charges of use of a false passport.

[5] 8098/77, (Dec.) December 13, 1978, 16 D.R. 11.

[6] *e.g. Kerr v UK*, 40451/98, (Dec.) December 7, 1999: a delay between arrest and charging did not raise any difficulty as it could be assumed that the applicant gained a reasonable idea of the suspicions against him during questioning a few hours after his arrest. See *Dikme v Turkey*, July 11, 2000, paras 54–57, where the applicant's obstructive conduct was apparently regarded as prolonging matters.

[7] *McVeigh v UK* 8022–25–27/77 Rep. March 18, 1981, 25 D.R.15.

[8] 10819/84, (Dec.) July 5, 1984, 38 D.R. 230 where an applicant informed that he was suspected of fraud and arrested for purpose of extradition to US; 23916/94, (Dec.) April 6, 1995, where a person was held for extradition, this did not involve the determination of a criminal charge so information given did not need to meet the requirements of Art.6, para.3: information from the judge that extradition was sought by US on charge of false billing was enough.

An applicant cannot claim any particular right to see the documents which initiated the investigation.[9] Nor does Art.5, para.2 not require the disclosure of the complete file, but must provide sufficient information to facilitate the pursuit of the remedy envisaged under Art.5, para.4.[10]

4. Promptly

The person must be informed at or soon after the time of arrest or be able to deduce the reasons from the questioning or circumstances within a few hours of arrest. In *Murray*, where the applicant was arrested at 7.00 and questioned from 8.20–9.35, this was sufficiently prompt. The Commission stated that no more than a few hours should elapse save in exceptional circumstances such as the serious incapacity of the arrested person to comprehend the reasons that might have been given. Thus, where an applicant was merely told that he was arrested under a particular provision and not questioned until next day, the Commission found that the alleged practical problems in assembling an interview team so late at night were not sufficient where the fundamental importance of the right to liberty was at stake.[11]

IIB–354

5. Access to legal representation or to contact family

Article 5, para.2 does not guarantee the right to call a lawyer.[12] Access to a lawyer is generally dealt with under Art.6 para.3(c) (see Pt IIA: Fair trial guarantees, Legal Representation in criminal proceedings) but as yet there is no automatic right to a solicitor from the first moment of arrest. Access to doctors and relatives were mentioned as elements in safeguards justifying derogation under Art.15 by the UK in respect of Art.5, para.3 concerning provisions allowing the detention of suspects for up to seven days without being brought before a judicial officer.[13] Inability of detained suspects to contact their wives in the *McVeigh v United Kingdom* case led to a finding of violation by the Commission of Art.8.[14]

IIB–355

Cross-reference

Part IIA: Information about the charge
Part IIB: Review of detention

---

[9] *e.g. Lamy v Belgium*, March 30, 1989, Series A, No.151, para.32, *i.e.* the allegedly tendentious report which had sparked off the judicial investigation: he had seen the arrest warrant and had an interview with the investigation judge.

[10] 9614/81 (Dec.) October 12, 1983, 34 D.R. 19, where a judge had removed certain documents from the case file to safeguard the investigation and the defence lawyers did not see them until a year later, the absence of the information did not hamper the exercise of an Art.5, para.4 remedy. In *Conka*, the Roma family were given sufficient information, with an interpreter, about the purpose of their arrest being to deport them to satisfy Art.5, para.2 though the circumstances, in particular the shortness of time before their expulsion, deprived them of a realistic possibility of applying to court for a Art.5, para.4 remedy (para.52).

[11] 12690/87, (Rep.) October 14, 1991, C.M. Resolution DH (95) 4 January 11, 1995.

[12] 8828/79, (Dec.) October 5, 1982, 30 D.R.93.

[13] *Brannigan and McBride v UK*, May 26, 1993, Series A, No.258–B, para.64.

[14] 8022–25–27/77, (Rep.) March 18, 1981, 25 D.R. 15.

Religion, thought and conscience

Key provision:

IIB–356   Article 9 (freedom of thought, conscience and religion).

Key case law:

Darby v Sweden, October 23, 1990, Series A, No.187; 13 E.H.R.R. 774; *Hoffman v Austria*, June 23, 1993, Series A, No.255–C; 17 E.H.R.R. 293; *Kokkinakis v Greece*, May 25, 1993, Series A, No.260–A; 17 E.H.R.R. 397; *Manoussakis v Greece*, September 26, 1996, R.J.D. 1996–IV, No.17; 23 E.H.R.R. 387; *Valsamis v Greece*, December 18, 1996, R.J.D. 1996–VI, No.4; 24 E.H.R.R. 294; *Kalaç v Turkey*, July 1, 1997, R.J.D., 1997–IV, No.41; 27 E.H.R.R. 552; *Larissis v Greece*, February 24, 1998, R.J.D. 1998–I, No.65; 27 E.H.R.R. 329; *Buscarini v San Marino*, February 18, 1999, ECHR 1999–I; 30 E.H.R.R. 208; *Serif v Greece*, December 14, 1999, ECHR 1999–IX; 31 E.H.R.R. 561; *Thlimmenos v Greece*, April 6, 2000, ECHR 2000–IV; 31 E.H.R.R. 411; *Cha'are Shalom Ve Tsedek v France*, June 27, 2000, ECHR 2000–VII; *Hasan and Chaush v Bulgaria*, October 26, 2000, ECHR 2000–XI; *Cyprus v Turkey*, May 10, 2001, ECHR 2001–IV; *Metropolitan Church of Bessarabia v Moldova*, December 13, 2001, ECHR 2001–XII.

1. General considerations

IIB–357   The relationship of churches and State has a troubled history in Europe. Where a State has a bias to a particular religion (for example, constitutional protection) there is potential for issues arising as regards the effect of this preference on other religious groups. It is questionable to what extent in multi-ethnic Europe one group can justifiably be given preferential treatment over another and what weight should be given to the history and traditions of the particular country. The arrival on the scene of other "religions" with differing cultural and social dimensions, poses special problems where practices conflict with expected ways of doing things.

Issues arise as to what may genuinely claim protection as a "religion" or matter of conscience; what may considered manifestations of those beliefs which require protection and what justifications exist for interfering with beliefs and practices. There are also questions as to what extent the State is under a positive obligation to protect the manifestation of religious beliefs from others.

2. Religion, thought and conscience

IIB–358   There has been little detailed discussion about the nature of the beliefs or principles which fall within the scope of these concepts. It is a sensitive area, what one person holds as sacred appearing absurd or anathema to another. The Commission showed a tendency to rely on other methods of rejecting cases based on the more controversial beliefs, using the justified exceptions under Art.9, para.2 and the possibility of finding that a particular claimed interference or restriction did not in reality prevent the manifestation of a particular religion, thought or belief.

For the Commission, it covered "the sphere of private, personal beliefs", religious creeds or the *"forum internum"*.[1] The Court emphasises its importance as a foundation of "democratic society and as part of the identity of believers and that their conception of belief is a precious asset to atheists, agnostics and the unconcerned.[2] The freedom guaranteed entails, *inter alia*, the freedom to hold or not to hold religious beliefs and to practise or not to practise a religion.[3]

More concretely, the Commission was prepared to assume that Veganism was a belief falling within Art.9[4]; pacifism was accepted as a philosophy involving the commitment in theory and practice to the securing of political and other objectives without the resort to the threat or use of force[5] Scientology was accepted without discussion[6]; Druidism was left open[7]; the Krishna consciousness movement was accepted without argument.[8] In the cases before the Court, Jehovah's Witnesses qualified.[9]

Article 9 does not cover mere "idealistic activities", for example the activities of a German legal association which gave advice to prisoners.[10] It also did not cover the stance taken by IRA prisoners with regard to "special category status"[11] or a lawyer's personal convictions which led him to refuse to carry out legal aid duty at police stations.[12] The Commission added that there is no right as such under Art.9 to "conscientious objection".[13]

3. Victim status

Individuals, churches and associations with religious and philosophical objects are capable of exercising Art.9 rights.[14] However a legal person cannot exercise freedom of conscience[15] and a corporate profitmaking body cannot rely on Art.9 rights.[16]

IIB–359

---

[1] *e.g.* 10358/83, (Dec.) December 15, 1983, 37 D.R. 142; "primarily" added in 11308/84, (Dec.) March 13, 1986, 46 D.R. 200.

[2] *Kokkinakis*, para.31.

[3] *Buscarini*, para.34.

[4] 18187/91, (Dec.) February 10, 1993.

[5] 7050/75, (Rep.) October 12, 1978, 19 D.R. 5.

[6] 7805/77, (Dec.) May 5, 1979, 16 D.R. 68.

[7] 12587/86, (Dec.) July 14, 1987, 53 D.R. 241: assuming Druidism was a religion, the closing of Stonehenge was a justified interference.

[8] 20490/92, (Dec.) March 8, 1994, 76–A D.R. 90.

[9] *e.g. Kokkinakis*.

[10] 11358/83, n.1 above.

[11] Nor was the wearing of non-prison uniform the manifestation of a belief under Art.9—8317/78, (Dec.) May 15, 1980, 20 D.R. 44.

[12] 37489/97, (Dec.) October 21, 1998.

[13] *e.g.* 7705/76, (Dec.) July 5, 1977, 9 D.R. 196: the Commission, unsympathetically noting the burden of military service to be shared equitably between citizens, found it legitimate for States to restrict exemptions (military or substituted) and acceptable under Art.14 together with Art.9 for total exemption to be applied only to members of religions whose position was well known *e.g.* Jehovahs Witnesses. Other persons, not so affiliated, had to suffer to avoid the possibility of shirkers!—10410/83 (Dec.) October 11, 1984, 40 D.R. 40.

[14] 7805/77, (Dec.) May 5, 1979, 16 D.R. 68; 8118/77, (Dec.) March 19, 1981, 25 D.R. 105; 12587/86, (Dec.) July 14, 1987, 53 D.R. 241; *Cha'are Shalom*, para.72, an ecclesiastical or religious body, such as a Jewish association promoting kosher rules, could exercise on behalf of its adherents the rights guaranteed by Art.9; *Metropolitan Church of Bessarabia*, para.101.

[15] 11921/86, (Dec.) October 12, 1988, 57 D.R. 81.

[16] 7865/77, (Dec.) February 27, 1979, 16 D.R. 85.

4. Manifestation and practice

IIB–360   Religion and beliefs pertaining especially to the inner sphere, the Commission has emphasised that the term "practice" as employed by Art.9, para.1 does not cover each act which is motivated or influenced by a religion or belief. There is a distinction between "manifestation" and motivation. There is also the idea that the act must directly express the belief. It protects acts intimately linked to beliefs or creeds such as acts of worship and devotion which are the aspects of the practice of a religion or belief in a generally recognised form.[17]

For example, the distribution of leaflets to soldiers may have been motivated by an applicant's pacifist ideals but was not a manifestation of her beliefs in the sense recognised by the Commission: rather it was specifically urging soldiers not to go to Northern Ireland.[18] Marriage, though considered desirable for muslims, cannot be regarded as a form of expression, thought or religion.[19] Non-payment of taxes by Quakers to prevent contribution to arms is not covered[20] nor the wish to have one's ashes scattered on one's own land,[21] or to have one's religion noted on an official identity card.[22]

Freedom to manifest one's religion has been found to include the right to try and convince one's neighbour[23]; kosher diet[24] and kosher slaughtering[25]; and it has been accepted that a high caste Sikh would transgress if he undertook such work as cleaning floors.[26]

Protection for organisation of religious communities may also be derived from Art.9, interpreted in light of Art.11 which safeguards associative life against unjustified State interference. Thus, in *Hasan and Chaush v Bulgaria*, the Court rejected the Government's argument that the alleged forced replacement of the leadership of the muslim community had no bearing on the rights of the applicants to manifest their religion personally.[27]

5. Interferences with Art.9 rights

IIB–361   Measures preventing a person from manifesting his belief in a manner recognised under Art.9 or penalising him for doing so will generally constitute a limitation requiring justification under the second paragraph, as for example, criminal

---

[17] *e.g.* 10358/83 and 11308/84, n.1 above.

[18] 7050/75, n.5 above; also 11567–8/85, (Dec.) July 6, 1987, 53 D.R. 150.

[19] *e.g.* 11579/85, (Dec.) July 7, 1986, 48 D.R. 253 where a muslim claimed an interference with his religion as English law prevented marriage to a 14–year-old girl. Marriage is governed by Art.12, which allows European notions of marriage, as provided in national laws, to prevail.

[20] 10358/83, (Dec.) December 15, 1983, 37 D.R. 132.

[21] 8741/79, (Dec.) March 10, 1981, 24 D.R. 137.

[22] 1988/02, 1997/02 and 1977/02, (Dec.) December 12, 2002.

[23] *Kokkinakis*, where a Jehovah's Witness had been convicted for proselytism (*e.g.* gaining entry to an orthodox christian's house to persuade her to convert) the Court acknowledged that where several religions co-existed some restrictions on this freedom might be necessary to reconcile their interests.

[24] 13669/88, (Dec.) March 7, 1990, 65 D.R. 245.

[25] *Cha'are Shalom*, para.74.

[26] 8231/78, (Dec.) March 6, 1982, 28 D.R. 5.

[27] paras 60–65—the first applicant was the Chief Mufti displaced by his state-supported rival and the second applicant a practising muslim. See also *Canea Catholic Church v Greece*, December 16, 1997, R.J.D. 1997–VIII: a breach of Art.14 in conjunction with Art.6 due to the inability of the church to take proceedings to defend its civil rights: no separate issue arose under Art.9.

sanctions imposed on the use of premises as a place of worship[28] or, as in *Kokkinakis*, where the Jehovah's Witness applicant was convicted for proselytising.[29] The refusal of the State to give official recognition to a church with the consequence that its priests cannot officiate or members meet to practise their religion was found to constitute an interference in *Metropolitan Church of Bessarabia v Moldova*, while severe restrictions on movement, with the consequence of curtailing the ability of enclaved Greek Cypriots in Northern Cyprus from attending places of worship outside their villages was found to infringe Art.9.[30] Conversely, the obligation to make a religious declaration or to participate in religious activities may constitute an interference.[31]

However, where an applicant's beliefs conflict with contractual and employment conditions, the Convention organs have adopted an approach of finding that the resulting dismissal does not necessarily interfere with the manifestation of religion. The alleged lack of protection of an applicant's beliefs, required to work on Sundays by her employer, did not disclose an interference with her beliefs since she was not dismissed for her beliefs but for failing to work certain hours.[32] While in *Kalaç v Turkey*, compulsory retirement of a military judge for his fundamentalist beliefs was not an interference with his freedom of religion but a disciplinary matter, the Court noting that he had joined the army knowing of the restrictions imposed on its members. Similarly, where religious beliefs clash with professional obligations, the applicant cannot expect to give precedence to the former, as where two Catholic pharmacists were convicted for their refusal to sell contraceptives, which were legal and could only be supplied on medical prescription from a pharmacy.[33]

Where a restriction is not shown in fact to prevent a particular manifestion of belief, no interference with Art.9 rights may arise, as in *Cha'are Shalom Ve Tsedek v France* where the refusal to licence the applicant Jewish association to carry out its form of ritual slaughter had not been shown to prevent its members from obtaining 'glatt' meat (*i.e.* from other sources).[34]

Requirements to act in a particular way will also not necessarily constitute an interference with Art.9 rights notwithstanding the person's objection to them on grounds of principle.

In *Valsamis v Greece*, where a child Jehovah's Witness was suspended from school for failure to participate with her school in a procession on a Greek national day, the Court noted that she had been exempted from religious education and the Orthodox mass, and considered that the obligation to take part in the school parade was not such as to either offend her parents' religious convictions under Art.2 of Protocol No.1 or amount to an interference with her right to freedom of religion. Although

---

[28] *Manoussakis.*

[29] Also *Larissis*, para.38; *Serif*, where the applicant was convicted for usurping the functions of a minister of religion (where he had assumed the position of mufti on election by the mosque congregation in opposition to the State-appointed mufti).

[30] *Cyprus v Turkey*, paras 244–6.

[31] *e.g. Buscarini*, where elected representatives were required to swear allegiance to the Gospels in order to take up their seats.

[32] Also 29107/95, (Dec.) April 9, 1997 89–A D.R. 104, citing 24949/94, (Dec.) December 3, 1996 where the applicant (member of the Seventh Day Adventists Church which forbade work after sunset on Friday) was dismissed from the Finnish State Railways for failing to respect working hour: this was not a dismissal for his beliefs either.

[33] *Pichon and Sajous v France*, 49853/99, (Dec.) October 2, 2001, ECHR 2001–X.

[34] See however the strong dissenting minority who saw no reasonable or objective justification for treating the applicant association differently from the mainstream Jewish body, which had been given by the State exclusive slaughtering rights, contrary to the notion of pluralism.

the applicants objected to participation on the grounds of their pacifist beliefs, the Court considered that there was nothing in the purpose or arrangements of the parade to offend them to an extent forbidden by the Convention provisions. Its own view was that the national day, which the Government stated commemorated Greece's attachment to democracy, liberty and human rights, served both pacifist objectives and the public interest and a military presence at some of the parades did not alter their nature.[35] This case seems to show that the offensiveness of particular measures to religious beliefs must meet a certain threshold of seriousness.

Whether the requirement imposed on a non-church adherent to pay a church tax constitutes an interference with rights under Art.9 will depend on the circumstances. It was compatible with freedom of religion if a person could avoid the tax by leaving the church.[36] In *Darby v Sweden*, where the applicant, a non-resident who worked in Sweden, had no possibility of exemption, the Commission considered that though the existence of a State Church system could not in itself be considered to breach Art.9, there there had to be safeguards that no-one be forced to enter or be prohibited from leaving. The Court commented that Art.9 protected everyone from being compelled to be involved in religious activities without being a member of the religious community concerned and thus the payment of a tax to a church for its religious activities could in certain circumstances be seen as such involvement. It considered however that the particular case disclosed primarily a discrimination problem in payment of taxes between residents and non-residents which was not founded on objective or reasonable justification. In a later case, the requirement of a non-church member to pay a portion of the tax to the Church of Sweden did not interfere with his freedom of religion since it was a contribution to the non-religious activities of the Church and its fulfilment of its civil responsibilities, such as burials.[37]

The requirement for elected representatives to take an oath on the Gospels was not regarded as necessary in *Buscarini v San Marino* as making the exercise of a mandate intended to represent different views of society within Parliament subject to a prior declaration of commitment to a particular set of beliefs was essentially incompatible with the democratic and pluralistic ethos of Art.9 and the Convention as a whole. On the other hand, in *McGuinness v United Kingdom*, where the applicant, an elected MP, was unable to use parliamentary facilities due to his refusal to take the oath of allegiance to the Queen, the Court considered that he was not thereby required to afffirm allegiance to any religion on pain of taking up his seat or obliged to abandon his republican convictions.[38]

6. Justified limitations

IIB–362   Restrictions on manifestations of belief or practice, where in conformity with the requirements of lawfulness,[39] may be justified *inter alia* on grounds of health and public safety (*e.g.* motorcycle helmets), security (access to certain publications where

---

[35] Dissenters in the Commission and Court considered that the applicants' perception of the significance of the parade to their own beliefs should be accepted unless obviously ill-founded or unreasonable, finding no need for the child's participation in a public event of this kind.

[36] 10358/83, (Dec.) December 15, 1983, 37 D.R. 142.

[37] *Bruno v Sweden*, 32196/96, (Dec.) August 28, 2001.

[38] 39511/98, (Dec.) June 8, 1999, ECHR 1999–V.

[39] "Prescribed by law": *e.g. Hasan and Chaush*, paras 85–89, where the chief mufti was removed, the law was insufficiently defined as to the circumstances in which disputed leadership could be resolved and without any procedural safeguards before an independent body concerning the exercise of the executive discretion in that regard). See Part 1C: "Convention Principles and Approach".

the applicant is in prison) or where there is a clearly perceived harm or threat to others.[40] The factors of necessity, pressing social need and proportionality apply.

Where an applicant Krishna society was subject to enforcement notices relating to the increased influx of pilgrims to the manor used as a religious centre, the Commission found the factor of their religious freedom was sufficiently taken into account by the planning authorities despite an unfortunate letter from the planning authorities referring to the religious factor not being "relevant" to the decision. However the Commission interpreted this in the positive sense that the decision was taken on proper planning grounds and not on the basis of objection to the religious activities.[41] Druids who are barred access to sites in or around Stonehenge have also found their complaints have been rejected as justified in the interests of protection of a historical site as well for public safety and the prevention of crime and disorder.[42] The refusal to dispense a child of Seventh Day Adventists from attending school on Saturday mornings was found to be justified in order to safeguard the coherence of the teaching programme as a whole and to ensure the education of the child concerned.[43]

Where a Jehovah's Witness was convicted for proselytism, the Court considered that a distinction had to be drawn between bearing witness and proseyltism by improper means (force, offering of material or social advantages by inducement, improper pressure on persons in distress or need). Since the liability of the applicant was established without any reference to whether he used improper means, but on the basis of a general prohibition and there was no indication of improper means on the facts,[44] the conviction was not justified by a pressing social need. In *Larissis v Greece* the Court found that the convictions of air force officers, members of the Pentecostal Church, for proselytising three airmen were justified to protect them from the risk of undue pressure, but not justified as regarded their proselytisation of civilians outside the hierarchical military structure. The imposition of criminal sanctions on Jehovah's Witnesses for using premises as a place of worship without authorisation was disproportionate where the framework of law and practice placed prohibitive conditions on the practice of religious non-orthodox movements.[45] The Court found that the relative leniency of the penalty immaterial. Exclusion of a Jehovah's Witness from appointment as a chartered accountant due to his conviction for refusal to wear a military uniform was found in *Thlimmenos v Greece* to be a disproportionate punishment.[46]

---

[40] *Manoussakis*, para.40—States are entitled to take steps to verify whether a movement, ostensibly for religious aims, carries on activities which are harmful to the the population. This did not apply to Jehovah's Witnesses, a "known religion".

[41] 20490/92, n.8 above.

[42] Also *Johannische Kirche and Peters v Germany*, 41754/98, (Dec.) July 10, 2001, ECHR 2001–VIII, where the refusal of permission to the church to use its land for a cemetery on planning grounds was justified under Art.9, para.2.

[43] *Casimiro and Ferreira v Luxembourg*, 44888/98, (Dec.) April 27, 1999, where the Court noted that special dispensation for particular religious events was permitted and found the right to education had to prevail in the circumstances against religious preferences.

[44] *Kokkinakis*—the Court appears to have accepted the applicant's arguments that the woman concerned was an experienced adult with intellectual abilities who was not unduly infuenced by the applicant's actions in calling at her door.

[45] *e.g.* the Minister was not subject to any requirement to give a decision in a particular time (the applicants' request was still pending without any explanation) and had wide discretion; the Orthodox church also played a role in consenting to authorisation being given.

[46] The Court found a breach of Art.14 in conjunction with Art.9.

While States have a legitimate interest in preventing tension in religious communities and in taking measures to protect those whose legal relationships can be affected by the acts of religious ministers (where such have legal and administrative powers to conduct marriages for example), the Court emphasised that their interventions should be guided by the principle of pluralism and aimed to ensure competing groups tolerated each other rather than to seek to eliminate one or the other and that in its relations with diverse religions and faiths, the State should remain neutral and impartial.[47] Nor does the State have to take measures to ensure that religious communities are brought under unified leadership.[48]

7. State obligation to protect religion from others

IIB–363   Positive obligations may arguably arise requiring the State to take steps to protect the exercise of religious freedom from others. However it would appear that this will only arise where the threat is of a particular severity. While in another context the Commission found the law of blasphemy an acceptable means of protecting the religious feelings of offended Christians,[49] it rejected complaints of an applicant muslim that the inability to prosecute blasphemous attacks on the Islamic faith was contrary to Art.9 and that it disclosed discrimination contrary to Art.14 as such protection was only available to Christians.[50] The Commission, in very brief reasoning, considered that the Government could not be said to have interfered in the applicant's right to manifest his beliefs and that Art.9 did not guarantee a right to bring proceedings against publishers of works that offended the sensitivities of any individual or group. Since this was found to render the complaint outside the scope of Art.9 (incompatible *ratione materiae*), the discrimination complaint was rejected on the same basis, without the necessity for finding any objective and reasonable justification in favouring the religious feelings of one group, albeit the historically dominant one.

Cross-reference

Part IIB: Army
Part IIB: Discrimination
Part IIB: Marriage and the right to found a family
Part IIB: Prisoner's rights

---

[47] *Serif*—the Court found that the conviction of the rival mufti was not justified since there had been no proof that the existence of two religious leaders was causing disturbances or that the non-officially appointed one had tried to exercise legal or administrative functions; *Metropolitan Church of Bessarabia*, paras 116 and 123, where the Government lacked neutrality and impartiality in refusing to give recognition to the applicant church without approval from the Moldovan Church which regarded it as schismatic.

[48] *Hasan and Chaush*, para.78, where the State intervened to appoint one of two rivals in the muslim religious community. The Court did not however rule on necessity or proportionality as the measure was not "prescibed by law".

[49] 8710/79, May 7, 1982, 28 D.R. 77 where the applicants were convicted in a private prosecution of the criminal offence of blasphemy for publication of a poem ascribing to Christ promiscuous homosexual practices, the Commission found the conviction pursued the legitimate aim of protecting the rights of others, namely the private prosecutor, not to be offended in religious feeling.

[50] 17439/90 (Dec.) March 5, 1991, concerning Salman Rushdie's "Satanic Verses".

Remedies

Key provision:

Article 13 (effective remedy before a national authority).

Key case law:

Delcourt v Belgium, January 17, 1970, Series A, No.11; 1 E.H.R.R. 355; *Klass v Germany*, September 6, 1978, Series A, No.28; 2 E.H.R.R. 214; *Silver v UK*, March 25, 1983, Series A, No.61; 5 E.H.R.R 347; *Abdulaziz v UK*, May 28, 1985, Series A, No.94; 7 E.H.R.R. 471; *James v UK*, May 11, 1984, Series A, No.98; 8 E.H.R.R. 123; *Lithgow v UK*, July 8, 1986, Series A, No.102; 8 E.H.R.R 329; *Leander v Sweden*, March 26, 1987, Series A, No.116; 9 E.H.R.R. 433; *Boyle and Rice v UK*, March 27, 1988, Series A, No.131; 10 E.H.R.R 425; *Kamasinski v Austria*, December 19, 1989, Series A, No.168; 13 E.H.R.R. 36; *Powell and Rayner v UK*, February 21, 1990, Series A, No.172; 12 E.H.R.R. 355; *Vereinigung Demokratischer Soldaten Österreichs v Austria*, December 19, 1994, Series A, No.302; 20 E.H.R.R. 56; *Chahal v UK*, November 15, 1996, R.J.D. 1996–V, 23 E.H.R.R. 413; *Aksoy v Turkey*, December 18, 1996, R.J.D. 1996–VI, No.26; 23 E.H.R.R. 553; *Valsamis v Greece*, December 18, 1996, R.J.D. 1996–VI, No.26; 24 E.H.R.R. 294; *D v UK*, May 2, 1997, R.J.D. 1997–III, No.37; 24 E.H.R.R. 423; *Halford v UK*, June 25, 1997, R.J.D. 1997–III, No.39; 24 E.H.R.R. 523; *Aydin v Turkey*, September 25, 1997, R.J.D. 1997–VI, No.50; 25 E.H.R.R. 251; *Kaya v Turkey*, February 19, 1998, R.J.D. 1998–I, No.65; 28 E.H.R.R. 1; *Smith and Grady v UK*, September 27, 1999, ECHR 1999–V;29 E.H.R.R. 493; *Z v UK*, May 10, 2001, ECHR 2000–V; *Kudla v Poland*, October 26, 2000, ECHR 2000–XI; *Hatton v UK*, July 8, 2003, ECHR 2003–VIII.

1. General considerations

Taking the principal consideration that it is the obligation first and foremost of Contracting States to secure to every individual their rights and freedoms,[1] Art.13 is the countervailing requirement that an individual has the opportunity to obtain redress for violations in the domestic system.[2] If a Contracting State fulfills this requirement, the Court's role will diminish. It may be said that observance of this provision is the most crucial to the effective protection of rights in Contracting States. It is however a technical and procedural provision and its role has been whittled away by interpretations and arguably not given its proper prominence.[3]

---

[1] Art.1.

[2] See, *e.g. Boyle and Rice*, (Rep.), para.73, citing *Handyside v UK*, December 7, 1976, Series A, No.24; 1 E.H.R.R. 737; para.48.

[3] There is perhaps a suspicion that the Convention organs were, and are, seduced by the more interesting questions arising under the substantive provisions (possibly trespassing on the role of the domestic authorities when involving themselves in rather detailed factual assessments) whereas they should have been encouraging domestic bodies to carry out this function.

Applicants are also sometimes reticent in raising Art.13 complaints, perhaps preferring to concentrate on what they see as the core substantives issues.[4]

2. Limitation to "arguable claims" of violations

IIB–366   Article 13 requires a remedy for everyone whose rights under the Convention have been violated. Thus the provision is linked to breaches of substantive rights. No breach of Art.13 is possible in isolation.

The words of the provision appear to require that a person must establish an actual breach of a substantive provision. The Court thought that this was unduly restrictive. Until a court or other body has investigated a claim, it will not necessarily be apparent whether there has been an unjustifiable interference with a right. Accordingly, it held that a remedy must be guaranteed to anyone who "claims" that his rights have been violated.[5] This was translated by the Court in *Silver* into the notion that a person with an "arguable claim" of being a victim of a violation of the rights in the Convention should be able to seek a remedy.[6]

The Commission, which was setting a high standard for the manifestly ill-founded inadmissibility criterion, applied the approach that Art.13 could be breached even if the substantive complaint was inadmissible, as there could still in the appropriate circumstances be an arguable claim.[7] The Court in *Boyle and Rice v United Kingdom* noted the Commission delegate's explanation that to be arguable a claim "only needs raise a Convention issue that merits further examination" and that a conclusion that a claim was manifestly ill-founded could be reached after considerable oral and written argument. It preferred its own view in *Airey v Ireland* that a finding of manifestly ill-founded meant that there was not even a *prima facie* case against the respondent State.[8] It held, bluntly, that on the ordinary meaning of the words it was difficult to conceive that a claim that was manifestly ill-founded could nevertheless be arguable. It declined to give an abstract definition of arguability, each case to be determined in the light of the particular facts and issues. It later commented, in face of Commission intransigence in *Powell and Rayner v the United Kingdom*, that different standards between the manifestly ill-founded inadmissibility criterion (now Art.35, para.1) and Art.13 would undermine the coherence of the system of enforcement since a State could not be required to make available a remedy at national level for a grievance which was so weak as not to warrant examination on its merits on the international. This approach had the practical effect of lowering of the threshold of admissibility on the manifestly ill-founded ground and of increasing the number of admissible cases.

Since then, it is also very rare to find a violation of Art.13 without the presence of a violation of a substantive provision,[9] and not at all without an admissible

---

[4] *e.g.* in *McCann v UK*, September 27, 1995, Series A, No.324, where there was an Art.2 violation but no complaint raised under Arts 6 or 13 by the relatives of the dead terrorists, who had been unable to pursue civil proceedings due to the nature of the case.
[5] *Klass*, para.64.
[6] para.113.
[7] *e.g. Boyle and Rice*, (Rep.), where the Commission had rejected as manifestly ill-founded Art.8 complaints but declared admissible the complaints about the lack of effective remedies for these complaints.
[8] October 9, 1979, Series A, No.32, para.18.
[9] *e.g. Hatton v UK*: no violation on Art.8 but a lack of effective remedy for an arguable claim under Art.13.

complaint. However, conversely, the fact that a complaint was declared admissible by the Convention organs did not require a finding of an arguable claim for Art.13. This still occurs where a number of complaints under different provisions are declared admissible together, the Court's practice being not to split issues based on the same facts, even if some complaints are clearly more substantial than others.[10]

3. Remedies for non-conformity of statute or law

The Commission took the view that Art.13 could not be interpreted as requiring a means by which the conformity of statute with the Convention can be examined at domestic law.[11] The Court endorsed this approach in *James v United Kingdom*.[12] To hold otherwise would be tantamount to requiring incorporation of the Convention in domestic law and this could not, in the Court's view, be imposed *de facto* by the Convention organs. In any event, it considered that if the substantive laws were found, as in *James*, to conform with Art.1 of Protocol No.1, it would be sufficient for the purposes of Art.13 that the aggrieved property owner could go to the courts to secure compliance with the relevant laws.[13] The new Court continues to apply this approach, where the applicant's complaints are directed against statutory provisions[14] or the state of domestic law.[15]

IIB–367

In relation to secondary legislation, the Commission found that the immigration rules in issue in *Abdulaziz v United Kingdom* did not attract the immunity of legislation; and in *Boyle and Rice* that the immunity did not apply to the prison rules, standing orders and administrative circulars, basing itself on the application of Art.13 in the *Silver* case to prison norms.[16] The Court agreed in *Abdulaziz*, finding that the applicants were victims of norms that were incompatible with the Convention and that there was no effective remedy as required by Art.13.

---

[10] *e.g. Valsamis*, where a girl Jehovah's Witness was suspended from school, the application was principally concerned complaints under Arts 9 and 2 of Protocol No.1 but the Art.3 complaint was also declared admissible: on the merits, arguable claims arose under the first two provisions but none under Art.3; *Halford v UK*, where complaints under Art.8 were admissible for claims of tapping of office and home phone, arguable claims under Art.13 arose in respect of the former alone.

[11] See *Young, James and Webster v UK*, (Rep.) December 14, 1979, interpreting the wording of Art.13 "notwithstanding that the violation has been committed by persons acting in an official capacity" as indicating that it was not meant to cover legislation.

[12] Referring to a dictum in *Swedish Engine Drivers' Union* case, February 6, 1976, Series A, No.20, para.50 and *Ireland v UK*, January 18, 1978, Series A, No.25; also *Lithgow*, para.206; *Observer and Guardian v UK*, para.76.

[13] See also concurring opinions in *James*, which added that this restrictive interpretation was supported by the existing legislation of Contracting States since it was improbable that the drafters intended to cover statute as few states had provision for constitutional challenge by individuals of legislation, and the dissenters, who saw see no reason to exempt acts of the legislature from Art.13 and considered that the approach of the Court in *Silver* and *Abdulaziz* should be maintained.

[14] *A v UK*, December 17, 2002, ECHR 2002–X, para.112.

[15] *Christine Goodwin v UK*, July 11, 2002, ECHR 2002–VI, para.113; *Hatton*, para.138, with a reference also to Art.13 not allowing a challenge to a general policy as such—the Court nonetheless found a violation of Art.13 due to the limited scope of judicial review proceedings concerning lawfulness of the scheme applicable to nightflying at Heathrow. Sir Brian Kerr, dissenting as *ad hoc* judge, considered that no violation arose as the applicants' complaints concerned the state of domestic law.

[16] *Boyle and Rice*, (Rep.), para.78; *Silver*, paras 124–127.

The approach was extended by the Commission in *Johnston v Ireland* where it held that Art.13 does not guarantee an effective remedy in respect of a constitutional provision.[17]

4. Relationship with procedural guarantees under Art.6 (fair trial) and Art.5 (liberty)

IIB–368 Where an alleged violation is alleged in respect of a court's decision, Art.13 does not require appeal to a higher court, having regard to the approach that Art.6 does not require courts of appeal to be set up.[18] Where the highest national court is alleged to have breached the Convention, the application of Art.13 is subject to a similar implied limitation.[19] Presumably, where the court proceedings are themselves in compliance with the requirements of Art.6, this is sufficient for the purposes of the Convention.

Where the more specific guarantees of Art.6 apply, Art.13 as the more general provision does not apply, its requirements being less strict and accordingly absorbed by Art.6 which is the *lex specialis*.[20] Thus where proceedings falling within the scope of Art.6 are involved, there is, in general, no possibility of issues arising under Art.13, whether or not there is a violation of Art.6.[21] The exception to this so far concerns complaints about length of proceedings under Art.6. In *Kudla v Poland*, the Court rejected the Government's argument that Art.13 was never applicable where the alleged violation had taken place in judicial proceedings. It considered that the application of Art.13 to complaints of excessive delay in court proceedings would fulfil the purpose of ensuring that individuals could obtain relief at a national level and therefore reinforce the safeguards of Art.6, para.1, rather than being absorbed by it. As the remedy was only required in respect of delay, this would not impose a right of appeal on the merits of the decision. It also rejected the argument that imposing the obligation to provide a remedy would add to the already existing delays since experience showed that it was not impossible to create such remedies and operate them effectively.[22] As regarded the type of remedy, there is the alternative of preventing the alleged violation or its continuation by providing for expedition or of providing adequate redress for past delays, such as compensation.[23]

---

[17] (Rep.), Series A, No.112, para.151: the complaint was dropped by the applicants before the Court.

[18] *Delcourt*, para.25; also 13135/87, (Dec.) July 4, 1988, 56 D.R. 268: where applicants could not require appeal to a higher court from the Land Tribunal's allegedly derisory compensation assessment.

[19] *e.g. Leander v Sweden*, (Rep.), May 17, 1985 (Art.13 not normally grant a further remedy against the decisions by the highest national court); 14739/89, (Dec.), May 9, 1989, 60 D.R. 296, no right to review by a higher court in criminal matters; *Pizzetti v Italy*, Series A, No.257–C, (Rep.) December 10, 1991, para.41: the Convention did not guarantee the right to a second level of jurisdiction and provisions of the Convention could not be held to oblige States to set up bodies to exercise supervision over judicial bodies.

[20] *e.g.* in *Kamasinki*, para.110; *W v UK*, July 8, 1987, Series A, No.121, para.86.

[21] *e.g.* only where there is a criminal charge or civil right is Art.13 superceded by Art.6 which is more stringent—8588/79, etc. (Dec.) December 12, 1983, 38 D.R. 18.

[22] *e.g. Gonzalez Marin v Spain*, 39521/98, (Dec.) October 5, 1999, ECHR 1999–VII, which rejected a length complaint length for non-exhaustion where the applicant had not sought statutory compensation for delay; *Tome Mota v Portugal*, 32082/96, (Dec.) December 2, 1999, where the New Code of Criminal Procedure had provided a legal remedy to end or expedite criminal proceedings; *Mifsud v France*, 61166/00, (Dec.) September 11, 2000, ECHR 2000– VIII: Art.L. 781–I (Code of Judicial Organisation) provided compensation for delays.

[23] *Kudla*, para.158. Remedies ineffective in, *e.g. Hartmann v Czech Republic*, July 10, 2003; *Doran v Ireland*,

Article 5, para.4 (review of the lawfulness of detention) is also *lex specialis* in the area covered by it.[24]

5. No separate issue: procedural rights contained in substantive provisions

Not infrequently, where the violation under a substantive provision involves findings **IIB–369** of lack of procedural safeguards, the Convention organs have found that no separate issues arise under Art.13. For example, in *Hokkanen v Finland*,[25] no separate issue was found under Art.13 since the complaints amounted in substance to those already dealt with under Arts 6 and 8 in regard to length of custody and child access proceedings and the non-enforcement of custody rights. However, in *Kaya v Turkey*, the Court held that its findings under Art.2 as regarded the procedural deficiencies of the forensic examination and. investigation into a death did not exclude a further finding of a breach of Art.13, the requirements of which were broader, including the availability of compensation where appropriate. In *Ergi v Turkey*, where the Commission had found a violation of the Art.2 procedural obligation to carry out an effective investigation and no separate issue left under Art.13, the Court found a violation of both, considering that a failure to carry out an effective investigation undermined the exercise of any remedies available under Turkish law.[26] Though there have also been cases where the Court has found a procedural violation under Art.3 regarding an inadequate investigation,[27] there are some indications that it may be more appropriate to consider this matter under Art.13 alone.[28]

6. Effectiveness

Where an individual has an arguable claim that he is the victim of a violation of the **IIB–370** rights set forth in the Convention he should have a remedy before a national authority which has the power both to decide his claim and if appropriate to give redress.[29] An absence of any possibility to seek relief at national level will disclose a violation.[30]

A remedy must also be effective in practice as well as in law.[31] However, the fact that an application to a court fails is not sufficient to indicate that the remedy was

July 31, 2003, where the constitutional remedy had not been shown to be sufficiently swift and no precedents of compensation existed; *Konti-Arvanti v Greece*, April 10, 2003, the possibility of suing in tort a tardy expert did not offer redress for a length problem; *Kangasluoma v Finland*, January 20, 2004, where mere delay was not a ground for compensation.

[24] *e.g. Chahal v UK.*

[25] September 23, 1994, Series A, No.299–A.

[26] *Ergi v Turkey*, July 28, 1998, R.J.D. 1998–IV, No.81, para.98.

[27] *Labita v Italy*, April 6, 2000, ECHR 2000–IV, paras 130–136 (procedural breach of Art.3); *Assenov v Bulgaria*, October 28, 1998, R.J.D. 1998–VIII, No.96 (procedural breach of Arts 3 and 13 on same basis).

[28] *Ilhan v Turkey*, (GC) June 27, 2000, ECHR 2000–VII, paras 89–93; dissenting opinion of Sir Nicolas Bratza in *Kuznetsov v Ukraine*, April 29, 2003.

[29] *Silver*, para.113; *Klass*, para.64.

[30] *e.g. Halford* (no remedy against telephone tapping of office phones); *Valsamis* (no remedy to challenge the requirement of Jehovah's witness pupils to participate in parades).

[31] *e.g.* not hindered by acts or omissions of the authorities, as in *Kaya*, para.106; *Ilhan*, n.28 above, para.97; *Iatridis v Greece*, March 25, 1999, ECHR 1999–II, where the applicant obtained a court order in his favour but the Minister of Finance refused to comply.

ineffective.[32] Where settled case law indicates that a person has no standing to lodge a complaint, the possibility to seek a review by the courts will not constitute an effective remedy.[33] An inability by a court to address the core elements of the alleged violation may also render the procedure ineffective, as in *Smith and Grady v United Kingdom*, where the courts' examination on judicial review of the Ministry of Defence policy on homosexuals in the army could only consider irrationality, to which a high threshold applied, and could not consider whether the interference with the applicants' rights was justified by a pressing social need and was proportionate, the principles at the heart of the Court's analysis under Art.8. The scope of review was also found inadequate in *Hatton v United Kingdom* where the courts were unable, on judicial review application, to examine whether the night flying scheme at Heathrow was a justified limitation on the private and family life rights of those living in the vicinity.

It does not necessarily have to be a judicial remedy although the powers and procedural guarantees are relevant in determining whether the remedy is effective.[34] A non-judicial body may for example have difficulties satisfying notions of independence which in some administrative spheres may undermine any real efficacy of a remedy.[35]

Effectiveness as a standard may vary depending on the subject matter, or nature of the Convention right relied on.[36]

Where secret surveillance was in issue, the Court took the approach in *Klass v Germany* that remedies only had to be as effective as they could be given the restricted scope for recourse inherent in such a system and referred to the possibility of an aggregate of remedies as satisfying the requirements of Art.13 (see below).[37] In the context of Art.9, the Court considered that a State's obligation could be discharged by making remedies in respect of registration of a religious community's leadership accessible only to certain representatives rather than to each individual believer.[38]

A more detailed and active scrutiny is required in cases concerning Arts 2 and 3. Generally, the Court has accepted that judicial review in the UK has sufficient scope as applied in expulsion cases to afford an effective remedy, since the courts have shown that they will apply a thorough scrutiny.[39] However, in *Chahal v United Kingdom*, where the applicant, a suspected terrorist, was found to risk torture or death on expulsion to India, the Court found that due to the irreversible damage which would be caused, the scope of the review was deficient since in the context of

---

[32] *e.g. Amann v Switzerland,* February 16, 2000, ECHR 2000–II, para.89; *Murray Family v UK,* October 28, 1994, Series A, No.300–A, para.100, where an action for trespass to property furnished an effective remedy for a search of a home by soldiers, despite the feeble prospects of success"; *Costello-Robberts,* where suit for assault was effective for corporal punishment at school notwithstanding the available reasonable and moderate chastisement defence, as "effectiveness" did not depend on the certainty of a favourable outcome.

[33] *e.g. Camenzind v Switzerland,* December 16, 1997, R.J.D. 1997–VIII, No.61, 28 E.H.R.R. 458.

[34] *e.g. Klass,* para.67; *Z v UK,* para.110. Also the Commission in *Powell and Rayner,* (Rep.), para.54 rejecting a submission that there was a general right to a court; 12573/86, (Dec.) March 6, 1987, 51 D.R. 283: effective remedy may be provided by non-judicial authority where it does not merely endorse decisions from below.

[35] *Chahal,* n.24 above, paras 153–154.

[36] *Hasan and Chaush v Bulgaria,* October 26, 2000, ECHR 2000–XI, para.99.

[37] para.70.

[38] *Hasan and Chaush,* n.36 above, paras 98–104.

[39] *e.g. Bensaid v UK,* February 6, 2001, ECHR 2001–I, paras 55–56, and authorities cited therein.

national security the courts did not carry out a scrutiny of the grounds and the possibility of review by the advisers who only had a power to recommend was insufficient.[40]

Where Arts 2 and 3 are concerned, a certain responsibility also lies on the authorities to take the initiative in respect of possible infringements. Thus, in *Aksoy v Turkey*, a violation was found in respect of the complete lack of reaction of the public prosecutor to the physical condition of the applicant who appeared before him after a long period in custody. In the series of cases arising out of the situation in south-east Turkey, where the public prosecutor played a central role in the system of criminal and civil remedies, the Court went so far as to state that Art.13 required the authorities to conduct a thorough and effective investigation capable of leading to the identification and punishment of those responsible, including effective access for the complainant to the investigation procedure.[41] In *Aydin v Turkey*, the lack of prompt reaction by the public prosecutor to an allegation of rape of a girl in gendarme custody, failing to obtain the necessary expert medical examination or to seek any factual corroboration, together with the deferential attitude disclosed towards the gendarmes, disclosed a violation. In respect of cases of killings by the security forces in the different context of Northern Ireland, the Court noted that generally an applicant who claimed the use of unlawful force had to exhaust domestic remedies by taking civil proceedings where the courts could establish facts, determine liability and award compensation. This process was not dependent on the proper conduct of criminal investigations as had been the situation in the Turkish cases. Thus, the Court found no violation of Art.13 as there was nothing to indicate that civil proceedings would not be capable of furnishing an effective remedy for alleged excessive use of force.[42] Insofar as the applicants' complaints disclosed defects in the inquest and criminal investigations these gave rise to breaches of the procedural obligation in Art.2 and no separate issue arose under Art.13.

Where complaints under Arts 2 and 3 of the Convention concern the failure of the authorities to protect the applicants from the acts of others, less stringent requirements are imposed as regards the investigative aspect of remedies. It may not always require the authorities to undertake the responsibility of launching an inquiry. There should be available a mechanism which the victim or victims' relatives can establish any liability.[43]

There are, in effect, two separate aspects of effective redress under Art.13, a procedure whereby the substance of the applicant's complaints under the substantive articles may be determined, including the finding of liability by the responsible Government body or authority and the provision of adequate redress, which includes compensation where appropriate for non-pecuniary, as well as pecuniary, damage.[44] The inability of children to sue the local authority for alleged negligence in failing to protect them from their parents breached Art.13 as it prevented them obtaining a

---

[40] paras 151–155: the procedures before the advisers were also lacking, *i.e.* no legal representation or information as to the grounds for expulsion.

[41] *Kaya*, para.107.

[42] *McKerr v UK*, ECHR 2001–III, para.173; *Hugh Jordan v UK*, May 4, 2000, para.162.

[43] *Z*, para.109.

[44] *e.g. TP and KM v UK*, May 10, 2001, ECHR 2001–V, para.107, concerning damages for allegedly negligent removal of child from home by social services.

determination of their allegations and denied them the possibility of obtaining an enforceable award of damages.[45]

As in the area of non-exhaustion of domestic remedies, there is a certain burden on the Government to show that the available remedies are effective. In *Vereinigung Demokratischer Soldaten Österreichs v Austria*, the Government alleged a number of remedies were available in the courts whereby the association could have had its journal distributed but the Court found that the Government had not put forward any example showing the application of the alleged remedies in a case similar to the present one and had therefore failed to show that the remedies would have been effective.[46]

7. Aggregate theory

IIB–371   The Court applied for a while a theory that where no single remedy may itself entirely satisfy the requirements of Art.13, the aggregate of remedies provided for under domestic law may do so. Thus, in *Leander v Sweden*, in respect of allegations of invasion of privacy through secret files, the Court found overall that the safeguards of the Chancellor of Justice, ombudsman and the presence of parliamentarians on the national police board sufficed.[47] This may be logical where in the context of secret surveillance the thrust of the Convention organs' concern has been to ensure an adequate framework to guard against abuse of power. It is not a satisfactory approach where an applicant is in a situation where he seeks a remedy which should have a more tangible result. Although, after a silence of some years the Court has made some recent reference to the principle, it has not been relied upon in a finding of non-violation.[48]

Cross-reference

Part IB: Admissibility, exhaustion of domestic remedies
Part IIB: Compensation for detention
Part IIB: Immigration and expulsion
Part IIB: Prisoners' rights
Part IIB: Review of detention

[45] *Z v UK*, paras 110–111. Breaches of Art.13 also found for lack of a practically available and enforceable right to compensation for the treatment of a mentally ill prisoner in *Keenan v UK*, April 3, 2001, and the inability of parents to obtain compensation for the death in custody of their son in *Paul and Aubrey Edwards v UK*, March 14, 2002, ECHR 2002–II.

[46] The Government also failed to show purported remedies were effective in *Rotaru v Romania*, February 4, 2000, ECHR 2000–V, paras 70–72 and *Wille v Liechtenstein*, October 28, 1999, ECHR 1999–VII, para.77 (absence of any precedent that court would entertain a claim).

[47] *cf.* the dissent of President Ryssdal noting no binding power of decision or specific responsibility to enquire into particular complaints.

[48] *e.g. Al-Nashif v Bulgaria*, June 20, 2002, para.132, violation for lack of appeal against an expulsion on national security grounds.

Review of detention

Key provision:

Article 5, para.4 (right to speedy review of lawfulness of detention by a court).　　IIB–372

Key case law:

De Wilde, Ooms and Versyp v Belgium, March 10, 1972, Series A, No.14; 1 E.H.R.R. 435; *Van Droogenbroeck v Belgium*, June 24, 1982, Series A, No.50; 4 E.H.R.R. 443; *Sanchez-Reisse v Switzerland*, October 21, 1986, Series A, No.107; 9 E.H.R.R. 71; *Weeks v UK*, March 2, 1987 Series A, No.114; 10 E.H.R.R. 293; *Bouamar v Belgium*, February 29, 1988, Series A, No.129; 11 E.H.R.R. 529; *Lamy v Belgium*, March 30, 1989, Series A, No.151; 11 E.H.R.R. 529; *E v Norway*, August 29, 1990, Series A, No.181–A; 17 E.H.R.R. 30; *Thynne, Wilson and Gunnell v UK*, October 25, 1990, Series A, No.190; 13 E.H.R.R. 666; *Toth v Austria*, December 12, 1991, Series A, No.224; 14 E.H.R.R. 551; *Megyeri v Germany*, May 12, 1992, Series A, No.237–A; 15 E.H.R.R. 584; *Herczegfalvy v Austria*, September 24, 1992, Series A, No.244; 15 E.H.R.R. 437; *Kampanis v Greece*, July 13, 1995, Series A, No.318–B; 21 E.H.R.R. 43; *Hussain v UK*, February 21, 1996, R.J.D. 1996–I, No.4; 22 E.H.R.R. 1; *Prem Singh v UK*, February 21, 1996, R.J.D. 1996–I, No.4; *RMD v Switzerland*, September 26, 1997, R.J.D. 1997–VI, No.51; 28 E.H.R.R. 224; *Chahal v UK*, November 15, 1996, R.J.D 1996–V; *Sakik v Turkey*, November 26, 1997, R.J.D. 1997–VII, No.58; 26 E.H.R.R. 662; *Assenov v Bulgaria*, October 28, 1998, R.J.D., 1998–VIII; *DN v Switzerland*, March 29, 2001, ECHR 2001–III; *Stafford v UK*, May 28, 2002, ECHR 2002–IV; *Hutchison Reid v UK*, February 20, 2003, ECHR 2003–IV.

1. General considerations

There is a right of review of the lawfulness of all the categories of detention　　IIB–373
provided for in Art.5, para.1, which is regarded by the Court as a crucial guarantee against the arbitrariness of detention.[1] However the scope of the obligation under Art.5, para.4 is not identical and its requirements will vary according to the kind of deprivation of liberty in question. It no longer applies once a person is released.[2]

2. Review of detention imposed by a court

Where sentences of detention are imposed by competent courts, the supervision is　　IIB–374
incorporated in the decision made by the court at the close of the judicial proceedings. Thus in respect of sentences imposed by competent courts within the meaning of Art.5, para.1(a), the review of lawfulness is inbuilt in the conviction and

---

[1] *e.g. Varbanov v Bulgaria*, October 5, 2000, ECHR 2000–X, para.58; *Benjamin and Wilson v UK*, September 26, 2002, para.33.
[2] *e.g.* 12778/87, (Dec.) December 9, 1988, 59 D.R. 158, concerning conditional release; persons in hiding or on the run, 25527/94, (Dec.) November 29, 1995.

appeal procedures.[3] Only where the decision of detention is taken by other authorities, administrative or executive, is there a right of recourse to a court pursuant to Art.5, para.4. No right to parole or release on licence can therefore be derived from Art.5, para.4.

This principle was initally applied to mandatory life sentences for murder which were seen as being imposed by a court as fixed sentences reflecting the gravity of the offence.[4] In *Stafford v United Kingdom*, the Court considered that the mandatory life sentence could no longer be considered as imposing imprisonment for life as a punishment and that after the expiry of the tariff period representing punishment and deterrence, the sentence fell to be regarded as justified by considerations of risk and dangerousness as in indeterminate, or discretionary life sentences (see further below).

3. Special types of sentences

IIB–375   Where sentences are passed with the aim of social protection and rehabilitation of offenders, since the grounds relied upon by the courts in sentencing (risk and dangerousness) are by their very nature susceptible of change with the passage of time, new issues may arise which affect the lawfulness of the detention. These types of sentence attract the right to review under Art.5, para.4. The principle was first applied in respect of sentences of detention imposed on recidivists in *Van Droogenbroeck v Belgium*[5] and then extended to the imposition of discretionary life sentences in the UK, which were found also to be based not only on the gravity of the offences but also on considerations of risk and dangerousness which could change with the passage of time.

In *Weeks v United Kingdom*, the applicant's recall after release on licence was compatible with Art.5, para.1(a) as derived from his original conviction when he was sentenced to a term of discretionary life imprisonment for robbery.[6] Nonetheless, Art.5, para.4 came into play as the Court found new issues of lawfulness in the Convention sense might arise if the decision not to release or to redetain was not based on grounds consistent with the objectives of the sentencing court. The right to review had to be wide enough to bear on those conditions which were essential for the lawful detention of a person subject to the special kind of deprivation of liberty both on recall to prison and at reasonable intervals during the course of his imprisonment. Thus the applicant whose sentence was imposed by the judge on the grounds of risk which his unstable personality presented, had the right to review on recall to prison after release to test that the legal basis for the detention still existed. Similarly in *Thynne, Wilson and Gunnell v United Kingdom*, three discretionary lifers, whose tariff had expired, could claim a review of their continuing detention.

Where minors convicted of murder were sentenced to detention at Her Majesty's Pleasure, the Commission and Court rejected the Government's argument that this

---

[3] *De Wilde*, para.76.
[4] *Wynne v UK*, July 18, 1994, Series A, No.294–A.
[5] See also 11082/84, March 4, 1988, 69 D.R. 27 where in respect of an offender placed at the disposal of the Government as a recidivist, an additional penalty of 19 years was left to the discretion of the executive after the expiry of a 4 year sentence, the judicial review required was not incorporated in the initial decision whereby the executive was empowered to order or not a deprivation of liberty.
[6] At age 17, he had stolen 35 pence using a starter pistol with blank cartridges.

was a fixed sentence imposed due to the gravity of the offence, finding that it had to be regarded as an indeterminate sentence based on a special factor subject to change over time. Indeed both adopted the argument of the applicant's counsel that if the sentence did intend that the child forfeited its liberty for the rest of its days there might be problems under Art.3. The Court had regard to the nature and purpose of the sentence, noting that the sentence was imposed because of the youth of the offender and held that an indeterminate sentence on a young person could only be justified by the need to protect the public which must take into account any developments in the personality or attitude as he grew older. There was accordingly a violation of Art.5, para.4 in the lack of any judicial review of continued detention for two applicants, *Prem Singh v United Kingdom* and *Hussain v United Kingdom*, who had both served their tariffs.[7]

As concerns mandatory life sentences imposed on adults for murder, the Court held in *Stafford v United Kingdom* that the tariff fixed by the Secretary of State comprised the punishment element of the sentence and once it expired continued detention depended on elements of dangerousness and risk associated with the objectives of the original sentence. As these elements could change over time, it could no longer be maintained that the original trial and appeal proceedings satisfied, once and for all, issue of compatibility of detention with Art.5, para.1. Such prisoners could therefore claim, after expiry of tariff, a right to review of the lawfulness of their continued detention by a body satisfying the guarantees of Art.5, para.4.

4. Access to court and scope of review

The "court" must be able to decide on the procedural and substantive conditions essential for "lawfulness". It is not required to cover every question and it does not guarantee a right to judicial control of such scope as to empower the "court" on all aspects of the case to substitute its own discretion for that of the decision-making authority.[8] However it is not enough for a court to confine itself to the existence of formal grounds for detention without examining the underlying lawfulness, such as the reasonableness of the suspicion underlying the arrest in remand cases and the legitimacy of the purpose of the varying types of detention.[9] Problems may also arise where the court treats as irrelevant, or disregards, concrete facts invoked by the detainee capable of putting in doubt the existence of conditions essential for the "lawfulness" in the Convention sense of the deprivation of liberty.[10] Security considerations, even relating to terrorism, do not provide a justification for a lack of

IIB–376

---

[7] See also *V v UK*, December 16, 1999, ECHR 1999–IX, paras 119–120: violation of Art.5, para.4, where after his conviction for murder, the 11 year old applicant's tariff was set by the Home Secretary but quashed by the House of Lords, leaving inchoate his entitlement to access to a tribunal for review of the lawfulness of his detention.

[8] *Weeks*, para.59; *Van Droogenbroeck*, para.49; *Toth*, para.87.

[9] e.g. *Jecius v Lithuania*, July 31, 2000, ECHR 2000–IX, paras 100–101; *Grauslys v Lithuania*, October 10, 2000, para.54: even in ordering release the court refused to examine the applicant's allegations of breaches of domestic law and specified no reasons for the release.

[10] e.g. *Nikolova v Bulgaria*, March 25, 1999, ECHR 1999–II, para.61, where the domestic court ignored the applicant's arguments concerning pre-trial detention, *inter alia*, that she had a permanent address and family and was in poor health; *Ilijkov v Bulgaria*, July 26, 2001, paras 97–98, rejecting the Government argument that the domestic court by ruling on the persistence of reasonable suspicion relevant to pre-trial detention would prejudice the merits and forfeit their impartiality.

judicial procedure to challenge detention as techniques are available to accommodate, for example concerns about confidential intelligence material.[11]

Judicial review in the UK was previously not wide enough for review of the continued detention of the discretionary lifer, as it was unable to verify whether detention was consistent with and justified by the objectives of the indeterminate sentence imposed on him.[12]

5. Procedural requirements of review

IIB–377 The review must be of a judicial character and give the individual the guarantees appropriate to the kind of deprivation of liberty in question.[13] The fact that the review is conducted by a court or judge is not decisive. For example, in *De Wilde, Ooms and Versyp v Belgium*, magistrates ordered the detention on vagrancy but in a summary procedure without the requisite guarantees necessary to the seriousness of what was at stake, which gave it the character of an administrative decision. To constitute a "court" for the purposes of Art.5, para.4, the authority must be independent from the executive and from the parties, as well as providing the fundamental guarantees of judicial procedure.[14]

Direct access to court is not always required. In *Sanchez-Reisse v Switzerland*, where the applicant argued that he could not apply directly to court without his request going via the police office, the Court found it was legitimate and necessary for the executive to have the power to comment, access not thereby being impeded or the power of the court hindered.[15] An applicant must however be entitled to apply to a court for review of detention himself, without relying on the permission or good will of the authorities.[16] Article 5, para.4 also presupposes the existence of a procedure in comformity with its requirements without the necessity of instituting separate legal proceedings in order to bring it about. Thus the Court rejected the argument of the Government in *Prem Singh v United Kingdom* that applicant could apply for judicial review of the Parole Board decision in order to obtain an oral hearing.

(a) *Power to release*

IIB–378 A power to release is necessary. In *Weeks*, the ability of the Parole Board to recommend release, which did not bind the Secretary of State, was not sufficient.[17]

---

[11] *e.g. Chahal*, para.131; *Al-Nashif v Bulgaria*, June 20, 2002, paras 94–98.

[12] *Weeks*, para.69. See, after the Human Rights Act 1998, *Stewart v UK*, 25185/02, (Dec.) December 16, 2002, where the prisoner's complaints were rejected for non-exhaustion for failure to invoke the Convention in judicial review proceedings.

[13] *De Wilde*, para.76; also, in *Weeks* there was no full disclosure of adverse material on recall to prison.

[14] *Varbanov*, n.1 above, paras 58–61, where the prosecutor who ordered detention was a party to the proceedings; *Dougoz v Greece*, March 6, 2001, para.62, where the applicant's appeal was to the leniency of Government ministers; *DN v Switzerland*, paras 50–57, concerning the lack of impartiality of a psychiatric panel member who had already expressed an opinion on key issues.

[15] para.45.

[16] *Rakevich v Russia*, October 28, 2003, paras 43–47 (mental health case) where the initiative lay with the medical staff.

[17] See also *Prem Singh* and *Hussain*; *Benjamin and Wilson*, n.1 above, where the practice of the Secretary of State in following the recommendation of the Mental Health Tribunal concerning the category of "technical lifers" did not alter the crucial fact that the decision to release was taken by the executive.

In *E v Norway*, the general power of the courts to review and rule invalid administrative decisions was found sufficient, notwithstanding no precedent of a court overriding such a decision. However, lack of precedents in successfully invoking an alleged remedy may indicate that the existence of the remedy is insufficiently certain, and that it is accordingly lacking the accessibility and effectiveness required for Art.5.[18]

(b) *Adversarial procedure*

The procedure should be adversarial, providing the applicant with the opportunity to present his case effectively. While Art.5, para.4 is not to be interpreted as identical with Art.6, para.1,[19] the Court has stated that this should allow to the largest extent possible the basic requirements of a fair trial, such as the right to an adversarial procedure.[20] While the Court has in some cases tended to acknowledge the need for a hearing before a judicial authority, the procedure required in each case is not identical.[21] Where in *Sanchez-Reisse* the applicant was challenging his detention with a view to extradition the Court found that he should have been provided in some way or other with an adversarial procedure. This could have included the possibility of submitting written comments on the objections of the Federal Police Office which went before the Federal Court with his request for release. It did not find any indication that his personal presence would have convinced the court about his release.

IIB–379

Failure to provide access to relevant documents and reports which deprives the applicant of the ability to participate properly in the proceedings has been found to render the review defective.[22] Where counsel was was unable to inspect documents in the file before the court ruled on whether to hold the applicant on remand, whereas Crown counsel was familiar with file, there was a failure to ensure equality of arms and the proceedings were not truly adversarial as required by Art.5, para.4.[23] Where prosecution counsel was present before the Court of Appeal whereas the applicant and his lawyer were not, the procedure did not ensure equal treatment and was not truly adversarial.[24] Procedures where submissions to the court by the prosecutor are not heard by or provided to the applicant or his lawyer, with an

---

[18] *e.g. Sakik*, where there was no example of any person in police custody having successfully invoked the Constitution or human rights provisions when applying to a judge for a release; *Sabeur Ben Ali v Malta*, June 29, 2000, paras 38–42; *Vodenicarov v Slovakia*, December 21, 2000, paras 41–44.

[19] *Megyeri*, para.22, *Assenov*, para.162.

[20] *Schops v Germany*, February 13, 2001, ECHR 2001–I, para.44; *Lietzow v Germany*, February 13, 2001, para.44.

[21] *De Wilde*, para.78.

[22] *Weeks*, paras 60–69; *Hussain*, para.58.

[23] *Lamy*, para.29; also *Schops*, n.20 above, paras 46–55: the Court rejected as over-formalistic the Government view that the applicant's lawyer should make requests to inspect the file at each stage of the proceedings, implying that the authorities should take some initiative in making files available; *Lietzow*, n.20 above, para.47, where the Court did not accept refusal of access to the file was justified to avoid compromising the on-going investigations as this imposed a substantial restriction on the rights of the defence.

[24] *e.g. Toth*. See (d) oral hearing and cases cited below.

opportunity to make comments, have also been found to infringe the principle of equality of arms.[25]

(c) *Oral hearing*

IIB–380   Equality of arms may require that the applicant be able to appear at a hearing, in addition to submitting written submissions, in particular where the prosecution is present.[26]

In *Hussein v United Kingdom* and *Prem Singh v United Kingdom*, having regard to what was at stake (a substantial term of imprisonment) and as questions of their personality and level of maturity were important to deciding on their dangerousness, Art.5, para.4 required an oral hearing in the context of an adversarial procedure involving legal representation and the possibility of calling and questioning witnesses.[27] Similarly hearings, attended by the applicant and/or counsel have been found necessary in cases dealing with review of detention on grounds of mental health[28] and hearings are required for review of persons detained pending trial (Art.5, para.1(c)).[29]

(d) *Legal representation*

IIB–381   Legal representation may be required depending on the nature of the proceedings and the capabilities of the applicant. It was found to be essential in *Bouamar v Belgium*, concerning a juvenile, that a lawyer be present at the hearings where he was remanded in custody in prison, otherwise an essential safeguard would be denied; and in *Megyeri v Germany*, concerning a person detained on ground of mental illness. The representation provided should be adequate.[30] Where the detainees are foreigners and unfamiliar with the legal system, legal representation affords an important guarantee.[31] In *Woukam Moudefo v France*,[32] where the appeal concerned questions of law, the Commission found that the applicant was unable, without a lawyer, to present his case properly and satisfactorily. It was not enough that the court addressed questions of public order of its own motion and it was the fundamental role of defence counsel to stress the crucial problems which may be raised by an appeal and which may otherwise not be examined by the court, as well as clarifying the applicant's submissions.

---

[25] *e.g. Trzaska v Poland*, July 11, 2000, para.78; *Wloch v Poland*, October 19, 2000, para.129.

[26] *e.g. Kampanis*: the applicant unable to attend the hearing although prosecutor was present; *Niedbala v Poland*, July 4, 2000, para.67, where the applicant and his lawyer had no right to attend even when the prosecutor attended; *Grauzinas v Lithuania*, October 10, 2000, para.34, where the applicant was not present at remand hearings to give instructions to his counsel or factual information.

[27] The Commission in *Prem Singh* had particular regard to the reasons for recall which were based on disputed facts relating to his conduct on which witnesses could have been heard. Also *Waite v UK*, December 10, 2002, where the applicant was recalled for alleged misuse of drugs, attempted suicide and relationship with a minor.

[28] See Pt IIB: Mental Health, Procedural Requirements.

[29] *Assenov*, para.162, *Sanchez-Reisse*, para.162.

[30] See *Magalhaes Pereira v Portugal*, February 26, 2002, where the applicant mental patient received ineffective legal assistance from a trainee lawyer and a hospital official. The Court stated that only in special circumstances would it be compatible not to provide legal assistance to such a detainee (para.56).

[31] *Sanchez-Reisse*, para.47.

[32] 10868/84, (Rep.) July 8, 1987 settled before the Court, October 7, 1988, Series A, No.141–B.

(e) *Effective access*

Where a time-limit or procedural requirements renders an apparent review **IIB–382** procedure theoretical, the Commission found that it did not comply with the requirements of Art.5, para.4. In *Farmakopoulos v Belgium*,[33] where the applicant was held in detention pending extradition, he had 24 hours from the service of the enforcement order to appeal though no mention of this possibility of appeal was included in the order. The Commission held that the shortness of time and lack of information made available did not afford the applicant a real opportunity to have the lawfulness of his detention reviewed, in particular noting the ignorance of aliens of language or procedures in this context.

Circumstances in which the applicant is detained which render practical use of a remedy ineffective or unrealistic may disclose problems, as in *RMD v Switzerland* where the applicant was transferred from canton to canton depriving him of any real or effective access to the review procedures available in each jurisdiction and in *Conka v Belgium*, where the applicant gypsies were arrested and expelled before their lawyer could lodge an application in the court.[34] Lack of clarity in domestic law and practice as to review of procedures may also raises issues where it impairs the exercise of the right under Art.5, para.4.[35]

(f) *Burden of proof*

The Court held that it is implicit in Art.5 case law that it is for the authorities to **IIB–383** prove that an individual satisfies the conditions for compulsory detention, not the converse. Thus it was contrary to Art.5, para.4 to require the applicant in *Hutchison Reid* to discharge the onus of proof that he was not suffering from a mental disorder rendering it appropriate for him to detained in a hospital for medical treatment.[36]

(g) *Appeals*

Article 5, para.4 does not require appeals from decisions ordering or extending **IIB–384** detention.[37] However, if domestic law allows for an appeal then in principle it must allow to detainees the same guarantees on appeal as at first instance. Therefore in *Toth v Austria*, where the applicant appealed to the Court of Appeal against a court ruling continuing his detention on remand, there was a violation where the procedure was not adversarial as the representative of the prosecution was present and would have been able to respond to questions, whereas neither the applicant or his lawyer were present. In *Hutchison Reid*, the time taken by the appellate levels was taken into account in assessing the speediness of the procedure.

---

[33] (Rep.), December 4, 1990, struck off before the Court, March 27, 1992, Series A, No.235.
[34] paras 45 and 55.
[35] *Shishkov v Bulgaria*, January 9, 2003, paras 89–90.
[36] paras 69–73. Also *Nikolova*, para.59 and *Ilijkov*, para.99, n.10 above, concerning incompatibility of a strong presumption that applicants held in pre-trial detention were likely to abscond or obstruct justice.
[37] *e.g. Jecius*, n.9 above, para.100; *Ilijkov*, n.10 above, para.103.

6. Speedily

IIB–385   A person taken into detention is entitled to a decision as to the lawfulness of that detention being taken with some expedition. In appropriate cases, Art.5, para.4 also requires the opportunity for review of continued detention at reasonable intervals, where such is not provided automatically.[38]

Different considerations will apply depending on the nature and circumstances of the detention. Release within three weeks was not sufficient to render a review unnecessary in relation to a person taken into detention on mental health grounds.[39] Regarding detention under Art.5, para.1(c), gaps of seven, 11 and six days before applicants were brought before the military court were not speedy.[40] The Court has stated that there is special need for a swift decision where a trial is pending.[41] Thirty-one days and forty-one days was not sufficient for review of lawfulness of detention for extradition in *Sanchez-Reisse v Switzerland* where the case was not complicated, did not require detailed investigation, and the case file and information about the applicant's health were to hand. Almost eight weeks was too long in *E v Norway*, where the Court rejected the excuse of a court vacation period, since it was for the State to organise necessary administrative arrangements to deal with urgent matters. Similarly in *AT v United Kingdom*,[42] a gap of almost 14 months between the expiry of the applicant's tariff and the first review by the new system of Parole Board hearings was not justified by the difficulties in introducing a new procedure and the need to establish priorities amongst the prisoners. In such cases, there was indeed a particular need for expedition in holding the first review.

Regarding the intervals at which reviews of continued detention should be made available, a gap of two years between the reviews for a discretionary lifer was not justified, particularly where he had completed the set rehabilitative work within eight months.[43] A period of nine months has been impliedly accepted by the Court in mental health cases.[44] Where detention on remand is concerned, the assumption is that the detention is to be of strictly limited duration and so periodic review at short intervals is called for.[45]

The dilatoriness of the applicant in pursuing proceedings may be a relevant factor, as in *Kolompar v Belgium*, where the Court noted the unusually long period but considered that the State could not be held responsible for the delays to which the applicant's conduct gave rise and that he could not complain validly of a

---

[38] *X v UK*, para.52.

[39] *Wassink v Netherlands*, September 27, 1990, Series A, No.185–A; see also *Rutten v Netherlands*, July 24, 2001, para.54: over 5 months at two instances for prolongation at a secure institution was too long.

[40] *De Jong, Baljet and Van den Brink v Netherlands*, May 22, 1984, Series A, No.77.

[41] *Jablonski v Poland*, December 21, 2000, para.93—43 days was too long; *GB v Switzerland*, November 30, 2000, 32 days for 2 instances too long; *Rehbock v Slovenia*, November 28, 2000, 23 days too long.

[42] 20488/92, (Rep.) November 29, 1995.

[43] *Oldham v UK*, September 26, 2000, ECHR 2000–X, paras 34–37—the Court commented that discretionary lifers appeared to be in a comparable position to mental health detainees; also *Hirst v UK*, July 24, 2001, periods of 21 months and 2 years between reviews. Exceptionally, a gap of 2 years was accepted in *Dancy v UK*, 55768/00, (Dec.) March 21, 2002, where the review system showed appropriate flexibility and due regard to the applicant's individual circumstances (a programme of offence-related work had been planned and a transfer to a Category C prison to facilitate further progress to release).

[44] *Herczegfalvy, Megyeri* (see section on Mental Health).

[45] *Bezicheri v Italy*, October 25, 1989, Series A, No.164, paras 20–21; *Assenov*, paras 162–165, where the applicant was only entitled to one review of his detention on remand over a period of two years.

situation which he had created.[46] However, the complexity of medical issues or the obtaining of expert opinions in accordance with wishes of the applicant did not provide a justification for delay of over one year and eight months in reviewing his detention on mental health grounds in *Musial v Poland* as the primary responsibility for obtaining such evidence rested with the State.[47] The Court commented that only exceptional grounds could justify such a delay. Where appellate instances are provided, the State has the obligation to organise its judicial system in such a way as to comply with the requirements of Art.5, para.4 concerning speediness.[48]

7. Relationship with Art.13

Together with Art.5, para.5 which provides for compensation, Art.5, para.4 is the *lex specialis* for remedies in respect of detention. Article 5, para.4 requirements are stated as being stricter than those of Article 13.[49]

IIB–386

Cross-reference

Part IIB: Compensation for detention
Part IIB: Extradition
Part IIB: Immigration and expulsion
Part IIB: Mental health
Part IIB: Pre-trial detention

[46] September 24, 1992, Series A, No.235–C: applicant held for extradition for 2 years and 8 months but had applied for postponements, successive applications for a stay of execution or for release. The Commission had found a lack of speed since despite the applicant's own conduct there was still an obligation on the State to take positive steps to expedite the proceedings. See *Magalhaes Pereira*, n.30 above, paras 47–51: the fact that the applicant absconded for 7 months was not taken into account as he was at his family home.

[47] March 25, 1999, ECHR 1999–II; also *Baranowski v Poland*, March 28, 2000, para.72, where the complexity of the medical issues could be taken into account but could not absolve the authorities from their essential obligations.

[48] *Hutchison Reid*, paras 74–80, (mental health case) violation for more than 3 years and 8 months for four instances; *Grauzinis*, n.26 above, para.32; *GB v Switzerland*, n.41 above, para.38, 32 days for 2 instances concerning pre-trial detention. See however *Letellier v France*, November 23, 1991, Series A, No.207, para.56 and *Touroude v France*, 35502/97, (Dec.) October 3, 2000, where, although expressing doubts as to the speediness of pre-trial detention decisions before the Court of Cassation, the Court found no breach of Art.5, para.4, as in the French system the applicant was able to make fresh applications at any time and had made use of this possibility.

[49] *De Jong*, para.60; *De Wilde*, para.95.

Right to life

Key provision:

IIB–387   Article 2 (right to life).

Key case law:

McCann, Farrell and Savage v UK, September 27, 1995, Series A, No.324; 21 E.H.R.R. 97; *Andronicou and Constantinou v Cyprus*, October 9, 1997, R.J.D. 1997–VII, No.52; 25 E.H.R.R. 491; *Kaya v Turkey*, February 19, 1998, R.J.D. 1998–I, No.65; 28 E.H.R.R. 1; *Güleç v Turkey*, July 27, 1998, R.J.D., 1998–IV, No.80; 28 E.H.R.R. 121; *Ergi v Turkey*, July 28, 1998, R.J.D., 1998–IV, No.81; 32 E.H.R.R. 388; *Yasa v Turkey*, September 2, 1998, R.J.D. 1998–VI, No.88; 28 E.H.R.R. 408; *Osman v UK*, October 28, 1998, R.J.D., 1998–VIII, No.95; 29 E.H.R.R. 245; *Ogur v Turkey*, May 20, 1999, ECHR 1999–III; 31 E.H.R.R. 912; *Cakici v Turkey*, July 8, 1999, ECHR 1999–IV; 31 E.H.R.R. 5; *Kilic v Turkey*, March 28, 2000, ECHR 2000–III; *Ilhan v Turkey*, June 27, 2000, ECHR 2000–VII; *Salman v Turkey*, June 27, 2000, ECHR 2000–VII; *Keenan v UK*, April 3, 2001, ECHR 2001–III; *Tanli v Turkey*, April 10, 2000, ECHR 2000–III; *Avsar v Turkey*, July 10, 2001, ECHR 2001–VII; *Calvelli and Ciglio v Italy*, January 17, 2002, ECHR 2002–I; *McKerr v UK*, May 4, 2001, ECHR 2001–III; *Paul and Aubrey Edwards v UK*, March 14, 2002, ECHR 2002–II; *Mastromatteo v Italy*, October 24, 2002, ECHR 2002–VIII; *Nachova v Bulgaria*, February 26, 2004, pending before the Grand Chamber; *Glass v UK*, March 9, 2004; ECHR 2004–II.

1. General considerations

IIB–388   This section concerns, principally, the use of force by State agents. This relates most obviously to the use of force by police, soldiers or other types of security forces which results in death of an individual. Allied to this aspect there may be circumstances where the respect for life may arguably impose an obligation on the State to take steps to protect life.

The right to life guaranteed under Art.2 is one of the most important rights from which no derogation is possible. The situations where deprivation of life may be justified are exhaustive and must be narrowly interpreted.[1]

The situations listed in the second paragraph are therefore the only exceptions possible: defence of others, lawful arrest or prevention of the escape of a person lawfully obtained of in action lawfully taken for the purpose of quelling a riot or insurrection. The use of lethal force for these purposes must be no more than "absolutely necessary". This necessity test indicates that a stricter and more compelling test must be applied than under other provisions of the Convention which refer to necessity alone. The use of force must be "strictly proportionate".[2] There should therefore be no, or at least less, scope for the use of the "margin of appreciation". The Commission and Court at least have not made reference to the term expressly in this context.

[1] 10044/82, (Dec.) July 10, 1984, 39 D.R. 162.
[2] *ibid.*

494

However as always, the Convention organs will have regard to the circumstances of the use of force, in particular, nature of the aim pursued, dangers to life and limb inherent in the situation and the degree of risk that the force employed might result in loss of life.[3]

Article 2 applies mainly to situations where a person is killed but may also in exceptional circumstances extend to life-threatening attacks where a person survives.[4] In *Ilhan v Turkey*, the Court found that Art.3, rather than Art.2, was violated by the excessive use of force on arrest which caused the victim serious brain damage. It commented that the degree and type of force, as well as the intention or aim of the perpetrators, would be relevant in assessing whether a particular use of force inflicting injury short of death infringed the object and purpose of Art.2.

Allegations that State agents were involved in the lethal use of force in circumstances infringing Art.2 must be established by proof beyond reasonable doubt,[5] though this may include sufficiently strong, clear and concordant inferences.[6] Special presumptions operate in the contexts of disappearances and deaths in custody.

2. Use of lethal force

(a) *Deliberate versus non-intentional infliction of loss of life*

Notwithstanding the use of the word "intentionally" in the first paragraph, Art.2   IIB–389
has been interpreted to cover the accidental deprivation of life by the use of lethal force. This question arose in the context of the death of a 13-year-old boy who was struck by a rubber bullet, fired by a soldier who was facing a barrage of missiles thrown by rioters. The domestic courts had found that the soldier had not intended to injure the boy; that he had aimed at a rioter standing next to him and his aim was deflected when a missile struck his shoulder. The Commission considered that Art.2 taken as whole must be interpreted as defining the situations where it is permissible to use force which may, whether intended or not, result in the deprivation of life. Any other interpretation would not, in the Commission's view, have been consistent with the object and purpose of the Convention or with a strict interpretation of the obligation to protect life.

---

[3] *ibid.*

[4] See *Ilhan*, paras 76–77. In three cases, concerning alleged positive obligations to protect life, Art.2 applied although the applicant was still alive: *Osman*, paras 115–122, where the applicant had been injured and his father killed by a teacher against whom they had sought protection from the police; *Yasa* paras 92–108, where the applicant had been shot 8 times by an unknown gunman; *LCB v UK*, June 9, 1998, R.J.D. 1998–III, paras 36–41 concerning complaints by the daughter of a service man exposed to radiation on Christmas Island, about lack of information from the authorities about the risks to her health.

[5] *Kaya*, para.76. Insufficient factual and evidentiary basis for complaints led to no violation where the applicant alleged that his brother, a farmer, was riddled with bullets in his fields while the security forces alleged that he was killed during a clash with armed terrorists.

[6] e.g. *Aktas v Turkey*, April 24, 2003, inferences were drawn from the Government's unsatisfactory response to Commission requests for information and witnesses and this together with evidence of injuries in the autopsy report, consistent with death by mechanical asphyxia, furnished proof beyond reasonable doubt that the victim was subjected in custody to violence that caused his death.

(b) *Standard of domestic law*

IIB–390 In *McCann v United Kingdom*, the applicants argued that the applicable domestic law should protect the right to life. The Commission agreed to the extent that this required national law to regulate in a manner compatible with the rule of law the permissible use of force by its agents. Both Commission and Court did not accept that the fact that domestic law imposed a test of reasonable as opposed to absolute necessity indicated a failure to comply with the Convention standard.[7] A State was not bound to use the same formulation, which would be tantamount to requiring incorporation into domestic law of the Convention. The Court noted that the Convention test appeared stricter but did not consider that the difference between the two standards was sufficiently great to found a violation alone.

It was also argued in *McCann* that domestic law was too general and that specific, clear and detailed rules were required, reference being made, *inter alia*, to the UN Basic Principles on the use of Firearms by Law Enforcement Officials. The Court however found that the rules of engagement for military and police personnel provided regulation of the use of force which reflected the domestic and Convention standard.

A case, however, where the criminal and/or civil courts rejected an applicant's claims on the basis of reasonable necessity in light of facts which the Convention organs found disclosed no justification under the Convention would cast doubt on the adequacy of the domestic law standard. Thus, in *Nachova v Bulgaria*, the Court found the standard was flawed where the authorities decided not to bring charges against an officer who shot dead two absconding conscripts as it was considered that the relevant regulations on the use of force had been complied with and no relevance was attached to the crucial fact that the two men, who had committed non-violent offences, did not pose any threat to the arresting officers.[8]

(c) *Procedural requirements*

IIB–391 While it may be permissible for a State to use lethal force in certain limited circumstances, the *McCann* case establishes that there must some form of effective official investigation. Otherwise the protection offered by Art.2 would be rendered nugatory if there was no form of open and objective oversight into the circumstances of a killing.[9] The nature and degree of the scrutiny which will satisfy the minimum threshold of effectiveness depends on the circumstances, some cases being undisputed and requiring a minimum formality, whereas in others the facts might be unclear or the situation suspicious.[10] The emphasis is on effective accountability and transparency to ensure respect for the rule of law and maintain public confidence.[11]

---

[7] The Government had argued that in practice the reasonable necessity test took into account all requisite factors. The Commission found that whether or not the application of the reasonable necessity standard permitted the use of force in contravention of Art.2 could only be determined by an examination of the case before it: 17579/90, (Dec.) February 13, 1993, 74 D.R. 139.

[8] paras 121–128. See also in the context of Art.3 the defective approach in domestic law on rape which required proof of resistance in *MC v Bulgaria*, December 4, 2003, ECHR 2003–XII, paras 171–174.

[9] para.161.

[10] *e.g. Velikova v Bulgaria*, May 18, 2000, ECHR 2000–VI, para.80.

[11] *Avsar*, para.393; *Gül v Turkey*, December 14, 2000, para.90 (lack of accountability for use of weapons).

The Court has refrained from specifying the exact form or procedures that should be involved.[12] However, cases from Turkey and Northern Ireland in particular have identified particular features necessary to an effective investigation. The onus is on the authorities to launch the investigation without for example relying on complaint being made by a relative.[13] The availability of civil proceedings, undertaken at the initiative of the relatives and not involving the identification or punishment of the perpetrator of an unlawful killing, cannot be taken into account.[14] The investigation should be conducted by an officer or body independent from those implicated in events, in a hierarchical, institutional and practical sense.[15] The notion of effectiveness requires that the investigation be capable of leading to a determination of whether the force used was justified and to the identification and punishment of those responsible.[16] The Court has specified that this is an obligation of means not result.[17] Lack of prosecution or conviction will therefore not be decisive, as long as the authorities have taken reasonable steps to secure the evidence concerning the incident, including, *inter alia*, eye witness and forensic evidence[18] and where appropriate an autopsy providing a complete and accurate record of injuries and an objective analysis of clinical findings including the cause of death,[19] and reach decisions supported by a careful analysis of the facts.[20] Thus, any defect in the investigation which undermines its ability to establish the cause of death or person responsible risks falling short of this standard.[21]

[12] *e.g. McKerr v UK*, para.159, where the Court rejected the applicant's arguments in favour of a Scottish model of inquiry instead of a system splitting the tasks of fact-finding, investigation and prosecution between various authorities.

[13] *Ergi*, paras 82–83; *Tanrikulu v Turkey*, July 8, 1999, ECHR 1999–IV, para.103; also *Tanli*, para.152, where onus was on the public prosecutor, not the family, to obtain a full autopsy; *Nachova*, para.131.

[14] *Hugh Jordan v UK*, May 4, 2001, para.141.

[15] *e.g. Ogur*, paras 91–82 (administrative councils lacking independence from governor, also head of the security forces); *McKerr v UK*, para.127 and *Hugh Jordan*, n.14 above, para.120 (lack of independence of RUC and ICPC investigations into shootings by RUC officers); *Kelly v UK*, May 4, 2001, ECHR 2001–III, para.114; *McShane v UK*, May 28, 2000, para.111–112 (RUC officers investigating deaths caused by soldiers were connected, albeit indirectly, with the operation); *Shanaghan v UK*, May 4, 2001, ECHR 2001–III, para.104, and *Finucane v UK*, July 1, 2003, para.76 (RUC investigators connected with those under suspicion of collusion).

[16] *e.g. Ogur*, para.88; *Aktas*, n.6 above, paras 301–307.

[17] *Avsar*, paras 394, 404; see, *e.g. Douglas-Williams*, No.56423/00, (Dec.) January 8, 2002, where all the relevant evidence and arguments had been aired at the inquest at which the family were represented, the fact that the jury reached a verdict of accidental, not unlawful death, did not deprive the procedure of its effectiveness.

[18] *e.g. Guleç*, para.79, failure to obtain witness evidence; *Tanrikulu*, n.13 above, paras 104–107 and *Gül*, n.11 above, para.89, superficial investigation at the scene and inadequate forensic testing; *Velikova*, n.10 above, paras 78–84, failure to collect key evidence.

[19] *Kaya*, para.89, perfunctory autopsy; *Ogur*, para.89; *Salman*, paras 106–107, defects in autopsy investigation (*e.g.* lack of proper forensic photographs, dissection and analysis of marks and injuries); *Tanli*, where defective procedure were not carried out by forensic experts.

[20] *Nachova*, paras 135–138, where the prosecutors omitted mention of "troubling facts", *e.g.* the location of cartridges and that one victim was hit in the chest, possibly while trying to surrender.

[21] *e.g. Yasa*, paras 105–107, exclusion from investigation of any consideration of security force responsibility; *Cakici*, para.80, general inertia; *Bilgin v Turkey*, November 16, 2000, para.144, inability of investigator to access police premises or obtain information about police officers; *Kiliç*, paras 82–83, limited scope of investigation excluding possible collusion by security forces; *Akdeniz v Turkey*, May 31, 2001, para.92, lack of serious effort to investigate and repeated jurisdictional transfers of file; *Tanli*, para.153, lack of proper autopsy findings led to acquittal of police officers; *Avsar*, paras 404–408, failure to investigate effectively alleged security force suspect. See, conversely, *Sabutekin v Turkey*, March 19, 2002, paras 100–104, where the investigation was adequate and the lack of promptness in one aspect did not deprive it of effectiveness.

While an investigation followed by a criminal trial with an adversarial procedure before an independent and impartial judge must be regarded as furnishing the strongest safeguards of an effective procedure for the finding of facts and attribution of responsibility, there may be circumstances where issues arise that were not or could not be addressed in the trial and where the aims of reassuring the public and the family were not met adequately, as in *McKerr v United Kingdom*, where there had been deliberate concealment of evidence and wider concerns about an alleged shoot to kill policy.[22]

The investigation must commence promptly[23] and be conducted with reasonable expedition to maintain public confidence in the rule of law and to prevent any appearance of collusion or tolerance of unlawful acts.[24] Those considerations also require sufficient public scrutiny of the investigation and its results, the extent of which may vary from case to case.[25] There is no automatic requirement that families have access to police files.[26] However, in all cases, the next of kin must be involved in the procedure to the extent necessary to safeguard their legitimate interests.[27]

Where a life-threatening disappearance is concerned, the State remains under a continuing obligation to provide an effective investigation, even where considerable time has elapsed since events occurred.[28]

In the context of Northern Ireland, the Court found problems arising from the inquest procedure into deaths implicating the security forces. The limited scope of the enquiry which, as the jury was restricted to the immediate facts surrounding the death and could not give any verdict as to the lawfulness or otherwise, was found to prevent the inquest from playing an effective role in the identification or prosecution of any criminal offences.[29] The inability to compel the security force personnel to give evidence also detracted from the inquest's capacity to establish the facts[30] as did the use of public interest immunity certificates to exclude certain potentially relevant

---

[22] See also *Gül*, n.11 above, para.94, where reliance on flawed security force report effectively deprived the court of the ability to decide the factual and legal issues.

[23] Delays in commencing inquests, *e.g.* 25 months in *Hugh Jordan*, n.14 above; over 4-year delay in re-opening inquest in *McKerr*, 8 years in *Kelly and others*, 4 and a half years in *Shanaghan*. Ten-year delay in opening inquiry and *Finucane*, para.80: n.15 above.

[24] *e.g. Timurtas v Turkey*, June 13, 2000, ECHR 2000–VI, para.89, delay in taking statements; *Mahmut Kaya v Turkey*, March 28, 2000, ECHR 2000–III, paras 106–107, delays in seeking statements and inactivity not excused by burden of work on public prosecutors as it was incumbent on authorities to respond actively and with reasonable expedition; *Avsar*, paras 405–408, dilatoriness in investigating security force suspect; *McKerr*, paras 152–155, frequent and lengthy adjournments in inquest.

[25] *e.g. Hugh Jordan*, n.14 above, paras 122–124, lack of reasons by the D.P.P. for decisions not to prosecute the killing of an unarmed man provided insufficient scrutiny and explanation to family; *McKerr*, para.141, reports from the independent police inquiry were not published; *Kelly*, n.15 above para.118, no reasons given for no prosecution where 9 men, at least 2 unarmed and one unconnected with the IRA, were shot, and the situation cried out for an explanation; *Finucane*, n.15 above, paras 82–83, no public explanation of decisions not to prosecute. See however *McShane*, n.15 above, paras 117–119, where the D.P.P. gave brief reasons and the applicant could have taken judicial review proceedings challenging their adequacy, it was not a problem that the family had to request the reasons.

[26] *e.g. Hugh Jordan*, n.14 above, para.121, as long as requisite access provided at other stage of the investigative procedure.

[27] *e.g. Ogur*, para.92—lack of access by family to case file or to administrative council proceedings.

[28] *Cyprus v Turkey*, paras 135–36.

[29] *Hugh Jordan*, n.14 above, paras 129–130; see also *Shanaghan*, n.15 above, paras 111–113, where the Coroner excluded evidence relevant to alleged RUC collusion in the targeting of the victim; *Finucane*, n.15 above, para.78, no examination of collusion issues at inquest.

[30] *McKerr*, para.144; *Kelly and others*, n.15 above, para.121.

evidence.[31] Non-disclosure of statements and evidence to the relatives of the deceased also showed failure to respect their interests.[32]

(d) *Justifiable exceptions*

(I) DEFENCE OF OTHERS (ART.2, PARA.2(A))

In *McCann*, SAS soldiers shot dead three IRA terrorists whom they said they believed were about to detonate a bomb in the centre of Gibraltar. In fact, there was no bomb in Gibraltar, nor were the terrorist carrying any arms or any object connected with any possible detonation of a bomb. Objectively therefore, three people were shot dead in circumstances where they posed no immediate risk and could have been taken into custody without difficulty. The case was surrounded by controversy. It was alleged that the security forces had deliberately executed the terrorists rather than bring them to trial.

    IIB–392

The Commission commented in strong terms on the alleged shoot to kill policy, which would be in flagrant violation of the Convention. A terrorist's right to life is also protected under Art.2 and also his or her right to fair trial on any allegations of criminal actions. Both the Commission and Court however, looking at the soldiers' actions, found that they were under an honest belief, due to the information given to them, that it was necessary to shoot the IRA suspects to prevent them detonating a bomb. Such an honest belief which is perceived for good reasons to be valid at the time could still be justified under Art.2 even if it turned out to be mistaken. To hold otherwise would put an unrealistic burden on law enforcement officers.

A standard of honest and reasonable belief also applied in *Andronicou and Constantinou v Cyprus*, where a security team shot both the hostage and the hostage-taker. The Court regretted the level of firepower used but giving allowance for "the heat of the moment" said the officers honestly and reasonably believed that they and the hostage were at risk from the armed hostage-taker and were entitled to open fire to eliminate that risk.[33]

The shooting of 50–55 bullets through a door, causing multiple and fatal injuries, on an unseen target in a residential block occupied by innocent civilians, women and children was found to be grossly disproportionate response by special team officers in *Gül v Turkey*,[34] where the Court found that they had no reasonable belief that their lives were at risk.

(II) TO EFFECT A LAWFUL ARREST OR PREVENT THE ESCAPE OF SOMEONE LAWFULLY DETAINED (ART.2, PARA.2(B))

There has been no case concerning the second limb. As regards the effecting of a lawful arrest, this was found to justify the use of lethal force by soldiers to stop a car of joyriders which drove through a Belfast checkpoint. The Commission accepted

    IIB–393

---

[31] *McKerr*, paras 150–151.
[32] *Hugh Jordan*, n.14 above, para.134; *Kelly*, n.15 above, para.128.
[33] Also *Brady v UK*, 55151/00, (Dec.) April 3, 2001, where a policeman killed a robber in the mistaken belief that the man had a gun, the Court found that this honest belief was explicable by "visual perception distortion" caused by stress and poor lighting.
[34] December 14, 2000, para.82.

that given a reasonable belief that the occupants of the case were terrorists (their manner of driving which put the soldiers at risk) the shooting at the car could be justified as absolutely necessary to effect a lawful arrest. This conclusion flew in the face of the domestic court's findings in the civil proceedings that the soldiers could not rely on the defence of arrest since the occupants of the car had not committed any serious offence when the incident arose. The Commission's decision does not explain this apparent contradiction. The level of force used to stop the car was also not found to be excessive or disproportionate, although the applicant had pointed out there was no attempt to fire at the tyres or take other steps to apprehend the vehicle and that no consideration was given to the known fact that cars going throught checkpoints were as likely to be joyriders, drunken motorists or inadvertent drivers. The Commission gave special regard to the difficult situation in Belfast and to the extreme circumstances of this case, where the soldiers had only seconds to react to an apparently determined effort to evade the checkpoint which had caused one soldier minor injury.[35]

Conversely in a Turkish case, where a soldier shot dead the driver of a car which passed through a checkpoint without stopping, the Commission distinguished it from *Kelly*, since the manner in which the driver, an ordinary civilian working for the State authorities, behaved was not shown to be suspicious.[36] The use of lethal force in attempt to arrest two absconding conscripts, who were unarmed and no record of violence, disclosed excessive force, in particular with regard to use of a rifle on automatic setting and the other options available to effect the arrest.[37]

(III) ACTION LAWFULLY TAKEN FOR THE PURPOSE OF QUELLING A RIOT (ART.2, PARA.2(C))

IIB–394   There is no Convention definition of a riot. Where a 13-year-old boy died from a plastic bullet striking his head and the applicant denied that there was a riot situation, the Commission considered that while definitions of what constituted a riot might differ between various jurisdictions 150 people throwing missiles at a patrol of soldiers such that they risked serious injury did fall within the term. As to the justification for the firing of the bullet, it had regard to the the continuous public disturbances which had given rise to loss of life in Northern Ireland, where such events were often used as cover for sniper attacks. Notwithstanding the arguments raised by the applicant as to the known risk to life from baton rounds, it concluded, given the threat facing the soldiers and the fact that the soldier's aim was disturbed when he fired, that the death resulted from the use of force no more than absolutely necessary for the purpose of quelling a riot.

In *Gülec v Turkey*, the Court for the first time considered this limb of Art.2 where the applicant's 15-year-old son had been killed by a bullet fired by gendarmes during a demonstration which had turned unruly. While it accepted that the use of force might be justified under para.2(c), it was axiomatic that the response by State agents had to use proportionate means. Despite the fact that the region was subject to disorder, the gendarmes had only machine guns to cope with the crowd, no truncheons, riot shields, water cannons, tear gas or rubber bullets available which

---

[35] n.7 above.

[36] *Aytekin v Turkey*, September 23, 1998, R.J.D 1998–VII: the Court did not consider the merits of the case however as material arose leading it to uphold the Government's preliminary objection on non-exhaustion.

[37] *Nachova*, paras 96–109.

the Court found incomprehensible and unacceptable. Unconvinced that armed terrorists had been amongst the crowd, the Court found the level of force used was not "absolutely necessary".

(e) *Planning and control of the use of lethal force*

The State has the responsibility in the planning and executing of operations to take steps to minimise the need for the use of lethal force. The Court has also referred to its role in evaluating whether the authorities were negligent in their choice of action.[38] Thus, in *McCann*, even though it was found that the soldiers' own actions did not contravene Art.2, the lack of care in evaluating and providing adequate information to the soldiers and the failure to allow for other contingencies were identified, in the context of using soldiers trained to shoot to kill, as not conforming with this standard. In *Andronicou and Constantinou v Cyprus*, the use of special teams, trained to kill, armed with sub-machines gun to intervene in a domestic dispute between a young couple was found by the Commission to increase the risk of injury and death. The Court, differing,[39] held that the decision to use the special team was a considered one of last resort and did not disclosed any lack of care, given that Andronicou was known to be armed, and with a capacity for violence and Elsie Constantinou had been screaming repeatedly that he was going to kill her. The Court saw no problem in the carrying of machine guns, since, *inter alia,* clear instructions had been issued as to their use and Andronicou was armed with a shotgun. It did not find that the officers had been supplied with misleading information as in *McCann*. Conversely, in *Ogur v Turkey*, where the security officers were operating in fog without means of communicating between themselves and without any loudhailers, gross negligence was disclosed by the situation in which a nightwatchman was mistakenly shot dead as an escaping suspect without any warning or warning shot being given.

Agents of the State are also expected to be trained to react with the degree of caution to be expected of law enforcement officers in a democratic society. Over-reaction was therefore a factor in finding a violation in *McCann*, where the suspects were shot repeatedly at close range and in the opinion of the Commission in *Andronicou and Constantinou* where officers reacted to two shots by a rate of firing which rendered almost inevitable the death of the hostage they were seeking to rescue.[40]

Where operations take place in the vicinity of civilian populations, necessary steps must also be taken to avert the risk of inadvertent death or injury in any ensuing clash. In *Ergi v Turkey*, where the security forces set up an ambush for the PKK at the entrance to a village, and a clash ensued with firing across the houses resulting in the death of a young mother, the Court agreed with the Commission's findings that, in the absence of direct evidence by the State authorities on the planning and conduct of the ambush, it could reasonably be inferred that insufficient precautions had been taken to protect the lives of the civilian population.

IIB–395

---

[38] *Andronicou and Constantinou*, para.181.
[39] However, it found no violation by a narrow margin of 5 votes to 4.
[40] See however *Brady v UK*, n.33 above, where an unarmed man was killed during a robbery, the Court found the ambush planned by the police did not render lethal force inevitable or highly probable and that although it could have perhaps been more efficiently executed, errors of judgement or mistaken assessments would not *per se* entail responsibility under Art.2.

3. Special contexts

(a) *Death in custody*

IIB–396   States are under a duty to protect detainees who are in a vulnerable position and have to account for injuries caused in custody. A particularly stringent obligation lies on the authorities to account for deaths in custody and strong presumptions of fact will arise in respect of injuried and fatalities occurring during detention.[41] Where the authorities therefore fail to satisfy the burden of proof lying on them to provide a satisfactory and convincing explanation, a violation of Art.2 arises, as in *Salman v Turkey* where the applicant's husband, with no prior history of heart disease, died in police custody, *inter alia*, with a broken sternum and bruising and swelling to the sole and ankle of the left foot. In *Tanli v Turkey*, where the 22-year-old, in prior good health, died during interrogation in police custody, the Court refused to accept the Government's assertion that he died of natural causes as providing a plausible or satisfactory explanation for his death, as the domestic *post mortem* was defective in fundamental respects and failed to establish the cause of death.[42]

As regards the obligation on the authorities to protect detainees from their own attempts to commit suicide or other inmates, see further below.

(b) *Disappearances*

IIB–397   The disappearance of a person in custody is not sufficient in itself to found a violation of Art.2 of the Convention.[43] The Court requires concrete evidence supporting the conclusion that the person has, beyond reasonable doubt, been killed by the authorities, though this can be provided by sufficient circumstantial evidence based on concrete elements, as first found in *Cakici v Turkey*, where the applicant's brother was established as having been the victim of serious ill-treatment while in unacknowledged detention and the authorities later claimed that he was dead as his identity card had been found, in unverified circumstances, on the body of an alleged terrorist after a clash.[44] The length of time over which the person has disappeared is a significant factor though it has not yet been found

---

[41] *Salman*, para.99.

[42] April 10, 2001, ECHR 2001–III, paras 143–147. Also *Aktas,* n.6 above, paras 292–294, where there were signs consistent with mechanical asphyxia; *Avsar*, paras 410–416, where the victim's body was found dead in a field after he had been taken into a gendarme station; *Velikova*, n.10 above, paras 71–74; *Anguelova v Bulgaria*, June 13, 2002, ECHR 2002–IV, paras 112–121, where the Court rejected as implausible the Government's claims that the fatal injuries were received before the deceaseds' arrest or from falling at the police station. See, conversely, *Douglas-Williams v UK*, n.17 above, where the applicant's brother died after arrest from positional asphyxia caused by the method of restraint used but the use of force had not been excessive to restrain a man armed with a knife and the evidence did not show that the police officers could have foreseen his sudden collapse.

[43] See *Kurt v Turkey*, May 25, 1998, R.J.D. 1998–III, No.74, paras 107–108.

[44] paras 85–87. Also *Ertak v Turkey*, May 9, 2000, paras 131–132, witness evidence that the applicant's son had been tortured and last seen dead or dying in detention; *Tas v Turkey*, November 14, 2000, paras 65–66 strong inferences drawn from the lack of documentary evidence from the authorities as to the location of the applicant's son after his acknowledged arrest and no satisfactory explanation for what had happened to him (the story of an escape while assisting a military operation was lacking in credibility and unsubstantiated by any reliable evidence); *Orhan v Turkey*, June 18, 2002, the men, missing for 8 years after their arrest, had been wanted by the security forces.

sufficient in itself.[45] The Court acknowledges that with the passage of time the likelihood of death becomes stronger and that can influence the weight to be attached to circumstantial elements.[46]

4. Protection from use of force or threat to life posed by others

(a) *Protection from the use of force or threat to life posed by others*

Article 2 has also been interpreted as requiring the State not only to refrain from taking life in unjustified circumstances but also to take appropriate steps to safeguard lives with its jurisdiction. Thus positive obligations may arise to protect an applicant from third persons or other threats to life.[47] This includes a primary duty to secure the right to life by putting in place effective criminal law provisions to deter offences against the person together with machinery for the prevention, suppression and sanctioning of such measures.[48] In early cases concerning Northern Ireland, where persons complained that the State had failed to protect them from terrorists, the Commission was not prepared to hold that a State was under an obligation to exclude all possible occurrence of violence, nor to examine in detail whether the UK had adopted appropriate and efficient measures to combat terrorism. It was sufficient that there were 10,500 soldiers in the area, that hundreds of them had lost their lives in the conflict and it did not consider that the State had been obliged to take any further steps to protect the applicant and her family. Where however in south-east Turkey there were serious allegations of collusion in counter-terrorist targeting of alleged PKK supporters, a failure in the system to hold security forces properly accountable for the use of force played a role the finding of Government responsibility in a number of so-called unknown perpetrator killings.[49]

Positive obligations to take preventive operational measures to protect life from the criminal acts of another may arise in certain well-defined circumstances. In

IIB–398

---

[45] *Timurtas*, n.24 above, paras 84–86, where the Court laid emphasis on the 6-year period as longer than the 4 year disappearance in *Kurt*, n.43 above. However, other elements included the fact that the applicant's disappeared son was wanted as a suspect terrorist, that the authorities had taken steps to conceal his apprehension and detention and findings in other Turkish cases on the lack of accountability of the security services in the region at that time. See also strong inferences drawn from lapse of over 7 years in *Akdeniz*, n.21 above, paras 87–88 (other inferences drawn from lack of documentary records of detention and the Government's inability to account for what had happened to the missing detainees); *Cicek v Turkey*, February 27, 2001, paras 146–147 and *Ipek v Turkey*, February 17, 2004, where there was very little by way of "concrete elements" beyond the respective 6 and 9-year lapse of time.

[46] *Bilgin v Turkey*, n.21 above, para.139: more than 6-and-a-half years had passed and the Court drew very strong inferences from witness evidence that the applicant's brother had been seen ill-treated and in bad physical condition in custody.

[47] 9438/81, (Dec.) February 28, 1983, 32 D.R. 190.

[48] *Osman v UK*, para.115. See also *Mastromatteo v Italy*, paras 72–73, where the Court examined whether the penal system provided sufficient protective measures when re-integrating prisoners into society.

[49] e.g. *Kiliç*, paras 71–77, *Mahmut Kaya*, n.24 above, paras 94–99 and *Akkoç v Turkey*, October 10, 2000: where the victims had been threatened with violence before their death to the knowledge of the authorities, the Court, in finding the Government's responsible under Art.2, took into account defects undermining the effectiveness in the investigative and judicial system in the south-east region and removing the protection which should have been available in law (*e.g.* limitation on the public prosecutor's ability to investigate certain offences by State officials, the role of non-judicial bodies in investigations, the lack of effectiveness of investigations generally as shown by the Court's numerous findings and the lack of independence of the State Security Courts assigned jurisdiction for terrorist crimes).

Osman v United Kingdom where the applicants' family was subject to a murderous attack by a school teacher whose behaviour had been increasingly bizarre and threatening, the Court held that failure to comply with such an obligation would arise where the authorities had not done all that could be reasonably expected of them to avoid a real and immediate risk to life of which they knew or ought to have had knowledge. However, on the facts of the case, the Court found that in the absence of any clear threat of serious violence or any evidence that would have supported arrest on reasonable suspicion of criminal offences or detention on mental health grounds, the police had not been shown to have known that the applicant family were at real and immediate risk or to have failed to have taken reasonable steps in that regard.[50]

The Court, as in other contexts, is careful in imposing positive obligations not to interpret Art.2 in such a way as to impose an impossible or disproportionate burden on authorities and has referred to the difficulties that arise in policing and issues of priorities and resources, as well as the need to respect other rights, in particular a respect for due process, the right to liberty and rights under Art.8 of the Convention.[51] Thus, while special duties are owed by the authorities to protect the lives of prisoners from harm, including self-harm, the measures imposed should take into account principles of dignity and self-determination, indicating that oppressive security measures may go too far.[52] The Court has also rejected the argument that every prisoner should be regarded at such risk: this would pose a disproportionate burden on the authorities and unnecessary and inappropriate restrictions on prisoners.[53]

The approach concentrates on the facts of each particular case and avoiding reliance on hindsight. Thus in *Keenan v United Kingdom*, where the applicant's son committed suicide in his cell, the Court found that the prison authorities were aware of his mental problems but took reasonable steps in response, placing him in hospital care and under close watch when he showed signs of suicidal tendencies. However, there had been no reason on the day of the incident for the authorities to suspect that an attempt was likely.[54] Conversely, in *Paul and Aubrey Edwards v United Kingdom*, the failures in communication and proper medical screening on entry to prison which led to a seriously disturbed prisoner being placed in the cell of the applicant's son who was then battered to death did lead to the Court finding that the authorities had failed to take reasonable steps to protect him from a man who should have been identified as a real and serious risk to others.

---

[50] Also *Dawn Bromiley v UK*, 33747/96, (Dec.) November 23, 1999, where the applicant's daughter was killed by a prisoner on home leave, the Court found no evidence that the authorities should have been aware that he was likely to commit a violent crime or that the daughter was at any risk; *Mastromatteo*, n.48 above, where the authorities could not have reasonably suspected that the release of two prisoners would lead to the death of the applicant's son during a robbery). *Cf. Kilic*, para.76, where the journalist had informed the authorities of threats to his life and requested protection but the authorities failed to take any steps, even by way of investigation.

[51] *Osman*, para.116.

[52] *Keenan*, para.91.

[53] *Younger v UK*, 57420/00,(Dec.) January 7, 2003, ECHR 2003–I.

[54] Also *Younger*, n.53 above, where the applicant's son hung himself in his cell, the Court found no evidence that his conduct, despite some signs of distress on remand in custody, should have alerted the authorities to a real and imminent risk of suicide.

(b) *Procedural requirements*

The obligation to carry out an effective investigation extends not only to those   **IIB–399**
deaths in which security forces are implicated but also to killings by use of force
generally, and arguably any suspicious or unlawful killing.[55] What form of
investigation will achieve the purposes required by Art.2 will again depend on the
circumstances.[56] Special vigour is required where there is a suspicion of racial
motivation.[57] It will not be in every case of tragic occurrence that special steps by
way of enquiry would be required. Where the authorities prosecute and convict the
perpetrators, this will generally show compliance with the requirements of Art.2 in
relation to the unlawful use of force.[58] In other contexts, such as medical negligence
it may be sufficient that the relatives have the opportunity to take civil proceedings
or that disciplinary proceedings are taken.[59] In *Mastromatteo v Italy*, where the
applicant's son was killed by two men released from prison, it was sufficient that the
State had tried and punished the two men and that the applicant could take civil
proceedings against the State alleging gross negligence. Art.2 did not require that
the State provide compensation on the basis of strict liability.[60]

Where investigations are required, similar considerations apply as to the elements
of effectiveness as in cases of the use of force by the authorities, namely promptness
and expedition,[61] access to material evidence and sufficient public scrutiny and
involvement of the relatives. Thus, in *Paul and Aubrey Edwards v United Kingdom*, the
lack of power of inquiry into a death in prison to compel prison officers to give
evidence diminished its effectiveness. The holding of the inquiry in private and the
inability of the parents of the deceased to attend also failed to comply with the
procedural requirements of Art.2.[62]

(c) *Medical services*

The extent to which a State is under an obligation to protect a person's state of   **IIB–400**
health is largely unexplored. It trespasses on an area of State health policy in which
matters of finance and policy are sensitive and controversial. Concerning complaints

---

[55] *Paul and Aubrey Edwards* (killing of prisoner by another detainee).

[56] *Paul and Aubrey Edwards*, para.69.

[57] *Menson v UK*, 47916/99, (Dec.) May 6, 2003, emphasis on impartial, effective investigations into racially-motivated killings, *inter alia* to maintain confidence of minorities in the ability of the authorities to protect them from racist violence; *Nachova*, paras 157–158.

[58] *Menson*, n.57 above, where the deceaseds' family complained about institutional racism in the investigation, the Court noted that nonetheless the perpetrators had been tried and convicted and that Art.2 did not guarantee as such a remedy in respect of alleged defects in the authorities' discharge of their obligations under that provision.

[59] *Calvelli and Ciglio*, para.51, concerning allegations that a doctor's negligence caused the death of the applicants' baby.

[60] See 23412/94, (Dec.) August 30, 1994, 79–A D.R. 127, where the authorities prosecuted the nurse for poisoning the applicants' children and there was the possibility to bring civil proceedings against the hospital for negligence, the Commission considered that Art.2 did not require a wide-ranging enquiry into the structural or policy defects in the national health system.

[61] *e.g. Paul and Aubrey Edwards*, para.86, while some delays in the inquiry could be criticised (the final report issued after 3 years), the Court found, due to the complexity and thoroughness of the investigation, that the authorities had not shown insufficient promptness.

[62] Contrast 23412/94, n.60 above, where an inquiry was held into a series of murders by the nurse Beverly Allitt in a hospital, the Commission had not found it incompatible with Art.2 that the enquiry was not open to the public and its membership not wholly independent from the health authorities.

that the vaccination of children was causing severe brain damage and even death, the Commission held that States were under an obligation to take adequate measures to protect life and that this might raise issues in the area of medical care.[63] However, in that case, it noted that there was no evidence that the vaccinations were administered poorly or that proper and adequate steps were not taken to avoid the risks of damage and death materialising. It appears to have given weight to the number of vaccinations which pursued the purpose of avoiding serious illness in comparison to the relatively few adverse reactions. It concluded that overall the system of supervision and control of those administering the vaccinations was sufficient to comply with the obligation. The Court recently adopted the Commission's view that Art.2 applied in the public health sphere, although no breach has yet to be found.[64]

The Court has stated in cases about medical malpractice that the State's positive obligation under Art.2 to protect life includes the requirement to have regulations for the protection of patients' lives.[65] In *Calvelli and Ciglio v Italy*, however, it found no violation arising from the failure to prosecute a doctor who allegedly had caused the death of the applicant's newborn baby through negligence, considering that the civil proceedings would serve to elucidate the issues of responsibility that arose. It also commented in *Cyprus v Turkey* that an issue could arise under Art.2 where it is shown that the authorities put an individual's life at risk through the denial of health care which they have undertaken to make available to the population generally.[66] No obligation arose on the authorities to refund the full price of life-saving drugs, where the applicant had had access to medical treatment and facilities under the Polish health service.[67]

In the absence of any real or immediate risk to life, it is unlikely that complaints about general standards or denial of medical care would be found to raise any issues.[68] In the case brought by the parents of children killed and injured by the nurse Beverley Allitt, the applicants sought to attack the system of national health as a whole. It was argued, *inter alia*, that the financial cutbacks and organisation of the local health services had lead to the situation in which an untrained and dangerous individual could be allowed to care unsupervised for children. The Commission did not consider that Art.2 extended to an examination of national health policy and practice in general. It was sufficient that Allitt had been prosecuted, that the applicants could sue the health authorities for negligence and that an inquiry had been held which had made public its findings with regard to the procedures at fault in the hospital in question.[69]

---

[63] 7154/75, (Dec.) July 12, 1978, 14 D.R. 31.
[64] *Calvelli and Ciglio*, paras 49–50.
[65] *e.g. Calvelli and Ciglio*, para.49.
[66] May 10, 2001, ECHR 2000–IV, para.219: it was not established however that the minorities in northern Cyprus had been denied access to hospitals or that any lives had been put at risk by the alleged delaying of requests for treatment in the south.
[67] *Nitecki v Poland*, 65653/01, (Dec.) March 21, 2002.
[68] 6839/74, (Dec.) October 4, 1974, 7 D.R. 78 where a mother complained of the denial of a medical card to her severely disabled daughter, the Commission found, whether Art.2 would apply or not, on the facts the daughter had been receiving medical assistance and her life had not been endangered.
[69] n.60 above.

Cross-reference

Part IIB: Abortion
Part IIB: Extradition, Death penalty
Part IIB: Torture, inhuman and degrading treatment (in particular, 5. Matters of proof and causation, dealing with the standard of proof and relevance of domestic factfinding)

Surveillance and secret files

Key provision:

IIB–401   Article 8 (private life).

Key case law:

Klass v Germany, September 6, 1978, Series A, No.28; 2 E.H.R.R. 214; *Leander v Sweden*, March 26, 1987, Series A, No.116; 9 E.H.R.R. 433; *Amann v Switzerland*, February 16, 2000, ECHR 2000–II; 30 E.H.R.R. 843; *Rotaru v Romania*, May 4, 2000, ECHR 2000–V; *Khan v UK*, May 12, 2000, ECHR 2000–V; 31 E.H.R.R. 1016.

1. General considerations

IIB–402   Under this section, the clandestine process of information-gathering and storing by democratic States is considered. While surveillance techniques will frequently involve interception of communications, this receives separate treatment under the Convention due to the specific protection of correspondence. Surveillance and intelligence gathering is a much wider and potentially unlimited field of activity. Many similar factors however come into play. The need for information gathering and storage is generally not questioned where it is in the context of police investigation or security, the legitimacy of the aims and the necessity of which is undoubted.[1] The concentration has been on lawfulness and procedural aspects to prevent arbitrariness or abuse.

2. Private life

IIB–403   Besides direct interception of phone and mail, there are a myriad of methods, from the use of listening devices or bugs in privately owned houses[2]; indirect information from intercepts in place on other persons[3]; collection of press reports, data from surveillance by Special Branch, photographs (usually from passport applications)[4]; long range cameras, drilling holes in wall.[5] Though doubt has been expressed whether the gathering of publicly accessible information or information relating to matters in the public domain (for example, press cutting files or criminal records) concern private life,[6] the Court has held that public information can fall within the

---

[1] *Leander*, para.49; even where the surveillance subjects are perhaps surprising as in *Hewitt and Harman v UK (No.1)* 12175/86 (Rep.) May 9, 1989, 67 D.R. 88, civil rights lawyers and Labour Party members or *Campbell Christie*, the trade union leader (21482/93 (Dec.) June 27, 1994 78–A D.R.119). See however the concurring opinion in *Rotaru*, which stated that the Court would have been entitled to find that unlawful and arbitrary collection and storage of information on the applicant's activities going back 50 years did not pursue a legitimate aim.
[2] *Redgrave v UK*, 20271/92, (Dec.) September 1, 1993.
[3] *Hewitt and Harman (No.1)*, n.1 above.
[4] *Hewitt and Harman, ibid.*
[5] *Govell v UK*, 27327/95, (Rep.) January 14, 1998.
[6] *e.g.* Judge Bonello's dissent in *Rotaru*. See *Zdanoka v Latvia*, 58278/00, March 6, 2003, where information about the applicant contained in public archives and public knowledge about her activities was considered information about her public, not private, life.

scope of private life where it is systematically collected and stored in files held by the authorities, particularly where such information concerns a person's distant past or where it is false and likely to injure reputation.[7] The Court has also stated that Art.8 corresponds with the Council of Europe's Data Protection Convention whose purpose is to secure for every individual his right to privacy with regards to the automatic processing of personal data relating to him and such personal data being defined as "any information relating to an identified or identifiable individual."[8]

A security check *per se* was not objectionable for the Commission which held in *Hilton v United Kingdom* that issues only arose where the check was based on information about a person's private affairs.[9]

3. Establishing an interference

While *Klass v Germany* concerned interception of communications in particular, it also referred to "surveillance measures" in more general terms. The Court stated that it was enough for there to be in existence a system permitting the use of such measures for Art.8, para.1 to be invoked by applicants as constituting an interference with private life. The Commission added a gloss in *Hilton v United Kingdom,* adopted later by the Court,[10] to the effect that it could not be open to anyone in the country to complain that they were subject to violations due to the activities of secret service activities: an individual had to show that there was a reasonable likelihood that he had been subject to such measures or was in a category of persons likely to be targetted. Once an applicant is in that category, it is not necessary to show that the information compiled and stored has been applied to his detriment.

IIB–404

In *Hilton*, the applicant did not establish a reasonable likelihood. It was only shown that the BBC had materials submitted in the context of her job application and that the Security Service objected due to her membership of a particular society. There was no indication that it had or continued to retain any information of a personal character about her. In *Hewitt and Harman v United Kingdom (No.1)*, where an MI5 operative made revelations in an affidavit, a reasonable likelihood that secret surveillance occurred and files compiled was established. While in *N v United Kingdom*, where the applicant was offered a post connected with an electronic warfare department working on defence projects, subject to "enquiries" which he was later told were not satisfactory, the Commission found there was a reasonable inference that he had been subject to security checks.[11]

The nature of an applicant's own activities may also render it reasonably probable that surveillance had been carried out and information gathered in secret files, as in

---

[7] *Rotaru*, paras 43–44.

[8] Convention for the Protection of Individuals with regard to the Automatic Processing of Personal Data, January 28, 1981, in force on October 1, 1985: *Amann*, para.65; *Rotaru*, para.43.

[9] 12015/86, (Dec.) July 6, 1988, 57 D.R.108; also *N v UK*, 12327/86, (Rep.) May 9, 1989, 67 D.R. 123. For example, a security check might involve scrutiny only of the materials given by the person in the application or reference to files where no entries exist.

[10] *Halford v UK*, June 25, 1997, R.J.D. 1997–III, No.39.

[11] Also *Esbester v UK*, 18601/91, (Dec.) April 2, 1993, *DE and F v UK*, 18600–2, (Dec.) October 12, 1992, concerning applicants who applied unsuccessfully for civil service posts—the Commission accepted the Government's submissions that for two applicants their residence abroad rendered a satisfactory security clearance impossible so that their applications were not checked; for the third, offered a post subject to enquiries which were unsatisfactory, the Commission found it was a reasonable inference that a security check had been carried out involving reference to recorded information falling within the sphere of private life.

the case of Vanessa Redgrave who found a bug on her premises which she alleged had been placed by the Government. The Commission noted that she was well-known for her involvement in a revolutionary party and controversial political causes, as well as evidence from documents showing US security interest over a considerable period of time.[12]

Once a file has been in existence, it is also likely that it will be presumed to exist at a later date, in the absence of rules for destruction.[13]

4. "In accordance with law"[14]

IIB–405   The basic principles have received significant examination in the area of interception of communications. It is established that the lawfulness criterion refers to the existence of a basis for the interference in domestic law, and the quality of the law, which must be accessible and render measures reasonably foreseeable, thus providing protection against arbitrariness. The requirement of foreseeability however is affected by the special context of secret controls of concerning national security. Thus in *Leander v Sweden* an individual did not have to be able to foresee precisely what checks would be made by the Swedish special police service. Nevertheless in a system applicable to citizens generally the law had to be sufficiently clear in its terms to give an adequate indication as to the circumstances in which and the conditions on which public authorities are empowered to resort to secret and potentially dangerous interference with private life.[15]

Lack of a proper basis in domestic law for the activities of the security service disclosed a violation in *Hewitt and Harman v United Kingdom (No.1)*, where there was only a 1952 Home Secretary directive, which though published did not have the force of law. A similar violation arose in *Govell v United Kingdom*, where there was no statutory system regulating the use of covert listening devices.[16]

In assessing the quality of the law, the Court may take into account instructions and administrative practices without status of substantive law and whether powers are adequately defined. Thus in *Leander*, there was no problem since, even though there was only one administrative instruction, it was public. Though there was a wide discretion as to what information could be entered, there were also significant limitations, *e.g.* no entry on the basis of expression of political opinion, detailed rules on how information on the register could be used and the system was subject to the necessity of measures for the purposes of national security. However this criterion was not met where the law defining the tasks of the Dutch Military Intelligence Services did not state the limits to be respected in carrying out their activities and

---

[12] n.2 above.

[13] *Hewitt and Harman v UK (No.2)* 20317/92 (Dec.) September 9, 1993. The Government ceded an interference for these applicants, in respect of whom files had already been found to have existed years before.

[14] See also Pt I, Convention Approach, Lawfulness.

[15] *e.g. Rotaru*, paras 56–63 (where the law provided no explicit, detailed provision concerning the persons authorised to consult the secret files or the use to be made of the files nor did the system provide supervisory safeguards against abuse); *Amann*, paras 75–80 (where the creation and storage of a card with information on the applicant lawyer from telephone interceptions of the Soviet embassy was not carried out under a law specifying the conditions in which the card could be created or the information which could be stored).

[16] n.5 above, paras 61–63. The Home Office Guidelines were neither legally binding on the police or publicly accessible.

there was no definition of categories of persons liable to be subject to measures of secret surveillance or the circumstances in which measures could be employed or the means to be employed.[17]

Provisions do not have to be subject to comprehensive definition. In *Esbester v United Kingdom* the Commission rejected the complaint that the phrase 'in the interests of national security' was only partially defined since the subject was inevitably couched in terms which had to be flexible and developed through practice. It was enough that there were express limits, in particular that the information could only be used where necessary to fulfil the specified functions. In *Hewitt and Harman (No.2)*, the Commission was not impressed that other systems limited powers more narrowly, for example, to those who advocated the use of force, as opposed to a definition which potentially covered actions intended to overthrow parliamentary democracy by non-violent means.[18]

5. Necessity and procedural safeguards

Regarding the necessity of measures, there is a wide margin of appreciation accorded to Contracting States in choosing the means of protecting national security.[19] The fact that a person finds himself subject to security checks which bar him from employment or is subject to secret surveillance is not enough to disclose a violation, whether justified on the facts or not.[20] The scrutiny of the Convention organs has concentrated rather on the existence of procedural safeguards, since the grant of such powers poses a risk of undermining, even destroying democracy on the ground of defending it. There must therefore be adequate and effective guarantees against abuse, and where these exist, there may be no violation. A pragmatic and not overly demanding approach, requiring an adequate framework of safeguards of a minimum level of protection, has been adopted.

In the context of procedural safeguards, the Court has referred to direct and regular control as constituting a major safeguard against abuse. It appears impressed by the involvement of judicial or parliamentarian bodies which can provide independent scrutiny of measures. In *Leander*, the safeguards which were found sufficient included the presence of parliamentarians on the National Police Board who participated in all decisions as to whether information should be released to a requesting authority and supervision by the Parliamentary Ombudsman and the Chancellor of Justice.

Following *Klass*, no problem arises from the failure to release information about past surveillance measures since it is the absence of communication which ensures at least partly the efficacy of the control procedure.

In *Esbester v United Kingdom*, where the applicant attacked the system set up under the Security Service Act 1989, the Commission found references to systems in other jurisdictions of limited relevance. While other arrangements might be more liberal, its role was to see if the system under examination in the concrete case passed the

IIB–406

---

[17] 14084/88, (Rep.) December 3, 1991.
[18] n.13 above.
[19] *Leander*, para.59.
[20] 35099/94, (Dec.) April 5, 1995, 81–A D.R. 136, where the Northern Irish applicant, living in Geneva, was subject to allegedly unjustified police surveillance but could only gain limited access to the files to refute their contents. Procedural safeguards were sufficient.

threshold imposed by Convention guarantees.[21] As a whole the 1989 Act provided adequate safeguards against abuse—an independent tribunal with lawyers of 10 years' experience and a Commissioner of high judicial office who made annual reports to Parliament and recommendations to the Secretary of State. It did not therefore consider that the inability of the Commissioner to make binding decisions, or the limited scope of the tribunal's review and its inability to verify or correct information recorded were decisive. In the absence of any indication that the system was not functioning as required by domestic law, it considered that the framework of safeguards achieved a compromise beween the requirements of defending democratic society and the rights of the individual. When further complaint was made in *Hewitt and Harman v United Kingdom (No.2)*, the Commission, in examining the Commissioner's reports, found that he was fulfilling his role actively and authoritatively, and therefore saw no reason to depart from its reasoning in *Esbester*, namely, the system functioned properly. The complaints, *inter alia*, that the tribunal did not hear witnesses on oath, its decisions were brief and that Commissioner could not order the destruction of records where he found it unreasonable to retain them, were not given weight.[22]

Regarding any right to consult the data held on files, for example to correct any erroneous entries, the cases do not indicate that this can be derived from Art.8 as yet. Though a right of consultation, even limited is commented on favourably in assessing the procedural safeguards available, no violation has yet been founded upon its absence.[23]

Cross-reference

Part IIB: Interception of communications
Part IIB: Private Life

---

[21] *e.g. Hewitt and Harman (No.2)*, n.13 above: comparison with other systems (Canadian and Australian) might indicate that the Government incorrectly assumed that other methods were not practicable but that did not assist in determining whether the concrete case passed the threshold.
[22] n.13 above.
[23] This point was raised unsuccessfully by *D, E, and F*, n.11 above, and the lack of any possibility to amend errors was referred to in *Hewitt and Harman (No.1)*. See also *Leander*, para.48, where the inability to check contents was part of the interference; 35099/94, n.19 above, where complete access was not necessary.

Tax

Key provisions:

Article 5, para.1 (right to liberty), 6 (access to court and fair trial) and Art.1 of   IIB–407
Protocol No.1 (right to property).

Key case law:

Darby v Sweden, October 23, 1990, Series A, No.187; 13 E.H.R.R. 774; *Bendenoun v France*, February 24, 1994, Series A, No.284; 18 E.H.R.R. 54; *Gasus Dosier GmbH v Netherlands*, February 23, 1995, Series A, No.306–B; 20 E.H.R.R. 403; *Benham v UK*, June 10, 1996, R.J.D. 1996–III, No.10; 20 E.H.R.R. 293; *National & Provincial Building Society v UK*, October 23, 1997, R.J.D. 1997–VII, No.55; 25 E.H.R.R. 127; *Ferrazzini v Italy*, July 12, 2001, ECHR 2001–VII; *Jokela v Finland*, May 21, 2002, ECHR 2002–IV; *Janosevic v Sweden*, July 23, 2002, ECHR 2002–VII.

1. General considerations

Tax receives special treatment under the Convention. Not surprisingly, in drafting   IIB–408
the Convention, the Contracting States did not intend to undermine the basis on which their financing depends. An individual's right to enjoyment of his property is accordingly subject to the State's right to assess, levy and enforce contributions by way of tax under the second paragraph of Art.1 of the First Protocol. The provision is to be interpreted in light of the underlying principle in the first sentence of the first paragraph of Protocol No.1, namely, to achieve a fair balance between the general interest of the community and the protection of the fundamental rights of the individual.[1]

There are few significant cases concerning the way in which States choose to tax or the levels of taxation. Where issues arise the ubiquitous margin of appreciation is present and wide. Arguable complaints arise more frequently in peripheral areas, as regards access to court and fairness of proceedings in tax-related matters. Peripheral issues may also arise where there is apparent discrimination in tax matters or where there is apparent discrimination in tax matters.

2. Imposition of tax: assessment and levels

It is for national authorities to decide in the first place what kind of taxes or   IIB–409
contributions are to be collected and the methods by which they are collected, such decisions commonly involving the appreciation of political, economic and societal questions which the Convention leaves within the competence of the Contracting States which enjoy a wide margin of appreciation.[2] The Commission found no problems arising as regards the imposition on employers of the costly PAYE

---

[1] *Sporrong and Lönnroth v Sweden*, September 23, 1982, Series A No.52, para.69.
[2] 11036/84, (Dec.) December 2, 1985, 45 D.R. 211; *Spacek sro v Czech Republic*, judgment of November 9, 1999, para.41.

system,[3] the increase of contributions on certain categories of persons to benefit others[4] and the imposition of retrospective tax measures.[5]

But there may be limits. The Commission stated that the imposition of tax would not generally be incompatible with Art.1 of Protocol No.1 unless it amounted to a *de facto* confiscation of some part of the taxpayer's possessions.[6] A financial liability might conceivably affect adversely the guarantee of ownership if it placed an excessive burden on the person concerned or fundamentally interfered with his financial position.[7] Reference is also made in cases to whether the imposition of a tax is disproportionate or an abuse of the State's power.[8] The cases indicate that gross arbitrariness or misuse of powers would be required for the Convention organs to find any violation. In *Jokela v Finland*, for example, the Court found a violation where the authorities, in levying inheritance tax on land, had given insufficient explanation for the highly inflated market value used in reaching the assessment.

3. Measures in enforcement of taxation and duties

IIB–410   Measures taken to ensure the payment of taxes or prevent defaulting are generally found compatible with the second paragraph. Consideration is given to whether the measure is of such a kind that it can reasonably be considered as necessary for the purpose and whether its application is grossly disproportionate.[9] The imposition of a mortgage on a defaulter in favour of the authorities to ensure payments was not disproportionate[10] and the prevention of the removal of property from the country by a person with outstanding tax liabilities fell within the second paragraph of Art.1.[11] The seizure by the tax authorities of a concrete mixer over which the vendor applicant had retained title was not a deprivation of property within the meaning of the first paragraph but a measure to secure the payment of taxes. In the circumstances the applicant company was involved in a commercial venture, which by its very nature involved an element of risk. Proportionality was satisfied since it could have taken measures of protection, such as stipulating payment in advance, which the tax authorities were not in a position to do in respect of defaulters, and the applicant was not without a measure of protection since it enjoyed priority over other creditors and an adequate review procedure before the courts.[12]

---

[3] 7427/76, (Dec.), September 27, 1976, 7 D.R. 148.

[4] 7995/77, (Dec.) July 11, 1978, 15 D.R. 198 where the imposition of additional N.I. contributions on some self-employed fell within the second paragraph of Art.1 of Protocol No.1 as justified in the general interest for financing the social security system for lower earners.

[5] 8531/79, (Dec.), March 10, 1981, 23 D.R. 203, concerning retrospective legislation to prevent deliberate trading losses to set off against tax—the measure was not excessive: tax liabilities for the previous year had not yet been settled and the losses were artificial.

[6] 9908/82, (Dec.) May 4, 1983, 32 D.R. 266: where the tax authorities upped the applicant's tax regarding large investments in companies as income unless shown to derive from capital or a gift.

[7] 11036/84, n.2 above: where a profit-sharing tax was introduced to the applicant's detriment but its level (not exceeding 1%) was not disproportionate or an abuse of the right to levy tax.

[8] 13013/87, (Dec.) December 14, 1988, 58 D.R. 163: concerning a 7% wealth tax on life assurance companies, the Commission noted the measure was introduced to tackle the budget deficit and inflation: it referred to the "sovereign power" of the State and found no lack of proportionality or abuse.

[9] 7287/75, (Dec.) March 3, 1978, 13 D.R. 27—the duties, fines and forfeiture were not so disproportionate in this case since the judge could have regard to applicant's economic means and, though very severe, were not excessive.

[10] 9889/82, (Dec.) October 6, 1982, 31 D.R. 237.

[11] 10653/83, (Dec.) May 6, 1985, 42 D.R. 224.

[12] *Gasus Dosier GmbH v Netherlands*.

4. Penalties and fines: failure to comply with tax authorities

Where a person is sanctioned for failure to comply with tax regulations, issues may arise where the sanction falls within the scope of "criminal charge" for the purposes of Art.6, para.1.[13] In *Bendenoun v France*, where a taxpayer, accused of not acting in good faith in relation to declared business receipts, was subject to tax surcharges (almost half a million francs) the Court agreed with the Commission that the tax surcharges concerned a "criminal charge" rendering the Art.6 guarantees applicable. It noted the charges were imposed under the Tax Code which applied to everyone; were not intended as pecuniary compensation for damage but essentially as a punishment to deter reoffending; were posed under a general rule whose purpose was deterrent and punitive; and there was liability of committal to prison for non-payment. However, tax surcharges may be regarded as a "criminal penalty" even where there is no risk of committal to prison, if they are nonetheless punitive and deterrent in character.[14] There is some authority that a surcharge of a small amount will not be regarded as sufficiently punitive.[15] Once Art.6 is applicable, the usual guarantees concerning effective access to court and fairness of procedures apply.[16]

Where a person is committed for failure to pay tax, this may constitute detention compatible with Art.5, para.1(b) as lawful arrest or detention in order to secure the fulfilment of an obligation prescribed by law. Issues have arisen in the context of poll tax, as to whether magistrates have complied with lawfulness criteria in exercising the power to commit defaulters.[17]

IIB–411

5. Civil rights

Article 6 does not apply to proceedings relating to the assessment or imposition of tax, including the consequences of a change in tax legislation. In *Ferrazzini v Italy*, the Court emphasised that tax matters still formed part of the hard core of public authority prerogatives. The fact that pecuniary interests of the tax payer might be at stake was not sufficient to remove tax from the public law sphere.[18]

In *National & Provincial Building Society v United Kingdom*, where the applicants were claiming restitution of monies paid under invalid tax regulations however, the Convention organs found that Art.6 applied. The restitution proceedings were regarded as private law actions decisive for private law rights to quantifiable sums of money and the judicial review proceedings were closely related to them.[19]

IIB–412

6. Retrospectivity

There is no express prohibition on retrospective legislation outside the criminal sphere. However, in respect of a retrospective removal of tax relief which aimed to prevent the avoidance of tax, the Commission held that a retrospective measure

IIB–413

[13] See, *e.g. Janosevic* and *Vastaberga Taxi Aktiebolag v Sweden*, July 23, 2002, where penalty surcharges were imposed on the applicants in addition to the amount of unpaid tax.
[14] *Janosevic*, para.68.
[15] *Morel v France*, 54559/00, (Dec.) June 3, 2003, concerning 10% increase of 4450 FRF.
[16] *Janosevic*, para.90; *Vastaberga Taxi Aktiebolag*, n.13 above.
[17] *Benham v UK*. See Pt IIB: Deprivation of liberty, In accordance with a procedure prescribed by law.
[18] paras 28–31, where the Court confirmed, tacitly, Commission case law.
[19] Also *Editions Periscope v France*, March 26, 1992, Series A No.234–B, para.40.

imposing a liability or removing a relief must be regarded as more severe due to the uncertainty which it engenders, in particular since it prevents a taxpayer arranging his affairs to mitigate new liabilities. On the facts of that particular case however, the measure was not excessive.[20]

7. Discrimination

IIB–414   Differences in treatment of persons in relevantly similar positions may raise issues under Art.14 in conjunction with Art.1 of Protocol No.1 since matters of taxation fall within the scope of that provision. The Commission considered that a wider margin of appreciation would apply in this area than in others, since taxation systems inevitably differentiate between groups of taxpayers and the implementation of any system creates marginal situations. It noted that attitudes and goals in taxation will change and a government may need to strike a balance between the need to raise revenue and to reflect other social objectives, the authorities being best placed to assess those requirements and the moment when it was appropriate to amend the tax system. Where the applicant was complaining of the inequal effect of taxation depending on whether the husband or the wife was the principal earner and pointed to the pending proposal to render the position of spouses identical, the Commission found that the anomaly resulted from measures of positive discrimination in favour of married women to encourage them into the job market and was proportionate and within the margin of appreciation. It also considered that for taxation purposes married and unmarried couples were not in comparable positions, marriage constituting a regime which attracted specific rights and obligations.[21]

Different tax rates can be justified by the consideration of avoiding too high a burden on lower earners.[22] Differences applied to taxpayers who live abroad may be justified, as in the case where civil servants working abroad were liable to pay Austrian tax on part of their salary but were unable to claim a single breadwinner's allowance. The Commission having regard to the margin of appreciation found that the difference could be justified since it was difficult for the Austrian authorities to verify what happpened outside their borders.[23] However in *Darby v Sweden* where the applicant was liable to pay church tax in Sweden even though he was not resident in the country but could not, unlike residents, apply for an exemption, the Court found no objective or reasonable justification in the alleged administrative difficulties that eligibility to non-residents would engender.

Cross-reference

Part IIA: General Principles, Fairness
Part IIA: General Principles, Civil rights and obligations
Part IIA: General principles, Criminal charge
Part IIB: Discrimination
Part IIB: Property

---

[20] 8531/79, n.5 above.
[21] 11089/84, (Dec.) November 11, 1986, 49 D.R. 181.
[22] 7995/77, n.4 above.
[23] 12560/86, (Dec.) March 16,1989, 60 D.R. 194.

Torture, inhuman and degrading treatment

Key provision:

Article 3 (prohibition on torture, inhuman and degrading treatment or punishment).   IIB–415

Key case law:

Ireland v UK, January 18, 1978, Series A, No.25; 2 E.H.R.R. 25; *Tyrer v UK*, April 25, 1978, Series A, No.26; 2 E.H.R.R. 1: *Soering v UK*, July 7, 1989, Series A, No.161; 11 E.H.R.R. 169; *Tomasi v France*, August 27, 1992, Series A, No.241–A; 15 E.H.R.R 1; *Herczegfalvy v Austria*, September 24, 1992, Series A, No.244; 15 E.H.R.R. 437; *Costello-Robberts v UK*, March 25, 1993 Series A, No.247–C; 19 E.H.R.R. 112; *Ribitsch v Austria*, December 4, 1995, Series A, No.336; 21 E.H.R.R. 573; *Chahal v UK*, November 15, 1996, R.J.D. 1996–V, No.22; 23 E.H.R.R. 413; *Aksoy v Turkey*, December 18, 1996, R.J.D. 1996–VI, No.26; 23 E.H.R.R. 553; *Aydin v Turkey*, September 25, 1997, 1997–VI, No.50; *Raninen v Finland*, December 16, 1997, R.J.D. 1997–VIII, No.60; 26 E.H.R.R. 563; *A v UK*, September 23, 1998, 1998–VI, No.90; 27 E.H.R.R. 611; *Assenov v Bulgaria*, October 28, 1998, R.J.D. 1998–VII, No.96; *Selmouni v France*, July 28, 1999, ECHR 1999–V; 29 E.H.R.R. 403; *Ilhan v Turkey*, June 27, 2000, ECHR 2000–VII; *Keenan v UK*, April 3, 2001, ECHR 2001–III; *Z v UK*, May 10, 2001, ECHR 2001–V; *Kalashnikov v Russia*, July 15, 2002, ECHR 2002–VI; *Ocalan v Turkey*, March 12, 2003, pending before the Grand Chamber; *MC v Bulgaria*, December 4, 2003, ECHR 2003–XII.

1. General approach

Article 3 sets an absolute prohibition. There are no stated exceptions and no   IIB–416
derogation is possible under Art.15. The Court has said that it enshrines one of the fundamental values of the democratic societies making up the Council of Europe[1] and calls for heightened vigilance.[2] It applies irrespective of the victim's conduct.[3]

That said, however, and perhaps as a result, the threshold for treatment falling within the scope of Art.3 was, at least initially, set high by the Convention organs. The Commission in the *Greek Interstate* case distinguished acts prohibited by Art.3 from a "certain roughness of treatment", which might take the form of slaps or blows of the hand on the face or head.[4] The Court distinguished between the use of

---

[1] *Soering*, para.88.
[2] *Ribitsch*, para.32.
[3] Governments have argued that in certain circumstances Art.3 does not have full effect. In *Chahal*, the argument was rejected that the expulsion of the alleged Sikh terrorist to India was justified due to the security threat which he posed to the UK if he stayed; in *Tomasi*, the argument it should be taken into account that the applicant was a terrorist and involved in a violent crime was smartly rejected by the Court which held that the fight against crime and difficulties with regard to terrorism could not justify limits on the protection to be afforded in respect of the physical integrity of individuals (para.115).
[4] *The Greek case*, 3321–3/67 and 3344/67, 11 YBK of the ECHR (Rep.) November 5, 1969, (1969), 501. More controversially, it commented that this was tolerated, even taken for granted by the detainees and that the point up to which people accepted physical violence as being neither cruel nor excessive

violence which is to be condemned on moral grounds and also in most cases under the domestic law of the Contracting States but which does not fall within Art.3.[5] The test established by the Court is that of attaining a certain minimum level of severity. The basic approach is:

". . . ill-treatment must attain a minimum level of severity if it is to fall within the scope of Article 3. The assessment of this minimum is, in the nature of things, relative; it depends on all the circumstances of the case, such as the duration of the treatment, its physical and mental effects and, in some cases, the sex, age and state of health of the victim."[6]

While in the early years of the Convention system there was perhaps a sentiment that to find a State in violation of this provision was particularly serious and not to be undertaken lightly, there has, since the new Court, been a certain evolution in the application of that minimum level and a more rigorous assessment is now considered appropriate.[7]

The Convention system has received, and continues to receive, many complaints of grave, distressing situations in which Art.3 is invoked. However, expulsion or extradition *per se* (without any risk to life or limb being involved), the taking into care and adoption of a person's children, the imposition of long sentences of imprisonment, while they may all entail significant personal distress are not such as to fall within Art.3, particularly where the distress is a collateral effect of measures primarily aimed at achieving other legitimate aims.[8] There would have to be special elements or circumstances bringing the case beyond the "usual" effect that the measure inevitably entails, such as discrimination based on racial grounds which degrade and stigmatise[9] or perhaps where the execution of the measure is unnecessarily and unjustifiably distressful.[10]

The principal Art.3 treatment cases have risen in the context of physical ill-treatment inflicted by the authorities or agents of the State—the archetypal police or prison brutality type case. This is gradually being extended to risk of severe physical or psychological harm where a State takes steps which may lead to a person being exposed to such harm, or even to the imposition of a positive obligation, to take steps

---

depended on societies and different sections of them: see also the Commission in *Ireland v UK*, in respect of conditions in holding centres, *i.e.* no bedding, compulsory physical "military drill" type exercises, even though some detainees were old and in poor condition—this was harsh, even illegal, a practice that was reprehensible and discreditable but not contrary to Art.3.

[5] *Ireland v UK*, para.167.

[6] *ibid.*, para.162.

[7] See *Selmouni*, para.101, and the cases on prison conditions, below.

[8] *e.g. V v UK*, December 16, 1999, ECHR 1999–IX, para.71.

[9] *East African Asians* case, 4403/70, etc. (Rep.) December 14, 1973, 78–A D.R. 5; however, see *Abdulaziz v UK*, May 28, 1985, Series A, No.94, para.91, where the difference in treatment in immigration matters did not denote any contempt or lack of respect for the personality of the applicants but was intended solely to achieve the aims of protection of employment, the economy and immigration control.

[10] *e.g.* 19579–82/92, April 4, 1993, the *Orkney* child care cases were communicated under Art.3 in relation to the dawn raid, the complete separation from families and familiar objects, intensive "interrogations"—the question would possibly have arisen whether these were accepted practices and without any therapeutic basis (applications later withdrawn); *V v UK*, n.8 above, para.79, where the traumatic effects of the murder trial on the 11-year-old defendant did not cause, to a significant degree at least, suffering going beyond what would inevitably have been engendered by an attempt by the authorities to deal with him after the commission of the offence.

to avoid such risk occurring. This is in the context of expulsion and extradition particularly but has been raised also in the context of punishment of children.[11]

Only individuals can invoke Art.3, not legal persons.[12]

2. Exhaustion of domestic remedies and administrative practice

Where an allegation is made of assault or ill-treatment in custody, a civil action for damages will generally be a remedy which should be exhausted for the purposes of Art.3.[13] However, States cannot buy their way out of their obligations, torturing freely and paying up in the courts.[14] Thus a civil remedy may cease to be regarded as an effective remedy where there is an "administrative practice" of treatment contrary to Art.3.[15] This requires

IIB–417

- a repetition of acts (a pattern such as the five techniques examined in *Ireland v United Kingdom*, see below);
- official toleration, at a senior level. Mere tolerance at the lower and middle level of the hierarchy is not of itself conclusive. It is necessary to examine what measures have been taken by the authorities to prevent the repetition of such treatment.[16]

It is not enough that the existence of an administrative practice be merely alleged, its existence must be shown by means of substantial evidence.[17]

While administrative practice was alleged in Turkish applications from South-East Turkey, the Commission did not find it necessary to make any findings in light of their view that in each case declared admissible the applicants had either done all that could be expected of them by way of exhaustion or that there were no effective remedies available.[18]

The difficulties of establishing an administrative practice outside an interstate case are illustrated by *Donnelly v United Kingdom*,[19] which was rejected on, *inter alia*, grounds of non-exhaustion shortly before the Court found a practice of ill-treatment existing in *Ireland v United Kingdom*.

3. Different categories of ill-treatment

Consideration is given to the particular circumstances of each case. Relevant factors include the manner and method of execution; the nature and context of the punishment[20]; premeditation and systematic organisation; age[21]; duration[22]; effect on

IIB–418

---

[11] *e.g. Soering; Chahal; D v UK*, May 2, 1997, R.J.D. 1997–III, No.37 (expulsion cases); as regards corporal punishment of children in school (see Corporal punishment) *Costello-Robberts* and *A v UK*.

[12] 11921/86, (Dec.), October 12, 1988, 57 D.R. 81.

[13] *e.g.* 8462/79, (Dec.) July 8, 1980, 20 D.R. 184.

[14] *Donnelly et al. v UK*, 5577–5583/72, (Dec.) December 15, 1975, 4 D.R. 4.

[15] *The Greek case*, n.4 above, paras 195–196.

[16] *Donnelly et al.*, n.14 above.

[17] Commission in *Ireland v UK*, (Dec.) October 1, 1972, 41 Coll. 3/85.

[18] *e.g.* the Commission's admissibility decisions in *Akdivar* and *Aksoy*.; the Court in *Aksoy*, para.57.

[19] n.14 above, where individual applicants who claimed to have been ill-treated in custody in Northern Ireland had either accepted settlements out of court or had civil claims pending.

[20] *e.g. Costello-Roberts*.

[21] Youth often puts into question the compatibility of measures under Art.3, *e.g.* it was an important

health[23]; state of health at the time[24]; public nature of the punishment[25]; whether alternative courses were open to the authorities[26] and the necessity and proportionality of measures taken for security reasons.[27]

(a) *Torture*

IIB–419   The Court in *Ireland v United Kingdom* held that torture involves suffering of a particular intensity and cruelty, attaching a "special stigma to deliberate inhuman treatment causing very serious and cruel suffering". It saw support in a resolution of the UN General Assembly referring to torture as an "aggravated and deliberate form of cruel, inhuman or degrading treatment of punishment". It found, overruling the Commission, that the five interrogation techniques used in holding centres in Northern Ireland did not constitute torture but inhuman and degrading treatment. The techniques involved keeping detainees' heads covered by a hood; submitting the detainees to continuous and monotonous noise of a volume calculated to isolate them from communication; deprivation of sleep; deprivation of food and water other than one round of bread and a pint of water every six hours; and making the detainees stand legs apart with their hands up against a wall for long periods. This was systematic but not sufficiently severe to be torture.

The Commission's approach attached weight to the character of the pressure involved, whether it intended to break or eliminate the will and the premeditated,

element in *Soering* concerning extradition to possible death penalty and detention on death row—the Court noted that the ICCPR and the American Convention on Human Rights prohibited the death penalty for those who commit the offence under 18—Soering was 18 at the time of offence; *Hussein v UK*, February 21, 1996, R.J.D. 1996–I, No.4, para.61—mandatory life sentences were acceptable as punishment for adults, but not for children. Advanced old age was a factor in *Henaf v France*, November 27, 2003, where the 75-year-old prisoner was chained to a hospital bed.

[22] The length of the wait on death row (six to eight years) "anguish and mounting tension" and long exposure to the stringent conditions on the death row was a significant factor in *Soering*; *mutatis mutandis*, the short cooling off period in which prison officers confined a teenage drug addict in her cell, combined with the lack of indications, physical or mental, as to likely ill-effects, did not disclose inhuman or degrading treatment in *Bollan v UK*, 42117/98, (Dec.) May 4, 2000, even though during this period she committed suicide.

[23] Significant effect on health, whether physical or mental, is usually required for inhuman treatment and for practical purposes generally requires substantiation and medical evidence of some kind. See, *e.g. Aerts v Belgium*, July 30, 1998, 1998–V, where the applicant, suffering from mental illness, was detained in a prison wing criticised as below acceptable standards by the CPT, the Court found no breach of Art.3 as he could not point to any serious effects on his mental health; *Ebbinge v Netherlands*, 47240/99, (Dec.) March 14, 2000, ECHR 2000–IV, where the Court criticised a special interrogation technique (involving the use of photographs of the murder victim and the applicant's own family) but did not find it established that use of the method resulted in mental pain or suffering attaining a minimum level of severity.

[24] *Soering* was suffering abnormality of the mind when he committed the murders, which was found relevant to the acceptability of "death row phenomenon" for a given individual; *Keenan*, para.115, punishment imposed on prisoner known to be a suicide risk.

[25] See *Tyrer*, below.

[26] In *Soering*, the Court took into account the possibility of achieving the purpose obtaining the trial of the applicant for serious crimes by extraditing him to Germany instead of the US. In *Chahal*, in response to the Government's allegations that he was a dangerous terrorist, it commented that it was open to the authorities to use the criminal justice system in the UK in respect of any offences committed.

[27] *e.g. Henaf*, n.21 above, para.56, chaining of 75-year-old prisoner to hospital bed disproportionate to alleged security risk.

systematic nature of the treatment.[28] In *Ireland v United Kingdom* it found that the five techniques caused some physical pain which stopped when the treatment ceased, exhaustion and a number of acute psychiatric symptoms, which it could not be excluded continued to exist for some time afterwards (anxiety, disorientation, isolation, etc.) While separately some of the techniques might not have fallen within Art.3, the techniques applied together were designed to impose severe mental and physical stress and suffering on a person in order to obtain information from him, which constituted torture.

In the subsequent findings of torture in Turkish cases, the Commission in particular emphasised the element of punishment or coercion.[29] In *Aksoy v Turkey*, the infliction of palestinian hanging in interrogation which left the applicant partially paralysed was, without discussion, torture. In *Aydin v Turkey*, where a 17-year-old girl was raped in gendarme custody, rape was found to be ill-treatment of an especially severe kind, "inherently debasing" striking at the heart of physical and moral integrity, aggravated by the fact that it was committed by person in authority and involving acute physical and psycholgical suffering in a punitive and coercive context.[30]

The new Court revised the applicable standard in *Selmouni v France*. Re-iterating the principle that the Convention was a living instrument which had to be interpreted in the light of present day conditions, it stated that an increasingly high standard was required in the area of human rights and that certain acts classified in the past as "inhuman and degrading treatment" as opposed to "torture" could be classified differently in future. It found in that particular case, where the applicant was assaulted and humiliated by police over a number of days with a view to inducing him to confess to the offence of which he was suspected, that the physical and mental violence was particularly serious and cruel and must be regarded as acts of torture.[31] Where however ill-treatment was inflicted on the applicant in *Egmez v Cyprus* over a short period of heightened emotions and there was some doubt as to the gravity of the injuries caused by the police officers and no indication of long-term consequences, the Court found that the ill-treatment could not be qualified as torture but was serious enough to be considered inhuman.[32]

---

[28] (Rep.) January 25, 1976, p.402; *The Greek Case*, 12/1 Ybk of the ECHR 461: where torture for the Commission implied inhuman treatment which had a purpose such as the obtaining of information or confessions or the infliction of punishment and that it was generally an aggravated form of inhuman treatment.

[29] e.g. in *Yagiz v Turkey*, (Rep.) May 16, R.J.D. 1996–III, No.13, it cited the UN Convention against Torture which in Art.1 includes elements of deliberatness for specific purposes of obtaining information or punishing or intimidating or coercing.

[30] (Rep.) para.189. The Court agreed that it was an especially cruel act amounting to torture, and was prepared to find torture separately for other aspects of ill-treatment, e.g. blindfolding, being kept naked, beaten and pummelled with high pressure water—paras 82–86. Also findings of torture in *Cakici v Turkey*, July 8, 1999, ECHR 1999–IV (electric shocks and beating); *Salman v Turkey*, June 27, 2000, ECHR 2000–VII (falaka and bruising to the chest); *Dikme v Turkey*, July 11, 2000, ECHR 2000–VIII, (severe beatings over lengthy interrogation beating, exacerbated by blindfolding); *Aktas v Turkey*, April 24, 2003, (crucifixion/palestinian hanging); *Akkoç v Turkey*, October 10, 2000, ECHR 2000–X (electric shocks, blows to the head and intense fear caused by threats to her children).

[31] Also *Ilhan*, where the severity of the beating and delay in obtaining treatment for brain damage was considered torture.

[32] December 21, 2000, ECHR 2000–XII, paras 78–79. See also, pre-*Selmouni*, *Tekin v Turkey*, June 9, 1998, R.J.D. 1998–IV, No.78, where treatment in police custody leaving wounds and bruises was regarded only as inhuman and degrading treatment.

Non-physical torture may also be possible, namely the infliction of mental suffering by creating a state of anguish and stress by other than bodily means.[33]

(b) Inhuman treatment and punishment

IIB–420   Inhuman treatment covers at least such treatment as deliberately causes severe mental and physical suffering.[34] The physical injuries in *Ireland v United Kingdom* fell within this notion (where individual detainees had been beaten and kicked by the security forces causing, for example, massive, substantial bruising, cuts to the head, a broken cheekbone, gross swelling) as did the injuries in *Tomasi v France*, in which medical reports indicated a large number of blows of sufficiently serious intensity (abrasions on face, chest and arms, haematoma on left ear) and their intensity. In *Ribitsch v Austria*, the applicant received bruises and haematomas on the arm caused while in police custody and there was a medical report that he was suffering from cervical syndrome, vomiting, violent headache and a temperature, after treatment in which the applicant alleged that he was punched repeatedly, kicked, and his head banged on the floor. The physical injuries and considerable psychological trauma constituted inhuman and degrading treatment. The Court added a very strong statement that in respect of a person deprived of liberty any recourse to physical force which has not been made strictly necessary by his own conduct diminishes human dignity and is in principle an infringement of the right in Art.3.

The use of force in the context of arrest although resulting in injury may fall outside Art.3, particularly if the circumstances disclose it resulted from the conduct of the applicant. In *Klaas v Germany*, where police officers used force to effect an arrest on the applicant, a 48–year old woman, who suffered a bruise to temple, concussion, contusion of left shoulder joint, in circumstances where the police alleged that she had tried to run away, the Court found nothing to lead it to depart from findings of fact of the national courts who had found the use of force not excessive and not unlikely to have been caused in her struggles.[35] Similarly in *Hurtado v Switzerland*, where the applicant received cracked ribs from the officer kneeling on him, the Commission accepted that the force used in the circumstances of the arrest did not contravene Art.3.[36] Where serious injury is inflicted during an arrest however, the Government will be required to furnish credible and convincing arguments to justify the degree of force and a violation will ensue if none is forthcoming, as in *Rehbock v Slovenia*, where the police accounts of how the applicant, unarmed and unresisting, came to suffer a double fracture were inconsistent and vague.[37]

---

[33] *The Greek Case*, n.4 above, pp.86 and 461; *Akkoç*, n.30 above, para.16, reference to intense fear caused by threats to children (though combined with physical torture elements).

[34] e.g. the Commission in *The Greek Case* and *Ireland v UK*, and the Court in *Ireland v UK*; as regards mental suffering see, e.g. the village destruction cases at 4(f) and the disappearance cases at 4(g).

[35] *Klaas v Germany*, September 22, 1993, Series A No.269; also *Douglas-Williams v UK*, 56413/00, (Dec.) January 8, 1002, use of positional restraint techniques was found justified by the applicant's violence on arrest, even where it contributed to his death from asphyxia; *Caloc v France*, July 20, 2009, ECHR 2000–IX, where there was nothing to call into question domestic findings as to the justified level of force used on the applicant, who it was undisputed had tried to run away; *Berlinski v Poland*, June 20, 2002, paras 62–64, where the applicants, bodybuilders, resisted the legitimate actions of the police, making recourse to physical force necessary by their own conduct.

[36] (Rep.) July 8, 1993, Series A, No.280–A (settled before the Court): the arrest took place during a planned police operation breaking into a drug ring, when there was reason to believe the suspects were dangerous and nothing to support allegations of beating.

[37] November 28, 2000, ECHR 2000–XII, paras 74–78.

Treatment was not sufficiently severe in consequences in *Tyrer v United Kingdom*, where three strokes of the birch which raised but did not break the skin; and in the context of school corporal punishment, three smacks from a shoe on the bottom through shorts causing no visible injury was not inhuman.[38] The Commission did find inhuman and degrading treatment in *Y v United Kingdom*[39] where the punishment resulted in four weals on the bottom from a cane, while in *A v United Kingdom* the corporal punishment inflicted by the stepfather of repeated caning causing significant bruising also reached this level.

(c) *Degrading treatment or punishment*

This consists of treatment or punishment which grossly humiliates a person or drives **IIB–421**
him to act against his will or conscience.[40] The five techniques in the *Ireland v United Kingdom* case were found to be degrading as well as inhuman since they were such as to arouse in their victims feelings of fear, anguish, and inferiority capable of humiliating and debasing them and possibly breaking their physical and moral resistance.[41] The purpose of the authority is particularly relevant, in the sense whether the measure denotes contempt or lack of respect for the personality of the person subjected to it and whether it is designed to humiliate or debase, instead of other aims.[42] However the absence of such a purpose does not conclusively rule out a finding of a violation.[43]

In *Tyrer v United Kingdom*, to distinguish between punishment which is generally humiliating to adults and degrading punishment within Art.3, the Court held that the humiliation or debasement involved must attain a particular level, beyond that usual element. This will depend on the circumstances of the case, in particular, the nature and context of the punishment, the manner and method of execution. While the public nature of the punishment might be relevant, its absence is not fatal, since a person may be sufficiently humiliated in his own eyes even if not in the eyes of others.[44] For the Court in *Tyrer*, it was "institutionalised violence" of the birching that was the crucial element, where the applicant was treated as an object in the power of the authorities and subjected to an assault on his personal dignity and physical integrity the protection of which is one of Art.3's main purposes. There was the element of delay, leading to the mental anguish of anticipation; the official aura attending the procedure and infliction of the punishment by strangers. The factor that the punishment entailed the stripping of clothes was only one aggravating element.

---

[38] *Costello-Roberts*.

[39] (Rep.) October 8, 1991, Series A, No.247–A settled before the Court.

[40] *The Greek Case*, n.4 above, p.186.

[41] para.67.

[42] *Raninen*: the Commission found degrading treatment where the applicant, a conscientious objector, was handcuffed publicly when unlawfully arrested by the military police. Notwithstanding the unjustified nature of the measure, the Court noted a lack of mental or physical effects on the applicant and found that the treatment did not attain the required level of severity. Also *Ocalan v Turkey*, paras 220–228, where the applicant was handcuffed and blindfolded on his arrest and transfer from Kenya to Turkey, the Court obviously considered this was justified by security considerations and was of relatively short duration.

[43] *V v UK*, n.8 above, para.71; *Peers v Greece*, April 19, 2001, ECHR 2001–III, para.74, violation where the exceedingly hot conditions or open toilet in the cell were not in any sense intended to humiliate or debase.

[44] para.32. See also *Yankov v Bulgaria*, December 11, 2003, paras 112–122: the visible and public stigma of headshaving a prisoner for arbitrary punitive reasons.

Where an applicant claimed that he had defecated on arrest, attributable to the use of a stun grenade, and had been unable to change clothes until the next day at the earliest, the Commission found that the wearing of soiled clothes for one day, during a hearing before a judge and on various journeys, due to the failure of the authorities to take the most elementary hygiene measures in making available clean clothes, was humiliating and debasing and therefore degrading.[45]

Humiliating circumstances of a sexual nature rendered the infliction on a teenage girl of corporal punishment by a male teacher in the presence of another male teacher degrading treatment though the severity of the punishment was not such as to render it inhuman.[46] In *Valasinas v Lithuania*,[47] requiring a male prisoner to strip naked in the presence of a female prison officer and touching his sexual organs and food with bare hands during a strip search diminished human dignity and disclosed degrading treatment. The imposition of strip searches, without any apparent security justification, may also humiliate and debase contrary to Art.3.[48]

Discrimination based on race, or membership of a national minority may be sufficiently severe to disclose degrading treatment.[49]

4. Particular contexts

(a) Punishment—type and length of sentence

IIB–422   Matters of length of sentence are generally outside the scope of this provision.[50] However elements of shocking disproportionality could raise an exception. In *Weeks v United Kingdom*, where the applicant aged 17 received a life sentence for robbery of 35 pence, the Court commented, in finding that discretionary life sentences attracted the right to review of lawfulness of continued detention, that otherwise a life sentence for such a minor crime by a young person would have been doubtfully compatible with Art.3.[51] The Commission has hinted that extradition where a person would be prosecuted for political offences or his political views or would receive an unjustified and disproportionate sentence would raise issues under Art.3.[52]

Extreme old age is not a bar as such to detention or imprisonment though the Court has not excluded that issues could arise and examines the individual circumstances of each case.[53] Detaining a severely disabled person, without requisite

---

[45] *Hurtado*, n.36 above.

[46] 9471/81, (Rep.) July 18, 1986, 60 D.R. 5: the applicant was caned on the hand.

[47] July 24, 2001, ECHR 2001–VIII, para.117.

[48] e.g. *Iwanczuk v Poland*, November 15, 2001, where the applicant, in order to use the voting facilities in the prison, had to strip for a body search before four guards who ridiculed him.

[49] *East African Asians* case, n.9 above; *Cyprus v Turkey*, May 21, 2001, ECHR 2001–IV, paras 305–311.

[50] e.g. 5871/72, (Dec.) September 30, 1974, 1 D.R. 54; also 11653/85, (Dec.) March 3, 1986, 41 D.R.231, where a drastic change in parole policy which dashed hopes of imminent release and increased effective length to be served was not covered.

[51] March 2, 1987, Series A, No.114, para.47.

[52] 10308/83, (Dec.), May 3, 1983, 36 D.R. 209; see however 11017/84, (Dec.) March 13, 1986, 46 D.R. 176 where the expulsion of a person claiming conscientious objection to military service with a risk of long sentence for refusal did not constitute such treatment.

[53] e.g. *Papon v France*, 64666/01, (Dec.) June 7, 2001, ECHR 2001–VI, where the applicant was 90 years old with serious heart problems, the Court found that he was under regular medical supervision and no indication that the inconveniences or constraints caused by the imprisonment were sufficiently severe to breach Art.3; *Sawoniuk v UK*, 63716/00, (Dec.) May 29, 2001 , ECHR 2001–VI, no problem *per se* from imposition of life sentence at 78.

provision for their needs, may raise problems, as in *Price v United Kingdom*, where the applicant, a four limb deficient thalidomide victim with numerous health problems, including defective kidneys was committed to prison for contempt.[54]

(b) *Compulsory medical treatment*

Where compulsory medical treatment, including force feeding, being strapped   **IIB–423** down, compulsory administration of drugs constitutes a therapeutic necessity in line with current medical practice, it cannot at the same time disclose inhuman or degrading treatment, according to the Court in *Herczegfalvy v Austria*. This was notwithstanding the "worrying" length of time that the applicant was handcuffed and held in a security bed. The Commission had found a violation, imposing the additional requirement that the manner of the application of the treatment must be compatible with Art.3. It found the timing and the use of massive force and the long term fettering were not so compatible.[55]

(c) *Prison conditions*

Until relatively recently, conditions of imprisonment had not been found to breach   **IIB–424** the requirements of Art.3. The early Commission cases, in particular, accepted significant levels of hardship, an approach reflecting an implicit acceptance that prison regimes require rigid discipline and severe restrictions on personal freedom. Any reluctance to criticise the conditions in which prisoners are held has now disappeared, though the Court continues to emphasise that issues only arise where the measures subject the prisoner to distress or hardship exceeding the unavoidable level of suffering inherent in detention.[56] Where a violation has been found, the Court has tended to categorise the treatment as degrading, rather than inhuman. It has had regard in particular to the length of time over which the prisoner has been obliged to endure the conditions[57] and taken account of the cumulative effects of the conditions, as well as specific allegations.[58] Offending features have included serious overcrowding, insufficient sanitary and sleeping facilities,[59] open unpartitioned toilets in shared cells,[60] high temperatures in unventilated cells[61] and pest infestation linked with recurring skin diseases and fungal infections.[62]

[54] July 10, 2001, ECHR 2001–VII—the cell was cold, without a bed which she could use and she suffered, *inter alia*, problems with fluid intake and had to be lifted on and off the toilet by male officers. See the separate opinion of Judge Bratza, who noted that the prison authorities did the best they could and laid responsibility on the judicial authorities for imposing detention on a severely handicapped person without at least verifying the existence of adequate facilities.

[55] paras 82–83; (Rep.) paras 247–254: See Pt IIB, Prisoners' rights, 5. Medical Treatment.

[56] *Kudla v Poland*, October 26, 2000, ECHR 2000–XI, paras 93–94; *Valasinas*, n.47 above, para.102, where the general conditions of detention were found, after a visit, not to attain the minimum level of severity, though an atmosphere of boredom due to lack of work and educational facilities and some regrettable shortcomings in toilet facilities was noted.

[57] *Dougoz v Greece*, March 6, 2001, para.48; *Peers*, n.43 above, para.75; *Kalashnikov*, para.102; while in *Valasinas*, n.47 above, para.108, the absence of toilet of partitions was noted to have been temporary.

[58] *Dougoz*, n.57 above, para.46; *Kalashnikov*, para.95.

[59] *Dougoz*, n.57 above; also severe overcrowding in *Kalashnikov*, where the applicant shared his bed on a rota with two other prisoners.

[60] *Peers*, n.43 above, para.75; *Kalashnikov*, para.99.

[61] *Peers*, n.43 above.

[62] *Kalashnikov*, para.98, where it was also a concern that the applicant was detained with persons suffering from syphilis and T.B.

Given the present-day rejection of capital punishment by European countries, the Court took a rigorous approach to the complaints of death row prisoners in Ukraine and found that the anxiety and uncertainty as to the effectiveness of the moratorium on executions together with, *inter alia*, the confinement 24 hours a day in a restricted cell space without natural light and little or no exercise or activities caused the applicants considerable mental suffering, diminishing their human dignity and disclosing degrading treatment contrary to Art.3.[63]

Special security regimes sometimes raise concerns about social or sensory isolation. The Court has not taken issue with the domestic authorities' assessment of the need for stringent precautions against escape in these cases and found acceptable quite serious limitations of visits and association with other prisoners.[64] In *Van Der Ven v Netherlands*, concerning the Extra-Security Institution (EBI), it was the almost automatic weekly strip search of the applicant over a three-and-a-half year period that appeared to tip the balance over the threshold of acceptable treatment.[65]

Lack of resources or economic problems cannot in principle justify prison conditions which offend the standards of Art.3.[66]

(d) *Lack of or delay in medical treatment*

IIB–425   Article 3 imposes an obligation on the State to ensure the health and well-being of persons deprived of their liberty, including providing them with the requisite medical assistance.[67] Serious ill-health does not necessarily render imprisonment incompatible with Art.3, where there is evidence that the prison authorities are providing appropriate care. It would appear to require however evidence of an identifiable shortcoming or defect in the treatment attaining a sufficient level of severity for the Court to find a violation in this respect.[68] In *McGlinchey v United Kingdom*, there was a failure by prison medical staff to monitor properly the state of the applicant who was vomiting repeatedly under withdrawal symptoms and dehydrated to the point of collapsing with multiple organ failure.[69]

Though due allowance is made for the practical exigencies of imprisonment, the strain imposed on an ill prisoner may attain the prohibited level of severity. In

---

[63] *Poltoraskiy v Ukraine*, April 29, 2003, ECHR 2003–V, paras 134–149; also judgments of the same date; *Kuznetzov*, paras 124–129, *Khokhlich*, paras 167–182, *Dankevich*, paras 125–145; *Aliev*, paras 133–152; *Nazarenko*, paras 128–145.

[64] *Van der Ven v Netherlands*, February 4, 2003, ECHR 2003–II, para. 55; see *Messina v Italy*, 25498/94, (Dec.) June 8, 1999, ECHR 1999–V: no violation of Art.3 concerning the special regime for mafia prisoners: severe restrictions on contacts with other detainees, and prohibition from communal recreation were justified by security requirements, the social isolation was not absolute and there had bee, no physically or pyschologically damaging effects.

[65] paras 52–63; also *Lorse v Netherlands*, February 4, 2003, where the applicant was subjected to the regime for over 6 years. There was also evidence in both cases of some mental side-effects of the prolonged period under these severe restrictions and a report from the CPT expressing considerable concern that the regime was having a harmful psychological effect on the detainees.

[66] e.g. *Poltoratskiy*, n.63 above, para.148, where the Court noted the serious socio-economic problems in Ukraine.

[67] *Kudla*, n.56 above, para.94.

[68] No failure to comply with necessary standards was found in *Kudla*; n.56 above, prison staff's failure to supply pain-killing medication on several occasions was insufficient in *Rehbock*, n.36 above, para.80.

[69] April 29, 2003, ECHR 2003–V, paras 57–58; see also *Keenan*, where the lack of effective monitoring and informed psychiatric input into the treatment of the mentally ill applicant, combined with the imposition of a disciplinary punishment following which he committed suicide, was found incompatible with the standard of treatment required in respect of a such a person; *Ilhan*, where there was a 36 hour delay in treating the victim's brain damage.

Mouisel v France[70], the Court found objectionable the way in which the applicant, suffering from cancer, had to be transferred to and from the prison to obtain external treatment, handcuffed throughout, which caused him suffering beyond that inevitably associated with either imprisonment or chemotherapy.

(e) *Expulsion and extradition*

The Convention organs, in *Soering v United Kingdom*, established that it would not be compatible with the fundamental principles underlying the Convention if a Contracting State were knowingly to surrender a fugitive to another State where he would be at risk of torture however heinous a crime he might have committed. This has since been extended to measures of expulsion generally and a potential breach of Art.3 will be found where there are substantial grounds for believing that an applicant faces a real risk of being subjected to torture or to inhuman and degrading treatment or punishment if expelled (see Pt IIB, Extradition; Immigration and expulsion).　IIB–426

(f) *Village destruction in Turkey*

The traumatic events alleged when Turkish security forces burnt houses in the south-east region, rendering villagers homeless and destitute, were found by the Commission to be sufficiently severe in their effects to constitute inhuman treatment, in particular where the applicants had been present, laying stress on the inherently violent nature of the experience and the anguish and distress caused in the process.[71] Although the Court showed an initial reluctance find such breaches,[72] it found found the circumstances in *Selçuk and Asker v Turkey* sufficiently traumatic to fall within the scope of Art.3 (namely, the burning was carried out without regard to the safety of the elderly applicants who witnessed the destruction of their home and all their possessions and were provided with no assistance afterwards).[73]　IIB–427

(g) *Disappearance*

The Court has rejected argument that the fact of a forced disappearance *per se* disclosed treatment contrary to Art.3.[74] In the absence of evidence of ill-treatment, it has so far declined to make any presumptions.[75] In special circumstances, the situation of uncertainty inflicted on the relative of the disappeared person may render him or her a victim of treatment contrary to Art.3.[76] The Court has given　IIB–428

---

[70] November 14, 2002, ECHR 2002–IX.

[71] *e.g. Mentes v Turkey*, 23186/94 (Rep.) March 7, 1996, R.J.D. 1998–VIII, No.59: where children were present and left without clothing, threats of physical force were made. The Court found it unnecessary to decide in view of the breach of Art.8.

[72] *e.g. Akdivar v Turkey*, September 16, 1996, R.J.D. 1996–IV, No.15.

[73] April 24, 1998, R.J.D. 1998–II, No.71; also *Bilgin v Turkey*, November 16, 2000; *Dulas v Turkey*, January 30, 2001, para.54.

[74] *Kurt v Turkey*, May 25, 1998, R.J.D. 1998–III, No.74, para.116; *Cicek v Turkey*, February 27, 2001, paras 155–157.

[75] *cf. Cakici v Turkey*, July 8, 1999, ECHR 1999–IV, paras 91–92 and *Akdeniz v Turkey*, May 31, 2001, where there was eye-witness evidence of ill-treatment of the victims who disappeared.

[76] *Cakici*, n.75 above, paras 97–99: the Court held that the finding an Art.3 violation on the part of the mother in the earlier case of *Kurt*, n.74 above, did not establish any general principle and referred to the need for "special features".

weight to the parent-child bond, to whether the relative witnessed the incident in which the victim was taken away, to the extent of the attempts by the relative to obtain information and the way in which the authorities have responded to those inquiries.[77] It has stated that the essence of the violation does not lie as such in the disappearance of the family member but rather the authorities' reactions and attitudes in respect of which a relative may claim directly to be a victim.[78]

5. Matters of proof and causation

(a) *Standard of proof*

IIB–429 The Convention organs adopted an approach of the free assessment of evidence, without any formal burden of proof on either party. The Court in *Ireland v United Kingdom* stated that it must examine all the material before it and may obtain evidence *proprio motu*. To assess this evidence it adopts, as the Commission did in *The Greek case*, the standard "beyond reasonable doubt".[79] Such proof may also follow from the coexistence of sufficiently strong clear and concordant inferences or of similar unrebutted presumptions of fact. In this context the conduct of the parties when evidence is being obtained has to be taken into account.[80]

In *Ireland v United Kingdom*, following complaints by the Irish Government that the UK had not afforded on occasion the necessary facilities for the effective conduct of the investigation, the Court considered this regrettable but this appeared to have no backlash on the assessment of the facts. However, a failure to produce relevant documents or witnesses has been taken into account by the Commission in drawing inferences and assessing facts in a number of Turkish cases.[81]

(b) *Injuries in custody*

IIB–430 As persons in custody are in a vulnerable position, the authorities are under a duty to protect them and to provide a plausible explanation for any injuries received.[82] Where a person held in custody suffers injury, there is accordingly a strong inference as to causation. This was applied by the Commission in *Ireland v United Kingdom*, where there was medical evidence of injuries received by detainees while under the responsibility of the security forces, with no other credible explanation, beyond

---

[77] e.g. *Kurt*, n.74 above, paras 133–134, *Cicek*, n.74 above, paras 173–174; *Timurtas v Turkey*, June 13, 2000, paras 96–97 and *Tas v Turkey*, November 14, 2000, ECHR 2000–XI, para.80, where, respectively, mothers or fathers of disappeared persons were victim of the authorities' complacency or callous disregard in face of their anguish; *Cyprus v Turkey*, n.49 above, para.157; conversely, *Cakici*, para.99, no violation in respect of the brother of the victim, who had neither witnessed the disappearance or been particularly involved in abortive contacts with the authorities; *Akdeniz*, n.75 above, para.102, no special features were found to exist.

[78] *Cakici*, n.75 above, paras 98–99; *Ipek v Turkey*, February 17, 2004, para.183.

[79] A reasonable doubt means not a doubt based on a mere theoretical possibility but a doubt for which reasons can be drawn from the facts presented—*Ribitsch*, (Rep.) para.104.

[80] *Ireland v UK*, para.161.

[81] e.g. *Aydin v Turkey*, (Rep.) where failure to provide a full plan of the custody area was found significant.

[82] *Selmouni*, para.87; *Salman*, n.30 above, para.99; *Berktay v Turkey*, March 1, 2001, para.167, where the applicant fell from a balcony while in the custody of six police officers; *Anguelova v Bulgaria*, June 13, 2002, ECHR 2002–IV, para.149, where the victim received injuries including a skull fracture in police custody.

vague, unsubstantiated references to the possibilities of fights or riots. In *Tomasi v France*, where the injuries clearly dated from the period in detention and the Government acknowledged that it could give no other explanation, the authorities were regarded as responsible.[83]

This presumption may be dislodged if there is some form of explanation by the authorities. In *Diaz Ruano v Spain*,[84] concerning the shooting of the applicant's son while in police custody, the Commission accepted that the police officer shot when attacked and in self defence. Although marks on the body supported the allegations of ill-treatment, there was no firm opinion as to timing from pathologists and the Commission did not find it established beyond reasonable doubt that injuries had been caused in police custody.[85]

(c) *Relevance of domestic factfinding*

While the Convention organs have always denied acting as a court of appeal or that they should substitute their opinion on the merits, they have not regarded themselves as bound by domestic courts' findings in any formal sense. Indeed, the Court has stated that in cases concerning allegations under Arts 2 and 3 it must apply a particularly thorough scrutiny.[86] The fact therefore that a domestic court has tried and acquitted an official concerning the same allegations will not prevent the Court finding a breach, as criminal law liability is distinct from international law responsibility under the Convention.[87]   IIB–431

Thus, in *Ribitsch*, the Commission and Court both found a violation of Art.3 in respect of the injuries suffered by the applicant in police custody although in the domestic proceedings the police officer's conviction was quashed on appeal and this decision was upheld at third instance. The Court proceeded to re-assess the evidence, giving significance to the existence of injuries, the fact that the injuries were not all explained by the policeman's story of a fall, the discrepancies in the police officer's versions of events and the lack of any other witness to the fall. It relied on the findings of the first instance court as to credibility and impliedly criticised the second instance's inadequate reasoning, *inter alia*, its references to the applicant's lack of credibility due to his past criminal record and personal extravagance, which the Court found irrelevant to events while he was in police custody.[88]

---

[83] See also *Aksoy*, where the injuries were alleged to have been received while in custody, and must have occurred at about that time and the Government gave no convincing explanation for their cause or what might have happened in the brief delay between release and the receipt of medical treatment.

[84] (Rep.) August 31, 1993, Series A, No.285–B settled before the Court.

[85] Also *Klaas, Berlinski, Caloc*, n.35 above.

[86] *Ribitsch*, para.32.

[87] *Avsar v Turkey*, July 10, 2001, para.284—the Court is dealing with the responsibility of the State, under the Convention, for the acts of its organs and agents, which is not the same as issues of individual criminal responsibility, or concerned with findings of guilt or innocence in that sense.

[88] In the Commission Report, see the then Mr. Bratza's separate opinion, stating that while he did not question the domestic decision to give the police officer the benefit of the doubt, the Government had not discharged the burden on them of providing a sufficiently convincing alternative explanation as to how the applicant came by his injuries. See also *Avsar*, n.87 above, where the courts convicted a village guard of the murder of the applicant's brother but the Court found that the applicant could still claim to be a victim of a breach of Art.2 as the authorities had failed promptly and effectively to investigate the possible involvement of a member of the security forces.

6. Positive and procedural obligations on the State

(a) The obligation to investigate

IIB–432   In order to render effective the fundamental safeguards enshrined in Art.3, the Court, as it has done with Art.2, interpreted the provision as requiring an effective, official investigation where an individual raises an arguable claim that he has been seriously ill-treated by the authorities.[89] This investigation should be capable of leading to the identification and punishment of those responsible. Thus in *Assenov v Bulgaria*, the cursory and defective investigation into allegations that police officers had beaten the 14-year-old applicant disclosed a breach of Art.3. The Court had found it impossible to establish from the evidence on the substantive complaints whether or not the boy's injuries had been caused by the police as alleged.[90]

In *Ilhan v Turkey*, the Court noted however that this approach might lead to an unnecessary overlap with Art.13 of the Convention, which requires an effective remedy for arguable breaches of the Convention and would generally impose the necessary procedural safeguards against abuse and possibility of redress. It considered that Art.2 differed significantly, both in the terms in which it was framed and in the problems with which it dealt.[91] Whether or not it was appropriate or necessary to find a procedural breach of Art.3 would depend on the circumstances, impliedly where the authorities' cursoriness or passivity, as in *Assenov*, hindered any possibility of making conclusive findings on the facts.[92]

The obligation was extended in *MC v Bulgaria* to punish rape and investigate rape cases generally. The failure of the prosecuting authorities to investigate the surrounding circumstances of the alleged rape of the applicant by two men on a date accordingly disclosed breaches of both Arts 3 and 8.

(b) The obligation to prevent ill-treatment

IIB–433   Article 3 has also been interpreted, in conjunction, with Art.1, to require States to take measures designed to ensure that individuals within their jurisdiction are not subjected to torture or to inhuman or degrading treatment or punishment.[93] This positive obligation to take protective measures applies particularly to children, or

---

[89] *Assenov*, para.102, citing Art.2 cases, in particular *McCann v UK*, September 27, 1995, Series A, No.324, para.161.

[90] See also *Labita v Italy*, April 6, 2000, ECHR 2000–IV where the lack of records and access by the prisoner to means of proving that he had been assaulted by prison officers also resulted in the Court finding insufficient evidence to disclose ill-treatment contrary to Art.3 and instead it found a procedural breach arising out of the tardy, inactive investigation by the authorities into the applicant's complaints; *Poltoratskiy*, n.63 above, paras 121–128, where there was insufficient evidence before the Court that the applicant had been beaten by prison guards but the prosecutors's investigation into the allegations had been perfunctory and superficial in breach of Art.3.

[91] paras 91–92.

[92] In *Ilhan*, the Court found it established by the evidence that the applicant had been hit on the head by a rifle butt by a gendarme and beaten, treatment severe enough to be torture. See Judge Bratza's separate opinion in *Poltoratskiy*, n.63 above, expressing doubt on the appropriateness of examining procedural complaints under Art.3 rather than 13.

[93] *A v UK*, para.22; *Al-Adsani v UK*, November 21, 2001, paras 38–40, where the ill-treatment took place in Kuwait without any causal connection to the UK and thus no positive obligation arose on the State to hold Kuwait to account in UK courts.

other vulnerable individuals.[94] It may require that adequate protection against severe ill-treatment exists in domestic law, such as protecting children from corporal punishment[95] or providing an effective criminal law system punishing all forms of rape and sexual abuse.[96]

It may also require that steps be taken to protect the individual against harm from third persons.[97] Taking the test applied in Art.2 positive obligation cases, the Court has held that the authorities should take reasonable steps to prevent ill-treatment of which they had or ought to have had knowledge.[98] The Court has stated that the scope of positive obligations must not be interpreted in such a way as to impose an impossible or disproportionate burden on the authorities and also should be compatible with the other rights and freedoms under the Convention.[99] On the other hand, the test does not require it to be shown that 'but for' the failing or omission of the public authority the ill-treatment would not have occurred. State responsibility is also engaged by a failure to take reasonably available measures which could have had a real prospect of altering the outcome or mitigating the harm.[100] So far, positive obligations have been found to arise concerning children, where the local authority has failed to protect children from serious abuse or neglect of which it knew or should have known[101] and prisoners, where the risk of harm came either from other prisoners or from the applicant's own vulnerable mental or health condition.[102]

7. Relationship with Art.2

Since Art.2 provides for judicial execution, the Court in *Soering* found that Art.3 **IIB–434** could not be interpreted as containing a general prohibition against the death penalty as inhuman punishment, though the manner of an execution, the personal circumstances of the condemned person or the disproportionality to the offence committed as well as conditions of detention while awaiting execution could be capable of bringing the treatment within Art.3. Since then the ratification by almost all member states of Protocol No.6, which bans the death penalty save in time of war, has led the Court in *Ocalan v Turkey* to consider that there has arguably been an abrogation or modification of Art.2 and that capital punishment may be regarded

---

[94] *A v UK*, para.22.

[95] *A v UK*, paras 23–24.

[96] *MC v Bulgaria*, para.182, undue emphasis in domestic law on the element of "resistance" in proving rape.

[97] *Z v UK*, para.73.

[98] *Z v UK*, para.73, citing *Osman v UK* October 28, 1998, Reports 1998–VIII, No.95, para.116.

[99] *Keenan*, paras 89–91, for example, there is a limit on the steps that can be taken, consistently with Arts 5 or 8 for example, to protect a person against deliberate self-harm.

[100] *E v UK*, November 26, 2002, para.99.

[101] *Z*, para.74, where the local authority failed to take effective steps, including removal, to protect the children from four and a half years of "appalling neglect" and physical and psychological injury; *E v UK*, n.100 above, paras 89–101 where the local authority failed to take effective measures which might have prevented the convicted abuser of the children of the family from returning to the home to continue sexual and physical abuse; conversely, *DP and JC v UK*, October 10, 2002, paras 110–114, where it was not established that the local authority had, or should have had, any suspicion of the long term abuse of the applicants by their stepfather.

[102] *Keenan*, para.115 (lack of monitoring of suicide risk); *Pantea v Romania*, June 3, 2003, ECHR 2003–VI, paras 188–196 (where the prison authorities failed to monitor the situation of the applicant, who had paranoid tendencies, or intervene effectively when he was suffering attacks from other detainees.

as an unacceptable, if not inhuman, form of punishment which is no longer permissible under that provision. It did not reach any firm conclusion on this point as, in any event, it found on the facts of the individual case that there had been a breach of Art.3 in imposing the death penalty in a trial which failed to comply with Art.6. It referred to the fear and uncertainty as to possible enforcement, which anguish could not be dissociated from the unfairness of the proceedings.[103]

Where accidental harm is the consequence of a use of force which complies with the requirements of Art.2, para.2, no issue arises under Art.3.[104]

Cross-reference

Part IIB: Corporal punishment
Part IIB: Extradition
Part IIB: Immigration and expulsion
Part IIB: Prisoners' rights

---

[103] Breaches of Art.6, paras 1 and 3 due, *inter alia*, to the composition of the court (a military member who could not be regarded as independent) and restrictions on the applicant's access and communication with his defence lawyers.
[104] *Stewart v UK* 10044/82 (Dec.) July 10, 1984, 39 D.R. 162.

Transsexuals

Key provisions:

Articles 8 (respect for private and family life), 12 (right to marry) and 14   IIB–435
(prohibition on discrimination).

Key cases:

Rees v UK, October 17, 1986, Series A, No.106; 9 E.H.R.R. 56; *Cossey v UK*,
September 27, 1990, Series A, No.184; 13 E.H.R.R. 622; *B v France*, March 25,
1992, Series A, No.232–C; 16 E.H.R.R. 622; *X, Y and Z v UK*, April 22, 1997,
R.J.D. 1997–II; 24 E.H.R.R. 143; *Christine Goodwin v UK*, July 11, 2002, ECHR
2002–VI; *I v UK*, July 11, ECHR 2002–VI; *Van Kuck v Germany*, June 12, 2003,
ECHR 2003–VII.

1. General considerations

The problems facing transsexuals in obtaining legal recognition of their change of   IIB–436
gender and the consequences on their enjoyment of the rights guaranteed under the
Convention was an area disclosing a marked divergence between the Commission
and old Court as to the application of the principles of the Convention. For the old
Court the matter raised legal, scientific, medical, social and ethical issues of a
controversial nature, and in the absence of any clear consensus in Contracting States
it accorded them a wide margin of appreciation.[1] Since it is an area in which
applicants tend to require States to take steps to ensure their rights, their complaints
also concern positive obligations by States, where the Court is generally more
reluctant to impose stringent requirements.[2] The recent cases of *Christine Goodwin*
and *I* show that the balancing exercise has at last tipped in favour of individual
rights and away from presumed public interests militating against change to the
existing status quo. There is an emerging emphasis on the right to personal
development and self-determination.[3]

2. Ability to change name and official documents

Inability to change name and amend official documents after a change of gender   IIB–437
disclosed a breach of Art.8 in the case *B v France*, where the applicant (male to
female transsexual) was unable to obtain a rectification of the civil status register,
with her masculine first name unchanged and recorded on all official identity papers,
sometimes accompanied by the indication that she was of the male sex. These
included documents which were in frequent use (*e.g.* cheque books, national
insurance no., driving licence, voting card, etc.) and placed the applicant in an
embarassing and humiliating situation on a daily basis which the Court considered
incompatible with the respect due to her private life.

[1] *Rees*, para.44; *Cossey*, para.40; *X, Y and Z*, para.44.
[2] See Pt IIB: Private life; 3. State obligations; Pt I: Convention Approach and Principles; 12. Positive
obligations.
[3] *Christine Goodwin*, para.90; *Van Kuck*, para.78.

3. Change of birth certificate

IIB–438 The right to respect for private life was held in in *Rees v United Kingdom* and *Cossey v United Kingdom* not to require that the national birth register amend birth certificates to record a transsexual's gender re-assignment.[4] In balancing the general interest of the community with the interests of the individual, the applicants' interests were given little weight since they had been able to change first names and official documents, which was at the time a situation more favourable than in some countries. On the other side of the scale, the Court considered that the UK could not be required to alter its entire birth registration system to a record of civil status as found in other Contracting States. It accepted the Government's argument that amendments to the register were not possible, save in the cases of clerical or medical mistake, since the system was based on recording facts at the time they occurred and that any subsequent changes would amount to a falsification of the record. It also accepted that measures protecting transsexuals from disclosure of gender re-assignment would have adverse effects, namely, an alleged risk of confusion and complication in family and succession matters, as well as apparently depriving third parties and government bodies of information which they might have a legitimate interest to receive.

This position, taken by the old Court, is not expressly overruled by the new Court's findings in *Christine Goodwin* and *I*. The UK Government was there found in breach of Art.8 for failing to accord legal recognition to the applicants' change of gender without the Court specifying what means should be employed to bestow such recognition.[5]

4. The right to legal recognition

IIB–439 A post-operative transsexual may now claim a right to official, legal recognition of his/her change of gender. While the failure to accord such recognition in the UK did not cause the daily humiliation suffered in *B v France*, the Court overturned its cautious approach to the subject in *Christine Goodwin* and *I*. It was in particular influenced by the fact that the applicant had undergone gender re-assignment surgery recommended, and carried out, by the national health services and found the general international recognition of the condition and of the need for the treatment was more significant than the lack of any clear scientific explanation as to the causes of the condition. Having regard also to the clear consensus in Contracting States to granting legal recognition, if not the means of achieving it, and the continuing international trend in that direction outside Europe (particular references to Australia and New Zealand), the Court found no detriment to the public interest identified which could outweigh the interest of the individual.[6]

---

[4] The Registrar adopted the biological approach as assessed at the time of birth without regard to later surgical intervention as in *Corbett v Corbett* [1971] P.83.

[5] *Christine Goodwin*, para.93: though the Court noted that providing for exceptions to the historic basis of the birth register had not been shown as likely to produce such a disastrous impact as previously assumed and that in any event the Government were proposing to introduce an ongoing civil registration system in the future (paras 86–88).

[6] *Christine Goodwin*, paras 76–93.

5. Right to marry

The old cases took the view that an individual who had received gender re-   IIB–440
assignment could not derive a right from Art.12 to marry a person of the biological
sex opposite to that with which he or she was attributed at birth.[7] In *Christine
Goodwin* and *I*, the Court expressly departed from the reasoning in those cases. It
rejected the argument that Art.12 was to be interpreted as the traditional marriage
between persons of opposite biological sex due to the reference in the same provision
to the founding of a family, pointing out that the modern right to marry could not
sensibly be held to be conditional on the capacity or intention to have children. Nor
could the reference to "men and women" any longer be regarded as referring to the
determination of gender by purely biological criteria. While the exercise of the right
was subject to the national laws of Contracting States, the Court considered that the
legal impediment imposed on post-operative transsexuals from marrying persons of
the sex opposite to their assigned sex impinged upon the essence of the right to
marry and could not be compatible with Art.12. The Court however phrased its
conclusion in terms which appear to leave a considerable margin of appreciation to
national legal systems as regards the formalities and conditions that can be imposed,
inter alia, regarding the information to be provided to the intended spouse and the
means by which a transsexual establishes that gender re-assignment has been
effected.[8]

Where however a State does provide for legal recognition of change of gender,
including for the purposes of marriage, a transsexual cannot complain under Art.12
of the resulting inability to marry a person of the same legal sex.[9]

6. Family life

In *X, Y and Z v United Kingdom*, the Court agreed with the Commission that *de facto*   IIB–441
family life falling within the scope of Art.8 existed where X, (a female to male
transsexual) had been in a stable relationship with a woman Y for over 15 years and
Y, with his support and involvement, had undergone artificial insemination by
donor (AID) treatment which resulted in the birth of a daughter Z. However, while
the inability of X under domestic law to have his name registered as the child's
father was found by the Commission to disclose a lack of respect for their family life,
emphasising the interests of the child and the family unit to security and legal
protection, against which it saw no convincing countervailing public interest, the
Court differed. It seemed influenced by what it perceived to be the controversial
nature of the AID treatment and found that while it had been not established that
legal recognition would harm any public interest it had neither been established that
it was in the interests of the child. Since the applicants were able to live together as
a family, the elements of practical detriment arising from the lack of legal
relationship between X and the child Z, such as succession rights, rights of support,

---

[7] *Rees, Cossey.*
[8] *e.g. Christine Goodwin*, para.103.
[9] 14573/89, (Dec.) November 9, 1989. Sweden did recognise changed gender but in this case the
transsexual (male to female) wanted to marry another female. The Commission found that Swedish law
was not lacking in respect for the right to marry since both persons were of the same sex and Art.12
covered only the right to marry someone of the opposite sex.

transmission of nationality or tenancy, were not considered to be significant, since they were either not relevant or steps could be taken to remedy them.[10]

The *X, Y and Z* judgment was given by the old Court, some five years before the recent findings in *Christine Goodwin* and *I* that transsexuals could claim, under Art.8, a right to legal recognition of their change of gender. It would appear likely that the consequent changes brought about by the UK Government to comply with these judgments will meet some of the difficulties experienced by a family in which one parent is a transsexual. It remains to be seen whether any residual differences in status will remain that would be found to cause sufficient concrete prejudice to breach the family life aspect of Art.8.

7. Reimbursement of medical expenses

IIB–442 Failure to give proper and appropriate consideration to a transsexual's condition in the context of a dispute with a private insurance company for reimbursement of her gender re-assignment surgery disclosed violations of both Arts 6 and 8 in *Van Kuck v Germany*. The Court purportedly did not make any finding about an entitlement to such expenses but found that the domestic courts' approach in requiring the applicant to prove the necessity of surgery and the "genuine nature" of her condition was disproportionate, inappropriate and in conflict with her right to self-determination.[11]

8. Discrimination

IIB–443 It is doubtful whether many issues will be found to arise here. If a violation is established under substantive provisions, such as Art.8, no separate issue is likely under 14 (as in *Christine Goodwin*). Conversely, if there is no lack of respect under Art.8, it is likely that any difference in treatment will be found to be be based on objective and reasonable justification. Where there is perhaps most scope for complaints by transsexuals of a difference in treatment, *e.g.* employment, access to services, such matters will fall outside the scope of the provision if they do not concern substantive Convention rights.

Cross-reference

Part IIB: Discrimination
Part IIB: Marriage and founding a family
Part IIB: Private life

---

[10] Concerning the lack of legal recognition of relationships between parents and children born out of wedlock, the ability to make *inter vivos* dispositions, etc. was not considered to remedy the disadvantages, *e.g. Johnston v Ireland*, December 18, 1986, Series A No.112; 9 E.H.H.R 203.
[11] The Court did not make a pecuniary award but for non-pecuniary damage happened to award a figure slightly above the amount of the claimed medical expenses.

Welfare benefits

Key provision:

Article 6, para.1 (fair hearing guarantees); Art.1 of Protocol No.1 (right to property) and Art.14 (prohibition against discrimination).

IIB–444

Key case law:

Feldbrugge v Netherlands, May 29, 1986, Series A, No.99; 8 E.H.R.R. 425; *Deumeland v Germany*, May 29, 1986, Series A, No.100; 8 E.H.R.R. 448; *Salesi v Italy*, February 26, 1993, Series A, No.257–E; *Schuler-Zgraggen v Switzerland*, June 24, 1993, Series A, No.263; 16 E.H.R.R. 432; *Schouten and Meldrum v Netherlands*, December 9, 1994, Series A, No.304; 19 E.H.R.R. 432; *Gaygusuz v Austria*, September 16, 1996, R.J.D. 1996–IV, No.14; 23 E.H.R.R. 364; *Duclos v France*, December 17, 1996, R.J.D. 1996–VI; 32 E.H.R.R. 86; *Van Raalte v Netherlands*, February 21, 1997, R.J.D. 1997–I, No.29; 24 E.H.R.R. 503; *Mennitto v Italy*, October 5, 2000, ECHR 2000–X; *Willis v UK*, June 11, 2002; *Koua Poirrez v France*, September 30, 2003, ECHR 2003–X.

1. General considerations

The omission of social and economic-type rights from the Convention gave the initial impression at least that complaints about welfare benefits fell outside the scope of the Convention. Gradually, however, the developing case law on the scope of civil rights under Art.6, para.1 and the approach to property rights under Art.1 of Protocol No.1 in conjunction with Art.14 (discrimination) have eroded the validity of this assumption. Generally, a complaint that a welfare benefit is not granted or that it is of a particular level will not be considered by the Court. However, as soon as eligibility criteria appear to single out persons unjustifiably on grounds of status (sex, nationality) or the proceedings dealing with disputes of entitlement show failure to conform to Art.6 requirements, the picture becomes problematic.

IIB–445

2. Applicability of Art.6

To attract the procedural guarantees of Art.6, there must be a dispute about a civil right or obligation. Whether a claim to a particular benefit or concerning levels of contributions concerns such right or obligation depends on a consideration of the nature and characteristics of the benefit concerned.

IIB–446

    The Convention organs initially gave particular consideration to the public and private law features of the benefit. In that context, the categorisation of the right in domestic law was only a starting point and not conclusive unless corroborated by other factors.[1] In a number of cases, the Commission rejected claims based on benefits which it considered to be essentially public law in character. Where a claim

---

[1] *Feldbrugge.*

of a previously self-employed person to unemployment assistance was based on a scheme wholly paid out of State funds without direct contributions from the workforce, the Commission found that this did not involve any insurance relationship between the beneficiary and the body paying the benefit or any direct contribution by beneficiaries to the unemployment insurance scheme, nor was there any connection with an employment contract. Thus public law features predominated notwithstanding the personal and economic nature of the right flowing from the specific rules laid down by the legislation in force.[2]

Disputes concerning entitlement to benefits were first found to fall within the scope of "civil rights" in *Feldbrugge v Netherlands* and *Deumeland v Germany*. Since those cases, the existence of public law features (*e.g.* the character of the legislation; the compulsory nature of the social security scheme and the assumption by the State or other public institution of full or partial responsibility for ensuring social protection) has tended not to be decisive and have been outweighed by private law features, including the individual, personal and economic nature of the right; the link between social insurance schemes and the contract of employment; and affinities with private insurance.

The fact that in *Feldbrugge* the State intervened to regulate health insurance and the scheme was compulsory was not enough in itself to bring the matter within the sphere of public law. The Court noted that other types of insurance (*e.g.* car or housing) was compulsory but the entitlement to benefits could not be qualified as public law. It also found an analogy between contributions to social security schemes and premiums for compulsory insurance.[3] In *Schouten and Meldrum v Netherlands* it noted that private insurance covering largely the same risks was available in the Netherlands to those not compulsorily affiliated to or entitled to benefit from those schemes primarily intended to benefit those likely to find private insurance beyond their means. In that case it was also not relevant that rules governing the deduction and payment of contributions corresponded to those governing the deduction of tax from wages, as it was inevitable that means used by government agencies to ensure payment bore such a resemblance.

Although the insurance scheme in *Feldbrugge* derived from statute and not from a contract, the Court considered that the provisions were effectively grafted onto the contract and formed part of the relationship between employer and employee. Insofar as the private and economic nature of the right is concerned, the Court has regard to whether there has been an interference with a means of subsistence and whether the applicant is claiming a right flowing from specific rules laid down by the legislation in force.[4] In *Feldbrugge* it found that it was of crucial importance where the employee, unable to work, had no other source of income and that the right was "personal, economic and individual". In *Mennitto v Italy*, where a non-discretionary statutory entitlement to an invalid carer's allowance was concerned, the Court referred merely to the economic nature of the right in finding Art.6 applicable.

---

[2] 10855/84, (Dec.) March 3, 1988, 55 D.R. 51; also 8341/78, (Dec.) July 9, 1980, 20 D.R. 161, where the payment of "military insurance" to soldiers injured on duty was regarded as a purely unilateral initiative, with no payments from the beneficiaries; 11450/85, (Dec.) March 8, 1988, 55 D.R. 142 where a claim for higher level sickness benefit was found to fall outside Art.6 since the the connection with employment was remote and assessment and collection conducted in the same legal framework as tax).
[3] *Schouten and Meldrum*, para.53.
[4] *e.g. Feldbrugge*, para.37.

In *Schuler-Zgraggen*, where the Government pointed out that sickness benefit did not derive from a contract of employment since affiliation was compulsory also for self-employed and unemployed, that the amount of pension depended entirely on degree of incapacity with no relation to amount paid in or level of income and that the Swiss system operated on a mixture of pay as you go, solidarity and drawing on tax revenues, the Court emphasised that State intervention was not decisive but that the most important consideration was that the applicant suffered an interference with her means of subsistence and was claiming an individual, economic right flowing from specific rules laid down in a statute. It found no distinction therefore between the applicant's right to an invalidity pension and the rights to social insurance benefits claimed by Mrs Feldbrugge and Mr Deumeland.

The Court has generally taken the approach that the State has been intervening in an area of private law allied closely to employment and acting as a form of insurance company.[5] In light of statements in *Schuler-Zgraggen* and *Salesi v Italy* and the emphasis given to the effect on subsistence, it would appear likely that Art.6, para.1 will be found to apply to most key benefits.[6] In *Duclos v France*, there was no dispute that it applied to the applicant's various disputes with the social security authority about the daily allowance for his disablement benefit; with an insurance company UAP about a disablement insurance policy his former employer had taken out with it; and with the family allowance body as to whether his drop in his earnings on unemployment should affect the calculation of the allowance.

As regards contributions to social security schemes, in *Schouten and Meldrum v Netherlands*, the Court found the approach would not necessarily be the same since in previous cases concerning claims to benefits the most important consideration had been the fact that the applicant had suffered "an interference with her means of subsistence" and was claiming an individual economic right, which did not apply automatically to disputes about contributions.[7] Also the fact that the obligation was "pecuniary" in nature would not be of the same decisiveness since pecuniary obligations exist *vis-à-vis* the State in public law, as taxes or part of other civic duties.

3. Application of the procedural guarantees under Art.6

Once Art.6, para.1 is applicable, in theory the usual guarantees as to, for example, independence and impartiality, length[8] and fairness[9] apply. The application of

IIB–447

---

[5] Art.6 was applicable in *Feldbrugge* (dispute as to entitlement to sickness allowance: insurance was compulsory for persons bound by contracts of employment and in case of unfitness entitlement flowed from statute, as a substitute for salary); *Deumeland* (claim by widow for pension on death of husband covered by compulsory industrial accidents insurance, closely linked to his status as an employee and an extension of his salary under the contract); *Salesi* (a refusal of disability allowance, a benefit funded entirely by the Government but under the jurisdiction of the labour magistrates' court); *Schuler-Zgraggen* (cancellation of invalidity pension following birth of child); *Schouten and Meldrum* (dispute about payment of contributions under health/unemployment insurance schemes covering employees).

[6] It is less apparent whether the considerations adverted to would apply to auxiliary benefits, such as mobility allowances, attendance allowances, etc.

[7] *Schuler-Zgraggen*, para.46.

[8] *e.g. Deumeland*, (over 11 years) the Court considered that particular diligence required in social security cases (para.90); *Duclos*, where the Government argued that the distinctive features of social security cases in the French system had to be taken into account (*i.e.* tribunals had no power to give directions, the parties had full control over the proceedings), the Court noted that tribunals were subject to the same

procedural guarantees may however affected by the nature of social security proceedings.

In *Schuler-Zraggen*, an exception appears to have been established to the general principle of providing a hearing. The Court found that the applicant could have asked for a hearing and since she did not, she waived her right unequivocally. As regarded whether nonetheless the nature of the proceedings required an hearing before a court, it found that the highly technical nature of the issues rendered proceedings in writing more effective and it was legitimate for national authorities to have regard to demands of efficiency, economy and the need for particular diligence in social security cases, in which context systematic oral hearings would be an obstacle.

4. Property rights

IIB–448   The Commission had doubted the applicability of Art.1 of Protocol No.1 to State benefits. Even assuming contributors to a social insurance system could derive a right to receive benefit, the Commission held that it could not be interpreted as giving a right to a pension of a particular amount.[10] Co-ordination by the State of pensions in light of benefits received from the social insurance system did not thereby deprive the applicant of any property right which he previously had. A claim to a disability pension was not a "possession" for the purpose of Art.1 of Protocol No.1, where the social security benefits in issue were part of general insurance system based on the principle of social solidarity, without any direct link between the level of contributions and benefits awarded and consequently a person did not have at any given moment an identifiable and claimable share in the fund.[11] Whether a claim to unemployment benefit constituted a property right was left open, since the Commission found that the applicant still had to satisfy domestic legal requirements governing the right to the benefit and thus no deprivation of possessions arose where her benefit was stopped for three weeks as she had left her job without lawful grounds.[12]

In *Gaygusuz v Austria*, benefits were treated for the first time as falling within the scope of Art.1 of Protocol No.1. While this was only in the context of Art.14, nonetheless the Court found that the right to emergency assistance was pecuniary in nature and linked to the payment of contributions to the unemployment insurance fund, which brought it within the scope of Art.1 of Protocol No.1. While it was left open for a while whether a social security benefit must be contributory in nature in order to constitute a "possession",[13] the Court has more recently held that a claim for a disabled adults' allowance, a non-contributory benefit, concerned a pecuniary

code of procedure as civil cases and the reasonableness of the time taken was to be judged as before civil courts—there was no mention of special diligence however—and periods of over 8 and 9 years disclosed a violation. In *Koua Poirrez*, para.62, over 7 years was acceptable where the applicant had meanwhile received an alternative benefit.

[9] *e.g. Feldbrugge*, where the procedure did not allow the applicant proper participation, *e.g.* the President of the Appeals Board neither heard the applicant nor gave her the opportunity to consult the evidence in the case-file and to submit written pleadings.

[10] 10671/83, (Dec.) March 4, 1985, 42 D.R. 229.

[11] 10971/84, (Dec.) July 10, 1985, 43 D.R. 190.

[12] 11285/84, (Dec.) December 7, 1987, 54 D.R. 88.

[13] *Willis*, para.35.

right for the purposes of Art.1 of Protocol No.1. The reasoning appears based on the fact that the applicant fulfilled the statutory criteria for the benefit, save for the element of nationality which discriminatory factor was in issue under Art.14.[14]

While in *Duchez v France*, the Court accepted that the right to family allowances payable to security force personnel, to the extent that it was provided for by statute, constituted a property right, it may be noted that in this case the domestic courts had already found claims to these allowances to be property rights.[15]

5. Discrimination

Differences in entitlements or in obligations to pay contributions may disclose discrimination in conjunction with either Art.6 or Art.1 of Protocol No.1.   IIB–449

Differences based on sex require very weighty reasons by way of justification in light of the importance of the goal of equality of the sexes. In *Schuler-Zraggen*, such reasons were not discerned by the Court where a decision as to entitlement of sickness pension was based on the assumption that general women gave up work when they had children. A violation was found in conjunction with Art.6, apparently on the basis that matters concerning the assessment and weight given to evidence fell within the scope of Art.6.

In *Van Raalte v Netherlands*, the obligation on the applicant, a man over 45, to pay a contribution to a child benefits scheme was discriminatory where women over 45 were not so obliged. The obligation to pay contributions to the social security system was found to fall within the scope of Art.1 of Protocol No.1 as part of the right of the State to "secure the payment of taxes or other contributions". In *Willis v United Kingdom*, discrimination arose where the applicant widower was unable to obtain benefits (Widow's Payment and Widowed Mother's Allowance) enjoyed by a woman in the same position. Arguably the Court would have been prepared to accept the entitlement to a bus pass on retirement was also sufficiently pecuniary and the differences in ages of entitlement of men and women unjustified. However, the case settled after admissibility.[16]

Refusal of benefits where the applicant would have qualified but for his status as a foreigner may also disclose discrimiantion. In *Gaygusuz v Austria*, as the applicant, of Turkish nationality, was lawfully resident in Austria and had worked and paid contributions on the same basis as Austrian nationals, there was no objective and reasonable justification to refuse emergency assistance exclusively on the fact of his nationality. Nor was the lack of French citizenship or any reciprocal agreement with the Ivory Coast found to justify the refusal of an allowance to the applicant in *Koua Poirrez v France*, where he was resident in France and son of a French citizen working in France.

---

[14] *Koua Poirrez*, paras 37–42: the Court's reasoning for this extension is somewhat thin, holding that the fact that the benefit in *Gaygusuz* was contributory did not mean, by converse implication, that non-contributory benefits did not qualify. See Judge Mularoni's dissent.

[15] 44792/98, (Dec.) September 26, 2002, ECHR 2002–VIII.

[16] *Matthews v UK*, 40302/98, (Dec.) November 28, 2000; June 24, 2002, struck out on change of legislation and compensation. See also pending admissible cases *Walker v UK*, 37212/02 (Dec.) March 16, 2004 and *Pearson v UK*, 8374/03 (Dec.) April 27, 2004, concerning age difference in entitlements and obligations to make contributions to State pensions between men (65) and women (60).

Cross-reference

Part IIA: Fair Trial, General Principles, Civil rights and obligations
Part IIB: Discrimination
Part IIB: Pensions

PART III—JUST SATISFACTION

A. General Principles

The grant of just satisfaction under Art.41 of the Convention[1] is dependent on the III–001
finding of a violation and the absence of total reparation in domestic law. When
only partial reparation is given, as in *Barbera, Messegué and Jabardo v Spain*, where the
domestic courts quashed the applicants' convictions, the Court may still award just
satisfaction.[2]

Just satisfaction is generally awarded at the same time as the finding of a
violation. Where however difficult questions of assessment arise, it may be
adjourned for further consideration.[3] When just satisfaction is adjourned and the
parties reach agreement as to the damages to be paid, the Court will verify that the
settlement has been reached on the basis of respect for human rights and, if it is
acceptable, it will strike the case out.[4]

Just satisfaction cannot be claimed by an applicant as a right: just satisfaction is
only to be granted if necessary and the matter falls to be determined by the Court at
its discretion, having regard to what is equitable.[5] The Court will also not raise any
just satisfaction issue of its own motion.[6]

The Court has no express jurisdiction under Art.41 to issue directions to
Contracting States on the measures or steps which they should take to rectify
violations. It considers that responsibility for supervising the execution of judgments
lies with the Committee of Ministers under Art.46 of the Convention.[7] It generally
declines therefore to impose any requirement such as, for example, quashing a
conviction.[8] In property cases however (see below), it has stated that the return of
the property would constitute *restituo in integrum*.[9] In certain cases, disclosing

[1] Formerly Art.50.
[2] (Art.50), June 13, 1994, Series A, No.285–C. The Court rejected the Government's arguments that the
quashing was total reparation since it did not compensate for the damage suffered from real loss of
opportunity to defend themselves at the original trial.
[3] *e.g.* where large pecuniary losses are involved with disputed value assessments as in *Papamichalopoulos v
Greece*, June 24, 1993, Series A, No.260–B; (Art.50), October 31, 1995, Series A, No.330–B. Parties
may be requested to nominate experts for a valuation report, *e.g. Belvedere Albighiera Srl v Italy (just
satisfaction)*, October 30, 2003.
[4] rr.62(3) and 43(2).
[5] *e.g. Sunday Times v UK (No.1)* (Art.50), November 6, 1980, Series A, No.38; see *X v U.K.* (Art.50),
October 18, 1982, Series A, No.55 where the applicant died, while noting that he may have suffered
distress from a breach of Art.5, para.4, the Court found that it was not necessary to award a sum to his
estate as it would not advance the cause of justice (para.19).
[6] *e.g. Francesco Lombardo v Italy*, November 26, 1992, Series A, No.249–B, para.25.
[7] *e.g. Finucane v UK*, July 1, 2003, ECHR 2003–VIII para.89, *Maestri v Italy*, February 17, 2004, ECHR
2004–I, para.47.
[8] *e.g. Schmautzer v Austria*, October 23, 1995, Series A, No.328–A, para.44; *Oberschlick v Austria (No.1)*,
May 23, 1991, Series A, No.204 (violation of Art.10 for defamation) where the applicant requested the
judgment to be set aside; *Vocaturo v Italy*, May 24, 1991, Series A, No.206 as regarded a request for a
judgment to be published in the Official Gazette; *Idrocalce v Italy*, February 27, 1992, Series A,
No.229–F request for a declaration that State should adopt legislative measures to ensure effective
protection of the human rights violated in the case.
[9] *Papamichalopoulos*, n.3 above; *Hentrich v France*, September 22, 1994, Series A, No.296, para.71.

flagrant unlawfulness or arbitrariness in detention, the Court has stated that the nature of the violation left no choice in the measure required and held that the State should secure the applicants' release at the earliest possible date.[10]

Just satisfaction is awarded under three heads: pecuniary loss, non-pecuniary loss and costs and expenses. The governing principle under all three heads is the notion of "equity".

An applicant must detail his claims: the Court will not examine possible damage of its own motion.[11] The Court has not proved unduly generous in its approach to awarding compensation under any of the heads. The emphasis is not providing a mechanism for enriching successful applicants but rather on its role in making public and binding findings of applicable human rights standards.

Since 2002, all awards are made in euros to enable direct comparison between cases from different countries.

B. Pecuniary Loss

III–002   There must be a causal link between the violation and the loss. Where the nature of the breach allows of *restituo in integrum*, it is for the State to effect it but if this does not occur the Court will award just satisfaction.[12] Loss must have been actually incurred.[13] While an applicant is generally expected to substantiate the pecuniary loss flowing from a breach, the Court acknowledges that in some cases a precise calculation, in particular of future losses, may not be possible and makes an equitable assessment.[14]

In cases of interference with property rights however, a distinction is drawn between cases of lawful and unlawful deprivations or dispossession. Where the breach results from inadequate compensation or procedural flaws, less than a full measure of compensation may be called for, particularly where the taking of property is linked to fundamental changes in the constitution or pursues economic reform and social justice.[15] In such cases, the Court may consider it appropriate to fix a sum "reasonably related" to the value of the property and which would have been found acceptable had the State compensated the applicants, or otherwise find an appropriate, equitable basis for compensation.[16] Where however there is "manifest unlawfulness" in the deprivation or dispossession, full restitution of losses is awarded.[17]

Where Art.6 violations are concerned, it is rare that a procedural failing is seen as causative of pecuniary loss following upon the subsequent conviction or from the

---

[10] *Assanidze v Georgia*, April 8, 2004, paras 203–204; *Ilascu v Moldova and Russia*, July 8, 2004, para.490.

[11] *e.g. Kostovski v Netherlands*, November 20, 1989, Series A, No.166; 12 E.H.R.R. 434, para.46; *Huvig v France*, April 24, 1990, Series A, No.176–B, para.37.

[12] In *Papamichalopoulos v Greece* (Art.50), n.3 above, paras 38–39 the Court held that the return of the expropriated land with award for loss of enjoyment would consitute *restituo in integrum* but if the land was not returned within six months, the State was to pay the value of the land; similarly in *Brumarescu v Romania (just satisfaction)*, January 23, 2001, ECHR 2001–I, paras 19–20.

[13] *e.g. Öztürk v Germany* (Art.50), October 23, 1985, Series A, No.85, para.8—there had been a breach of Art.6, para.3(e) but the applicant's insurance company had paid the interpretation fees.

[14] *Smith and Grady v UK (just satisfaction)*, July 25, 2000, ECHR 2000–IX, paras 8–9.

[15] *e.g. The Former King of Greece v Greece* (just satisfaction), November 11, 2002; *James v UK*, February February 21, 1986, Series A, No.98.

[16] *e.g. The Former King of Greece*, n.15 above; *Beyeler v Italy (just satisfaction)*, May 28, 2002; *Sovtransavto Holding v Ukraine (just satisfaction)*, October 2, 2003.

[17] *Iatridis v Greece (just satisfaction)*, October 19, 2000, ECHR 2000–XI, para.35; see also *Belvedere Albighiera Srl (just satisfaction)*, n.3 above.

decision affecting civil rights or obligations.[18] The Court usually finds itself unable to speculate on the outcome if the breach had not occurred. In rare cases, it may find that there has nonetheless been a real loss of opportunity which requires an award. In *Barbera, Messegué and Jabardo v Spain*, following a finding of a violation of Art.6 in a criminal trial in a number of fundamental aspects, the Court considered that there was a real loss of opportunity for the applicants to defend themselves in accordance with the requirements of Art.6 and thus a clear causal connection between the damage claimed and the violation. It did not however accept the calculations of loss of earnings and career prospects during their period of detention, awarding a sum on an equitable basis together with non-pecuniary damage.[19]

In cases of unreasonable length of proceedings, pecuniary loss may be granted where it is attributable to the delay rather than the fact that the proceedings were instituted or brought.[20]

Fines imposed and costs incurred in domestic proceedings directly linked to the violation are covered.[21]

Interest can be claimed from the dates on which each recoverable element of past pecuniary damage accrued.[22]

Applicants cannot be required to exhaust domestic remedies to obtain compensation for pecuniary loss in light of the Court's judgment since this would prolong the procedure before the Convention organs in a manner incompatible with the effective protection of human rights.[23]

---

[18] *e.g.* claims were unsuccessful in *Findlay v UK*, February 25, 1997, R.J.D. 1997–I, No.30 (lack of independent and impartial court martial) claim for loss of salary/pension following army discharge; *Saunders v UK*, December 17, 1996, R.J.D. 1996–VI, No.24 (breach of privilege against self-incrimination) claim of over £3 million for loss of salary; access to court cases where no causal link found with loss of trade, fees, etc., *e.g. Tre Traktorer v Sweden*, July 7, 1989, Series A, No.159 (revocation of license to sell alcohol); *Fredin v Sweden*, February 18, 1991, Series A, No.192 (revocation of permit to exploit gravel pit).

[19] (Art.50), June 13, 1994, Series A, No.285–C :It accepted the original claim based on the minimum salary in their respective fields of employment for the period held in closed prison plus one million pesetas for loss of career prospects, plus increase by retail price index. It rejected the later claim based on daily rates awarded by Spanish courts for incapacity to work. Pecuniary awards also made in *Teixiera de Castro v Portugal*, June 9, 1998, R.J.D. 1998–IV, No.77; *Pelissier and Sassi v France*, March 23, 1999, ECHR 1999–II.

[20] *e.g. Laine v France*, January 17, 2002, para.41.

[21] *e.g.* where journalists were fined, required to pay costs or incur costs of publishing in defamation proceedings found in breach of Art.10 (*Lingens v Austria*, July 8, 1986, Series A, No.103; *De Haes and Gijsels v Belgium*, February 24, 1997, R.J.D. 1997–I, No.30; *Association Ekin v France*, July 17, 2001, ECHR 2001–VIII; *Nikula v Finland*, March 21, 2002, ECHR 2002–II).

[22] *e.g. Smith and Grady*, n.14 above, para.24.

[23] *e.g. Papamichalopoulos* (Art.50), n.3, para.40; *Barbera* (Art.50), n.19 above, para.17.

Examples of Court findings of pecuniary loss

III–003

Main issues	Case	Just satisfaction awards
ARTICLE 2		
Deaths for which State responsible	*Gulec v Turkey*	No award. Father of teenage victim could not show any financial loss
	Salman v Turkey	£35,000 loss of earnings of deceased taxi driver. Based on actuarial calculation
	Gul v Turkey	£35,000: loss of earnings for work in family petrol station. The Court found the claimed sum of £740,000 was not supported by any evidence and had regard to awards in similar cases
	Avsar v Turkey	£40,000 to family for deceased business man. The Court rejected highly speculative claims as to future profits
	Aktas v Turkey	€225,000 to family for loss of future earnings of shop-keeper
State failure to protect life	*Akkoç v Turkey*	£35,000 loss of earnings of of deceased teacher
	Mahmut Kaya v Turkey, Kilic v Turkey	No award as applicant was not financially dependent on deceased brother
Disappearances	*Cakici v Turkey* *Ertak v Turkey* *Akdeniz v Turkey*	£11,000 £15,000 £10–80,0000 for loss of earnings from farming activities. This included sum for loss of contribution to work on farm of a minor and loss of service pension
Procedural breach	*Semse Onen v Turkey*	No award. No causal link between breach and loss
ARTICLE 3		
Serious assault by soldiers	*Ilhan v Turkey*	GBP 80,600. Loss of earnings (based on acturial calculation), past medical expenses. Claimed future medical expenses too vague

Main issues	Case	Just satisfaction awards
Failure to protect children from abuse	*Z v UK*	£8,000; 100,000; 80,000; 4,000. Sums to cover future counselling and psychotherapy and for two boys, sums to reflect damage to future wage-earning capacity. Based on medical reports of damage. The Court rejected statistical claims as to future mental illness
	E v UK	£16–32,000. Pecuniary and non-pecuniary together, to reflect some loss of future earning capacity. Took into account an award made by the Criminal Injuries Compensation Board
ARTICLE 5		
Unlawful deprivation of liberty	*Tsirlis and Koloumpas v Greece*	7.3 and 8 million GRD. Award for pecuniary and non-pecuniary together. Fact of unlawful detention must have produced damage of both kinds
	Assanidze v Georgia	€150,000 for loss of opportunity to work over three year period
Procedural defects, etc.	*Baranowski v Poland* *Jecius v Lithuania*	Loss of earnings rejected due to lack of causal link with breach
ARTICLE 6		
Lack of fair trial (criminal)	*Barbera, Messegue and Jabardo v Spain* (Art.50)	8 million pesetas for pecuniary/non-pecuniary including loss of earnings
	Teixiera de Castro v Portugal	10 million PTE pecuniary/non-pecuniary together. The Court found that the term of imprisonment would not have been imposed but for the police entrapment: loss of earnings during detention and of opportunities when the applicant came out of prison were actual
	Pelissier and Sassi v France	FRF 90,000 each: while the Court could not speculate as to result if breaches had not occurred, in the circumstances the applicants had suffered a real loss of opportunities

Main issues	Case	Just satisfaction awards
	Sander v UK *Kreps v Poland*	No earnings award as no causal link between breach and detention
Lack of access to court	*De Geouffre de la Pradelle v France*	100,000 FRF for loss of opportunities
Length of proceedings	*Union Alimentaria v Spain*	Award for depreciation of the value of the debt
	Probstmeier v Germany, Pammell v Germany	15,000 DEM for real loss of opportunity from the effect of delay on applicability of rent provisions
	Laine v France	€50,155, *e.g.* effect of liquidation proceedings, destruction of property
ARTICLE 8		
Gays in the army: investigation and dismissal based on sexual orientation	*Smith and Grady v UK* *Lustig-Prean and Becket v UK* (Just satisfaction)	Loss of past earnings: £30–34,000 Loss of future earnings: £7–25,000 Loss of benefit of non-contributory service pension: £14–30,000
Turkish village destruction cases	*Akdivar v Turkey* (Art.50); *Mentes v Turkey Selcuk and Asker* (Art.50); *Bilgin; Dulas; Ayder Ozkan*	Awards between GBP 12,000–€97,000—in light of findings that homes were destroyed but taking into account lack of independent or decisive evidence about their property or previous income, sums awarded, *e.g.* for home, possessions, foodstuffs, fuel, costs of alternative accommodation, livestock, loss of income from land. No awards for land itself as it was not expropriated
ARTICLE 10		
Prohibition of counselling service	*Open Door Counselling v Ireland*	£25,000 IR loss of earnings on equitable basis
Conviction of publisher and seizure of book	*Ozturk v Turkey*	USD 10,000 for fine and equitable amount for destruction of books. Alleged loss of future sales too speculative
Ban of sales of book	*Association Ekin v France*	250,000 FRF though speculative, some undoubted losses

Main issues	Case	Just satisfaction awards
Refusal of registration of periodical	*Gaweda v Poland*	10,000 PLZ some loss of opportunities from inability to sell periodical
ARTICLE 11		
Dismissal due to closed shop	*Young, James and Webster v UK*	£17,626, £45,215 and £8706 for loss of earnings and travel privileges
ARTICLE 14 in conjunction with ARTICLE 1 of Protocol No.1		
Denial of legal standing to pursue proceedings to protect property	*Canea Catholic Church v Greece*	5 million GRD losses incurred in dismissal of action
Liability to pay church tax	*Darby v Sweden*	8,000 SEK for tax paid plus interest
Racial discrimination in eligibility for unemployment assistance	*Gaygusuz v Austria*	200,000 ATS
Invalid planning permission	*Pine Valley v Ireland* (Art.50)	£1.2 million IRL in respect of value of the land if it had been immediately developed, taking into account reduction for rental value and uncertainties in land development
Sexual discrimination in obligation to pay welfare contributions	*Van Raalte v Netherlands*	Finding did not entitle the applicant to retrospective exemption of contributions
Discrimination in inheritance rights to child born out of wedlock	*Mazurek v France*	376,000 FRF difference between sum inherited and that which hewould have received if legitimate
Difference in levels of benefits due to national origin	*Koua Poirrez v France*	€20,000 pecuniary and non-pecuniary
Lack of eligibility for benefits on death of wife	*Willis v UK*	£25,000, for sums which would have been paid to bereaved widow, including interest
In conjunction with ARTICLE 4		
Obligation on men to pay fire levy	*Karl-Heinz Schmidt v Germany*	225 DEM for levy paid over 2 years
In conjunction with ARTICLE 6		

Main issues	Case	Just satisfaction awards
Sex discrimination in court refusal to award benefits	*Schuler-Zgraggen v Switzerland*	25,000 CHF for interest over 8 years until courts paid her claims
In conjunction with ARTICLE 8		
Lack of rights for child born out of wedlock	*Vermeire v Belgium*	22,192 BEF for loss of inheritance to which applicant would have been entitled if legitimate
ARTICLE 1 of Protocol No.1		
Deprivation of property		
Expropriation of land/ housing	*Papamichalopoulos v Greece*	4,200 million GRD for land 1,351 million GRD for buildings erected on land as award for loss of enjoyment
	Belvedere Albighiera Srl v Italy (Just satisfaction)	€763,391 loss of value of land, revenue, depreciation
	Lallement v France	€75,000 loss of revenue €75,000 future losses
Pre-emption on purchase of land by tax authorities	*Hentrich v France*	1 million FRF for current market value less sums paid
Pre-emption on purchase of painting	*Beyeler v Italy*	€1.3 million. As breach flowed from unfair procedures, award was not based on value of painting
Confiscation of coins/ jewellery	*Vasilescu v Romania*	60,000 FRF
Demolition of house	*Allard v Sweden*	€100,000
Overruling of final judgments on property rights:	*Brumarescu v Romania*	USD 136, 205: value of house and land
	other cases, *e.g.* *Anghelescu* *Stoicescu*	award for loss of rent €270,000 value of property (based on Government expert report showing current market value)
Delays		
—in paying compensation for expropriation	*Akkus v Turkey—series of cases* (e.g. *Aka, Yasar*) *Hatzitkakis v Greece*	Award to cover depreciation due to inflation Award of interest for delay period
—in proceedings for redistribution of agricultural land	*Piron v France*	100,000 FRF

Main issues	Case	Just satisfaction awards
Legislative annulment of award	*Stran Greek Refineries v Greece*	Amount of award plus interest
Lack of enforcement of tenancy evictions	*Italian cases: Scollo, AO, Palumbo, etc.*	Awards for loss of rent and/or expenses incurred to rent another apartment and bailiffs/lawyers' fees for enforcement proceedings
Long term restrictions on use of land/loss of use of land	*Sporrong and Llonroth v Sweden*	800,000/200,000 SEK for uncertainty and lack of opportunities
	Matos E Silva v Portugal	10 million PTE pecuniary/non-pecuniary
	Elia Srl v Italy	€1 million (based on legal rate of interest on value of land over period of ban on development)
	Loizidou v Turkey (Art.50)	300,000 CYP for loss of use of land in the north: equitable basis due to absence of real data and uncertainties in property market
	Iatridis v Greece (Just satisfaction)	loss of earnings until end of the lease (based on past tax declarations)
Other interferences with property rights		
Disproportionate imposition of VAT	*SA Dangeville v France*	Repayment of tax concerned
Excessive valuation of expropriated land for inheritance tax purposes	*Jokela v Finland*	€1,600 per applicant (the Court did not grant the difference expropriation and tax values)
Declaration of invalidity of option to renew building lease	*Stretch v UK*	€31,000 based on consideration paid for entering into agreement. Future profits claim too high and did not necessarily flow from the breach
Failure to demolish building cutting out light	*Antonetta v Italy*	Award to reflect loss of commercial value of property (based on architects' report)
Failure to provide proper/fair procedure to protect property rights	*Sovtransavto Holdings v Ukraine* (Just satisfaction)	€500,000 based not on loss of value of shares but on real loss of opportunities

Main issues	Case	Just satisfaction awards
Unreasonable valuation of expropriated property/ inadequate compensation	*Platakou v Greece*	Award of difference between full market valuation and that paid
	Malama v Greece (Just satisfaction)	Award for failure to take long period of delay in fixing compensation (based on 6 per cent of value over part of the period)
	The Former King of Greece v Greece (Just satisfaction)	€12 million /€900,000 /€300,000 for estates and possessions. Both parties provided widely differing valuations of expropriated estates. The Court took as starting point the objective value, making deductions for past tax and other financial benefits enjoyed by the applicants
ARTICLE 2 of Protocol No.1		
Suspension from school	*Campbell and Cosans v UK*	£3,000 for pecuniary/non-pecuniary. The Court accepted some effect on loss of education and job prospects

C. Non-Pecuniary Loss

III–004   An award for non-pecuniary damage may be made in respect of pain and suffering and physical or mental injury, including feelings of anxiety, helplessness or frustration, where such can be regarded as causally linked to the breach. The latter has led to damages in child care cases for example but not in respect of many procedural breaches of Art.6 cases or where terrorist suspects have been involved.[24] The Court makes awards on an equitable basis, generally without any explanation of its quantification or more than brief reasoning. It often appears to take a moral stance, as in the cases of terrorist suspects and reacts with evidently more sympathy to certain applicants or where there has been a clearly arbitrary use of power. In length of proceedings cases, it awards standard low sums reflecting to some degree

---

[24] See Art.8, child care cases below. Terrorist cases: see *McCann v UK*, February 24, 1995, Series A, No.324 (breach of Art.2); *Brogan v UK* (Art.50), May 30, 1989, Series A, No.152–B (Art.5, para.3); *Fox, Campbell and Hartley v UK* (Art.50), March 27, 1990, Series A, No.190–B (Art.5, para.1(c)).

the length of the delay, but may on occasion show some regard to significant hardship or effect on employment or career.[25] It does not make large awards, rarely going above GBP 30,000 even in cases of death or torture and has declined invitations to impose exemplary or punitive damages.[26]

The Court also considers whether there has been a real loss of opportunity from a breach, in the absence of any strict causal link, for example, lack of access to court in child care cases where it could not be established that an application for custody would have been successful but the loss of opportunity to apply is given weight. It has in certain cases referred to the effect on reputation or damage to career.[27]

In the absence of any of the above features, the Court generally finds that a finding of a violation in itself constitutes just satisfaction. It may award a sum in respect of pecuniary and non-pecuniary loss together, on an equitable basis, without distinguishing respective proportions.[28] Although it initially expressed doubts that a company could suffer non-pecuniary damage,[29] it has stated that it may make awards taking into account effects on a company's reputation, uncertainty in decision-planning, disruption in the management of the company and the anxiety and inconvenience caused to the members of the management team.[30]

Even where Court judgments are binding on domestic courts, an applicant cannot be expected to bring new proceedings for compensation on the basis of a judgment finding a violation. The Court thus awarded non-pecuniary damage in *Philis v Greece (No.2)* for length of proceedings, notwithstanding the Government argument that the applicant could apply for compensation to the domestic courts on the basis of the Court's finding of a violation.[31]

---

[25] *e.g. Triggiani v Italy*, February 19, 1991, Series A, No.197–B.

[26] *e.g. Akdivar v Turkey* (Art.50), April 4, 1998, R.J.D. 1998–II, No.69, para.38; *Orhan v Turkey*, June 18, 2002, para.448.

[27] *e.g. Darnell v UK*, October 26, 1993, Series A, No.272 (length case); £5,000 for damage to career during the long legal battle; *Helmers v Sweden*, October 29, 1991, Series A, No.212–A, where the applicant university lecturer's claims of discrimiation and defamation were rejected but he nonetheless received 25,000 kroner for a lack of public hearing.

[28] As in *Allenet de Ribemont v France*, where the applicant and the Commission unsuccessfully sought interpretation of the Court's judgment awarding two million francs for both heads. It was relevant to the applicant's claims in domestic proceedings that the award was immune from attachment in respect of other liabilities. The Court explained that it did not feel bound to identify proportions in making aggregate awards and that it was often difficult or impossible to make distinctions—August 7, 1996, R.J.D. 1996–III, No.12.

[29] *Manifattura v Italy*, February 27, 1992, Series A, No.230–B.

[30] *Comingersoll S.A. v Portugal*, April 6, 2000, ECHR 2000–IV, paras 35–36; award also made in *Sovtransavto Holding v Ukraine, (just satisfaction)* October 2, 2003, paras 79–82.

[31] February 27, 1997, R.J.D. 1997–IV, No.40, para.59. See however *Clooth v Belgium*, December 12, 1991, Series A, No.225, where the Court reserved Art.50 as it wished to take into account the award that the applicant might receive in domestic proceedings for the breach of Art.5, para.3 and (Art.50), March 5, 1998, R.J.D. 1998–I, No.66, where it found the domestic court award of non-pecuniary damage provided just reparation.

Court findings of non-pecuniary loss

III–005   (FOVIS: finding of violation was just satisfaction in the circumstances of the case)

Principal issues	Case	Findings
ARTICLE 2		
Excessive use of force on arrest	*McCann v UK*	No damages appropriate (IRA suspects killed while on bombing mission)
	Nachova v Bulgaria	€20,000 (also procedural breach of Art.2 and breach of Art.14)
In house search	*Gul v Turkey*	£20,000 to heirs; £10,000 to father as injured party
In riot	*Gulec v Turkey*	50,000 FRF (also procedural breach of Art.2)
Lack of control and planning	*McCann above* *Ergi v Turkey*	No award £5,000 to daughter, £1,000 to brother (applicant)
	Ogur v Turkey	FRF 100,000
Death and disappearance	*Cakici v Turkey*	€£25,000 to heirs (also breaches of Arts 3, 5, 13) £2,500 to applicant (brother) as injured party
	Tas v Turkey	€£20,000 (also breaches 3, 5, 13); £10,00 to applicant (father) as injured party and victim of Art.3 treatment
	Cicek v Turkey	£20,000 to heirs (also breaches Arts 3, 5, 13) £10,000 to mother as injured party and victim of Art.3 treatment
	Ertak v Turkey	£20,000 to heirs (also breach Art.13) £2,500 to father as injured party
	Akdeniz v Turkey	£20,000 (also breaches of Arts 3, 5, 3); £2,500 to applicant relatives as injuried parties
	Timurtas v Turkey	£20,000 to heirs (also breaches of Arts 3, 5, 13); £10,000 to applicant mother as injured party and victim of Art.3 treatment
	Ipek v Turkey	€10,000 per son (also breaches of Art.5)
	Orhan v Turkey	16,800 and €14,900 (also breaches of Arts 2 (investigation), 5, 8 Art.1 of Protocol No.1

Principal issues	Case	Findings
Death in custody	*Salman v Turkey*	£35,000 (also breaches of Arts 3, 13)
	Ozalp v Turkey	€25,000 (also breach of Arts 2 (procedural), 13.
	Ozkan v Turkey	€68,100 (also breach of Arts 2 (procedural), 3, 5, 8
	Tanli v Turkey	£20,000 to heirs; £10,000 to father as injured party (also breach of Art.13)
	Aktas v Turkey	€58,000 (also breaches of Arts 2 (procedural), 3,13)
	Orak v Turkey	€22,500 to heirs (also breaches of Arts 3, 13); €4,000 to father as injured party
	Anguelova v Bulgaria	€19,050 (also breaches of Arts 2 (procedural and lack of medical care) 3, 5, 13)
	Aktas v Turkey	€58,000 to heirs (also breaches Arts 3, 13, 38). €4,000 to brother as injured party
Failure to secure medical treatment	*Ozkan v Turkey*	€47,600 (death of child from injuries during operation: also breaches of Arts 2 (procedural), 3).
Lack of protection		
From known threats of violence	*Mahmut Kaya v Turkey*	£15,000 to heirs; £2,500 to applicant (brother) as injured party
	Kilic v Turkey	£15,000 to heirs (also breach of Art.13); £2,500 to applicant (brother) as injured party
	Akkoc v Turkey	£15,000
From risks on an operation:	*Demiray v Turkey*	USD 40,000 (allegations used to spring boobytrap on arms cache)
From fellow prisoner	*Paul and Aubrey Edwards v UK*	£20,000 (+ Arts 2 procedural breach and 13)
From environmental dangers	*Oneryildiz v Turkey*	€133,000 (failure to enforce health/building regulations near rubbish tip/methane explosion)
Procedural breaches		
—in the UK	*Hugh Jordan v UK, McKerr v UK, Kelly v UK, Shanaghan v UK, Finucane v UK*	£10,000
	McShane v UK	£8,000

Principal issues	Case	Findings
—elsewhere	*Tankrikulu v Turkey* (killing)	£15,000
	Yasa v Turkey (wounding and killing)	£6,000
	Kaya v Turkey (killing during operation)	£10,000
	Tahsin Acar v Turkey (disappearance)	€10,000
	Nuray Sen v Turkey (No.2) (abduction and killing)	€14,600
	Ulku Ekinci v Turkey (abduction and killing)	€15,590
	Onen v Turkey (raid on house)	16,000/€13,000
ARTICLE 3		
Assault by security forces	*Ilhan v Turkey*	£25,000 (brain damage from beating)
	Rehbock v Slovenia	€12,782 (violent arrest—double jaw fracture, etc.)
	Berktay v Turkey	€£55,000 (applicant thrown off balcony during police raid)
	Denizci v Cyprus	€34,686 (beatings on forcible expulsion to north)
Torture/ill-treatment in custody	*Selmouni v France*	€76,224.51 for repeated kicking, sexual humiliation over several days, etc.
	Dikme v Turkey	€30,489 for large number of blows. Also breach of Art.5, para.3
	Akkoc v Turkey	£25,000 for electric shocks, blows to head, hot and cold water, threats to children
	Satik v Turkey	£5,000 beating with batons and sticks
	Egmez v Cyprus	£10,000 violent arrest and detention, *e.g.* bruises, beating, lacerations and whip marks
	Büyükdag v Turkey	€15,244 blows and bruising on arm
	Hulki Gunes v Turkey	€25,000 beating. Also breach of Art.6
	Ayse Tepe v Turkey	€20,000 beating, palestinian hanging
	Esen v Turkey	€17,718 maltreatment, beating
	Yaz v Turkey	€32,000 falaka, beating, palestinian hanging

Principal issues	Case	Findings
	Elci v Turkey	25,500/€36,000 torture over 17–24 days (assault, hosing, stripping, etc) with lack of investigation and breach of Art.5 10,200–€15,000 inhuman treatment over 17–24 days with lack of investigation and breach of Art.5
Conditions of detention	*Dougoz v Greece*	€14,673.51 *e.g.* overcrowding, absence of sleeping facilities
	Peers v Greece	n.14, €673.51, *e.g.* overcrowding, lack of ventilation in heat, lack of toilet privacy
	Price v UK	£4,500 three day detention of severely disabled person in cold, inadequate sleeping and toilet arrangements
	Kalashnikov v Russia	€5,000 *e.g.* severe overcrowding, insanitary conditions, no toilet privacy
	Poltoratskiy; Kuznetzov; Nazarenko; Dankevich; Aliev; Khokhlich v Ukraine	€2,000 Restricted confinement on death row, no access to natural light, no outdoor exercise, little activity or human contact
Strip searches	*Valasinas v Lithuania*	€1,746 Also breach of Art.8
	Iwanczuk v Poland	€8,267 Also breaches of Arts 5 and 6
	Van der Ven v Netherlands (weekly routine search)	€3,000
	Lorse v Netherlands (weekly routine search) token claim	€453.78
Threat of expulsion	*Hilal*	FOVJS Proposed expulsion to Tanzania
Destruction of home:	*Bilgin*	£10,000 also breaches of Arts 8, 13 and P1–1
	Dulas	£10,000 ditto
	Yöyler	€14,500 ditto
For effect of disappearance on family	See above *Timurtas, Tas, Cicek, Orhan*	
Lack of prompt/adequate medical care or supervision	*Ilhan v Turkey*	See above
	Keenan v UK	£7,000 to estate for punishment and segregation of mentally ill prisoner who committed suicide

Principal issues	Case	Findings
	Mouisel v France	€15,000. Conditions of detention and transfer in handcuffs of prisoner with cancer
	McGlinchey v UK	€11,500. Failure to monitor/ treat drug withdrawal symptoms (leading to fatal dehydration)
Inadequate investigation	*Labita v Italy*	€38,734.27 (also breaches of Arts 5, 8, P1–3, P4–2)
	Sevtapveznedaroglu v Turkey	€2,606.18
	Indelicato v Italy	€36,151.98
	Kmetty v Hungary	€4,700
Failure to protect	*Z v UK*	£32,000 children not protected from long term neglect and abuse of parents
	E v UK	€16,000 and €32,000. No protection from known sexual abuser (pecuniary and non-pecuniary together)
	Pantea v Romania	€40,000. Applicant locked up with inmates who attacked him; delay in medical care Also breaches of Art.5, paras 1, 3, 4, 5 and Art.6, para.1
	MC v Bulgaria	€8,000. Shortcomings in domestic law on rape
	Yankov v Bulgaria	€8,000. Punitive head shaving of prisoner (also breach of Art.10)
Other: Imposition of death sentence after unfair trial	*Ocalan*	FOVJS
ARTICLE 5		
Para.1: no lawful or Convention basis for arrest or detention	*Lukanov v Bulgaria*	115 days : 40,000 FRF
	Tsirlis and Koulompas v Greece	13 months : 8 million GRD 12 months: 7.3 million GRD (pecuniary and non-pecuniary together)
	Amuur v France	FOVJS: 20 days for asylum seekers in airport zone
	Shamsa v Poland	€4,000: 14 days for asylum seekers in transit zone
	Raninen v Finland	10,000 FIM for 2 hours' unlawful arrest of conscientious objector

Principal issues	Case	Findings
	Labita v Italy	75 million ITL—continued detention one day after acquittal: also breach of Arts 3 (procedural) 5, para.3, 8, P1–3, P4–2: 38
	Engel v Netherlands	token 100 guilders for 2 days' arrest
	KF v Germany	FOVJS (a few hours)
	Jecius v Lithuania	€16,243 (preventive detention without Convention basis, no legal basis for 7 weeks detention on remand —also breaches of Arts 5 paras 3 and 4)
	Grauslys v Lithuania	€11,518, (no legal basis 3 months detention on remand). Also breaches Art.5, paras 4 and Art.6 para.1
	Baranowski v Poland	10,000 PLN (lack of legal basis—detention on remand)
	Kawka v Poland	4,000 PLN (3 months' remand—lack of legal basis)
	Goral v Poland	€2,000, (also breaches Arts 5, paras 3, 4 and 6 1)
	GK v Poland	€3,500. Also breach 5 paras 3/4, Art.6 para 1, 8
	Riera Blume v Spain	250,000 ESP (detention for cult deprogramming purposes)
	Aerts v Belgium	50,000 BEF—detention of mentally ill person in inappropriate penal location
	Erkalo v Netherlands	FOVJS (delays in procedure extension of detention)
	Conka v Belgium	€10,000: use of ruse to bring applicants into custody for peremptory expulsion. Also breach of Arts 5, para.4, 4P-4 and 13
	Nikolov v Bulgaria	€2,000—7 day delay in release of juvenile. Also breaches Art.5, paras 3 and 4
	Butkevicius v Lithuania	€5,700—no lawful basis for detention on remand Also breach of Art.5, paras 3 and 4
	Stasaitas v Lithuania	€21,700. Also breach of Arts 5, para.4 and 6
	Zeynap Avci v Turkey	€10,000—six days' prolongation of remand over statutory limit. Also breach of Art.5 paras 3 and 4

Principal issues	Case	Findings
	Assanadze v Georgia	€150,000 for over three years of detention after the order for his release
Disguised extradition	*Bozano v France*	100,000 FRF
Para.1(a)	*Stafford v UK*	€16,500 Recall of mandatory lifer not linked to original conviction — also breach of Art.5 para.4
	Grava v Italy	€8,000. Failure to apply reduction to term of applicant's sentence
Para.1(b)	*Nowicka v Poland*	€10,000. 83 days detention for compulsory medical examination (also breach of Art.8 — visiting restrictions)
	Vasileva v Denmark	€500 overnight detention for failure to give identity
Para.1(c) Standard of suspicion on arrest	*Fox, Campbell and Hartley v UK*	FOVJS
No reasonable suspicion to base arrest	*Berktay v Turkey*	£55,000 (plus breach of Art.3)
	Pantea v Romania	€60,000 (plus breaches of Arts 3, 5 paras 3 and 4, 6 (length)
Para.1(d) 119 days placement of minor in prison rather than educational establishment	*Bouamar v Belgium*	150,000 BEF (by agreement)
1 month placement of minor in prison	*DG v Ireland*	€5,000 (also breach of Art.5 para.5)
Para.1(e) Delayed release from mental hospital	*Johnson v UK*	£10,000 for over 3 years' delays, taking into account the applicant's own negative attitude
Lack of medical opinion and basis in domestic law for detention in mental hospital	*Varbanov v Bulgaria*	4,000 BGN (also breach of Art.5, para.4)
	Kepenerov v Bulgaria	€2,200
Failure to conform with domestic legal procedures: time-limits for hearings/ service delay in court review	*Tcacik v Slovakia*	€1,000
	Rakevich v Russia	€3,000 (also breach of Art.5 para.4)
	Wassink v Netherlands	FOVJS (absence of registrar at hearing)
Arbitrary detention of person as "alcoholic"	*Witold Litwa v Poland*	€2,013.57

Principal issues	Case	Findings
Para.1(f): Breach of lawfulness and length	*Quinn v France*	10,000 FRF (11 hours' no legal basis of detention) 50,000 FRF (length—almost 2 years)
Breach of "lawfulness" criteria for detention pending expulsion	*Dougoz v France*	5 million GRD (also breaches of Arts 3, 5 para.4)
Para.2	*Van der Leer v Netherlands*	150,000 guilders for all three heads together, including frustration and fear of return to hospital
Para.3		
Arbitrariness/lack of reasons for detention on remand No "judicial officer"	*Smirnova v Russia* *Pauwels v; Belgium, Huber v Switzerland; UK court martial cases: Hood, Stephen Jordan; Nikolova v Bulgaria, Aquilina v Malta, TW v Malta, Polish cases: Eryk Kawka, Salapa etc.*	2,000/€3,500. Also breaches of Art.5 paras 1, 6 (length), 8 FOVJS
	Brincat v Italy	1,000 maltese lira—adverse effect on lawyer's reputation/ feelings of insecurity
	Sabeur ben Ali v Malta	€2,454. Also breach of Art.5, para.4
	Niedbala v Poland	€2,103. Also breach of Arts 5, para.4, 8
	HB v Switzerland	€1,309.
	Shishkov v Bulgaria	€1,500. Also reliance on statutory presumption as justifying detention on remand
	Nikolov v Bulgaria	€2,000
Automatic denial of bail	*Caballero v UK*	£1,000. Also breach of Art.5, para.5
	SBC v UK	FOVJS. Also breach of Art.5, para.5
Promptness	*Koster v Netherlands, Brogan v UK* (over 4–6 days), *O'Hara* (6 days)	
	Ocalan v Turkey	FOVJS
	De Jong, Baljet and Van den Brink v Netherlands	300 NLG
Turkish cases	*Sakik v Turkey* (12–14 days)	25,000/30,000 FRF
	Igdeli (5 days)	€1,830. Also breach Art.5, para.4
	Nuray Sen (11 days)	€3,600
	Dalkaliç v Turkey (15 days)	€5,500. Also breach Art.5, paras 4 and 5
	Zeynep Avci v Turkey (21 days)	€10,000

Principal issues	Case	Findings
Length of detention on remand	*Toth v Austria*	FOVJS (entire period deducted from sentence)
	Scott v Spain (+4 yrs)	FOVJS (to be taken into account in eventual sentence)
	Muller v France (+3 yrs); *Debboub alias Husseini v France* (+4 yrs) *Czesky v Czech Republic* (+3 yrs), *Trzaska v Poland* (+3 yrs); *PB v France* (+4 yrs); *Szeloch v Poland* (+4 yrs) *Lavents v Latvia* (+6 yrs)	FOVJS
	Kemmache v France (No. 1) (+2 yrs)	75,000 FRF although period deducted from sentence. Also breach Art.6 para.1
	Punzelt v Czech Republic (+2 yrs)	€5,112
	Barfuss v Czech Republic (+3 yrs)	€2,811. Also breach of Art.6, para.1
	Kudla v Poland (+2 yrs)	+€7–8000. Also breach of Arts 6, paras 1, 13
	Vaccaro v Italy (+4 yrs)	€5,164
	Jablonski v Poland (+3 yrs)	€+6,000. Also breach of Arts 5, para.4,6 para.1
	Ilijkov v Bulgaria (+3 yrs)	€3,055. Also breach of Arts 5, paras 4, 6 para.1
	Zannouti v France (+5 yrs)	€7,622. Also breach Art.6, para.1
	Ilowiecki v Poland (+1 yr)	+€6,000. Also breach Art.5, para.4, 6, para.1
	Olstowski v Poland (+3 yrs)	+€5,000
	Demirel v Turkey (+7 yrs)	€6,000
	Klamecki v Poland (No.2) (+2 yrs)	€13,000. Also lack of "judicial officer" and breach of Art.5, paras 4 and 8
	Hristov v Bulgaria (+3 yrs)	€3,000. Also breach of Arts 5, para.4 and 6, para.1
	Mihov v Bulgaria (+3 yrs)	€4,000. Ditto
Delay in setting bail	*Iwanczuk v Poland* (+4 mths)	+€8,000. Also breach Arts 3, 6 para.1
Para.4		
Lack of review	*De Wilde, Ooms and Versyp v Belgium, Thynne, Gunnell and Wilson v UK Hussein v UK, Singh v UK, Rutten v Netherlands* (17 days); *Nikolova v Bulgaria Soumare v France*	FOVJS: No indication applicants would have been released earlier

FOVJS |

Principal issues	Case	Findings
	Curley v UK (HM Pleasure)	£1,500; feelings of frustration, uncertainty, etc.
	Oldham v UK (discretionary lifer)	£1,000. Ditto
	Hirst v UK (discretionary lifer	£1,000. Ditto
	Von Bulow v UK (mandatory lifer)	€1,500
	Hill v UK (mandatory lifer)	€2,200
	Vodenicarov v Slovakia	60,000 SKK
	Al-Nashif v Bulgaria	€7,000. Also breach of Arts 8 (expulsion), 13
	Rakevich v Russia	€3,000. Also breach of Art.5, para.1
	Yankov v Bulgaria	€8,000. Also breaches of Arts 3, 10, 5, paras 3, 5 and 6, para.1
Recidivist case	*Van Droogenbroeck v Belgium*	20,000 BEF—some loss from absence of guarantees
Procedural defects: Absence of/inadequate lawyer	*Megyeri v Germany*	5,000 DEM for feelings of isolation/ helplessness
	Magalhaes Pereira v Portugal	€6,000 (also breach of Art.5, para.4 for delay)
Lack of access to file	*Lamy v Belgium, Lietzow v Germany, Garcia Alvez v Germany, Migon v Poland:*	
	Shishkov v Bulgaria	FOVJS
		€1,500. Also breach of Art.5, para.3
Lack of appearance at hearing	*Kampanis v Greece*	FOVJS
	Grauzinis v Lithuania	5,000LTL
No oral hearing	*Waite v UK*	€2,500
Lack of procedural equality	*Niedbala v Poland*	2,000 PLN. Also breach of Art.5, paras 3 and 8
	Trazka v Poland	FOVJS. Also breach of Art.5 para.3
	Lanz v Austria	€3,000. Also breach Art.6 paras 1, 3b and c
	Ilijikov v Bulgaria	6,000 BGN. Also breach Art.5 para.3, Art.6 para.1
	Mihov v Bulgaria	€4,000. Also breach Art.5 para.3
	Hristov v Bulgaria	€3,000. Also breach Art.5 para.3 (period partly justified)
Lack of impartiality/ independence	*DN v Switzerland*	2,000 CHF
Breach of speed requirement	*Luberti v Italy, Koendibjbiharie v Netherlands, Bezicheri v Italy, E v Norway, Kawka v Poland, Wloch v Poland, Salapa v Poland Konig v Slovakia*	FOVJS—in Luberti, the applicant's own dilatory conduct taken into account

Principal issues	Case	Findings
	Herczegfalvy v Austria	100,000 ATS. Also violations of Arts 8 and 10
	RMD v Switzerland	50,000 CHF for undoubted non-pecuniary damage. Pre-trial detention
	Musial v Poland	15,000 PLN
	Baranowksi v Poland	30,000 PLN. Also violation of Art.5 para.1
	GB v Switzerland	2,000 CHF
	Delbec v France	€3,500 (delay in review of mental health committal)
	DM v France	€6,500 (delay in review of mental health committal)
	LR v France	€6,000 (delay in review of mental health committal)
Para.5 Right to compensation for arrest and detention	*Ciulla v Italy, Brogan v UK Fox, Campbell and Hartley v UK, Thynne, Gunnell and Wilson v UK, Hood, Stephen Jordan, SBC, O'Hara.*	Generally no awards made
Awards made in some cases with other violations	Art.5, para.1: *DG v Ireland*; Art.5, para.3: *Cabellero*; Art.5, para.4 *Curley v UK, Waite v UK, Hill v UK*	
ARTICLE 6		
Lack of a fair hearing	*Barbera, Messegué and Jabardo v Spain*	See pecuniary damages above: real loss of opportunities
Lack of clarity in court's procedural rules	*Coeme v Belgium*	200,000 BEF
Civil: lack of access to documents in court file	*Kerojarvi v Finland*	FOVJS
Breach of adversarial principle/equality of arms Criminal	*Bonisch v Austria*	(inequality of status of experts): 700,000 ATS prolonged uncertainty/feelings of inequality
	Reinhardt and Slimane-Kaid v France; Slimane Kaid v France (reporting judge's report not communicated to applicant on appeal); *Rowe and Davis v UK, Atlan v UK* (non-disclosure of documents by prosecution); *Goc v Turkey* (non-communication of prosecutor's submissions)	FOVJS

Principal issues	Case	Findings
Civil	*Kerojarvi v Finland* (non-communication of documents from court file); *Niderost-Huber v Switzerland* (not informed of lower court's comments on appeal); *Mantonovelli v France* (inequality vis-à-vis court expert report); *Lobo Machado v Portugal* (role of Attorney General's department); *Vermeulen v Belgium* (unable to reply to advocate general's submissions); *Foucher v France* (lack of access to case file); *Van Orshoven v Belgium* (inability to reply to procureur's submissions):	FOVJS
Lack of communication of documents	*KP v Finland*	15,000 FRF
	KS v Finland	5,000 FIM,
	Hirvisaari	20,000 FIM
No opportunity to comment on evidence obtained by court	*Krcmar and others v Czech Republic*	1,350,000 CZK—pecuniary and non-pecuniary together for real loss of opportunity
No adequate opportunity to answer case	*Pellegrini v Italy*	10 million ITL
Applicant not invited to make submissions	*Karakasis v Greece*	2 million GRD (also lack of adequate reasoning)
Inequality of time-limits	*Platakou v Greece*	300,000 GRD (also breach of Art.6 length and Art.1 of Prot. No.1)
Access to court	*Golder v UK, Benthem v Netherlands, Boden v Sweden, Austrian administrative offence cases (Schmautzer, Umlauft, Gradinger, Pramstaller, Palaoro, Pfarrmeier and Mauer), Perez de Rada Cavanilles v Spain*	FOVJS
	Pudas v Sweden	(revocation of taxi licence) 20,000 SEK
	Fredin v Sweden (No.1)	(refusal of licence to exploit gravel pit) 10,000 SEK
	Matts Jacobsson v Sweden	(building restrictions) 10,000 SEK
	Skarby v Sweden	(building prohibition) 30,000 SEK (for 6 appts.)

Principal issues	Case	Findings
	Philis v Greece (No.1)	(engineer's contract claims) 1 million GRD for frustration anxiety at financial position
	Bellet v France; FE v France	AIDS compensation case):1 million FRF
	O v UK (child care case)	5,000 GBP: some loss of opportunity and feelings of frustration and helplessness
	De Geouffre de la Pradelle	100,000 FRF some loss of opportunity
	Annoni di Gussola v France	50–100,000 FRF (pecuniary/ non-pecuniary together)
	Tinnelly and McElduff v UK	£10–15,000 for loss of opportunity
	(similar cases Devlin/Devenney	£10,000)
Overly technical procedural bars	*Leoni v Italy*	10 million ITL
	Sotiris and Nikos Koutras Attee v Greece; Platakou v Greece:	3 million GRD
	Zvolsky and Zvolska v Czech Republic:	FOVJS
Lack of legal aid	*Airey*	£3,000 IR offered by Government for anxiety frustration, etc.
Prohibitive costs	*Kreuz v Poland*	(prohibitive costs requirement): 30,000 PLN
	Ait- Mouhoub v France	FOVJS
Entrapment	*Texeira de Castro v Portugal*	10 million PTE pecuniary and non-pecuniary together
Legislative interference with court proceedings	*Papageorgiou v Greece*	2.5 million GRD
	Zielinski and Pradal v France	80,000 FRF pecuniary and non-pecuniary together. Plus breach of Art.6 (length)
	Agnastapoulos and others v Greece	500,000–1,000,000 GRD. Also breach of Art.6 length
	Agoudimos and Cefallonian Sky Shipping	2.5 million GRD
	Smokovitis v Greece	€2,900 (also breach of 1–P1)
	Kutic v Croatia	€10,000
	Acimovic v Croatia/Multiplex v Croatia	€4,000
Failure to enforce judgments	*Antonetta v Italy*	15 million ITL (also breach of 1–P-1)
	Eduaordo Palumbo v Italy	30,000 ITL (also breach of 1–P-1)
	Lunari v Italy	15, million ITL (also breach of 1–P–1)
	Sorrentino Prota v Italy	€3,000 (also 1–P-1)

Principal issues	Case	Findings
Overruling final judgments	*Jasiuniene v Lithuania* *Burdov v Russia* *Kyrtatos v Greece* *Brumarescu*	€9,000—pecuniary and non-pecuniary together) €3,000 (also breach of 1–P-1) €10–20,000 (also breach of Art.6 length) 15,000 USD (also breach 1–P-1) (following cases, *e.g. Vasiliu v Romania*—€19,000; *Lindner and Hammermayer v Romania*—€5,000, €15,000 (unable to use property for over 50 years)
Right to silence		
Customs fine for failure to disclose documents	*Funke v France*	50,000 FRF
Use of incriminatory materials obtained by compulsion	*Saunders v UK*	FOVJS
Judge' direction on adverse inferences not respect right to silence	*Beckles v UK*	FOVJS
Use of coached informant to pressurise applicant in his cell while held on remand	*Allan v UK*	FOVJS
Conviction of applicants for refusal to give incriminating information to police	*Heaney and McGuinness v Ireland* *Quinn v Ireland"*	4,000 IRL ditto
Lack of reasons/inadequacy of reasoning	*Ruiz Toriga v Spain; Hiro Balani v Spain; Georgiadis v Greece* *Dulaurans v France* *Karakasis v Greece* *Hirvisaari v Finland* *Lindner and Hammermeyer v Romania* *Suominen v Finland* *HAL v Finland*	FOVJS 100,000 FRF (pecuniary and non-pecuniary together) 2 million GRD 20,000 FIM €5,000 (also breach of 1–P-1) €2,000 €4,000 (medical certificate for stress)
Lack of independence or impartiality	*Hauschildt v Denmark; Langborger v Austria; Demicoli v Malta; Pfeiffer and Plankl v Austria; De Haan v Netherlands; Stallinger and Kuso v Austria; Gautrin v France; Castillo Algar v Spain; Buscemi v Italy; McGonnell v UK; Daktaras v Lithuania; Kingsley v U..K; Perote Pellon v Spain; Lavents v Latvia*	FOVJS

569

Principal issues	Case	Findings
	De Cubber v Belgium	100,000 BEF legitimate misgivings on judge who sat
	Tierce v San Marino	12 million ITL also lack of a hearing
	Rojas Morales v Italy	10 million ITL real loss of opportunity
	Werner v Poland	10,000 PLZ distress from dismissal as liquidator
	Sigurdsson v Iceland	€25,000. Supreme Court judge's husband financially involved with other party to civil case
	Pescador Valero v Spain	€2,000 judge's professional links with university party in employment dispute
Turkish National Security Court cases		
With breach of Art.10	*Incal v Turkey; Surek (No.4): Sener; Surek and Ozdemir*	30,000 FRF
	Karatas; Gerger	40,000 FRF
With breaches Art.6, paras 3(a)(b) and (d)	*Sadak and others:*	USD 25,000 each
With breaches of Arts 6 and 7	*EK v Turkey:*	€10,700
Alone	*Ciraklar v Turkey, Surek (No.1); Surek (No.3):*	FOVJS
UK court martial cases	*Findlay, Coyne, Hood, Cable, Morris*	FOVJ
Jury cases	*Holm v Sweden; Remli v France; Sander v UK*	FOVJS
Lack of public/oral hearing	*Le Compte v Belgium, Ekbatani v Sweden, Diennet v France, Stallinger and Kuso v Austria, Gautrin v France, Scarth v UK Ashan Rushiti v Austria, Riepan v Austria, Malhous v Czech Republic*	FOVJS
	Helmers v Sweden	25,000 SEK noting allegations of discrimination and defamation
	Fredin v Sweden (No.2)	15,000 SEK Also breach of Art.6 (access to court)
	H v Belgium	250,000 BEF also lack of adequate reasons
	De Moor v Belgium	400,000 BEF ditto
	Serre v France	10,000 FRF (disciplinary proceedings suspending a vet)

Principal issues	Case	Findings
	Stefanelli v San Marino	10 million ITL (criminal proceedings)
	Tierce v San Marino	12 million ITL (with lack of independence); 10 million ITL to other applicants (criminal proceedings)
	Guisset v France	100,000 FRF criminal proceedings (damaging to career)—also breach of Art.6 length
	AT v Austria	€1,500 (Media Act proceedings)
	Bakova v Slovakia	€1,000 property case: reference to applicant being personally affected by the breach)
	De Biagi v San Marino, Forcellini v San Marino:	€4,000 criminal trial
Lack of public delivery of judgment	*Werner v Austria, Szucs v Austria*	FOVJS
Length of proceedings	A non-pecuniary award is generally made in length cases in a relatively small amount, geared to the overall length of the proceedings and number of instances. Other factors taken into account: prolonged uncertainty, effect on profession (*Konig v Germany; Darnell v UK*), anxiety, stress and impact on health (*e.g. Martins Moreira v Portugal, H v France, Weisinger v Austria*), in criminal proceedings if the sentence has been in some way mitigated or proceedings discontinued due to the length (*e.g. Eckle v Germany*, FOVJS; *Howarth v UK*), whether applicant contributed to delays (*A. v Denmark; Muller v Switzerland* FOVJS); the importance of the proceedings of the applicant due to impact on health, compensation, employment or pensions issues (*e.g. Gocer v Netherlands* (benefits case, *Halka v Poland* (labour camp compensation claim))	

571

Principal issues	Case	Findings
	The awards also are geared to some extent to cost of living index in Member States, awards being adjusted downwards for those countries at the lower end of the scale	
Awards in recent UK cases		
Criminal		
	Howarth + 4 years:	£750
	Stephen Jordan (No.2) +4 years	€2,500
	Mellors + 3 years	€2,800
Civil	*Davies* (director's dis-qualification proceedings) + 5 years	€4,500
	Somjee (employment tribunal proceedings + 8 years	€5,000
	Foley +14 years	€4,000 (not all the fault of the authorities)
	Mitchell and Holloway + 9 years	€5,000
	Obasa + 7 years	€5,000
	Price and Lowe + 12 years	€1,000 (failure of applicants to take steps to expedite proceedings)
Para.2		
Comments by courts on costs or compensation proceedings linked to criminal case	*Minnelli v Switzerland, Ashan Rushiti v Austria Baars v Netherlands*	FOVJS
	Y v Norway	€20,000
	O v Norway	€5,000
Statements of guilt to press	*Allenet de Ribemont v France*	2 million FRF: statements widely reported. Also breach of Art.6 (length)
	Butkevicius v Lithuania	€5,700 (also breaches Art.5 paras 1 and 4)
	Lavents v Latvia	FOVJS
Racist remarks of juror	*Remli v France*	FOVJS
Breach of privilege against self-incrimination	*Heaney and McGuinness v Ireland*	4,000 IRL
	Quinn v Ireland"	ditto

Principal issues	Case	Findings
Presumption of involvement as owner of car in accident Contempt proceedings	*Telfner v Austria* *Kyprianou v Cyprus*	20,000 ATS €15,000 (also breach Art.6 paras 1 and 2)
Para.3(a)	*Pelissier and Sassi v France* *Mattocia v Italy* *Sadak and others v Turkey (No. 1)* *Kyprianou v Cyprus*	90,000 FRF for pecuniary/ non-pecuniary Also breach of Art.6 para.3(a)–(b) and 1 length 27 million IRL Also breach of Art.6 para.1 (length) 25,000 USD for all heads together Also breach of Art.6, paras 1, 3(b) and (d) €15,000. Also breach of Art.6 paras 1 and 2
Para.3(b)		
See cases under 3(a) above	*Vacher v France* (also breaches of Art.6 paras 1, 3(c)); *Ocalan* (also breaches of Arts 3, 5 paras 3 and 4, 6, paras 1,3(c)); *Fitt v UK, Dowsett v UK* *GB v France* *Lanz v Austria (also Art.5 para.4, Art.6 paras 1, 3(c)*	FOVJS 90,000 FRF €3,000
Para.3(c)		
Lack of free communication with counsel No legal aid lawyer	*S v Switzerland* *Lanz v Austria* *Ocalan v Turkey* *Brennan v UK* *Pakelli v Germany* *Alimena v Italy* *Benham v UK, Perks v UK*	2,500 CHF: frustration from surveillance of visits €3,000; 2 months super-vision by investigating judge (also breaches of Arts.5 para.4 and Art.6 para.1) FOVJS presence of security forces during lawyers' visits and restrictions on number and length of visits FOVJS presence of police officer during solicitors' visit No legal aid/lawyer (no lawyer on appeal) FOVJS (no notification of appeal to lawyer) FOVJS (no legal aid for com-mittal proceedings)

Principal issues	Case	Findings
one year without a lawyer	*Artico v Italy*	3 million ITL
absence of lawyer on appeal	*Goddi v Italy*	5 million ITL real loss of opportunity, *i.e.* could have made a difference
no lawyer during investigation or trial	*Quaranta v Switzerland*	3,000 CHF though received partial pardon, some anxiety
no legal aid for appeal with complex issues later cases no lawyer for appeal no legal aid on appeal	*Granger v UK* *Boner v UK, Maxwell v UK* *Pham Hoang v France* *Twalib v Greece* *Biba v Greece* *RD v Poland*	£1,000 FOVJS FOVJS 1.5million GRD 3 million GRD 10,000 PLZ
no lawyer for first year on remand inability to have lawyers at prison disciplinary hearing:	*Berlinski v Poland* *Ezeh and Connors v UK*	€2,000 FOVJS
lack of access to lawyer after arrest	*John Murray v UK, Magee v UK, Averill v UK*	FOVJS
Lawyer barred on trial/appeal due to absence of applicant	*Poitrimol v France, Lala v Netherlands, Pelladoah v Netherlands, Van Geyseghem v Belgium, Van Pelt v France, Krombach v France*	FOVJS
Absence of applicant at trial	*Zana v Turkey* *Yavuz v Austria*	40,000 FRF (also breach of Art.6 length) €2,000 (also breach of Art.6 length)
Absence of applicant on appeal	*Cooke v Austria* *Belziuk v Poland*	1,000 GBP FOVJS
Applicant not informed of hearing of appeal	*Vacher v France*	FOVJS
Ineffective lawyer on appeal	*Daud v Portugal* *Czekalla v Portuga*	FOVJS €13,000
Para.3(d)		
Principal witnesses not appear at trial Anonymous witnesses	*Unterpertinger v Austria* *Kostovski v Netherlands* *Windisch v Austria*	100,000 AS 6 months in prison as result of guilt established in manner not complying with Art.6 150,000 NLG by agreement FOVJS (rehearing had occurred)

Principal issues	Case	Findings
	Van Mechelen v Netherlands *Visser v Netherlands*	25,000 NLG to first applicant 20,000 NLG to others[32] €6,000
Failure of court to call/hear witnesses	*Vidal v Belgium* *Delta v France* *A.M. v Italy* *Luca v Italy* *Hulki Gunes v Turkey*	250,000 BEF for real loss of opportunity 100,000 FRF for real loss of opportunity 50 million ITL; ditto 15 million ITL; ditto €25,000 (also breach of Arts 3, 6 para.1)
Lack of confrontation with witnesses	*Bricmont v Belgium, Said v France, Craxi v Italy, Rachdad v France*	FOVJS
Refusal to hold hearing with witnesses	*Yavuz v Austria*	€2,000
Failure to produce evidence necessary for proper examination of witnesses and forgery issues	*Papageorgiou v Greece*	€20,000. Also length breach
ARTICLE 7		
Retrospective penalties	*Welch v UK* *Jamil v France*	FOVJS
Unforeseeable extension of prison sentencing provisions (also breach of Art.10)	*EK v Turkey* *Baskaya v Turkey*	€10,700 45,000 FRF
ARTICLE 8		
Unjustified police entry to home search of lawyers' office	*McLeod v UK* *Niemietz v Germany* *Roemen and Schmidt v Luxembourg*	FOVJS; FOVJS €4,000
customs searches and seizures	*Cremieux v France; Miailhe v France:*	50,000 FRF
search of company premises	*Ste Colas Est v France*	€5,000
search of journalists' homes and offices	*Ernst v Belgium*	€2,000

[32] The Government argued unsuccessfully that since the release of the applicants after the finding of a violation was just satisfaction enough.

Principal issues	Case	Findings
Other interferences with home Refusal of residence permit for house	*Gillow v UK*	GBP 10,000
Eviction from caravan site	*Connnors v UK*	€14,000
Destruction of home cases (also breaches of Arts 3, 13 and 1–P–1):	*Mentes v Turkey* (Art.50)	GBP 8,000
	Selcuk and Asker v Turkey; Bilgin v Turkey; Dulas v Turkey	GBP 10,000
	Yoyler v Turkey, Ayder	€14,500
Child care cases		
Unreasonable delay in proceedings	*H v UK*	GBP 12,000—breaches of Arts 6 and 8: some loss of real opportunity, feelings of frustration and helplessness
	Schaal v Luxembourg	€10,000—breaches of Arts 6 and 8
Lack of procedural protection/procedural defects	*W v UK, B v UK*	£12,000. Lack of consultation—also breach of Art.6 (access to court)
	R v UK	£8,000
	Keegan v Ireland	£10,000 IRL—breach of Arts 6 and 8 (natural father)
	McMichael v UK	£8,000 for evident trauma, anxiety and feelings of injustice (despite no real effect on result of case)
	Elsholz v Germany	35,000 DEM (lack of hearing and calling of expert witness) —some possible effect on future relationship with child
	Buchberger v Austria	80,000 ATS (failure to disclose evidence) also breach of Art.6
	TP and KM v UK	(non-disclosure of video evidence)—£10,000 each to mother and child. Loss of opportunity to shorten separation
	PC and S v UK	€12,000 to each parent (lack of legal assistance in hearings and manner of implementation of emergency care order at birth)
	Venema v Netherlands	€15,000 lack of involvement prior to decision to remove at birth
Restrictions on contact	*Margareta and Roger Andersson v Sweden*	50,000 SEK

Principal issues	Case	Findings
	Scozzari and Giunta v Italy	100 million ITL to mother, 50 million to children (also breach of Art.8 as regarded the placement in a special community)
Removal of children/ restriction on contacts	*Kutzner v Germany*	€15,000
Delay in returning child	*Eriksson v Sweden*	200,000 SEK
Placement of children at long distances	*Olsson v Sweden*	200,000 SEK—considerable anxiety, distress and inconvenience
Lack of rehabilitation/ enforcement of orders	*Olsson v Sweden No.2*	50,000 SEK
	Hokkanen v Finland *K and T v Finland*	100,000 FIM for distress 80,000 FIM. Also breach due to lack of justification for emergency removal
	Ignaccolo-Zenide v Romania *Sylvester v Austria*	100,000 FRF €20,000 to mother (FOVJS for child)
	Iglesias-Gil v Spain, Maire v Portugal *Covezzi and Morselli v Italy*	€20,000 FOVJS (no violations for removal and restrictions on contact in case with grounds for taking action to protect children from sexual abuse)
	Hansen v Turkey	€15,000 (non-enforcement of contact visits)
Other family life issues		
Delay in returning child's body after autopsy	*Pannullo and Forte v France*	100,000 FRF
Lack of recognition of family links	*Marckx v Belgium, Johnston v Ireland, Kroon v Netherlands*	FOVJS
Restrictions on family visits in prison in mental hospital	*Lavents v Latvia* *Nowicka v Poland*	FOVJS €10,000 (also breach of Art.5)
Refusal to allow prisoner to attend parents' funeral	*Ploski v Poland*	€1,500
Private life		
Criminalisation of homosexual acts	*Dudgeon v UK (Art.50); Norris v Ireland; Modinos v Cyprus*	No awards FOVJS
Transsexuals		
—inability to change name and identity documents —lack of legal recognition of gender change	*B v France* *Christine Goodwin v UK, I v UK*	100,000 FRF FOVJS

Principal issues	Case	Findings
—failure of courts to respect transsexual's private life in rejecting insurance claim for surgery expenses:		€15,000 (breaches of Arts 8 and 6)
Prosecution for homosexual acts	*ADT v UK*	£10,000
Investigations and dismissals of gays in the army:	*Lustig-Prean and Beckett v UK* (Just satisfaction) *Smith and Grady v UK* (Just satisfaction) *Beck, Copp and Bazeley Perkins and R. v UK*	£19,000 €30,300
Lack of protection in criminal law		
—for rape —for rape (together with breach of 3)	*X and Y v Netherlands* *MC v Bulgaria*	3,000 NLG €8,000
Lack of protection from environmental nuisance	*Lopez Ostra v Spain*	4 million ESP
Lack of information about environmental threat	*Guerra and others v Italy*	10 million ITL
Lack of access to personal records: (social services)	*Gaskin v UK* *MG v UK*	£5,000 €4,000
Rendering public details of HIV status of witness in criminal proceedings	*Z v Finland*	100,000 FIM
Disclosure of CCTV film (showing applicant's attempted suicide)	*Peck v UK*	€11,800
Delay in proceedings to settle affiliation	*Mikulic v Croatia*	€7,000
Repeated orders for compulsory psychiatric examinations	*Worwa v Poland*	€3,000
Failure to obtain court ruling on appropriate medical intervention for child	*Glass v UK*	€15,000
Confiscation of passport necessary for everyday life	*Smirnova v Russia*	€3,500 (also breaches of Arts 5 and 6)
Expulsion/exclusion orders	*Slivenko v Latvia* *Mehemi v France; Yildiz v Austria; Jakupovic v Austria Mokrani v France* *Yilmaz v Germany*	(expulsion due to Russian origin): €10,000 FOVJS €2,500 (strong family links with France) €3,000 (minor applicant; offences not too serious)

Principal issues	Case	Findings
Telephone tapping/ surveillance		
Lack of legal basis/ unlawfulness	Kruslin v France, A. v France; Kopp v Switzerland; Amann v Switzerland; Khan v UK, Armstrong v UK, Taylor-Sabori v UK, Hewitson v UK, Chalkley v UK	FOVJS
	Halford v UK	£10,000—interception to use material against her in sex discrimination proceedings was a serious infringement of her rights
Inability to challenge tapping on third party line	Lambert v France	10,000 FRF
Longterm storage/use of secret files on applicant	Rotaru v Romania	50,000 FRF
Covert taping for voice analysis	PG and JH v UK	£1,000
Covert taping in police station/ use of informant in cell	Allan v UK	€1,642
Covert video'ing for identification	Perry v UK	€1,500
Leak to press of taped telephone conversations and reading at trial	Craxi v Italy (No.2)	€2,000
Correspondence		
Restrictions/interference with prisoners' correspondence	Silver v UK, Schonenburger and Durmaz v Switzerland, McCallum v UK, Golder v UK, Campbell v UK, Domenchini v Italy, Calegoro Diana v Italy, Niedbala v Poland; Messina v Italy (Nos.2 and 3); William Faulkner v UK; Lavents v Latvia; Salapa v Poland	FOVJS
Interference with correspondence with European Commission of Human Rights, with breach of former Art.25 (now 34) from threats by prison officers	Petra v Romania	10,000 FRF
Opening of/ban on letters from lawyers, courts, Strasbourg	Demirtepe v France	5,000 FRF
	Valasinas v Lithuania	6,000 LTL (also breach of Art.3)
	AB v Netherlands	€3,500

Principal issues	Case	Findings
	Puzinas v Lithuania *Radaj v Poland:* *Klamecki v Poland (No.2)* *Poltoratskiy; Kuznetzov;* *Nazarenko; Dankevich; Aliev;* *Khokhlich v Ukraine*	€300 €500 €13,000 together with breaches of Art.5 paras 3 and 4, restrictions on contact with wife €2,000—also breach of Art.3)
Delays, opening, restriction in writing materials to Court (also breach of Art.34)	*Cotelet v Romania*	€2,500
Interference with bankrupts' correspondence Italian cases (also breaches of 1–P-1, 6, 2–P-4)	*Foxley v UK; Narinen v Finland* *Luordo* *Bottaro* *Bassani*	FOVJS €31,000 €27,000 €48,000
ARTICLE 9		
Convictions for proselytising Conviction for using place of worship without authorisation	*Kokkinakis v Greece* *Manoussakis v Greece*	400,000 drachmas FOVJS
Conviction for acting as mufti	*Serif v Greece* *Agga v Greece (No.2)*	2 million GRD FOVJS
Removal as chief mufti	*Hasan and Chaush v Bulgaria*	10,000 BGN to mufti (with Art.13 breach) FOVJS to member of community
Refusal to recognise a church	*Metropolitan Church of Bessarabia v Moldova*	€20,000
Requirement on M.Ps to take religious oath	*Buscarini v San Marino*	FOVJS
ARTICLE 10		
Sanctions imposed on, *inter alia*, journalists, politicians, *e.g.* injunctions, convictions	*Goodwin v UK, Oberschlick v Austria; Castells v Spain; Weber v Switzerland, Jersild v Denmark; De Haes and Gijssels v Belgium; Vereinigung demokraticher soldaten v Austria; Piermont v France;*	

Principal issues	Case	Findings
	Grigoriades v Greece; Lopes Gomes da Silva v Portugal; Du Roy and Lemaurie v France; Jerusalem v Austria; Thoma v Luxembourg; Maronek v Slovakia; Perna v Italy; Lehideux and Isorni v France, News Verlags Gmbh and Cokg v Austria; Krone Verlag v Austria	FOVJS
Prosecution for leaflets about electoral candidates	*Bowman v UK*	FOVJS
Defamation conviction	*Dalban v Romania* *Feldek v Slovakia*	20,000 to widow for loss of reputation 65,000 SKK for inconvenience of proceedings and measures to publish the defamation findings
Ban on publication of book	*Association Ekin v France*	50,000 FRF
Private prosecution of defence counsel for statements during trial	*Nikula v Finland*	€5,042
Seven hours' detention for protest	*Steel v UK*	£500
Interference with renewal of judicial appointment due to expression of views	*Wille v Liechtenstein*	10,000 CHF
Suspension of teacher for political views	*Vogt v Germany*	117,639.55 DM by agreement for loss of salary, etc.
Turkish cases concerning eg.convictions for separatist propaganda, etc.	*Polat; Ceylan; Karatas* *Incal; Erdogdu and Ince* *Erdogdu* *Kucuk* *Gunduz* *CSY v Turkey* *Abdullah Aydin* *Yagmurderli*	40,000 FRF (applicant served sentence/spent time in prison) 30,000 FRF (sentence suspended); 20,000 FRF (only 6 hours in custody) €4,000 €5,000 reference to severity of sentence (2 years) FOVJS (company) €10,000 prosecution for speech at public meeting (sentenced to prison) €7,500 (spent time in prison)
Ban on advertising	*Barthold v Germany*	FOVJS

Principal issues	Case	Findings
ARTICLE 11		
Loss of jobs due to closed shop	*Young, James and Webster v UK*	£200, £6,000 and £3,000
Employer's use of financial incentives to give up trade union rights	*Wilson, NUJ v UK*	€7,730 per applicant
Disciplinary sanctions	*Ezelin v France* *NF v Italy , Maestri v Italy*	FOVJS (lawyer's participation in demonstration) 20 million ITL, €10,000 (sanction on judge for freemason membership)
Dissolution of political parties	*United Communist Party v Turkey* *Socialist Party of Turkey v Turkey* *Freedom and Democracy Party (OZDEP) v Turkey*	FOVJS FOVJS 30,000 FRF
Refusal of registration of association	*Sidiropoulos v Greece*	FOVJS
Forcible membership of hunting association	*Chassagnou v France*	30,000 FRF each applicant (also breaches of Art.1 of Protocol No.1 and Art.14)
Requirement on officials to declare not a freemason	*Grande Oriente d'Italia v Italy*	FOVJS
ARTICLE 12		
Prohibition on marriage	*F v Switzerland*	FOVJS
Bar on transsexual marriage	*Christine Goodwin v UK*	FOVJS
ARTICLE 13		
	Chabal v UK, Valsamis v Greece (no substantive breach), *Camenzind v Switzerland (no substantive breach),* *Khan v UK, Jabari v Turkey, Messina v Italy (No.2), Hatton v UK* (no substantive breach)	FOVJS
no remedy for alleged disappearance together with breach of former Art.25	*Sarli v Turkey*	GBP 5,000
for inability to pursue remedy for alleged local authority negligence in child protection duties (abusive step parent)	*DP and JC*	€5,000

Principal issues	Case	Findings
Also breaches of Art.5 para.3 and Art.6 para.1 (length)	*Kudla v Poland*	30,000 PLN
Length breach	*Horvat v Croatia*	20,000 HRK
With procedural breach of Art.2	*Yasa v Turkey*	£6,000
	Kaya v Turkey	£10,000
	Semse Onen v Turkey	13,000 and €16,000
With substantive and procedural breach of Art.2	*Paul and Aubrey Edwards v UK*	£20,000
With breach of Arts 8 and 6 (secret files/surveillance)	*Rotaru v Romania*	50,000 FRF
Inability to obtain remedy for inhuman treatment of son/ relative in prison (breach of Art.3)	*Keenan v UK*	£3,000
	McGlinchey v UK	€3,800
ARTICLE 14		
In conjunction with ARTICLE 2 Use of lethal force tainted by racism against roma	*Nachova v Bulgaria*	€20,000 (also breach of Art.2)
In conjunction with ARTICLE 6 Sex discrimination	*Schuler-Zgraggen v Switzerland*	FOVJS
In conjunction with ARTICLE 8 Sex discrimination in immigration entry	*Abdulaziz v UK*	FOVJS: while some distress and anxiety, the applicants knew that they had no right of entry and were able to live together elsewhere
Procedural discrimination against unmarried fathers in child contact applications	*Sommerfeld v Germany, Sahin v Germany*	€20,000
Discriminatory reasoning in child care case concerning Jehovahs witness parent	*Palau-Martinez v France*	€10,000
Criminalisation of homosexual acts with males under age of 18	*BB v UK*	€7,000
/for acts with males 14–18	*L and V v Austria*	€15,000 (applicants were convicted)
	S and L v Austria	€5,000

Principal issues	Case	Findings
Discrimination against child born out of wedlock	*Camp and Bourimi v Netherlands*	NLG 6,750
Differences in security of tenure for tenants	*Larkos v Cyprus*	CYP 3,000
In conjunction with ARTICLE 1 of Protocol No.1		
Lack of inheritance rights—birth out of wedlock	*Inze v Austria* *Mazurek v France*	150,000 AS loss of real opportunity FRF 20,000
Liability to church tax	*Darby v Sweden*	FOVJS
Sex discrimination in social security contributions	*Van Raalte v Netherlands*	FOVJS
Discriminatory planning refusal	*Pine Valley v Ireland*	£150,000 on equitable basis to (inability to proceed with development compounded personal and financial difficulties)
Requirement on landowners to join hunting association	*Chassagnou v France*	FRF 30,000 (breaches also of Arts 11 and 1 of Protocol No.1)
ARTICLE 1 of Protocol No.1		
Length of tenancy eviction proceedings/lack of enforcement of property rights, *e.g.*	*Scollo v Italy* *AO v Italy* *Palumbo v Italy* *More recent cases: average 3000€, e.g.: Marini v Italy*	30 million ITL: with reference to effect on applicant's own living conditions 6 million lira ITL 30 million ITL: applicant wanted property for own living accommodation €3000; €10,000, *e.g. Carloni and Bruni v Italy* (over 10 years delay)
Refusal to execute demolition of building cutting out light to property	*Antonetta v Italy*	15 million ITL—profound feeling of injustice
Ban on developing property	*Elia SRL v Italy*	FOVJS (large pecuniary award)
Delay in paying compensation for expropriation	*Akkus v Turkey*	USD 1,000 for hardship, practical difficulties (other similar cases, *e.g. Aka v Turkey* USD 1,000)

Principal issues	Case	Findings
Loss of use of land since 1974	*Loizidou v Cyprus*	(Art.50): 20,000 CYP for feelings of anguish, helplessness and frustration in being unable to use her property: Court resisted claims to make large reward to reflect discriminatory policies of excluding Greek Cypriot owners, aggravating factors of international public order, etc.
Deprivation of property (gold coins and jewellery) over 30 years	*Vasilescu v Romania*	30,000 FRF
—overruling of judgment for return of house and land	*Brumarescu v Romania* (Art.41)	USD 15,000 (also *Anghelescu* €20,000; *Oprea* €7,000 *Falcoianu* €40,000; *Mosteanu* €4,000)
	—*Zwierzynski v Poland*	occupation of property by police authority 15,000 PLN
	—*Lallement v France*	€15,000 deprived of his "outil de travail" (60 per cent of his working farm) and undoubted anguish and stress
	—*Motais de Narbonne v France*	—over 3.2 million euros for expropriation of land (value of land at expropriation plus interest on the sum)
	—*Zvolsky and Zvolska v Czech Republic*	FOVJS
	—*Allard v Sweden* (demolition of house)	FOVJS
	—*Belvedere Aberghiera Srl*: blatantly unlawful expropriation so award justified to company for considerable inconvenience to company officials and administrators and effect on its ongoing business	€25,000
	—*Iatridis v Greece* (Just satisfaction)	5 million GRD for manifest unlawful occupation of his leased property by municipal authority
Non-enforcement of judgment	*Burdov*	€3,000
	Bocancea v Moldova	€800–1000 for stress and frustration, fact that pensions at stake were their only income

Principal issues	Case	Findings
Excessive inheritance tax:	*Jokela v Finland*	€1,300 to heirs, FOVJS to applicant not directly affected
Unfair procedure for compensation for expropriated procedure:	*Platakou v Greece*	3 million GRD for some anxiety and stress
Invalidity of lease renewal option: Failure to protect property rights in judicial procedure:	*Stretch v UK,* *Sovtransavto Holding v Ukraine* (Just satisfaction)	€5,000 suffered feelings of frustration and inconvenience company got €75,000 taking into account effect on decision-making capacity, inconvenience, effect on reputation of clients, prolonged uncertainty
ARTICLE 3 of Protocol No.1		
Forfeiture of Parliamentary seats	*Sadak v Turkey (No.2)*	€50,000 (pecuniary and non-pecuniary together
Ineligibility to stand for Parliament	*Podkolzina v Latvia*	€7,500
Prisoner's inability to vote	*Hirst v UK (No.2)*	FOVJS
ARTICLE 2 of Protocol No.4		
Restriction on movement	*Raimondo v Italy* *Luordo v Italy* *Bottaro v Italy*	5 million ITL (violation of Art.1 of Protocol No.1) €31,000 (also breaches of Arts 6 and 8) €27,000 (also breaches of Arts 6 and 13)
Monitoring of movements	*Denizci and others v Cyprus*	20,000 CYP (also breaches of Arts 3 and 5)

D. Legal costs and expenses

III–006   This head potentially covers not only the cost of proceedings before the Court but expenses incurred in domestic proceedings in order to prevent the violation or to obtain redress.[33] The Court applies the test whether the costs and expenses were

---

[33] *Le Compte v Belgium* (Art.50), October 18, 1982, Series A, No.54, where the appeal proceedings against the disciplinary sanctions were not part of a procedure to obtain redress for the lack of public hearing but the applicants' application to the Court of Cassation where the lawyers pleaded the Convention as part of the process of exhaustion of domestic remedies was taken into account and costs awarded. However in *Sunday Times v UK (No.1)* (Art.50), November 6, 1980, No.38 where the parties in the domestic proceedings agreed to pay their own costs, the Court made no award in this respect.

actually[34] and necessarily incurred in order to prevent, or obtain redress for, the matter found to constitute a violation of the Convention and were reasonable as to quantum.[35] The Court does not consider itself bound by domestic scales and practices in assessing what is reasonable by way of fees, although it may derive assistance from them.[36] It resisted the invitation by the Commission to impose a uniform approach to the assessment of fees since there is too great a disparity between the rates applicable in Contracting States.[37]

Where the Court finds one or more of the applicant's complaints of violation unfounded, it may reduce the amount of costs awarded.[38] It will not do so where a violation is found on the principal matter in issue as in *Soering v United Kingdom*, where the essential concern and bulk of the argument was on Art.3, although complaints under Art.6, paras 3(c) and 13 were rejected.[39] Where an applicant's claims for pecuniary and non-pecuniary damage are rejected in Art.41 proceedings, the legal costs for that part may not be granted.[40]

While an applicant is not required to agree to joint legal representation with other applicants before the Court, the Court will reduce claims that fail to take sufficient account of the similarity of cases or the potential for efficient co-ordination between the various representatives.[41] An applicant is not required to instruct counsel within his own country but may use lawyers from another Contracting State even if this has the result of increasing legal expenses.[42]

Awards are made subject to deduction of any sums granted by way of legal aid from the Council of Europe, unless stated otherwise.

The UK Government is active in querying fees which exceed domestic norms or which appear excessive. The Court has shown itself responsive to its objections to the level of fees or hours claimed, or to the number of representatives involved.[43] In *Young, James and Webster v United Kingdom*, the Court noted high litigation costs might themselves constitute an impediment to effective human rights protection

---

[34] Fees to be paid on a contingency basis have been discounted as they were not legally enforceable, *e.g. Dudgeon v UK* (Art.50), February 24, 1983, Series A, No.59; also *Mc Cann v UK*, September 27, 1995, Series A, No.324, where legal representatives acted free of charge at an inquest, the applicants could not claim to be under any obligation to pay the solicitor and the inquest costs could not be said to be "actually" incurred.

[35] *e.g. Sunday Times v UK (No.1)* (Art.50), cited above, para.23.

[36] *e.g. Silver v UK* (Art.50), October 24, 1983, Series A, No.67, para.20. See also *Abdulaziz v UK*, May 28, 1985, Series A, No.94 where the Government contested the rate of fees for junior counsel as higher than the domestic rate but the Court found the amount reasonable as to quantum; *Hadjianstassiou v Greece*, December 16, 1993, Series A, No.252 where the Court discounted the Government's complaints that fees claimed exceeded domestic rates.

[37] *Tolstoy v UK*, July 13, 1995, Series A, No.316–B, para.77.

[38] *e.g. Le Compte*, n.33 above, award reduced where most of the complaints were rejected; reductions also in *Tolstoy*, n.37 above where claims only partly successful. However the Court rejected in *Sunday Times v UK (No.1)* (Art.50), n.5 above, para.28 the Government argument that amounts should be reduced due to the fact that not all submissions under Art.10 were successful, *i.e.* criticising the length and detail of the applicant's case. The Court noted that a lawyer must present his case as fully as he is able and may not anticipate what arguments will convince.

[39] July 7, 1989, Series A, No.161. Also *Observer and Guardian v UK* and *Sunday Times (No.2)*, November 26, 1991, Series A, No.216, where there was no reduction despite no findings of violations of Arts 13 and 14 since the bulk of the argument had been on Art.10.

[40] *Welch v UK* (Art.50), February 26, 1996, R.J.D. 1996–II, No.5.

[41] *e.g. IJL v UK (just satisfaction)*, September 25, 2001, para.19.

[42] *e.g. Kurt v Turkey*, May 25, 1998, R.J.D. 1998–III, No.74, para.179, where the applicant instructed UK lawyers with expertise in international human rights.

[43] *e.g.* the Court accepted the Government objections to hourly rates in *Fox, Campbell and Hartley v UK* (Art.50), March 27, 1991, Series A, No.190–B and *Gaskin v UK*, July 7, 1989, Series A, No.160.

and considered it wrong to give encouragement to such a situation in costs awards under Art.41.[44] High costs claims have almost always been subject to reductions, on an equitable basis. The highest awards for awards in UK proceedings have been in the *Observer and Guardian, Sunday Times (No.2), Saunders* and *Tolstoy* cases (see below). In cases concerning length of proceedings or following a lead judgment, the Court is likely to reduce any high costs claims as unjustified by the issues or procedures and to make relatively small awards.[45]

Failure to itemise costs properly may lead to no award being made, or to a reduction in the award.[46] An applicant representing himself cannot claim to have incurred legal fees but may be paid costs of postage, photocopying, etc.[47]

Awards of legal costs and expenses

Recent selected UK cases

	Case	Court Awards (A: applicant; G: government; Ct: court)
III–007	P, C and S v UK	A: claimed €113,000
		G: objected as excessive, proposing €60,000
		Ct: awarded €60,000 noting overlapping and duplicating of work by multiple representatives
	Stafford v UK	A: claimed £18,000
		G: did not object
		Ct: awarded in full
	Paul and Aubrey Edwards v UK	A: claimed over £33,000
		G. objected
		Ct: while noting the factual and legal complexity, it found the claims on the high side when compared with other cases and in light of the fact that there had been no oral hearing: awarded GBP 20,000
	Z v UK	A: claimed £52,000
		G: objected, *e.g.* as after a certain date they had conceded breaches of Arts 3 and 13. Proposed £36,000
		Ct: awarded £39,000, noting unsuccessful on Art.6 claims but allowing for costs on Art.41 issues

---

[44] The Court awarded the £65,000 proposed by the Government, finding the applicant's claims for additional representation by a French legal firm debatable and criticising the applicant's refusal of the Government's offer to have the costs taxed domestically.

[45] *e.g.* telephone tapping, court martial. See table below.

[46] See r.60(2), *e.g. Zubani v Italy*, June 16, 1999, para.23 (no award); *Wilson and others v UK*, July 2, 2002, ECHR 2002–V (reduction in award).

[47] *e.g. Foley v UK*, October 22, 2002.

Case	Court Awards (A: applicant; G: government; Ct: court)
IJL v UK	As: claimed over £65,000, 40,000 and 117,000 for Convention procedure; over £500,000 for domestic procedures
	G: objected, criticising time-consuming arguments that failed
	Ct: awarded £40,000, noting similar issues for all three applicants based on established case and unconvinced by domestic claims
Keenan v UK	A: claimed over £38,000
	G: objected proposed £15,000
	Ct: awarded £21,000, noting excessive amount for counsel's fees for one memorial
Oldham v UK	A: prisoner claimed £1,600 for own costs
	G: accepted reasonable costs payable
	Ct: awarded £500
Halford	A: claimed £119,500 for solicitors (£239 rate for 500 hours) and £14,875 for counsel's fees
	G: objected to rate (£120–150 applicable in domestic proceedings) and excessive hours considering narrow range of issues and that the applicant chose to put in submissions of 200 pages of irrelevant annexes). Proposed £25,000
	Ct: awarded £25,000 as it was not satisfied all costs claimed necessarily incurred or reasonable as to quantum
D v UK	A: claimed £49,443 plus 13,811 FF
	G: objected as excessive (unreasonable number of lawyers involved)—proposed: £29,000 plus 9,194 FF
	Ct: £35,000 plus VAT
Findlay	A: claimed £23,956
	G: objected to inclusion of Divisional Court application costs of £1,250 (solicitor and counsel)
	Ct: found it reasonable to make application seeking redress for violation and granted claim in full
Saunders	A: claimed over £336,000
	G: objected as excessive and to amounts claimed for advisers beyond solicitor and junior and leading counsel
	Ct: not satisfied necessarily incurred or reasonable as to quantum: £75,000 on equitable basis

Case	Court Awards (A: applicant; G: government; Ct: court)
Chahal family	A: claimed £77,700 VAT incl.
	G: proposed £22,000
	Ct: found applicant's claim excessive: £45,000 VAT incl.
Benham	A: claimed £26,000
	G: objected—excessive
	Ct: granted £10,000, *e.g.* applicant only partly successful
Goodwin	A: claimed £49,500
	G: proposed £37,595
	Ct: considered sum conceded by Government to be adequate in the circumstances
Hussain	A: claimed £32,459 (VAT included)
	G: objection as excessive
	Ct: granted £19,000
Singh	A: claimed £22,058 (VAT included)
	G: objection as excesive
	Ct: £13,000 granted
McCann	Court awarded £22,000 solicitor, £16,700 counsel
Tolstoy	A: claimed £149,000 and 70,000 CHF approx
	G: objected as excessive
	Ct: was not satisfied all costs necessarily incurred and applicant only partially successful on the merits: awarded £70,000 and 40,000 CHF on an equitable basis
Welch (Art.50)	A: claimed £13,852
	G: no objection
	Ct: granted in full
Campbell	A: claimed £9,257.69
	G: no objection
	Ct: granted in full

Case	Court Awards (A: applicant; G: government; Ct: court)
Keegan v Ireland	A: claimed IR £42,863 supported by costs accountants' view I/ *Ireland* reasonableness
	G: proposed reduction without substantiation of its basis
	Ct: awarded claim plus VAT
Open Door Counseling v Ireland	A: Open Door claimed for domestic and Convention' proceedings: £68,985 IR Well Woman claimed £63,302: for domestic proceedings; £21,084 and £27,116 for Strasbourg
	G: accepted domestic costs for both. For Strasbourg proceeding, it made no objection to Open Door's claim but considered it excessive to pay Well Woman's costs for this same proceeding
	Ct: granted Open Door's claims in full. Awarded IR £100,000 in total to Well Woman, finding its claim excessive in light of the similarity of the cases
Pine Valley Developments v Ireland (domestic proceedings)	A: claimed £42,655
	G: thought inflated
	Ct: found it was not contested that sums actually and necessarily incurred and considered interest was warranted:-granted in full
Pine Valley (Strasbourg proceedings)	A: claimed IR £406,760 for Strasbourg
	G: objection as excessive (proposed IR £80,455)
	Ct: agreed with Government that claims excessive: £70,000 paid after legal aid deduction
Observer and Guardian (Domestic proceedings)	A: claimed: £137,825
	G: objected
	Ct: not agree with Government that applicants should have instructed the same solicitors since they were free to choose own representatives. But since their interests were the same, the number of fee earners involved was not "necessarily" incurred and agreed with the Government that solicitors' fees not reasonable as to quantum. Discounted period where found no violation. Granted £65,000

Case	Court Awards (A: applicant; G: government; Ct: court)
Observer v Guardian (Strasbourg proceedings)	A: claimed £74,605
	G: objection to size of fees
	Ct: reduction made for finding of no violation for one period and solicitors' fees unreasonable: granted £35,000
Sunday Times No.2 (*Domestic proceedings*)	A: £84,219 claimed
	G: objected to solicitors costs over £30,000
	Ct: agreed that solicitors' costs not reasonable and doubted all items necessarily incurred; also counsel's fees not reasonable (£30,590). Granted £50,000
Sunday Times (Strasbourg proceedings	A: claimed £140,120
	G: objection
	Ct: granted £50,000
Repetitive cases Telephone tapping *Taylor-Sabori v UK; Chalkley v UK:*	Ct: awarded €4,800
Court martial *Thompson v UK*	€5,000; *GW* €2,900
Length cases *Obasa v UK*	A: claimed over £92,000
	Ct: awarded €5,000
Mitchell and Holloway v UK	A: claimed over £58,000
	Ct: awarded €15,000

E. DEFAULT INTEREST

III–008   Interest in default of payment of awards after three months from the date of delivery of judgment is set, since 2002, to reflect the use of the euro as reference currency, namely, at three percentage points above the marginal lending rate of the European Central Bank.[48]

---

[48] See *Christine Goodwin v UK*, July 11, 2002, ECHR 2002–VI, para.124.

APPENDICES

APPENDIX 1

The 1950 European Convention for the Protection of Human Rights and Fundamental Freedoms, as amended by Protocol No.11, (Arts 1–49) and Protocols Nos 1, 4, 6 and 7

The governments signatory hereto, being Members of the Council of Europe, A–001

Considering the Universal Declaration of Human Rights proclaimed by the General Assembly of the United Nations on December 10, 1948;

Considering that this Declaration aims at securing the universal and effective recognition and observance of the rights therein declared;

Considering that the aim of the Council of Europe is the achievement of greater unity between its Members and that one of the methods by which that aim is to be pursued is the maintenance and further realisation of human rights and fundamental freedoms;

Reaffirming their profound belief in those fundamental freedoms which are the foundation of justice and peace in the world and are best maintained on the one hand by an effective political democracy and on the other by a common understanding and observance of the Human Rights upon which they depend;

Being resolved, as the governments of European countries which are like-minded and have a common heritage of political traditions, ideals, freedom and the rule of law, to take the first steps for the collective enforcement of certain of the rights stated in the Universal Declaration;

Have agreed as follows:

Article 1

The High Contracting Parties shall secure to everyone within their jurisdiction the rights and freedoms defined in section 1 of this Convention.

SECTION 1

Article 2

1. Everyone's right to life shall be protected by law. No one shall be deprived of his life intentionally save in the execution of a sentence of a court following his conviction of a crime for which this penalty is provided by law.

2. Deprivation of life shall not be regarded as inflicted in contravention of this Article when it results from the use of force which is no more than absolutely necessary:

    (a) in defence of any person from unlawful violence;
    (b) in order to effect a lawful arrest or to prevent the escape of a person lawfully detained;
    (c) in action lawfully taken for the purpose of quelling a riot or insurrection.

Article 3

No one shall be subjected to torture or to inhuman or degrading treatment or punishment.

Article 4

1. No one shall be held in slavery or servitude.

2. No one shall be required to perform forced or compulsory labour.

3. For the purpose of this Article the term "forced or compulsory labour" shall not include:

   (a) any work required to be done in the ordinary course of detention imposed according to the provisions of Article 5 of this Convention or during conditional release from such detention;
   (b) any service of a military character or, in case of conscientious objectors in countries where they are recognised, service exacted instead of compulsory military service;
   (c) any service exacted in case of an emergency or calamity threatening the life or well-being of the community;
   (d) any work or service which forms part of normal civic obligations.

Article 5

1. Everyone has the right to liberty and security of person. No one shall be deprived of his liberty save in the following cases and in accordance with a procedure prescribed by law:

   (a) the lawful detention of a person after conviction by a competent court;
   (b) the lawful arrest or detention of a person for non-compliance with the lawful order of a court or in order to secure the fulfilment of any obligation prescribed by law;
   (c) the lawful arrest or detention of a person effected for the purpose of bringing him before the competent legal authority on reasonable suspicion of having committed an offence or when it is reasonably considered necessary to prevent his committing an offence or fleeing after having done so;
   (d) the detention of a minor by lawful order for the purpose of educational supervision or his lawful detention for the purpose of bringing him before the competent legal authority;
   (e) the lawful detention of persons for the prevention of the spreading of infectious diseases, of persons of unsound mind, alcoholics or drug addicts or vagrants;
   (f) the lawful arrest or detention of a person to prevent his effecting an unauthorised entry into the country or of a person against whom action is being taken with a view to deportation or extradition.

2. Everyone who is arrested shall be informed promptly, in a language which he understands, of the reasons for his arrest and of any charge against him.

3. Everyone arrested or detained in accordance with the provisions of paragraph 1(c) of this Article shall be brought promptly before a judge or other officer authorised

by law to exercise judicial power and shall be entitled to trial within a reasonable time or to release pending trial. Release may be conditioned by guarantees to appear for trial.

4. Everyone who is deprived of his liberty by arrest or detention shall be entitled to take proceedings by which the lawfulness of his detention shall be decided speedily by a court and his release ordered if the detention is now lawful.

5. Everyone who has been the victim of arrest or detention in contravention of the provisions of this Article shall have an enforceable right to compensation.

Article 6

1. In the determination of his civil rights and obligations or of any criminal charge against him, everyone is entitled to a fair and public hearing within a reasonable time by an independent and impartial tribunal established by law. Judgment shall be pronounced publicly but the press and public may be excluded from all or part of the trial in the interest of morals, public order or national security in a democratic society, where the interests of juveniles or the protection of the private life of the parties so require, or to the extent strictly necessary in the opinion of the court in special circumstances where publicity would prejudice the interests of justice.

2. Everyone charged with a criminal offence shall be presumed innocent until proved guilty according to law.

3. Everyone charged with a criminal offence has the following minimum rights:

   (a) to be informed promptly, in a language which he understands and in detail, of the nature and cause of the accusation against him;
   (b) to have adequate time and facilities for the preparation of his defence;
   (c) to defend himself in person or through legal assistance of his own choosing or, if he has not sufficient means to pay for legal assistance, to be given it free when the interests of justice so require;
   (d) to examine or have examined witnesses against him and to obtain the attendance and examination of witnesses on his behalf under the same conditions as witnesses against him;
   (e) to have the free assistance of an interpreter if he cannot understand or speak the language used in court.

Article 7

1. No one shall be held guilty of any criminal offence on account of any act or omission which did not constitute a criminal offence under national or international law at the time when it was committed. Nor shall a heavier penalty be imposed than the one that was applicable at the time the criminal offence was committed.

2. This Article shall not prejudice the trial and punishment of any person for any act or omission which, at the time when it was committed, was criminal according to the general principles of law recognised by civilised nations.

Article 8

1. Everyone has the right to respect for his private and family life, his home and his correspondence.

2. There shall be no interference by a public authority with the exercise of this right except such as is in accordance with the law and is necessary in a democratic society in the interests of national security, public safety or the economic well-being of the country, for the prevention of disorder or crime, for the protection of health or morals, or for the protection of the rights and freedoms of others.

Article 9

1. Everyone has the right to freedom of thought, conscience and religion; this right includes freedom to change his religion or belief and freedom, either alone or in community with others and in public or private, to manifest his religion or belief, in worship, teaching, practice and observance.

2. Freedom to manifest one's religion or beliefs shall be subject only to such limitations as are prescribed by law and are necessary in a democratic society in the interests of public safety, for the protection of public order, health or morals, or for the protection of the rights and freedoms of others.

Article 10

1. Everyone has the right to freedom of expression. This right shall include freedom to hold opinions and to receive and impart information and ideas without interference by public authority and regardless of frontiers. This article shall not prevent States from requiring the licensing of broadcasting, television or cinema enterprises.

2. The exercise of these freedoms, since it carries with it duties and responsibilities, may be subject to such formalities, conditions, restrictions or penalties as are prescribed by law and are necessary in a democratic society, in the interests of national security, territorial integrity or public safety, for the prevention of disorder or crime, for the protection of health or morals, for the protection of the reputation or rights of others, for preventing the disclosure of information received in confidence, or for maintaining the authority and impartiality of the judiciary.

Article 11

1. Everyone has the right to freedom of peaceful assembly and to freedom of association with others, including the right to form and to join trade unions for the protection of his interests.

2. No restrictions shall be placed on the exercise of these rights other than such as are prescribed by law and are necessary in a democratic society in the interests of national security or public safety, for the prevention of disorder or crime, for the protection of health or morals or for the protection of the rights and freedoms of others. This Article shall not prevent the imposition of lawful restrictions on the exercise of these rights by members of the armed forces, of the police or of the administration of the State.

Article 12

Men and women of marriageable age have the right to marry and to found a family, according to the national laws governing the exercise of this right.

APPENDIX 1

Article 13

Everyone whose rights and freedom as set forth in this Convention are violated shall have an effective remedy before a national authority notwithstanding that the violation has been committed by persons acting in an official capacity.

Article 14

The enjoyment of the rights and freedoms set forth in this Convention shall be secured without discrimination on any ground such as sex, race, colour, language, religion, political or other opinion, national or social origin, association with a national minority, property, birth or other status.

Article 15

1. In time of war or other public emergency threatening the life of the nation any High Contracting Party may take measures derogating from its obligations under this Convention to the extent strictly required by the exigencies of the situation, provided that such measures are not inconsistent with its other obligations under international law.

2. No derogation from Article 2, except in respect of deaths resulting from lawful acts of war, or from Article 3, 4 (paragraph 1) and 7 shall be made under this provision.

3. Any High Contracting Party availing itself of this right of derogation shall keep the Secretary General of the Council of Europe fully informed of the measures which it has taken and the reasons therefore. It shall also inform the Secretary General of the Council of Europe when such measures have ceased to operate and the provisions of the Convention are again being fully executed.

Article 16

Noting in Articles 10, 11 and 14 shall be regarded as preventing the High Contracting Parties from imposing restrictions on the political activity of aliens.

Article 17

Nothing in this Convention may be interpreted as implying for any State, group or person any right to engage in any activity or perform any act aimed at the destruction of any of the rights and freedoms set forth herein or at their limitation to a greater extent than is provided for in the Convention.

Article 18

The restrictions permitted under this Convention to the said rights and freedoms shall not be applied for any purpose other than those for which they have been prescribed.

SECTION II—European Court of Human Rights

Article 19—Establishment of the Court

To ensure the observance of the engagements undertaken by the High Contracting Parties in the Convention and the Protocols thereto, there shall be set up a European Court of Human Rights, hereinafter referred to as "the Court". It shall function on a permanent basis.

Article 20—Number of judges

The Court shall consist of a number of judges equal to that of the High Contracting Parties.

Article 21—Criteria for office

1. The judges shall be of high moral character and must either possess the qualifications required for appointment to high judicial office or be jurisconsults of recognised competence.

2. The judges shall sit on the Court in their individual capacity.

3. During their term of office the judges shall not engage in any activity which is incompatible with their independence, impartiality or with the demands of a full-time office; all questions arising from the application of this paragraph shall be decided by the Court.

Article 22—Election of judges

1. The judges shall be elected by the Parliamentary Assembly with respect to each High Contracting Party by a majority of votes cast from a list of three candidates nominated by the High Contracting Party.

2. The same procedure shall be followed to complete the Court in the event of the accession of new High Contracting Parties and in filling casual vacancies.

Article 23—Terms of office

1. The judges shall be elected for a period of six years. They may be re-elected. However, the terms of office of one-half of the judges elected at the first election shall expire at the end of three years.

2. The judges whose terms of office are to expire at the end of the initial period of three years shall be chosen by lot by the Secretary General of the Council of Europe immediately after their election.

3. In order to ensure that, as far as possible, the terms of office of one-half of the judges are renewed every three years, the Parliamentary Assembly may decide, before proceeding to any subsequent election, that the term or terms of office of one or more judges to be elected shall be for a period other than six years but not more than nine and not less than three years.

4. In cases where more than one term of office is involved and where the Parliamentary Assembly applies the preceding paragraph, the allocation of the terms

of office shall be effected by a drawing of lots by the Secretary General of the Council of Europe immediately after the election.

5. A judge elected to replace a judge whose term of office has not expired shall hold office for the remainder of his predecessor's term.

6. The terms of office of judges shall expire when they reach the age of 70.

7. The judges shall hold office until replaced. They shall, however, continue to deal with such cases as they already have under consideration.

Article 24—Dismissal

No judge may be dismissed from his office unless the other judges decide by a majority of two-thirds that he has ceased to fulfil the required conditions.

Article 25—Registry and legal secretaries

The Court shall have a registry, the functions and organisation of which shall be laid down in the rules of the Court. The Court shall be assisted by legal secretaries.

Article 26—Plenary Court

The plenary Court shall:

- (a) elect its President and one or two Vice-Presidents for a period of three years; they may be re-elected;
- (b) set up Chambers, constituted for a fixed period of time;
- (c) elect the Presidents of the Chambers of the Court; they may be re-elected;
- (d) adopt the rules of the Court, and
- (e) elect the Registrar and one or more Deputy Registrars.

Article 27—Committees, Chambers and Grand Chamber

1. To consider cases brought before it, the Court shall sit in committees of three judges, in Chambers of seven judges and in a Grand Chamber of seventeen judges. The Court's Chambers shall set up committees for a fixed period of time.

2. There shall sit as an ex officio member of the Chamber and the Grand Chamber the judge elected in respect of the State Party concerned or, if there is none or if he is unable to sit, a person of its choice who shall sit in the capacity of judge.

3. The Grand Chamber shall also include the President of the Court, the Vice-Presidents, the Presidents of the Chambers and other judges chosen in accordance with the rules of the Court. When a case is referred to the Grand Chamber under Article 43, no judge from the Chamber which rendered the judgment shall sit in the Grand Chamber, with the exception of the President of the Chamber and the judge who sat in respect of the State Party concerned.

Article 28—Declarations of inadmissibility by committees

A committee may, by a unanimous vote, declare inadmissible or strike out of its list of cases an application submitted under Article 34 where such a decision can be taken without further examination. The decision shall be final.

Article 29—Decisions by Chambers on admissibility and merits

1. If no decision is taken under Article 28, a Chamber shall decide on the admissibility and merits of individual applications submitted under Article 34.

2. A Chamber shall decide on the admissibility and merits of inter-State applications submitted under Article 33.

3. The decision on admissibility shall be taken separately unless the Court, in exceptional cases, decides otherwise.

Article 30—Relinquishment of jurisdiction to the Grand Chamber

Where a case pending before a Chamber raises a serious question affecting the interpretation of the Convention or the protocols thereto, or where the resolution of a question before the Chamber might have a result inconsistent with a judgment previously delivered by the Court, the Chamber may, at any time before it has rendered its judgment, relinquish jurisdiction in favour of the Grand Chamber, unless one of the parties to the case objects.

Article 31—Powers of the Grand Chamber

The Grand Chamber shall:

(a) determine applications submitted either under Article 33 or Article 34 when a Chamber has relinquished jurisdiction under Article 30 or when the case has been referred to it under Article 43; and

(b) consider requests for advisory opinions submitted under Article 47.

Article 32—Jurisdiction of the Court

1. The jurisdiction of the Court shall extend to all matters concerning the interpretation and application of the Convention and the protocols thereto which are referred to it as provided in Articles 33, 34 and 47.

2. In the event of dispute as to whether the Court has jurisdiction, the Court shall decide.

Article 33—Inter-State cases

Any High Contracting Party may refer to the Court any alleged breach of the provisions of the Convention and the protocols thereto by another High Contracting Party.

Article 34—Individual applications

The Court may receive applications from any person, non-governmental organisation or group of individuals claiming to be the victim of a violation by one of the High Contracting Parties of the rights set forth in the Convention or the protocols thereto. The High Contracting Parties undertake not to hinder in any way the effective exercise of this right.

Article 35—Admissibility criteria

1. The Court may only deal with the matter after all domestic remedies have been exhausted, according to the generally recognised rules of international law, and within a period of six months from the date on which the final decision was taken.

2. The Court shall not deal with any application submitted under Article 34 that:

   (a) is anonymous; or

   (b) is substantially the same as a matter that has already been examined by the Court or has already been submitted to another procedure of international investigation or settlement and contains no relevant new information.

3. The Court shall declare inadmissible any individual application submitted under Article 34 which it considers incompatible with the provisions of the Convention or the protocols thereto, manifestly ill-founded, or an abuse of the right of application.

4. The Court shall reject any application which it considers inadmissible under this Article. It may do so at any stage of the proceedings.

Article 36—Third party intervention

1. In all cases before a Chamber or the Grand Chamber, a High Contracting Party one of whose nationals is an applicant shall have the right to submit written comments and to take part in hearings.

2. The President of the Court may, in the interest of the proper administration of justice, invite any High Contracting Party which is not a party to the proceedings or any person concerned who is not the applicant to submit written comments or take part in hearings.

Article 37—Striking out applications

1. The Court may at any stage of the proceedings decide to strike an application out of its list of cases where the circumstances lead to the conclusion that:

   (a) the applicant does not intend to pursue his application; or

   (b) the matter has been resolved; or

   (c) for any other reason established by the Court, it is no longer justified to continue the examination of the application.

However, the Court shall continue the examination of the application if respect for human rights as defined in the Convention and the protocols thereto so requires.

2. The Court may decide to restore an application to its list of cases if it considers that the circumstances justify such a course.

Article 38—Examination of the case and friendly settlement proceedings

1. If the Court declares the application admissible, it shall:

   (a) pursue the examination of the case, together with the representatives of the parties, and if need be, undertake an investigation, for the effective conduct of which the States concerned shall furnish all necessary facilities;

   (b) place itself at the disposal of the parties concerned with a view to securing a friendly settlement of the matter on the basis of respect for human rights as defined in the Convention and the protocols thereto.

2. Proceedings conducted under paragraph 1.b shall be confidential.

Article 39—Finding of a friendly settlement

If a friendly settlement is effected, the Court shall strike the case out of its list by means of a decision which shall be confined to a brief statement of the facts and of the solution reached.

APPENDICES

Article 40—Public hearings and access to documents

1. Hearings shall be in public unless the Court in exceptional circumstances decides otherwise.

2. Documents deposited with the Registrar shall be accessible to the public unless the President of the Court decides otherwise.

Article 41—Just satisfaction

If the Court finds that there has been a violation of the Convention or the protocols thereto, and if the internal law of the High Contracting Party concerned allows only partial reparation to be made, the Court shall, if necessary, afford just satisfaction to the injured party.

Article 42—Judgments of Chambers

Judgments of Chambers shall become final in accordance with the provisions of Article 44, paragraph 2.

Article 43—Referral to the Grand Chamber

1. Within a period of three months from the date of the judgment of the Chamber, any party to the case may, in exceptional cases, request that the case be referred to the Grand Chamber.

2. A panel of five judges of the Grand Chamber shall accept the request if the case raises a serious question affecting the interpretation or application of the Convention or the protocols thereto, or a serious issue of general importance.

3. If the panel accepts the request, the Grand Chamber shall decide the case by means of a judgment.

Article 44—Final judgments

1. The judgment of the Grand Chamber shall be final.

2. The judgment of a Chamber shall become final

    (a) when the parties declare that they will not request that the case be referred to the Grand Chamber; or

    (b) three months after the date of the judgment, if reference of the case to the Grand Chamber has not been requested; or

    (c) when the panel of the Grand Chamber rejects the request to refer under Article 43.

3. The final judgment shall be published.

Article 45—Reasons for judgments and decisions

1. Reasons shall be given for judgments as well as for decisions declaring applications admissible or inadmissible.

2. If a judgment does not represent, in whole or in part, the unanimous opinion of the judges, any judge shall be entitled to deliver a separate opinion.

Article 46—Binding force and execution of judgments

1. The High Contracting Parties undertake to abide by the final judgment of the Court in any case to which they are parties.

2. The final judgment of the Court shall be transmitted to the Committee of Ministers, which shall supervise its execution.

Article 47—Advisory opinions

1. The Court may, at the request of the Committee of Ministers, give advisory opinions on legal questions concerning the interpretation of the Convention and the protocols thereto.

2. Such opinions shall not deal with any question relating to the content or scope of the rights or freedoms defined in Section I of the Convention and the protocols thereto, or with any other question which the Court or the Committee of Ministers might have to consider in consequence of any such proceedings as could be instituted in accordance with the Convention.

3. Decisions of the Committee of Ministers to request an advisory opinion of the Court shall require a majority vote of the representatives entitled to sit on the Committee.

Article 48—Advisory jurisdiction of the Court

The Court shall decide whether a request for an advisory opinion submitted by the Committee of Ministers is within its competence as defined in Article 47.

Article 49—Reasons for advisory opinions

1. Reasons shall be given for advisory opinions of the Court.

2. If the advisory opinion does not represent, in whole or in part, the unanimous opinion of the judges, any judge shall be entitled to deliver a separate opinion.

3. Advisory opinions of the Court shall be communicated to the Committee of Ministers.

The Substantive Protocols to the Convention

PROTOCOL No. 1
MARCH 20, 1952

The Governments signatory hereto, being Members of the Council of Europe,

Being resolved to take steps to ensure the collective enforcement of certain rights and freedoms other than those already included in section 1 of the Convention for the Protection of Human Rights and Fundamental Freedoms signed at Rome on November 4, 1950 (hereinafter referred to as "the Convention"),

Have agreed as follows:

Article 1

Every natural or legal person is entitled to the peaceful enjoyment of his possessions. No one shall be deprived of his possessions except in the public interest and subject to the conditions provided for by law and by the general principles of international law.

The preceding provisions shall not, however, in any way impair the right of a State to enforce such laws as it deems necessary to control the use of property in accordance with the general interest or to secure the payment of taxes or other contributions or penalties.

Article 2

No person shall be denied the right to education. In the exercise of any functions which it assumes in relation to education and to teaching, the State shall respect the right of parents to ensure such education and teaching in conformity with their own religious and philosophical convictions.

Article 3

The High Contracting Parties undertake to hold free elections at reasonable intervals by secret ballot, under conditions which will ensure the free expression of the opinion of the people in the choice of the legislature.

PROTOCOL No. 4
SEPTEMBER 16, 1963

The Governments signatory hereto, being Members of the Council of Europe,

Being resolved to take steps to ensure the collective enforcement of certain rights and freedoms other than those already included in Section I of the Convention for the Protection of Human Rights and Fundamental Freedoms signed at Rome on November 4, 1950 (hereinafter referred to as "the Convention") and in Articles 1 to 3 of the First Protocol to the Convention, signed at Paris on March 20, 1952,

Have agreed as follows:

Article 1

No one shall be deprived of his liberty merely on the ground of inability to fulfil a contractual obligation.

Article 2

1. Everyone lawfully within the territory of a State shall, within that territory, have the right to liberty of movement and freedom to choose his residence.

2. Everyone shall be freed to leave any country, including his own.

3. No restriction shall be placed on the exercise of these rights other than such as are in accordance with law and are necessary in a democratic society in the interests of national security or public safety, for the maintenance of *ordre public*, for the prevention of crime, for the protection of health or morals, or for the protection of the rights and freedoms of others.

4. The rights set forth in paragraph 1 may also be subject, in particular areas, to restrictions imposed in accordance with law and justified by the public interest in a democratic society.

Article 3

1. No one shall be expelled, by means either of an individual or of a collective measure, from the territory of the State of which he is a national.

2. No one shall be deprived of the right to enter the territory of the State of which he is a national.

Article 4

Collective expulsion of aliens is prohibited.

PROTOCOL No. 6
APRIL 28, 1983

The Member States of the Council of Europe, signatory to this Protocol to the Convention for the Protection of Human Rights and Fundamental Freedoms, signed at Rome on November 4, 1950 (hereinafter referred to as "the Convention"),

Considering that the evolution that has occurred in several Member States of the Council of Europe expresses a general tendency in favour of abolition of the death penalty,

Have agreed as follows:

Article 1

The death penalty shall be abolished. No one shall be condemned to such penalty or executed.

Article 2

A State may make provision in its law for the death penalty in respect of acts committed in time of war or of imminent threat of war; such penalty shall be applied only in the instances laid down in the law and in accordance with its provisions. The State shall communicate to the Secretary General of the Council of Europe the relevant provisions of that law.

PROTOCOL No. 7
NOVEMBER 22, 1984

The Member States of the Council of Europe signatory hereto,

Being resolved to take further steps to ensure the collective enforcement of certain rights and freedoms by means of the Convention for the Protection of Human Rights and Fundamental Freedoms signed at Rome on November 4, 1950 (hereinafter referred to as "the Convention").

Have agreed as follows:

Article 1

1. An alien lawfully resident in the territory of a State shall not be expelled therefrom except in pursuance of a decision reached in accordance with law and shall be allowed:

(a) to submit reasons against his expulsion,

(b) to have his case reviewed, and

(c) to be represented for these purposes before the competent authority or a person or persons designated by that authority.

2. An alien may be expelled before the exercise of his rights under paragraph 1(a), (b) and (c) of this Article, when such expulsion is necessary in the interests of public order or is grounded on reasons of national security.

Article 2

1. Everyone convicted of a criminal offence by a tribunal shall have the right to have his conviction or sentence reviewed by a higher tribunal. The exercise of this right, including the grounds on which it may be exercised, shall be governed by law.

2. This right may be subject to exceptions in regard to offences of a minor character, as prescribed by law, or in cases in which the person concerned was tried in the first instance by the highest tribunal or was convicted following an appeal against acquittal.

Article 3

When a person has by a final decision been convicted of a criminal offence and when subsequently his conviction has been reversed, or he has been pardoned, on the ground that a new or newly discovered fact shows conclusively that there has been a miscarriage of justice, the person who has suffered punishment as a result of such conviction shall be compensated according to the law or the practice of the State concerned, unless it is proved that the non-disclosure of the unknown fact in time is wholly or partly attributable to him.

Article 4

1. No one shall be liable to be tried or punished again in criminal proceedings under the jurisdiction of the same State for an offence for which he has already been finally acquitted or convicted in accordance with the law and penal procedure of that State.

2. The provisions of the preceding paragraph shall not prevent the reopening of the case in accordance with the law and penal procedure of the State concerned, if there is evidence of new or newly discovered facts, or if there has been a fundamental defect in the previous proceedings, which could affect the outcome of the case.

3. No derogation from this Article shall be made under Article 15 of the Convention.

Article 5

Spouses shall enjoy equality of rights and responsibilities of a private law character between them, and in their relations with their children, as to marriage, during marriage and in the event of its dissolution. This Article shall not prevent States from taking such measures as are necessary in the interests of the children.

APPENDIX 2

Dates of entry into force

States	Convention CETS 005	Protocol No. 1 CETS 009	Protocol No. 4 CETS 046	Protocol No. 6 CETS 114	Protocol No. 7 CETS 117	Protocol No. 13 CETS 187
Albania	02/10/96	02/10/96	02/10/96	01/10/00	01/01/97	—
Andorra	22/01/96	—	—	01/02/96	—	01/07/03
Armenia	26/04/02	26/04/02	26/04/02	01/10/03	01/07/02	—
Austria	03/09/58	03/09/58	18/09/69	01/03/85	01/11/88	01/05/04
Azerbaijan	15/04/02	15/04/02	15/04/02	01/05/02	01/07/02	—
Belgium	14/06/55	14/06/55	21/09/70	01/01/99	—	01/10/03
Bosnia and Herzegovina	12/07/02	12/07/02	12/07/02	01/08/02	01/10/02	01/11/03
Bulgaria	07/09/92	07/09/92	04/11/00	01/10/99	01/02/01	01/07/03
Croatia	05/11/97	05/11/97	05/11/97	01/12/97	01/02/98	01/07/03
Cyprus	06/10/62	06/10/62	03/10/89	01/02/00	01/12/00	01/07/03
Czech Republic	01/01/93	01/01/93	01/01/93	01/01/93	01/01/93	—
Denmark	03/09/53	18/05/54	02/05/68	01/03/85	01/11/88	01/07/03
Estonia	16/04/96	16/04/96	16/04/96	01/05/98	01/07/96	01/06/04
Finland	10/05/90	10/05/90	10/05/90	01/06/90	01/08/90	—
France	03/05/74	03/05/74	03/05/74	01/03/86	01/11/88	—
Georgia	20/05/99	07/06/02	13/04/00	01/05/00	01/07/00	01/09/03
Germany	03/09/53	13/02/57	01/06/68	01/08/89	—	—
Greece	28/11/74	28/11/74	—	01/10/98	01/11/88	—
Hungary	05/11/92	05/11/92	05/11/92	01/12/92	01/02/93	01/11/03
Iceland	03/09/53	18/05/54	02/05/68	01/06/87	01/11/88	—
Ireland	03/09/53	18/05/54	29/10/68	01/07/94	01/11/01	01/07/03
Italy	26/10/55	26/10/55	27/05/82	01/01/89	01/02/92	—
Latvia	27/06/97	27/06/97	27/06/97	01/06/99	01/09/97	—
Liechtenstein	08/09/82	14/11/95	—	01/12/90	—	01/07/03
Lithuania	20/06/95	24/05/96	20/06/95	01/08/99	01/09/95	—
Luxembourg	03/09/53	18/05/54	02/05/68	01/03/85	01/07/89	—
Malta	23/01/67	23/01/67	05/06/02	01/04/91	01/04/03	01/07/03
Moldova	12/09/97	12/09/97	12/09/97	01/10/97	01/12/97	—
Netherlands	31/08/54	31/08/54	23/06/82	01/05/86	—	—
Norway	03/09/53	18/05/54	02/05/68	01/11/88	01/01/89	—
Poland	19/01/93	10/10/94	10/10/94	01/11/00	01/03/03	—
Portugal	09/11/78	09/11/78	09/11/78	01/11/86	—	01/02/04
Romania	20/06/94	20/06/94	20/06/94	01/07/94	01/09/94	01/08/03
Russia	05/05/98	05/05/98	05/05/98	—	01/08/98	—
San Marino	22/03/89	22/03/89	22/03/89	01/04/89	01/06/89	01/08/03
Serbia and Montenegro	03/03/04	03/03/04	03/03/04	01/04/04	01/06/04	01/07/04
Slovakia	01/01/93	01/01/93	01/01/93	01/01/93	01/01/93	—
Slovenia	28/06/94	28/06/94	28/06/94	01/07/94	01/09/94	01/04/04
Spain	04/10/79	27/11/90	—	01/03/85	—	—
Sweden	03/09/53	18/05/54	02/05/68	01/03/85	01/11/88	01/08/03
Switzerland	28/11/74	—	—	01/11/87	01/11/88	01/07/03
the former Yugoslav Republic of Macedonia	10/04/97	10/04/97	10/04/97	01/05/97	01/07/97	—
Turkey	18/05/54	18/05/54	—	01/12/03	—	—
Ukraine	11/09/97	11/09/97	11/09/97	01/05/00	01/12/97	01/07/03
UK	03/09/53	18/05/54	—	01/06/99	—	01/02/04

APPENDIX 3

Article 63 Declaration

Reservations/Declarations
ETS No. 5

Declaration contained in a letter from the Permanent Representative, dated November 8, 1983, registered at the Secretariat General on November 9, 1983—Or. Engl.

A–003 I have the honour to refer to Article 63 of the Convention for the Protection of Human Rights and Fundamental Freedoms, under which the Convention was extended to the Leeward Islands (including St. Kitts-Nevis) in 1953.

On instructions from Her Majesty's Principal Secretary of State for Foreign and Commonwealth Affairs, I now have the honour to inform you that since the independence of St. Kitts-Nevis from September 19, 1983, the Government of the United Kingdom is no longer responsible for this territory.

Declaration contained in a letter from the Permanent Representative, dated April 3, 1984, registered at the Secretariat General on April 3, 1984 — Or. Engl.

I have the honour to refer to Article 63 of the Convention for the Protection of Human Rights and Fundamental Freedoms, under which the Convention was extended to Brunei on September 12, 1967.

On instructions from Her Majesty's Principal Secretary of State for Foreign and Commonwealth Affairs, I now have the honour to inform you that since Brunei Darussalam resumed full international responsibility as a sovereign and independent State on December 13, 1983, the Government of the United Kingdom is no longer responsible for her external affairs.

List of territories for whose international relations Her Majesty's Government in the United Kingdom are responsible and to which the European Convention on Human Rights has been extended:

Anguilla	Guernsey
Bermuda	Isle of Man
British Virgin Islands	Jersey
Cayman Islands	Montserrat
Falkland Islands	St. Helena
Gibraltar	Turks and Caicos Islands

April 1984

APPENDIX 4

Voir Notice explicative
See Explanatory Note

COMMISSION EUROPÉENNE DE DROITS DE L'HOMME   A–004
EUROPEAN COMMISSION OF HUMAN RIGHTS

Conseil de l'Europe — *Council of Europe*
Strasbourg, France

REQUÊTE

APPLICATION

présentée en application de l'article 25 de la Convention européenne des Droits de l'Homme,
ainsi que des articles 43 et 44 du Règlement intérieur de la Commission

under Article 25 of the European Convention on Human Rights
and Rules 43 and 44 of the Rules of Procedure of the Commission

IMPORTANT: La présente requête est un document juridique et peut affecter vos droits et obligations.
This application is a formal legal document and may affect your rights and obligations.

I— LES PARTIES
THE PARTIES

A. LE REQUÉRANT
THE APPLICANT
(Renseignements à fournir concernant le requérant et son représentant éventuel)
(*Fill in the following details of the applicant and any representative*)

1. Nom de famille .... 2. Prénom(s) ....
    Name of applicant   *First name(s)*

3. Nationalité .... 4. Profession ....
    Nationality   *Occupation*

5. Date et lieu de naissance ....
    Date and place of birth

6. Domicile ....
    Permanent address

    .... 7. Tel. No ....

8. Adresse actuelle ....
    At present at
    ....

    Le cas échéant, (*if any*)

9. Nom et prénom du représentant* ....
    *Name of representative**

10. Profession du représentant ....
    Occupation of representative

11. Adresse du représentant ....
    Address of representative

    .... 12. Tel. No ....

A. LA HAUTE PARTIE CONTRACTANTE
THE HIGH CONTRACTING PARTY

    (Indiquer ci-après le nom de l'Etat contre lequel le requête est dirigée)
    (*Fill in the name of the Country against which the application is directed*)

13. ....

---

* Si le requérant est représenté, joindre une procuration signée par le requérant en faveur du représentant.
  A form of authority signed by the applicant should be submitted if a representative is appointed.

II— **EXPOSÉ DES FAITS**
STATEMENT OF THE FACTS

(Voir chapitre II de la note explicative)
(*See Part II of the Explanatory Note*)

14.

III— **EXPOSÉ DE LA OU DES VIOLATION(S) DE LA CONVENTION ALLÉGUÉE(S) PAR LE REQUÉRANT, AINSI QUE DES ARGUMENTS À L'APPUI**
STATEMENT OF ALLEGED VIOLATION(S) OF THE CONVENTION AND OF RELEVANT ARGUMENTS

A. (Voir chapitre II de la note explicative)
See Part III of the Explanatory Note

15.

Si nécessaire, continuer sur une feuille séparée
Continue on a separate sheet if necessary

IV— EXPOSÉ RELATIF AUX PRESCRIPTIONS DE L'ARTICLES 26 DE LA
CONVENTION
STATEMENT RELATIVE TO ARTICLE 26 OF THE CONVENTION

(Voir chapitre IV de la note explicative. Donner pour chaque grief, et au besoin sur une
feuille séparée, les renseignements demandés sous ch. 16 à 18 ci-après)
*(See Part IV of the Explanatory Note. If necessary, give the details mentioned below under points 16 to
18 on a separate sheet for each separate complaint)*

16. Décision interne définitive (date et nature de la décision, organe — judiciaire ou
autre — l'ayant rendue)
Final decision (date, court or authority and nature of decision)

17. Autres décisions (énumérées dans l'ordre chronologique en indiquant, pour chaque
décision, sa date, sa nature et l'organe — judiciaire ou autre — l'ayant rendue)
*Other decisions (list in chronological order, giving date, court or authority and nature of
decision for each one)*

18. Le requérant disposait-il d'un recours qu'il n'a pas exercé? Si oui, lequel et pour
quel motif n'a-t-il pas été exercé?
*Is any other appeal or remedy available which you have not used? If so, explain why you
have not used it.*

V— EXPOSÉ DE LA REQUÊTE
STATEMENT OF THE OBJECT OF THE APPLICATION

(Voir chapitre V de la note explicative)
(See Part V of the Explanatory Note)

19.

VI— AUTRES INSTANCES INTERNATIONALES TRAITANT OU AYANT
TRAITÉ L'AFFAIRE
STATEMENT CONCERNING OTHER INTERNATIONAL PROCEED-
INGS

(Voir chapitre VI de la note explicative)
(See Part VI of the Explanatory Note)

20. Le requérant a-t-il soumis à une autre instance internationale d'enquête ou de
règlement les griefs énoncés dans la présente requête? Si oui, fournir des indications
détaillées à ce sujet.
Have you submitted the above complaints to any other procedure of international investigation
or settlement? If so, give full details.

VII— PIÈCES ANNEXÉES   **(PAS D'ORIGINAUX,**
LIST OF DOCUMENTS   **UNIQUEMENT DES COPIES)**
                                      (*NO ORIGINAL*
                                        DOCUMENTS
                                    ONLY PHOTOCOPIES)

(Voir chapitre VII de la note explicative. Joindre copie de toutes les décisions mentionnées
sous ch. IV et VI ci-avant. Se procurer, au besoin, les copies nécessaires, et, en cas d'impos-
sibilité, expliquer pourquoi celles-ci ne peuvent pas être obtenues. Ces documents ne vous
seront pas retournés.)
(See Part VII of the Explanatory Note. Include copies of all decisions referred to in Parts IV and VI
above. If you do not have copies, you should obtain them. If you cannot obtain them, explain why not.
No document will be returned to you.)

21. a) . . . .

b) . . . .

c) . . . .

Si nécessaire, continuer sur une feuille séparée
Continue on a separate sheet if necessary

VIII— LANGUE DE PROCÉDURE SOUHAITÉE
STATEMENT OF PREFERRED LANGUAGE

(Voir chapitre VIII de la note explicative)
(*See Part VIII of the Explanatory Note*)

22.   Je préfère recevoir la décision de la Com-   anglais/français*
mission en: *English/French**
I prefer to receive the Commission's decision in:

IX— DÉCLARATION ET SIGNATURE
DECLARATION AND SIGNATURE

(Voir chapitre IX de la note explicative)
(*See Part IX of the Explanatory Note*)

23.   Je déclare en toute conscience et loyauté que les renseignements qui figurent sur la présente formule de requête sont exacts et je m'engage à respecter la caractère confidentiel de la procédure de la Commission.
I hereby declare that, to the best of my knowledge and belief, the information I have given in the application is correct and that I will respect the confidentiality of the Commission's proceedings.

24.   S'il n'est pas indiqué clairement ci-après que le requérant désire garder l'anonymat à l'égard du public, il sera considéré qu'il n'a pas d'objection à ce que son identité soit révélée:
It will be assumed that there is no objection to the identity of the applicant being disclosed unless it is stated here in unambiguous terms that the applicant does object:

Lieu/*Place* .... Date/*Date* ....

....
(Signature du requérant ou du représentant)
(*Signature of the applicant or of the representative*)

---

* Biffer ce qui ne convient pas.
Delete as appropriate.

Explanatory Note

for persons completing the Application Form
under Article 25 of the Convention

Introduction

These notes are intended to assist you in drawing up your application to the Commission. **Please read them carefully before completing the form**, and then refer to them as you complete each section of the form.

The completed form will be your application or "petition" to the Commission under Article 25 of the Convention. It will be the basis for the Commission's examination of your case. It is therefore important that you **complete it fully and accurately even if this means repeating information you have already given the Secretariat in previous correspondence.**

You will see that there are nine sections to the form. You should complete all of these so that your application contains all the information required under the Commission's Rules of Procedure. Below you will find an explanatory note relating to each section of the form. You will also find at the end of these notes the text of Rules 43 and 44 of the Commission's Rules of Procedure.

Notes relating to the Application Form

I. The Parties—Rule 44, para.1(a), (b) and (c)
(1–13)

If there is more than one applicant, you should give the required information for each one, on a separate sheet if necessary.

An applicant may appoint a lawyer or other person to represent him. Such representative must be resident in a Convention country, unless the Commission decides otherwise. When an applicant is represented by another person, relevant details should be given in this part of the application form, and the Secretariat will correspond only with the representative.

II. Statement of the facts—Rule 44, para.1(e)
(14)

You should give clear and concise details of the facts you are complaining about. Try to describe the events in the order in which they occurred. Give exact dates. If your complaints relate to a number of different matters (for instance different sets of court proceedings) you should deal with each matter separately.

III. Statement of alleged violation(s) of the Convention and of relevant arguments—Rule 44, para.1(d) and (e)
(15)

In this section of the form you should explain as precisely as you can what your complaint **under the Convention** is. Say which provisions of the Convention you

617

rely on and explain why you consider that the facts you have set out in Part II of the form involve a violation of these provisions.

You will see that some of the articles of the Convention permit interferences with the rights they guarantee in certain circumstances — (see for instance sub-paras. (a) to (f) of Article 5, para. 1 and para. 2 of Articles 8 to 11). If you are relying on such an article try to explain why you consider the interference which you are complaining about is not justified.

IV. Statement relative to Article 26 of the Convention—Rule 44, para.2(a) (16–18)

In this section you should set out details of the remedies you have pursued before the national authorities. You should fill in each of the three parts of this section and give the same information separately for each separate complaint. In part 18 you should say whether or not any other appeal or remedy is available which could redress your complaints and which you have not used. If such a remedy is available, you should say what it is (e.g. name the court or authority to which an appeal would lie) and explain why you have not used it.

V. Statement of the object of the application—Rule 44, para.1(d) (19)

Here you should state briefly what you want to achieve through your application to the Commission.

VI. Statement concerning other international proceedings—Rule 44, para.2(b) (20)

Here you should say whether or not you have ever submitted the complaints in your application to any other procedure of international investigation or settlement. If you have, you should give full details, including the name of the body to which you submitted your complaints, dates and details of any proceedings which took place and details of decisions taken. You should also submit copies of relevant decisions and other documents.

VII. List of documents—Rule 44, para.1(f) (No original documents, only photocopies) (21)

Do not forget to enclose with your application and to mention on the list all judgments and decisions referred to in sections IV and VI, as well as any other documents you wish the Commission to take into consideration as evidence (transcripts, statements of witnesses, etc.). Include any documents giving the reasons for a court or other decision as well as the decision itself. Only submit documents which are relevant to the complaints you are making to the Commission.

VIII. Statement of preferred language—Rule 44, para.2(c) (22)

The official languages of the Commission are English and French. Although the Secretariat conducts correspondence in a number of other languages as well, documents such as the Commission's decision will be communicated to you in one of the two official languages. Indicate which you prefer.

IX. Declaration and signature—Rule 44, para.2(d) and (e) (23–24)

The declaration includes an undertaking to respect the confidentiality of the Commission's proceedings. Under Article 33 of the Convention the Commission meets *in camera*. This means that the contents of all case-files, including all pleadings, must be kept confidential. The Commission's decisions on the admissibility of your case may, however, be made available to the public. If you have any objection to your name being made public, you should inform the Secretariat of this.

If the Application is signed by the representative of the applicant, it should be accompanied by a form of authority signed by the applicant himself (unless this has already been submitted) — Article 43, para. 3.

Rules 43 and 44 of the Rules of Procedure of the Commission

Institution of Proceedings

Rule 43

1. Any application made under Articles 24 or 25 of the Convention shall be submitted in writing and shall be signed by the applicant or by the applicant's representative.

2. Where an application is submitted by a non-governmental organisation or by a group of individuals, it shall be signed by those persons competent to represent such organisation or group. The Commission shall determine any question as to whether the persons who have signed an application are competent to do so.

3. Where applicants are represented in accordance with Rule 32 of these Rules, a power of attorney or written authorisation shall be supplied by their representative or representatives.

Rule 44

1. Any application under Article 25 of the Convention shall be made on the application form provided by the Secretariat, unless the President decides otherwise. It shall set out:

- (a) the name, age, occupation and address of the applicant;
- (b) the name, occupation and address of the representative, if any;
- (c) the name of the High Contracting Party against which the application is made;
- (d) the object of the application and the provision of the Convention alleged to have been violated;
- (e) a statement of the facts and arguments;
- (f) any relevant documents and in particular the decisions, whether judicial or not, relating to the object of the application.

2. Applicants shall furthermore:

   (a) provide information enabling it to be shown that the conditions laid down in Article 26 of the Convention have been satisfied;

   (b) indicate whether they have submitted their complaints to any other procedure of international investigation or settlement;

   (c) indicate in which of the official languages they wish to receive the Commission's decisions;

   (d) indicate whether they do or do not object to their identity being disclosed to the public;

   (e) declare that they will respect the confidentiality of the proceedings before the Commission.

3. Failure to comply with the requirements set out under paragraphs 1 and 2 above may result in the application not being registered and examined by the Commission.

4. The date of introduction of the application shall in general be considered to be the date of the first communication from the applicant setting out, even summarily, the object of the application. The Commission may nevertheless for good cause decide that a different date be considered to be the date of introduction.

5. Applicants shall keep the Commission informed of any change of their address and of all circumstances relevant to the application.

APPENDIX 5

Cour Européenne des Droits de L'Homme
European Court of Human Rights

Legal aid rates
applicable as from 1 January 2004

A. <u>FEES</u>   Average   A–005

1. Preparation of the case €337

2. Filing written pleadings at the request of the Court

    (a) observations on the admissibility
    or merits of the case €303

    (b) supplementary observations at the request of the Court
    (on the admissibility or merits of the case) €168

    (c) submissions on just satisfaction
    or friendly settlement €107

3. Appearance at an oral hearing before the Court
    or attending the hearing of witnesses (including preparation) €306

4. Assisting in friendly settlement negotiations €173

B. <u>EXPENSES</u>

Normal secretarial expenses
(for example telephone, postage, photocopies) .... lump sum €61
                                                (prior authorisation needed for
                                                any claims above given sum)

Travelling costs incurred in connection with appearance at an oral hearing or
hearing of witnesses or with friendly-settlement negotiations .... according
to receipts

Subsistence allowance in connection with appearance at an oral hearing or hearing of
witnesses or with friendly-settlement negotiations .... per diem

APPENDIX 6

Practice Direction

Requests for Interim Measures

(Rule 39 of the Rules of Court)

A–006   Applicants or their legal representatives who make a request for an interim measure pursuant to Rule 39 of the Rules of Court, should comply with the requirements set out below.

Failure to do so may mean that the Court will not be in a position to examine such requests properly and in good time.

I. Requests to be made by facsimile, e-mail or courier

Requests for interim measures under Rule 39 in urgent cases, particularly in extradition or deportation cases, should be sent by facsimile or e-mail or by courier. The request should, where possible, be in one of the official languages of the Contracting Parties. All requests should bear the following title which should be written in bold on the face of the request:

"Rule 39—Urgent/Article 39—Urgent"

Requests by facsimile or e-mail should be sent during working hours unless this is absolutely unavoidable. If sent by e-mail, a hard copy of the request should also be sent at the same time. Such requests should not be sent by ordinary post since there is a risk that they will not arrive at the Court in time to permit a proper examination.

If the Court has not responded to an urgent request under Rule 39 within the anticipated period of time, applicants or their representatives should follow up with a telephone call to the Registry during working hours.

II. Making requests in good time

Requests for interim measures should normally be received as soon as possible after the final domestic decision has been taken to enable the Court and its Registry to have sufficient time to examine the matter.

However, in extradition or deportation cases, where immediate steps may be taken to enforce removal soon after the final domestic decision has been given, it is advisable to make submissions and submit any relevant material concerning the request before the final decision is given.

Applicants and their representatives should be aware that it may not be possible to examine in a timely and proper manner requests which are sent at the last moment.

III. Accompanying information

It is essential that requests be accompanied by all necessary supporting documents, in particular relevant domestic court, tribunal or other decisions together with any other material which is considered to substantiate the applicant's allegations.

Where the case is already pending before the Court, reference should be made to the application number allocated to it.

In cases concerning extradition or deportation, details should be provided of the expected date and time of the removal, the applicant's address or place of detention and his or her official case-reference number.

Practice Direction

Institution of Proceedings

(individual applications under Article 34 of the Convention)

I. General

1. An application under Article 34 of the Convention must be submitted in writing. No application may be made by phone.

2. An application must be sent to the following address:

> The Registrar
> European Court of Human Rights
> Council of Europe
> F–67075 STRASBOURG CEDEX.

3. An application should normally be made on the form referred to in Rule 47 § 1 of the Rules of Court. However, an applicant may introduce his complaints in a letter.

4. If an application has not been submitted on the official form or an introductory letter does not contain all the information referred to in Rule 47, the Registry may ask the applicant to fill in the form. It should as a rule be returned within 6 weeks from the date of the Registry's letter.

5. Applicants may file an application by sending it by facsimile ("fax"). However, they must send the signed original copy by post within 5 days following the dispatch by fax.

6. The date on which an application is received at the Court's Registry will be recorded by a receipt stamp.

7. An applicant should be aware that the date of the first communication setting out the subject-matter of the application is considered relevant for the purposes of compliance with the six-month rule in Article 35 § 1 of the Convention.

8. On receipt of the first communication setting out the subject-matter of the case, the Registry will open a file, whose number must be mentioned in all subsequent correspondence. Applicants will be informed thereof by letter. They may also be asked for further information or documents.

9. (a) An applicant should be diligent in conducting correspondence with the Court's Registry.

(b) A delay in replying or failure to reply may be regarded as a sign that the applicant is no longer interested in pursuing his application.

10. Failure to satisfy the requirements laid down in Rule 47 §§ 1 and 2 and to provide further information at the Registry's request (see paragraph 8) may result in the application not being examined by the Court.

11. Where, within a year, an applicant has not returned an application form or has not answered any letter sent to him by the Registry, the file will be destroyed.

II. Form and contents

12. An application must contain all information required under Rule 47 and be accompanied by the documents referred to in paragraph 1 (h) of that Rule.

13. An application should be written legibly and, preferably, typed.

14. Where, exceptionally, an application exceeds 10 pages (excluding annexes listing documents), an applicant must also file a short summary.

15. Where applicants produce documents in support of the application, they should not submit original copies. The documents should be listed in order by date, numbered consecutively and given a concise description (e.g. letter, order, judgment, appeal, etc.).

16. An applicant who already has an application pending before the Court must inform the Registry accordingly, stating the application number.

17. (a) Where an applicant does not wish to have his or her identity disclosed, he or she should state the reasons for his or her request in writing, pursuant to Rule 47 § 3.
    (b) The applicant should also state whether, in the event of anonymity being authorised by the President of the Chamber, he or she wishes to be designated by his or her initials or by a single letter (e.g. "X", "Y", "Z", etc.).

Practice Direction

Written Pleadings

I. Filing of pleadings

General

1. A pleading must be filed with the Registry within the time-limit fixed in accordance with Rule 38 and in the manner described in paragraph 2 of that Rule.

2. The date on which a pleading or other document is received at the Court's Registry will be recorded on that document by a receipt stamp.

3. All pleadings, as well as all documents annexed thereto, should be submitted to the Court's Registry in 3 copies sent by post with 1 copy sent, if possible, by fax.

4. Secret documents should be filed by registered post.

5. Unsolicited pleadings shall not be admitted to the case file unless the President of the Chamber decides otherwise (see Rule 38 § 1).

Filing by facsimile

6. A party may file pleadings or other documents with the Court by sending them by facsimile ("fax").

7. The name of the person signing a pleading must also be printed on it so that he or she can be identified.

II. Form and contents

Form

8. A pleading should include:
   (a) the application number and the name of the case;
   (b) a title indicating the nature of the content (e.g. observations on admissibility [and the merits]; reply to the Government's/the applicant's observations on admissibility [and the merits]; observations on the merits; additional observations on admissibility [and the merits]; memorial etc.).

9. A pleading should normally in addition
   (a) be on A4 paper having a margin of not less than 3.5 cm wide;
   (b) be wholly legible and, preferably, typed;
   (c) have all numbers expressed as figures;
   (d) have pages numbered consecutively;
   (e) be divided into numbered paragraphs;
   (f) be divided into chapters and/or headings corresponding to the form and style of the Court's decisions and judgments ("Facts" / "Domestic law [and practice]" / "Complaints" / "Law"; the latter chapter should be followed by headings entitled "Preliminary objection on . . ."; "Alleged violation of Article . . .", as the case may be);
   (g) place any answer to a question by the Court or to the other party's arguments under a separate heading;
   (h) give a reference to every document or piece of evidence mentioned in the pleading and annexed thereto.

10. If a pleading exceeds 30 pages, a short summary should also be filed with it.

11. Where a party produces documents and/or other exhibits together with a pleading, every piece of evidence should be listed in a separate annex.

Contents

12. The parties' pleadings following communication of the application should include:
   (a) any comments they wish to make on the facts of the case; however,
      (i) if a party does not contest the facts as set out in the statement of facts prepared by the Registry, it should limit its observations to a brief statement to that effect;

(ii) if a party contests only part of the facts as set out by the Registry, or wishes to supplement them, it should limit its observations to those specific points;

(iii) if a party objects to the facts or part of the facts as presented by the other party, it should state clearly which facts are uncontested and limit its observations to the points in dispute;

(b) legal arguments relating first to admissibility and, secondly, to the merits of the case; however,

(i) if specific questions on a factual or legal point were put to a party, it should, without prejudice to Rule 55, limit its arguments to such questions;

(ii) if a pleading replies to arguments of the other party, submissions should refer to the specific arguments in the order prescribed above.

13. (a) The parties' pleadings following the admission of the application should include:

(i) a short statement confirming a party's position on the facts of the case as established in the decision on admissibility;

(ii) legal arguments relating to the merits of the case;

(iii) a reply to any specific questions on a factual or legal point put by the Court.

(b) An applicant party submitting claims for just satisfaction at the same time should do so in the manner described in the practice direction on filing just satisfaction claims.

14. In view of the confidentiality of friendly-settlement proceedings (see Article 38 § 2 of the Convention and Rule 62 § 2), all submissions and documents filed within the framework of the attempt to secure a friendly settlement should be submitted separately from the written pleadings.

15. No reference to offers, concessions or other statements submitted in connection with the friendly settlement may be made in the pleadings filed in the contentious proceedings.

III. Time-limits

General

16. It is the responsibility of each party to ensure that pleadings and any accompanying documents or evidence are delivered to the Court's Registry in time.

Extension of time-limits

17. A time-limit set under Rule 38 may be extended on request from a party.

18. A party seeking an extension of the time allowed for submission of a pleading must make a request as soon as it has become aware of the circumstances justifying such an extension and, in any event, before the expiry of the time-limit. It should state the reason for the delay.

19. If an extension is granted, it shall apply to all parties for which the relevant time-limit is running, including those which have not asked for it.

IV. Failure to comply with requirements for pleadings

20. Where a pleading has not been filed in accordance with the requirements set out in paragraphs 8–15 of this practice direction, the President of the Chamber may request the party concerned to resubmit the pleading in compliance with those requirements.

21. A failure to satisfy the conditions listed above may result in the pleading being considered not to have been properly lodged (see Rule 38 § 1 of the Rules of Court).

INDEX

INDEX